The Crucible of War

WESTERN DESERT 1941

BARRIE PITT

The Crucible of War

Western Desert 1941

JONATHAN CAPE
THIRTY BEDFORD SQUARE LONDON

First published 1980
Copyright © 1980 Barrie Pitt
Jonathan Cape Ltd, 30 Bedford Square, London WC1

British Library Cataloguing in Publication Data

Pitt, Barrie
The crucible of war.
Western Desert, 1941
1. World War, 1939–1945 – Campaigns – Africa, North
I. Title
940.54'23   D766.82
ISBN 0 224 01771 3

491213002

Photoset by Rowland Phototypesetting Ltd
Bury St Edmunds, Suffolk
Printed in Great Britain
by Richard Clay (The Chaucer Press) Ltd
Bungay, Suffolk

To Ann
who makes it all worth while

Contents

Illustrations

65 Litter of the battlefield
66 German artillery prepares to strike back
67 Panzergruppe moves forward again
68 Panzer IV in the lead
69 Major the Reverend Wilhelm Bach
70 Major-General Jock Campbell

MAPS

FIGURES

The author and publishers wish to thank the following for permission to reproduce photographs: the Imperial War Museum, for figs 1, 3, 6–9, 12–19, 21–2, 24–8, 31–2, 35–6, 39–52, 54–5, 57–8, 62–3, 67, 69 and 70; Zennaro, Rome, for figs 2, 5, 10 and 11; Major Michael Crichton-Stuart, for fig. 4; Australian War Memorial, for fig. 20 (neg. no. 5414); the Trustees of the Rifle Brigade Museum, for fig. 23; the National Archives, Washington, for figs 29, 37 and 66; Bundesarchiv, Koblenz, for figs 33, 53 and 56; Rijksinstituut voor Oorlogsdocumentatie, for figs 30, 34, 38, 59, 64, 65 and 68; and the South African National War Museum, for figs 60 and 61.

They would also like to thank Mr John Batchelor for permission to use his line drawings, figures 1–7.

Author's Note

No book such as this can be written without the help of others – librarians, fellow historians, archivists, survivors of the various actions – and to attempt to list all who so freely made available to me their time, their expertise or their memories would add pages to an already long book. I hope that they will therefore forgive me if I do not particularise, but accept once again my gratitude for their contributions.

There are some, however, whose help was either unique or continuous and to these I would like to express especial thanks. General Sir Richard O'Connor was kind enough not only to lend me his own unpublished account of the planning and execution of *Operation Compass* (smuggled with great ingenuity out of an Italian prison-camp in 1941) but also to spend time clarifying various aspects of the battle which had puzzled me before, as did Field Marshal Lord Harding of Petherton and the late Major-General Eric Dorman O'Gowan. To the same extent I am indebted to Colonel C. A. H. M. Noble, M.C., who lent me the diary he kept, first as adjutant to the 2nd Camerons during *Operation Compass*, and later as a staff officer with H.Q. 4th Indian Division.

During conversations we had together many years ago, Generale Giuseppe Mancinelli did much to explain to me the Italian attitudes to the War in the Desert and especially the psychological problems besetting Italians fighting with the Germans against the British, while Generals Walther Nehring and Walter Warlimont helped considerably towards an understanding of the views taken at Panzergruppe Headquarters and in Berlin.

At a different level, Colonel D. T. L. Beath has been kind enough to read through the typescript and point out the various military solecisms I had committed, and to Mr John Keegan I owe an especial debt, both for his expert critique of the chapters dealing with *Operation Crusader* and for his vital intercession at a crucial moment.

I would also like to thank Mrs Jane Caunt who completely retyped the book, Christopher Harrison who drew the maps,

Deborah Shepherd who has so expertly clarified the text, and Anthony Colwell and Graham Greene for the energy and enthusiasm they have given to its publication.

Prologue: September 12th, 1882

The advance parties moved out westward at dusk and well before midnight the entire force was on the march – Cameron, Seaforth and Gordon Highlanders plus the men of the Black Watch on the left along the line of the Sweetwater Canal, Royal Irish Fusiliers, Royal Marines and the York and Lancasters on the right with forty-two pieces of artillery trundling between the two divisions. The Household Cavalry and two batteries of the Royal Horse Artillery trotted to the right rear, while to the south of the canal on the left flank and deliberately an hour behind on the march came the Pathan mountaineers, the Baluchis and the Oudh Sepoys with the Sikh Lancers in front. There was no moon but the stars were bright; the night warm, almost velvety.

Along the railway line and between the canal and the Highlanders came the Royal Naval detachment hauling the trolley with padded wheels and the 40-pounder aboard, keeping abreast of the Indian Brigade.

Well in front of the main artillery between the divisions rode the General and his staff while out in front of them marched Lieutenant Rawson of the Royal Navy, piloting the entire force by the stars. Some 11,000 bayonets, 2,000 sabres, 61 guns and six machine-guns were on the move against fortifications manned, it was believed, by 20,000 regular troops supported by 6,000 irregulars, 2,500 cavalry and 60 guns.

Dawn was at 0540 and the North Star and Great Bear, veering very slightly north-west as they set, drew the marching columns some seven degrees off their route so that they were approaching the enemy lines in slight echelon with the Highlanders ahead; but to offset this disadvantage nature had supplied a westerly wind, which took the sounds of the tramping men away back into the desert.

With just over 200 yards still separating the Camerons from the first line of defence, the right wing on the far side of the marching divisions bumped a cavalry picket who fired on them, and as a scattered fusillade followed, a bugle sounded the alarm in front.

The General dismounted and ran forward to peer through the

growing but still dim light, a hostile shell screeched overhead to bury itself between him and his horse, the enemy cavalry picket galloped across in front and then raced off into the morning mist – and with the need for silence at last gone, barked orders and bugle calls rang out all around, followed by a myriad clicks as bayonets slotted home.

To the left the Highlanders and to the right the Irish and the English broke into a run and surged forward towards the sandheaps and the main defensive ditch, ten feet wide and six feet deep, while behind them the Guards – Grenadiers, Coldstream and Scots – tore open their pouches and loaded their rifles, carried empty so far in pursuit of the order for total silence. Solid ranks, crested with steel, swept forward on to the black mounds under a lilac sky. A line of fire sparkled along the top of the mounds, but in their frenzy the defenders fired high, and bullets and balls whined out into the desert to furrow the distant sand-drifts.

The Highlanders were first into the ditch, and first out, cheering and shouting, climbing on one another's shoulders to reach the top and charge the first defence line, gun-butt and bayonet at work in desperate hand-to-hand battle wherever they found the white-clad enemy standing. Enfiladed from redoubts, the Scotsmen still in the ditch rushed or climbed to the loop-holes, thrusting in with bayonet and sword while the first of their comrades to reach the top swung back into the shelters to club or cut the gunners to the ground, thus releasing the main attack.

A hundred yards further on they found another line of entrenchments from which the defenders from the first line who had dropped back and now recovered from the first shock of battle were firing, quite coolly and deliberately, picking off the now-tiring Highlanders. As the front line melted into the ground, the second line wavered – but as they did so their pipers at last got wind into the bags and *The March of the Cameron Men* wailed out, to be followed by the skirl of Irish pipes from the north as the right-hand division, held back by the error in navigation, stormed into the attack.

They had further to go but found a comparatively soft spot in the line, and excitement and some degree of desperation was now affecting the Egyptian infantry and gunners (though the Sudanese troops among them fought with an exemplary steadiness) and the shots flew high. With few casualties, Royal Marines and Royal Irish Fusiliers charged down along the line of the second entrenchments and the York and Lancasters mopped up with bayonet and club behind them. The artillery, having found their own separate ways across the main ditch, opened fire, to be joined almost immediately by the batteries of their mounted brothers to the north, while to the south the Indian Brigade, having cleared the southern bank of the canal, crossed it and with their lancers well in front flung themselves against the unprotected Egyptian flank.

And it was at this moment that the Household Brigade, lost for twenty minutes out on the right wing, rode in from the north over the Egyptian guns in a thunderous cascade of heavy horses and gigantic men, to turn what had been until then an orderly and well-fought withdrawal into a disorganised rout.

The Battle of Tel el Kebir was all over in thirty-five minutes. That very model of a modern Major-General, Sir Garnet Wolseley – small, neat and highly professional – had won yet another small, neat and highly professional victory at the end of a well-conducted campaign, and by the following day the first British troops were in Cairo. Arabi Pasha and his chief lieutenant surrendered without further ado, the Egyptian Army quietly dispersed homeward to take up their pathetic, poverty-stricken civilian lives again, and Wolseley and his staff moved into the Abdin Palace. The following day, the General sent a message to London: 'The war in Egypt is over; send no more men from England.'

But in the event, many more men did come out and the British were in Egypt to stay. Although the Liberal Government in general and Mr Gladstone in particular were delighted with General Wolseley's message *in toto*, the second part was to receive little practical application.

The campaign had been fought in order to ensure that the interest on the vast Egyptian national debt of £10,000,000 was paid to the international bondholders, and for that to be possible it quickly became obvious to European eyes that Egypt's administration must be placed upon a far more practical basis. Lord Dufferin arrived as High Commissioner to report upon the entire situation, Sir Evelyn Baring came out as British Agent and Consul-General, Sir Evelyn Wood arrived to organise a new 4,000-strong Egyptian Army, to be officered in the main by British gazetted regulars with himself as Sirdar or Commander-in-Chief. And in order to maintain the good order and discipline considered essential while these reforms were being carried out, a British Army of Occupation of some 14,000 men settled down in barracks between Suez and the Nile.

Long before it could be felt that their presence there was unnecessary the fanatical followers of the Mahdi in the south rose in revolution, and the ensuing assassination of General Gordon in Khartoum in 1885 resulted firstly in the increase of the British forces and then in the launching of relief columns and the general pacification of the Sudan, all of which kept more and more British troops quartered in Egypt during the closing years of the nineteenth century.

After the Sudan was pacified, the regiments stayed because they might be needed in the troubles down in the Transvaal, and when the Boer Wars were over they stayed because the events of the past few decades had demonstrated both the importance and the convenience to Britain of control of the eastern Mediterranean in respect of her communications with India and Australasia. As Lord Palmerston had put it many years before:

> We do not want Egypt or wish it for ourselves any more than any rational man with an estate in the north of England and a residence in the south would have wanted to possess the inns on the North Road. All he would want would have been that the inns should be well-kept, always accessible, and furnishing him, when he came, with mutton chops and post horses.

The possibility that the apparently obsequious, invariably subservient, frequently devious and generally poverty-stricken Egyptians might object to their country being regarded as a hostelry, however convenient and well-managed, seems rarely to have occurred to the inheritors of a solidly Victorian tradition, who shouldered their responsibilities firmly and regarded the growing evidence of their unpopularity with resignation and national phlegm.

And there was always, of course, the matter of the Suez Canal, of which Britain had been a bitter opponent until it was built, but a large shareholder increasingly insistent upon control ever since. If Lord Palmerston had not wanted Egypt, he and his successors were equally clear that no one else should have it, and it was a national axiom that the vital link with India and the southern dominions must always remain under British control.

This became even more evident in 1914 when the passage of the canal became essential for the transport of Australian and Indian troops to France, although in the event fewer Australians or Indians used it to reach the Western Front than British troops sent in the opposite direction to deal with the proliferation of troubles which then ensued (though these were by no means entirely the fault of the Egyptians). By 1918, as a result of the Middle East campaigns, a huge British military base had been built up.

Nevertheless, after prolonged – and often caustic – discussion, the British protectorate of Egypt ended on February 28th, 1922, Egypt being declared an independent sovereign state, with just four matters reserved to the British Government until agreement could be reached upon them: the security of British communications with her Empire, the defence of Egypt itself, the protection of foreign interests and minorities in Egypt, and control of the Sudan.

But as the years between the wars went by, the Royal Air Force grew in size, parts of the British Army became mechanised, and following that astonishing era of maritime revolution inspired by Lord Fisher during the turbulent 1900s, the Royal Navy stopped using coal and relied entirely upon oil-fired turbines. All of this meant that without the products of the Mosul oilfields at the head of the Persian Gulf, Britain would be powerless to wage war.

Egypt thereby became the western shield of an area of vital importance to Britain, especially as her own western border with Libya was demarcated by a 200-mile triple fence supported on five-foot metal stakes embedded in concrete and closely woven with barbed wire, erected by the Italians as security for their Libyan empire. And although Italy had fought alongside Britain in the First World War, it had become evident by the late 1930s that her sympathies would lie initially elsewhere in the event of a second.

Thus, early in September 1939 a British official found himself explaining to King Farouk (younger, slimmer and much better-looking than he is now remembered) that British control of Egypt would now have to be both retained and increased until the Axis had been defeated.

'Oh, all right!' replied the King, moodily. 'But when it's all over, for God's sake *lay down the white man's burden, and Go!*'

1 · The First Adversaries

Upon the outbreak of war, the responsibilities of the Commander-in-Chief, Middle East, had been substantially increased. From the day of his appointment in August 1939, General Sir Archibald Wavell had commanded all British land forces in Egypt, the Sudan, Palestine, Transjordan and Cyprus, but when Britain's ultimatum to Hitler ran out on September 3rd the Army formations in British Somaliland, Aden, Iraq and along the shores of the Persian Gulf also came under his command. The area for which he had thereby accepted military responsibility thus measured some 1,800 miles by 2,000 and included nine different countries in two continents.

Moreover, in the event of actual armed conflict taking place in the area – probably against Italy and possibly against Germany – troops stationed in Kenya would have to be involved in actions under his command, as would South African troops coming up from the other end of the continent – with, of course, the consent and approval of the South African Government.

There were other governments and governmental authorities as well from whom Wavell would have to secure co-operation, if not 'consent and approval'. His instructions were that he must keep in 'close touch and sympathy' with the rulers of Egypt and Iraq; with the High Commissioner for Palestine and Transjordan and the Governor-General of the Sudan; with the Governors of Cyprus, Aden and British Somaliland, the Political Resident in the Persian Gulf, the British Ambassadors in Cairo, Baghdad, Istanbul, and Athens, together with the chief representatives of Britain's allies adjoining his area of command. As at that time France was Britain's chief ally, this meant that he must on all matters of military significance consult the French military commanders in Algeria and Tunisia, in Syria and the Lebanon, in French Somaliland and quite possibly in French Equatorial Africa.

More practically, he had also to work closely with the Royal Naval Commanders-in-Chief in the Mediterranean and the East Indies, and with the Air Officer Commanding-in-Chief, Middle East.

As the general shortage of military equipment with which Great Britain faced the outbreak of war precluded the allocation of a personal aircraft to anyone, however exalted his rank or extensive his responsibilities, it can be seen that whoever fulfilled the duties of General Officer Commanding-in-Chief in the Middle East would need to be a remarkable man. Fortunately for Britain, he was.

General Sir Archibald Percival Wavell was fifty-six years of age when he arrived in Cairo to set up his Headquarters (with a staff of five in addition to his A.D.C.) and he had spent his life in the military world. The only son of an officer in the Norfolk Regiment, he had been commissioned at the age of eighteen into the Black Watch and had seen almost immediate service in South Africa and then on the north-west frontier of India. He had applied to go on the Staff College course at Camberley and after completing it had spent a year in Russia learning the language. He had already passed professional examinations in French, Urdu and Pushtu.

When the First World War broke out, Acting Captain Wavell had managed to evade the pressure to remain safely on the Staff until after the Second Battle of Ypres in 1915, during which he won the Military Cross and lost his left eye doing so. After convalescence, he spent two years shuttling between Russia, where he was sent to report on the probability of continued Russian participation in the conflict, and G.H.Q. France where he spent what he later described as the 'dullest ten months' of his life – before being sent out to the Middle East to join the staff of General Allenby. As a result of this, he took part alongside Colonel T. E. Lawrence in the entry into Jerusalem and the advance to Damascus, ending in 1918 with a brigadier-general's appointment and a clear understanding of the qualities of generalship which had enabled Allenby to win one of the most notable victories of that war. Wavell wrote later:

> In less than six weeks Allenby's army had captured 75,000 prisoners and 360 guns, and had moved its front forward 350 miles. Its own casualty list had been little over 5,000. The most advanced troops, the 5th Cavalry Division, had actually covered some 550 miles in the thirty-eight days from the breaking of the line to the occupation of Aleppo. The greatest exploit in history of horsed cavalry, and possibly their last success on a large scale, had ended within a short distance of the battlefield of Issus (333 B.C.), where Alexander the Great first showed how battles could be won by bold and well-handled horsemen.[1]

Peace brought a year's regimental duty with his beloved Black Watch (as a major) followed almost inexorably by another nine years' progression up the ladder of Staff promotion. The Adjutant-General's Department, the Directorate of Military Operations, the

Headquarters of the 3rd Infantry Division knew him well and appreciated his services, and then in 1930 he had been given command of an experimental infantry brigade at Aldershot. Three years later he had been promoted to Major-General, in 1935 he commanded an infantry division at Aldershot and in 1938 as a Lieutenant-General he was G.O.C.-in-C. Southern Command, United Kingdom. His appointment to the Middle East in August 1939 had been accompanied by promotion to full General.

So much for the bones of his military career. But a man capable of shouldering the enormous burdens which command of Britain's armies in the Middle East would entail required elements of greatness not revealed by a catalogue of appointments. Although he was perfectly prepared to model his outward behaviour along the lines of obdurate taciturnity which had come to be expected of British generals since Haig had set the pattern, Wavell's was a many-faceted character which presented all who knew him with considerable surprises.

Later, during one of the more crucial periods of the war, he astonished Winston Churchill with the casual announcement that during what leisure time he had he was editing a book of poems, and during the second half of the war he organised and judged a poetry competition for men in his command. And this was not, in Wavell's particular pattern of character, anything greatly to be marvelled at. 'Music, mystery and magic are the essence of the highest poetry,' he was to write – and the second and third of these qualities he also considered essential for successful military command.

He took a refreshingly caustic view of his profession, despite his own deep interest in it. In a letter to a fellow officer, he wrote:

The main ethical objection to war for intelligent people is that it is so deplorably dull and usually so inefficiently run. 'I see no reason why the human race, so inefficient in matters of peace, should suddenly become efficient in time of war.' I've forgotten where I saw that but it has always seemed to me that most people seeing the muddles of war forget the muddles of peace and the general inefficiency of the human race in ordering its affairs. War is a wasteful, boring, muddled affair; and people of fine intelligence either resign themselves to it or fret badly, especially if they are near the heart of things and can see matters which ought to be done, or done better, and cannot contrive to get them set right.[2]

Humour, robustness and sound common sense were the qualities which sustained him through life, and they were evident in everything he did – in the solidity of his stance as he watched his troops

in training, in the lines which furrowed his brow and the corners of
his eyes as he spoke, in the wry iconoclasm of the advice he gave.

I would give you a word of warning on the so-called principles
of war, as laid down in Field Service Regulations.

For heaven's sake don't treat those as holy writ, like the Ten
Commandments, to be learned by heart, and as having by their
repetition some magic, like the incantations of savage priests.
They are merely a set of common-sense maxims, like 'cut your
coat according to your cloth,' 'a rolling stone gathers no moss,'
'honesty is the best policy,' and so forth. Those in F.S.R. are not
necessarily complete or the best. They omit for instance the
importance of information in war. Clausewitz has a different set,
so has Foch, so have other military writers. They are all simply
common sense, and are instinctive to the properly trained
soldier . . .

Lastly, I do advise you to study the human side of military
history, which is not a matter of cold-blooded formulas or
diagrams, or nursery-book principles such as:

Be good and you will be happy.

Be mobile and you will be victorious.

Interior lines at night are the general's delight.

Exterior lines in the morning are the general's warning, and so
on.

To learn that Napoleon in 1796 with 20,000 men beat combined
forces of 30,000 by something called 'economy of force' or
'operating on interior lines' is a mere waste of time. If you can
understand how a young, unknown man inspired a half-starved,
ragged, rather Bolshie crowd; how he filled their bellies; how he
out-marched, outwitted, out-bluffed and defeated men who had
studied war all their lives and waged it according to the textbooks
of the time, you will have learnt something worth knowing. But
you won't get it from crammers' books . . .

But as a final word, I suggest you put this ideal of an infantryman
before you:

Quick-footed, quick-minded and, as far as possible, light-
hearted . . .[3]

Here, it was evident, was none of the prodigal habit of mind
which had led to the murderous holocausts in France of the First
World War, and would again in Russia in the Second. The new
Commander-in-Chief, Middle East, was well aware of the value of
each human life, and of the shortage of trained soldiers, sailors and
airmen with which Britain faced perhaps the greatest trials in her
long and arduous history.

This was an aspect of affairs which in any case was daily confronting him, for despite the crucial importance of his own command, he had hardly enough troops to police it, let alone defend it from attack. One incomplete and not fully trained armoured formation, twenty-one infantry battalions, two regiments of horsed cavalry, four regiments of artillery with sixty-four field guns, forty-eight anti-tank guns and eight anti-aircraft guns made up the force immediately under his command, while down in the Sudan there were three more infantry battalions and twenty companies of the Sudan Defence Force. In British Somaliland was the Sudan Camel Corps of 500 men, in Kenya were two brigades of the King's African Rifles (native troops officered by British regulars) and two light batteries, while at Aden there were two Indian battalions of garrison troops.

So far as his allies were concerned, there were apparently some 5,000 native troops in French Somaliland under the experienced command of Colonel Legentilhomme, an expeditionary force of three newly raised divisions and some 40,000 troops engaged on frontier defences and tribal control in Syria and the Lebanon under the veteran Général Weygand, while to the west in Tunisia under Général Noguès were eight divisions – six infantry, one fortress and one light cavalry. But most of these, Wavell considered, might well be too occupied with their own problems to be able to spare him much support in time of emergency, despite the politicians' promises.

As for the forces ranged against him, despite inter-war financial stringency in intelligence matters and a degree of disapproval of spying in Italian territories by his political masters (in view of the danger of upsetting Mussolini), interception of political and military wireless traffic combined with a quite sophisticated cryptanalytical organisation had been sufficient to provide him with some relevant figures.

According to these, there were nine Italian divisions in Tripolitania facing Général Noguès's force, and five divisions in Cyrenaica in a position to threaten Egypt and the theatre of Wavell's most immediate attention. In the area encompassing Eritrea, Italian Somaliland and the recently conquered Ethiopia, there were about a quarter of a million troops under command of the Duke of Aosta, equipped with some 400 field and mountain guns, 200 light tanks and about 100 armoured cars. There were also in both Cyrenaica and in the Italian East African Empire many thousands of colonists, a large proportion of whom might well be called to arms if and when hostilities began.

Thus, the 40,000 British and native troops under his own command appeared to be rather neatly sandwiched between

250,000 enemy troops on the eastern side and 70,000 on the western, with an extra 122,000 available to join in from the Tunisian border if French attention became engaged elsewhere. Whatever his opinion of the quality of the opposition, against such odds Wavell had no choice but to press as hard as possible for reinforcements – which, to be fair to them, the Government were as anxious to give as he was to receive. But requirements in 1939 and early 1940 were obviously most urgent in France.

None the less, during the winter of 1939/1940, help did arrive. By spring 1940 two brigades of the 4th Indian Division had arrived with much of their artillery, New Zealand provided an infantry brigade, a machine-gun battalion, a field regiment of artillery and the best part of a cavalry regiment, while Australia had sent two infantry brigades, two regiments of field artillery and some divisional troops. From the United Kingdom had come the 1st Cavalry Division complete with most of its horses but with a considerable Territorial Army element, which was hastily training in Palestine to take over the duties of the regular cavalry already stationed there.

Even this increase in numbers, however, made little apparent difference to the enormous disparity between his own forces and those ranged against him; and if he suspected that his own regular and volunteer force might, man for man, possess more military ardour and skill than the conscript Italian and Libyan levies across the frontiers, this was not a factor upon which he might count until it had been demonstrated.

Something else would be required, something which T. E. Lawrence had called 'the irrational tenth . . . like the kingfisher flashing across the pool . . . that is the test of generals.'

Bluff would certainly have to be part of it, as would imagination and audacity.

But even these qualities would be of little avail without a sound base from which to operate, a solid administrative structure from which to draw support for exploitation of success, or protection if things went wrong.

Before Wavell had arrived, the senior officer commanding British troops in Egypt was Lieutenant-General H. Maitland Wilson, a soldier of wide experience, of calm and placid appearance which, however, masked considerable energy and determined attitudes on many matters, and so vast a bulk as to have earned him fairly early in his career the soubriquet 'Jumbo'. He had been appointed in the early summer of 1939, leaving Britain, as he later rather sadly recorded, 'on the day of the Ascot Gold Cup'.

His instructions had been to make an examination of the potential defences of the area under his command, and to do what was necessary to build them up – a task he quickly found comparable to a combination of those allocated to Hercules and the Children of Israel.

There was, for instance, the matter of some important roads which under an Anglo-Egyptian treaty signed in 1936 should by now have been completed. Investigations revealed a twenty-mile gap in the road between Alexandria and the forward advance base of Mersa Matruh (though the rail-track – single line – had been completed during the emergency created by the Italian invasion of Ethiopia in 1935) while those roads intended to link the Canal with Cairo and Alexandria were virtually non-existent. So, also, was the road across the Sinai Desert linking Egypt with the British protectorate of Palestine, which would obviously be needed to carry fast and heavy reinforcement traffic in the event of action on either the southern or the western front.

Another matter was that of co-operation in the event of war between the British and Egyptian Armies, also provided for in the 1936 treaty. Although at first sight much seemed to have been achieved, examination revealed some disturbing aspects. For example, although the Egyptian anti-aircraft artillery and searchlight batteries in the Delta appeared well equipped and of sound if not high morale – as did the infantry and artillery units – those units patrolling the Libyan Frontier or occupying the frontier posts, and thus most likely to meet the enemy at the outset of any hostilities, seemed curiously uninterested in their work.

It did not take long for Wilson to find out why. Serving out in the desert, the Egyptian High Command explained with an air of sweet reasonableness, was less expensive than serving in Cairo or Alexandria – so the Sudanese soldiers and especially the Egyptian officers engaged on border duties were paid less than when serving nearer the delights of home; indeed officers were generally posted to such services as a result of some social or economic misdemeanour. Wilson protested to the somewhat puzzled Army Chief of Staff, Azziz el Mashri Pasha, but six months later heard that yet another young officer unfortunate enough to be overheard making a tactless remark about one of his seniors had been posted to Williams Pass, an important post north-west of Siwa. It was obviously going to take some time for old customs to be changed.

But by no means all the problems facing Wilson were of Egyptian responsibility. Little remained of the huge military bases of 1918, for the 1922 agreement with Egypt had resulted in the reduction of British military presence in the country by over 75 per cent, and since then governmental parsimony on defence matters had reduced the accommodation, the administration and training facilities, even the transport and weaponry for what remained, to an absolute minimum. It all had to be built up again, and at first by inexperienced hands. When the first bulk stores arrived there was very limited storage capacity in which to house and protect them; when transport and trucks arrived they invariably had to be modified for use in the desert as the specifications to which they had been manufactured had been based upon European conditions.

Tank tracks designed for English roads or rough ploughland cracked and split on the desert rubble; dust clogged air-intakes, and in lorry radiators the precious water boiled away under a combination of high temperatures and soft 'going' over sand where the roads petered out; and in the event of sufficient armour and transport to defeat an enemy eventually becoming available, where was the petrol to be stored?

Where were the workshops for repair and maintenance? Where were the skilled men to carry out the maintenance? Where were the barracks for the men to live in, the messes and canteens where they would eat and drink, the stores for them to use, the food for them to eat, the doctors to treat them when they got sick, the hospitals and staff to look after them, the chaplains to bury them if they died? And this was just the base staff.

Where were the replacements for the tanks when they broke up, wore out or were wrecked in battle? Where were the ammunition dumps? Where were the artillery parks? Where was the transport to bring the infantry to the front and sustain it while it was there? Where were the bricks, the cement, the asbestos sheets, the beds, the bedding, the tentage, the oil, the petrol, the gelignite, the tools, the pipes, the plumbing, the roadmaking equipment, the workshop plant, the cargo-handling plant at Port Said, Alexandria and Suez? The cargo-handling plant for unloading bigger and better cargo-handling plant at Port Said, Alexandria and Suez?

And above all, where was water and how could it be brought to where it was needed?

All Egypt's water seemed at first glance to come from the Nile; undrinkable, not even safe to wash in. Water-purification plant was needed; men to run water-purification plant; men to guard men running water-purification plant. Men and equipment to sink wells in the forward areas; surveyors to find the places to sink the wells; equipment for the surveyors to find the wells; pumps to pump the water out when it was found; pipes to pipe the water even further forward when it had been purified.

General Wilson was by no means the first to find that the desert was the tactician's paradise but the quartermaster's hell – but it was while he was coping with and solving many of the consequent problems that war against Germany was declared. Within a week he was instructed by his new Commander-in-Chief first to make preparations to receive into Egypt another six divisions, and secondly to ensure that everyone on his staff worked henceforward on the assumption that the Allies would be at war with Italy within six months.

Thirdly, Wilson was to have plans drawn up for the invasion of Libya, the capture of both Bardia at the northern end of the frontier Wire and Jarabub 200 miles to the south, with a corps consisting of one armoured and two infantry divisions. He was also to look into the possibilities of raising, training and putting to good use a specially chosen body of troops to be transported by air and possibly dropped into action by parachute – for which, of course, he would additionally require aircraft and parachutes.

The practice which 'Jumbo' Wilson had recently acquired in building bricks without straw was apparently to be put to good use.

If the two men with the greatest responsibilities for safeguarding British interests in the Middle East were deeply worried by the realities with which they were faced (and, needless to say, neither gave the slightest outward sign of doubt or hesitation) most of the troops they commanded felt no such qualms. Few in number they might have been and well aware that parsimony on the part of the British public had left them acutely short of up-to-date arms and equipment – but they were professionals, used to soldiering in rough, exacting conditions, and a large proportion of them were quite accustomed to the whine of the sniper's bullet above their heads, the sudden violent explosion of land-mine or bomb.

This was still part of the age when, to use the most apt phrase of a leading American historian, Joseph Lehmann, 'the blood never dried on the British Empire' – and a great deal of it was British blood. Since Easter 1936, British troops in Palestine had been engaged in suppressing the Arab rebellion, policing the roads, searching villages, chasing guerrilla bands and being in turn ambushed, shot at and blown up by them. Many men under General Wilson's command wore campaign ribbons and a number of them had quite recently won decorations for bravery.

And the Arabs were by no means the only enemy against whom some of these men had fought. To the tribes of the north-west frontier of India intermittent warfare against the British (and one another) was part of an accepted way of life, and for a hundred years British battalions had marched and counter-marched, manned pickets, been sniped at by Mahsuds and Afridis, and kept watch and ward from the Khyber Pass to Baluchistan. The 1st Battalion Hampshire Regiment, for instance, had gained the Indian General Service Medal with clasp 'N.W. Frontier 1935', followed by a second with clasp 'N.W. Frontier 1935–1937' – and it was then posted to Palestine where it gained yet another campaign medal; and these were not awarded just for being in the area, they were earned in action by the regiments concerned.

British regular troops of the 1930s signed on for a minimum of seven years 'with the colours' followed by five years on the reserve, but many of them remained with their battalions for much longer, making a lifetime career of soldiering. From these 'long-service' men came the majority of the warrant officers and senior N.C.O.s, and many of these came from regimental families whose names appeared on the rolls of their chosen battalion for periods going back well into the last century. For them, the reason for joining the Army was obvious; for many others in the 1930s it had been the sole alternative to unemployment, and although they may not at first have shown much enthusiasm for the military life, a surprisingly large number remained with the colours even when they might have successfully returned to 'civvy street'.

Yet others had joined the Army because they had believed the recruiting posters, and they stayed in it because the posters had not lied. They 'saw the world', or at least more of it than if they had remained at home, and quite often they had the adventure and excitement that was promised. One young man in the early 1930s who had no wish to become part of his father's hairdressing business ran away and joined a famous cavalry regiment. Within six months he had taken part in a cavalry charge against Afghan tribesmen, wielding a sabre to some effect, and shortly after that he was engaged in the far more humanitarian but just as dangerous task of pulling out survivors of the disastrous Quetta earthquake of 1935. At no time did he feel the slightest regret at his decision to abandon the barber's calling.

Above all, the British Regular Army in the 1930s offered opportunity for sport – football, both soccer and rugger, hockey, cricket, swimming if the station was by the sea, shooting, running, and for the cavalry regiments riding, or perhaps learning to drive a motor vehicle, an accomplishment not, in those days, quite so common as it has since become. Many people have judged that the British Army's dedication to sport was at the expense of profession-alism, but any lack of military efficiency in the late 1930s was due as much to lack of equipment as to any other factor. The Army would willingly have trained with tanks and guns had they been available; in 1939, the anti-tank guns of at least one regular battalion in England were still represented on exercises by green and white flags.

In any case, the physical toughness and teamwork engendered by playing rugby football on a sand-covered, rock-hard pitch on the borders of Afghanistan or in the Western Desert were not qualities which would be found useless in the days to come.

And if the life led by the 'other ranks' was strenuous, rarely dull and often exciting, for the officers there was the added bonus of a social life and a degree of luxury varying with the regiment and with the size of private income available to augment their pay. In 1935 a subaltern's pay was £230 a year (and a major-general's £1,100) and the mandatory expenses of a commission necessitated at least a parental allowance to most young officers. As Correlli Barnett put it so pungently, 'Nothing could have suited the British public better than an army in which it did not have to serve, officered by a narrow clique of men of private means who did not demand a living salary.'

To a great extent the officers came from middle or upper classes (although, as always in the British Army, there were the occasional exceptions who had risen through the ranks) and they had all gone through the mill of Sandhurst or Woolwich; and for the infantry and cavalry officers, Sandhurst had been a great leveller in which the sons of royalty were subject to just the same scarifying and often humiliating treatment at the hands of drill sergeants as the poorest ex-Grammar school boy. Sandhurst may not have taught them a great deal of military law or history – though the opportunities to learn about such matters were there for those who wished to take advantage of them – but it did expose them to the appraising eyes of their coevals with whom, one day, they would be facing battle.

Sandhurst also gave them, though not as part of the academic curriculum, some idea of the violence in which they might find themselves embroiled as a result of their choice of career. The tales of room-wrecking, of tarring and feathering of unpopular cadets, of setting fire to shirt-tails (Field Marshal Montgomery was responsible for one such episode during his time at Sandhurst) are legion, and occasionally news of some particularly flagrant piece of hooliganism would reach the outside world. John Masters has told of one episode in his autobiographical *Bugles and a Tiger*:

In the previous affair a couple of hundred cadets had battled up and down the corridors that lay between two companies' quarters, for the space of an hour or so. Brass knuckle-dusters, loaded canes, chairlegs, and practically any other weapon that came to hand had been used; two cadets were injured for life, and thousands of pounds' worth of damage was done. News of this episode reached the newspapers, and people asked what the authorities were about to permit such hooliganism.

It was a good question. I do not think any good answer was given in public. The answer, though satisfactory to realists, might not have been thought so by the parents of the injured cadets. That answer was: 'War is a dirty business, and we are training these young men for war; we are not running a kindergarten; we do not intend to snoop around seeing whether the cadets treat one another like Little Lord Fauntleroys; we have learned that a wild young man can learn wisdom as he grows older – if he survives – but a spiritless young man cannot learn the dash that wins battles. And, finally, we believe that a man's contemporaries are his fairest judges.'[4]

Thus, the officers of the regular British regiments in the Middle East as war came ever nearer during the late 1930s shared in the main one important formatory experience, had all been exposed to influences likely to shape them towards a common attitude of mind, and those who were still with their regiments or battalions after four or five years – for it was quite easy for an officer to resign his commission – were there because they liked the life, physically hard and demanding though it often was.

One lesson which they had all learned – and their instructors and senior officers made quite certain that they understood it thoroughly – was that Britain did not possess, as had at one time been believed, an unlimited supply of soldiers' lives upon which they could draw. Not only was the health and well-being of every man committed to their care in peacetime a solemn responsibility, but in any future war there were to be no more holocausts such as the British Army had suffered on the Somme or at Passchendaele. From this it followed that the best way a young officer could ensure that the lives of his men – and his own, come to that – were not wasted, was to see that they were well trained, and no thought of his own social superiority, more expensive education or more patrician antecedents must be allowed to interfere with this aim.

Thus the gap which had divided officers from other ranks right up to the First World War was, by the outbreak of the Second, if not entirely bridged, at least considerably narrowed. Although up to the time of mechanisation of the cavalry units – and some famous regiments did not begin this until 1938 – officers merely oversaw the grooming of the horses, the polishing of the saddlery, the care and maintenance of stable equipment, once they became part of a tank crew they 'mucked in', as the saying went, as able to clean an oil filter or lift a cylinder head as the drivers, their overalls as oil-stained, their hands as filthy. In the field, they were to share guard with their crews, eat with them and if they rarely actually helped prepare the food, this would generally be passed off as because they weren't very good at it.

What a number of them were becoming quite good at, however, was finding their way around the desert, and this was an art which in those days was developed by very few people.

Very little of what was to become known as the Western Desert – originally just the Egyptian Desert west of the Nile but in due course usage extended the term to cover an extra 150 miles west as far as Gazala – bears much relation to the romantic view of the desert, the Hollywood scenery of wind-formed sand-dunes with occasional oases fringed with palm. Areas such as these do exist, in the Nile Valley, along the coastal plain bordering the Mediterranean and in the vast sand seas to the south where the dunes are sculpted into fantastic shapes, but the greater part of the area is a plateau standing on average some 500 feet above sea level, barren, rubble- and boulder-strewn, dark brown in colour, occasionally dotted with scrub and, at first sight, flat.

It was upon this plateau that, in the summer of 1935 as a response to Mussolini's invasion of Abyssinia, a British 'Mobile Force' formed from the Cairo Cavalry Brigade began its first tentative attempts at desert manoeuvres, and the fact that its sardonic participants quickly redubbed it the 'Immobile Farce' was sufficient reflection upon its need for more realistic training and much more practice. This, its commanders quickly and systematically organised, and within the limits imposed by the chronic shortage of equipment and even of petrol or spare parts for the vehicles, soon achieved remarkable results.

At the beginning of 1935, it had taken three and a half days of worry, frustration and bad temper for one squadron of the 11th Hussars to make a 200-mile journey from Cairo to the oasis of Baharia. Punctures, soft sand in which the lorries buried themselves to their axles, broken springs and uncertainty of navigation had all helped to make the trip a nightmare, and they had needed two days for servicing and reappraisal before they felt confident enough to begin the trip home. But by the following November they were driving their Rolls-Royce armoured cars ('1920–24 pattern') quite confidently from Mersa Matruh across the coastal plain, up the Escarpment to the plateau, on to the Siwa Oasis and back again, all within three days.

In the training exercises which from then on became the programme for all the mechanised units of the Cairo Cavalry Brigade, both officers and men learned to dispense with even the faintly marked tracks which did exist and to find their way across the featureless wastes by stars, sun and compass, plus a combination of keen observation and good memory which made up such a crucial part of what became known as 'desert sense'. They learned to live in the desert.

They learned that it is not flat. They learned to find cover for men and guns in the slightest undulations, they learned to recognise and take advantage of 'hull-down' positions for tanks behind dunes from which only their turrets would be visible to the enemy; they learned that the scrub patches gave concealment for machine-gun or observation posts, and from these they learned to judge what constituted reality and what was more likely to be mirage.

A great deal of their training was devoted to movement, and here the techniques of desert driving were paramount. Although the 'going' – a word which was to become of supreme importance during the years to come – was generally good for both wheeled and tracked vehicles on the plateau, there were many traps for the inexperienced or unwary. With a burning sun overhead it was difficult to see a sudden hollow down which the vehicle would drop at the cost of broken springs; sharp rocks would rip tyres, a boulder not seen until too late could buckle a wheel or crack a sump. For the tracked vehicles there were often large and unavoidable areas strewn with rocks and studded with outcrops which strained their springs and ruined their tracks; for the wheeled vehicles, the constant hazard of deep and soft sand in which the wheels quickly became embedded to the axles, necessitating hours of 'unsticking' with spades and sandmats, and often of unloading the stores and equipment carried and reloading when the vehicle was clear.

Above all, the squadrons learned to conserve water, food and petrol in the face of the basic, unalterable fact that everything they needed for existence – or would need for battle – had to be taken with them. The desert supplied nothing but an arena.

However, such training among separate units, even with the friendly rivalry and traditional co-operation which existed between several of them, would not serve to weld them all into a military formation capable of taking the field in anything but a skirmishing role. It took the Munich crisis to begin a process which would bring this about.

Major-General Percy Cleghorn Stanley Hobart, D.S.O., M.C., had been appointed Director of Military Training at the War Office in 1937, a post he had taken up with some reluctance as he was well aware that those with whom he would have to work most closely disapproved of his appointment and distrusted what they knew of his ideas. They believed, with some justification, that he was a 'tank fanatic', and thought this meant that he saw tanks as the only essential weapons, 'tank warfare' as the only course of future battles, and considered tank units capable of winning wars without the assistance of other arms.

His critics were, in fact, mistaken in this suspicion, for Hobart was well aware of the necessity for both infantry and artillery on the field of battle, and he had far more advanced ideas for air co-operation above it than they had; but his was an abrasive, abrupt and occasionally violently argumentative personality, and those senior officers who shared none of his enthusiasms and preferred a quiet life – and there was a large number of them – wished to have as little as possible to do with him. In this they were generally successful, as he did not suffer those who disagreed with him gladly, believing that he had sound precedent for his attitude.

Pat Hobart, as his friends called him (he was also widely known, but rarely addressed in the army, as 'Hobo'), had joined the Army as a Royal Engineer, risen to the rank of Brevet Major by the end of the First World War during which he had served in France both in the trenches and on the Staff, and in Mesopotamia where he had won his D.S.O., been wounded and spent an uncomfortable three days as a prisoner of the Turks. At the time of the Armistice he was G.S.O.2 (General Staff Officer, second grade) to the 53rd Division in Jerusalem, and the despondent subject of a tale which was to dog him through the remainder of his military career and, indeed, in the end find place in his entry in the *Dictionary of National Biography*.

This was to the effect that during September 1918 while acting as Staff Officer with the 8th Brigade, he had taken the blind-eye technique somewhat too far. In the words of his biographer, Kenneth Macksey:

> At one vital moment, when his brigadier wished to make a last-minute change of plan before an attack, Hobart refused to pass the order and made doubly sure it would not be sent by seizing possession of the telephone until the attack had gone successfully ahead to the original plan. It is said that this incident brought his association with 8th Brigade to an end, and the purists will agree, with justification, that for a staff officer to defy his commander is poison to the roots of discipline and confidence.[5]

That there may have been more than a vestige of truth in the tale is supported by advice given to the young Lieutenant Michael Carver many years later. 'The secret of success in the Army', Hobart said, 'is to be sufficiently insubordinate, and the key word is *sufficiently*.'

But whatever his attitude to the conventions of the military world, the lesson which had been burned into his mind throughout the welter of the First World War battlefields had been the values of mobility and of the element of surprise that mobility gives. With these in mind he had transferred in 1923 to the Tank Corps, and during the following years been second-in-command of the 4th Battalion, Royal Tank Corps, and commanding officer of the 2nd Battalion.

In 1933 he became Inspector of the Royal Tank Corps and a year later commanded the Tank Brigade in the annual manoeuvres – a task to which he had looked forward with immense enthusiasm but which, for reasons not unconnected with his personality, ended in near disaster. Kenneth Macksey tells the story:

On its own the Tank Brigade did all that Hobart said could be done, but co-operation with other arms led into deep waters, even when the other arm happened to be the 7th Experimental Infantry Brigade commanded by his fellow armoured enthusiast, Lindsay. A combined exercise in September fell under the control of the G.O.C.-in-C. Southern Command, General Sir John Burnett-Stuart, a forward-looking soldier but one endowed with a destructive sense of humour ('anything for a laugh,' was Hobart's comment), and the chief umpire was Major-General A. P. Wavell.

For the first time mechanised artillery, a mechanised infantry brigade, an armoured car regiment and a tank brigade, were brought together, forming the earliest recognisable shape of an armoured division of the future – all under the command of Lindsay. But the exercise devised by Burnett-Stuart paid scant heed to the future: instead it concentrated on hampering the Tank Brigade as a fillip to the morale of the infantry – the very opposite of the spur of which they were in need. The embryo armoured division was launched on a raid along a circumscribed route towards a limited objective, tied to a schedule that gave insufficient time for the approach to be made at night. Furthermore, Lindsay was told he was not to incur heavy losses during the raid in order that the force might be preserved for use in another more important task later on. In consequence the enemy had only to block one route and the surprise inherent in the mobility of the force was sheered off.

Lindsay tried to solve an almost insuperable conundrum by expedients, not one of which satisfied Hobart or himself. Both were loath to split up the armour, both convinced that speed was essential and that, if possible, the direction of their thrust should be disguised. The sheer speed of their first plan, in which, as it happens, a battalion of tanks was grouped with the infantry, achieved complete success, by taking the 'enemy' and, above all, the umpires, by surprise, catching everybody unprepared and forcing the exercise controllers to adopt bogus measures (by means of an enforced halt for the tanks to allow the enemy infantry to get in position) to restore the situation.

From that moment the umpires under Wavell lost sight of reason in their effort to hamper the mobile force with measures outstripping subterfuge, and as the farce dragged on Hobart got angrier and refused to take part in what appeared to him to be a charade. The knowledge that officers' wives had been employed to guide the 'enemy' into position and that infantry had been told to lie in the road to prevent his tanks passing drove him to fury. This, to him, was a vital experiment upon which the future of armour depended – to make a mockery of it was a senseless waste of time and opportunity.[6]

It is easy to sympathise with Hobart, and easier still to see how his enemies – and these were accumulating rapidly as he hammered his way towards his objectives with no thought or consideration for anything or anyone in his path – made him appear childish and ill-tempered in their subsequent reports. 'Hobart's Tantrums' were the subject of many a barbed comment over cocktails during the months that followed.

Not only was Hobart unpopular, but so was the circle in which he moved and from whom he drew the sparks which set alight his own ideas. Both Captain Liddell Hart and Major-General J. F. C. Fuller had by now been edged by one means or another out of the Army, while within it other tank enthusiasts such as Charles Broad, 'Tim' Pile and G. M. Lindsay were being posted to appointments in which they could have no influence on military development. All three were promoted to major-general and then sent respectively to Administration at Aldershot, command of the 1st Anti-Aircraft Division, and an obscure appointment in Calcutta.

But Hobart was immovable, perhaps because the removing force did not have confidence to match his in their own irresistibility. In the meantime he continued his assaults on some of their more cherished traditions by acidly inquiring why tank soldiers should waste their time on infantry drill when it was their task to acquire the modern techniques needed to fight in machines. He could turn a good phrase, too, when he wished and 'military buffoonery' was an expression first accredited to his inspiration:

I dislike all this dressing up. This emotional intoxication produced by bagpipes and bearskins, and the hypnotism of rhythmical movement and mechanical drills. The glorification of the false side of war. This is not the gay flaunting of danger that I greatly admire. It is the deliberate inebriation to avoid seeing things as they are.[7]

In 1937 came a sudden upsetting of the conventional military coterie in Whitehall. Mr Leslie Hore-Belisha was appointed Secretary of State for War with a brief from Prime Minister Chamberlain to do what he could to make Britain ready for a confrontation which even Mr Chamberlain could see was a strong possibility, despite his discussion with Herr Hitler; and to the horror of the High Command Mr Hore-Belisha invited Captain Liddell Hart to become his personal adviser on military matters. One result of the ministerial appointment was that before the end of the year General Lord Gort became Chief of the Imperial General Staff in place of the elderly and hidebound Field Marshal Sir Cyril Deverell, and another of the advisory appointment was that Hobart went to the War Office as Director of Military Training with the strict understanding that in the event of war looming he would be given command of a 'Mobile Division'.

The Munich Crisis provided the reason, Gort the instruction – in person. On the afternoon of September 25th, 1938, Hobart was ordered to go to Egypt immediately and form an armoured division to hold off the Italians, who were expected to attack across the Libyan–Egyptian frontier immediately war was declared, if not before.

On September 27th, Hobart arrived at Alexandria in company with the British Ambassador and several senior officers who were to carry out an examination of the entire Middle East situation. They were met by General Wilson's immediate predecessor as G.O.C.-in-C, British Troops in Egypt, Lieutenant-General Sir Robert ('Copper') Gordon-Finlayson, who was considerably taken aback to see Hobart, and greeted him with, 'I don't know what you've come here for, and I don't want you anyway.'

The tone for Hobart's relationship with Cairo Headquarters was thereby set, and it was hardly to vary.

In the field, Hobart's appearance was at first greeted with curiosity mingled with much scepticism, but once the officers and men became accustomed to an unexpected demand for speed in all their activities, they began to appreciate the qualities of the man now in charge of them, and the advantages they might gain from his leadership.

Hobart found that the force from which he was expected to form a modern armoured division consisted entirely of units equipped with old, outdated weapons and equipment, and however enthusiastically trained the personnel they were never up to strength. For instance, the Cavalry Brigade (Hobart soon arranged for it to be renamed 'Light Armoured Brigade') consisted of three Hussar regiments, each of which was over a hundred men short of establishment. The 7th Queen's Own Hussars consisted of two instead of three squadrons and were equipped with light tanks which varied in age and pattern from Marks III to VIB but had no ammunition for their 0·5-inch guns; but they were in better case than the 8th King's Royal Irish Hussars, who practised their light tank manoeuvres in 15-cwt Ford pick-up trucks with Vickers-Berthier guns mounted in them. The 11th Hussars (Prince Albert's Own) still had most of their Rolls-Royce armoured cars of 1920–4 vintage, for which they were very grateful as they were excellent machines, and they were just receiving new models of a Morris car which promised well for reconnaissance work – better than the Rolls in soft sand though the suspension and steering proved not so robust when it came to the rough work among the boulders.

The Tank Group which was intended to form the main striking force – to be called the Heavy Armoured Brigade – consisted of the 1st Battalion Royal Tank Regiment, recently arrived from England with fifty-eight light tanks but with little track mileage left in them and pathetically few track replacements, and the 6th R.T.R. which had both light and medium tanks, though they had to be left behind in Cairo for Hobart's first exercises, for 'internal security' duties. (When Maitland Wilson inspected the tanks of this battalion some time later, he was horrified. They were, he wrote, 'the same medium tanks which one had seen performing at the Aldershot Tattoo for many years and whose armour was questionably proof against anti-tank small arms'.)

As for the 'Pivot Group', whose role was to supply the artillery and infantry support which Hobart considered essential (despite his critics' belief that he professed total independence for tanks), the 3rd Regiment Royal Horse Artillery was almost up to strength even though their 3·7-inch howitzers may not have been ideal weapons for their role (but new anti-tank guns were on their way) but the 1st Battalion King's Royal Rifle Corps were not even in Egypt. They were still in Burma, and would be without any form of transport when they did arrive.

The making of bricks without straw was apparently still considered the local speciality.

Nevertheless, Hobart set to work with his usual application and as his appointment also gave him responsibility for the Garrison Troops at Abbassia Barracks in Cairo, he squeezed and scraped from them enough signals and administrative personnel to put together a divisional headquarters, and a company of Royal Army Service Corps to help with the supply problems. Based on Mersá Matruh, he carried out a series of exercises to test the quality of his new command.

He was not dissatisfied, and as the autumn and winter of 1938 went by without war and more men and equipment arrived, the force – it could hardly yet be called a division – began to take shape. The infantry component arrived, and more light tanks for the Hussars; anti-tank guns and 25-pounders replaced the howitzers of the Royal Horse Artillery and the first ten cruiser tanks (A9s) were taken over by the 6th Royal Tank Regiment, which was also released from its Cairo-bound duties. Hobart wrote:

> I decided to concentrate on dispersion, flexibility and mobility this season: to try and get the Division and formations well extended, really handy, and under quick control. To units unused to the speed and wide frontages made possible by mechanisation these matters present considerable difficulties.
>
> There is the isolation due to the wide intervals necessary in the desert, involving the necessity of being able to keep direction, to navigate a unit, to keep a dead reckoning, to learn to watch for small indications and to use one's eyes in spite of mirage, etc.[8]

Such lessons had of course, to be learned by every unit as it arrived in the desert and this would constitute a problem for every commander-in-chief while the desert war raged; there was always to be a great disparity between the number of troops which arrived in the Delta, and that which could be put into the battle-line. Other problems with which Hobart had to wrestle arose from the recent mechanisation of some of the cavalry units:

> Maintenance in newly mechanised units is not, of course, of a high standard, but great interest is being taken and as knowledge increases the standard of inspection, which is the secret of good maintenance, will improve.
>
> It must be a matter of course for all officers not only to wear overalls but also to take part in the maintenance work on their vehicles.
>
> It has not yet become instinctive for crews and commanders to get down at every halt and look round their vehicles at once. If this were the case many oil leaks, loose bolts etc., would be seen and remedied and many subsequent demands on fitters avoided.
>
> I am certain that we have to encourage in all crews the sense of ownership which makes it a point of honour that they should be able to keep their vehicles running without assistance from outside; even if we have to do it at first at the cost of some damage by unskilled enthusiasts.[9]

Gradually, the separate pieces of the force began to learn their positions and carry out their roles. The 11th Hussars formed a wide screen in front and along the flanks to provide reconnaissance and the first delay to an attacking enemy, the tank group learned to manoeuvre for attack or counter-thrust, the artillery to swing into action to break up a threatened attack before it developed. At all key positions, the infantry dug themselves weapon pits to hold ground won, and to guard the brains and nerve centres which controlled them all.

Thus, if there was still an acute shortage of everything from supply transport and ammunition to radio sets, there was now a growing ability to improvise and a rapidly developing integral spirit. By the middle of 1939 the days of the 'Immobile Farce' were long gone, and by the outbreak of war Hobart's command constituted a force with far greater striking power than any other formation of comparable size in Africa. Certainly the Italian commanders on the other side of the frontier wire had good cause for concern at its rapid development.

As it happened the Italian Command at the outbreak of war had a very exaggerated idea of Allied – and particularly British – strength, and it is interesting to analyse why. Basically, there seems to have been a marked reluctance among the Italian people, with the exception of the ruling Fascist hierarchy, to go to war against the British. This reluctance shows in practically every report on their own readiness for war submitted to Mussolini by the heads of the armed services. Even the Italian Navy, which at that time was undoubtedly the most efficient and up-to-date of the three services and was to score some notable triumphs, especially with its smaller units, decried its own ability. One report from the Chief of the Italian General Staff read:

> The British naval forces (stationed in the Mediterranean) represent an amount of power which compared with ours cannot be described other than 'of crushing superiority'. It is not possible to nourish any hopes of achieving positive results in a struggle with this power since our navy is only a spearhead without any bulk behind it . . . The British battleships, escorted by a considerable number of destroyers, could cruise at will in the Mediterranean inflicting all the damage they wanted on our ill-defended coasts. Nor can we make much use of the air force which finds itself in a state of crisis and whose older material, which is the bulk of it, would be out of action after a few days . . .[10]

It is interesting that there is no mention in this report of the existence of the French Fleet, upon which the Royal Navy was placing great reliance in the coming struggle for naval control of the Mediterranean.

As for the military situation in North Africa, whereas the British saw themselves hemmed in and sandwiched between large military forces in Libya and Eritrea, the Italian Command saw only the dangers to which their Libyan Armies were exposed, of being crushed between the overwhelming powers of the French Army in Tunisia and the '100,000 strong Anglo-Egyptian Army' backed up by an unknown but presumed potent and vigorous force consisting of 'General Wavell's British troops in the Near East'.

It seems likely that the very number of Italian agents, amateur and professional, resident in Egypt added to the confusion, and that one column of tanks leaving Abbassia and reported to Rome by fifty different enthusiasts became a division by the time it arrived at Mersa Matruh. Certainly the powers, both defensive and offensive, of the British forces east of the Libyan frontier were considered great enough to cause Maresciallo d'Armata Balbo to add his voice to that of Mussolini's son-in-law Count Ciano, in late August 1939, entreating Mussolini not to let Hitler drag their country into a war which they were in no condition to fight. Despite his willingness to sign the Pact of Steel in May 1939, Ciano had become thoroughly disenchanted with Hitler and the whole of Nazi Germany during the following three months.

But if the Italians in general and Maresciallo Balbo in particular exaggerated the power against them, they took a realistic attitude to their own military strength. Despite the numbers of men they deployed, despite also their recent military successes in Ethiopia and Albania, the Italian Armies were in no condition to fight a modern war abroad.

Generale di Divisione d'Armata Giuseppe Mancinelli of the Comando Supremo Staff, who had already spent a term as military attaché in Berlin and had seen enough of the Wehrmacht on manoeuvres to recognise military reality when he saw it, found the outlook depressing in the extreme:

At the moment of the declaration of war in 1939, the army consisted of seventy-three divisions, of which twenty-four were deployed in the [Aegean] islands and in the overseas commands. In 1938, the division, through the unhappy initiative of the then Chief of Staff, Generale Pariani, had been transformed from 'ternary' to 'binary': this meant that the infantry component had been reduced from three to two regiments. This was a strange operation which certainly did not do any good to the general efficiency of the army. In the new units, the infantry–artillery ratio had been raised but the result could not be considered satisfactory since the division became too small a unit to be able to undertake and successfully terminate a tactical action of any importance; it was subject to quick deterioration and was incapable of any prolonged effort. Possibly in this decision was involved the more or less conscious aim of 'bluffing' – not so much as regards other countries but for the Duce himself, as a gesture of prestige, an apparently miraculous multiplication of the forces at his disposal.

Modernity in the composition of our army was represented by the 9th Army – the Army of the Po – which with its three armoured divisions, three 'rapid movement' divisions and two motorised divisions was to constitute the 'mass of manoeuvre' for a war of rapid movement. But the tanks of the armoured units were already largely obsolete, little more than pretty mechanical toys from six to ten tons, to be offered as targets to the enemy anti-tank guns. The 'rapid movement' divisions were a romantic and obsolete combination of horsed cavalry and Bersaglieri cyclists, and the so-called motorised divisions did have motor transport of a kind, but were all wheeled vehicles incapable of movement off roads.

In general, the problem of mechanisation, or more appropriately non-mechanisation, of our army represented one of the largest gaps in our organisation, a canker which excluded any capacity for large manoeuvres and which lay at the heart of the very painful losses suffered in the course of the various campaigns, especially those in North Africa . . . For instance, the Italian 'binary' infantry division disposed of one hundred and thirty-five vehicles; the German 'ternary' division had over one thousand.[11]

What of the men who made up the Italian Armies? Except for the Blackshirt Divisions where, as Generale Mancinelli comments acidly, promotion was more likely to be as a result of political enthusiasm than military efficiency, there were now few volunteers joining the Italian Army. By 1939, it had been on a warlike footing for five years, with many units engaged in action or on garrison duties in hostile lands. Ethiopia, Eritrea, Spain, Libya and Italian Somaliland had all called for sacrifices of blood and effort and in all of them the Italian soldier had obeyed his orders, patiently, under a discipline often lax but sometimes harsh, with varying comprehension as to the battle's necessity and rarely with a great deal of enthusiasm. Now he was to be called upon to fight an enemy he did not hate, armed with weapons and equipment which were quickly and effectively demonstrated to be unequal to war against any but a colonial, tribal enemy. In addition, his allies were of a race for whom he felt little affection, however great his admiration for their martial prowess might be.

The Italian private soldier was drawn from traditionally sturdy peasant and worker stock, and so far as it is possible to generalise upon so large a subject, these are hard-working, adaptable, sensible people, with a strong feeling for home and family, a natural gaiety and capacity for happiness, combined with a thoroughly Latin distrust of violent enthusiasms. They respond to friendliness,

recognise natural good manners and, given the slightest encouragement, will be cheerful and co-operative. The world can always do
with such qualities, and in the late 1930s and early 1940s they were
at a premium.

Although the man who commanded the Italian forces in Libya was by
no means of worker or peasant stock, he nevertheless epitomised
their qualities. Italo Balbo was gay, handsome, possessed of great
charm, imagination and courage of a typically Italian brand. He had
served with distinction as an Alpini officer in the First World War,
had joined the Fascist movement soon afterwards and led the
militia in the March on Rome in 1922. He had been promoted
General of Militia in 1923 but then played a leading part in the
building up of the Regia Aeronautica, making many long-distance
flights which gave him an international reputation. But by 1933
when Mussolini promoted him to Marshal and sent him as
Governor-General to Libya, he had incurred considerable unpopularity in Rome as a result of his strongly pro-British views,
coupled with his outspoken criticism of the growing *rapprochement*
between his own country and Germany.

He, like so many of his countrymen who had visited Britain, had
felt at home there, and as so many of them were to find in the years to
come in British company they could relax, chatter, laugh and get on
with their work. Perhaps they sensed a shared fecklessness, a
similar attitude of casual scepticism to the accepted values of
ambition and worthiness.

All this did not, of course, prevent Maresciallo Balbo carrying
out his duties as instructed when war was declared between
Germany and the two western allies, Britain and France. Regroup-
ing and reinforcement of the units under his command duly took
place, all the native troops were re-formed into two divisions, the
three army corps of nine divisions on the Tunisian border were
strengthened and inspected, as were the two army corps of five
divisions facing Egypt. In the Saharan hinterland were posted
special groups at strategic points such as the Kuffra Oasis, Jarabub
150 miles down the frontier Wire south of Sollum, Jalo on the
western edge of the great Libyan Sand Sea, and Murzuk 500 miles
south of Tripoli.

Balbo also conscientiously endeavoured to bring home to the
highest authorities in Rome one basic fact of which they seemed to
be losing sight – that the term 'motorised' as applied to some of his
army corps did not mean that they actually had been motorised. It
meant, as the authorities should remember, that it had been agreed
that 'they had the capacity for motorisation' but that very little had
as yet been done to convert them from their original classification as

infantry corps. As for the request by the High Command for his plans for an invasion of Egypt, he felt that before he could undertake this he should be able to deploy along the frontier at least thirteen divisions – so he would need another eight; of which in his opinion two should be armoured to a degree equating them with the German panzer divisions, and two airborne – with, of course, the necessary adjunctive air support.

With this force, he was quite confident that he could advance through the Wire as far as the edge of the Escarpment running south-east from Sollum. Here, his forces would be able to block any attempted British invasion of Libya, and also to undertake the advance to the Nile and the complete subjugation of Egypt once further reinforcements had arrived, particulars of which would be sent to Rome as soon as they had been worked out.

Oddly enough, Mussolini was neither infuriated nor aggrieved when Balbo's appraisal of the situation in North Africa arrived on his desk, as he was still suffering a sense of outrage at his fellow dictator's totally unilateral activities. Mussolini had had no more warning of the probabilities of the outbreak of war than any other European outside Hitler's immediate entourage, and in view of his own recently well-tried philosophy that it was possible to get everything a reasonable man could want by simply rattling the sabre without actually drawing it, he was perhaps even more taken aback than most.

His immediate reaction was a declaration of non-belligerency, followed by an order to Maresciallo d'Armata Badoglio, the Chief of the Italian General Staff, to take up a defensive attitude on every front, an instruction followed with great alacrity on one front in particular – along the Breonie Alps where the fortifications guarding the Brenner Pass into Austria were strengthened. As for taking the field alongside his partner in the Pact of Steel, he had specifically warned Hitler that Italy would be in no condition to make war against a European power until 1943 at the earliest, and then only with a considerable amount of aid and equipment from Germany.

He thus felt justified in taking a far cooler tone in his communications with Berlin than he had of late, together with an air of detached statesmanship which he was sure would impress the rest of Europe and both Americas, probably leading in due course to everyone soliciting his aid and judgment at some soon-to-be-convened conference table. After all, had this not recently occurred at Munich where both Mr Chamberlain and M. Daladier had been almost fulsome in the attention they had paid him?

The outbreak of war in 1939 was thus followed by something of a diplomatic and military hiatus so far as Italy was concerned, during which it gradually became clear to Il Duce and his immediate circle that perhaps the world was not, after all, hanging on his word. From Berlin came no sign that Hitler was even aware of Mussolini's chagrin (a much worse interpretation of the air of bland friendliness which emanated from Berlin was that Hitler *was* aware, but totally unconcerned about it) and as details of the success of the German Blitzkrieg in Poland began to reach Rome, doubts as to the value of non-belligerency arose. In December, Balbo received from the newly appointed Army Chief of Staff, Maresciallo Graziani, instructions to draw up a more detailed plan for offensives against both Tunisia and Egypt 'to be applied in exceptional circumstances', while during the early part of 1940 Mussolini's pronouncements grew ever more anti-France and Britain who, he informed the Council of Ministers on January 23rd, 'can no longer win the war'.

In February 1940 he forbade sales of any further goods to Britain (much to his Commercial Minister's disgust as the Italian budget was in its usual precarious state and the cancelled deals had been expected to bring in some £20 million worth of much-needed sterling) but insisted that obligations to Germany must be fulfilled. 'Governments, like individuals, must follow a line of morality and honour,' he announced, presumably hoping that Hitler would take the hint and see that the 3,500 tons of copper about to be extorted from the Italian people by the confiscation of their cooking-pots, and sent across the Alps, would be paid for. (They weren't.)

During March, another 80,000 men were sent to North Africa and Mussolini declared 'England will be beaten. Inexorably beaten. That is the sure truth,' while at another Council of Ministers in early April, he claimed that for Italy to remain neutral would 'lose her prestige among the nations of the world for a century as a Great Power and for eternity as a Fascist regime'.

It was, of course, the events of April 1940 which brought the whole situation to a head. As German troops flooded into Denmark and across the Skagerrak to Norway, stamping the Swastika across the face of yet another subjugated country and expelling the hastily committed and ill-organised French and British troops, Mussolini's exasperation grew and his fears that he would not even be invited to sit at a Peace Conference took a harder outline. Then, on May 10th, the panzer columns roared across the frontiers of Belgium and Luxembourg and Il Duce was reduced to a frenzy.

'We Italians are already sufficiently dishonoured,' he declared three days later. 'Any delay is inconceivable. We have no time to lose. Within a month I shall declare war. I shall attack France and Great Britain in the air and on the sea!' And when his military advisers pointed out to him that the lack of almost every sort of military equipment made the carrying out of this declaration virtually impossible, he muttered defiantly but gloomily, 'Then we will do what we can!'

The next day, cheering up, he began manoeuvres to persuade the reluctant King Victor Emmanuel that he, Mussolini, was the best person to assume the Italian Supreme Command, especially as he was even then in communication with his friend Hitler as to the best timing for the Italian declaration of war against the decadent democracies – and by 'best' he meant the timing likely to bring Italy most profit when the French and British empires came to be divided up.

The rest of May passed in a flurry of meetings, conferences and correspondence until at last on the evening of June 10th he read a speech from the balcony of the Palazzo Venezia to a markedly un-enthusiastic crowd, detailing the enormous provocations their country had been subjected to by both England and France, and declaring war on them.

Among his listeners was his son-in-law Count Ciano, who, when he confided the day's events to his diary that night, concluded the entry with 'May God help Italy!'

Whatever Balbo thought of the events of that epochal week, he was sufficiently realistic to know that with the virtual elimination of France from the war, Tunisia would no longer hold threat on the west and he would soon be under pressure from Rome to transfer divisions from there to the east and put matters in train for a march to the Nile.

'It is not the number of men', he wrote to Mussolini in order to damp down too great an excess of martial zeal, 'which causes me anxiety, but their weapons. With two big formations equipped with limited and very old pieces of artillery, lacking in anti-tank and anti-aircraft weapons, I need to be able to depend on the closing of ways of access to Tripolitania, and on the perimeters of Tobruk and Bardia. To have fortified works without adequate weapons is an absurdity. Another urgent necessity is anti-aircraft defences – batteries and organisation. It is useless to send more thousands of men if then we cannot supply them with the indispensable requirements to move and fight.'

But this slightly confused *cri de cœur* did him little good, and quite shortly he received further instructions to proceed with plans for an invasion of Egypt, together with a promise that all the war materials he required would be immediately dispatched. This he countered with a detailed list: a thousand motor vehicles would be the minimum requirement, he claimed, together with a hundred water-tankers, medium tanks for two divisions, a mass of radio equipment and, again, batteries of both anti-tank and anti-aircraft guns.

He was immediately promised all of them, and perhaps a few items arrived quite soon – which he may have had time to regret, for on June 28th, having carried out a reconnaissance flight over Sidi Barrani and Maaten Baggush, he was shot down and killed by one of his own anti-aircraft batteries as he came in to land at Tobruk. The following day, the R.A.F. dropped a note of genuine regret and a wreath on to the landing ground above which Maresciallo Balbo had died. Britain and her allies had lost a good friend in their fight against totalitarian dictatorship.

Appointed in Balbo's place was Maresciallo d'Armata Rodolpho Graziani, who had been responsible for the 'pacification' of Libya between 1930 and 1934 and who enjoyed little local popularity as a result.

2 · Skirmish and Circumspect Advance

Twenty-four hours after Mussolini had concluded his speech from the balcony of the Palazzo Venezia, six troops of the 11th Hussars, each consisting of three armoured cars, left Dar el Hamra, a barren location some thirty miles from the coast and about the same distance east of the frontier, and set out westwards across the plateau for the Wire. They reached it at four different places between Fort Maddalena and Fort Cápuzzo just as the light was fading, and as there was no sign of life on the other side, began the process of 'gapping'.

This was accomplished by a very simple method which they had devised back in the training area around Mersa Matruh. The first armoured car nosed its way up to the nearest picket-post, and in low gear gradually pressed it down until it was almost flat. It then drove over it towards the middle and third posts (there were three lines of upright fencing with barbed wire strung along and also coiled and tangled between them) and repeated the operation, trailing a mass of attached wire behind. Following closely, the second armoured car drove with its wheels actually on the iron picket-posts, pressing them flat to the ground and in some cases snapping them off. It then followed on through, tearing away more of the wire, and the three cars of the troop then drove slowly back and forth across the wire until it gradually disintegrated, while crew members dragged the mass clear with ropes.

It was all much simpler than expected for the wire was older and rustier than that upon which they had practised, the posts more fragile (in one place they were found to be of wood and these just snapped off straight away) and none of the fence was electrified. The rubber-soled shoes which crews of the leading cars had worn thus proved to be unnecessary, though later in the campaign they were to come in useful for foot patrols.

In the north, B Squadron troops fanned out and made for their objectives up around Fort Capuzzo, while the squadron commander, Major Geoffrey Miller, held back a small section of the

Headquarter Troop to guard the gap. It was a cloudless night, warm and with only a light breeze, and the intoxication of this first penetration of enemy territory kept everyone keen and alert. The sounds of the other armoured cars driving off – the gritting of the tyres on sand, the clunk of changing gears – died away and only the murmured conversation of Miller's own section disturbed the taut silence. There was little to do once the immediately surrounding area had been searched.

As the hours passed, there came occasionally to over-anxious ears the sounds of aircraft a long way off – and surely that was the crackle of a Bren-gun? – then shortly before 0200 the northern horizon came dimly alight and in due course the headlamps of a lorry came waveringly into view. Miller and his men watched in silence as a lorry-load of extremely fortunate Italian troops

Map 1   The frontier area

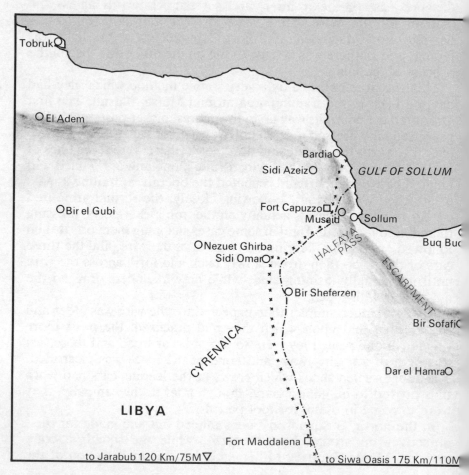

lumbered by, presumably bound for Sidi Omar, revealing to the Hussars the whereabouts of the track normally followed.

With the idea of ambushing the lorry as and if it returned before he and his men withdrew, Miller took his attenuated section across to the track and began disposing them for an attack on a small target approaching from the south; so he was somewhat disturbed when four more lorries appeared from the north and rumbled on down towards them, headlights ablaze. Whether anybody even considered withdrawing in the face of such greater odds is doubtful, and as the lorries came into short range the Hussars opened up with every weapon they had.

There was a babble of outrage, cries of pain and terror, a few wild shots loosed off from the black caverns over the tailboards, and then the unmistakable shouts of officers calling for a cease-fire. Cab

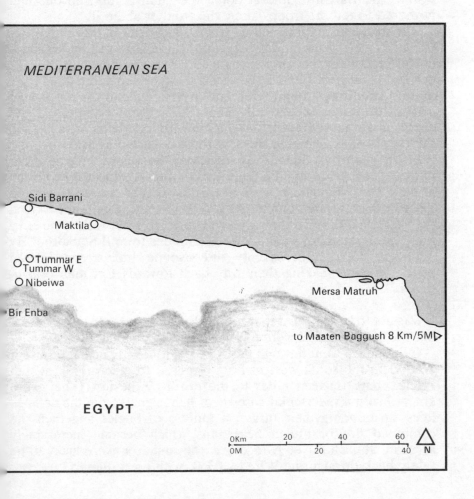

doors burst open and officers and drivers jumped down, dropping their arms as the Hussars rushed out of the darkness with revolvers and sub-machine-guns at the ready; then the tailboards were down and a flood of astonished and frightened Libyans poured out, hands high in the air, rifles left aboard the lorries.

The next few minutes were chaotic as Major Miller and his men rushed from lorry to lorry, herding the prisoners away, quickly searching for small arms any officers or men who looked capable of recovery from shock, and policing the gap between the jettisoned weapons and their now vociferous former owners.

It all made a very tidy haul to be captured by half a section – two officers, fifty N.C.O.s and privates, nine Breda automatics, sixty rifles and several boxes of hand-grenades; but one of the interesting facts which emerged when Miller had time to listen to the indignation of the two officers was that despite Mussolini's proclamation of war to the Italian people at home the night before, no one had bothered to tell the troops along the frontier about it.

But in the meantime, other troops had been at work. At Sidi Omar, No. 2 Troop under Sergeant-Major Howarth had made a useful reconnaissance and exchanged a few random shots with its occupants, at Fort Capuzzo Sergeant Bowyer had had a good look around and lifted a number of land-mines, while to the north-west of Fort Capuzzo, Second Lieutenant Halliday had ambushed and captured a Lancia-Diesel 10-ton lorry with its occupants, all in the same state of exasperated shock as those collected by Miller.

Further south, A Squadron had gapped the wire in three different places, cut a large number of telephone lines, skirmished briefly around Fort Maddalena with an unidentified armoured truck and loosed off a few Bren-gun bursts at a low-flying aircraft; after which they returned through their gaps to Hamra to greet with some envy their exhilarated but slightly awed comrades from B Squadron. By noon on June 12th, seventy disconsolate Italian and Libyan prisoners were making their way back towards Egyptian prison-cages.

It was not to be expected that so simple a success could be repeated, but the next few days were to produce some notable results.

C Squadron went through the Wire the following night and swept around to the south-west of Fort Capuzzo to take a look at Sidi Azeiz, some thirteen miles to the north of the fort. They were greeted with a spectacular cascade of light signals from the defence lines surrounding their target, a fanfare of bugles and then the combined fire of fifteen field guns which became increasingly accurate at each salvo. Altogether, the squadron were lucky to be safely back through the Wire by 0300, with no casualties.

Three troops of A Squadron went in again the following night and drove to Sidi Omar, to find a situation reminiscent of the *Marie Celeste* affair. Everywhere were signs of hasty evacuation – books and documents left lying about, clothing and even arms and ammunition; an unfinished meal was black with a cloud of flies, a sight to confirm Lieutenant Friend in his decision to set fire to the two main posts. They were back through the Wire by dawn with no sign of Italian interference, though their detached troop was having its first experience of a new type of harassment.

Sergeant-Major 'Nobby' Clarke had been sent off with No. 4 Troop to take another look at Fort Maddalena, and with perhaps a little too much confidence drove directly – almost flagrantly – towards the main gate. Machine-guns opened up on the three cars from along the wall, and when this failed to divert the troop, air-craft suddenly appeared and began strafing and bombing them, at which, intelligently, the Hussars turned and fled. In the end, no less than six Caproni bombers and nine Fiat fighters had joined the attack, fortunately without armour-piercing bullets; but their bombs had been a different matter and the cars had had some narrow escapes, only violent swerving on their part and the lack of teamwork between Capronis and Fiats saving them from damage.

On June 14th, the biggest incursion into Libya took place, the capture of both Fort Maddalena and Fort Capuzzo being under-taken by the 4th Armoured Brigade, as Hobart's 'Heavy Armoured Brigade' had now been renamed.

Again, A Squadron of the 11th Hussars attacked Fort Maddalena after a period of 'softening up' by a flight of R.A.F. Blenheims, and with the whole squadron moving together in a wide encircling movement to surround the fort, a sense of great excitement per-vaded them all in this, the regiment's first battle-charge of the war. And again, it was all rather a let-down. There was no sign of opposition, a white flag was run up as the cars converged and the Hussars went in without a shot being fired, taking prisoner the five Italians and thirteen native troops who were all that remained of the garrison.

The Hussars found the fort well designed and soundly built, with such luxuries as a refrigerator and an electric-light plant, a radio transmitter and receiver which they wrecked, and a well-stocked store and arsenal (including the twelve machine-guns which had opened up on Sergeant-Major Clarke the day before) which they ransacked, removing the guns for later use against their original owners.

But further north, where the attack on Fort Capuzzo was taking place, the picture was more complicated.

Brigadier J. R. L. Caunter (nicknamed, rather sardonically, 'Blood' Caunter by his troops) had decided that although the main strength of his column should attack Fort Capuzzo itself, a lighter force should capture Sidi Azeiz beyond in order to prevent any reinforcement of the Capuzzo garrison, and then continue northwards to carry out a daylight reconnaissance of the small port of Bardia.

This lighter force consisted of B and C Squadrons of the 11th Hussars, a squadron of light tanks from the 7th Hussars and a battery of 25-pounders from the Royal Horse Artillery, the whole force led by the commanding officer of the 11th Hussars, Lieutenant-Colonel John Combe. As he had further to go, Colonel Combe took his leading elements through the Wire at 0800 on the morning of the 14th, and half an hour later C Squadron was under fire from the same batteries which had chased them away two nights before.

The two 11th Hussar squadrons thereupon diverged to run along the flanks of the position, while between them the light tanks of the 7th Hussars swept in to overrun the infantry defences. At first, this appeared a task as easy as any the Hussars had faced to date, for the Libyan infantry promptly climbed out of their weapon-pits and fled over the ridge behind – but when the tanks pursued them up the slope they found themselves in the middle of a minefield in which three of their tanks blew up and the rest were either stuck or forced to pull back. They then came under fire from Italian artillery skilfully sited on the reverse slope of the ridge, and shells burst all around them occasionally exploding mines alongside. Those crew members who had not jumped or been pulled clear were trapped inside their tanks, praying that the steel was thick enough and thanking God that the Italians were not using armour-piercing shells, while the 11th Hussars raced up and down the flanks, desperately trying to draw fire away from their more unfortunate colleagues, hoping that the flashes of the Italian guns could be pinpointed by the R.H.A. batteries and their observers now in position but with their view masked by the rise.

It was all, however, to little effect. The sun was up, the glare off the desert surface blinding and aswim with mirage, and the 25-pounder crews well aware that not only were they in action and under fire for the first time, but that another battle was going on somewhere behind them. Above all, the Italian artillery was being directed with efficiency and admirable coolness. By noon John Combe was in doubt as to whether he should break off this part of the action and proceed with the second part – the reconnaissance – and it was with considerable relief that at 1500 he heard the news that the main target of the attack, Fort Capuzzo, had surrendered.

(As a result of an R.A.F. attack – in which no bombs had landed inside the target area – followed by a few 2-pounder shells from the guns of the cruiser tanks present, which penetrated the walls. Again, a bloodless victory.)

With his rear therefore safe, Combe divided his force, drew the remaining tanks and guns off and dispatched them back to the Wire, left B Squadron to screen Sidi Azeiz and sent C Squadron northward to descend the Escarpment and take a look at the defences of Bardia.

Three significant episodes filled the rest of the day. Three troops of C Squadron found and negotiated quite easily a pathway up and down the Escarpment, one drove quite unobstructed along the road at the bottom as far as the outskirts of Bardia which they found ringed with well-sited infantry defences, while the others explored towards Sollum and guarded the way back.

Back on the plateau, the first troop approached the wasps' nest of Sidi Azeiz again, only to find it apparently quiet, with the dust of a convoy leading away from it. As they turned to investigate, a white flag was run up – but as the troops deployed to race forward and take over, the flag came down and the guns opened up on them. Whether this event was a deliberate flouting of the rules of war or a misunderstanding overruled by the pugnacity of the Italian gunners was never established, but C Squadron beat a hasty retreat and was extremely lucky to suffer no casualties.

The third event concerned B Squadron. While screening Sidi Azeiz, Halliday's troop had suddenly been attacked by six Italian Fiat-Ansaldo L3 light tanks, and Halliday, with considerable misgivings, opened up on the nearest with a weapon viewed with great scepticism by all familiar with it – a Boyes anti-tank rifle. To the astonishment of all watching, the L3 promptly fell out of the attack, the others scuttled off 'like a lot of little pigs' to quote Halliday's report, while the two-man crew of the disabled tank climbed out and gave themselves up. Closer examination revealed that the L3 was very thinly armoured, carried no wireless and was little but a death-trap for those within. Halliday promptly set this one alight and returned triumphantly through the Wire.

Two days later, between Sidi Omar and the now-deserted Fort Capuzzo, occurred the quite astonishing Battle of Nezuet Ghirba.

Two troops of C Squadron were 'swanning about' on the Libyan side of the Wire north of Sidi Omar when the leader of one troop saw an Italian column of twelve L3 tanks and thirty lorries, apparently full of infantry, moving north along the track towards Capuzzo – presumably to re-garrison the fort. He reported to Squadron H.Q. on the other side of the Wire by radio, but at the same time the leader of the second troop reported another column, east-bound, consisting of forty lorries and seventeen L3s, on a course obviously aimed to converge with the first.

Realising that his men would soon be heavily outnumbered (the first troop had only two cars that morning), Major Miller from his covering position ten miles inside Egyptian territory ordered their withdrawal and asked for some of 4th Armoured Brigade's anti-tank guns to come up in case they should be needed.

But by this time, Second Lieutenant Vyvyan Gape, commanding the first troop to report, had gaily driven up to the first column and opened fire on the thin-skinned lorries and luckless infantry within; and as the twelve supporting L3s – six in front of the column and six at the rear – swung inwards to attack these two incredibly impudent armoured cars, the noise of the battle reached the ears of Second Lieutenant Dier, the other troop commander, who was already withdrawing from his Italian column but who now promptly drove towards the sound of the guns.

By the time Dier arrived, Gape had managed to knock out two of the L3s but was being harried by the rest who between them had managed to puncture a tyre on his second car, thus slowing them both down enough for the L3s to get between the Hussars and their exit through the Wire. Dier now opened fire, knocked out another L3 and frightened the others off (to be fair to the crews, the L3s were probably the most ineffectual fighting vehicles ever put into production), but by this time an Italian field gun hitherto concealed within the column had come into action and both Hussar troops wisely fled to the shelter of a small rise, from which position Gape radioed back the latest developments.

John Combe, who had now come up to take command, mustered all his own reserve troops and alerted the others still on the western side of the Wire. He then set off to meet the support which Brigadier Caunter was sending down, and soon a mixed squadron of light and cruiser tanks, an anti-tank troop of the Royal Horse Artillery and more armoured cars of the 11th Hussars were converging on the gap, while from both north and south beyond it came hastening in other troops of the 11th which had been reconnoitring further afield.

Soon they had concentrated, and Geoffrey Miller led them all forward to the slight rise from which Gape and Dier were watching the Italians below with fascinated disbelief. Soon both Miller and Combe were registering the same stunned astonishment.

Some three miles distant, on a flat plain totally devoid of cover, the Italian column (the second and bigger one never put in an appearance) had marshalled their lorries and infantry into a formed square – a combination of Wellington's infantry at Waterloo and

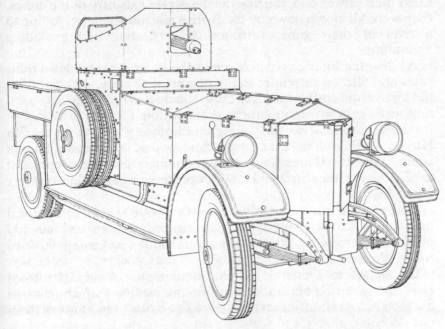

Figure 1   Rolls-Royce armoured car: weight 4 tons; armour 8mm.; engine
50 h.p.; maximum speed 45 m.p.h.; armament one ·303 Vickers m.g.; crew 3

the prairie laager beloved by Hollywood – which the L3s patrolled
outside but looking towards the British as though the Indians and
Palefaces had joined forces.

Two thoughts crossed John Combe's mind   who do they think
they're fighting, and do they have any concealed artillery?

There was only one way to find the answer to the second and most
immediately important of those questions, and he sent the 7th
Hussars' tanks down to do so with one of his own regiment's Morris
armoured cars to provide a radio link. As the tanks rolled up and
over the crest, they were subjected to a number of near-misses from
the one known piece of Italian artillery, and then valiantly attacked
by seven of the L3s which came forward to defend their infantry.
Knocking these out with one shot each, the advancing tanks then
circled the square, exactly like Red Indians attacking a ring of
covered wagons, pouring fire into the unfortunate and virtually unprotected infantry.

For some reason never disclosed, they were allowed to make two
complete and uninterrupted circuits before the Italians revealed
their hidden punch – field guns at each corner of the square. The
battle now briefly became four separate conflicts between guns and
tanks but the action was really at too close a range for the guns to

exert their power and, despite the desperate gallantry of the crews, they were all mown down by the British machine-gun fire, falling to a man at their guns, surrounded by blazing and exploding ammunition.

At this, the square broke. Some of the infantry threw down their rifles and offered surrender to the nearest tank crew, others ran for the lorries and endeavoured to escape, only to be rounded up by the armoured cars which now raced down to join the fray. The last of the Italian tanks tried unavailing conclusions with one of the 7th Hussars' two cruiser tanks on the field, whose commander merely waited until the Italian had virtually rammed him, then depressed his 2-pounder gun, fired and totally wrecked his gallant but helpless adversary.

In the end, a force of nearly 200 soldiers with 30 lorries, four guns and 12 tanks was wiped out, leaving only 12 lorries and 100 prisoners to make the sad journey across the Wire. Among the dead was Colonello D'Avanso from whose coat pocket an order was taken signed by Generale Sibille, commander of the 1st Libyan Division, ordering him to 'destroy enemy elements which have infiltrated across the frontier, and give the British the impression of our decision, ability and will to resist'.

There were no British casualties, and indeed the day had seen yet another success for the 11th Hussars, further to the north.

The previous night, C Squadron had gone back through the Wire and retraced their steps around Sidi Azeiz to the edge of the Escarpment, this time to the west of Bardia. At dawn two troops descended to the road below and at the bottom set up an ambush, while the remainder watched from the top to provide guard and covering fire if necessary. First the advanced crews cut all telephone and telegraph lines and then, remembering their own experiences in Palestine, they cut down a telegraph pole and manhandled it across the road to form a block. The armoured cars then moved into cover 'where', according to the report, 'the crews settled down to await their first customers'.

They did not have long to wait. A convoy led by a big diesel lorry with a heavy machine-gun mounted on top came up, and at the roadblock the gunner, of all people, dismounted to remove the telegraph pole. As the Hussars opened fire the vehicles behind either crashed into the one in front or were bumped by the one behind, and chaos and confusion followed with panic engulfing the convoy as the true situation became apparent. Another Hussar troop rushed down from the Escarpment to help deal with the prisoners, and as these were being marshalled up the rise 'carrying peculiar suitcases and giving out the overwhelming smell of a Latin army short of water', the original troops worked their way along the road to catch new arrivals. According to the regimental history:

> Altogether they had a splendid morning. Time and again the lorries would come bowling down the road all oblivious of the fate of their forerunners, would stop short of the last one in the queue, and usually dismount the passengers to find out what was holding up the convoy. The sequel was always the same: each in turn found himself confronted by the gun-muzzle of a grinning 11th Hussar, to make the uncomfortable but undeniable discovery that he was 'in the bag'. There was practically no resistance, and the game went on unchecked to the tune of forty vehicles in all.
>
> The chief prize was a Lancia car containing a general and his staff officer – and, to the infinite diversion of the 11th Hussars, two lady friends![1]

One of the lady friends turned out to be pregnant and her baby was eventually safely delivered in Alexandria Hospital, but the general was Generale di Corpo Lastucci, Engineer-in-Chief of the Tenth Army, and he carried with him excellently marked maps of the defences of Bardia. He was also a personal acquaintance of the new commander of the forward troops on the Egyptian side of the Wire, Lieutenant-General Richard O'Connor, for at the time of the Battle of Nezuet Ghirba, Hobart was serving as a lance-corporal in the Gloucestershire Local Defence Volunteers, soon to be renamed the Home Guard, from which exalted position he was grimly reorganising the defence of Chipping Campden.

There had been changes at high level among the British Forces. Hobart had been replaced eight months before, partly as a result of a general lack of communication with and understanding of his superiors, specifically as a result of an undignified row with Maitland Wilson, all the more unfortunate in view of the apparently good relationship established between Hobart and Wilson once Gordon-Finlayson had gone.

In July 1939, almost as soon as Wilson had taken over from Gordon-Finlayson, he visited Mersa Matruh and, in company with Hobart (with whom he had been a fellow-student at Staff College twenty years before) made a journey south into the desert, which he later described:

> The Western desert of Egypt rises gradually from the coast until Quattara depression is reached; the first major rise, in the form of an escarpment varying in height from 100 to 300 feet, runs from south of El Alamein, duplicating itself at times as far

west as Tmimi in Cyrenaica. The distances of these escarpments from the coast varied from cliffs overhanging the sea, as at Sollum and Bardia, located inside the Egyptian and Italian frontiers respectively to in other places some four or five miles [*sic*] . . .

A force with thorough knowledge of such conditions possessed a great advantage over an adversary which was new to the country. We spent two days travelling over the country to the south, enabling one to get acquainted with desert conditions including navigation and location finding. One was at once struck with the fascination of those open spaces, devoid of outstanding landmarks, the only features being low, flat-topped ridges with striking similarity so that every small object such as a cairn of stones or an empty tar barrel assumes great importance.[2]

In order to confirm what would seem to have been a good impression, Wilson then attended the closing phase of an exercise Hobart held at the end of the month and spoke later to the officers of the Mobile Force, praising the way in which it had been carried out and urging further training along the same lines.

Hobart then went on leave to England (leaving on the same day that Wavell arrived) but an early recall in view of the developing situation brought him hurrying back to Mersa Matruh and the deployment of the Mobile Force in case Italy immediately followed Germany's lead. During the uneasy months which followed, some patrolling of the frontier took place (but not much, so as not to annoy Mussolini) and exercises and training continued on the plateau until it became evident that tracks and vehicles were being worn out at too rapid a rate in relation to replacement possibilities.

Wilson quite reasonably decided upon a recall to base for at least the armoured sections of the Mobile Force for rest and refit, but announced that before they returned he would hold a signals exercise to test progress. This exercise began with a misunderstanding between Wilson who wanted to test communications and Hobart who thought it was to try out the whole Mobile Force, progressed through chaos as a result of an important code-key being retained at the wrong place (for Hobart led his force from the front instead of the rear, where Wilson assumed he would be) and ended in consuming ill-temper caused to a very great extent, as one of the Rear H.Q. Staff was to write, by Wilson's A.D.C. who 'did not seem to want to understand the instructions given him regarding map references and compass bearings which were essential to enable him to guide his General to General Hobart'.[3]

Heat, frustration and confusion all led inexorably to high blood-pressure, and in the end to a confrontation over the exercise analysis which became vituperative in the extreme, grossly unfair to all concerned and highly embarrassing to those who witnessed it.

There was a short interval during which Hobart wrote a letter to Wilson rebutting the few purely military criticisms which Wilson had made, but these were no longer of much import. The quarrel had become a personal one and on November 10th, Wilson sent to Wavell a letter which began, 'I regret to report that I have no confidence in the ability of Major-General P. C. S. Hobart, C.B., D.S.O., O.B.E., M.C., to Command the Armoured Division to my satisfaction,' and ended, 'I request therefore that a new Commander be appointed to the Armoured Division . . .'[4]

To what extent Wavell agreed with Wilson is not known – and he could have remembered the 1934 annual manoeuvres at which he had acted as umpire – but one fact was quite clear. Despite the vast size of the area now under his command, there was not room in it for both Lieutenant-General H. Maitland Wilson and Major-General P. C. S. Hobart.

The immediate reaction in the Mobile Force was one of widespread dismay, and two of his staff officers, Horace Birks and 'Strafer' Gott who was later to win great fame in the desert war, urged Hobart to fight the order, but as his biographer put it:

> Nothing of this sort could be of avail, as Hobart knew. Since he could not stay, the best course was to go with dignity. In the event he went in triumph, for as his car drove the mile and a half from his H.Q. to the airstrip it was to find the route lined by the men of his division, gunners, rifle, cavalry and tankmen, all cheering their general in a spontaneous and unforgettable farewell. They none of them knew why he was going – simply that he was and they must pour out to see him off with a demonstration of outright confidence and affection. To the General and his wife came a flood of letters from the C.O.s of all the units expressing their shock and dismay at his departure, and from Major-General Richard O'Connor, commanding the 8th Infantry Division at Matruh, who had found co-operation with Hobart easy and with whom he had worked in close accord, a sorrowful letter saying of the Mobile Division: 'It is the best trained division I have ever seen.'[5]

Fortunately for Britain and the Royal Armoured Corps, Hobart's services were not irretrievably lost as a result of this deplorable affair. Almost exactly a year after Wilson's letter had been written, he was called on Churchill's insistence for an interview with the Chief of the Imperial General Staff (by then Sir John Dill) to discuss his future employment. There was a slight conversational hiatus when Hobart inquired acidly if he should come in the uniform of a lance-corporal in the Home Guard or of a major-general, or even in civilian clothes, but that having been settled the interview took place and in due course Hobart was to raise and train the 11th Armoured Division and then the 79th (Specialised) Armoured Division which drove the 'Funnies' (the Flails which blew paths through minefields, the Crocodiles which scorched out enemy strongpoints with liquid fire, the Buffaloes which swam ashore) on to the Normandy beachhead and acted as 'tin-opener' for the British side of 21st Army Group under General Sir Bernard Montgomery who had, incidentally, been married to Hobart's sister until her tragic death in 1937.

Hobart's place was taken by Major-General Michael O'Moore Creagh, M.C., who had served most of his army career with the 15th and 19th Hussars, and who thoroughly appreciated the good fortune which had come his way. On February 16th, 1940, the Mobile Division – ex 'Mobile Force' and ex 'Immobile Farce' – became the 7th Armoured Division, and under that title was to win renown enough for twenty divisions, to make it the most famous armoured division in the British Army and one of the most famous in the world. But while there were still members of the Mobile Force alive to serve in the division, when problems arose would be heard the words, 'Well, Hobo always used to say . . .'

A much more significant appointment, however, had been that of Lieutenant-General Richard O'Connor to command the entire Western Desert Force. Shortly after the outbreak of war, Maitland Wilson had asked Cairo H.Q. for help in dealing with the growing administration of the forward troops at Mersa Matruh, and O'Connor – who had been in Jerusalem since 1937 – had come over as a major-general on a presumed temporary basis. He had returned to Palestine in early 1940 and three days before Mussolini's declaration from the Palazzo Venezia had been at Sarafan, the Headquarters of the southern district. There he received a cable summoning him to Cairo again and the following day was given orders by Maitland Wilson to go back to Mersa Matruh to assume permanent command of all forces there, and undertake the task of protecting Egypt from Italian attack.

These instructions he received, he later recalled, 'with surprise, and of course pride', adding, 'My recollection is that I was given very sketchy instructions as to policy. I did not object, really, as I don't mind being left on my own.'

The two men made an almost ludicrous contrast – Jumbo Wilson massive, heavy in jowl, deep-voiced, slow and almost majestic in gesture, filling his chair and the space to his desk almost to over-flowing; O'Connor small, bird-like, sitting nervously on the edge of his chair rather like a shy schoolboy at his first interview with his housemaster. His voice was light and clear, only the ribbons of the D.S.O. and bar, the M.C., the First World War campaign ribbons and, ironically, the Italian Silver Medal for Valour awarded him in 1918 belying this gentle manner and reminding the observer that here was a professional soldier of thirty years' service. After brilliant war service as a junior officer (in addition to his awards he had been mentioned in dispatches nine times), he had recently held very active commands indeed – the Peshawar Brigade 1936–1938, then in Palestine appointments which included the onerous and somewhat exposed post of Military Governor of Jerusalem.

Perhaps in this contrast between manner and achievement lay the key to the man. In the military world an impressive physique is an advantage, the ability to fill a uniform splendidly and gaze levelly over the top of everyone else's head an undoubted help towards promotion – and on occasion those possessed of such attributes have filled high office with great distinction. But quite often the tall, handsome general proves to possess brawn in too great a proportion to brain, and in the years to come large numbers of these, in all armies, were to achieve active command and then pass rapidly to static governorships or even back to civilian life, after a phase of battle in which other men's blood had had to pay the price for their own lack of brain.

This had never been, and would never be, the case with O'Connor. The delicate head held a cool and logical brain which saw to the heart of a problem with a certainty and quickness which could make other quite sound soldiers seem slow-witted; the slight body had already unconcernedly endured battle in Alpine snows, in Ypres mud and the heat of India, and the gentle manner masked a will and determination as firm as Wavell's. Here again was an example of the British regular soldier in the Wolseley mode – small, neat and highly professional.

But there was something else about O'Connor which Correlli Barnett was the first to note – at any rate for the benefit of the non-military world. Although others might draw more immediate attention in a company, 'no-one could talk a quarter of an hour with him without being aware of unusual qualities of character and personality'. Imagination? A more than usually acute perception? A combination of both?

Perhaps here was that 'irrational tenth' that Wavell was seeking.

By the evening of June 8th, 1940, O'Connor had reached his new headquarters at Maaten Baggush thirty miles east of Mersa Matruh, a tented camp though with H.Q. offices well dug in under sand-dunes and thus, it was hoped, bomb-proof. Inland and only a few hundred yards away was the landing-strip and headquarters of the

Desert Air Force under Air Commodore Collishaw, and even nearer, to the north, were two small and pleasant beaches for swimming. It was not so luxurious as Jerusalem had been, but perhaps the coming months would give little opportunity for soft living; in the meantime, the most important things to do would be to get to know the ground, the men under his command (he already knew most of his officers, and they knew him), their state of training and their resultant state of mobility.

Within days of taking command General O'Connor received the best possible indications of the morale of the men under him in the shape of the reports of those first brushes with the enemy, and it was with considerable relish that he greeted his acquaintance Generale Lastucci and sped him on his way towards the prison-camp in which he was to languish for many months; but as the days of June passed, worries arose as a result of the shortages of both men and material, and the strain to which both were being subjected.

On June 19th, the first war-time *khamsin* blew – a hot wind from the heart of Africa like a blast from an opened oven laden with a seemingly unending sandstorm, of which the Arabs maintain that after five days murder is thoroughly excusable. This one caught one troop of the 11th Hussars well behind the Italian lines in the vicinity of El Gubi where it was believed lay the headquarters of the 1st Libyan Division, and another at Jarabub, the oasis at the southern end of the Wire, eighty miles south of Fort Maddalena and on the edge of the Great Sand Sea.

It was here, according to the regimental history, that the effects were felt most horribly:

> On June 25th the *Khamseen* blew its very worst. It was the hottest day the 11th Hussars had yet experienced – and in fact it was probably the hottest one they ever knew. For the time being the weather transcended all considerations – with the possible exception of the growing air attacks which the squadrons were now drawing down each day. Together the two seemed calculated to defeat every attempt they made to carry on: for the heavy armoured cars were scarcely able to move owing to the water shortage, while the unarmoured Rhodesian scout cars which were trying to fulfil their role became an easy prey to the Italian fighter-bombers. In these bare open plains they were desperately vulnerable. 'One had to decide in a second either to stay quite still or to make for a patch of scrub, if available, and hope that one's car would suddenly take on the appearance of a camel-hump,' wrote one of their officers.

Looking back upon it in after years, many of the Regiment maintained that fortnight was the hardest to endure of any they experienced throughout the whole course of the war . . . it is difficult to realize from afar the intensity of the physical strain which it imposed. It was not uncommon for men to collapse unconscious on the floors of their cars . . .

Colonel John Combe, travelling round his scattered squadrons, was horrified to find the men becoming really frightened of their continual thirst under the piercing heat. For the first, and only, time in his life, he said, he saw a hunted look in their faces, as the *khamseen* went on blowing all day long and every day until the armoured cars became too hot to touch. For most of the time the exhausted crews lay sweating underneath them, for now one patrol alone would use more water than the daily allowance for a whole Troop. Bully beef and biscuits was the only fare, and the men's personal water ration had sunk to pitiful proportions. Shaving and washing had long become a rare treat, and even when it was possible pathetic attempts were made to clean used water time and time again by draining it through a perforated petrol tin filled with sand.[6]

A report back to H.Q. to the effect that the capture of Jarabub would require the support of tanks brought down to the troop the second-in-command of 4th Armoured Brigade, who was escorted forward and into the basin which held the oasis.

As they climbed back again in the full blast of the sun, the colonel said he would certainly not hear of bringing his tanks into such a furnace and that he considered the conditions entirely precluded any further operations there. Back at R.II.Q. he was just telling John Combe how he hoped to get the armoured cars withdrawn, when the heat claimed him, too, as a victim and he fell down at John Combe's feet in a dead faint. Soon afterwards General O'Connor himself arrived . . .[7]

and the operation was for the moment abandoned.

But it is interesting to note that two weeks after taking command, O'Connor was 200 miles from his base, and well behind enemy lines. Shortly afterwards, one of the advanced cars of the 11th Hussars already over fifty miles into enemy territory, met the general in his staff car coming towards them from even further west.

When the matter was reported to Brigadier Caunter, supposedly in command of the forward area, he remonstrated with his general; who apologised. But as O'Connor needed to know even more about the ground he wished to make his battle area, neither the brigadier's remonstrance nor his polite acceptance prevented him from going well past the Wire again.

As July passed, two developments became clear: the Italian

forces near the frontier were being strengthened and the British forces were tiring, despite their psychological dominance of the area. Although more men were arriving at the frontier, it took time for them to learn the lessons already absorbed by those who had been there from the beginning and common sense demanded a slackening of pressure, a cool reappraisal of potentialities. The 4th Armoured Brigade were relieved by the 7th; the 11th Hussars – still the only reconnaissance unit available – were ordered to halve their activities so that at least two troops could be resting by the sea at Buq Buq (one of C Squadron's operations had gone wrong and they had lost four men killed and fourteen taken prisoner), and a reinforced Support Group deployed to cover the whole front and act as a delaying force should the Italians attack.

This Support Group, commanded now by Brigadier W. H. E. (Strafer) Gott, consisted of three battalions of motorised infantry – 1st King's Royal Rifle Corps (originally the Royal Americans), 2nd Rifle Brigade and 3rd Coldstream Guards – two 25-pounder batteries of the Royal Horse Artillery, each battery of twelve guns; two anti-tank batteries; a troop of medium artillery; and detachments of engineers and machine-gunners. With an incomplete battalion of cruiser tanks in reserve, this force constituted the shield, and the duty squadron of the 11th Hussars the eyes, of British power in Egypt; behind them the bases were growing, the men training, the tanks and supply vehicles being repaired and maintained, the odds calculated.

These, by any count, were still formidable. Against the known five divisions which Balbo had had facing the Egyptian border plus however many Graziani intended to bring across from the Tunisian front, the Western Desert Force could marshal only the 7th Armoured Division with but 65 of its full complement of 220 cruiser tanks (and these suffered from lack of spare parts and even lack of full armament) and the 4th Indian Division, still short of one complete brigade and of much of its artillery. The Australian and New Zealand troops which had arrived, though full of enthusiasm and courage, were desperately short of all types of equipment, and the only defence against low-flying aircraft was a battery of twelve Bofors guns at Alexandria. As for air cover, there were virtually no modern bombers or fighters anywhere in the area.

With this tatterdemalion collection as his instrument, O'Connor drew up his plans for the defence of Egypt against an Italian attack. Incredibly, he was neither discouraged nor depressed by his conclusions, and quietly confident that if and when an Italian army crossed the frontier and advanced towards the obvious first objective – Mersa Matruh – he would be able to launch out of the desert against its flank a force strong enough to cut through and reach the sea, thus isolating the main enemy force and perhaps defeating it by starvation. How long his own force would be able to hold against attacks which would then almost certainly develop from both directions, was something in the lap of the Gods; perhaps they would be kind.

In the meantime, the thing to do would be to continue intensive training, to use every day that Italian dilatoriness gave him to strengthen his force qualitatively and hope that Britain or India would help him quantitatively.

Maresciallo d'Armata Graziani had arrived in North Africa at the end of June, the recipient of an order intended for his predecessor Balbo but which, as it had been dispatched the day he was killed, had never reached him. Mussolini had concluded that the invasion of Great Britain was imminent, that the first German soldiers would be ashore on Britain's embattled coasts by July 15th and that Italian troops must cross the Libyan–Egyptian frontier on the same day. However, any support Graziani had given this proposal when he had been Army Chief of Staff in Rome, evaporated during the next few days as he hurriedly inspected his inheritance in Libya.

His first communication back to Comando Supremo announced that not only would he require every item on Balbo's list, but that Balbo had lamentably failed to appreciate the paralysing inadequacy of the Italian air force in Africa. Of the 350 aircraft on strength on June 10th only 60 were still effective after three weeks of war, and of these most were obsolescent compared with the modern, fast, hard-hitting fighters which the enemy would be able to range against them. (Air Commodore Collishaw would have been surprised and gratified to read that signal.) Many more fighters, reconnaissance aircraft and transport planes were essential before an attack into Egypt could be mounted, and new techniques along the lines of the German Stuka dive-bombing must be worked out and practised.

Graziani was probably not particulary surprised at the response he received from Badoglio – to the effect that the attack *must* begin on the specified day, that he must if necessary strip the Fifth Army facing Tunisia of equipment and transport and give it all to the Tenth Army, and that in the meantime seventy medium tanks had been dispatched together with other items on Balbo's list which had become available; but he could not have been very heartened by it either. The message ended on a note of combined encouragement and entreaty. 'In Somalia, you overcame very great difficulties; you will overcome similar ones now. Give me an assurance of this!'

Gloomily, Graziani called a conference with his senior commanders and their staffs and on July 5th he forwarded their conclusions and plans for action as requested. It would be taking an enormous risk, his report declared, but in accordance with the wishes of Il Duce as transmitted by the Comando Supremo, Tenth Army would advance through the Wire on July 15th, cross the frontier, descend the Escarpment at its northern end – and occupy Sollum. Here a new base could be set up and, once the expected furious reaction of the enemy had been fought off, the resultant casualties in men and material replaced and reinforcements brought up, a further advance could be considered. Of course, it would be quite impossible to advance much further along the widening coastal belt without the tanks, water-carriers, anti-aircraft and anti-tank batteries plus other miscellaneous equipment which Maresciallo d'Armata Balbo had wisely requested, together with the aircraft which had been the subject of his own latest communication – and now also plus a force of new armoured cars without which any sort of manoeuvring action would be impossible.

What happened during the next ten days is somewhat obscure, but July 15th came and went without either a reply from Rome (though one had been drafted) or, not surprisingly, an advance through the Wire. When Badoglio's letter did at last arrive, it was to the effect that Comando Supremo thought that the trouble and effort of moving forward at all required a greater reward than just the occupation of a small post at the bottom of the hill, and that as it now seemed unlikely that German troops would be fighting on British soil as early as had been expected, it would be better to await the arrival of the required material and then advance in strength upon a more ambitious plan. A convoy carrying 'a great part' of the equipment which Balbo and Graziani had requested should arrive in Tripoli on July 27th, and the advance might be expected to commence in early August.

Two ships duly arrived, and in addition a personal letter to Graziani from Il Duce, spurring him on to greater glories both for his country and himself and ending in a cloud of metaphor: 'I hope and feel sure that having been the anvil for several weeks, it will be possible quickly to become the hammer – which, held in your staunch hands, will deal out resolute blows to the enemy!'

Time, however, had been given to Graziani for consideration of several factors which had perhaps not been quite so clear to him before his arrival in Tripoli. In his reply to Badoglio's letter suggesting a deeper advance into enemy territory than just down to Sollum, there is a note of surprise, tinged with reproof for a lack of understanding of practical realities. 'Such an operation [as was suggested] cannot be considered as other than impossible during this season, given the physical and topographical environment.' The summer heat alone apparently precluded physical effort of the magnitude necessary for such an advance, not to speak of the water shortage – which would now be exacerbated by the enormous number of vehicles which Comando Supremo were promising him, each one of which would require even more water than the men it carried. 'An action of this nature can only be effected, even though still presenting grave difficulties, at the end of the hot season, towards the end of October' – upon which note of sweet reason the letter ended.

The result of this was a curt summons back to Rome where on August 5th occurred an acrimonious exchange of views, ending in a compromise. A 'limited objective' offensive (though presumably not so limited as Sollum) would now be launched in order 'to relieve troublesome British pressure' along the Cyrenaican frontier, to establish a base below the Escarpment and to raise the morale of the Italian troops, now depressed by prolonged inaction.

But a clearer view of the reasons for the proposed advance is revealed in a letter Mussolini sent Graziani on August 10th:

> The invasion of Great Britain has been decided on, its preparations are in the course of completion and it will take place. Concerning the date, it could be within a week or within a month. Well, the day on which the first platoon of German soldiers touches British territory, you will simultaneously attack. Once again, I repeat that there are no territorial objectives, it is not a question of aiming for Alexandria, nor even for Sollum. I am only asking you to attack the British forces facing you. I assume full personal responsibility for this decision of mine.

As a recipe for military disaster, that must rate high in the annals of politico-military incompetence, but it gave some comfort and relief to Graziani who immediately assured Mussolini that his orders would be obeyed. The next day he issued instructions to Generale d'Armata Berti, commanding Tenth Army, to be ready to move on August 27th with as first objective the Sollum Escarpment (top or bottom?), and the final objective, 'should maximum exploitation be achievable', of Sidi Barrani.

As Hitler's invasion of Britain was apparently to be postponed for some time, the date of attack was allowed a little elasticity but, on Mussolini's strict injunction, was not to be later than September 9th. And at dawn on September 13th, it actually did begin – 'with', as one of the generals was later to record, 'much dedication on everyone's part'.

Five days beforehand, an Italian fighter had swooped low over the Advanced Headquarters of 7th Armoured Brigade and dropped a message-bag; it contained the names of all the British soldiers who had been taken prisoner by the Italians to that date (mostly 11th

Hussars) with a report on their health and a letter from the senior British officer among them, confirming all details, giving surprisingly full explanations of how they had all been taken prisoner, and assuring their colonel, John Combe, that they were being well looked after. One sergeant who had died of wounds had been buried with full military honours.

There were, apparently, to be no hard feelings on either side at this stage of the desert campaign.

On the Italian side there was also to be a total lack of subtlety or deception. Graziani's original plan was for an advance along the coast by the XXI (Metropolitan) Corps, with two divisions in front and one held back in reserve near Tobruk, while two motorised Libyan Divisions augmented by a mobile group under command of Generale di Corpo Maletti (who had won renown in the Ethiopian Campaign and a reputation as a 'fire-eater') swung across the Escarpment to the south as a shield for the main infantry.

This was still the plan on September 9th, but during September 10th and 11th, the Maletti Group lost its way to the assembly point near Sidi Omar and had to be searched for by aircraft diverted from planned attacks on the British advance posts, while the Libyan divisions, watched curiously by the ever-present 11th Hussars, had taken an unconscionable time to rendezvous near Fort Capuzzo. Moreover, Graziani about this time received word of 'massive British armoured forces' augmented by the 'excellent and omnipresent Camel Corps' deployed to strike at his southern flank, so he decided to guard against this threat by giving the lead of the coastal advance to the Libyan Divisions (62nd Marmarica and 63rd Cyrene) and instructing Maletti to follow a more northerly course, thereby sheltering the advancing infantry more closely and perhaps moving out of reach of the threatening enemy. If battle casualties among the Libyans at the head of the main advance became too heavy, then that exposed position could be taken over by 1st Blackshirt (23rd March) Division, while the 4th Blackshirt and the 64th Catanzaro Divisions could now both remain in reserve near Tobruk. It was necessary to safeguard the lives of native sons as far as was possible.

So, at dawn on September 13th the Italian invasion of Egypt began with a spectacular artillery bombardment of the old Egyptian barracks at Musaid on the edge of the Escarpment (which had been empty for some days) followed by their occupation by a column which entered Egypt through the gaps in the Wire left obligingly by the 11th Hussars. Once there, the artillery was then deployed nearby and opened up another barrage on the old barracks at Sollum and the landing-grounds just below them. When the dust of this second barrage cleared, the head of the main coastal thrust was revealed, drawn up as though on Sunday parade, lines of motor-cycle troops in front, light tanks and staff cars behind, lorries stretching back into the distance.

With a roar of engines starting up, the whole cavalcade began to move majestically forward to the top of the winding pass which led down to Sollum, while the troops who had occupied Musaid in their turn moved further along eastwards until they came to the top of what was to become one of the most famous and contested passages in Egypt, Halfaya Pass. Meanwhile, the only British troops in the area – a single platoon of the 3rd Coldstream Guards who had been watching all this panoply of war with fascination – closed down the signal net upon which they had been reporting it all, unobtrusively but rapidly left Sollum itself and activated the mines sown along the tracks leading eastwards.

The Italian descent of both passes thereupon became hazardous. As the motor-cyclist advance guards roared around the hairpin bends, rifle shots cracked overhead and an understandable nervous astonishment tweaked their handle-bars to send them shooting over the edge or swerving dangerously in front of their compatriots behind; tank tracks were blown off on mine-fields and at certain bends in the track, lorries would arrive simultaneously with British 25-pounder shells, the guns having been fired as sunlight caught the lorry windscreens on previous bends. (The Royal Horse Artillery had one of the most successful days in its history.)

From above came whistling fragmentation bombs from R.A.F. Blenheims while slow but agile Gladiators zoomed along the routes machine-gunning the stalled lorries and marching troops. High above it all, the few Hurricanes in Egypt fought it out with the Fiats and Macchis, stricken planes wheeling down in flame and smoke to end with a dull thump away in the desert.

And all the time, the marching Italian infantry columns built up behind and began inexorably to overflow down the passes, scrambling around the blocked lorries, over the wrecked tanks, past the scars left along the verges by exploding mines. They were joined by the lorried infantry escaping from the baulked and dangerous caverns of their vehicles, and a khaki-grey flood built up, lapping all the time towards the white-topped stone huts and abandoned dumps of the port area of Sollum.

Here a neat but harmless comedy was being played out. Royal Engineers had mined most of the buildings and dumps, retiring down the coast a short distance with their detonating wires. They had been about to start blowing up the buildings when an Italian artillery observation plane appeared above the port and shortly afterwards a barrage opened up from over the rim of the Escarpment. Appreciating the situation, the sapper officer instructed his men to wait until they heard a gun fire, then, just as the shell was due to land, to blow up one of their charges. Inevitably, the blown charge was not in the same place as the gun-fire had been directed, and the air-observer became obviously more and more confused as too many explosions took place, few of which he could identify as his own. Eventually the British charges were all exploded, the engineers retired, the plane flew off and what remained of Sollum after two armies had tried to destroy it was slowly occupied by weary Libyan infantry. By late afternoon lorries, tanks and more motor-cyclists were arriving and the advance eastward along the coast had begun. As there was no surfaced road at that time between Sollum and Sidi Barrani fifty miles to the east, and British army traffic and now shell-fire had crushed the surface into an even finer dust than before, it was a choking, blinding and tongue-searing experience for all.

Up on the plateau, the Italian troops who had attacked Musaid, together with another division which had come up from Sidi Omar, also spent a tiring and frustrating day, their transport boiling in the hot sun and the enforced slow pace, the thirsty infantry trudging desperately and miserably alongside, the motor-cyclists bumping across rocks or stuck in soft sand, rarely able to show the speed and flair for which they were intended. And all the time they were subjected to machine-gun attacks and occasionally to shelling from the marauding and infuriatingly elusive enemy, cruising always just beyond their grasp with an ease and confidence of movement which appeared magical.

On arrival at the top of Halfaya Pass they found even worse conditions reigning, for enormous traffic jams had built up in the gathering darkness and by nightfall thousands of Italian and Libyan soldiers were crowded into formed leaguer, with lorry headlights and searchlights sweeping the desert approaches to help guard against more enemy onslaughts. These made excellent and rewarding aiming points for the guns of the Support Group detachment, which Brigadier Gott had left up on the plateau.

From the British point of view, despite the undoubted success of their harassing tactics and the boost to their already high morale of this clear demonstration of their superiority, man for man, in desert fighting, one overwhelming and sobering fact emerged. Three battalions of infantry plus assorted artillery, tanks and armoured cars, however well handled, cannot hold up for long a force of five divisions, however lethargic they may be.

Strafer Gott commanding the Support Group and Lieutenant-Colonel Jock Campbell commanding the 25-pounder batteries of the Royal Horse Artillery might have had an exciting and successful day – as had the officers and men of the K.R.R.C., the Rifle Brigade and Coldstream Guards – but to Wavell and O'Connor watching from Headquarters the nagging questions were, 'When would the grey tide stop flowing?' and, 'How many divisions are there still in Libya to back up the five divisions which have now been identified in this first attack?' They were fairly confident that they could hold the first thrust on Mersa Matruh, and the heavier tank units of 7th Armoured Division were now poised to strike northwards from the plateau as soon as the enemy lines of communication were sufficiently exposed – but how long could the tanks and guns of one division hold out against those of at least five divisions, especially in view of the chronic shortage of vehicles and ammunition which plagued them all?

Even now, the gunners of the Support Group were looking anxiously at their ammunition stocks, and although the supply columns had no trouble in racing up when required, the 25-pounders were being fed from ever-diminishing dumps; not that that stopped them on the morrow from repeating and even exceeding their exploits of the previous day, when movement started again and the two Italian columns met and merged (became, in fact, inextricably mixed) at the foot of Halfaya Pass. Batteries of both 3rd and 4th Royal Horse Artillery plastered the concentration as it formed and eddied, spilling out over the plain and re-forming into columns to move forward again to the slight rise where the Coldstream Guards awaited it, to fight the first of that day's series of delaying actions.

All through September 14th, the pattern was the same; the R.H.A. batteries would fire at the plodding mass as it edged forward on wider and wider fronts until the risk of being overrun became real, then they would limber up and move back to the next position. The Coldstream Guards held the line until the guns opened up again, when they in their turn could slip away; by evening, tired and hot but still quite confident, all were back east of the salt-pan by the sea at the miserable location rejoicing in the singular name of Buq Buq. Further east and behind them at Sidi Barrani waited the remainder of the Support Group, with the exception of C Squadron of the 11th Hussars still watching the gap at Bir Shefersen south of Sidi Omar.

And there was no change on September 15th except that in the early afternoon the R.H.A. completely ran out of ammunition and were quickly withdrawn through the supporting infantry, which in turn watched and waited for the moment when they would themselves have to retreat through the line of the 11th's armoured cars, right back to the last defences at Mersa Matruh. Meanwhile, the main weight of the 7th Armoured Division moved a little closer towards its attack position and girded itself for its first major action – apparently to be fought on or about September 17th and 18th. All were quite confident that they would be able to give good account of themselves.

Then at dusk on the 16th the Italian forward troops reached Sidi Barrani, probed a little further on as far as Maktila where they waited for the main mass to settle in behind them, and to the only British troops still in contact (the 11th Hussars, needless to say) it gradually became evident that this was where they intended to stay. The following evening, while the tank crews of 7th Armoured Division were beginning to relax with some degree of disgust, Rome radio concluded a long panegyric on the glorious advance of their Tenth Army in Libya against fanatical but out-manoeuvred British troops with the announcement that 'All is now quiet in Sidi Barrani, the shops are open and the trams running again' – which would have come as a surprise to the inhabitants, most of whom had never seen a tram in their lives.

A few days later, Sergeant Peacock of the 11th Hussars edged his way to within 200 yards of an outlying Italian post under cover of the morning mist, and watched an Italian officer talking to a civilian dressed in suit and trilby hat, both poring over a civil-engineering blue-print. Behind them waited a gang of labourers carrying picks and shovels, and there was curiously little evidence to suggest that here lay the forward outpost of a thrusting military empire. Solid fortifications were undoubtedly to be constructed, but it looked as though a further advance was not for the moment under consideration.

Soon after that, Gladiator pilots reported work commencing on the construction of a well-surfaced road between Sollum and Sidi Barrani, the laying of water-pipes and the arrival of tons of supplies at the end of the Bir Sofafi track, well to the south, where Generale Maletti's group had also come to rest. Evidently, Graziani's much-vaunted attack had ground to a halt, and there was for the moment to be no further thrust towards Mersa Matruh or continuation of the Drive to the Nile.

'It was all', said General O'Connor as he withdrew the tanks of the 7th Armoured Division and redeployed the Support Group, 'rather a disappointment.'

3 · The Pace Quickens

'Nobody', wrote Wavell's son many years later, 'would call my father a chatty general' – a delightful comment but one whose truth occasionally makes things difficult for the historian endeavouring to pierce the screen of inscrutability behind which Wavell so often hid his immediate reaction to events.

Because of his Olympian viewpoint of Middle East affairs at this time, his reactions inevitably differed from those of his subordinates, aware only of their own immediate problems. O'Connor and the Western Desert Force were intent only upon events along the Libyan border; Wavell had at least four frontiers to watch – with Libya, East Africa, Syria and Iraq – intricately balanced political situations in the last two to judge, and, ever since hostilities had commenced in Europe, a highly imaginative, demanding and often aggressively argumentative political master in Winston Churchill at home.

The withdrawal of France from the war against the Axis Powers had monumentally increased Wavell's problems. Not only had he now lost any hope of support from Tunis in the battle against Graziani's forces, but by the end of June 1940 it had become obvious that Général Mittelhauser (who had succeeded Weygand in command of the French armies in Syria and the Levant) was prepared to accept the Franco-German Armistice terms, and the announcement to this effect was almost immediately followed by the attack by the Royal Navy upon the French Fleet at Mers el Kebir and Oran.

Whatever the justification for this – and as Churchill said, 'Who in his senses would trust the word of Hitler [that he would not use the French Fleet against their former allies] after his shameful record and the facts of the hour?' – it had the effect of fanning the always latent French Anglophobia into open hatred, and strengthened the hand of the Vichy Government in any anti-British attitudes they cared to adopt. These were quickly indicated by the replacement of Général Mittelhauser by the rabidly anti-British Général Fougère, and then further demonstrated by instructions to the pro-British Général Legentilhomme in French Somaliland to cease all communications with his neighbours to the east, and prepare instead to collaborate with the representatives of the Duke of Aosta away to his west in Addis Ababa. When it became obvious that Legentilhomme had few sympathies with his country's new rulers in Vichy a replacement was sent out who was likely to prove more amenable, and Legentilhomme crossed the narrows from Djibuti to Aden where he received a friendlier welcome than he was likely to get at home.

The hostility from across the Syrian and Levantine frontiers was to pose a problem for some time to come; that from French Somaliland was fairly quickly resolved, though not in the manner Wavell would have preferred.

The Italian forces in East Africa – in Eritrea, Abyssinia and Italian Somaliland, all under command of the Duke of Aosta – had not been entirely inactive, but neither had they exhibited much

Map 2   Italian East Africa

more aggression than had their compatriots in Libya. Caproni bombers had occasionally attacked Port Sudan on the Red Sea coast, Atbara, the inland road junction, Kassala, the small provincial town near the Sudan–Ethiopian border, and Kurmuk further south, but there had been little ground activity. However, on July 4th, somewhat to the surprise of the two companies of the Sudan Defence Force there, Kassala was attacked by three columns of Italian and native troops, consisting of two colonial brigades, four cavalry squadrons with some twenty-four light tanks and armoured cars, together with ten batteries of artillery.

The ensuing action was brisk but shortlived, and the result was inevitable. By evening the defending companies had retired some twenty miles to the next rail-stop at Butana Bridge having suffered ten casualties, while the Italian command was reporting occupation of an important stronghold at a cost of 117 dead and wounded.

This had not been all. Nearly 200 miles south at Gallabat (again, virtually on the Sudan–Ethiopian frontier) an Italian colonial battalion had driven a platoon of No. 3 Company Eastern Arab Corps away, while during the next few days the police posts at Karora and Kurmuk were attacked and occupied, and their Sudanese occupants dispersed, in every case after a spirited defence and well-conducted retreat.

From these successes the Italians made valuable tactical gains, for in Kassala they now possessed a springboard for any further advance into the Sudan, and in Gallabat they had secured a block against any British intentions against Ethiopia.

They had also, inevitably, given hostages to fortune, for they now held outposts which could become targets for that speciality of the British and especially the Indian Army, infantry patrolling – a disadvantage which became only too evident in the weeks that followed.

Then, as July ended and the enormous heat of equatorial Africa in August began to build up, it became evident that in the Duke of Aosta, Britain had a more determined antagonist than the one on the Libyan border. Despite the heat, the Duke intended to rid himself of hostility on at least one border and had concluded that the enclave formed by British Somaliland, now neatly invested on three sides, could be eliminated by the expulsion of the occupying forces out through the fourth side and into the Gulf of Aden.

To Wavell it had always been a cardinal principle that territory should not be given up without a fight, but now, with the acute shortage of men throughout his vast command, he had to compromise and accept the classic dictum to the effect that a soldier saved is a soldier won. He was well aware of the probable size of the force which Aosta was massing along an extremely vulnerable frontier, while his own forces were so exiguous that in July they were still commanded by a lieutenant-colonel of the Royal Marines. Hastily promoting him to brigadier, Wavell endeavoured to amass for him the force of at least five battalions which he would require to put up any worthwhile defence, and by the beginning of August Brigadier A. R. Chater had under his command 1st Battalion North Rhodesia Regiment, 2nd Battalion King's African Rifles, 1st/2nd Punjab Regiment, 3rd/15th Punjab Regiment and the 1st East African Light Battery with four 3·7-inch howitzers. He also had elements of the lightly armed Camel Corps which had recently been augmented by officers and N.C.O.s from the Southern Rhodesia Regiment, while the 2nd Battalion the Black Watch was en route from Aden.

Against this, the Italian Force Commander, Generale di Corpo Nasi, had twenty-six Italian and Colonial battalions, twenty-one batteries of mixed artillery, assorted tanks, armoured cars and aircraft (of which Chater had none at all) and five groups of 'irregulars' – who might or might not fight, but who would undoubtedly prove highly dangerous to a defeated or retreating force.

The Italian forces crossed the British Somaliland frontier on August 3rd in the form of a trident, the main force under Generale di Divisione de Simone advancing towards Hargeisa, his left flank guarded by a column under Generale di Corpo Bertoldi moving on to Zeila (and thus masking the frontier with French Somaliland, just in case some of the departed Général Legentilhomme's supporters might wish to help the beleaguered British), his right flank guarded by a similar column under Generale di Brigata Bertello whose first objective was Odweina.

By August 5th, the Camel Corps screens and a company of the Northern Rhodesia Regiment which had been operating with them had withdrawn on all attacked frontages, and the Italian forces had reached their objectives – at which point Bertoldi sent light patrols eastwards along the coast while the other two columns began an amalgamating move on the small town of Adadle. From this area would be launched the main attack across the only natural defence between the Ethiopian frontier and the sea, a range of rugged hills which ran parallel to the coast, about fifty miles from it. A wide gap existed here through which ran the main road from Hargeisa to the capital and only port, Berbera, and here, at the Tug Argan as it was called, would be fought the battle for British Somaliland.

Numbers made the result a foregone conclusion, numbers combined with a lack of artillery on the part of the defenders illustrated by the offer from H.M.A.S. *Hobart*, part of the naval contingent standing by to aid the inevitable evacuation, of a 3-pounder saluting gun with thirty rounds of ammunition – an offer which was grate-

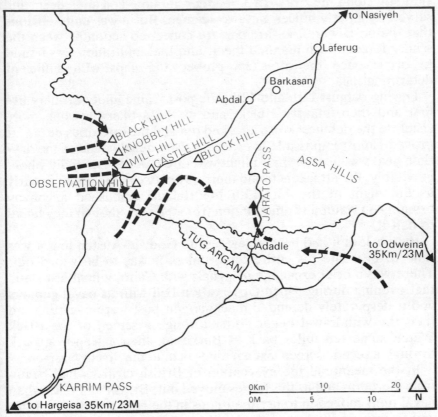

Map 3 The battle of Tug Argan

fully accepted. The only other artillery available were the four light howitzers mentioned above, although Wavell, once he had realised that the Italians were invading in strength, had ordered two anti-tank guns to be sent to Berbera by special convoy, together with some of the 4th Indian Division's guns from the hardly less threatened Western Desert. He also requested the Command in India to dispatch immediately the first convoy of the 5th Indian Division, already earmarked for the Middle East, and then in view of the build-up in strength in the area should it all arrive in time to stem the Italians, he diverted Major-General A. R. Godwin-Austen from his journey to East Africa where he was about to take command of the 2nd African Division.

The general arrived on the evening of August 11th and found that virtually the entire force under his command was already in action. Five hills in the Tug Argan gap – Black Hill, Knobbly Hill, Mill Hill, Observation Hill and Castle Hill – had been prepared for defence with barbed wire and machine-gun posts, and on Observation Hill stood the *Hobart*'s 3-pounder, mounted on an oildrum and served by a petty officer and two seamen. But it was quite obvious that the posts were too far apart for concerted action between the scanty forces which manned them, and that infiltration was bound to occur once the attackers probed the gaps with sufficient determination.

During August 11th and 12th, the posts came under artillery fire first and then infantry attack, and as the artillery became more accurate the defences were knocked out and the casualties began. It proved almost impossible to evacuate them quickly, and as the day-time heat was intense their plight was dire indeed, especially when, inevitably, the attackers found their way between the posts; as early as the night of the 13th/14th the Italians ambushed a convoy bringing up water and ammunition from the rear, though they failed to halt it.

By the 15th it had become evident to Godwin-Austen that it was time to evacuate his entire force unless it was to be wiped out. There was a brief exchange of signals with Cairo, a final last stand that evening during which Observation Hill with its naval gunners and a desperately defended machine-gun post were overrun, and then the withdrawal began – first through a screen of the Black Watch some ten miles back at Barkasan, then a leap-frog back through a second screen sixteen miles behind the first at Nasiyeh.

In the meantime the evacuation of British civilians had begun from Berbera, and as the ferries moved out, British and Australian naval units moved in to use their guns in the final perimeter battles and to pick up the last of the troops as they reached the coast. By 1400 on August 18th all survivors of the action (together with the civilians they amounted to about 7,000 souls) were safely aboard and away, although H.M.A.S. *Hobart* with Force Headquarters aboard remained until the morning of the 19th in order to be certain that no lone individuals were still arriving. She was also on hand to greet with a final salvo the first Italian troops to approach the port.

The defence of British Somaliland had cost 260 casualties, of which some were later to be recovered, and as the Italians were at that time still broadcasting their losses, the British had the satisfaction of finding out that they had cost their attackers 2,052 in dead and wounded together with a great deal of military equipment. The whole operation had undoubtedly been carried out with great skill and efficiency, under testing conditions, and the co-operation between the Royal Navy, the Army and the Royal Air Force once operations had come within range of the Aden-based bombers had been professional in the extreme.

It was a great pity that this truth was not more evident in Whitehall.

Although Wavell was back in Cairo by the time the evacuation from Berbera was complete, he had just spent eight days in London, a substantial portion of them in the company of the Prime Minister. These meetings had not been an unqualified success.

It was hardly likely that they would be, for the two men – both of enormous strength of character – were poles apart in attitude to the common problems and in background and training to overcome them. Churchill, bearing then the enormous burdens of a Prime Minister at the time of his country's greatest danger – and revelling in them – was using his great qualities of courage, imagination and unflinching optimism to sweep his countrymen out of their desperate plight on a tide of emotion and oratory. His attitude to military problems was greatly affected by his tendency to simplify arithmetic by dealing only in round figures – and optimistically rounded at that – allied to a belief that practically any member of any military formation, if issued with a rifle, was perfectly fit and able to take his place in the front line.

To those entrusted with the tasks of actually fighting and winning the battles upon which Britain's existence depended, the Prime Minister's viewpoint therefore posed many problems, though few commanders – and certainly not Wavell – ever forgot the vital impulse which Churchill was contributing to their joint effort or believed that their own part in the war was more important than his.

Even more significant, however, than the differences in technical training between Churchill and the majority of his service advisers – and Wavell was typical of them in this – were their different attitudes to personal behaviour

Churchill was a politician and parliamentarian – some would claim the greatest parliamentarian of his age – and he had climbed to the peak of power by the use of his great parliamentary gifts. Every facet of the art of verbal persuasion, from sweet reason through flattery, sarcasm, Ciceronian irony, mordant wit, plain verbal bullying and personal abuse, was his to command, and as he was quite rightly convinced of the justice of the great cause upon which he was engaged, he had no hesitation in using all his skills upon every occasion when he felt that his own way was the best. As these occasions were frequent, so were those upon which he used the full range of his talents, and when occurring in the House of Commons or in Cabinet they were accepted by his parliamentary colleagues as part of the day to day cut-and-thrust of the business of government.

But when they occurred in debate with his service advisers, the results were by no means so happy. At this period of the war, the Chief of the Imperial Staff was Sir John Dill, a sensitive and at that time extremely anxious man who was also a great personal friend of

Wavell's; and his sessions with Churchill, which the Prime Minister enjoyed so much, exhausted and sickened Dill.

But at least Dill would answer Churchill's verbal attacks, and endeavour to parry the master's thrusts with some kind of argument. Wavell met them with taciturnity or, even more frustrating for Churchill, with one of his formidable but total silences, followed in due course by a lucid and cogently argued paper in which many of the Prime Minister's most attractively presented verbal points were revealed as impractical and sometimes patently absurd fancies.

Not only did this difference in behaviour create great tension between the two men, but it stirred unfortunate memories in Churchill's mind. Twenty-four years before, Lloyd George had been confronted with just such a façade of impassive silence by General Haig at their meetings, and much later the latter revealed in his diaries a contempt for his political master only equalled by Lloyd George's distrust of the general. As Lloyd George was in many ways Churchill's political model and exemplar, the idea cannot have escaped the Prime Minister that the commander of the only army which Britain had in the field did not hold him in very high esteem. There would also have arisen in the Prime Minister's mind the possibility that Wavell might repeat Haig's performance as a military commander, which in Churchill's opinion would be disastrous.

Nevertheless, the discussions progressed, based to a large extent upon a detailed exposition of the situation in the Middle East given by Wavell on the second day of his visit to the Chief of Staff's Committee, and if there was disagreement between politician and soldier on the distribution and use of military manpower in the area, there was total agreement on the need for further reinforcement and, even more important, for a swift and considerable build-up of supplies and arms of every sort.

Considering the fact that the Battle of Britain was at that very moment reaching its climax and that all over England men were drilling with armbands instead of uniforms, with pikes instead of rifles and still with flags instead of anti-tank guns, Churchill and the War Cabinet showed admirable courage in the decision they took the day after Wavell's dissertation to the Committee – to send to the Middle East a convoy bearing a Cruiser Tank Battalion, a Light Tank Battalion (both of 52 tanks), an Infantry Tank Battalion of 50 tanks, 48 anti-tank guns, 20 Bofors light anti-aircraft guns, 48 25-pounder field guns, 500 Brens, 250 anti-tank rifles and as large a supply of ammunition for all of them as could be assembled in time.

There followed a brisk exchange of memoranda between the Admiralty who held doubts about the wisdom of convoying so valuable a shipment through the Mediterranean, and Churchill who had a keen and justifiable sense of the importance of time in military matters and felt that the risk should be accepted. The argument was not entirely resolved when the time came for Wavell to return to Cairo where he arrived on August 16th, but his reflections upon his meetings with the Prime Minister were perceptive and prophetic:

> I do not think Winston quite knew what to make of me and whether I was fit to command or not. He was determined that something must be done to put the defence of Egypt on a sound basis; and in providing reinforcements of tanks and sending a convoy through the Mediterranean was bold in overriding the views both of those who wished to keep all armoured forces for home defence . . . and of the First Sea Lord . . .
>
> On certain details the P.M. was difficult. He did his best to make me move both South African and West African troops from East Africa to Egypt or the Sudan; and he never realised the necessity for full equipment before committing troops to battle. I remember his arguing that because a comparatively small number of mounted Boers had held up a British division in 1899 or 1900, it was unnecessary for the South African Brigade to have much more equipment than rifles before taking the field in 1940. In fact I found that Winston's tactical ideas had to some extent crystallised at the South African War, just as his ideas on India's political problems . . . had not advanced much from his impressions as a subaltern in the nineties . . .
>
> In the end . . . I succeeded in convincing him that it would not be advantageous or politic to move the African troops from East Africa. At least I convinced him that I wouldn't do it. I am pretty sure that he considered my replacement by someone who was more likely to share his ideas, but could not find any good reason to do so.[1]

Unfortunately, there then followed an incident which deepened the dislike which Wavell felt that Churchill had already conceived for him. As Wavell was leaving Britain there had occurred the exchange of signals between Generals Godwin-Austen and Wilson which had resulted in the evacuation of British Somaliland – a decision to which Wavell gave his full support as soon as he reached his headquarters; but within hours Mussolini was trumpeting loudly his army's victory over British military might in this, their first major encounter, and on August 20th he proclaimed that Italian forces were now exercising a 'total blockade' of all British possessions in the Mediterranean and in Africa.

Although Churchill was well aware of the basic facts of the situation, this propaganda victory by Il Duce annoyed him considerably. At that same moment there arrived on his desk the statistics of the retreat, revealing that British casualties had amounted to a mere 260 dead, wounded and missing, and reverting to a habit of thought of a previous age which had often interpreted a battle's success by the size of the resultant casualty list (on one's own side) he dashed off what Wavell later described as 'a red-hot cable' demanding the suspension of Godwin-Austen from command and the immediate assembly of a court of inquiry into an episode which he clearly regarded as tinged with disgrace.

Wavell replied with a cable refusing both the suspension of a competent general and the holding of an unnecessary inquiry, pointing out that the troops had fought well and hard and, as the Italians had themselves admitted, had inflicted far more casualties than they themselves had suffered. The cable ended with the gravid admonition, 'A big butcher's bill is not necessarily evidence of good tactics.'

For somebody who was used to dealing in the language of both praise and rebuke, Churchill took this very badly; perhaps because it was on paper. The great neck flushed deep red, the baby-blue eyes glowered, and General Dill, who was present, later wrote to Wavell that he had never seen the Prime Minister so angry. It was a reaction which would later exact its toll, but in the meantime Churchill had composed the first of what was to be a long series of directives to the generals in the field. It reached Cairo late on the afternoon of August 23rd as a signal which when deciphered covered three and a half pages of close typing – and as Wavell later wrote, 'It showed clearly that Winston did not trust me to run my own show and was set on his ideas.'

The directive first analysed the military situation in the Middle East as Churchill saw it, then with a series of tables proved that by October 1st Wavell would have under his command a force of thirty-nine battalions altogether totalling 56,000 men with 212 guns, not including any security troops. It was not an analysis with which Wavell agreed, especially as the Prime Minister had again reverted to the suggestion that South and West African troops should be moved up from Kenya, despite Wavell's expressed determination not to carry this out.

The last part of the directive gave detailed and explicit instructions as to how this force of thirty-nine battalions was to be deployed for the defence of the Delta and then went on:

> In this posture, then, the Army of the Delta will await the Italian invasion. It must be expected that the enemy will advance in great force, limited only, but severely, by the supply of water and petrol. He will certainly have strong armoured forces on his

right hand to contain and drive back our weaker forces, unless these can be reinforced in time by the armoured regiment from Great Britain. He will mask, if he cannot storm, Mersa Matruh. But if the main line of the Delta is diligently fortified and resolutely held he will be forced to deploy an army whose supply of water, petrol, food, and ammunition will be difficult. Once the army is deployed and seriously engaged, the action against his communications, from Mersa Matruh, by bombardment from the sea, by descent at Sollum, or even much further west, would be a deadly blow to him.

All this might be put effectively in train by October 1, *provided we are allowed the time*. If not, we must do what we can. All trained or Regular units, whether fully equipped or not, must be used in defence of the Delta. All armed white men and also Indian or foreign units must be used for internal security. The Egyptian Army must be made to play its part in support of the Delta front, thus leaving only riotous crowds to be dealt with in Egypt proper.[2]

In view of the lack of information of Italian strengths and intentions at this time (for it must be remembered that Graziani had not moved when the directive was written) there is much of truth and value in the overall analysis of the situation as set out in the directive; but it also demonstrated, as perhaps nothing else could, the wide gap between the viewpoint of a political leader – however gifted – looking at the situation from Whitehall, and that of a military technician dealing with practicalities on the spot.

Later, Wavell was to write, 'I carried out such parts of the directive as were practical and useful, and disregarded a good deal of it' – which, in view of the fact that this was obviously the best thing to do, throws an interesting light on the basic tenet of our democracy that the military must always be subordinate to the elected representatives of the people.

Wavell replied to the directive in four cables sent over the next five days, diplomatically sidestepping some issues, avoiding others as best he could, and only entering the difficult arenas of categorical rejection in the matters of demonstrable statistics. Upon Churchill's figures of strength, he commented:

Approximate total of forces excluding Egyptian for defence of Egypt by 8th October is 38 battalions, 156 field guns, 18 medium guns, 90 anti-tank guns, 1,000 anti-tank rifles, 239 Bren-carriers, 40 A.A. guns, 12 light A.A. guns. Above includes reserves. Please note that proper proportion equipment for force of this size should be 380 field guns, 50 medium guns, 320 anti-tank guns, 2,100 anti-tank rifles, 730 carriers universal. Above does not include reserves.[3]

And in a letter to Dill, Wavell echoed the plea which Balbo had made to Mussolini – 'It is material, especially artillery and anti-tank weapons, that is required rather than men. The enemy will not reach the Delta [just] with large forces of infantry, but only if he can bring up superior armoured force.'

But by the time these exchanges had taken place the convoy carrying the promised arms and reinforcements had reached Gibraltar, and as there seemed little sign of immediate Italian aggression across the Libyan border it was decided that the ships should all make the long haul around the Cape, arriving at Suez by the end of September. By then, Graziani *had* moved and Wavell was facing an entirely different situation in the Middle East, acutely aware of the need for the reinforcements up in the battle area but also aware of the time factor. To unload and disperse the equipment, to test the vehicles and adapt them for desert conditions, to train and acclimatise the men to withstand the heat and sand in which they would have to fight, would require a minimum of six weeks.

And he knew that the Italian force must not be left undisturbed for that length of time.

By a quite simple computation, Sergeant Lamb knew that within five minutes he must turn back; otherwise all three cars of the troop would be caught at dawn, still within the arc of Italian camps curving south-westwards from Maktila on the coast down to Sofafi forty miles inland. The question uppermost in his mind was whether he had led his men into a trap – for they seemed to have come a hell of a long way in without seeing anyone, and there was no way of knowing for certain that they were not, themselves, being watched.

The troop – with two Rolls-Royce armoured cars and his own Morris – had been briefed the previous afternoon to patrol north-westwards as far as Bir Enba (which they should not reach before midnight at the earliest) and then to probe as far forward as possible, off the track, retiring immediately any contact with the enemy was made and in any case in time to be clear of the encampments by daylight. It was a cold, clear night, the going had been good all the way – flat and not particularly bumpy – and during the entire time the horizons had remained spectacularly empty. From each side and behind came the creaks, the tyre-gritting, the occasional clunk of metal against metal from the other two cars, the random curse.

They must now be at least ten miles into the gap, and had seen no sign of life whatsoever. No camp, no minefield, no sign of activity except for reflected lights in the sky from the known camps to north-east and south-west, no traffic of any kind – not even the tracks of an Italian patrol. It was slightly uncanny, and had it not been for such similar experiences ever since the 11th Hussars began probing the Italian lines back in June, unbelievable.

Time was up. To grunted orders the cars stopped, closed, the crews muttering between themselves, scanning the empty, faintly luminous darkness around them. Lamb made a last sweep of the horizon, checked his watch again, nodded to the others and the troop swung around and headed back. They passed the lonely pile of stones which marked the bir (a well) about half an hour before dawn, and were far out in the desert before full daylight. They stopped in a shallow gully to brew up tea and eat their meagre breakfast ration, then pressed on, removing layers of clothing as the sun built up strength. By midday they'd be down to shirtsleeves.

They were about twenty miles out when they heard the planes coming, and as the roar grew they scattered – but they had been seen long before they could reach any cover and the whole world was suddenly full of the howl of dive-bombers, the crack of bombs bursting on the hard surface followed by the squeal of splinters through the air, the rattle of their own Brens as they replied. There were twelve dive-bombers up there, swooping down on them as they dodged, and in the short gaps as the Bredas climbed back for height, two Caproni fighters would come in strafing, the machine-gun bullets cutting lines of thrown dust on the desert floor.

The drivers spun the wheels, wrenching the cars around in response to shouts from the gunners fighting the aircraft off, watching for the moment when the bombs swung away from under the bellies. They'd all done it before, they all knew the drill, they all knew the odds; and with fourteen aircraft against them with perhaps others coming to join the fray, these were not very high. It was just a question of who would run out of ammunition first – combined, of course, with who would run out of luck.

Sergeant Lamb's Morris was the first casualty. Two Bredas screamed down on him, and as his driver wheeled to miss the bomb coming down behind, he drove over the one already down in front which went off almost exactly between the axles. As it also went off in what must have been the only patch of soft sand anywhere around, some of the force of the explosion was thus absorbed, and the Morris just bucked violently into the air and crashed down again, its bottom blown out, its engine and chassis wrecked, its crew severely shaken but otherwise unharmed.

And still efficient. As a third Breda, confident now of complete destruction of the smoking and stationary car, screamed in for the kill, Lamb opened up with the Bren at point-blank range and a feeling of some familiarity, for he had done the same only a few days before. He saw the bomb swing away far too early to be dangerous, the dive-bomber flatten out and instead of climbing away, hurtle overhead to crash into the desert only thirty yards away – giving him a personal score of two dive-bombers shot down in just a month.

He reached the wreck seconds before it burst into flames and with his crew pulled the pilot clear – to find the man dead with two bullets through his skull and papers in his pocket revealing that he had been commander of the squadron, which had itself been especially formed to hunt the armoured cars of the 11th. There were other papers, too, which would prove full of interest when they reached headquarters.

And in the meantime, silence had fallen over the battlefield, either because the attackers had run out of ammunition or because they had decided not to interfere with the attempted rescue of their late leader.

It was some hours later that the two remaining armoured cars of Sergeant Lamb's troop reached C Squadron H.Q. and not until the following day that a full report of his exploit reached General O'Connor; but when it did it served to crystallise many conclusions which had been forming in the general's mind.

There were several points to be considered, one of which was that the 11th Hussars were taking far too much of a hammering. Apart from the loss of Lamb's Morris, B Squadron had had two men wounded by shell-fire a few days previously, one of the old Rolls cars had been blown up on a minefield and the sergeant-major who went to get it out killed – the kind of loss which no unit can suffer without some effect on its morale, especially when strain on both men and equipment had been as continual and prolonged as it had been on the Cherrypickers. Even Rolls-Royces cannot be expected to operate properly if they have too little maintenance, and if the 11th's crews were – quite justifiably – taking pride in the fact that they could claim to have seen more action against the enemy than the rest of the Army of the Nile put together, that action was nevertheless taking its toll.

But the 11th were still the only experienced reconnaissance unit in O'Connor's force, and there was still a great deal to find out about Italian dispositions, about Italian movements, about Italian plans. What, for instance, was the significance and extent of those gaps reported by every patrol which went out, stretching between the various fortified camps? How wide were the minefields around each camp? How much artillery was apportioned to each camp and how mobile was it? Were there many tanks within the camp perimeters and – much more important – was there a strong armoured force held in reserve at the back of those tempting gaps, waiting to pounce on those unwary enough to venture too far?

The 11th Hussars just could not be spared from the vital part they were playing in finding answers to these questions, or indeed in the other task which O'Connor deemed essential and for which the Support Group under Strafer Gott had accepted responsibility – the complete and continual domination of the seventy-mile-wide strip of no-man's-land which separated the two armies. In that space, only the men of the Western Desert Force must move; no Italian was to pass the lines of the Support Group except as a prisoner.

Very well – if the 11th Hussars could not be spared at least they could be protected, and at a conference between the various commanders, the tactics were hammered out.

Some of the armoured cars had been lost through shell-fire; then they must have mobile artillery to protect them. Some, like Sergeant Lamb's, had been attacked and damaged by aircraft; as it happened, a few Italian anti-aircraft guns had been captured recently at sea, and these could be put to good use. And as there were undoubtedly Italian tanks in the area which might, one day, come out and offer battle, anti-tank guns must also be made available.

All this artillery would need infantry protection at night, so this too must be an integral part of such a force – and indeed, the same infantry could carry out even closer patrolling than was possible by armoured cars, up to and perhaps through the minefields. As communications would obviously play a vital part in any operations carried out by such a force, signallers would be needed – and sappers as well in case mines had to be lifted.

Such a force of mixed arms would need a single commander accompanied by a staff officer, both of whom would need to combine imagination, a distinct taste for adventure, and a great deal of hard, professional skill. As at the meeting there was one officer who appeared to combine not only all those qualities, but was also still junior enough to command so small a unit, he was given the task of assembling and leading the first column. Thus occurred the first significant step in the career of Lieutenant-Colonel J. C. 'Jock' Campbell, Royal Horse Artillery, towards fame and an enduring devotion among the men he led. The 'Jock Column' had been born.

Two of them were in action by the end of October with artillery and infantry both drawn from Strafer Gott's Support Group, and one or other of them was out most nights probing the Italian defences, lifting the mines, harassing the rear areas and communication lines. Many of the raids were highly successful, even profitable; some were uneventful and a few were totally bewildering. On October 14th, the armoured cars of the column in the northern sector were scouting ahead when they saw dust-clouds rising to the west and reported back that some thirty Italian vehicles and guns were approaching, apparently the advance spearhead of a much larger force. Perhaps this was the beginning of another main advance, so the infantry and artillery component prepared quickly for a sharp defensive action and the signallers immediately contacted H.Q. But all that happened was that the Italian guns opened fire and shelled the armoured cars out of their wadi, after which the spearhead veered off to the south-west and after a couple of hours of indeterminate activity, retired to Maktila leaving the watchers wondering what it had all been about.

Not all the actions fought during this period were by Jock Columns, of course, and not all were successful – except that from the failures some important lessons were learned.

Quite a heavy raid was planned for the night of October 23rd on the camp at Maktila, and as the place was believed to contain 'a battalion or perhaps even a brigade' of Libyan troops, the men of the Cameron Highlanders and the tank crews of the 8th Hussars who made up the assault force were quite prepared for a stiff fight. But café gossip in Cairo had been full of the attack for three days beforehand, much of the chatter had been unusually accurate, and as Egypt had been the home of many Italian nationals for years before the war and still undoubtedly harboured many Italian sympathisers, if not actual agents, it was hardly surprising that the entire Marmarica Division who actually comprised the Maktila garrison were alert, ready and waiting.

Seven minutes after the leading troops had moved across the start-line there was a shout from a listening-post just in front, a figure was seen darting back towards the garrison pursued by a bellicose 'Gie a hold on him!' from one of the Jocks and a burst of Bren-gun fire, all of which served as a signal to the waiting defenders, who put down a positive deluge of fire on the unfortunate Highlanders:

> It sounded as though every gun, machine-gun, rifle and revolver in the Camp opened up. Down came their defensive fire, and, coupled with mortar bombs exploding, the din was terrific. What was most impressive however was the display of tracer, which seemed to be attached to every sort of missile. Things like 'flaming footballs' floated out across the desert, and the fixed lines of the machine-guns were most noticeable.[4]

In the circumstances, it was hardly surprising that the assault company which had run into the listening-post was pinned down and remained so for the rest of the action, or that of the other company only one platoon actually managed to break into the camp. Inside, these took a few prisoners, smashed up some transport and then stole a diesel lorry in which they endeavoured to get back to their own lines, but the lorry attracted a storm of anti-tank fire which wrecked it – fortunately causing no casualties – and in the ensuing mêlée all the prisoners got away. The platoon itself escaped and by 0400 had returned to their start-line, where they found most of their comrades awaiting them, aggrieved but relatively unharmed.

It could not be said that the raid achieved much of significance, but both Wavell and O'Connor knew that the lapse in security which had contributed so much to its failure must not be repeated.

If O'Connor and the men of the Western Desert Force were intent upon embarrassing the Italians on a narrow, tactical front, the Commanders-in-Chief back in Egypt had wider, strategic fields to consider. So, come to that, had their opposite numbers in Rome who had an added disadvantage in the close proximity of their political master, still urging military action for disputable reasons.

During the month of October 1940, Mussolini was becoming more and more frustrated with his military commanders, principally as a result of the comments and actions of his fellow-dictator in Berlin. The tardiness of the advance across the Egyptian border had not passed unnoticed and, following reports to Berlin from the German Military Attaché in Rome, one of the leading German tank experts, Generalleutnant von Thoma, had been sent to tour the desert battle areas and the assistance of a panzer division offered.

But Il Duce was well aware of the atmosphere of patronage in which the offer was made, and also that his request for arms without the men had no chance whatsoever of being met; and although Italy was dreadfully short of aircraft, guns and tanks, she was not sufficiently short in his opinion that she need welcome men of the Wehrmacht into her prospective zones of influence and profit, from which they might prove difficult to eject once they had played their part.

This was a point which had been approached but delicately skirted around when the two dictators had met on the Brenner Pass on October 4th, when Mussolini had the uncomfortable feeling that only a combination of circumstances exceptionally favourable to himself had prevented a bruising and sarcastic tirade from Hitler. As it was, he had been able to dilate upon the glorious victories won by Italian arms in Africa, confident that whatever scepticism his brother-in-arms might feel, he could hardly give much expression to it in the light of the failure of the much-vaunted Luftwaffe to defeat the Royal Air Force, and thus open the way for the promised invasion and conquest of the homeland of the common enemy.

As it was, Hitler had remained somewhat subdued on the subject of the British (though confirming the offer of fully manned and equipped ground and air forces to assist in the drive to the Nile), neutral in his opinion of the possibilities of worthwhile collaboration from either France or Spain and only rising to his more accustomed heights of vituperation on the subject of Bolshevism. It was in Russia, apparently – despite the continuation of the Soviet–German Non-aggression Pact which had been signed in August 1939 to the astonishment of the watching world, including Mussolini – that the real danger for the Axis Powers lay; and if Il Duce had not been so full of Italian triumphs he might have wondered what the Führer intended to do about it.

For not one word of German intentions to the east was mentioned during that meeting on the Brenner Pass, and it was thus with an anger which made him feel physically sick that Mussolini learned, only three days later, that German troops had entered Rumania. The excuse that they had done so 'to reorganise the Rumanian Army' was obviously nothing but cover for actual occupation of the country, as his own observers quickly reported back as soon as he had managed to have them admitted – with Hitler's casual permission – on October 14th.

As a result, Il Duce determined upon at least two courses whereby he might level the score. First of all, Graziani must be goaded to further action in Egypt, with which object a memo was dispatched containing the passage:

> Forty days after the capture of Sidi Barrani, I ask myself the question – to whom has this long halt been of most use? To us or to the enemy? I do not hesitate a minute to answer – it has been of more use, and rather exclusively, to the enemy! Is it not time to ask yourself whether you feel you wish to remain in command?
>
> At the peace table, we shall bring home whatever we shall have conquered militarily. Will it have been worth sixteen months at war to bring home just Sidi Barrani?

Mussolini then turned his gaze immediately eastwards to where, since an onset of aggression eighteen months before, Italian troops had been occupying with varying degrees of success the Adriatic kingdom of Albania.

'Hitler always faces me with a *fait accompli*,' he announced to his immediate entourage. 'This time I am going to pay him back in his own coin. He will find out from the papers that I have occupied Greece. In this way the equilibrium will be re-established.'

It is one of the recurrent ironies of fate that although the subsequent advance of Italian troops across the Albanian–Greek border was to result immediately in yet another humiliation for him, in the end his directive to his Commander-in-Chief in Albania was probably the greatest contribution he ever made to the Axis Powers' attempt to achieve world domination.

To the British Commanders-in-Chief in the Mediterranean, Mussolini's attack into Greece, despite the theoretical drawing-off of enemy attention from the Western Desert Front, despite also the sharp rebuff which Greek forces administered to the invading Italians, was by no means an unmixed blessing. Churchill's reaction was predictable and almost immediate. 'We will give you all the help in our power!' he cabled the Greek Government, and although the Greek dictator, General Metaxas, was of the opinion that unless Britain could send a force of really worthwhile strength – say, six divisions – it would be better if she were to send nothing and so avoid attracting German military attention to the area, the Prime Minister ordered troops to be sent to Crete, airforce units to Greece itself and a Royal Naval presence into Greek waters.

All this could only come, of course, from forces already in the Middle East or en route and eagerly awaited there; and both Wavell and Air Chief Marshal Longmore dutifully scraped the bottoms of their respective barrels and sent units to Crete (particularly for the defence of Suda Bay), and to other Greek islands. As Admiral Cunningham already considered the whole of the Eastern Mediterranean his bailiwick, the only extra burdens thrown immediately upon his forces concerned additional convoying of troops and stores, and for these his existing plans could be fairly conveniently adapted. But this further complication of the situation in the Eastern Mediterranean did serve to crystallise in the Admiral's mind certain plans for aggressive action which he had been nurturing for some time.

For weeks past, Royal Naval units had been trailing their coats off Italian ports, trying to draw the Italian battlefleet into action, preferably piecemeal, but the ships of the Italian Navy had remained obstinately in port for most of the time, and temptingly out of range whenever they did proceed to sea. Now, large numbers of them were concentrated within the well-protected confines of the harbours at Taranto, offering a splendid target for any plan ingenious enough to provide means for penetrating the very strong defences.

There was obviously no hope of shelling the Italian base in the way that the French Fleet had been attacked at Mers el Kebir, first because that episode had been observed and lessons drawn from it by both sides, and secondly because of the presence of Italian air bases grouped around the port and throughout the length and breadth of the Italian 'foot' from which units of the Regia Aeronautica had already inflicted damage on British ships, both merchant and naval. Besides, there were strong rumours of a growing Luftwaffe presence in the area.

A submarine attack was out of the question, too, for once Gunther Prien in U47 had penetrated Scapa Flow and sunk the *Royal Oak*, no navy in the world neglected harbour defences around their most powerful units. Air reconnaissance revealed quite clearly that even if a submarine penetrated the Mar Grande at Taranto, sea walls and torpedo-nets closely screened the only worthwhile targets.

Attack, therefore, could only come from the air – and Taranto was far beyond the range of what few bombers the Royal Air Force had in the Middle East. Cunningham must rely upon the forces under his own immediate control.

During October and the early days of November there was a great deal of traffic throughout all the waters of the Mediterranean, as men and materials were ferried both from the Italian mainland to Albania and from British bases to British outposts. Generally speaking the Italian moves were beyond the striking distance of British forces, but the Royal Navy and its charges were subject to fairly continuous attention from Italian aircraft and were also well aware that Ammiraglio Campioni was watching their every move, waiting to pounce upon any weak detachment which ventured too close to the Italian mainland. It all made for rather complicated manoeuvres but perhaps their very complication might provide a key.

There was no doubt that the garrison on Malta must be strengthened, and by November 7th, some 2,000 infantrymen and gunners were distributed aboard the battleship *Barham*, the cruisers *Berwick* and *Glasgow* plus half a dozen destroyers, and en route between Gibraltar and the embattled island. At the same time, a convoy carrying stores and weapons from Alexandria for both Crete and Malta was at sea, closely escorted by cruisers and destroyers, while the main Mediterranean Fleet consisting of the aircraft-carrier *Illustrious*, four battleships, two cruisers and thirteen destroyers patrolled in the central basin between Crete and Sicily.

By November 9th, the Alexandria convoys had reached Malta and were being unloaded by an anxious and extremely grateful populace, while the main fleet went on and rendezvoused with the Gibraltar force. Swordfish aircraft from the *Ark Royal* carried out a small raid on Cagliari in Sardinia and during the afternoon the combined forces were subjected to quite a heavy and concentrated attack by Italian land-based planes which, although they hit nothing, scored a number of unpleasantly near misses, especially alongside the *Barham*. After the reinforcing troops had been landed on Malta, those naval vessels due to return to Gibraltar (where they were later to win fame as Force H) sailed off to the west while the others joined the main fleet from Alexandria, and by dawn this augmented force was steaming north-eastwards towards Taranto.

By late afternoon they were about 200 miles from their target, and aboard *Illustrious* an intent group of officers was studying the latest photographs of the harbour, just delivered from Malta where three R.A.F. Marylands were stationed, one of which had flown over the target area that morning. Overhead, fighter aircraft patrolled and efficiently shot down the two Italian scouting planes which had come within sighting distance of the force below. By early evening, Cunningham knew that six of the most powerful Italian battleships – the *Duilio*, the *Littorio*, the *Cesare*, the *Doria*, the *Vittorio Veneto* and the *Cavour* – were anchored in the Mar Grande together with several assorted cruisers and destroyers, while the Mar Piccolo beyond contained more cruisers and was surrounded by valuable shore installations such as oil storage depots, repair sheds and aircraft hangars.

Ammiraglio Campioni had thus unexpectedly placed all his most valuable eggs in one basket and had also – though Cunningham was not to know this – lost track of the British forces; at that moment the Italian admiral was very close to assuming that the entire Mediterranean Fleet was on its way back to Alexandria.

Shortly before 2100 the first wave of Swordfish – the 'Stringbags' as their crews derisively called them – climbed awkwardly off *Illustrious*'s decks and up towards the clouds which would shelter them for at least part of the way; twelve aircraft, six of them with huge torpedoes slung beneath their bellies, four with six 250-pound bombs, two with four bombs and heavy illuminating flares, all under command of Lieutenant-Commander Kenneth Williamson of 813 Squadron, Fleet Air Arm, each carrying a pilot and an observer. None of the men aboard any of the aircraft could have been buoyed up by much beyond hope and a belief in the luck of the Navy, for their Stringbags were cumbersome, underpowered, years out of date and now some of them were expected to undertake the unlikely role of dive-bombers.

But at least they had been given the range to carry out this extremely hazardous mission, for half of the rear cockpit of each torpedo-carrier was taken up by a sixty-gallon petrol-tank (to the great discomfort of the observers) while similar extra fuel capacity for the bombers was strapped on outside the fuselage. Those among

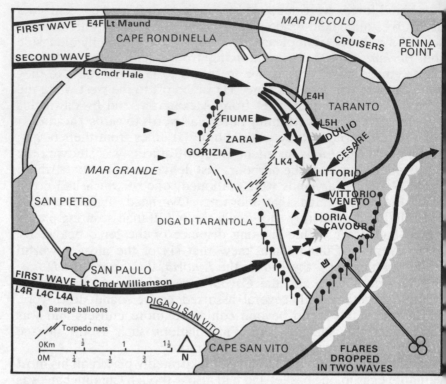

Map 4   Taranto: November 11th, 1940

the crews with strong imaginations kept them under very tight control.

Williamson led them up into cloud at 4,500 feet and immediately lost all contact with the others, for it was very thick cloud; when he emerged at 7,500 feet into clear moonlight it was to find that one torpedo-plane and three bombers were no longer with him, and as this was in the days before such refinements as radio-telephones, he had no choice but to accept that they would now all make their own separate ways to the target area. This, after another ninety minutes' droning flight, became only too visible, spread out beneath them.

Together, the two anchorages of Mar Grande and Mar Piccolo make up one of the finest harbours in the Mediterranean. The outer one, Mar Grande, is a westward-facing bay embraced by the two arms of Cape Rondinella to the north and Cape San Vito to the south, while two islands between the capes, San Pietro and San Paulo, are joined to each other and to Cape Rondinella by breakwaters. A curved mole, the Diga di San Vito, runs out from the south for nearly a mile, and between the end of the Diga and San Paulo is the only entrance to the anchorage – studded at this time with floating anti-aircraft positions.

The main warship anchorage was in the eastern curve of the bay, and here another mole, the Diga di Tarantola, formed a shield a mile and a half long for the vessels behind it. Lines of deep nets between the groups of ships extended the protection of the Diga and added further to the complications facing the attackers, whose torpedoes must either be dropped inside the Diga or the nets – or so far outside the nets that they would pass underneath them in which case they might pass underneath their targets as well, although in theory the Duplex fuses with which the torpedoes were armed would be activated by the change in magnetic field when this happened.

From the northern edge of the bay, a narrow channel led through the town of Taranto itself into the Mar Piccolo – an inner, completely land-locked harbour which sheltered more naval vessels, all armed with anti-aircraft weapons of various calibres and surrounded by dockyard installations similarly protected.

In all, the Swordfish attack was to take place through fire from defences consisting of twenty-one batteries of 4-inch guns and nearly 200 machine-guns, all supported by a thoroughly adequate searchlight system. As the intention was to launch the torpedoes from a height of not more than thirty feet, the machine-guns and the searchlights were likely to be just as distracting as the heavier armament. And to make the manoeuvre even more awkward, lines of barrage balloons were deployed across the most promising axes of attack, making it essential for most of the Swordfish to attempt to fly between the steel cables attaching the balloons to their anchors.

It did not seem to the men flying beside and behind Lieutenant-Commander Williamson, therefore, that there was a very high chance of all of them getting back that night to the *Illustrious*, now waiting anxiously some 180 miles astern like a mother hen worried about her chicks. The only support they had (in addition to nature's built-in comfort that 'it won't happen to me') was the expectation of surprise on their side, an expectation dashed at 2250 when even above the drone of their own engines they heard the shriek of Taranto's air raid warning sirens, followed almost immediately by an eruption of multicoloured fairy lights as the heavy batteries put up a barrage, the machine-guns threw out strings of tracer in every direction and the searchlights swung their beams around the sky like spillikins sticking up from a dark blue tablecloth.

Through it all, the torpedo-bombers must dive.

They were coming in from the south, and just off Cape San Vito the two Stringbags with flares aboard swung away to starboard while Williamson in L4A led the torpedo-bombers away to port to line up for an attack from the south-west. Two followed him directly – L4C piloted by Sub-Lieutenant Peter Sparke and L4R by

Sub-Lieutenant A. S. D. Macauley – and as they curved down through the ceiling of tracer and swinging light to straighten up for an attack line across the Diga di Tarantola, the flares dropped by Sub-Lieutenants Kiggell in L4P and Lamb in L4B burst like candelabra in the sky, silhouetting immediately in front and below them the spectacular outline of the battleship *Cavour*.

They went in line ahead across the first mole jutting out towards San Paulo, through the line of barrage balloons – incredibly, without noticing them – at thirty feet as they streaked in across the Diga di Tarantola. Peter Sparke saw the fire of at least two destroyers converging on Kenneth Williamson's plane ahead and, although he had also seen and set his heart on the magnificent target of the *Vittorio Veneto* just away to port, he held on for the more certain prize. Williamson's torpedo dropped away, a final burst of fire caught L4A and she vanished in a pillar of water and then the *Cavour* was there, exactly ahead of him and unprotected. As he felt the Stringbag jump when the weight of his torpedo was released, he swung away to port, over the unscathed *Vittorio Veneto*, through a cross-fire of tracer like a three-dimensional mesh and up towards a moonlit haven – listening as he did so to the honey-sweet voice of his observer screaming triumphantly that whoever was responsible, *Cavour* had been hit at least once abreast her foremost turret. Behind them Macauley, too, had dropped his torpedo, turned, and was now braving the curtain of steel cables below the barrage balloons on his way home.

While those three attacks on *Cavour* had been taking place, both *Littorio* and *Vittorio Veneto* had been under attack. Lieutenant H. I. A. Swayne was piloting the torpedo-bomber which had been lost in the clouds, but he caught up with the others just as they were going into their dives, veered to port – as Sparke had intended to do – as he crossed the Diga di Tarantola, and released his torpedo about four hundred yards short of the *Littorio*, flying ahead right over it as a huge explosion ripped a twenty-three-foot hole in the battleship's port quarter. Just seconds before, Lieutenant N. Kemp in L4K had swung around the far end of the northern balloon barrage, skirted the edge of the harbour (where he had seen some of the shot fired at him from the cruisers and destroyers arching over and actually exploding amid shore establishments and merchant-ships berthed close in), swooped close down on *Littorio* as well and launched his torpedo to strike the battleship on her starboard bow. Both Kemp and Swayne cleared the combat area – as did the others who got away – within five minutes of Williamson's first attack dive, leaving behind them two badly hit battleships for the price of one plane shot down. Later, it was learned that both Williamson and his observer had miraculously escaped unhurt, and, after some rough handling by the dockyard workers who found them, were treated kindly and chivalrously by the Italian navy.

The last of the first wave to go in was E4F piloted by Lieutenant M. R. Maund, who used both an approach and an escape route all his own. He came in over Cape Rondinella, swung slightly north over Taranto town itself and dived down on the *Vittorio Veneto* – which was to lead a charmed life that night, for Maund's torpedo dived too deep and exploded as it hit the bottom, close to the *Littorio* which seemed to attract all the attention. Curling around hard to starboard, Maund then baffled the machine-gunners frantically trying to get a bead on him by zig-zagging through the masts of the merchant-ships moored along the north shore until he, too, was clear of the area and safely on his way back to *Illustrious*.

But by now the second wave was approaching, fascinated by the cluster of fireworks erupting beneath them and grimly aware that they had now to fly down into it without the slightest element of surprise on their side. Again, two flare-dropping Swordfish detached, swung in over Cape San Vito and behind the main targets, while Lieutenant-Commander 'Ginger' Hale led the five torpedo-bombers in a wide curve over Cape Rondinella to sweep down from 5,000 feet across the neck of land, behind the northern balloon barrage and into a cone of fire coming up at them from the shore-based 4-inch batteries behind, from flak-ships and cruisers to starboard and from the multiple guns of the main battleships ahead of them.

Through it all, the first two Stringbags dived straight on to the doomed *Littorio*, their torpedoes going down straight and cleanly, one to blow yet another hole in the battleship's bow, the other to leave a deep dent in her starboard quarter before sinking to the sea-bed without exploding. Immediately astern of the two leaders, Lieutenant C. S. C. Lea in L5H had swerved slightly to port until he was low over the entrance to the narrow channel leading into Mar Piccolo and he could see the *Duilio* admirably silhouetted against the slowly descending flares. His torpedo thudded home almost exactly amidships, the explosion tearing a hole in the battleship's side some thirty feet by twenty-five and well under water, through which the sea flooded into the main magazines. As the tracers screamed up at him from every angle (each flaming ball with at least three unseen projectiles close behind it), he banked sharply, dodged between two cruisers each erupting fire at him, and fled out across the end of the Diga di Tarantola, between the unseen cables of the balloon barrage into the peace and quiet of the seas beyond San Pietro.

Behind him came frustrating failure and, for the British, the one tragedy of the whole night.

Lieutenant T. W. G. Welham piloting E5H seemed perfectly placed to break the shield which fortune had thrown over the massive flagship of the fleet, the *Vittorio Veneto*. He had come in behind Lea, glimpsed the latter's successful attack on the *Duilio* and then seen, dead ahead and across his path, the huge looming shape of the finest target in the bay; he had steadied on her, let his torpedo go at exactly the right moment, pulled E5H up right over the battleship and was away across the rest of the harbour through the maelstrom of fire with but two machine-gun bullets through the fabric of one wing. But what happened to his torpedo no one ever found out; whether it went too deep or whether it failed entirely to explode is still unknown; *Vittorio Veneto* came through the entire raid unscathed.

But Lieutenant Bayley flying E4H, with Lieutenant Slaughter as his observer and navigator, was last to go in and perhaps by then the incredible luck which had attended the operation so far had run out. They were caught by a concentration of fire as they flew in from the north and crashed in flames in the middle of the Mar Grande, both men dead before the flames were extinguished – a poignant but hardly unexpected price to be paid for such otherwise unqualified success.

At the cost of two elderly and out-of-date aircraft and two young and sadly missed lives, three Italian battleships had been put out of action, *Cavour* permanently, *Littorio* and *Duilio* for many months.

Moreover, that was not the whole of the night's work. In their role of providing distraction and illumination, the Swordfish dropping flares had been highly successful and they had also scored some minor hits with bombs; an aircraft hangar had been left blazing and the cruiser *Trento* had been hit fair and square by a bomb which, like so many dropped in those days, failed to explode though it split decks and did some damage.

Further afield, three cruisers and a pair of destroyers had been detached by Cunningham and sent up through the Straits of Otranto to prey upon Italian traffic crossing the Adriatic. Just about the time that Taranto was recovering from the second wave attack, they turned south and in bright moonlight saw a convoy of four merchant-ships with two escorts making for Brindisi; the action which followed was sharp and conclusive, though the Italian escorts seem to have contributed little. They managed to escape themselves without damage, but all four merchant ships, totalling nearly 17,000 tons, were sunk.

Thus the events of the night of November 11th/12th, 1940, tilted the balance of naval power in the Mediterranean much in favour of Britain, an adjustment which was to be significant for several very important months. The immediate problems of reinforcing the

Middle East were eased, the domination of the Royal Navy at sea confirmed, and the gap between Italian and British morale increased. It was now up to the army to increase it still further.

The idea of an attack against the Italians in the desert had never been far from either Wavell's or O'Connor's minds and even while Graziani was actually advancing, the 7th Armoured Division had been held in a position from which, had the Libyan Division pressed on towards Mersa Matruh, a very heavy counter-attack could have been launched. As time went by and the Western Desert Force grew in both manpower and equipment, the intention to go over on to the offensive hardened, especially in view of the evident domination the Support Group had achieved in the no-man's-land between Mersa Matruh and Maktila on the coast, and in all the country south of Sofafi.

Several plans were discussed in September and October but each was to be abandoned in the light of increased reinforcements arriving in the Delta, and further intelligence of Italian dispositions coming in from the patrols carried out first by the 11th Hussars, and then by the infantry patrols and the Jock Columns. The wide and apparently deep gap between the southernmost Italian posts now proliferating around Sofafi and Rabia, and the next one up at Nibeiwa, held everyone's attention, for a strong force inserted into that gap could strike up to the coast towards the water-point at Buq Buq thus cutting off the main Italian force at Sidi Barrani, and quite possibly isolating all the forward garrisons from their main bases further back, and from the Sofafis in the south. If a force attacking westwards from Matruh succeeded in holding enemy attention to the requisite degree, this raiding force at the rear could well wreak considerable havoc for perhaps as long as five days before withdrawing either through the same gap or directly through the Italian positions to the protection of the holding force.

Because of the need for high security demonstrated on many occasions and highlighted by the failure of the Jock Column raid in early October, this idea of a five-day raid was discussed in very narrow circles – at first, in fact, just by Wavell, Wilson and O'Connor – and with past experience of the Prime Minister's enthusiasm and ebullience in mind, Wavell carefully avoided mention of it in his signals to London. This caution, though understandable, had the unfortunate result of increasing Churchill's dissatisfaction with Wavell's performance as commander of Britain's only army in the field, especially as it was still not deployed as he, Churchill, considered best. Malta was obviously short of troops, there were still in the Prime Minister's opinion far too many inactive soldiers in Kenya, and although reinforcements were arriving in the Delta at an average of a thousand men a day, Wavell seemed to have no plans for using them.

As a result of these factors, the Secretary of State for War, Mr Anthony Eden, arrived in the Middle East on October 4th, had long talks with various Government officials in Cairo, accompanied Wavell to Khartoum on October 28th where he had further discussions with both the South African leader Field Marshal Smuts and the Ethiopian Emperor Haile Selassie, but all the time learned nothing whatsoever of Wavell's intentions in the Western Desert. However, immediately following the Italian invasion of Greece on October 28th came demands from London that Wavell release quantities of men and material – to such an extent that plans for even the smallest raid against Graziani would have been jeopardised. Wavell wrote later:

> All this meant a considerable drain on my resources, and led to my disclosing to Eden my plans for an early attack on the Italians. I had not intended to do so until the plans were further advanced, since I realised Winston's sanguine temperament and desire to have at least one finger in any military pie. I did not want to arouse premature hopes, I did not want Winston to make detailed plans for me, and I knew that absolute secrecy was the only hope of keeping my intentions from the Italians, who had so many tentacles in Cairo. But Eden was proposing to sap my strength in aircraft, A.A. guns, transport, etc., in favour of Greece, thinking I had only a defensive policy in mind, to such an extent that I had to tell him what was in my mind to prevent my being skinned to an extent that would make an offensive impossible.[5]

The reaction when on November 8th Eden was able to tell Churchill of Wavell's plans was far better than had been expected, for if the Prime Minister was put out at first by the revelation of Wavell's secrecy, he 'purred like six cats' as the details of the plan were unfolded, and future events were to demonstrate that there were no security leaks from Whitehall. However, it was too much to expect an entirely passive reaction to the plan, and if Churchill sent no suggestions for different tactics he was quick to insist that, as always, time was of the essence, and that any success achieved should be thoroughly exploited:

> I am having a Staff study made of possibilities open to us, if all goes well, for moving fighting troops and also reserves forward by sea in long hops along the coast, and setting up new supply bases to which pursuing armoured vehicles and units might resort . . .

As we told you the other day, we shall stand by you and Wilson in any well-conceived action irrespective of result, because no one can guarantee success in war, only deserve it.[6]

But other passages in the same cable – and other cables – did reveal one ominous difference in attitudes between the political and military chiefs. Whereas Churchill hoped for a quick success in the desert to release men and material for an approaching confrontation in the Balkans, Wavell wanted one so that he could clean up the situation on his own *eastern* front, in particular down in Somaliland, perhaps leading to a further campaign in Ethiopia. Wavell saw the reduction of all Italian influence in Africa as his immediate and overriding task; Churchill's attitude was summed up in a sentence in his cable which read, 'One may indeed see possibility of centre of gravity in Middle East shifting suddenly from Egypt to the Balkans, and from Cairo to Constantinople . . .

But above all, Churchill wanted as fully exploited a victory as it was possible to achieve, as soon as possible, and his doubts as to Wavell's intentions were exacerbated when he learned the contents of a cable Wavell sent to Sir John Dill on December 6th:

1. If weather permits preliminary move night 7th/8th December, approach march night 8th/9th December, attack morning 9th December.
2. Feel undue hopes being placed on this operation which was designed as raid only. We are greatly outnumbered on ground and in air, have to move over 75 miles of desert and attack enemy who has fortified himself for three months. Please do not encourage optimism.
3. Creagh is in hospital and may not be available which is unfortunate since so much depends on handling of armoured division.[7]

Sir John Dill's explanation of the guarded nature of this message – that Wavell was merely trying 'to write down his intended operation to avoid disappointment' – did nothing to restore Churchill's confidence, but there was by this time little that the Prime Minister could do as the moment for the attack – by now code-named *Operation Compass* – was fast approaching. His reply to Dill's memo was thus blunt and sceptical:

Naturally I am shocked at paragraph 2, and I trust that your explanation of it will be realised. If, with the situation as it is, General Wavell is only playing small, and is not hurling on his whole available force with furious energy, he will have failed to rise to the height of circumstances.[8]

His doubts would have been greatly increased had he known of a meeting held in Cairo four days previously at which had been present Lieutenant-Generals Platt and Cunningham, General Officers Commanding respectively in Sudan and Kenya. At this meeting, plans for at least containing and at best eliminating Italian influence in East Africa had been thoroughly discussed and a decision taken for the early recapture of the railhead at Kassala – for which reinforcements of at least one trained and experienced infantry division would be required from Egypt, together with their transport and artillery. This division, Wavell promised Platt, would begin the move down to the Sudan about the middle of December.

But as there was only one infantry division in Egypt which could possibly be described as 'trained and experienced' – the 4th Indian Division – it would obviously already be playing a vital part in *Compass*; and if *Compass* should succeed to any marked degree, in the light of these new proposals the division would have to be withdrawn at what could well be a crucial point in the exploitation of General O'Connor's attack.

With this fact very much in mind, Wavell enjoined full secrecy upon both Platt and Cunningham before sending them back to their posts, and also upon the only other man in Egypt who was let into the secret, Lieutenant-General H. Maitland Wilson.

4 · The 'Five-day Raid'

It was quite cool in the office at O'Connor's Headquarters at Maaten Baggush on the evening of November 26th, and the men attending the conference were glad of their sweaters, pulled over the khaki drill they had been wearing all summer. There were five of them – the two lieutenant-generals, Wilson and O'Connor himself, and three brigadiers – John Harding, O'Connor's senior staff officer, as small and neat as O'Connor himself, as polite, as determined; 'Sandy' Galloway, Wilson's senior staff officer, lean and hard, quick-tempered, quick-witted and with a caustic tongue; and Eric Dorman-Smith, concealing a fertile and original mind behind the rabbit teeth and soft moustache of the caricaturist's dream of a languid British officer, a man with a cutting wit and an impatience with orthodox doctrine unleavened by imagination and administered by seniority, which had already earned him enemies in high places and would continue to do so.

'Training Exercise No. 1' had just been completed and the troops were now back in their garrison areas, as unconcerned as ever with what it had all been about. Their officers were still engaged with the usual reports and details which always remain to be cleared up after any extensive military movement, and any doubts or conclusions they might wish to draw about the events of the past two days would have to wait until the paperwork was done.

Only the men at the conference knew the whole picture, only they could draw the right conclusions.

The exercise had consisted of attacks upon fortified localities laid out in the desert to the south of Matruh, and although very few knew or even suspected it, the localities had been replicas of the Italian camps at Nibeiwa and Tummar. The attack plans had been based upon perfectly orthodox lines as laid down in the official pamphlet *The Division in Attack*, and the men at the conference knew they would not do.

The two-hour wait after the infantry had arrived at their assembly areas, during which the artillery had registered on the defences, would undoubtedly prove disastrous in the reality of battle, as the troops – keyed up and ready for action – would be completely exposed to inevitable attack from the air, with its consequent casualties, disorganisation and effect on morale. Moreover, the artillery bombardment itself would rob the attack of any chance of surprise – and with the disparity in forces which existed between the two sides, surprise must be a key factor in any British offensive.

According to the information at O'Connor's disposal, the Italian forces in the arc of camps opposite consisted of five divisions – one Blackshirt Division in Sidi Barrani, two Libyan Divisions divided between Maktila on the coast and the two Tummar camps, General Maletti's force at Nibeiwa and a Metropolitan Division in the Sofafi and Rabia camps. One Blackshirt Division was in reserve at Buq Buq while further back at Sollum, Bardia and Tobruk waited the equivalent of four more divisions; and the units of the Regia Aeronautica in the area gave Graziani a superiority in numbers of aircraft over the R.A.F. of about five to one.

O'Connor's own forces in the Western Desert consisted still of just the 7th Armoured Division and the 4th Indian Division, plus 'Corps Troops' and the Matruh garrison. In manpower they amounted to a meagre 36,000 men (against 80,000 enemy in the area of attack) but in addition to their already demonstrated high morale, they did possess some very real advantages.

The 7th Armoured was now up at least to paper strength, with two armoured brigades and the Support Group. The Support Group consisted of one battalion each of the King's Royal Rifle Corps and the Rifle Brigade, with the 1st and 4th Batteries of the Royal Horse Artillery, each with forty 25-pounders – decidedly better guns than the Italian 75mms against which they would be pitted. Working with the group, as always, were the 11th Hussars, now augmented by an extra squadron of ten R.A.F. Rolls-Royce armoured cars and their crews who had spent the previous months, indeed years, pottering up and down the Iraqi pipeline guarding it from the attentions of curious Arab pyromaniacs, or gloomily patrolling the Saudi-Arabian frontier. Now, at last, they were to see some action and bring very welcome aid to the hard-pressed 11th Hussars.

The two armoured brigades – the 4th and the 7th – each of three regiments, made up the main battle strength of the division, and between them could put nearly 200 light tanks into the battle, together with 75 cruiser tanks (A9s, A10s and A13s) which, although many were approaching the end of their track mileage, were more than a match for the Italian M11s or M13s, of which Graziani had a total of about 60. (The remainder of Graziani's 300 tanks were the almost useless L3s.) Normal engineer complements, signals and ambulance sections, recovery and repair organisations and, most importantly, Royal Army Service Corps companies for the supply columns, made up the rest of the divisional strength.

The 4th Indian Division had been made up to a full complement of three infantry brigades each consisting of three infantry battalions, by the attachment to it of the 16th British Infantry Brigade. It would thus put into the field the 5th Indian Brigade – 1st Royal Fusiliers, 4th/6th Rajputana Rifles and the 3rd/1st Punjab Regiment; the 11th Indian Brigade – 2nd Queen's Own Cameron Highlanders, 4th/7th Rajput Regiment and the 1st/6th Rajputana Rifles; and the 16th British Brigade – 1st Queen's Regiment, 2nd Leicester Regiment and the 1st Argyll and Sutherland Highlanders, plus, of course, its own divisional artillery, field ambulance units, engineers, supply columns and a machine-gun battalion of the Northumberland Fusiliers.

But it was with the 'Corps Troops' that lay the most potent weapon in the arsenal of the Western Desert Force, for in addition to three batteries of 25-pounders, one battery of 6-inch howitzers and one of 4·5s, they included the 7th Royal Tank Regiment which possessed forty-eight heavy 'I' (Infantry) Tanks – the Matildas. The Italians had nothing even faintly comparable and, so O'Connor had every reason to believe, not the slightest inkling of their presence in the Delta.

These unwieldy mastodons were the product of the second line of British tank philosophy between the wars, which had concentrated on trying to produce first a family of cruiser tanks in which armour had been sacrificed to speed and range in order to provide an offensive thrust force, and second an armoured support for the infantry. Armour 78 mm thick rendered the Matildas practically impervious to anything the Italian artillery could fire at them, and their twin 87-horsepower engines gave them in theory a speed of fifteen miles an hour and in practice, by the time they arrived in the desert, about eight miles an hour, which was fast enough for their major tasks of guarding their own infantry and spreading alarm and despondency among the enemy.

But, of course, the Matildas might well prove vulnerable to concentrated attack by dive-bombers, and their tracks could undoubtedly be blown off by mines; and how were they to make their own way across seventy miles of open desert without being seen and having their potentiality for shattering surprise thus dissipated?

The first and third problems could only be solved by the Desert Air Force making sure that enemy aircraft never reached the battle areas, but the Air Officer Commanding-in-Chief, Air Marshal Longmore, was under considerable pressure from Whitehall to send more and more of his units to Greece, and he was by now in some doubt as to whether the R.A.F. would be able to play its part in any

attack in the desert. Only by stripping air defences in the rest of his
command to an alarming degree could he manage to accept even a
portion of the responsibilities which were to be asked of him – and
thus for many weeks Aden and the Sudan were without their
Blenheim and Gladiator squadrons, and at one time Alexandria
was so denuded of its fighter defence that it had to rely completely
upon two Sea-Gladiators of the Fleet Air Arm.

By such means a force of 48 fighters – two squadrons of Hurricanes and one of Gladiators – and 116 bombers – three squadrons
of Blenheims, three of Wellingtons and one of Bombays – was
placed at the disposal of Air Commodore Collishaw, operating
from his Headquarters alongside O'Connor's at Maaten Baggush,
while a further Army/Air Component was placed directly under
O'Connor's command through an air liaison officer. This consisted
of two squadrons plus one flight of mixed fighter and reconnaissance aircraft, whose task would be to provide O'Connor with eyes,
both before and during the battle. The task of the main R.A.F.
contingent, however, would be to blind the eyes of the enemy, to
keep the Italian aircraft on the ground or at least away from the
area between the two armies, and to ensure that any Italian pilot
who did filter through their net and thus catch sight of the
converging British forces did not return to base to tell the tale.

But how about the minefields? How could the Matildas get
through them?

Even more important, how could 36,000 men, complete with
their arms, their armour, their food, their water, their petrol and
their ammunition – enough for five days – reach, without being
seen, an assembly line close enough to the Italian positions from
which to launch a storming attack?

The nights were getting colder now, and the patrol were glad of
their balaclavas, their scarves, their thick pullovers, even of the rags
wrapped around their boots. As they marched towards the night-
glimmer and occasional flares of the Italian camp, they thought of
the truck they had just left behind them and the journey up through
the Enba Gap to the dropping point behind their objective, and
wondered how soon they would be back within the safety of its dark
cavern. Despite the number of times they had scouted up to the
Italian perimeters, it always felt very naked out here on the desert
at night, within the arc of the enemy camps.

There were fourteen in the patrol tonight – quite usual. Two
scouts ahead and fifteen yards apart, platoon sergeant between and
behind them, officer with compass behind him with a pace-counter
alongside, three men in arrowhead formation on each flank and a

three-man rearguard. Just like in training – except that the bullets weren't blanks.

After nearly an hour's march the camp perimeter looked just ahead and the pace-counter touched the officer on the shoulder; the whole patrol halted, without a word the formation changed, the officer and the two scouts went forward, and the rest melted into the ground.

So did the officer and the two scouts when they were some 200 yards short of the camp perimeter, now visible as a low wall punctuated every fifty yards or so with sangars in which were mounted machine-gun posts. Some fifty yards nearer them was the line of outer sentry posts – they could see the sentries silhouetted against stars, moving, stopping, occasionally gesturing among themselves, then returning to the posts with the slightly self-conscious, slightly apprehensive, thoroughly bored air of men on stag. Even closer was the anti-tank ditch which led towards tonight's reconnaissance area, and between the ditch and the wall, they already knew, were the minefields.

About half an hour later, crawling northwards in the ditch, they came to a blank end and beyond it stretched a rutted surface covered with the dust of continual traffic. They climbed out on to it, turned right and began to crawl in towards the camp along what seemed very likely to be the approach to the main entrance. But if it were, was it mined – and how and where?

The officer signalled, then went on alone. He could hear sentries ahead and occasionally see their outlined, shadowed forms but they were moving between dark, vaguely familiar humps randomly distributed along this wide and apparently much used thoroughfare. As he reached the vicinity of the nearest, he realised that the humps were tanks – M11s and M13s with an occasional L3 – stationed out here to cover the main entrance to the camp and to act, in effect, as a roadblock. From this he deduced that the sentries were posted here to check traffic – not that the Italians as a rule travelled much at night – and if mines were sewn in this entrance gap, they must be marked in so clear a manner that the tanks would not drive over them when they were taking up their night positions, or when they withdrew into the camp at daybreak.

He and the two scouts spent the next hour wriggling to and fro along the ruts, keeping the tanks always between themselves and the sentries, finding the edges of the main minefields, searching for indications of mines in the actual approaches to the camp entrance. When eventually they dropped back into the shadows of the ditch, they had good reason to feel satisfied.

They crawled back along to their previous entry point, chose a suitable moment to climb out again and were soon moving back over their own tracks until, thankfully, they were silently greeted by the rest of the patrol. Soon, they were jolting back through the Enba Gap to Battalion H.Q., breakfast, and an hour or so's sleep.

It had been a good patrol. Lieutenant Liddell now knew pretty certainly the limits of the gap in the minefield through which the normal supplies reached the garrison, and through which any attacking force could also make its way. Quite soon the report would be on the planning desk at Maaten Baggush.

It was, in fact, one of the last pieces of a huge jigsaw to fall into place, and it served to confirm that only a very indirect approach to the problems which faced O'Connor and his staff held much chance of success. The weakest faces of the defences were, not all that surprisingly, the ones furthest away from the direction of expected attack – so far as an attack was expected at all; and the essential thing was to keep that expectation down as low as possible. No inkling of British offensive plans must reach the Italians and in a country riddled with their agents, this made security of the utmost importance. O'Connor's very strict instructions were issued to the following effect:

1   Only the two Senior Staff Officers at Western Desert Force H.Q., the two Divisional Commanders and their Senior Staff Officers (one each), the Brigade Commanders and the Brigade Majors were to be informed of the plan initially, and others only if and when some specific action was required of them for which no acceptable cover story could be devised.

2   Nothing at all was committed to paper until a few days before the offensive began. (Even Wilson's directive to O'Connor was not written until four days before the attack went in.)

3   The fighting troops were not to be informed until three days before the action commenced, and when they were already on the way to the assembly areas.

4   The formation of the essential forward dumps was explained as a purely precautionary and defensive move.

5   Leave was not stopped until the move forward had begun.

6   No warning was given to the medical services to expect anything but the usual run of accident casualties and illness.

To help matters along, Sir Archibald and Lady Wavell embarked upon a full programme of social events, and were especially looking forward to a race meeting at the Gezira Sporting Club in Cairo on the afternoon of December 7th, followed by a dinner party for fifteen senior officers of his command in the evening.

Bluff, deception and rigid security would all play their parts in cloaking the intentions and movements of the attack; but what would succour it? Even given the organisation – and luck – which would be necessary for the troops to reach their assembly areas un-detected and launch their attacks, how could they be kept supplied with water, with petrol and with ammunition for even a five-day battle, from a railhead seventy-five miles from the enemy front lines – when they were already behind those enemy lines?

All day and all night long, the lorries churned back and forth across the desert – those on the northern run from the railhead dump at Matruh out along the main Sidi Barrani track for some forty miles until they pulled off into the desert where the military police waited, into the ever-growing camp, draped with netting until it resembled nothing so much as a vast, twenty-acre dilapidated marquee, stacked like a supermarket with giant-sized crates and cans, and pyramids of what might have been long tins of cold drink lying on their sides, but weren't. On the side of one of them, some wag had chalked 'Duck, Duce!'

But it was the southern route that was real trouble. The drivers would pick up their loads at the dump just south of Qasaba and strike out south-westwards across the desert until they reached the line of the Escarpment, then swing westwards along it, without – thank God – trying to get to the top. But even the route along the bottom was fraught with trouble, especially for the newcomers just out from England who, in trying to avoid the deep dust as the traffic ground away more and more of the surface, would almost inevitably run into a pocket of soft sand – and sink to the axles as panic drove the foot further down on the accelerator, the wheels spun, the tyres smoked and the sand flew out in a huge spray; while other, more experienced drivers swung their lorries away and past, laughing; or sweating in the heat and thinking 'Poor bastard!'

Then would begin the awful grind of lightening the lorry, digging out the wheels, backing and filling, sweating and cursing – often for hours on end until, by one means or another, the lorry came back on firm ground again.

'If all the desert's like this,' one newcomer was heard to say bitterly, 'it's going to be a bloody long war!'

Then on across the Matruh–Siwa track, still holding the bottom of the Escarpment (now looming higher and higher like a cliff the further westward it went) until at last Field Supply Depot No. 4 was reached, and all the unloading could start again, into dim-lit, gloomy, canvas- and camouflage-covered caverns until, the lorry empty, the drive back could start. Back to Qasaba, where it would all begin again.

One way and another, the drivers and mates, the loaders and un-loaders, the storemen and military police and the supply depot guards, hardly had time or leisure to reflect that the reasons given

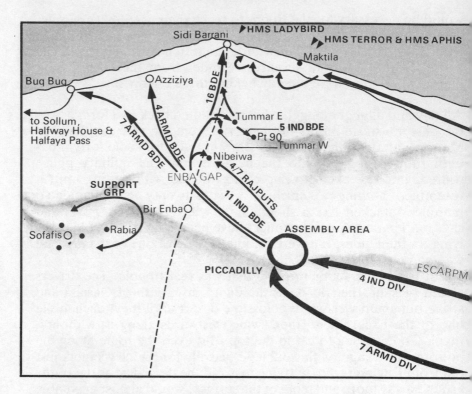

Map 5　*Operation Compass*: the opening moves

for forming these dumps – that if the Italians began moving forward again, these dumps could be drawn upon for the defence – hardly made sense. If 7th Armoured, who were the only ones out there, started retreating, they wouldn't have time to use the stuff in the northern dump (though they'd find the petrol useful) before Graziani was breathing down their necks and they had to retire to the main defences at Matruh; which would be a better idea, anyway. As for the southern dump, it was totally exposed if the Italians made a really forceful drive towards the Nile – and indeed, would prove extremely valuable to them on their way if it fell undamaged into their hands.

But who were the likes of them at the bottom to question the decisions of those at the top? 'We are all', as the drill sergeants at the depots continually reminded them, 'just tiny little cogs in a bloody great big machine.'

'Training Exercise No. 2' began for the 4th Indian Division on the morning of December 6th when they moved out from Gerawla, heading westwards for Bir el Kenayis on the Matruh–Siwa track. It

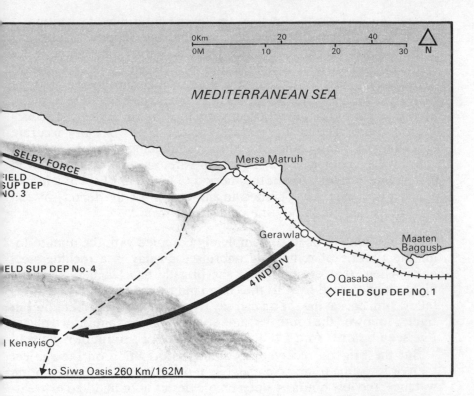

was chilly and overcast, a rising wind whipping the sand first into dancing spirals and then into a continual, infuriating, blinding drift; coat collars were pulled up, the troops huddled together cursing cheerfully and uncomfortable in whatever shelter they could find inside the jolting, heaving lorries. Everything was covered in a fine dust – but 'everything' included the entire movement during the day of 5,000 vehicles which thus arrived at their destination unnoticed by hostile eyes.

The units then scattered out over some thirty or forty square miles giving the impression to all concerned that here was a division about to commence an ordinary training session.

In the meantime, 7th Armoured Division, whose base area had for weeks past been not far from where 4th Indian had just arrived, were now getting ready to play their allotted role in the exercise. One of the young tank commanders in 4th Armoured Brigade was Lieutenant Cyril Joly, who later wrote:

> The second exercise started on 7th December. The same routine was to be followed, and we expected to return after three

days and to settle down again to the interminable waiting. I noticed with no particular interest that the Support Group had moved out earlier across our front and were now some miles ahead. Behind us I could see the dust raised by more vehicles. But soon a mist settled over the desert which shrouded all but the nearest vehicles and hid the country over which we were moving, so that I could not even occupy my time by surveying the scenes around me. The mist was thick enough to prevent any accurate reading of a sun compass and so, to my annoyance, I could not follow the course of our move. In wireless silence, shrouded in mist and resigned to another period of boredom, I spent a lonely and dispiriting day perched in the cupola of the turret, in discomfort and chilled by the cold winter wind.[1]

But not all had been so completely occupied with the minute-to-minute routine of remaining unbruised all day in a rocking steel box. When, that evening after the brigade had leaguered for the night, Joly crossed over to the command truck, he heard one of his fellow officers saying, 'You can say what you like but I bet you I'm right. I followed the route we came and I recognised one or two places I've seen before. And I tell you we're now just south of Nibeiwa.'

But the brigade received no official information on the subject then or for some hours to come. Night passed with the usual routine watches, the few hours of sleep on the desert floor huddled in greatcoats, seeking shelter from the cold and from the drifting wind in the lee of tanks, or in the scanty protection of grooves in the ground that only experienced and wary eyes would have seen. But when daylight came and orders were given that no fires were to be lit that day and that no one should move about unnecessarily, some thoughtful glances were exchanged and every move by adjutants or company commanders was watched by curious eyes.

By now the 4th Indian Division was closing up. They had spent nearly thirty-six hours around Bir el Kenayis, and on the Saturday morning, December 7th, one of the brigade padres had held a communion service. It had been very well attended and when an Italian aircraft had appeared overhead, no one had moved though a few lips were seen muttering supplications unconnected with those in the prayerbooks; and by early afternoon, the orders had come through. Now everyone knew that this training exercise was likely to prove more eventful than most.

But they stayed where they were for the moment and passed the first hours of the bitterly cold night which followed, chilled and cramped beneath their vehicles or in hastily scraped slits, sometimes sleeping, often lying awake and thinking of what the next forty-eight hours were likely to bring. Indian sepoy, Scottish infantryman, fusilier from London, all now waited for the time when their years of professional training would be put to the test, when they too would learn the price of the traditions which their fathers and grandfathers had formed over the years, on so many foreign fields, so many hundreds of miles from their homes.

The division was on the move before dawn. The wind had dropped, the sky was clear and as daylight grew it seemed totally impossible that this vast concourse of over 5,000 vehicles could cover the necessary 60 miles – all directly towards the enemy – without being seen by some prowling reconnaissance plane. Deliberately, they drove slowly to keep down the dust; and every now and then they would see an aircraft – but it was always one of their own Lysanders, sauntering slowly and almost casually up and away, checking on their progress and doubtless assuring the anxious Staff that all was well.

By four o'clock in the afternoon of December 8th, 4th Indian Division was concentrated about fifteen miles south-east of Nibeiwa, five miles east of 4th Armoured Brigade and not quite four miles from the Corps Troops – including forty-five Matildas of 7th Royal Tank Regiment.

As this was long before the days of tank transporters, the Matildas – and indeed all the tanks of the force – had had to make their way from their bases (indeed, some from their points of disembarkation) on their own tracks. In view of the vital part the Matildas had to play, therefore, 7th Royal Tank Regiment had commenced their journey some time before the others, arriving above the southern dump (Field Supply Depot No. 4) as early as December 5th, and spending thirty-six hours there on rest and maintenance of engines and tracks, before moving off again to their rendezvous point for the last evening before the attack. As the whole regiment had only been in Egypt since the end of September, very few officers and even fewer men had been 'up the blue' before and for security as well as mileage reasons their Matildas were also paying their first visits to this lunar landscape in which they were to get their first taste of action.

There was, therefore, a certain amount of apprehension visible in the bearing and expression of many members of the regiment, though humour and ribaldry played their normal part at such times and there was also, of course, a solid underlying confidence in the tanks themselves. All crews were well aware of the thickness of armour which would protect them, and had no reason to doubt the assurances they had been given that the enemy had nothing to throw at them likely to cause much damage.

They all now knew what was expected of them, and were confident of their ability to carry it out.

O'Connor had moved his headquarters from Maaten Baggush (where Wilson had now installed himself) forward to a point quickly to be dubbed Piccadilly Circus, at the top of the Escarpment about fifty miles west of the Matruh–Siwa road, slightly above and behind the concentration of his forces in the plain below. All seemed to be going well. Reports coming in from Collishaw's H.Q. still at Maaten Baggush informed him that no extra activity on the part of forward formations of the enemy had been noticed, that the previous night Wellingtons from Malta had bombed the Italian Air Force base at Castel Benito and destroyed twenty-nine aircraft on the ground, and that a force of his own bombers would shortly be on their way to attack the air base at Benina near Benghasi. More importantly, the remaining bombers and all his fighter aircraft would be over the immediate target area for most of the night, keeping Italian attention in the skies, cloaking the sounds of approaching attack.

As for the one Italian aircraft which had managed to get through over the concentration area about noon that day, either the pilot had seen nothing or he had failed to make an adequate report. (In fact he had conscientiously reported what he had seen, and for his pains was told to 'take more water with it'.)

The Royal Navy were also playing their part. The monitor H.M.S. *Terror* was closing Maktila and about to begin a bombardment with her two 15-inch and eight 4-inch guns in which the comparatively small armament of the gunboat *Aphis* would assist, while further along the coast her sister gunboat *Ladybird* would lob a few shells into Sidi Barrani – an exercise intended not only to cause annoyance inside the target areas but, like the R.A.F. flights over the inland camps, to distract attention from more vital angles. For a third force was moving this evening towards an unsuspecting prey, though its intentions were not quite so aggressive as those of the forces further south.

Part of the garrison had moved out of Mersa Matruh (but only very few of the New Zealand Brigade, to their intense fury) under command of Brigadier A. R. Selby, with some artillery, a machine-gun company of the Northumberland Fusiliers and the 3rd Battalion Coldstream Guards. Their tasks were to engage the attention of the Libyan units at Maktila immediately the attack began and thus to ensure that none of them was available to offer help and reinforcement to their compatriots further south, and then, if matters progressed well, to get behind those units and prevent their retirement into Sidi Barrani. As Selby Force was only some 1,800 men strong this last requirement might seem a little much, but at least the drivers of their transport were determined to get as far along the coast as they could. These drivers, and some others carrying out the same chores for 4th Indian Division, were the only New Zealanders allowed to take part in *Operation Compass*, and they had no intention of allowing anyone to overlook their presence.

As for the 7th Armoured Division, all units were now in place and well aware of their tasks. While 4th Indian Division and the Matildas stormed into the camps north of the Enba Gap from the rear, 7th Armoured would form a shield to guard them from any attempts to interfere by Italian units from further west – from Rabia or the Sofafi camps, from the post along the top of the Escarpment at Halfaya, or from Capuzzo, Buq Buq, Sollum or Bardia. When the attacks went in, 4th Armoured Brigade would move up towards Azziziya and the coast road, the Support Group with its artillery would attack Rabia, and the 7th Armoured Brigade would wait between them as a reserve for emergency or exploitation.

And with regard to that last phrase, General O'Connor now had another problem to consider. In accordance with his orders he had been planning for a five-day raid, but a day or so previously he had been made aware of the contents of a memo received by Wilson from Wavell some ten days before. This read:

I know that you have in mind and are planning the fullest possible exploitation of any initial success of 'Compass' operation. You and all Commanders in the Western Desert may rest assured that the boldest action, whatever its results, will have the support not only of myself but of the C.I.G.S. and of the War Office at home.

. . . It is possible that an opportunity may offer for converting the enemy's defeat into an outstanding victory . . .

I am not entertaining extravagant hopes of this operation, but I do wish to make certain that if a big opportunity occurs we are prepared morally, mentally and administratively to use it to the fullest.[2]

It was a little bit late in the day to let the commander in the field know that he might launch a full-scale campaign aimed at driving the enemy back a considerable distance instead of just conducting an 'in-and-out' raid; but as he had always been of the opinion that something of a more permanent nature could be made out of *Compass*, O'Connor – as soon as he could take his mind off more immediate problems – was quite ready to adapt his thinking towards more satisfying ends. So far as the 'moral' and the 'mental' preparations were concerned there was little problem; he could expand his horizons and so would his staff when pressed. But the administration, like the impossible, might take a little longer.

How far would he really be able to go with just two divisions, even those as well trained and experienced as the 7th Armoured and the 4th Indian? Perhaps their casualties would be light, perhaps they might capture enough petrol and water to keep going, to keep up the essential momentum. Perhaps, too, the Navy would be able to rush supplies along the coast to Sollum, to Bardia or even to Tobruk (stretching imagination and optimism only a little further than reason might allow). But what about weapons and ammunition? Even if the 4th Indian sepoys and gunners could adapt to the use of Italian automatic weapons and artillery quickly enough, the 7th Armoured's losses could not be replaced by the useless Italian M13s and L3s. Where would replacements for the cruiser tanks come from? What about replacement tank tracks for the Matildas? What about the men? One brigade of the 6th Australian Division were apparently the only trained reserve available, whatever happened, and they were already moving up to take the place of the New Zealand Brigade who for political reasons O'Connor was not allowed to put into action. Could one brigade, added to a force of two divisions, give it sufficient impetus to expand a five-day raid into a victorious advance?

Not impossible . . . perhaps. But highly unlikely.

The final moves into the attack positions began very shortly after dusk, when guides from the 7th Armoured arrived at the Advanced Headquarters of both the 4th Indian and the 7th R.T.R to take them forward. By midnight, selected units were moving towards their final assembly positions under a clear sky, the desert gradually silvering as a full, saucer-shaped moon rose to splodge the landscape with dark blue shadows. It was again bitterly cold though this was not so noticeable to the moving men, absorbed in their own private worlds of fear and confidence, of apprehension and eagerness.

Ahead was Nibeiwa camp, and from it came the crump of bombs as the R.A.F. harried the inmates, keeping their attention upwards, cloaking the sounds of the approaching tanks beneath the roar of their own engines. There were flares mushrooming, occasional parabolas of tracer, once or twice the brief glow of an explosion. There were also, inevitably, the much more immediate crises of minor mistake and misunderstanding.

'Where the hell's the Enba track . . . I'm lost!'

'For God's sake, get those damned guns out of our way . . . You're a bigger bloody nuisance than Hitler.'

'If you're the 8th Hussars, old boy, one or both of us is travelling in the wrong direction.'

But they were all quite quickly sorted out – in fact in some ways the slight errors and the distractions they caused were rather comforting – and overall the movements took place in a manner which said much for both the staff work and the troop training. By 0200 the 4th/7th Rajput Regiment were moving up towards the eastern perimeter at Nibeiwa, while the rest of the infantry of the 11th Indian Brigade with their artillery and forty-five Matildas were swinging up through the Enba Gap towards the unmined entrance explored by Lieutenant Liddell and his scouts, and checked again but a few hours previously. They dropped the artillery some five miles short of the entrance, and the infantry and tanks then went on for another mile, settling down for their last wait at about half-past four. The feint by 4th/7th Rajputs had gone in at 0300 and for an hour the rest of the brigade had listened to the continual rattle of rifle and machine-gun fire coming across the desert from the far side of the enemy camp. The R.A.F. light bombers and fighters were still picketing the skies above, the growl of their engines giving both security and comfort, while from far away to the north they had heard the muffled thumps of the naval bombardment. Dawn would be at 0630.

Away to the west, the 7th Armoured Division were also now in position, the riflemen and gunners of the Support Group in an arc around Rabia with the Sofafis further west also masked, the 4th Armoured with (who else?) B and C Squadrons of the 11th Hussars in the lead were high up in the Enba Gap waiting to probe towards the Sidi Barrani–Sollum road, to cut water-pipes and telegraph lines, to establish roadblocks, and also to locate any Italian armour which might be waiting in the desert behind Sidi Barrani. Lower in the gap waited 7th Armoured Brigade with D Squadron of the 11th available as reserve if required, hoping to be allowed to push on to Buq Buq and attack the Italian garrison there.

Selby Force, leaving behind them a complete brigade of dummy tanks spread in the desert to attract the attention of the Italian fighters when events at last forced them into an appearance over the battlefield, had closed up to the south-west of Maktila, listening to the crash of *Terror*'s shells landing in the comparatively confined spaces of the Maktila post. Northumberland Fusiliers talked between themselves in their clipped, northern accents, the Coldstream Guards muttered together in their own highly individual slang, a *lingua guarda* virtually incomprehensible to non-members of the Household Brigade.

Now, for all of Western Desert Force, there was nothing to do but wait.

Back in Tripoli, Maresciallo Graziani had been made aware of the Italian pilot's report of lorries moving just south-west of Nibeiwa and took sufficient notice of it to issue instructions that the matter should be brought again to the attention of Tenth Army H.Q., fifty miles behind the front at Bardia. But he could not give it a great deal of thought himself, as he had other problems to consider.

At the end of the previous month, Maresciallo Badoglio had been forced by pressure of events to resign as Chief of Staff in Rome – a resignation of which Graziani thoroughly approved. But, of course, the question of who succeeded Badoglio was just as important to the commander of the Italian Army in Libya as the fact that he had gone, and the intrigues of the Fascist court in Rome during the ensuing few days had been worthy of the days of the Borgias. However, just two days previously, Generale d'Armata Cavallero had emerged as victor, and Graziani had at first drawn a breath of relief for the new Chief of Staff was a man after his own heart.

But now second thoughts were interposing. The news from the Balkans where, incredibly, the Greeks were showing not only a resolute defence but also an offensive spirit which bade fair to push the Italian invaders back behind the Albanian frontier, was so bad that very soon Mussolini would assuredly be pressing for counter-balancing good news from somewhere else. And Cavallero, unable to make much contact with the Duke of Aosta far away in Addis Ababa, would therefore be turning his eyes towards Tripoli and exhibiting all the expected characteristics of a new broom. Thus, Graziani's December offensive towards the Nile, which he had been hoping to put off at least until after Christmas, would now become the subject of the same infuriating probing and general interference which had plagued his life before the last advance, but which had mercifully eased with the start of the Greek affair.

Fortunately, planning for the offensive was well under way and he could always point again to the lack of material and the continued late delivery of reinforcements and stores; but a new man in a new job would not be placated for very long, and the advance to the Nile must soon restart.

There were, of course, few solid reasons why it should not. The British, however much they might like to roam the desert and however many trifling attacks they might care to deliver against his flanks, were obviously far too weak to put up much resistance – especially as all the intelligence sources were unanimous in their opinion that British strength in Egypt was being drained away to help the Greeks; however little the Greeks might be needing it at the moment. *Perfide Albion* was at this particular moment apparently set on honouring her commitments to Greece, and although it was difficult to see why, it was not a matter upon which he need waste much thought. The main thing was to exploit British weakness to his own advantage, and to avoid criticism from Rome, preferably by forestalling it.

However, the news that Luftwaffe units were now to move in

strength into the Mediterranean area was worth pondering. Perhaps he should put off the advance until they were available to give him air cover? He must talk to Porro about it and find out how the 5th Squadra would feel about flying alongside the Luftwaffe to the Nile. And also about more defences for the airfields; those losses at Castel Benito would be difficult to replace.

He must go forward again, too, and talk to Gariboldi at Bardia and find out how he was getting on while Berti was away ill. It was always a nuisance when generals went sick, but at least Tenth Army was without its commander in a slack period. He would certainly want Berti back before the next phase of the advance began, together, of course, with Pastucci of the 4th Blackshirts who was also in Rome, on leave.

Those camps right at the front must be pretty uncomfortable, despite the fact that he had seen to it that the officers were properly supplied and that the defences were well and logically constructed. But it must be very cold – and very boring. Even that fire-eater Maletti at Nibeiwa would be finding it hard to keep on his toes, with only an occasional pin-prick raid from the enemy to repulse. Something must be done about the officers and men in those camps, otherwise an atmosphere would be generated there of lack of interest and listlessness.

Graziani was quite right. In most of the camps, that night, there was an air of listlessness, coupled with annoyance that the British were again making a thorough nuisance of themselves. Maktila had suffered casualties and damage from the shells of the Royal Navy, the Tummar camps had been briefly disturbed by aircraft overhead and a few ineffective but noisy bombs, and so had the camps right down in the south on the other side of the Enba Gap, Rabia and the Sofafis. Doubtless, the British were again carrying on their interminable patrols up and down the gap and morning would bring yet more reports of sentries shot or lost – presumably into a prison camp – and of more minefields disturbed. And doubtless, tomorrow would be as boring, as uneventful, as thoroughly uncomfortable as all the days which had preceded it.

In Nibeiwa, however, the atmosphere was different in degree, if not in kind. The British were really being a *bloody* nuisance tonight, the R.A.F. especially. Except for an hour or so after three o'clock their planes had been overhead all the time – and during that brief interlude had come an inexplicable attack by some unidentifiable but quite sizeable force of infantry along the south-east face of the camp. What sort of raid was that meant to be, with not even the artillery support that the raiding columns in the gap always had?

The possibility that it might have been a serious attack, as it was on the side that would first receive the full force of any hypothetical British offensive, had of course occurred to some of the senior officers; but when the shooting died away after little more than an hour, it was realised that it had probably all been the result of a part of one of the raiding columns getting lost – which God knows was easy enough out there in that forsaken, featureless wilderness.

With which thought, those not on duty went back to sleep, the sentries resumed their cold and thankless duties, the perimeter machine- and anti-tank gunners huddled back into their sangars with a prayer that dawn and breakfast would come soon, and Generale Maletti and his aide-de-camp – who was also his son – had a quick nip of cognac and also retired to their tents. Breakfast, as usual, would be served to them at 0730.

It was actually in course of preparation when the opening salvoes of the demoralisation fire from the 25-pounders crashed out and shells burst among the tents and vehicles, trenches and foxholes along the southern perimeter; but the scurry of activity down there had hardly begun coping with these problems before the real danger was revealed. Ponderous and irresistible, the lines of Matildas appeared over a crest half a mile from the main entrance to the Nibeiwa camp and proceeded with almost contemptuous accuracy to reduce to smoking rubbish the only defence between them and the camp – the twenty or so M11s and M13s of the roadblock. Only a few of these had even the chance to start up their engines, let alone fire at the approaching hordes – and hordes the attackers now appeared to be to the startled Italian tank and gun crews, shocked out of sleep, in all states of undress, surrounded suddenly by the violence and chaos of battle.

As usual, it was the Italian artillery who reacted fastest and fought most effectively – or rather least ineffectively, for they had nothing which could hurt the Matildas.

These, having brushed aside the Italian tanks, burst through the entrance and fanned out across the camp area like avenging furies. Their 2-pounders had little to fire at once they were in the camp, but their machine-guns chattered interminably cutting down first anyone who moved above ground, then concentrating on the gun crews as these proved the most determined enemies. Often the brave met fearful deaths in that first charge, for as their shells bounced harmlessly off the Matildas' armour the tanks came on and on to crush both gun and crew beneath the awful weight of steel. And all the time British artillery was still pouring high explosive into the camp with occasional smoke to increase the confusion, and huge plumes of sand would vomit upwards to add to blindness and

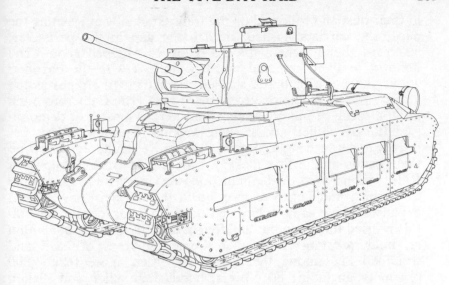

Figure 2 Infantry tank Mark II (Matilda II): weight 26·5 tons; armour
20mm.–78mm.; engine 174 h.p.; maximum speed 15 m.p.h.; armament one
2-pdr, one 7·92 Besa m.g.; crew 4

dismay, while shards of steel and stone screamed across the wastes
or sliced horribly into yielding flesh.

At first the Libyan infantry, once they realised the dangers on the
surface, stayed in their trenches and cowered away from the storm
above – but when the Matildas had smashed their main enemy, the
guns, they were free to harry the remaining occupants of the camp
and this they did, 'like iron rods probing a wasps' nest' as the 4th
Indian's regimental history puts it. Everywhere the Matildas ranged
they flushed dazed, frightened but often desperate Italians and
Libyans from covered trenches and slits, from open holes in the
ground – some without weapons at all, some with weapons which
they dropped as they put their hands up; some with bombs which
they threw or weapons which they fired before being cut down by
immediate reply from the tanks. One such was Generale Maletti
himself, emerging from his tent with his son just behind him and a
light machine-gun in hand; he was caught by a burst and flung back
across his bed, his son falling badly wounded beside him.

Impervious and implacable, the tanks ground forward, trampling
down every obstacle, leaving death and disorder in their
wake.

Fifteen minutes after the tanks struck the camp, a shout rang
over the radio: 'CAMERONS – GO!' The Highlanders' carrier
platoon shot ahead in screen; the troop-carrying lorries wheeled

in their dust and followed on the trail. Gradually quickening the pace, the carriers flashed through the gap in the perimeter; 500 yards behind them the troop lorries whipped about. The infantry tumbled out and raced in hotfoot with the bayonet; above the noise of battle shrilled the skirl of the pipes as the gravely pacing pipers played in the charge. The Camerons burst upon a scene of indescribable confusion, as masses of demoralised Italians milled about, some seeking to escape, others belatedly endeavouring to organize resistance. Hundreds threw up their hands at the first flicker of the bayonets. 1/6 Rajputana Rifles, riding hard to the hunt, followed in, passed through the Camerons, and began to mop up in the northern and eastern expanses of the camp. Here and there brave or hysterical handfuls refused the summons and fought until shot down, but within an hour resistance was over. Some hundreds of dead and wounded lay among the débris and litter; more than 4,000 prisoners, including 80 officers, huddled in sullen and shaken groups. 23 tanks, together with some scores of lorries and guns, represented material captures. British and Indian losses had been trifling.[3]

The 4th Indian Division had been well and truly blooded, and its historian given a remarkable scene to report.

By now the leading elements of 4th Armoured Brigade were approaching the Sidi Barrani–Sollum road, having seen no sign as yet of Italian armour. No. 3 Troop, B squadron of the 11th Hussars under, coincidentally, Sergeant J. Cameron (the clan were to do very well this morning), reached the road just before 0900, and ten minutes later had captured eight lorries containing fifty men endeavouring to make their way back over the border from what had shown signs of being a thoroughly hostile environment. They gave no trouble to Cameron and his men, but shortly afterwards the troop came under fire from some anti-tank guns on the Escarpment and had to withdraw after three cars had been hit, one of the Hussars killed and two wounded. But they lost none of their prisoners.

Behind the Hussars came the bulk of 4th Armoured Brigade, with Lieutenant Joly in the leading troop on the right flank.

However preoccupied I was with the stark, ominous desert to my right, I could not resist occasionally glancing at the scene on my left. As far as the eye could see, stretching across the horizon to my left front and flank and rear, there were vehicles moving: the tanks of the leading and the other flanking regiment to my front and left, and behind me the other two squadrons of my own regiment. Each tank was followed by a plume of sand, lit and highlighted by the slanting rays of the early sun, as it pitched and rolled and tossed over the uneven, stony surface of the desert. Within the three-sided box formed by the tanks were the supply vehicles, the fitters' lorries, the doctors' trucks, the ambulances. In the centre of the whole array I could see the few vehicles of the Brigade Headquarters. In front of them, and behind the centre of the leading regiment, was the small group of tanks from which I knew the Brigadier was controlling the whole move and ready to give instant orders the moment the enemy was met.[4]

They reached the area around Azziziya with hardly an exchange of shots and no interference at all from the Regia Aeronautica. In Azziziya itself the garrison of about 400 gave themselves up without a murmur of protest, so within a very short time the brigade were firmly across the Sidi Barrani road, collecting prisoners as these either tried to retreat from Sidi Barrani or came up from the west to investigate. The news that Nibeiwa had been captured arrived about 1030 – but then followed a long and uneasy wait, with 4th Armoured Brigade virtually stationary but acutely aware of the fact that battles were being fought between themselves and their base.

Tummar West was proving a tougher nut to crack than Nibeiwa, for the simple reason that surprise was no longer possible.

As the noise of battle in Nibeiwa died and the Camerons and the Rajputs of 11th Indian Brigade began the tasks of marshalling their prisoners and examining their haul, the infantry of the 5th Indian Brigade were driving past on their way to the main entrance of Tummar West – again at the north-west point, again unmined – preceded by all but six of the Matildas which had now pulled out of Nibeiwa. The missing six had had their tracks blown off as they drove rather too enthusiastically towards the new battle, over the edge of a minefield.

Tummar West was of roughly the same size and shape as Nibeiwa – about two miles long by just over a mile wide, roughly oyster-shaped – and an anti-tank ditch encircled its low perimeter wall, studded with machine-gun posts as at Nibeiwa but with many gaps. Its commander was obviously not so sedulous a soldier as Generale Maletti had been.

But Tummar West had one protection which Nibeiwa had lacked, and it was to extend its life for a few extra hours. The wind had now risen and the haze of battle thickened as a sandstorm developed – made worse than usual by the violence which was breaking up the desert surface all the time. Italian aircraft arrived overhead and added to the confusion by dropping bombs into the murk below; some even attempted dive-bombing attacks and so blinded were they that three of them crashed into the ground as they tried to level off.

All this, of course, caused the British reconnaissance groups considerable difficulty, and when one of them blundered out of the murk to be confronted by a low wall lined with Italian soldiery peering anxiously at them and obviously aware only of general menace but not specific danger, the officer in charge reacted too late to stop his exasperated driver shouting, 'Are you lot Tummar West or East?'

The answer is not recorded, but doubtless one of the Italians was polite enough to have replied.

But gradually, the attack force was assembled, the targets identified, the guns lined up. At 1330, two hours later than ordered by the commander of the 4th Indian Division, General Beresford-Peirse, the guns crashed out, the Matildas headed in for the entrance shooting up everything before them, the Italian artillery reacted quickly – and just as quickly found out that their guns were virtually useless against the steel carapaces of the irresistible tanks. However, some anti-aircraft crews swung the barrels of their high velocity guns down and when their shells hit the Matildas between turret and hull they jammed the turrets.

Twenty minutes after the tanks went through the entrance, the infantry troop carriers drove up at the unheard-of rate across desert of some thirty miles an hour and to within 150 yards of the perimeter – to the considerable surprise of the men inside, especially of the officers who had ordered the move and who had expected to find themselves with over 500 yards still to go. But this was the transport driven by the New Zealanders of No. 4 Reserve Motor Transport Company, and they had no intention of allowing the Royal Fusiliers they were carrying to go on without them; neither did they see the point of going further on their feet than they had to. Deserting their carriers to a man, they borrowed bayonets from the platoon Bren-gunners and charged alongside the infantry, slightly diluting their swift popularity by their warcries which seemed in a large number of cases to be 'Come on then, you Pommie bastards!'

But the attackers now ran into far more trouble than their comrades at Nibeiwa had experienced. As they hurtled across the perimeter wall, they were met by a fusillade of rifle and machine-gun bullets which cut down the leaders and drove the rest of the first wave to ground. Then the grenades came out and systematic advances with bomb and Bren-gun fire began; the quick rush, the murderous work with bayonet, rifle butt and boot. In the centre of the camp, a line of dug-outs was the scene of several vicious and bitter clashes until the Matildas were brought back to crush their implacable way over the defence – and there were still some of the gallant Italian artillerymen standing and fighting around their wrecked guns.

Then the second wave of infantry – the 3rd/1st Punjabis – swept in to attack through the pinned-down Fusiliers, right across the central areas until at last their Sikh Company penned those Italians who had not surrended or been killed into the south-east corner of the camp. Shortly afterwards the immaculate form of an Italian general emerged from a concrete dug-out, accompanied by thirteen equally immaculate senior officers, and after a short parley during which it was suggested that the prisoners should be allowed to retain their arms in order to protect themselves against the savage Indian natives, Tummar West surrendered. Another 2,000 prisoners were taken and although the Royal Fusiliers had lost several officers and N.C.O.s in that first rush, the casualties for the attackers had again been unbelievably low.

While Tummar West was being fought over, another battle had been in progress but a short way away. 4th/6th Rajputana Rifles had not been put into the same battle as their comrades from 5th Brigade, but in their troop carriers and Bren-carriers had swept past the embattled entrance and across towards the south-west face of Tummar East. As they did so, two Italian M11 tanks followed by quite a large force of Italian infantry on foot emerged from Tummar East to confront them, while six lorries obviously crammed with infantry began to drive across their front in a well-intentioned attempt to help the Tummar West garrison.

These last had little hope against the Northumberland Fusilier machine-gunners attached to Rajputana Rifles, who had their guns in action pouring bullets into the soft-skinned lorries and their hapless contents long before they could debus – and the lorry drivers reacted understandably but fatally by trying to drive as quickly as possible out of range, thus allowing their infantry no chance to escape the torrent of bullets tearing them apart.

The 4th Indian troop carriers, however, had screeched to a stop the moment the enemy had been seen and identified; the sepoys poured out and flung themselves behind cover or to the ground, and within seconds were directing rapid and accurate fire upon the advancing tanks and their marching support. The M11s had already demonstrated their vulnerability to fire from the Boyes anti-tank rifles with which the Rajputanas were still armed, and so were not much longer in a condition to offer protection to their accompanying infantry; these turned and fled, thus offering an even easier target to the riflemen behind them.

Some 400 killed and wounded were left behind on this particular

field of battle, with not even a flesh wound inflicted on the victors -
and by this time the British artillery had been released from their
tasks on Tummar West and were registering on Tummar East.
Moreover, the Matildas had now carried out their main duties in
Tummar West and the sixteen runners still left came out to attack
Tummar East – but arriving at the assembly line before the delayed
infantry, they went straight into the attack without waiting. Again,
they wrought havoc through the camp, again there was nothing the
unfortunate Italians could do against them; but by this time, the
murk of sandstorm and battle had thickened unbearably and the
early December dusk was falling. Beresford-Peirse, with every
reason to feel pleased with the activities of his division, recalled the
Matildas, held back the still eager Rajputana Rifles and ordered
everyone into night leaguer between the two Tummar camps.

Unbelievably, this tactic proved to be the cheapest method of
achieving victory on that extraordinary day. Probably because of
the time allowed them for reflection during that cold and sinister
night, the entire garrison of Tummar East surrendered at first light
the following morning, without another shot being fired.

In the meantime, the Highlanders and sepoys of 11th Brigade still in
Nibeiwa had had time to examine their booty, to take stock of the
extraordinary haul which had fallen into their hands.

The Italian garrisons may not have been supplied with very
efficient arms with which to defend themselves, but the officers at
least lived in splendid style up until the moment of attack. The
astonished eyes of the victors were greeted, as they made their way
through well-built subterranean tunnels from grotto to grotto, with
hanging wardrobes full of superbly cut uniforms, glittering with
gold lace and silver epaulettes; with dressing tables covered with
silver-mounted toilet sets, each with regimental or Fascist embossed crests; with polished and tasselled jack-boots, with sashes
and belts and embroidered caps. There was enough military finery
in Nibeiwa camp alone to hold a grand pageant and parade in St
Peter's Square, and all the exquisite niceties to set it off – perfume,
manicure sets, hair lotions, bootbrushes and polishes, soft cloths
and cleaning sets to remove stains from the smooth, pale blue
cavalry cloaks which would drape romantically from padded
shoulders to gold-spurred heels.

And those on parade would not have been suffering from either
lack of sleep or sustenance as they broke all hearts in Rome. Alongside the dressing tables were comfortable beds with clean sheets
obviously made up by servants, the linen replaced each day from
the full chest of drawers which made up the last item of apparently
regulation equipment with which each officer and many of the

1 Sollum bay, at the northern end of the Wire

2 Jarabub at the southern end

3 11th Hussars in one of their old Rolls-Royce armoured cars, about to go through the Wire

4 The desert: in the foreground, an L.R.D.G. truck

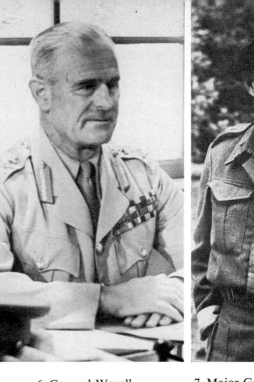
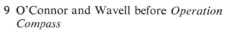

5 Maresciallo Balbo   6 General Wavell   7 Major-General Hobart

8 Lieutenant-Generals O'Connor and Maitland Wilson, and Brigadier Selby

9 O'Connor and Wavell before *Operation Compass*

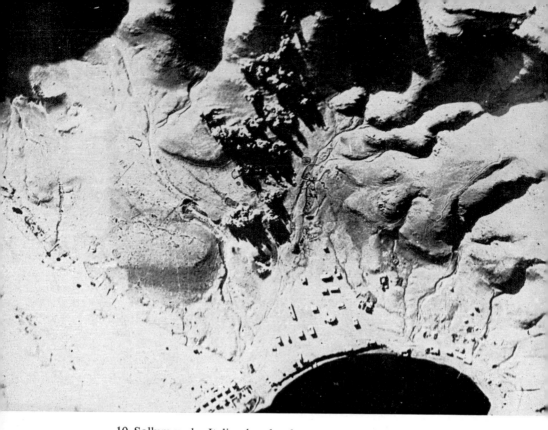

10 Sollum under Italian bombardment

11 Libyan troops in one of the Sofafi camps

warrant and non-commissioned officers were supplied by a generous but unwise command. Italian corporals in Nibeiwa – and in the Tummar and Sofafi camps, too, as was later revealed – lived far more comfortable, indeed luxurious, lives in their front line than had O'Connor at his Western Desert Headquarters.

As for food, Alan Moorehead arrived at Nibeiwa with the first party of journalists and had this to say:

> We sat down on the open sand and ate from stores of bottled cherries and greengages; great tins of frozen hams and anchovies; bread that had been baked somehow here in the desert; and wines from Frascati and Falerno and Chianti, red and white, and Lacrimae Christi from the slopes of Vesuvius above Naples. There were wooden casks of a sweet, heady, fruity brandy, and jars of liqueurs of other kinds wrapped carefully in envelopes of straw. For water the Italians took bottles of Recoaro minerals – the very best in Italy – and these, like everything else, had been carted out to them in hundreds of cases across a thousand miles of sea and desert by ship and car and mule team.
>
> The spaghetti was packed in long blue paper packages and stored with great sacks of macaroni and other wheat foods as numerous as they used to be in the shops of Italy before the war. Parmesan cheeses as big as small cart-wheels and nearly a foot thick lay about in neat piles except where some hungry soldier had slashed one open with his sword. Ten-pound tins of Estratto di Pomidoro – the tomato extract vital to so many Italian dishes – formed the bulk of the tinned stuff, which also contained many excellent stews and delicate tinned tongue and tunny fish and small round tins of beef. The vegetables were of every kind. Potatoes, onions, carrots, beans, cabbages, leeks, cauliflowers, pumpkin and many other things had been steamed down into a dry compact that readily expanded to its old volume when soaked in warm water – a fine food for the desert. We sampled one package that seemed at first to contain dry grass, but brewed itself over a stove into a rich minestrone soup.[5]

An Aladdin's cave was opened to the tired, hungry, thirsty but still exhilarated Scots and Indian troops, and one would have thought that discipline would have cracked and an orgy of feasting taken place; but oddly, once immediate thirst and hunger had been satisfied, curiosity, and a rather pitying affection for a race which apparently needed such luxuries even in war, became the prevailing mood. The alcohol had little attraction for the Indian troops who were forbidden it by their religion, and although the Scots could appreciate both the Italian wine and the highly spiced foods, they were for the moment too tired to take the fullest advantage of their good fortune.

But they did appreciate some of the equipment. The small, beautifully made pistols all disappeared quite quickly – though those that weren't sold in the Cairo back streets were thrown away once their ineffectiveness in combat had been demonstrated – and so did the ornamental daggers. The light, aluminium water-bottles were snapped up and remained in use until they split, and many of the leather belts and straps accompanied their finders right through the North African campaign. Cameras and binoculars found at Nibeiwa and the Tummars were still up for sale or barter in Cairo and Alexandria when the war ended, and possibly still are.

The one large beneficence which was admired by all who saw and especially those who needed its ministrations, was that provided by the hospital tent and medical services in each camp. Cool, spacious tents, with stores of bandages, sheets, folding beds and every sort of drug, appliance or instrument for the treatment of wounds or sickness, now provided relief for vanquished and victor alike, both Italian and British doctors working together and on each patient as he needed help, irrespective of rank or nationality. But even this service for the fighting troops was, in reality, impractical for the front line. Such lavish accommodation and equipment should have been located much further back, certainly as far back as Sollum and probably better at Bardia.

Shortly after Beresford-Peirse had given the order to the 5th Indian Brigade to leaguer for the night he was joined by General O'Connor, who, as reports of the last of the day's fighting came in, confessed to being 'very pleased with the excellent progress made'.

He had left the advanced headquarters on the Escarpment as soon as it became obvious that the main action was moving north and away from him, and his first call had been at 7th Armoured Division where 'Blood' Caunter was in temporary command as General Creagh had succumbed to an abscess on the tongue and been forced into hospital in Cairo. There O'Connor had learned of the progress of the 11th Hussars and the 4th Armoured Brigade, that the Support Group had achieved its purpose by totally screening Rabia and the Sofafi camps from which there had been little sign of life – or even curiosity – all day; and that 7th Armoured Brigade, having had virtually nothing to do but wait and listen to the sounds of battle around them, were showing a tendency to chafe at the bit.

To temper their impatience, O'Connor told Caunter to release the 8th Hussars and send them to the west of the Sofafi camps to ensure that the whole of that garrison would be ripe for capture when the time came – and also to send a senior staff officer to

Beresford-Peirse's Headquarters so as to make certain that the smooth co-operation between the two divisions which had distinguished the battle so far would continue during the more uncertain days ahead. The opening phase of the battle – the only one which can be planned in detail – was now almost over; from now on improvisation and exploitation would be the watchwords, flexibility and co-operation the keys.

Now, in 4th Indian Division's H.Q., he recast the battlefield for the following day.

The fall of the remaining inland camps – Tummar East and Point 90 – could now be assumed to be but a matter of time and 5th Indian Brigade could be left in position to deal with them; the Sofafis in the south would have to wait. Sidi Barrani was obviously the next target for attack, in many ways the most important of all. There was no news as yet from Selby Force, but as 4th Armoured Brigade across the road to the west of Sidi Barrani had not been subjected to anything heavier than isolated attacks from small and uncoordinated groups probably dispatched by the garrison merely in order to find out what was happening, it was reasonable to assume at least that no spectacular failure had taken place.

And there was still the 16th British Brigade under Beresford-Peirse's command, uncommitted during the first day's fighting, waiting alongside 7th Armoured Brigade for the call to action. Sidi Barrani should be theirs.

During the night they moved north – Argyll and Sutherland Highlanders in the lead, the Leicesters and the Queen's Regiment in echelon behind; and behind them those of the 11th Brigade who could be released from guarding prisoners and counting stores in Nibeiwa. By dawn they were in position.

Brigadier C. E. N. Lomax, commanding the 16th British Brigade, was in something of a dilemma. Although his infantry were now in a position from which to launch the attack, he had little idea of the whereabouts of his artillery or any of the Matildas which were supposed to be in support, principally because of the appalling weather conditions. For British troops who had grown up under the impression that Egypt was a land of blistering heat, brilliant blue skies and golden sands, the bitter winds of the morning of December 10th sharpened by the myriad grains of sand and pulverised clay which stung their faces and hands and reduced visibility at times to but fifty yards, were a savage disappointment.

But unfortunately, although the wind remained cold and the sand stung, the one potentially useful concomitant of the weather – the fog – was infuriatingly variable. Although it cloaked the artillery and armour from view on the flanks (they were in fact both within a thousand yards of Lomax's Headquarters) it had already faded sporadically and given him glimpses of the Italian positions in front, and by the same token would expose his troops to the enemy artillerymen whenever they happened to look in the right direction. There was therefore as much danger in waiting for the arrival of gun and tank support as in going in without it, so just after 0600 he gave the order to move forward and the troop lorries started off. They had covered about half the three and a half miles to the Italian gun-line when the wind slackened again, the fog parted and with the efficiency and accuracy which all had learned to expect, the Italian artillerymen opened fire.

The Argylls poured out of their troop carriers and hit the ground, Leicesters coming up on the flank swung out slightly but then were caught and forced to do the same, anti-tank guns raced up and opened their puny fire on the dug-in enemy guns now firing over open sights, and the whole area was engulfed in the kind of set battle-piece which had characterised the plains of Flanders twenty-five years before. Behind the pinned-down infantry their lorries blazed amid plumes of sand and smoke, alongside them the 2-pounders barked and coughed while all around the dust and smoke thickened, the shells crashed, their own machine-guns chattered.

But on their left flank, the reserve battalion, the 1st Queen's, were coming up into position and with them – guided solely in the still opaque storm by the sound of guns – were the ten surviving Matildas in one of which was crouched their commanding officer, Lieutenant-Colonel R. Jerram, released from administrative duties by the gradual whittling down of his command and able at last to get into action. Sweeping forward past the line of the Argylls and Leicesters they crashed into the western face of the defences just south of the road – and were immediately enveloped in an even thicker fog as the wind rose again and all the powdered dust of their own activities was whipped upwards.

In it were fought unnumbered small, close, vicious battles. A dozen shadows would rise out of the ground in front of the half-blinded cockneys of the Queen's to be shot or bayoneted before it was known whether they had intended to fight or surrender; a machine-gun would bark, unseen from ten yards away, to cut down half a dozen men before the crash of randomly thrown grenades ended its life and those of its crew; a lumbering Matilda would catch a line of puzzled and frightened Italians trying to give themselves up and chase them away back into the gloom – and then, identifying the crash of an Italian gun nearby, turn like a mastodon and waddle in its direction until it overwhelmed it from flank or rear.

In the meantime, sensing the diversion of Italian attention,

Lieutenant-Colonel R. C. B. Anderson of the pinned-down Argyll and Sutherland Highlanders called for a charge, just as the British artillery wheeled at last through the fog into position, opened up with a barrage intended for the Italian gun-line but – fortunately for the Matildas – crashed down well beyond it. Up from the ground rose the Highlanders, their pipe-major frantically trying to sound the charge through sand-choked pipes, and swept on and on through the murk until, having cleared a series of small hummocks which had been Colonel Anderson's main objective, they found themselves so close under the Italian gun-line that the hostile shells screamed overhead and no attempts at deflection by the gunners could reach them.

Now the Leicesters were on their feet and at some time just after 1000 (no investigation has ever been able to fix exactly when), under a growing weight of artillery support, the whole of 16th Brigade moved forward – Queen's on the left, Argylls in the centre, Leicesters on the right. The crash and thunder of battle rose to sudden fury, the infantry pace quickened along almost the whole line – and the wind and sand dropped to reveal 2,000 Blackshirt troops rising from their trenches just in front, formed up, apparently, for a mass attack.

But as Scot and Englishman launched forward for what looked to be that crisis of infantry fighting, hand-to-hand bayonet work, it was realised that the majority of the foe were unarmed and had their hands in the air. They had had enough. Within two hours all the first objectives for the infantry of 16th Brigade had been taken, a brigade line had been established along the whole of the western side of Sidi Barrani and a part of the southern side, and the outer line of Italian artillery had been overrun. Moreover, the 4th/6th Rajputana Rifles of the 5th Brigade were now closing up on the right of the Leicesters – and the surrender of the Tummar East garrison that morning had also released the 2nd Camerons to join the western flank of the line, north of the Sidi Barrani–Buq Buq road. Everything now turned on the still obscure position of Selby Force.

The Guardsmen and gunners of the Matruh garrison had had a trying and frustrating twenty-four hours. Brigadier Selby had received no word of the progress of the attacks on Nibeiwa and Tummar West until nearly 1530 the previous afternoon, and it was only then that he had felt secure enough to detach a part of his holding force – which had been rather statically engaging the attentions of the men of the 1st Libyan Division in Maktila all day – to advance north-westwards and try to cut the road leading back to Sidi Barrani. But bad going and darkness held up the move until the following dawn, which broke to reveal columns of Libyan infantry with their transport and guns marching stolidly westwards to join their comrades fifteen miles back in Sidi Barrani.

As this was specifically what O'Connor had planned to avoid, it was now up to Selby Force to close up quickly and hinder the Libyan retreat and this, to some extent, they achieved. By advancing as quickly as possible along the flank, they delayed the rear and middle of the marching Libyans who moved into the sand-dunes north of the road and took up defensive positions from which it soon became obvious that they would prove difficult to eject.

It was now that O'Connor's recommendation that a senior liaison officer from 7th Armoured Division should be attached to Beresford-Peirse's H.Q. bore excellent fruit, and immediately the situation became clear, this officer set about its resolution. As 4th Armoured Brigade's task of shielding the 4th Indian Division's infantry from attacks from the west was obviously unnecessary in view of the total lack of any Italian initiative from that direction, then some at least of its units could be employed actively helping the infantry attacks – especially as the Matildas were being steadily reduced in numbers (by the afternoon of the 9th, they were down to seven runners, though very few were in need of repair work taking more than four hours). 2nd Royal Tank Regiment could thus be used to augment the Matildas remaining in 7th R.T.R., while the cruiser tanks of the 6th R.T.R. could go east and help Selby Force.

As Lieutenant Joly was commanding one of these, we have an interesting light on the atmosphere and movements. He had just been helping with first aid to three badly wounded infantrymen, and then watched the remaining Matildas lead in for another spell of mopping up:

In the next moment I heard the Colonel's voice again calling Kinnaird and giving him further orders:

'. . . As the relations have passed through your front you will lead behind them. As soon as you are through the enemy defended area, swing right. Take no notice of the relations, as they are to go left. We are to go east until we have joined up with other friends about whom you have heard. Off.' . . .

Waiting until the Matildas were about 500 yards ahead, Kinnaird then gave the order to advance and to follow, as closely as possible, in the wake of the heavier tanks, so that we could take the best advantage of the gap they made in the line of guns. Once through, we swung east, being fired at whenever the sand-storm cleared, by a further line of guns on another ridge to our left.

It was here that I had my first experience of being hit squarely by a shell, though, luckily for us, it was not armour piercing and did no internal damage to the tank. Nevertheless it was an unpleasant occurrence and served to give me a clear indication of what would happen when the day came when I was unfortunate enough to have my tank penetrated . . . On this morning we were hit by two shells in fairly rapid succession. It was true that these hits jammed the turret so that we could not traverse it, and damaged the gunner's telescope so that, until he had replaced it with the spare one, he was unable to engage any targets. But for the rest, except that the dull metallic thud of the hit and the following crash of the explosion stirred up all the dust in the tank, making it difficult for a few moments for us to see each other, I and the other members of the crew only suffered from headaches for a short while afterwards.[6]

Having completed the switch to the east of Sidi Barrani, still in a blinding sandstorm which necessitated their all keeping very close station, 6th R.T.R. tanks swung north at about 1715, put in a shattering attack on the Libyan defences in the sand-dunes and completely overran them. They then made contact with the Selby Force guardsmen, and just before midnight the combined force went into action again, continuing the pressure and harassment on the unfortunate enemy.

The Italian forces left in the area – the remainder of 4th Blackshirt Division and the 1st and 2nd Libyan Divisions (less one detachment at Point 90, still holding out in Tummar East) – were now penned against the sea in an enclave measuring less than ten miles long and about five miles deep; and neither O'Connor nor Beresford-Peirse had any intention of allowing the escape of a single soldier. Perhaps the inflexibility of this resolve permeated to Generale di Divisione Gallina, commanding the trapped forces, adding considerably to his deep depression and that of his staff.

On the afternoon of the 9th, Gallina had signalled Graziani to the effect that the entire area of his command was 'infested by a mechanised army against which I have no adequate means' – and since then the news of ever-growing disaster to the south had been supplemented by every survivor who staggered in. The rot which set in early in the 4th Blackshirt Division spread quickly and there was obviously no hope of further defiance from them when the British next attacked; and even if the Italian artillery were still prepared to show their gallantry and resolve by throwing back the midnight attack with some success (6th R.T.R. suffered an unexpected bloody nose and were temporarily reduced to seven cruisers and six light tanks), it was quite certain that the Italian infantry had had enough.

And it really was enough. Whether any instructions went out from Gallina's H.Q. that night is not known, but when the British guns opened fire first thing on the morning of December 11th, their advancing infantry were greeted everywhere with white handkerchiefs waved by apathetic soldiers, tired of battle, weary of separation from their homes, no longer interested in the promises of Fascism or its posturing leadership.

Only at Point 90 did a legion of the 2nd Libyan Division still defy their besiegers, occasionally lobbing a few shells towards the positions held by the remainder of the 5th Indian Brigade. According to the 4th Indian Division history:

> Brigadier Lloyd sent a captured Italian officer under a flag of truce with a demand for surrender. The Point 90 commander reiterated his resolve to die fighting. Whereupon 1 and 25 Field Regiments registered and 3/1 Punjabis escorted by 5 'I' tanks moved forward. (By dint of feverish exertions, two crocks from workshop caught up with their hale brethren and seven actually waddled to the attack.) The Punjabis advanced in skirmishing order and closed on Point 90 to find 2,000 Libyans lined up with kitbags and suitcases packed for travel. Honour had been satisfied.[7]

By the evening of December 10th, it had become obvious to O'Connor that his original plans for the 'five-day raid' had succeeded to an unbelievable extent. Now, in accordance with those orders which had come to him so late, he must turn his mind to the enormous problems – and excitements – of that 'fullest possible exploitation' expected of him.

With everything between Sidi Barrani and Nibeiwa in British hands and some basic organisation started for the evacuation of the 20,000 prisoners (British and Indian losses to date had been less than 700, of whom nine officers and 144 other ranks had been from the Argyll and Sutherland Highlanders that morning) the next targets were obviously Rabia and the Sofafi camps, followed by the Italian posts along the top of the Escarpment at such places as Halfway House and Halfaya Pass, and the garrisons at Buq Buq and Sollum on the coast – in other words, the reduction of all enemy forces in Egypt.

The Support Group of 7th Armoured Division could move almost immediately, though if the Hussars from 7th Armoured Brigade had succeeded in bottling up all enemy troops in Rabia and Sofafi, it would be unwise to presume, even in the face of the evidence so far, that all the Italian forces would give up so easily that Gott's riflemen and Campbell's gunners could do the job entirely on their own.

Beresford-Peirse must therefore bring his 5th and 11th Brigades down to just south of Nibeiwa as soon as they could be disengaged, to provide any necessary support, leaving 16th British Brigade and Selby Force to cope with the prisoners in the north – and as soon as they had handed them over to the Australians and any New Zealanders still at Mersa Matruh, they could move forward along the coast road behind the 7th Armoured Brigade.

The 1st Royal Tank Regiment and the 3rd Hussars under Brigadier Russell must move on Buq Buq as quickly as possible, preferably arriving there in time to catch the Italian garrison before it tried to escape back to Sollum; 11th Hussars must try to get around Buq Buq and repeat their old trick of cutting the road, the telegraph and the water pipelines. That would give 4th Armoured Brigade just enough time to reassemble west of the Tummars and then to move up on to the Escarpment and clear the posts along the edge as far as the Wire – and possibly go through it and on to Capuzzo, Maddalena and Sidi Azeiz; though something would have to be done about screening them from the Italians in Sidi Omar or further south along the way to Jarabub. Perhaps by the time those alternatives had to be faced, the Support Group and 4th Indian Division would have cleared up the Sofafis, the road-block of prisoners at Matruh would be clear and the Anzacs could come further forward to take over.

That would release 4th Indian's 5th and 11th Brigades to deal with any threats from the south, so perhaps plans should be drawn up for an attack on Bardia; or even on Tobruk.

With which pleasant, imaginative and exciting prospects in mind, General O'Connor took an hour or so's well-deserved rest.

He was woken before first light on December 11th with a message from General Wavell via General Maitland Wilson to the effect that the two brigades of the 4th Indian Division, plus their transport and divisional artillery, were to be withdrawn from the battle as quickly as possible for dispatch to the Sudan.

'It was a tremendous shock,' he was to write later. '. . . I had had no previous intimation of it and it came to me as a bolt from the blue.'

The fact that the 16th British Brigade attached to the 4th Indian would remain with him was small consolation.

5 · First Battle for Tobruk

However great the immediate shock, it seems that General O'Connor had no intention of allowing it to upset his plans for that day. He left his headquarters as soon as he had swallowed a hasty breakfast, called at Caunter's headquarters and arranged for 7th Armoured Brigade to move as quickly as possible towards Buq Buq and Sollum, hoping to cut off the Italian forces there before they could escape back into Libya, while the Support Group moved against Rabia. Once 4th Armoured Brigade could be disentangled from the Sidi Barrani area, it was to reorganise itself in the Enba Gap and then sweep around to the south to trap the remnants of the Cyrene Division in Sofafi.

He then went on to Beresford-Peirse's headquarters south of Sidi Barrani, to find that solid and imperturbable figure still chain-smoking the cheroots of which he seemed to have an inexhaustible supply, already concerning himself with the problems of with-drawing his two brigades from battle, and transporting them together with their artillery first back to the Delta and then down into Ethiopia. He had apparently been aware of the planned move for rather longer than had O'Connor, and regarded it quite philosophically as just a transfer from one theatre of battle to another; and in the meantime, at least 4th Indian's transport would be moving in a direction which should help with the ever-growing problem of evacuation of the prisoners. When should they go?

It did not take O'Connor long to decide, for the cold facts of administration and supply were unarguable; if 4th Indian were not to continue fighting under his command, then the sooner they were off his ration strength the better. Until they could begin the move, however, would they please do what they could to tidy up the area of the last two days' fighting, help with the wounded and prisoners, and keep their sticky fingers out of the Field Supply Depots.

With which prescient admonition, O'Connor returned to 7th Armoured H.Q. to receive his second disappointment that morning. The efforts of the 8th Hussars to hem in – or at least to give warning of the escape of – the garrisons at Rabia and Sofafi had been neither determined nor continuous enough, and early that morning Sergeant Holland of the King's Royal Rifle Corps had probed forward with his carriers to find Rabia deserted except for two stragglers whom he took prisoner. His reports quickly brought up other carriers and, pressing further forward, they found the main Sofafi camps empty except for about a hundred Libyans totally uninterested in resistance, or indeed anything but sampling the luxuries with which these camps, too, had been stocked, apparently for the sole delight of the Italian N.C.O.s and officers. The rest of the Cyrene Division had stolen out of camp during the night and were now toiling along the top of the Escarpment towards Halfway House and the outpost at the top of Halfaya Pass, with the distant refuge of Fort Capuzzo in mind.

They were harried during the early part of their flight by a squadron of the 11th Hussars who had been posted out south of the Escarpment as a backstop for the proposed drive of 4th Armoured, but the Hussars themselves were caught about noon by two excellently led and conducted flights of 5th Squadra fighters. The second flight were using armour-piercing explosive bullets which effectively put the Hussars out of action for the time being and allowed the Sofafi garrison the rest of the day to continue a virtually uninterrupted retreat.

On the coast, however, matters were proceeding somewhat differently. Early in the morning, 7th Armoured Brigade had been launched towards Buq Buq with B Squadron of the 11th Hussars on its desert flank and C Squadron even further west, patrolling between Buq Buq and Sollum. C Squadron's reports quickly convinced their C.O., John Combe, that the Italians had no intention of making a stand there, and after a delay caused by wireless difficulties and the breakdown of the tank carrying 7th Armoured's commander, Brigadier H. E. Russell, 7th Armoured swept through Buq Buq and eventually found the best part of the 64th Catanzaro Division among the sand-dunes between the coast road and the sea, its guns well placed, its flanks resting on salt-pans and mudflats.

The first charge by a squadron of the 3rd Hussars in light tanks presaged ill for the battle, for in attempting to reach the outer line of guns they tried to cross a dried salt marsh which looked firm enough but broke under their weight, bogged the Hussars down and left them easy targets for the Italian artillerymen – as always both efficient and brave. But the cruiser tanks of the 8th Hussars swung in across firm ground on the seaward flank, the armoured cars of the 11th darted in from further along the coast road and the Italian infantry then broke and fled. Many got away briefly towards

Sollum, but sufficient were rounded up for a report to go in, when the extent of the bag was requested, to the effect that there appeared to be 'twenty acres of officers and about a hundred acres of men'.

By the end of this third day of the battle, there were another 14,000 prisoners, another 68 guns and an uncounted number of lorries to add to the profits of *Operation Compass*. The guns, lorries and other assorted war materials were, of course, extremely welcome to O'Connor who could use every gun and shell, every vehicle, every pint of petrol or water his troops could capture; but the prisoners were an acute embarrassment, even given their native charm, their friendliness and their willingness to help. The second-in-command of 7th Armoured Brigade that day, Colonel Alec Gatehouse, wrote:

> No defeated army has ever co-operated with its opponents to the extent that the Italians did on this day. They assembled their own lorries, refuelled them with their own fuel, and drove them full of their own prisoners to Maktila, and they came back for more – all without escort of any kind.[1]

It was certainly one way of redeeming Mussolini's promise that they would spend Christmas in the Delta.

Even with all this help, however, O'Connor's problems were many and serious, for it would seem that his easiest way out never entered his mind. *Operation Compass* had already vastly exceeded the highest hopes which anyone had placed on it. In three days, Western Desert Force had captured 38,000 Italian and Libyan prisoners, 237 guns, 73 light or medium tanks and over 1,000 vehicles. (The full count of captured vehicles was never made due to an old-fashioned army practice of hanging on to anything which might be useful, and only reporting it to Higher Authority if Higher Authority actually saw it.) Many of the enemy soldiers had been killed, and a high proportion of enemy equipment had been destroyed; all the enemy camps which had been the objectives of the 'five-day raid' had been annihilated in three days – and now half O'Connor's trained fighting strength and more than half of his serviceable transport was to be taken from him.

History would thus hardly have criticised him had he thereupon insisted on reverting to the original plan and withdrawing all his forces to their start positions before the raid began, especially in view of the fact that his Field Supply Depots were now down to two days' stock, and the track mileage left to the armour – his only remaining striking force – was perilously small.

Instead, on December 12th O'Connor was planning not for a retreat, not even for completion of the very acceptable operational target of the expulsion of all hostile forces from Egypt (for that would obviously be attained within days if not hours) – but for an immediate advance into Cyrenaica by the 7th Armoured Division and the investment of the first sizeable enemy stronghold, the port of Bardia. Along the coast road, 7th Armoured Brigade augmented by Rifle Brigade companies from the Support Group must press on into Sollum, while along the top of the Escarpment, 4th Armoured must mop up any Italian resistance which might show itself on the Egyptian side of the Wire, shoulder aside anything across the Wire and cut down the Escarpment and across the Bardia–Tobruk road as quickly as possible.

As 4th Armoured's role in this was obviously the more important, and as Creagh was still in hospital and Caunter thus still commanding the whole division, his second in command, Horace Birks, would have the honour of leading the first invading thrust of British armour into hostile territory. In order to help him, a light striking force was formed consisting of 11th Hussars less two squadrons, two batteries of the Royal Horse Artillery and the 2nd Royal Tank Regiment with light tanks, all under command of the 11th's C.O., Lieutenant-Colonel John Combe. The other two 11th Squadrons remained with Birks.

It was bitterly cold that night along the edge of the Escarpment whether on top or below, with a full moon and a freezing wind. The men were very tired now after three days' continuous fighting, but buoyed up with triumph; there was little comment and no complaint when orders for an advance to the frontier were given which included the words, 'Owing to this change of plan we shall have to be short of food and water so that we can continue to be supplied with the ammunition and petrol we shall need.'

Some of the tanks still carried items from the larders of the Sofafi camps, though the armour had not in fact had much to do with the occupation of any of these and therefore had not done so well as the infantry. Anyway, there was no water with which to cook the soups, which would have been the most welcome form of nourishment in those conditions.

To get forward was the main thing. By the afternoon of December 13th, all of Birks's command were concentrated around Khereigat about twelve miles south of Halfaya, and ready to move. They crossed the frontier shortly after midnight and knifed through between the Italian posts to reach their first rendezvous twenty miles west of Bardia by 0700 on the morning of the 14th. Then Combeforce went forward to find the route down the Escarpment that C Squadron's Sergeant Lamb had used six months before.

It was there that the Italian fighters caught them.

This was the squadron which had been especially formed to find the 11th Hussars, and now they were firing explosive bullets. They came screaming in at just above ground level and in twenty minutes of violent action wrecked five armoured cars, a fitter's lorry and a truck, killed another of the 11th's squadron sergeant-majors, badly wounded an officer and five of the men. Then they were gone again, leaving a scene of smoking desolation, with cars burning, ammunition exploding, blood and oil soaking into the uncaring, absorbent sand. The Cherrypickers were paying the price always exacted of those who choose the sharp end.

But the survivors were ready to move within a quarter of an hour, and there then followed one of the more bizarre incidents in what was to prove a bizarre campaign. One of the Rolls-Royce armoured cars commanded by Sergeant Charles Galpin descended the Escarpment and reached an apparently deserted stretch of the Bardia–Tobruk road along which the sergeant intended to cut the telephone lines. Unfortunately, as he negotiated the ditch which bordered the road, the hump broke the timing gear of his car and totally immobilised it; and at that moment Galpin became acutely conscious of the fact that there was an Italian tank half a mile away along the road, whose crew were watching him with considerable interest.

Very shortly, the Italian tank crew's interest quickened to the extent of their climbing into their vehicle and starting along the road towards him – at which point the sergeant heard the sound of another vehicle, this time an ambulance, approaching in the other direction, from Bardia. He and his crew were therefore sandwiched rather neatly between two hostile units, though as one was probably non-combatant, his danger lay mostly in the immobility of his own vehicle.

Stepping smartly into the middle of the road, he held up the ambulance, highwayman fashion, and within a very short time the astonished driver and his passengers were locked in the back while Galpin and his crew hurriedly fastened a tow-rope between his capture and his car. Three minutes later an onlooker would have been granted the astonishing sight of an Italian ambulance with a British driver at the wheel, towing a British armoured car in the direction of Bardia, pursued by an Italian tank whose crew could apparently do nothing but shout and wave their arms in a positively operatic frenzy.

Unfortunately for Galpin, he had overlooked a small square opening in the partition behind him, through which the driver normally communicated with his passengers – and just as his driving mirror was providing sound evidence that he was drawing away from his pursuer despite the 4-ton weight he was pulling, an arm came through the opening and a hand fastened around his throat. There followed a frantic few minutes while Galpin tried to draw his revolver with one hand and break the grip which was choking him with the other, at the same time keeping the now violently swaying ambulance and its tow on the road. Immediately behind him he could hear at least two of the passengers trying to smash their way through the partition, and he also caught a split-second view in the mirror of the expression of total bewilderment on the face of his driver, struggling with the wheel of the armoured car.

Then his gun came free, he fired immediately back through the opening and felt the grip on his throat relax, put another four shots through the partition until the hammering stopped – and saw immediately ahead of him an approaching convoy.

He and his crew fled into the sand-dunes, watched their late charges being driven back towards Bardia, and eventually reported back to their own squadron headquarters. These, however, had been bombed three more times that morning (in all, the 11th Hussar squadrons were bombed over twenty times that day and were so reduced in strength that they had been withdrawn from the action).

But by now, 2nd R.T.R. had come down the Escarpment and were firmly established across the road. Bardia was cut off from reinforcement, at least from the west.

Needless to say, not all went as well on every front.

When it became evident that 4th Armoured's thrust was likely to meet with success, O'Connor realised that the Italian commander in Bardia, Generale di Corpo d'Armata Bergonzoli, would be very likely to call for the retreat of the Italian garrisons in both Capuzzo and Sollum to Bardia, in order to strengthen his own garrison. O'Connor therefore ordered 7th Armoured Brigade first of all to capture Sollum and then to cross the Wire and get between Capuzzo and the coast, thus holding back Bergonzoli's reinforcement.

But neither of the moves took place in time and both Italian garrisons, travelling at night, safely reached their destinations; and O'Connor was very annoyed, especially when he divined the reasons for the delays and realised that they were also the ones which had allowed the escape of the Sofafi garrison. Admittedly, 7th Armoured Brigade had lost some transport to 4th Armoured by arrangement and was not quite so experienced as 4th, but, O'Connor later wrote:

> I feel that this question of preventing the movement of enemy columns at night must be tackled. I think the main difficulty arises from the fact that our training suggests that armoured units

should not be used at night, and I have noted a distinct dis-inclination of tank units to be used in any [such] capacity. I have a strong feeling that the real objection is due to a lack of decen-tralization as regards maintenance and messing – in particular below a squadron basis. In the case of the 11th Hussars, I have met no such disinclination. This unit decentralized its messing arrangements down to single cars, and was constantly employed at night.[2]

Whether the Italians in Capuzzo actually escaped while 7th Armoured Brigade were sitting down to dinner or not, it would seem that the commander of one of the 1st R.T.R. Squadrons felt unhappy about the situation, for that night he pressed hard on the heels of the retreating Italians, chased them as far as the outskirts of Bardia and then, with perhaps too keen a sense of opportunism, tried to rush the last gap in the defences before it closed.

'I gave the order to advance with all speed,' he wrote afterwards, 'and as my tank was travelling on the road I was soon well in the lead.'

But again, the Italian artillerymen were on watch, every gun in the sector opened up and when he was about half a mile from the entrance, the whole desert exploded about him. Soon his own tank had been hit repeatedly, the ammunition was blazing and a track broken, while behind him the rest of his command was turning away under heavy fire. He and his crew ran for it and got away – but the defences around Bardia were now closed and as secure as the garrison could make them.

The defences were, in fact, formidable, and now Bergonzoli had over 45,000 men and some 400 guns to support them. The eighteen-mile perimeter defences around Bardia had been planned and constructed many months before, and kept in good condition since. Along its entire length ran a thick, double-apron barbed wire fence, and for most of the way it was accompanied by a sheer-sided anti-tank ditch four feet deep and as much as twelve feet wide; and only where natural wadis at the extreme northern and southern ends of the defences made the approaches totally impossible for tanks was the anti-tank ditch not continued. Immediately behind these defences was a line of strongholds, each containing artillery and machine-gun posts housed in concrete-lined trenches and shelters, and each protected by a ditch and barbed wire; further back was a second line of wired posts while between the lines were six well-dispersed minefields under good artillery cover. Extra isolated strongholds covered points of especial importance or vulnerability, and behind the southern arc of the defence line there was even an extra 'switch line' of duplicated defences, across the most direct road from the frontier, and here also was the greatest artillery concentration.

By December 16th Generale Bergonzoli had under his command in Bardia the 1st and 2nd Blackshirt Divisions, the 62nd Marmarica Division and parts of the 63rd Cyrene and 64th Catanzaro Divisions, plus the original fortress troops and the frontier guards from the Wire. He had also a dozen M13 tanks held as central reserve and, for what they were worth, a hundred or so L3s scattered about the area behind the main line defences; but it was in the 300 medium and field guns, the 100-plus light guns and especially in the calibre of his artillerymen that the main shield of his command area lay.

The paper comparison between the defending force and those now grouping outside for attack was therefore such that Bergonzoli's reply to one of Mussolini's more supplicatory exhortations would have appeared totally justified. Mussolini had addressed him:

> I have given you a difficult task, but one suited to your courage and your experience as an old and intrepid soldier – the task of defending the fortress of Bardia to the last. I am certain that 'Barba Elettrica' and his brave soldiers will stand at whatever cost faithful to the last.

The reference to Bergonzoli's beard recalled his service in the Spanish Civil War during which he had won this apparently acclamatory cognomen, somewhat devalued among the British who had translated it as 'Electric Whiskers'. He, in turn, had replied to his Duce:

> I am aware of the honour and I have today repeated to my troops your message – simple and unequivocal. In Bardia we are and here we stay.

The trouble with this splendidly Roman sentiment was that it was not held higher up the line. Maresciallo Graziani was already questioning the advisability of trying to hold Bardia against the hordes of British, Commonwealth and Imperial troops which his overheated intelligence service – aided by a similarly excited imagination on his own part – was conjuring forth. How could the pitiful garrison of tiny little Bardia stand up to the hammering about to fall from skies dominated by the massed air fleets of the R.A.F. – to say nothing of bombardments from the sea by the huge guns of the concentrated and unconquerable Royal Navy?

According to his *cris de cœur* to Rome, the treachery of Badoglio had left Bardia – and perhaps Tobruk and all Cyrenaica – virtually unprotected; so what was Graziani expected to do now? Where was the promised aid from the Luftwaffe? Where were the anti-aircraft batteries he had long been requesting? Where all those promised reinforcements?

In any case, there was only sufficient water in Bardia to withstand a month's siege, so would it not be wise to withdraw all forces at least to Tobruk, thus presenting an even stronger defence to the ravening invaders when they arrived there? In the meantime, he had begun withdrawing the Italian colonists in Cyrenaica back towards Benghasi, and would forward them to Tripoli and the homeland as and when circumstances dictated.

As there exists in all armies a kind of spiritual osmosis whereby lack of confidence seeps inexorably from higher to lower levels, neither the general commanding the garrison in Bardia nor the troops of which it consisted were regarding the solicitations from Rome with much enthusiasm. They knew quite well that from higher up the line and further back in safety, their own situation was regarded as disastrous, their plight unfortunate, and their cause and fate insignificant except in so far as it affected the High Command.

The odds were never really on the side of the defenders of Bardia.

It is doubtful if General O'Connor or the men of the Western Desert Force gave much thought to the odds for or against them during the next few days, for they were all far too busy. With 7th Armoured Brigade obviously for the moment better fitted to undertake the more static role, O'Connor brought them forward to hold the ring around Bardia, while he sent 4th Armoured – now at last again under command of Brigadier 'Blood' Caunter as Creagh had been released from hospital – back towards the Wire where the garrison of Sidi Omar was still holding out.

The camp around Sidi Omar was laid out much as had been the camps further forward, but in this instance the central feature was a picturesque white *Beau Geste*-type fort surrounded, as was normal, with wire, trenches and an unknown area of minefields. As there were no 4th Indian infantry to support the armour, the attack opened with a brisk bombardment from the 25-pounders of the R.H.A. batteries, followed immediately, under the dust-cloud thrown up by the shelling, by a 'glorious gallop' by the tanks of the 2nd R.T.R. and the 7th Hussars. Captain Patrick Hobart – Hobo's nephew – commander of C Squadron, 2nd R.T.R., wrote a vivid description of the charge:

> We drove around to avoid the enemy shelling while the 25-pounders did their bombardment, then formed up in line and

advanced at full speed on the fort in what I imagined to be the best traditions of the *arme blanche*. The enemy must have suffered pretty severely from the attentions of the R.H.A., for in we went unscathed, with every gun and machine-gun firing. My orders to the squadron were to drive straight through the perimeter, doing as much destruction as possible, out the other side, and then to return again and rally back on the near side. I was in the centre of the squadron line, and in an excess of zeal and enthusiasm charged the fort itself. The outer wall was built of solid blocks of stone, and in breaking it I knocked off my near-side idler, so that I found myself inside the courtyard of the two-storey fort, with an immobilised tank . . . There were some hectic minutes, particularly as my second-in-command, David Wilkie, was shelling the fort from outside with his close-support tank. During this time I had inadvertently left my No. 9 set switched to 'send', so that all my frenzied orders and exhortations to my crew were going out over the regimental net – which caused considerable pleasure to my brother officers and later embarrassment to me![3]

The rest of the story is best given by a quotation from the report later written by the driver of David Wilkie's tank, Sergeant Bermingham:

After circling the fort once, my commander gave the urgent order 'sharp left'. This turn placed the tank facing a large breach in the fort. I sailed across it, with all machine-guns blazing, and came to rest beside the squadron commander's tank . . . Looking through the visor, I could see Captain Hobart, with steel helmet on, shooting away over the top of his cupola with a pistol. The sight of a second tank inside the fort must have been too much for the Italians and very soon they were appearing from nooks and crannies everywhere to give themselves up.[4]

It was all over in ten minutes, due in great part to the fact that the Italian guns and crews had been concentrated along the eastern side of the fort facing across into Egypt, and the attack came from behind them. And there had not been time for the lessons taught the Italians at Nibeiwa and the Tummars, even if absorbed, to be put into effect.

The fall of Sidi Omar now cleared the area to the east for O'Connor, and he could concentrate upon his primary – and enormous – problems of supply and reinforcement.

As the New Zealand Government was solidly supporting the attitude of the commander of their troops in Egypt, Major-General Bernard Freyberg, V.C., in his determination that the New Zealand

Division would only go into action as a complete formation, O'Connor could still not call forward the men of the 4th N.Z. Brigade behind Matruh, much to the frustrated fury of the infantrymen, forced now to listen to the patronising tone of their transport drivers telling them how battles were really won.

Fortunately, neither the Australian Government nor the general commanding the 6th Australian Division, Major-General Iven Mackay, took the same attitude, and 16th Australian Brigade had already moved up as far as Sollum and was more than anxious to get even further forward. Moreover, their 17th Brigade was spoiling for a fight and would move up as soon as transport became available to them, while the 19th Brigade made it quite clear that there would be something very close to mutiny if, despite their comparative lack of training and total lack of transport, they were not present when the rest of their division went into action.

But as at every stage in the battle so far, and every stage to come, it was greatly a matter of transport; this was to be the war of the 3-tonners.

O'Connor and Mackay had already met when both were serving in Palestine and had established very friendly relations so there was little to resolve between them but the practical problems. They had a brief conference at Mackay's headquarters at Sidi Barrani during which Mackay took command of the Sollum area and also assumed responsibility for the attack on Bardia. They then planned the necessary moves forward and very shortly 16th Australian Brigade was on its way:

> A little before midnight on the 19th–20th the column reached the frontier wire and before dawn the 2/2nd Battalion had taken over positions astride the Capuzzo–Bardia road held by the 1/King's Royal Rifle Corps, one of the two motorised battalions of the armoured division. When dawn came they found themselves deployed on a wide flat dusty plain. Bardia lay ahead over the straight horizon. A bitterly cold wind blew and the infantrymen wore every garment they possessed. The ground was so stony that it was difficult to find places where trenches could be dug even with crowbars; soon the men learnt to look for places where the desert rats had dug their holes because there the soil was likely to be softer and with fewer stones. On the night of the 20th December the 2/3rd Battalion went into position on the left of the 2/2nd.[5]

On 16th Australian Brigade's right were the remnants of the 16th British Brigade, brought up very shortly after the leading elements of 7th Armoured Brigade had taken over from 4th Armoured. The British infantry were still licking their wounds from the Sidi Barrani battles, tired after Herculean efforts to tidy up the battlefield and help in the unending task of bringing forward supplies, and O'Connor wanted them rested and in reserve, for already his eyes were on the next target – Tobruk; but nothing could be moved for a while, so Christmas Day was spent around the besieged town in a manner not untypical of national characteristics. The Italian troops were given many reminders of home – wine, pastas with rich sauces, solemn pageantry in religious services held in the justifiable belief that on this day their civilised enemies would not attack too seriously. The Australian troops each received a Comforts parcel containing plum pudding and tinned cream, cake, fruit and cheese and there was some tinned beer available. The British received another delivery of petrol and ammunition, coupled with warnings to the artillery to hoard their shells for the main attack, and to everyone that shortages of both food and water were likely to continue.

Then on December 27th, 17th Australian Brigade arrived to release the 16th British who went back to Buq Buq, the Support Group of the 7th Armoured Division reclaimed most of their transport which had been given to the Armoured Brigade for the move across the Wire and closed in on the north-western edge of Bardia; and O'Connor, having received word from Colonel Jerram of the 7th R.T.R. that by supreme efforts the fitters had now put twenty-two Matildas back on the road, approved Mackay's plans for the attack and fixed the time for dawn, January 3rd. He also asked Mackay not to use his 19th Brigade unless it was absolutely necessary, as he wanted it in support for the first move on Tobruk by 7th Armoured Brigade two days later.

Nobody could call O'Connor a pessimistic general, even on the diet he was sharing with his men.

If the men of the 6th Australian Division lacked the hard professionalism of the long-service regular soldiers of the 4th Indian, they made up for it in sheer size and physical strength. Far and away the greater part of soldiering, especially infantry soldiering in battle and in preparation for battle, is a matter of sweat and blood – and as military lore has long had it, the more sweat, the less blood. The infantryman, despite motorisation, marches a long way carrying a load often as much as a third of his body weight; before the actual clash of battle, he digs slit trenches for himself and larger chasms for the administration services which will sustain him while away from a more permanent base, and when battle is joined, he is usually called upon to attack before dawn. The battle almost invariably continues throughout the following daylight hours, and even if it slackens at dusk, the second night will be just as short as the first and punctuated frequently by bursts of violence.

Wrenched and aching muscles, fatigue and strain, sweat and thirst make up more of a soldier's life than do fear, anger, blood-lust or death, and the man who can carry most ammunition is often the one with the last, vital shot left at the end of the day.

The Australians were big men. To one startled observer it seemed that those who weren't well over six feet tall made up for it by being three feet wide; and if they were three feet thick as well, it was all bone and muscle. Rifles in their huge hands looked like boys' airguns, they handled light machine-guns as though they were rifles and later in the war would carry anti-tank weapons as easily. A column of marching Australians shook the foundations of the road, and two of them seemed to fill a bar especially if an argument developed.

And these first Australians into action in the Second World War had something else as well; an immense pride in the traditions of military valour set twenty-five years before at Gallipoli and in France, where some of their battalion commanders and senior officers had themselves fought, together with the fathers and uncles of the men who now marched towards Bardia. The battalion numerals reflected this attitude – 2nd/1st, 2nd/2nd, 2nd/3rd, 2nd/8th, the prefix '2nd' indicating that this was the second time the battalion had been formed, the first being the First World War formations. These were the men who, despite an anti-military atmosphere between the wars coupled with the peacetime parsi-mony towards military matters, had nevertheless joined Australia's citizen army and were now determined to prove they were as good soldiers as their fathers had been.

In France between 1915 and 1918 the men of the Australian Imperial Force had earned for themselves a name for aggressive and continual patrolling, and within twenty-four hours of the arrival of 16th Brigade their sons dominated the no-man's-land opposite (against little opposition it must be admitted) and were feeding back the intelligence upon which their attack would be based. According to their official history:

In the following week patrols went forward each night and, unnoticed by the Italians, continued to measure the ditch and wire at various points along the western side of the enemy's line, or else were detected and drew a deafening fire from the posts. When this occurred the men merely lay still, sometimes for two hours, until the fusillade ceased and then made their way back to their company's area, perhaps 6,000 yards away. Eventually men who went out on patrol wore sandshoes rather than muffled boots and, because they might have to lie motionless for hours at a time, dressed warmly, with sweaters over their jackets, balaclavas under steel helmets, mittens, scarves and long woollen underpants if they had them. From 22nd December onwards two or three engineers would generally accompany each infantry patrol to search for and disarm land mines and to reconnoitre the ditch and the wire through which they would have to make a passage for the infantry when the attack was made.[6]

As the reports came in, the plans were laid. Surprise to the degree achieved at Nibeiwa was of course impossible now, but the timing could be masked and so could the direction of the main thrust. As the Italians had obviously planned their defences with the thought of a direct attack from the Wire at their south-eastern flank in mind, there was no harm in encouraging the idea – so the most blatant patrolling was carried out here by the 2nd/6th Battalion along the line of the Wadi Muatered. Elsewhere, discovery and violence were kept to a minimum, but a ditch of the same dimensions as that running southwards from the Bardia–Tobruk road was dug well back behind the Australian lines, and much effort was spent finding out how long it would take men of the 2nd/1st and 2nd/3rd Battalions to fill it in and which was the best method.

Generale Bergonzoli and his men were allowed little peace during this period, even if they weren't stationed in the outer defences, for O'Connor wished every man in Bardia to know what he was in for. Every night Air Commodore Collishaw's bombers were over the little port, and if most of their bombs fell on the stony desert (for there were very few buildings in Bardia) they made a great deal of noise and their splinters, howling through the night air and smacking against rocks or walls, at least reminded the inhabitants of battle's imminence.

The Royal Navy played her part, too, the monitor H.M.S *Terror* bombarding the port and its defences with her huge 15-inch guns, while on December 17th the gun-boat *Aphis* steamed right into Bardia harbour and for an hour cruised around firing at shore establishments, sinking three small craft and damaging others. But this was a sight unappreciated by the Italian artillerymen, and when *Aphis* tried a repeat performance the next day, she was briskly chased off and along the coast by mobile guns until she was out of range.

With the infantry closing up and the plans developing, O'Connor's next preoccupation was with the materials of war, especially guns and ammunition. His strictures to 4th Indian with regard to the inviolability of the contents of his Field Supply Depots had been observed,

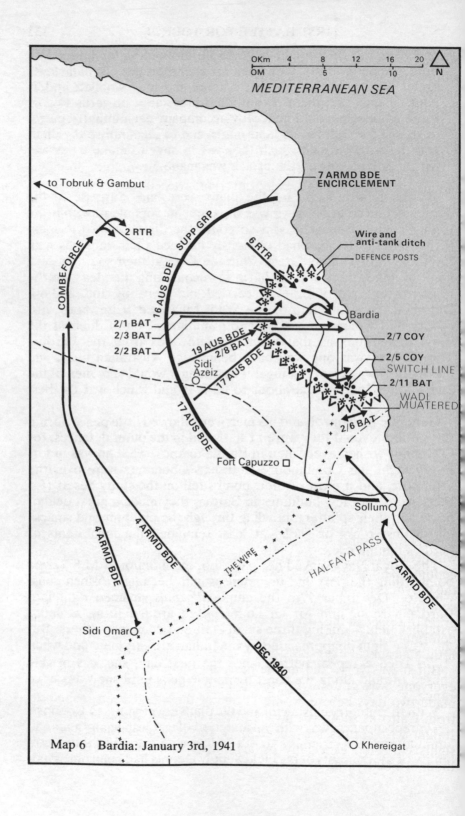

Map 6   Bardia: January 3rd, 1941

but he was soon to learn that they had not been wide enough in scope, and with annoyance tinged with reluctant admiration he had had to send bleakly worded orders to Beresford-Peirse to the effect that although his division were entitled to take with them their own field artillery, they were *not* also entitled to take the medium guns and howitzers of the Corps artillery. Would he please instruct his C.R.A. to return them in short order?

It was, as he realised, a piece of quite normal military larceny, though on rather a grand scale; but it had wasted time and used up petrol and vehicle mileage, all in short supply.

The guns were back with him by Christmas Day, bringing his total up to 120 to support two brigades – 96 supporting the main attack into the western border, 24 supporting the feint in the south – and when given these figures, General Mackay made the interesting comment that the 96 guns on an 800-yard front gave only a slightly smaller artillery concentration than that at Messines in 1917, which had been one gun or howitzer every seven yards; but the Messines Front had been six miles long.

Support Group had another forty 25-pounders up in the northern sector.

At the moment when 1940 became 1941, Western Desert Force, in consequence of the rapidly growing build-up of forces in the Middle East, was redubbed XIII Corps (the Roman numerals were an essential part of this new designation) but the weather in which it operated remained the same; vile. Records for the district are hard to come by, but local memory united in agreeing that the winter of 1940/1941 was the worst in recall. Rain fell in unremembered quantities, cold and with traces of sleet, filling the slit trenches with gritty slop and turning the powdered clay which had been mistaken for sand to glue; yet when the rain stopped and the icy wind continued, as it did all the time, it still managed to scrape up genuine sand to sting exposed hands and faces, and at times to turn the greyness into yellow fog. Misery abounded and only a species of confirmed optimists, such as infantry soldiers, could have found any grain of solace in the world at large. 'Who wants Bondi Beach?' one determinedly happy warrior was heard to ask, adding with only a little anatomical exaggeration, 'Sharks and sun-blistered arses!'

But it was very cold in the early morning of January 3rd, and everyone was grateful for the issue of sleeveless leather jerkins made two days before. Some 11,500 of these had been rushed up from Cairo as soon as they had been checked, together with 350 Italian wire-cutters scavenged from the camps in Egypt, mortar sights collected especially by an officer sent back 400 miles for them, 10,000 yards of white tape to mark the boundaries of the attack (too late; they used strips of four-by-two rifle-cleaning flannelette instead) and 300 pairs of gloves for the men who would cut through the wire – issued as the men were actually moving up.

O'Connor was still operating on a knife-edge.

The men of the leading companies of the 2nd/1st Battalion began moving forward just before 0430, almost grotesque in size and shape. Over their tunics they wore the leather jerkins and on top of these their greatcoats, buttoned back from the waist down like old-style Foreign Legionnaires to give freedom of movement. They wore steel helmets, respirators on their chests, and in pouches, haversacks and pockets they each carried 150 rounds of ammunition, grenades, tinned beef and rations for three days; this in addition to their rifles or Bren-guns, and the picks, shovels and Bangalore Torpedoes (twelve-foot-long pipes stuffed with explosive) which the leading patrols would need. Only men built on imposing lines could have stood up under the burden, let alone moved and fought.

From ahead came the sounds of the customary R.A.F. bombardment, for the moment no heavier than on the previous few nights, and around them just the gritting of boots on the desert, the occasional swish as they moved through camel-brush. It was pitch dark, the men following the guides, who in turn watched their compasses, looked out for the white strips of flannelette – and prayed.

Then, as the leading platoons reached the start line just before 0530, the artillery crashed out, shells screamed overhead and an area some 2,500 yards by 500 yards in front of them and just beyond the wire erupted in violence. Immediately, groups of engineers went forward, first to the anti-tank ditch where some began tearing down the almost vertical sides to make passages for the Matildas, while seven groups each of three men went forward with the Bangalore Torpedoes to push them through under the double-apron wire at about sixty-yard intervals. Behind them more engineers were tearing up mines while, with shattering irrelevance, the infantry were singing 'South of the Border'.

There was a slight delay due to the fact that one of the few Italian shells to come back in reply to the assault had knocked out the lieutenant in charge of the blowing party, but his second-in-command gave the order, the torpedoes exploded and as the wire ripped up and away the infantry charged forward, some still singing, some shouting both encouragement to each other and defiance at the enemy.

There was, however, very little sign of the enemy for the moment, for those Italians in the posts who had not been stunned by the artillery bombardment were apparently morally shattered by the sight of these huge figures lumbering up to their posts out of the gloom, cutting their way through the wire as though it didn't exist, firing their Brens from the hip and tossing grenades into trenches and shelters like ping-pong balls. Very soon a stream of shaken prisoners was trotting out through the gaps in the wire towards the ditch where, until an officer arrived who had rather more acquaintance than his men with the provisions of the Geneva Convention, they were employed helping the engineers fill it in.

Behind them, the rest of 2nd/1st Battalion were now through the wire and fanning out to the north up towards the Bardia–Tobruk road, leaving in their wake half a dozen reeking strongposts and two artillery sangars – the guns wrecked, the shells scattered, the crews to a man shot or bayoneted. Within twenty minutes over 400 prisoners were on their way back, but encountering a new danger as their own artillery put down an accurate barrage along the wire which effectively destroyed all of it that was left, and raised a dust cloud like a London fog.

Through it waddled the Matildas, along six passages made for them across the ditch, on and through the wire to turn south accompanied by the men of the 2nd/2nd Battalion. There then followed a period of close, storming actions which must have put some of the older men in mind of trench warfare in 1918 – prowling, cautious advances followed by a swift rush when the target post was identified, and then a chaos of noise, of cries of anger and fear, of thud of boot or rifle-butt, of crash of bomb and crack of bullet; of sudden silence and whimper of surrender.

Sometimes a tank would roll towards a post and, at the crack of its 2-pounder, men would pour out with their hands up to be roughly directed to the rear; sometimes machine-guns would answer the tank, the bullets ricocheting away on a high note, sometimes to thud into one of the accompanying infantry. Then the charge would go in and the close, set-piece battle would be fought, invariably over in fifteen minutes or less. And as progress continued and the light grew, an excitement gripped the Australians which seemed to transfigure them into total irresistibility, the more adventurous pressing further and even further ahead, quite confident that they could take posts single-handed. One patrol approached a post at a run, lobbed in a grenade and were about to follow it with more when the voice of another patrol's sergeant issued forth from inside bidding them desist in language of which only the gist is given in the *Official History*; but Sergeant Skerrett had been bombing his way along the line in isolated exhilaration for some time.

Behind 2nd/2nd as they swung to the south came 2nd/3rd, pressing forward directly towards the fortified area and the port itself, marching at first through dust so thick that they could hardly see the men around them, while the officers led by compass despite the fact that it was by now broad daylight. A few sangars briefly held their attention, there were three gun positions which were charged, but without casualty for the dust cloud hid the attackers until the last moment – and all the time the prisoners were coming in, to be briefly checked, then escorted by two riflemen back to the Wire. But at two riflemen to a hundred prisoners, the company strengths were dropping too fast for the tasks which might yet face them, for from ahead came the crack of the redoubtable Italian artillery and there was still a long way to go before the port would be reached.

Then another menace appeared, so unexpected that the result had elements of the ludicrous. On the left flank of the line of the 2nd/3rd objective (which had almost been reached by noon) six tanks suddenly arrived, and at first the Australians assumed that they were British. Then Captain Hutchinson noticed that they were painted grey and not khaki, and a moment later came a burst of fire from the leader not more than thirty yards away which killed Hutchinson's runner and shot his own rifle out of his hand. At the same moment one of Hutchinson's lieutenants who had been casually walking towards the rear tank (which he, too, thought was British), realised his mistake, jumped on to the back, emptied his revolver into the open turret and raced away into the shelter of a nearby sangar.

At this, the tanks moved off towards a group consisting of half a dozen Australians guarding about 500 Italian prisoners whom they freed, sending one of the ex-guards to a nearby Australian post with the suggestion that they all surrender. As the reply was a concentrated burst of rifle and machine-gun fire, the tanks moved away (leaving the Italian infantry to be taken prisoner all over again), and a little while later their presence was reported to the crews of two Matildas resting over a rise out of sight. The phenomenon of Italian tanks going into action was so unbelievable, however, that the British crews dismissed the information as a product of Antipodean technical ignorance and the M13s might well have gone on to reach one of the battalion headquarters, had not three 2-pounder truck-mounted anti-tank guns arrived on the scene. One of them, commanded by a Corporal Pickett, opened fire with such lethal accuracy that within minutes four of the tanks were out of action, but the remaining two tanks scored a couple of hits on Pickett's portée (as the truck was called) and put it out of action before the other guns silenced them too.

The end of enterprising Italian tank crews was sad and grisly. The 2-pounder solid shot smashed through the armour with ease – but then lacked the velocity to pass out through the far side of the tank and thus ricocheted around inside until all momentum was lost, with bloodily fatal results.

By midday, the 16th Brigade were thus on their first objectives, holding the perimeter of a deep bridgehead, and 17th Brigade were following in through the gaping entrance along the western flank of the Bardia defences. On their approach to the gap they had been astonished by the apparently unending column marching towards them – and at first some rather uncharitably thought it was 16th Brigade retreating after a savage defeat; but the growing number of prisoners was proving an embarrassment to everybody and the roughly constructed prison-cages were soon overfull. It had been assumed at O'Connor's H.Q. that the entire garrison of Bardia had consisted of about 25,000 men, and the reports by Mackay's Intelligence section by noon on the first day that they had already captured 30,000 brought a swift and ironic query from O'Connor's B.G.S., John Harding – which was soon withdrawn with apology.

The men of the 17th Brigade were to have a tougher time than those of the 16th, for by now surprise had gone again. Nevertheless, they drove south along the fence line taking each strongpost as they came to it, then swung eastwards to take the Switch Line from the rear. By early afternoon they were pushing ever further eastward towards the coast, but several factors were beginning to tell against them.

They had always been chronically short of transport and so had already marched some fifteen miles up from the south, before even passing into the battle area. Moreover, by this time, the Matildas were either out of action through damage, or out of fuel or ammunition or both; only two of them could accompany the men of 17th Brigade, and those only for purposes of morale as their guns were useless. Thus the advances had to take place with only the support of mortar fire and of the heavy machine-guns of a company of Northumberland Fusiliers who had been attached to them – and now the infantry were coming up against the concentration of Italian artillery in the south which had had ample time and warning to make themselves ready for attack.

The result was a bitter battle indeed, during which only the indomitable and highly competitive spirit of the Australians kept them going despite severe losses – including that of many of their most experienced officers and senior N.C.O.s. Time and again they found themselves pinned down in narrow wadis, time and again they found themselves committed to a charge across open country towards Italian guns firing over open sights.

And again, their situation was all the time complicated by the apparently unending accumulation of prisoners. As the Australians drove further and further in, they began uncovering the same picture as that found by the Indians below Sidi Barrani. At a turn in one wadi, they came across an amphitheatre with almost vertical sides, in which had been carved by man or nature a number of deep caves. According to the official history –

At first there were no signs of life but, when Morse fired a shot into the pit, about seventy Italians, including twenty-five well-dressed officers, began to appear at the openings of a dozen caves and dugouts waving white flags. It was the headquarters of an artillery group, where the staff had been living in complete security against shell fire from the landward side and in considerable luxury. There were enamelled baths, silken garments and cosmetics. The notepaper in the offices was embossed and the glasses in the messes were engraved.[7]

But this was a lighter moment in 17th Brigade's fight that day; generally, it was bitter and grim and as the day went by their casualty figure rose – in one sector, unnecessarily.

The 2nd/6th Battalion had, since the arrival of 17th Brigade, been carrying out the deliberately exhibitionary patrolling along the Wadi Muatered down in the south, and their orders for the day were to bring them to a pitch of noisy activity; but as they were not really intended to do much but keep Italian attention away from the areas of the central thrusts to the north, they were not supplied with armour (which would in any case have been unable to cross the deep ravine of the wadi) or even with much artillery.

Despite this, and their orders, 2nd/6th were determined to make a name for themselves that day and when the battle opened, their leading platoons scaled the sides of the wadis and attempted to break through the lines of outposts opposite them to attack the strongholds behind, backed as these were by strong concentrations of artillery. The results were predictable and tragic. Although some survivors of the first wave reached the posts, all except four were badly wounded in the next few minutes and those four were driven to take shelter in an empty sangar where two hours later they were taken prisoner.

It was the same all along that sector – not surprisingly, for that was how it had been foreseen, though apparently the plan had not been made sufficiently clear to the officers and men of the 2nd/6th. They had little support and no armour, no plan for the attack which they carried out – nothing, in fact, but their romantic determination to outshine their fathers' exploits of twenty-five years before, and those of their brothers now to the north, despite the fact that they were supposed to attract violence but not instigate it. The battlefield is a place for ruthlessness, fear, anger and hatred; not for romance.

At the northern end of the arena there was stalemate, too, but only a portion of it was unexpected. Three battleships and four destroyers of the Royal Navy had arrived off the port early in the morning, and for forty-five minutes had poured their thunderous broadsides into the sector to the north of Upper Bardia – more as a demonstration to lower Italian morale than as a practical contribution to the battle. However, an attack was put in on one small sector with six light tanks of the 6th R.T.R., but a party of Free French Marines who had been assigned as supporting infantry declined to follow the tanks, four of which were forced as a result to withdraw, while two pressed on until they ran out of fuel and their crews were taken prisoner.

But the main thrust by the Australians in the centre was proving irresistible and both brigades were advancing all the time, though this was not always evident further back at Headquarters. The reports of the bitterness of the fighting on the 17th Brigade front worried Mackay's staff to such a degree that, despite O'Connor's request, they persuaded Mackay to put in one battalion of the 19th Brigade – the 2nd/8th – which came in on the right of 16th Brigade, releasing some of the 2nd/2nd men to move even further forward.

This move had, apparently, a most impressive effect, and the first one section of the Northumberland Fusiliers knew of it was when their corporal turned around and shouted, 'Christ! Look at this!'

Behind them, silhouetted against the setting sun, was what appeared to be a whole plain full of advancing giants, huge under their flapping greatcoats, their weapons held casually in their hands, their helmets pushed back above their grinning, sand-blurred faces, equipment, bandoliers and shovels hanging apparently unnoticed from their slab-like shoulders as they trotted like friendly Neanderthals past the Fusiliers and on towards the edge of the next wadi.

'Poor bloody Wops!' said one of the machine-gunners, feelingly.

The fighting went on all night in one sector or another, and everywhere the Australians moved forward, the prisoners came in and after a brief inspection were dispatched – generally under their own N.C.O.s when these could be identified – back towards the gap. Their methods of surrender varied from the dropping of arms and the raising of white flags almost as soon as the Australians came in sight, through a brisk exchange of shots before giving in, to the staunch defence, often to the death, of the artillerymen. One extremely foolish infantryman popped up out of a concealed trench, shot an Australian company commander through the chest, threw down his rifle and climbed out with his hands up and a broad smile on his face. He was promptly thrown back into the trench and a Bren-gun was emptied into him – and only the swift action of the company second-in-command stopped the immediate slaughter by the incensed Australians of all the other prisoners in the area.

But this appears to have been the single incident of its type, and by morning well over 30,000 prisoners were herded in and around the cages outside Bardia perimeter, while inside it the area left in Italian control was restricted to the town itself and the artillery concentration in the south.

At 1100 the drive to the town was launched, 2nd/3rd Battalion driving up across the Bardia–Tobruk road, 2nd/2nd with 2nd/8th on their right flank driving east towards the lower town and the headland above the port – and although only six Matildas were now available in support, the infantry drove forward so fast that the collapsing Italian defence had no time to destroy the water supply plant (if, indeed, they ever entertained any idea of doing so) or to increase the amount of damage in the small harbour over that already caused by *Aphis*. The attackers were now in what the official history calls 'the soft centre' of the Italian garrison, and the results predictable.

> . . . the column of prisoners streaming back to the south was soon a mile in length. It was led by dapper officers, wearing swords, pith helmets or 'Mussolini caps', and knee boots, and shaven and scented. When they were halted for lunch the Australians, dusty, unwashed and weary, collected bottles of champagne from the dugouts these Italians had abandoned and drank it from enamel pannikins.[8]

As one trooper from the Support Group was heard to say as they closed in from the north:

'What we want is more Wine, Women, and War with the Wops! —— the bloody songs!'

All defence north of the Switch Line had collapsed by nightfall on the 4th, and the following morning the 2nd/11th Battalion drove southwards with another half-dozen hastily repaired Matildas, and after a brisk battle with the remaining artillery posts were able to hand over to the weary 17th Brigade who mopped up. By 1300 all opposition was at an end and the entire area stained with the detritus of war – abandoned trucks, empty shell-cases, smouldering rubbish, fly-covered bodies; and paper everywhere. No army in history had received so many letters as this one and now they were littered about, blowing in the wind, impaled on the thorn bushes, covering the floors of trenches, dug-outs and strongposts; and in the buildings the floors were deep in official forms.

12 *Above*, Matildas on the way up. 13 *Below*, cruisers of 4th Armoured Brigade.

14 Western Desert Force infantry

15 Australian post outside Bardia

16 The interminable crocodiles of disconsolate prisoners

17 *Above*, one of the 3rd Hussars' light tanks trapped in the Buq Buq salt marshes.
18 *Centre*, Bren-gun carriers at Fort Capuzzo. 19 Little sign of trams in Sidi Barrani.

20 *Left*, the hoisting of the Digger's hat on the Tobruk flagpole. 21 *Right*, one of the Italian M13s captured before Bardia and used by the Australians in the capture of Tobruk.

22 Tobruk harbour, first time through

Everywhere roamed the soldiers – disconsolate groups of Italian privates looking for a few of their belongings or something to salvage from the ruins; sometimes a batch of elegant officers trudging along, accompanied by servants carrying their suitcases and occasionally chivvied by a lone Australian, weary, dirty and sardonic, longing to get back to his own sort, and to some sleep.

In three days' fighting, these first Australians into action in the Second World War had taken over 40,000 prisoners, captured over 400 guns and a few serviceable tanks. They had lost 130 officers and men killed and 326 had been wounded; and those few taken prisoner during the action were, of course, released – indeed many of them had exchanged roles with their captors at their captors' request. One of the tank commanders who had been taken prisoner in the north, when he had been isolated without the support of the French Marines, had to look after the whole of the batch who in their turn had surrendered to him as the nearest Australian formation could handle no more; there were, he had rather apologetically explained, about 1,500 of them.

But one of the Italians who got away was Generale di Corpo 'Barba Elettrica' Bergonzoli, who had left on foot for Tobruk on the morning of the last day, accompanied by several of his staff officers. It took them five days to reach Tobruk, and they had to pass through enemy lines to get there – for O'Connor had begun the investment of this major stronghold and port even before Bardia had fallen.

General O'Connor's supply problems were now reaching a pitch of complexity exceeded only by those of maintenance. The country through which his troops were fighting provided nothing – absolutely nothing – except a floor upon which to fight; no food, no fuel, not even water for washing or drinking despite the atrocious weather. A limited amount of warlike materials had been captured from the enemy, but against this slight advantage was the embarrassment of the vast numbers of prisoners; and even had he adopted towards them a totally inhuman attitude (a solution which, it is fairly safe to say, never crossed his mind) he would still have faced enormous problems. Some 40,000 starving and thirst-maddened Italians across his lines of communication would have proved only slightly more hazardous to his enterprise than the disease, corruption and disgust emanating from the same number of corpses.

The problem of prisoners apart, his main preoccupation was with the supply of ammunition, petrol, food and water to keep his men not only in the field, but continually advancing further and further away from their main bases. As he was later to write:

There are always two possible methods of supply which may be adopted in a situation of this sort, depending entirely on the amount of transport available.

(i) Using a number of echelons of transport to carry forward the supplies from the advanced Base to the forward troops. As each echelon has in general a radius of action of not more than 40 miles, the adoption of this method depends on whether there are sufficient echelons to cover the required distance.

(ii) Making dumps or Field Supply Depots with issue sections at stated intervals along the axis of the advance.

As we never had anything like sufficient transport for (i) we were forced to adopt (ii). This method meant that a formation's radius of action was dictated by the position of its most forward F.S.D., which in the case of the Armoured Division was 75 miles . . . in advance.[9]

The day after the Sofafi camps had been occupied, 7th Armoured Division's F.S.D. (No. 4), was already a hundred miles behind the troops it was supplying, and No. 5, set up within two days just east of the Sidi Barrani–Siwa track was another seventy miles behind two days later. By concentrating all 4th Indian Division at Sidi Barrani and putting them to work there forming F.S.D. No. 7, while he used their transport to lift supplies for the armour even further forward to a new F.S.D. at Fort Capuzzo (No. 9), O'Connor gave the arriving Australians a slight degree of security, but it would not have sufficed for the Bardia battle had not 16th British Brigade set up F.S.D. No. 8 at Sollum itself. This depot was fed at first by the Navy bringing supplies up from Alexandria which had to be unloaded by sheer human effort, for the port had only two tiny piers and no heavy-duty facilities whatsoever. Pioneer companies rushed forward from Cyprus and Palestine carried out the bulk unloading and the supplies were then lifted off the beaches by men of No. 4 New Zealand M.T. Company, all within range of heavy guns in Bardia whose shells killed or wounded seventy of them on Christmas Eve.

But now, with 7th Armoured Division and the Australians about to move up to Tobruk, two more Field Supply Depots would be needed – No. 10 half-way between Capuzzo and the Italian airfield at El Adem (which would obviously be 7th Armoured's first objective) and No. 11 for the Australians at Gambut where O'Connor himself was setting up his headquarters. Unfortunately, port facilities at Bardia were soon seen to be virtually useless (as a result, ironically, of the successes of the *Aphis*) so until Tobruk fell, all supplies for any further advance had still to come partly via Sollum from Alexandria but mostly by road from the railhead back at Matruh. What few stocks were left in the Field Supply Depots en route were being quickly eaten down, and some must be left to fuel the transport now engaged on longer and ever-longer hauls.

Moreover, as events had forced upon them all a veritable hand-to-mouth existence, stores had to come forward as they were needed for immediate use, not in accordance either with good storage principles (for there was less and less time for storage) or even with forecasts of needs made a week before; weather conditions and the inexperience of the transport drivers wrecked any system based on forethought, for sandstorms delayed convoys – on one occasion for four days – and only too often exhaustion, inexperience and the plain technical difficulty of finding the way across an unmarked, open, rough-surfaced desert led young drivers far off into wastes, sometimes to be missing for days, on occasion for ever, their ammunition-filled lorries found months later by far-ranging patrols, radiators dry, the bodies of the drivers lying ten yards or ten miles away.

Yet despite conditions of such haphazard chance, O'Connor's men had to have fuel when they needed it, ammunition in time for the attacks, spare tyres when the originals wore through (and on the desert surface, this was every few hundred miles), spare wheels when boulders had been impassable, spare tank tracks after every action; spare carburettors, spare magnetos, spare plugs, spare filters; spare sprockets, spare track pins, spare gun-sights, spare fans, spare fanbelts, spare engines. And water all the time; every ship which sailed into Sollum brought water, even the monitor *Terror* bringing in 200 tons which went straight into water-carts on the beach and off up to the front.

When Capuzzo had been taken it was found that the water in the storage tanks was too salt for use and 12,000 gallons had to be brought forward from Matruh – by road, again, which used up mileage in the battered and now-labouring 3-tonners – but some help was provided by pump-holes at Sidi Barrani and Buq Buq, and a pipeline to the tanks at Capuzzo was run from Sollum so that they could be topped up once the salt water had been cleaned out. Then Bardia fell, and although the water-plant had not been destroyed its product was found to be brackish and almost undrinkable – and there were another 40,000 prisoners to be watered; and fed.

However much the Navy were willing or able to co-operate, Sollum was a bottleneck through which only one-tenth of the necessary supplies could pass, so the vast bulk of everything needed had to come by lorry and truck from the railhead, either along the narrow and increasingly potholed coast road or across the desert above the Escarpment on the southern route. One reserve transport company was fitted out with captured Italian diesel trucks, and fifty lorries and their drivers were brought down from Palestine to join the transport pool – but by the end of December the vehicle wastage in the desert had reached 40 per cent, due in some case to age, in others to inexpert handling by drivers trained on the firm roads of Britain (though they learned quickly), but chiefly to the continual driving in clouds of dust which often thickened into sand-fogs, clogging every moving part and choking every filter and feed-pipe. The journey from railhead to Field Supply Depot and back could now take five days, and just as the exhausted driver would need a rest, so the truck would need a workshop maintenance; and neither would get either.

As for the men who were doing the fighting, the tank crews, gunners and infantrymen of 7th Armoured Division had by January 5th been operating in front line conditions for nearly a month, had advanced nearly 200 miles and played a not inconsiderable part in the destruction of eight Italian divisions – all in vehicles which had been perilously close to the end of their track mileages when they started out. Machines are rarely as efficient as men well trained to handle them, if only because they have no inborn repair and maintenance system; an exhausted tank crew can lie down beside their broken-down vehicle at night and with luck wake up next morning feeling refreshed – but the tank is still just as unusable as when they went to sleep.

In fact, of course, the crews got very little sleep, for no maintenance or repairs could be carried out during the day when action was unremitting, and all servicing and most refuelling and restocking with ammunition had to be done in leaguer at night – generally in almost complete darkness so that enemy attentions would not be attracted, especially those of the artillery. And while such duties were being carried out, guards had always to be mounted and any hot food available to the crews had to be cooked and eaten then. Quite often a choice had to be made whether to use the few snatched moments to assuage the pangs of hunger or to give way to the aching need for sleep, and many a time men were found slumped over congealing plates of bully stew, their one hot meal for twenty-four hours slopped in a glutinous mess into the sand.

But despite the exhaustion, the hunger, the thirst so continuous that life without it became almost beyond recall, despite also the beginnings of boils as a result of lack of fresh vegetables and the continual plague of 'desert sores' caused by the unremitting rubbing of sand-choked serge on sun- or windburnt skin, the men of XIII Corps were buoyed up by a sense of victory. If they sometimes thought of home before sleep claimed them or muttered scathingly of base troops hogging the Cairo fleshpots, few of them would have taken any opportunity to change their lot; they were professionals, this was the life they had chosen and most realised that war had little better to offer its votaries than the confidence of a winning streak.

General O'Connor had hoped, perhaps rather fancifully, to take Tobruk 'on the bounce' but that amount of fortune was not to be his, largely because of lack of transport. Although 7th Armoured Brigade had swept around through El Adem and cut the western approaches to Tobruk by the time the last Italians at Bardia had surrendered, and the 19th Australian Brigade was sealing off the eastern side of the Tobruk perimeter twenty-four hours later, it was not until January 9th that investment of the entire thirty-mile-long defence line was complete and by that time it had become obvious that a deliberate, phased attack would be necessary. Although there were only about 25,000 men in the Tobruk garrison under the command of Generale Petassi Mannella, and they had a longer line to hold than had Bergonzoli's men at Bardia, that line was well conceived and apparently well held. The first patrols both on the west by riflemen of the Support Group and on the east by the Australians had been greeted with accurate and sustained fire, and many casualties had been caused by a new factor in this war – booby traps. The explosion of these, moreover, often brought Italian patrols to the scene and some sharp and bitterly fought skirmishes resulted, complicated for the attackers if they were hampered by the problems of bringing back men wounded by the traps.

But every night the patrols went out and a picture of the defences was built up, including the booby-trap line running some one hundred yards in front of the anti-tank ditch. The engineers also brought back some of these unpleasant weapons   canisters filled with small pieces of metal or ball-bearings which would spray out to about waist height when the canister was detonated by a trip wire – and found a quick and simple way of 'delousing' them; so plans for an attack were laid and the date decided. By which time, of course, General O'Connor's mind was much occupied with what would happen after Tobruk had fallen:

Some time in the second week of January, I flew into Cairo and attended a conference at G.H.Q., General Wavell, the A.O.C.-in-C. [Air Chief Marshal Longmore], and Brigadier Galloway B.G.S., B.T.E. being present. When asked what my proposals were after the fall of Tobruk, I said I considered the occupation of Mechili of great importance, as it immediately caused a threat to the enemy positions in the hilly coastal belt. General Wavell agreed and asked me to come and see him the next day. At this meeting he discussed with me the possibility of a raid on Benghazi and asked me to study an 'appreciation' of his on the subject. I was very much in favour of an advance on Benghazi but would have liked it to have been on a permanent basis rather than a raid. However, I was delighted to think that there was the possibility of an attempt of some sort.[10]

When he returned to his own headquarters, O'Connor had first to come to grips yet again with his supply problems, which had unfortunately become even more complicated by the assumption of all responsibility for his lines of communication by an Advanced H.Q. set up at Baggush by General Wilson. In theory – and indeed in intent – this should have relieved O'Connor of much worry and labour, but in practice the supplies sent forward were those considered desirable for storage by men 200 miles from the front line, instead of supplies immediately required by men about to go into battle; O'Connor very quickly decided that for any future advance, all control must remain in his own hands. He told General Wilson of this problem as soon as he returned (for Wilson and he had exchanged places while O'Connor went back to Cairo) and also about the plans for an advance to Benghasi; and was thus rather nonplussed when he received during the days that followed a series of telegrams from Wilson's Cairo H.Q. to the effect that no advance towards Benghasi was to be considered, and that not only would no further transport be made available to XIII Corps for such an advance but that some might have to be taken from them and sent to Greece.

As this was completely at variance with what General Wavell had told me, I wired B.T.E. for an explanation and received an answer that the Benghazi project was not being proceeded with. I wrote in and said that I should like to see the C. in C. on the subject as I found it difficult to carry on with the different policies and I would like to know how I stood.[11]

Two days later both Wavell and Galloway arrived at Gambut, and by the time they departed, O'Connor was working directly under Wavell, Benghasi was confirmed as an objective for permanent occupation and it was clearly established that O'Connor's authority over all stages of XIII Corps activities was supreme and unquestioned.

I would like to record here what very great assistance was always given me by H.Q., B.T.E. and by Brigadier Galloway . . . throughout the entire operation. General Wilson also was most helpful whenever I saw him, and I am very grateful to him for all his sound advice.

This period of working directly under G.H.Q. was the most
effective and happiest time of my command[12]

– O'Connor was to write later. But generals are human beings and
if the practice of going over the head of one's superiors on occasion
gives immediately happy results, it also invariably breeds resentment.

At 0540 on the morning of January 21st, the crash and thunder of
the heaviest bombardment the Western Desert had known up to
that time rolled out, and a rectangle some 2,500 yards wide and 800
yards deep erupted along the southern stretch of the Tobruk
perimeter, about three miles east of the El Adem road. Well in
front of the guns, the men of 2nd/3rd Battalion with their attached
engineers were already moving forward from their start lines across
the flat approaches to the perimeter – so flat, indeed, that they
could look back and see the flashes from the gun-muzzles, hear the
shells scream overhead and watch the explosions in front.

They reached the ditch – shallow here and unfinished – and
while they waited for the moment of the next advance, began filling
it in for the Matildas when they came up. In the meantime, the
engineers went forward to find and clear the booby-trap line, to
delouse the minefields in front and to blow five lanes through the
wire with Bangalore Torpedoes. From far ahead came the sounds of
a heavy naval bombardment on the town itself, from overhead the
roar of R.A.F. bombers engaged in their customary task of
distraction of enemy attention and now, inevitably, there came
from in front the first barking crashes from the Italian artillery.
Away to the east a battery of R.H.A. 25-pounders was putting
down a deception barrage on the defence posts on each side of the
Bardia road, where waited the 2nd/5th Battalion of the 17th
Brigade – allotted the same type of task as that given the 2nd/6th at
Bardia, but with stricter instructions limiting their role.

There was an explosion away to the right as one of the flanking
platoons, coming up late, veered too far west and kicked a trip wire
still connected to a batch of booby-traps. ('It was a quite beautiful
sight,' someone reported afterwards with perhaps too keen a sense
of the artistic. 'In the flash you could see twenty or more men
peeling back like a flower opening.') Then, ludicrously, a bugle
sounded from about 400 yards in front across the perimeter. As the
wire and front posts were only some fifty yards away, the crouching
infantrymen tensed themselves for an immediate counter-attack of
some sort, but the last notes of the bugle died away and were
followed by an uncanny silence.

Then a red Very light soared into the air, four Bangalore

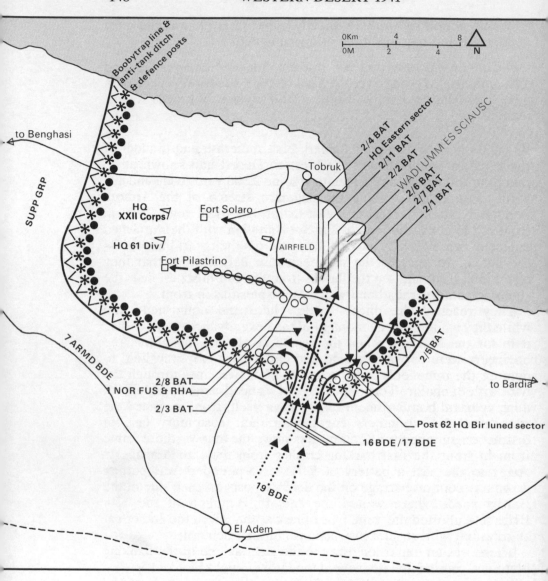

Map 7   Tobruk: January 21st, 1941

Torpedoes exploded and in the slight pause while the commander waited for the fifth to go, the voice of a young and overkeen lieutenant was heard shouting 'Go on, you bastards!' followed by cheers as the men started climbing out. There then came one of those hints of chaos which dot the course of even the best-run attacks, with the company commander calling them all back and the colonel urging them forward, but eventually the engineers confirmed that there were four clear gaps in the wire, and through these the 2nd/3rd charged – more rapidly than at Bardia for they had left their greatcoats and respirators behind and now carried only their weapons, ammunition and a haversack with the barest rations. They wore their leather jerkins inside out to hide the shine on the leather.

Within minutes they were through the wire and fighting in the first-line posts, and backed by their experience at Bardia they were moving very fast – so fast indeed that only the unmistakable Australian language used by one platoon as it swept towards a second objective saved it from attack by another platoon which had already secured its prime objective and was looking for further prey. As before, resistance varied and some of the platoons had very hard fights, suffering casualties as a result – but by 0645 the projected gap in the perimeter defences was open and eighteen Matildas accompanied by the leading companies of 2nd/1st Battalion were coming through.

Three Matildas turned left and joined the 2nd/3rd fighting their way westwards towards the El Adem road, three turned right and with the 2nd/1st began attacking posts down towards the Bardia road at a steady and apparently irresistible progress of two and a half miles an hour. They had taken twenty-one posts by 0900 – some easily, some only after heavy and sustained attacks mostly with bayonet and grenade; and they had to leave one post, No. 62, which held the Headquarter troops of the Italian Bir Iuned sector, for the attention of the next troops coming up. These were men of the 2nd/6th Battalion (of 17th Brigade which was following in to form and hold the eastern side of the bridgehead) and before they could force this post out of action they had to bring up their Pioneer Platoon to pour a mixture of crude oil and kerosene into the outer trenches and set fire to it.

The Italians manning Post 62 thus held up an important sector of the advance for over three hours and they lost eleven men killed before the other thirty-five gave up in the face of liquid fire. It showed, as one of the attackers pointed out later, what could have happened if all the enemy had been really determined.

The other 16th Brigade battalion, the 2nd/2nd, had come through behind the Matildas and, accompanied by nine of them, pressed forward to cross the Bardia road, wiping out three groups of Italian guns on the way and thus removing the immediate dangers to the flanks of the other two drives. They had been at first blinded by the thick sand-fog stirred up by the battle so far and whipped by a rising breeze, and then helped by it as they approached their first targets; whether the bombardment had severely shaken the Italian gunners or whether they too had been blinded by the sand, this was almost the first occasion when Italian artillery had been easily overrun.

By 0910, 2nd/2nd were on their objective along the Bardia road, 2nd/1st had crossed it well to the east near the perimeter and 2nd/6th, having eliminated the resistance at Post 62, had also crossed the road and held a line between the other two. The 2nd/7th with a company of the 1st Cheshires (machine-gunners) were now following down along the eastern end of the perimeter, mopping up any lingering traces of resistance and engaged upon the now-familiar task of organising the columns of prisoners. The eastern end of the garrison was thus under control and the Bardia road as far as the central crossroads where the Bardia, El Adem and Tobruk main roads joined was strongly held.

To the west, towards the El Adem road, the picture was similar. Despite some firm resistance in places, 2nd/3rd Battalion had fought their way to high ground overlooking the road and now rested there for the moment, sniping at Italian batteries on the other side. To their right were two companies of their old friends from 1st Northumberland Fusiliers, a battery of the Royal Horse Artillery and three troops of the Divisional Cavalry, brought up in their carriers.

Into the gap between the cavalry and the 2nd/2nd came the men of the 19th Brigade, commanded by Brigadier H. C. H. Robertson, a red-haired Digger in the classic mould who had set his mind not only on taking the crossroads against what were known to be well-constructed inner defences, but also on smashing his way through to Forts Pilastrino and Solaro, five miles further on, where he believed he would find the Command Headquarters for the entire garrison.

'If we capture Solaro and Pilastrino tonight, we should have all the Italian generals in the bag,' he told a group of journalists who had at last caught up with the campaign. 'I hope to bring my tally up to six. I captured one major-general in the last war and I've now got two in this campaign.'

19th Brigade had left its start line at 0830, was through the gap well inside the timescale with its three battalions quickly deployed and moving steadily in open order behind a barrage from 78 guns, lifting 200 yards every two minutes. The men of the 2nd/11th Battalion reached their objective beyond the Bardia road to link with the left flank of 2nd/2nd without a single casualty, but the 2nd/4th on their left ran into trouble as they neared a suspected Italian Sector Headquarters just to the north-east of the crossroads. Despite the fact that 2nd/4th had been supported by more elements of the Divisional Cavalry, including one made up of captured and reserviced Italian M13s (each with a gigantic white kangaroo painted on both sides of the turret) their leading company on the left had been caught by heavy machine-gun fire from the defences arced around the crossroads and several men had been hit, including the company commander who suffered two badly smashed legs.

But it was the 2nd/8th Battalion on the left flank of the brigade advance which ran into the fiercest and best-organised resistance, and had no choice but to swing immediately into action and remain committed to it until a considerable local victory had been won. It had been known that a line of defensive posts existed in this area, but the men of C Company soon discovered that the posts actually consisted of dug-in tanks in which were mounted twin machine-guns. At first C Company went to ground to wait for their artillery to open up and give them cover but unfortunately a platoon from D Company had become detached from the main company on their right and, caught in the open, had had no choice but to charge into the defence line without further delay.

There could thus be no artillery cover for C Company who now joined the battle, the platoons taking it in turns to give light covering fire and then to leap-frog ahead. They met spirited resistance from every tank but they had an advantage in the fact that the line of tanks had been formed to meet an attack from the south instead of the east, and as they were thus attacking from the flank, each objective shielded them from the fire beyond. It thus became a series of separate fire-fights in which the Australians soon realised that their winning card was the width of their platoon front. If the men were well strung out abreast, and the last fifty yards of the attack were carried out in a rush, the opposing machine-guns could not possibly sweep from one end to the other with total effect and there would always be some attackers left to finish the fight with rifle, bayonet and bomb; but it was equally certain every time that not all would reach the target. It became, as one of them was heard to remark, 'a bit bloody rough!'

North of this line of attack the other companies of the 2nd/8th, hearing the sounds of battle, had swung west and soon found themselves engaged in another series of close battles, through strongpoints, blockhouses and more tanks, some dug-in but some mobile. One company fought its way out to the right flank of the battle (though it had started in the middle) and its leading element took cover in some apparently empty concrete trenches, only to find that they led down into deep dug-outs where they surprised and took prisoner the artillery commander, Generale di Divisione Umberto Berberis, and his entire staff.

But above ground and in the centre of the battle area, the fighting was still fierce and the casualties on both sides mounting. Three companies of the 2nd/8th were now battling from strongpost to strongpost armed with nothing heavier than their Bren-guns and

some Boyes anti-tank guns of doubtful value except at short range
and only against thin armour; and if their progress was continual, so
were their casualties. Rifles stuck bayonet down into the ground
alongside Australian dead and wounded marked their progress like
a forest of burnt saplings, stripped, blackened, the smoke of battle
drifting between them to heighten the impression. By early afternoon, only one officer, one corporal and nineteen men of C
Company were left, and away on their northern flank A and B
Companies were losing men at a rate not experienced before.

But at least this phase of the fighting was leading in the right
direction – directly towards Fort Pilastrino – though perhaps the
first people to realise this were the Italians who hurriedly put
together the forces for a counter-attack. Not surprisingly, it caught
the Australians off balance, and the first they knew of it was the
bursting of shells among them from a barrage put down by Italian
artillery as cover. The 2nd/8th Intelligence Officer, Lieutenant
Allan Fleming, described it:

> We saw several hundred Italians moving towards us from
> Pilastrino, led by more than a dozen medium tanks covered by a
> barrage. The barrage lifted – either by design or because our
> guns got on to theirs. The Italian infantry seemed to waver but
> the tanks kept moving towards our left company . . . [who took]
> the first brunt of the attack by seven of the enemy tanks, and for a
> while they had a sticky time.

Major A. S. Key took up the story:

> As the tanks came on we couldn't check them because we had
> no 2-pounders and most of the men with anti-tank rifles were hit
> before the tanks got close enough for our weapons to do much
> damage. The forward platoon was over-run and several men were
> forced to surrender. The rest of us took cover in sangars and
> shallow trenches, and fired at the tanks whenever we could. In
> several cases, men played hide and seek with a tank, sheltering
> behind sangars, moving as it moved, to keep clear of its fire, and
> then taking a quick shot with a Boyes rifle. The tanks came up so
> close that we disabled several – even though they were M13s.[13]

But at last one of the 2nd/8th sergeants arrived dragging a
captured anti-tank gun followed by a couple of the R.H.A.
2-pounders, men from one of the flanking companies charged the
already hesitant infantry behind the tanks and chased them back
and – to clinch the matter – two Matildas came lumbering up
from the south, at the sight of which the remaining M13s turned
and fled.

At this the surviving Australians rose from the ground and, in Fleming's words:

> With wild yells and fixed bayonets, the troops went for the sangars from which rifles, machine-guns and small mortars were still firing. Some of the enemy were bayoneted; the rest crumbled and so did the counter-attack.[14]

One Italian, however, made an unfortunate mistake. Concealed among a group surrendering with their hands raised, he threw a grenade which killed one of the men walking towards them – and Bren-gun fire cut down the whole group before an officer could hold back the fury of the dead man's friends. Already the Australians were finding it difficult to restrain their anger when, having been pinned to the ground and losing comrades in a fiercely contended scrap, their final charge would be met over the last ten yards by a cessation of fire and the sight of their opponents rising to their feet with their hands in the air and, as often as not, a deprecating smile of welcome on their faces.

With the counter-attack dispersed the close fighting still went on, but as the attackers neared Fort Pilastrino they came under fire from a battery of about twelve guns apparently stationed there as an H.Q. protection. Again the charges went in, again the line of defence was gradually whittled away, but then a group of four heavy anti-aircraft guns began firing shrapnel on them from about half a mile away. Fortunately, F Battery of the R.H.A. came up and when one of their officers inquired what they could do to help, was crisply told to 'Get those bloody guns up there.'

Within ten minutes, to the enormous relief of the infantry, a salvo of R.H.A. shells went over, followed by a terrific explosion which

> sent a column of smoke and debris three hundred feet into the air and dulled all other sounds . . . Later we found our shells had hit a magazine and the guns had been lifted from their concrete emplacements and left twisted wrecks.[15]

There was still some hard fighting to be done by 2nd/8th before they were in the Fort, but it was now just a matter of time. However, when at dusk they eventually broke into the buildings they found them merely a collection of empty barracks – and moreover they were themselves now under fire from a position 600 yards away; but as the enemy were as tired as they were, the firing died as nightfall deepened. The 2nd/8th had advanced twenty miles since they had left their start line at 0430, and since 0900 had been in continuous action against an enemy more determined to resist than any encountered before in this campaign. No wonder the survivors slept.

In the meantime, the other Australian battalions had been moving forward too, against varying opposition. On 2nd/8th's right flank, 2nd/4th had crossed the main road from the crossroads to the port, swept through the fire of some anti-aircraft guns on the airfield (one platoon was detailed off to take them after the divisional artillery had softened them up) and moved on towards Solaro where the leading company commander saw six Italian trucks presumably full of men making off in the direction of the harbour. He and Private F. Wright, both mounted on captured motor-cycles, raced ahead to cut them off but were diverted by machine-gun fire from the nearest building, whereupon Wright rode straight at it and, with astonishing expertise, lobbed a grenade through the window without dismounting. But the next few minutes, as the rest of the battalion arrived at the run, revealed that Fort Solaro, too, was just a collection of barrack huts, empty of anything remotely connected with headquarter functions.

It was now growing dark, and the men of 2nd/4th were almost as tired as their comrades of 2nd/8th – but the barracks they were occupying then came under fire from four machine-gun posts on the edge of the Escarpment where the track leading down from Solaro to Tobruk crossed it. Somewhat wearily, Captain McCarthy led his men out to deal with them (which they did by firing the heavy bullets of the Boyes anti-tank rifles at the edge of the sangars, thus producing a highly dangerous fragmentation of the rocks) only to find that they had been grouped around the entrances to caves dug in the face of the Escarpment. Almost by habit, the Australians drove on in and were soon shepherding prisoners out into the open; eventually, an immaculately dressed Italian major arrived and requested the presence of an officer who, when produced, was first carefully examined for his credentials – for Lieutenant Copland was as dust-begrimed and filthy as any of his men – and then led further into the underground labyrinth until he was confronted by a dignified and quiet old man.

'Officer?' queried the old man.

'Oui, officer,' replied Copland, with the justifiable hope that there would be some strand of common meaning between his own schoolboy French and the general's language. Whereat the old man drew his pistol from its holster and handed it to him, tears streaming from his eyes.

There was a moment of deep embarrassment while the young Australian strove frantically for some commiseration to offer, and in this he was at last aided by luck and memory. The only complete French phrase he remembered would do very nicely.

'C'est la guerre,' he offered gently.

'Oui,' replied Generale Petassi Mannella, 'c'est la guerre.'

The Command Headquarters of the Tobruk garrison had fallen to one of Brigadier Robertson's men just as the day ended.

But not yet the port itself, and whatever Robertson's demands, the old man refused pointblank to issue orders that the whole garrison was to lay down its arms without further opposition. It seemed that another day's battle would be necessary before Tobruk was firmly in Allied hands, but the end was certain. The brigades had become mixed to a small extent, but by the end of that first day Australian formations held a line joining the heads of all the coastal wadis from the eastern end of the perimeter as far as the Wadi Umm es Sciausc four miles to the west, from which point the 19th Brigade battalions controlled everything in a wide arc from Sciausc back through Solaro to Pilastrino and on towards the southern arc of the perimeter where 2nd/3rd Battalion held the El Adem road. According to the official history:

> To most of the weary men in the forward companies it seemed that the battle was won. At Bardia the Italian guns were firing vigorously at the end of the first day; at Tobruk they were now almost silent. Over the harbour black plumes of smoke were rising. Ahead of Solaro and Pilastrino there was no sound except of rumbling explosions as the enemy blew up stores of ammunition and fuel. Along the line of Australian outposts the desert was lit up eerily after darkness fell by the fires that blazed in the west and by intermittent flashes from burning dumps, bright enough to make patrolling difficult. Farther south a cluster of fires showed where some 8,000 Italian prisoners who had been herded along the road to a fenced enclosure three miles north of El Adem were trying to keep themselves warm. Late at night, while the line of battle was still, a squadron of Italian aircraft, in futile response to Tobruk's appeals for help, saw the fires, and dropped their bomb loads on them. The number of prisoners killed was reported at various figures between 50 and 300; the Italians were huddled together and the effect of the bombs was appalling.[16]

The Italians in this campaign had reached that unenviable state which is seen so often on the football pitch, when nothing the losing side tries to do works properly and however fumbling the winners' moves may seem, they always come off.

During the night, General Mackay issued orders for the continuation of the battle. To Brigadier Robertson and his 19th Brigade was allotted the task of clearing the southern edge of Tobruk harbour, taking the town itself and the northern headland, while 17th Brigade on their right cleared the remainder of the eastern half of the garrison area up the edge of the sea. The three battalions of 16th Brigade would be reunited during the night along the line of the El Adem road to continue the drive westward towards the positions of the Support Group of the 7th Armoured Division, still blocking the exits to the west. The 7th's armoured brigades had already left for the next stage of the advance.

There was some desultory patrolling throughout the night, and the approach of dawn was awaited with curiosity; would there still be much fighting to be done? Some indication was given at half-light, when the figures of two Italian officers were seen approaching the positions of 2nd/8th at Pilastrino, waving a piece of white cloth. They announced that Generale della Mura of the 61st Sirte Division was ensconced with his headquarters in a wadi just behind Pilastrino and was prepared to surrender, but when Lieutenant Phelan went forward to assist him in this design, he protested ungraciously that no such junior rank would suffice. He was not particularly pleased even with the production of Major Key to officiate, but by now a brusqueness equalling his own was entering the Australians' attitude and under Key's direction several thousand Italian officers and men trooped away back towards the prison-cages.

In the meantime, 2nd/4th were getting ready to move down into Tobruk itself, and in order to probe the defences two carriers under Lieutenant Hennessy and Sergeant Mills set off along the road leading down the Escarpment. They met no sign of opposition until they were practically in the town, when they came to a roadblock consisting of an iron girder supported on sandbags. Mills and his crew began dismemberment – a task in which they were assisted by two Italian soldiers who ran forward to help – and after a burst from Hennessy's Bren at another Italian who for a brief moment looked as though he might have offered some form of remonstrance at their activities, the carriers pressed on into the town, Hennessy's leading:

> As we drove through, a truck loaded with Italians was moving back into the town. A couple of bursts from my Vickers stopped it and the occupants were taken prisoner. As the carriers moved towards the centre of the town an immaculately clad Italian officer came to meet us and eventually made me understand that he had been sent to lead us to the naval H.Q., where the admiral was waiting to surrender.[17]

Sitting the officer on the front of his carrier as a guarantee of good faith, Hennessy drove on to a large building facing a wide courtyard where, sure enough, Ammiraglio Massimiliano Vietina was waiting to offer him his sword. With an unusually proper respect for protocol, Hennessy declined and the formalities had to wait until Brigadier Robertson himself arrived to accept the last official surrender of the Tobruk garrison. There then followed orders and assurances with regard to mines and booby traps, the sounds of further dumps being blown up away on the far side of the harbour and the occupation of the hulks of three large Italian ships which had been sunk by the R.A.F. in the harbour but which had still been usable as gun-platforms – the *Marco Polo*, the *Liguria* and the cruiser *San Giorgio*.

Perhaps the most satisfactory act of these proceedings, however, was the hoisting to the top of the main flagstaff outside the Admiral's headquarters, by an exuberant Digger, of an Australian slouch hat.

There was still some mopping up to be done during the afternoon, and the battalions of the 16th Brigade continued their wide sweep through the western half of the perimeter, like a bent arm pivoting on Tobruk, until they met the riflemen of the Support Group who had encountered a certain amount of resistance along the western side, mostly from men determined to escape back towards the Jebel Akhdar.

Among the successful escapees had been Generale di Corpo Annibale Bergonzoli.

The port of Tobruk, this first time through, was still a pleasant place of wide streets, white colonial-style buildings, gardens with flamboyants and small green trees. There was an hotel, some shops, well-constructed offices and barracks for the military and naval garrisons, a restaurant and those other staples of Italian service life, garages and at least one brothel.

In the port area itself were found a power station virtually intact, at least one totally undamaged jetty, many large pontoons and a veritable flotilla of schooners, lighters and motor launches. Most important of all were the two water distilleries and the sub-artesian wells which between them could produce nearly 40,000 gallons of water every day and which were completely undamaged; and if the water was brackish, there were thousands of cases of Recoaro mineral water to make a pleasant change for the victors while the supply lasted, though for the first few days champagne slaked a lot of thirsts. There was also enough of the usual high-quality tinned foods to have lasted the garrison of 25,000 men for two months, though a great deal was wasted and very little indeed went to the men for whom it had been originally intended.

Tobruk yielded 27,000 prisoners (in addition to 200 guns and 200 vehicles) and now the accumulation was passing the stage of embarrassment and becoming a major problem for O'Connor's administration. His forces had now captured over 100,000 prisoners (more than three times their own peak strength) in forty-five days, and the distance back to the Delta for this latest batch would be 250 miles, much of it, in view of the acute transport problem, to be travelled on foot. The sight of long crocodiles of weary prisoners trudging from horizon to horizon in interminable zigzags was already only too familiar, and the duty of escorting them (two guards armed just with their rifles to every 500 prisoners) a chore dolefully but philosophically accepted by men much in sympathy with their charges.

But the task of administering the prison-cages at Tobruk and the life inside them until dispatch to the rear could be organised beggared description. All too many of the British and Australians who saw the conditions in the prison-cages at Tobruk were themselves to experience the life of prison camps – from Tunis through Italy to Upper Silesia – but there is some agreement among them that conditions at Tobruk were the worst they ever saw.

At the beginning, over 20,000 Italians were herded into a cage about 800 yards long by 400 yards wide, which they themselves had erected near the crossroads to house prisoners they had expected to take; some of them must have reflected that it was rather a pity that the British had had neither the opportunity nor the foresight to take such precautions themselves. One of the observers wrote:

> There was a terrific dust storm blowing, and the limited area of the enclosure was so full of men that there was hardly room to move. All officers had been removed and 20,000 or more men were a completely unorganised and panic-stricken rabble. Many had not had anything to drink, let alone a meal, for many hours. I found 200 to 300 lying on the ground outside a small building in which an Italian doctor was working. They appeared to be dead but apparently they were acute cases of exhaustion and thirst, and I think nearly all recovered. The first attempt to get water into the cage ended in a wild stampede; I had not thought that a crowd of men could so resemble a stampeding herd of cattle . . . [We] managed to obtain concrete tubs filled with water and, to some extent, to regulate the rush . . . The sanitary conditions were indescribable. After we had fed and watered the prisoners the greatest possible efforts were made to provide trenches and insist on their use. Drastic punishment was meted out to offenders . . . I don't know how we managed to avoid a major epidemic.[18]

It was a problem which the Germans had faced after Dunkirk, with 30,000 British and over 100,000 French, but at least they had been doing so in an environment which offered some facilities, and they had to help them their own superb organisational talents; but in the empty desert, all the British had were their own gifts of improvisation, aided by the sympathy felt by the common soldier for his fellows in distress. The Australians, with something like a stroke of inspiration, organised mass singing in the camp – and to help, they even sang back, though what they sang is unrecorded. One of the first problems facing the men of 2nd/2nd Battalion in the days immediately following the fall of Tobruk was providing each prisoner with a bottle or tin of some sort in which to collect water, and then with a greatcoat or a blanket – and many Diggers spent what spare time they had searching the buildings in Tobruk for such articles for their recent enemies, thereby laying the foundations of the reputation they gained for pillage and looting.

Gradually the numbers in the camp decreased, but by the end of February others began to arrive from points further west; it was going to be quite a long time before O'Connor's lines were cleared of this worrying and vexatious problem. But one point does emerge from every examination of this facet of the first Libyan campaign; O'Connor and his administrators received little help from any of the Italian officers who, according to the records, never protested at being separated from their men and, indeed, would seem in most instances to have climbed aboard their transports and left them with some degree of relief.

Perhaps this explains why their men often lacked enthusiasm in fighting for them.

6 · Beda Fomm: The Narrow Victory

'I could hardly believe my eyes', wrote General O'Connor of the moment when he saw the maps built up by his Intelligence staff of the Italian positions which faced his forces after the fall of Tobruk.

There was not much left of the huge Tenth Army with which he had been faced less than two months before, and what there was seemed so dispersed as to make their destruction in detail, even by the exhausted men of XIII Corps and their worn-out equipment, as easy as possible. Tenth Army Headquarters under Generale d'Armata Tellera was apparently at Cyrene, some sixty miles from any possible battle area, while XX Corps Headquarters – the command for the Italian troops nearest to Tobruk – was at Giovanni Berta, nearly twenty miles behind its main defences. Those defences were anchored on the small port of Derna behind a formidably deep and long wadi, and at Mechili to the south, well out in the desert at the meeting point of a whole network of camel tracks.

Forty miles separated those two points, and if British Intelligence was to be believed, in Derna was concentrated the 60th Sabratha Division less one regiment, while grouped around Mechili was the one detached Sabratha regiment and an armoured brigade consisting of two battalions of medium tanks under command of Generale di Divisione Babini; and there was very little indeed between them. Doubtless there were Sabratha units along the line of the Wadi Derna, and it was known that Babini's force was extended northwards along the line of a wadi which led from Mechili back into the foothills of the Jebel Akhdar towards Chaulan and Slonta – but at least twenty-five miles separated the right flank of the Derna force from the left flank of the Mechili force, and it should certainly not be beyond average military competence so to engage the attention of one force that it could do nothing to avert the total destruction of the other.

As the armoured brigade at Mechili was obviously the more important of the two, it was equally obviously both the main target and the prey for 7th Armoured Division. General Creagh was summoned for a conference in which O'Connor impressed upon him the necessity for the total destruction of Babini's force, while General Mackay was asked to detach one of his brigades from Tobruk as quickly as possible and to send it along the coast to attack the Italian forces in the approaches to Derna and in the port itself.

Time as always was of the essence but some factors were in XIII Corps's favour, in that even before the fall of Tobruk, 7th Armoured Brigade had moved westwards and come up against some Italian defences at Martuba, while 4th Armoured were already away to the south of Mechili scouring the tracks leading up to it. Needless to say, since mid-January patrols of the 11th Hussars had been probing well to the west of Mechili and up into the Jebel Akhdar past Bomba and between Derna and Chaulan, and indeed it had been largely upon their reports that the Intelligence Summary had been based; some confirmation had also been provided by the R.A.F., whose aircraft now completely dominated the skies, their opponents having been forced off their forward airfields by the army's advance, and heavily battered on their fields around Benghasi and at Barce by bombers from Alexandria and Malta.

It all promised well – and by January 24th, signs abounded that proper progress was being made. Robertson's 19th Brigade, flushed with their victories at Pilastrino and Tobruk, were now fighting their way up towards Derna and totally occupying the attention of all Italian forces in that area, while 4th Armoured Brigade were circling around and making directly for the position O'Connor had urged upon Creagh as the most vital of all – north of Mechili and across the only line of retreat of Babini's forces into the Jebel. Behind them, 7th Armoured Brigade were streaming down from the north to form the southern arm of the pincers closing on Mechili fort and the crossroads.

That night, reports arrived on O'Connor's desk of a brisk tank battle to the north-east of Mechili in which eight medium tanks of Babini's force had been destroyed and one captured for the loss of one of 4th Armoured's cruiser tanks and six light tanks, at the conclusion of which the Italian forces had retired back towards Mechili. Urging 4th Armoured on and detaching immediately two regiments of corps artillery to give them increased holding power in the block across the escape route, O'Connor repeated his instructions to Creagh to see that no part of Babini's force got away, and he then sat back to await events with a justifiable degree of confidence.

Nothing of great import occurred on January 25th or 26th, and as O'Connor's mind was greatly occupied with the unremitting problems of bringing up fuel and ammunition (just showing signs of easement as the harbour at Tobruk came into use) he assumed that the lull was being used to consolidate the block to the north of

Mechili and to prepare for the attack on the southern flank. It was good that the Italians were allowing time for his forces to move into position, for both armoured brigades were severely handicapped by shortages of fuel, ammunition, food and water, not to speak of the condition of their vehicles and the unreliability of their maps, most of which had been acquired during the search of the Italian Headquarters in Tobruk. But doubtless Creagh and his men were fulfilling their tasks admirably.

O'Connor was thus considerably perturbed when on the night of January 26th a report came in from A Squadron of the 11th Hussars that a long column of Italian vehicles had been sighted making for the foothills of the Jebel some twenty-five miles north of Mechili, and even more so when, on the following morning, patrols of the 7th Armoured Brigade went forward and entered Mechili to find it completely empty. And all this with not a shot fired – for 4th Armoured had *not* been sitting across Babini's escape route as Creagh had been instructed, the bulk of the brigade having spent those parts of the night when they had not been on guard soundly asleep.

'General Creagh was also very disappointed,' reads O'Connor's report with marked restraint, and then goes on to list the excuses he was given – bad maps, difficulty of getting the armour across the wadi which ran northwards from Mechili, shortage of fuel. But this section ends with a distinct note of acidity concerning the 'disinclination of armoured forces to take any action at night . . . If the Italians were able to move their tanks away at night, I see no reason why we should not have been able to operate ours.'

He was, he later admitted, very angry indeed.

There was some attempt to make up for the failure the following day when 4th Armoured turned and frantically chased after the withdrawing enemy, but the defiles through which the pursuit had to take place favoured the rearguards, petrol was undoubtedly short and heavy rain descended to turn the ground into red mud. The pursuit was called off on January 29th, 4th Armoured turning back to Mechili and events doubtless justifying O'Connor's cryptic closing remark on this episode: 'I am sure that General Babini must have breathed a sigh of relief on reaching Slonta . . . '

There was better news from the north, however. After the first engagement by the Australian 19th Brigade south of Derna, they had pressed on towards the lip of the Wadi Derna which curled away south and south-westwards from the port and formed a formidable barricade against their attack. It was very deep – 700 feet in places – and as much as a mile wide from lip to lip; and along the coast to the east one side was continued in the form of an escarpment over 400 feet deep which dropped almost vertically to the beach. Derna itself filled the mouth of the wadi and could be approached only by a road which wound snakelike down one escarpment, through the port and up the other.

The fighting along the line of the wadi was extremely tough during the days which followed, not only because of the sheer difficulty of moving men and equipment across such a wide chasm but also because, perhaps heartened by their evident advantages, the Italians fought here more determinedly than elsewhere – and certainly much better than their seniors deserved. Attempts by the Australian Divisional Cavalry to move inland in carriers and turn the end of the wadi were thwarted by well-concealed minefields and well-placed heavy machine-gun posts, and here the Australians lost several of their most promising young officers and N.C.O.s, including Sergeant Mills who had removed the roadblock into Tobruk. The Australian official history gives a moving footnote:

> After the fall of Derna Onslow found the carriers. Ferguson was dead in his seat, Mills dead beside his carrier with a note of farewell scrawled in his diary; Townshend lay dead fifty yards away.[1]

The main object at this stage of the battle was the pinning down of the Sabrathas in the area to prevent their going to the help of Babini's armoured force, and if the core of O'Connor's plan had not gone well, the role played by the men of Robertson's 19th Brigade gave no grounds for criticism. For four grim and heartbreaking days, in cold, wet and appallingly muddy weather, they battled it out with the Italian defenders, at the beginning with nothing much heavier than 3-inch mortars to support them; and even when their guns came up, there were not so many of them as there were of the defenders', and they could not be so well placed.

But if 19th Brigade could not cross the wadi at least they stayed hard up along its nearest lip, and 2nd/11th Battalion took and held the heights overlooking Derna and the sea on the right flank.

Then on the evening of January 29th, which had been on the whole a comparatively quiet day, the Italian artillery along the whole front opened a long and continuous bombardment which, when Robertson's men had moved to positions from which they could watch it in some degree of safety, excited considerable curiosity amongst them. It could not be cover for an Italian attack up the side of a 500 foot wadi (against Australians waiting at the top) and there was certainly no sign of another Australian attack being mounted for the Italian guns to be dispersing. So what was it all in aid of? After a while they began to guess – and a feeling of cheerful certainty overcame the watching men; they grinned at each other and smoked their wet and bedraggled cigarettes with growing enjoyment.

A patrol started down the escarpment when the artillery fire showed signs of slackening; but was seen, fired upon, turned and came back. So was a second which tried to repeat the probe before dawn.

But just after daylight, a party of Libyans climbed the Escarpment with the news that the Italians had gone, and when the 2nd/11th went forward they found the entire town deserted except for a gathering posse of Arabs piling heterogeneous loot – sewing machines, tables, chairs, sideboards full of china and cutlery – on to the backs of diminutive donkeys.

Derna was theirs – and at Derna, the desert ends. From here on, stretching west and south around the Cyrenaican bulge to Soluch, was the country of the Jebel Akhdar, the Green Mountains. Rising in places to over 2,500 feet, these hills were covered with sufficiently fertile soil for olive trees and even some orange and lemon groves to grow; for cultivation and colonisation, for a high degree of comfort and civilisation to attract families from southern Italy to settle there, and to form happy, hard-working farming communities.

In Derna, the Australians found streets of well-designed, single-storey houses standing in green, shady gardens, well-watered from the wadi behind, fragrant with flowers and planted with cauliflowers, radishes and onions – the first fresh vegetables they had seen for months. In the hills to the west were the houses and settlements of 90,000 Italian colonists, and plans existed in Rome for the formation of more settlements to contain double that number. This could indeed be a pleasant place, warm enough in summer to remind the inhabitants that they were in Africa, but with Mediterranean breezes, winter rains to swell their produce and a red soil rich enough to bear it. And until their Duce, who had sent them there in the first place, sent them war as well, the indigenous Arab population could be persuaded by one means or another to help them with the hardest part of the labour.

But through the curtains of rain which at the end of January were turning the fields into bogs of red mud and the roads and tracks into churned up, treacherous quagmires, it did not look particularly attractive to the Australians. Even their physique had taken a hammering during the last few days, especially below the knees; broken ankles were a common cause of hospitalisation, and sprained and bruised ankles, cut and barked shins, blistered feet, broken toes and cut and swollen heels the commonest complaints. The desert might have been dry, gritty and monotonous, but the battles ahead in the Jebel were obviously going to be just as rough for the P.B.I. – and in the Jebel it was certainly going to be an infantry battle, for armour would be virtually useless in attack with only narrow roads upon which to move, and little or no room for dispersal or manoeuvre. On the other hand, it would be excellent for defence.

This was a point which, once he had swallowed his chagrin at the escape of Babini's force, was exercising General O'Connor.

In the Jebel were the armoured formations under Babini, the complete Sabratha Division and, as far as could be judged, elements of two more divisions, the 17th Pavia and the 27th Brescia, around Cyrene and Slonta. There were even rumours that German units had disembarked at Benghasi, although O'Connor felt that, if they existed at all, they would be only anti-aircraft formations.

Well, however hard-worked the 7th Armoured Division might have been since Mussolini declared war eight months before, they had not distinguished themselves recently on two or three rather critical occasions, and if they wished to be considered a military formation of serious worth they had better take full advantage of their next, and greatest, opportunity. Quite obviously the division could not be sent to harry the Italians in the close country of the Jebel, so their most useful move now would be to cut off enemy forces which might attempt to escape out of the Cyrenaican bulge into Tripolitania when the Australians, as O'Connor had every intention they should, chased them out of Benghasi.

Could the 7th Armoured, in their present condition and in spite of their recent failures, cut across the southern limits of the Jebel Akhdar and block the exits leading down southwards from Benghasi, around the Gulf of Sirte and into Tripolitania?

On the face of it – no; and certainly not without the establishment of more of the essential Field Supply Depots. Work on bringing these forward, however, was well advanced, aided not only by growing expertise on everyone's part but also by the unexpectedly rapid opening up of Tobruk harbour by the Royal Navy. F.S.D. Nos 12 and 13 were already in action, one at Tmimi and the other for the armour about twelve miles south, and O'Connor would open No. 14 somewhere south-west of Mechili to service the thrust to the coast as soon as possible. Ten days' supply of food and petrol should be enough, two refills of ammunition and a continual water supply to organise – say 3,000 tons, plus the water; it should take twelve days.

This time-lapse would also give occasion for repairs to 7th Armoured's vehicles of all classes, though the fifty remaining cruiser tanks really required major overhauls. This, however, would not be possible without a return to Abbassia workshops, but some relief other than routine maintenance could be offered. Units of the 2nd Armoured Division had just arrived in the Delta from England and if the C-in-C agreed, two cruiser regiments could come forward in time to join the 7th by February 8th, be given three or four days to become acclimatised and absorbed and then take part in the chase. In the meantime, in order to concentrate what forces he had, O'Connor decided that 4th Armoured Brigade should take over the most reliable of 7th Brigade's tanks and thus be better fitted to lead the advance when it began.

Having discussed these plans with General Creagh, with Brigadier Harding and with Brigadier Dorman-Smith, O'Connor sent the last-named back to Cairo to obtain permission for the move from General Wavell, who immediately granted it with his blessing. As it happened, Wavell had just received a cable from the Chief of the Imperial General Staff inquiring when London might expect news of the fall of Benghasi, and after his talks with Dorman-Smith he was able to reply that this major port should be in British hands by the end of February.

Dorman-Smith returned to Mechili with the good news, arriving back on February 2nd, by which time the Australians in the Jebel had taken Giovanni Berta, while a patrol of the 11th Hussars had entered Chaulan fifteen miles to the south-west to find it unoccupied. This was somewhat unexpected, but the following day the Australians found to their astonishment that they were out of touch with the enemy along their entire front; Graziani had finally lost his nerve and ordered the complete withdrawal of all Italian forces in the Cyrenaican bulge back towards Tripoli.

The immediate result of this is best summed up in the regimental history of the Rifle Brigade. After recounting the part played by one company in the pursuit with 4th Armoured of the Babini force, it continues:

> The rest of the Battalion followed up and concentrated at Mechili on the 3rd of February. It seemed that administration had at last been outrun: it was said that there would be no move before the 15th. The Battalion settled down to rest.
>
> The Battalion had some two hours' rest. Every truck had its bonnet open; for they had most of them already exceeded the useful mileage of their make. Washing operations were everywhere in progress as far as one gallon of water a man a day allowed. Hair was being cut; vehicles were being unloaded. Hugo Garmoyle went on leave and Brigadier Gott was due to leave the next day, Colonel Callum Renton having actually taken over command. The Adjutant had already been overtaken by piles of paper. Then General Wilson drove up. The enemy were showing

signs of quitting Benghazi, of giving up Cyrenaica altogether. The plan was to send an armoured force straight across the desert for a good one hundred and fifty miles to cut the road from Benghazi to Tripoli where it ran along the edge of the Gulf of Sirte. The Battalion would take part in this gallop. There was no time to lose.[2]

There was also no time to await the 3,000 tons of stores, the organisation of a better supply of water, the arrival of enough petrol to be sure of getting to the critical point in sufficient strength, or of enough ammunition to be able to enter battle with confidence if they did so; there was quite certainly not enough time to await the arrival of the fresh 2nd Armoured Division regiments and their comparatively unused cruiser tanks. From the reports of Italian withdrawal coming in from every section of the Jebel Akhdar, it was evident that if the formations of the 7th Armoured Division were to block the escape of the enemy forces already beginning to stream south from Benghasi, they would have to move now, and move fast. Administration arrangements would have to comply, improving on the fashionable saying by doing the impossible, as well as the difficult, at once.

The first departures from Mechili shortly after dawn the following day were of A and C Squadrons of the 11th Hussars, augmented by a squadron of the King's Dragoon Guards which had just arrived in the Middle East. Their task was to 'break the trail' for so as not to betray intention it had been decided that reconnaissance of tracks leading westwards, first to Msus and then on towards the coast, would not be carried out until just before the proposed advance, that is, on previous planning, about February 9th or 10th.

Behind the armoured cars came the striking force of 4th Armoured Brigade, its fifty cruisers and ninety-five light tanks stocked with two days' supply of food and water, just enough petrol to complete their journey and as much ammunition as they could find room for. Behind them came the artillery and the 2nd Battalion, Rifle Brigade – the only elements of the Support Group ready in time.

They had been warned by the R.A.F. (who were now down to a flight of Hurricanes and the Lysanders from 208 Army Co-operation Squadron, practically all other fighters having been withdrawn as there were no replacement Merlin engines anywhere in the Middle East) that the going in front of them was rough, but they had certainly never before experienced anything as bad as the first fifty miles or so. Lieutenant Joly, in the leading troop of the leading squadron of the armoured brigade, was, in common with all the tank commanders, desperately worried about the state of his tank tracks and the likelihood of their being disabled before arrival:

> For mile after mile I was faced with a vista of huge, forbidding rocks and boulders through which I had to pick my way carefully to avoid the risk of shedding a track. All the time I was being nagged and harried by Kinnaird and the Colonel to speed up and press on. In the mind of every one of us was the vision of the Italians streaming out south of Benghazi, every moment more and more of them eluding the trap which was gradually closing in
> Revived by the short period of rest [about noon], I found that the fever of the chase kept me at a pitch of excitement throughout the day, despite the many frustrations of the incredible country through which we were passing and the uncertainties of the highly inaccurate maps on which we were forced to pin our faith . .
> Where the ground improved we accelerated in frantic anxiety to make the best possible time. Where the ground was again cut up by slabs of rock and out-crops of boulders, we learnt to contain ourselves in patience and to pick a slow, laborious route through the obstacles, trying desperately to keep the number of mechanical failures to a minimum.[3]

But it soon became obvious to General Creagh that other, even more precipitous steps must be taken to ensure the arrival, in time and at the right place, of some form of block to Italian intentions, and he therefore took the decision to split his force. All the wheeled portion – which could travel just that little bit faster than the more cumbersome tracked element – must be released to surge ahead and join the armoured cars, by now nearly a hundred miles in front; so the Royal Horse Artillery batteries and the infantry, all under temporary command of Colonel Jock Campbell, were sent off to catch the Hussars and, in effect, to reconstitute Combeforce.

Meanwhile, by a remarkable feat of driving and navigation, for they had not been spared the daily sandstorm, the forward squadrons of armoured cars had reached Msus by 1500 and by 1530 had chased the very surprised Libyan garrison out of the fort, without, however, managing to capture them. Retaining his own H.Q. Squadron and the King's Dragoon Guards in Msus, John Combe sent A and C Squadrons of 11th Hussars on towards Antelat – for it seemed to him that the lower down he struck the coast road, the greater would be the proportion of escaping Italians cut off. It also meant that he would be attempting with a totally inadequate force to block the escape of an unprecedented number of enemy soldiers, all desperate to get home.

He then sat back to await the arrival of the main force, the first intimations of his new responsibilities being the arrival after

midnight of Jock Campbell in his staff car with headlights ablaze –
a phenomenon he explained as necessary in order to see the
'thermos bombs' which had been scattered across the tracks by
low-flying Italian aircraft just before dusk, and which had effectively
held up the infantry and guns some twenty miles back. These nasty
little devices, resembling Thermos flasks, were a perpetual plague
during the desert war; they were designed to withstand the shock of
hitting the ground, but would then go off at the slightest touch and
maim or blind the curious but uninformed investigator, or blow the
wheel off a lorry or the track from a tank.

They held up not only the wheeled Support Group element but
also the 4th Armoured Brigade tanks, by now out of the really
rough country and at last willing, perhaps with O'Connor's
strictures in mind, to try travelling at night. It was not an experience
which Lieutenant Joly enjoyed, though it had, apparently, some
visual compensations:

> When night fell . . . we continued the advance in the moon-
> light. To me this was a new experience . . . It was bitterly cold,
> so that my face soon became frozen and raw and was painful to
> touch . . . Occasionally I glanced down into the turret to reassure
> myself that I was not dreaming the whole situation. In the eerie
> light cast by the single red warning bulb of the wireless set I could
> see, beyond the glinting metal of the gun-breech, the huddled
> figure of Tilden. At my feet, crouched forward peering through
> the gun telescope – his only view of the outside world – sat
> Holton, on the alert, as he had to be, since we were one of the
> leading tanks of the Division. Beyond, and farther down and
> forward, I could see Sykes' head and shoulders silhouetted
> against the panel and instrument lights on the forward armoured
> bulkhead.[4]

It must have been extremely uncomfortable, with perhaps only
for the tank commanders the full excitement of the chase to offset
it, and it became even more uncomfortable later when, in addition
to the cold, a fierce wind sprang up bringing with it torrential rain.
This, and the growing awareness of the danger from the thermos
bombs, eventually forced a halt – during which the crews had first
of all to carry out their routine maintenance in the bitter weather,
and then prepare their only meal since the previous morning; cold,
of course, for there could be no fires.

General Creagh reached Msus on the morning of February 5th,
hustled the remainder of Combeforce on down to Antelat with
instructions to get across the coast road as quickly as possible; and
then, as reports came in from the R.A.F. that columns of Italian
transport were thickening on the road south from Benghasi through

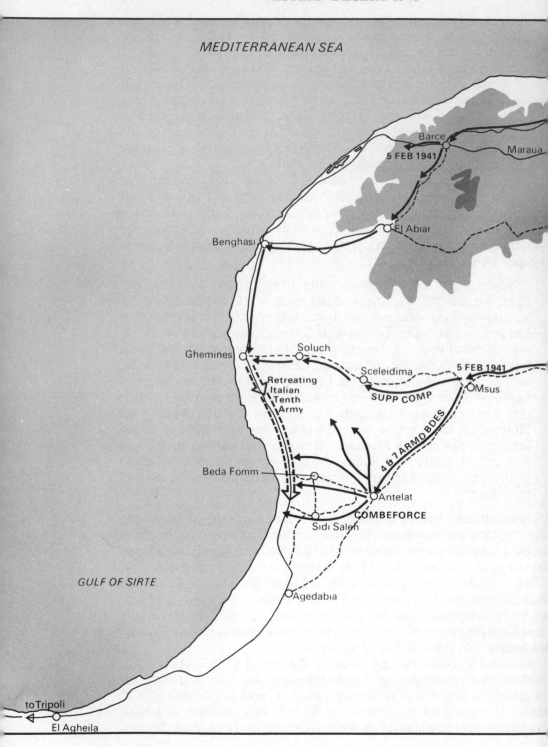

MEDITERRANEAN SEA

Barce

5 FEB 1941

Maraua

El Abiar

Benghasi

Ghemines

Soluch

Sceleidima

5 FEB 1941

SUPP COMP

Msus

**Retreating
Italian
Tenth
Army**

4 & 7 ARMD BDES

Beda Fomm

Antelat

COMBEFORCE

Sidi Saleh

GULF OF SIRTE

Agedabia

to Tripoli

El Agheila

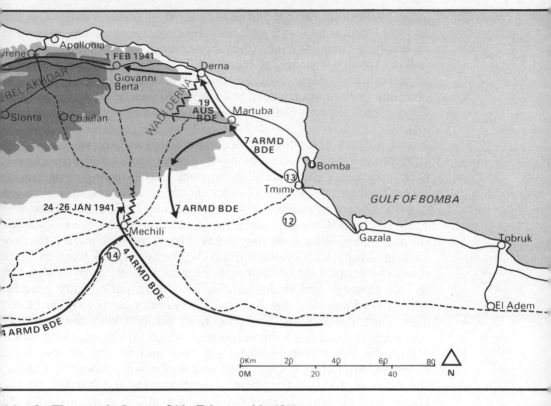

Map 8   The pursuit: January 24th–February 6th, 1941

Ghemines, decided that his own force had better follow Combe and not try for a block across the road higher up.

One small force he did detach, though – the rump of the Support Group which had now come down from Mechili and the 7th Armoured Brigade with what remained of their tanks – which he sent off due west, first to attack the fort and garrison at Sceleidima, then to press on to Soluch and Ghemines if opportunity and advantage so indicated.

Now all that remained was the practical problem of getting his battered tanks and well-worn guns across the path of the retreating Italians as fast as possible – and then keeping them supplied with ammunition throughout the tough battle which would undoubtedly follow.

As for the northern arm of the pincers up in the Jebel, the Australians were by now in sight of Barce, having found Cyrene, above the beautiful, broken ruins of the old Graeco-Roman city and its port of Apollonia, totally deserted. It had been very rough going for they were in a hurry and just as short of sound transport as the rest of O'Connor's force; in theory the brigades of 6th Division were to leapfrog through each other's positions, the pooled and canni-balised transport switching from one command to the other, but in practice the greater part of the advance was made on the chafed and bleeding feet of weary men who nevertheless would not give up. They found not only their second wind, but third and fourth winds, too.

The physical toughness of the Australians and the tide of victory kept them going. Since leaving Giovanni Berta they had clawed their way along the sides of hills, over wadis, through minefields, across broken bridges, over blown and cratered roads; their forward patrols always in danger of ambush, losing their scouts time and again to the last burst of machine-gun fire as the enemy rearguards slipped away. Wherever they went they were welcomed either by looting Arabs who greeted them as liberators and tried to offer them the hospitality of their own regained lands, or by frightened Italian farmers and their families who were pathetically grateful when they found that the Australians were not going to join or even encourage the looting, and who then pleaded with them to stay and protect them from the vengeance which now surrounded them.

But the Australians had to get on – and by the afternoon of February 5th (while Creagh's armour was moving down from Msus) the men of 2nd/8th Battalion were breasting the last hill before Barce, and elements of the Divisional Cavalry in their carriers were already in the town. Accompanied by the Italian mayor, the officer commanding the detachment was in the process of inspecting this, the last main enemy garrison before Benghasi, and had just left a large ammunition dump in the centre when it exploded with astonishing force, sending a huge opalescent ball of flame into the sky followed by a column of smoke which billowed out until it resembled a vast toadstool – the first recorded time this particular phenomenon was seen.

The infantry moved in at dusk and spent the first few hours driving Arab looters away from their plunder, but there were many random explosions during the night and several stores were found burnt out and wrecked in the morning. Not that the Australians had much time to concern themselves with such matters; Robertson's orders had been issued during that night and as soon as dawn broke, the culminating drive on Benghasi would commence.

The leading cars of C Squadron, 11th Hussars, had reached the coastal road at Sidi Saleh, about ten miles south of Beda Fomm, just after midday, and their reports to John Combe were that only light, administrative traffic appeared to be moving along it. By 1400 one company of the Rifle Brigade was in place across the road with the Hussars on their right flank to guard against any enemy units trying to get around the inside of the block, while two more rifle companies formed protective screens around the gun positions to the rear, where the R.H.A. under the enthusiastic direction of Jock Campbell were preparing for the most concentrated shoot of their careers so far.

Ammunition was stacking up around them, but they were all very conscious of the fact that there would be no more arriving for at least twenty-four hours, possibly for forty-eight; as always, after the first onslaught much would depend upon supply.

The first onslaught was not long in coming. Within half an hour of the riflemen taking up their positions, they saw the head of what proved to be the leading column of the Italian Tenth Army on their way out of Cyrenaica, bowling unconcernedly along the road towards them, apparently oblivious of the presence of hostile forces.

The ensuing action was brief and conclusive for the guns of the Hussars on the right caught the few escorting tanks in the flank and so surprised the crews that they immediately baled out, while the rifle and Bren-gun fire from the infantry scattered the lorries and their bewildered cargo into the sands on each side of the road; from which position they could shortly afterwards watch some 200 of their compatriots, following about ten minutes behind them in thirty lorries, give themselves up practically without firing a shot. Not long afterwards Jock Campbell and his gunners were apprehensively watching the first prisoners making their way towards them (they were occupying, after all, the only 'positions to the rear' in this particular action) and wondering what on earth to do with them; they eventually solved the problem by sending the Italians along the track towards Antelat, assuring them that there they would find someone to look after them.

Then just after 1700 the head of a much larger column came into view and it was obvious that a major action was about to begin. Despite the initial surprise when the R.H.A. batteries opened fire, there were soon signs of a serious attempt being mounted to burst a way through the block – an apparent 'mushrooming' at the head of the column as infantry was dispersed into the sands to the west of the road and towards the sea, followed by a shake-out among the vehicles, evidently in order to bring artillery up to the front.

Fortunately by this time the colonel of the Rifle Brigade, Callum Renton, had appreciated the dangers of the open flank on the left, and filled it with a Support Company on the beach and B Company immediately on A Company's flank; so the Italian infantry soon came under brisk and accurate rifle and machine-gun fire, while the

R.H.A. batteries brought down a discouraging blast on the vehicles at the head of the column and on the artillery coming up alongside.

Moreover, some thirty minutes before, John Combe had sent off a signal to 4th Armoured requesting their presence in the neighbourhood of Beda Fomm, ten miles north of his own position, and 'Blood' Caunter, in command at Antelat and scenting action, had quickly dispatched the 7th Hussars in their light tanks, and six fast A13s from 2nd R.T.R. This force reached the rear of the column forming up to attack Combeforce just before 1800 after a 30 m.p.h. dash over rough tracks, smashed quickly through what proved to be a transport section and in the light of the petrol fires which this brisk *tour de force* produced, caught up and attacked the rear of the artillery concentrating against Combeforce.

This timely arrival relieved Combeforce of increasing pressure, for the sight of the British tanks rampaging up and down alongside the column persuaded many in it to throw down their arms and offer themselves up to anyone willing to take them prisoner. They may have been influenced in this by the large number of civilians in their ranks, but their decision did nothing to help Jock Campbell and the reserve company of the Rifle Brigade who now had over 5,000 prisoners to deal with – and a hard battle to fight on the morrow.

This anticipation was confirmed by the sight of yet another column approaching which, despite the sight of the burning disarray on each side of the road, was pressed forward apparently by the weight of men and vehicles building up behind. Again the tanks of 7th Hussars and 2nd R.T.R. sallied up and down the eastward side of the road, spraying the soft-skinned transport with their machine-guns, saving their shell for the Italian armour when it showed itself; and in this they were helped by a patrol from the Rifle Brigade, sent out by their colonel on the other side of the road, which had with it two anti-tank guns.

Between them, these two groups did a lot of physical damage, but their greatest effect was on Italian morale, giving the hapless survivors of Graziani's Tenth Army a greatly exaggerated idea of the strength ranged against them – which was still, considering the task with which it was faced, positively minuscule. Not that this fact was evident to the majority of British troops present, and the differences in outlook between the two sides at this stage in the battle is fascinatingly illustrated in a letter written afterwards by a tank crew member, Trooper 'Topper' Brown:

> My recollections of Beda Fomm start with the thirty-six hour run across the desert to the area. The day before a Hurricane fighter had dropped a message (lead-weighted) slap on the back of

our tank. Apparently it was information that the Italians had left Benghazi. I can't remember the exact date; I only know that it was February 1941, and that I had been on patrol and on guard every night since December 8th 1940. I had also been 'Up the Blue' since September and had knocked out three or four M13s at Mechili some time previously. My feelings were ones of complete indifference. I was just utterly fed up, absolutely filthy and badly underfed. The terrain we crossed to cut off the Italians was terribly rocky. As we approached Beda Fomm my commander brought me to my senses by telling me to shoot up an enemy staff car, but the range was too great and the tank was bouncing all over the place – whether I hit it or not I don't know, but some of my tracer certainly surrounded it . . .

It was now quite dark, and after some time my commander told me that we had to go out to spike some deserted enemy guns; this was going to be my job. We mounted and advanced along the convoy of enemy trucks. When we got to the end we saw two Italian M13 tanks stationary, and we approached them from the side until we were about fifteen yards away. The operator, Taff Hughes, was then ordered to get the crews out. I offered to get them out with my 2 pounder, but Lt Plough rejected this, because the flash would have shown up our position.

Taff got out, went over to the tanks and knocked on the outside with his pistol. Seven enemy got out, Hughes took them prisoner and began to walk down the convoy with them. I told my commander that there should be eight and that if he would let me put a shell in the tank where the other man was, he would either get out or stay there permanently, but he again refused my offer. We then followed Hughes and the prisoners down the convoy. As we passed one large truck the driver, who was still in the cab with two others, switched his headlights on us. Lt Plough shouted to me to put the lights out, but I had already started firing: the three of them must have been dead within two seconds of the lights going on. We then returned to the squadron with Hughes, who was later awarded the D.C.M. for this exploit.

It rained very heavily for most of that night – my duty was the second half of the guard and I was soaked, even wearing my greatcoat.[5]

Despite Topper Brown's initial indifference and the discomfort in which he passed the rest of the night, he was not so discouraged as the Italians, again the victims of their own propaganda and convinced that they were surrounded on all sides by overwhelming numbers of heavily armoured, highly efficient and savagely ferocious British and Australian troops.

In fact, of course, although by the morning of February 6th the Italians *were* surrounded, it was by a line so thin as to be in places virtually non-existent. Combeforce still blocked the road to the south, the rest of 4th Armoured Brigade had now moved in from Antelat and was waiting hull-down behind the ridge nearest to the road and on the eastern flank, while the rump of the Support Group was poised to attack Sceleidima and the 7th Armoured Brigade had changed direction and were on their way down to Antelat, for it had become evident that even the most well-worn armour could come in useful down there in the morning. On a map it would look convincing – but Caunter had only twenty-nine cruiser tanks left and events would demonstrate that over a hundred Italian M13s waited in the dip below; and against M13s the light tanks of the 3rd and 7th Hussars could do little but make impudent gestures, and even those only so long as their petrol lasted. Every Italian vehicle captured had already had its petrol siphoned into British tanks, and the fuel situation was so desperate that the artillery was now immobile, its petrol having also been appropriated by the armour. Some fuel came up during the night, but once that was gone, none cared to say when the next would arrive.

What remained of 7th Armoured Division was thus, on the night of February 5th/6th, 1941, at Beda Fomm, in the situation of the hungry boxer; either it must win or starve – and starve to death.

It was still raining hard when daylight came, and the first rush by the head of the Italian column against the roadblock would seem to have been prompted by little more than a fit of early morning pique, exacerbated as much by the gross discomfort of the night as by the desperation of the situation. It was most ineptly mounted, consisting of little but an advance by Bersaglieri units under sparse artillery cover, with a few L3s in attendance and a number of thin-skinned vehicles revving their engines furiously in the background and edging slowly forward, presumably in order to bring up more infantry support if required, or to be ready to spring away towards Tripoli if by any chance the British had disappeared during the night.

But Combeforce was still there (with all their petrol requisitioned they had no choice but to stay), the R.H.A. batteries had had ample time to check the fall of their shot the previous evening and now had a reasonable view of what was happening, despite the weather. Their opening salvo crashed down upon the bunched vehicles at the head of the column, one of their following salvoes completely destroyed an Italian gun and severely shook the rest of the battery (so far as the rather loose collection of artillery the Italians had marshalled could be called a battery) and the Bersaglieri were quickly forced to ground by the cold and bedraggled, but well-dug-in and still expert riflemen in the front line. Another frontal attack on the roadblock fizzled out, and Combeforce could relax and prepare their frugal breakfast.

Seven miles north of the roadblock was a low, round hillock dubbed by the British the 'Pimple', while about a mile to the east was a low ridge topped by a conspicuous white tomb referred to as the 'Mosque'. Nineteen of Caunter's 2nd R.T.R. cruiser tanks were around here, while the 3rd and 7th Hussars, each with a mixture of light tanks and a few cruisers, were away to the north trying to find the tail of the column to continue their harassing tactics of the night before. This, however, as growing daylight revealed, was likely to prove more difficult than expected, for the column of Italian traffic packed three deep on the road and lining the sand on both sides stretched up towards Ghemines and Benghasi as far as the eye could see. Caunter's tactics were therefore dictated by circumstance; in order to keep as much pressure as possible off Combe's light forces to the south, he must form another roadblock here on the Pimple and use every other ounce of power he could muster for attacks along the inviting and virtually unprotected flank – bearing in mind all the time, however, that the very length of the flank might in the end prove the decisive factor. Even if every Italian were prepared to stand where he was and be shot, there would still be a large number left when 7th Armoured had run out of ammunition and the Italians then would win the day

To Bergonzoli, now in charge of the attempt to break through to Tripolitania, the situation looked much more complicated, primarily because of the usual lack of Italian reconnaissance. He had virtually no air cover (neither had the British for this stage of the battle) and thus no intelligence based on anything seen from above ground level – and since no one had expected the British to appear so far west of Mechili, few ground-level reports either. He therefore subscribed to the general view that large and powerful enemy forces encompassed him on all sides, strengthening a growing conviction that Rome had completely failed either to foresee the problems which would face the Italian Army in the field, or to provide them with adequate equipment with which to overcome them. And in this he was undoubtedly correct; eau-de-Cologne and Parma hams have little protective value against bullets or shells, especially when fired by bloody-minded soldiers after a cold night in the wet.

Bergonzoli was thus half defeated already as dawn broke – tactically blind, desperately worried by his lack of real knowledge of the situation, and resentful at his appointment as the heir to chaos. Although it was obvious that he must somehow organise a hammer-head to smash a way out to the south, he dare not move that part of his command most suitable for this task – the Babini armoured brigade – down from the north where it now constituted the only shield against the menace of the Australians driving for Benghasi. As a result, he gave instructions that whatever armour was available should proceed towards the head of the column, exploring the areas to the east in case there should be a way around the roadblock, but holding themselves in readiness to concentrate wherever and whenever he required them once he had obtained sufficient information to make a sound decision.

The first group of ten M13s to move did so from a point about two miles north of the Pimple, edging out into the desert a short way, then running down parallel to the main column with the intention of

Map 9   Beda Fomm: February 6th, 1941

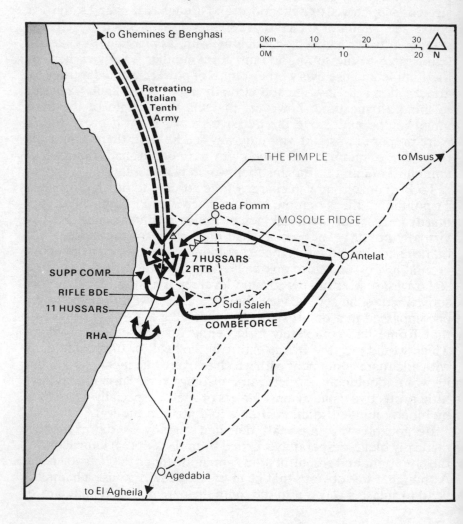

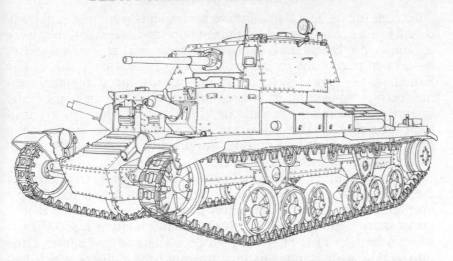

Figure 3   Cruiser tank Mark I (A9): weight 12·5 tons; armour 6mm.–14mm.; engine 150 h.p.; maximum speed 25 m.p.h.; armament one 2-pdr, three ·303 Vickers m.g.; crew 6

breasting the Pimple in order to see what lay beyond. As they were moving forward in diamond formation, their drivers and commanders suddenly saw rising purposefully above the crest 600 yards in front of them the turrets and 2-pounders of over a dozen British cruiser tanks from which, after the briefest moment for correction of aim, came the flash of gunfire, followed for only a few of the M13 crews by the whip-crack passage of high-velocity shells; eight M13s were turned into blazing coffins in an instant, and as the other two desperately wheeled in order to escape, they too were caught in flank, and disabled.

Before a single Italian shot could be fired in reply, the cruisers had reversed back down the slope of the Pimple and disappeared, never having exposed their main hulls to enemy sight, let alone fire (the perfect 'hull-down' position, in fact). In response to a curt order from the Squadron H.Q., they moved quickly across to the Mosque ridge, from behind which they destroyed another seven M13s which had moved far out from the road in order to probe to the east. As this action was concluding, more R.T.R. cruisers came up on the right, caught another formation of M13s moving unguardedly between the crest and the road and then swung across and down to reoccupy the Pimple from the north. In the meantime, the cruisers originally on the Pimple had moved rapidly down from the Mosque ridge to chase after that part of the Italian column which had crossed the Pimple during their absence and were now bearing down on Combeforce.

Except for the fact that all these movements were taking place in driving rain across a marsh of churned-up sand – and that they were leaving behind them trails of death, anguish and fire – they could all have been part of the formal movements of an intricate dance. The British tank crews were operating against uncoordinated and ineffective opposition, in country which in its low undulation and openness resembled the Salisbury Plain across which so much of their training had taken place, and almost every crew member was a professional soldier now putting into practice those months of hard work, largely inspired by Hobart.

But now another element of professionalism entered the battle; the Italian artillery was getting itself organised and the Pimple erupted under salvoes of accurately placed shells. Two of the British tanks there were quickly hit, though their situation eased slightly when a battery of R.H.A. 25-pounders attached to Caunter came into action with counter-battery fire, and the cruisers which had gone south completed their task and rejoined those on the Pimple; but now an already difficult problem was becoming crucial, as another part of Topper Brown's letter reveals:

> Practically all morning we never stopped firing, at wagonloads of infantry or tanks. I haven't a clue how many enemy I killed, but it must have run into hundreds. We definitely had a score of twenty M13s at the end of the day . . .
>
> At times we were getting overwhelmed and had to keep withdrawing to the Pimple. One time we came around to the right of the Pimple and stopped. My orders were to traverse left and I then saw at about 600 yards an M13 coming towards me on absolutely flat ground. Just as I was about to fire Taff said, 'There are only two rounds left.' I cursed him soundly, but fortunately hit the tank with both. Taff and I immediately had a good fall-out. We had started out with 112 rounds of 2 pounder, 97 in the racks and 15 extra. Hughes had let us get down to the last two. If I had not been so well trained (I mean this), we could have died . . . I was also nearly out of BESA, so you can understand the amount of firing that I had done.[6]

Topper Brown was by no means the only tank gunner whose racks were empty, and a temporary solution was found by feeding those in front from the H.Q. squadron racks; but how long would that give them and where were the main supply lorries? In an effort to win time, Caunter sent an urgent message north to the 3rd and 7th Hussars that they must increase their harassment of the column wherever they might find themselves and whatever the calibre of the opposition, and received back almost immediately the welcome news that they had at last found the tail and were destroying it piecemeal and rapidly – a relief which proved very short-lived indeed as within a few minutes the Hussars saw over their shoulders the head of yet another enormous column coming up behind them, preceded, unbelievably, by a captured Rolls-Royce armoured car of the 11th's. This was rammed and put out of action in short order – but now other Italian M13s appeared from the north-east, as the result (although this was not realised at the time) of the Support Group's attack on Sceleidima; Bergonzoli, informed of this new threat from a different direction, had ordered the withdrawal of the garrison and its armour and artillery to join the main column of retreat, soon after the first token attack by Strafer Gott's infantry.

With over twenty M13s now moving against the 3rd and 7th Hussars in the gap between the two columns, these had no choice but to retire, and with the cruisers on and around the Pimple both under heavy artillery fire and almost out of ammunition, the situation for the hard-pressed British – however successfully they may have been fighting individually – was, as the R.H.A. battery commander commented, 'decidedly tricky'. There was no point in the 2nd R.T.R. cruisers staying up on the Pimple if they had nothing to fire, and by now they had lost four of their number to the Italian artillery; reluctantly, they came away, holding on as long as possible if only for the sake of morale, until in due course the light tanks of the Hussars which had been chased away from the north came down and they all became aware of an unrealised bonus presented by the weather. It had now become so murky and the visibility so inconsistent that their enemies could no longer distinguish between one British tank and another and so reacted as though every one were a cruiser, and withdrew as quickly as possible.

At 1300 came at last the news that the ammunition lorries had arrived just behind the Mosque.

The next hour was perhaps the most confused and critical of the entire day, as the cruisers made their way in turn back to the Mosque – and three of them broke down, one with a seized engine. Meanwhile the light tanks of the Hussars played an effective but risky game of bluff along the sides of the column, delicately balancing their act so that they wasted none of their ammunition – which itself would run low soon – and also that their pressure was just enough to hold the Italians without threatening the head of their column to such an extent that it might lunge forward in panic, and thus discover the tenuous nature of the only block now remaining between itself and the haven of Tripolitania.

As for Combeforce themselves, their situation was now slightly ludicrous. Despite the precariousness of their general position and the fact that they had been first in action on both days of the battle so far, the effectiveness of 4th Armoured's tactics to the north meant that they had had little to do but marshal prisoners since the end of the early morning's engagement. Any potentially dangerous concentration of enemy forces in their area had been quickly broken up by Jock Campbell's gunners, and so little serious business had come their way that the commander of the Rifle Brigade H.Q. Company, worthily endeavouring to find work for idle hands, had put some of the men to erecting the Officers' Mess tent a few hundred yards to their rear where, although it provided little sustenance or comfort for the officers, it was to provide a convenient aiming mark for the Italian artillery when action did come close.

For the moment, the battle raged to the north. Although the main force, 2nd R.T.R., were down to ten cruisers, they were at least stocked with ammunition and their fuel tanks were full. But the Pimple had fallen into Italian hands by default and everywhere the British tanks moved between the Mosque ridge and the road, they were in view of the Italian artillery there, which, although showing signs of tiring, was still a force to be reckoned with. Desperately, Caunter sent request after request for the cruisers of 7th Armoured Brigade to hasten from Antelat, but communications were not of the highest standard between the two brigades and 4th Armoured had to battle on alone.

Their luck varied. A perfect example was given when 7th Hussars mounted one of their dashes from behind the Mosque ridge against an apparently vulnerable section of the Italian column, only to see when they were half-way across towards the road that there were several M13s opposite them, though on the western side of the road, together with some guns. They were just about to reassess the situation when the sole cruiser in the squadron broke a track and for twenty-five hair-raising minutes they all milled around creating as much dust as possible and a troop of 25-pounders came up to offer support if necessary, while the crew sweated on the repairs. Nobody dared fire anything lest they should draw attention to themselves – but now their luck returned and the enemy column ignored them completely.

By 1500, it was obvious that the crisis of the battle was approaching. Up to the north, 7th Hussars had now found the tail of the column and were again chewing it up piecemeal; 3rd Hussars had been caught by a concentration of M13s coming down the eastern flank, about mid-column, and had been ordered to remain in contact with the enemy – not to withdraw and let them through but to try to hold them by bluff and manoeuvre; the R.H.A. battery were in trouble as their forward observation post had been hit; the remaining tanks of the 2nd R.T.R. had been foiled in an attempt to get around the front of the column and try to attack the Pimple from the other side, and were grimly assessing their chances of knocking out the now-dominating artillery on it by a frontal charge.

It began to look very much as though, despite all the damage they had done, 4th Armoured's cordon would be burst by the sheer weight of the Italian column which would then lurch on through the Combeforce roadblock and away to the open spaces beyond – leaving 7th Armoured Division to face O'Connor's annoyance yet again. The likelihood of this outcome was increased by the arrival at last of 7th Armoured Brigade's commanding officer at Caunter's H.Q. – in a staff car but with no radio. He was thus unable, even when he eventually appreciated the seriousness of the position, to communicate with his forces, still making their painful way across the broken country from Antelat.

Already Combeforce was in danger. Many Italian units had attempted to bypass the Rifle Brigade lines by crossing westwards through the dunes and slipping past along the edge of the sea, and as the head of the main Italian column closed down towards them, the riflemen's attention was held more and more to their front and away from the flank by which more groups of Italians managed to escape. True, these were only small groups – but it was all too possible that the trickle could become a stream and the stream a torrent. The only place the battle could be won by the British was to the north.

Here, the action was reaching crisis-point. The Hussars had been inevitably driven back towards the Pimple, the 2nd R.T.R. were edging in towards it, drawn by an almost centripetal force in spite of the suicidal effect that a frontal, uphill charge against the Italian guns would have for them; and all around the sound and fury of battle echoed back and forth, the smoke and din and drifting sand confusing the vision, terrifying those on the periphery of the action, infuriating those within it.

Then, at last, two new elements joined. Away to the north, the cruisers and light tanks of 7th Armoured Brigade, having driven to the sound of the guns, came over the last ridge and lumbered down to take the pressure off the Hussars and drive the M13s there westwards back through their own column which, denied the protection of their tanks, was then thoroughly torn apart by the new arrivals and the rejoicing Hussars.

And with their observation post at last back in communication, the gunners on the Mosque ridge were suddenly touched by inspiration and blanketed the Pimple with so accurate a concentration of fire that when a brief lull fell, the overjoyed but rather shaken observers in the British tanks could see that the Italian artillery had been completely wiped out. Within ten minutes, the nearest R.T.R. squadron – now reduced to but four tanks – was in command of the Pimple again, and the battle paused while both sides adjusted to yet another tactical change.

But the overall situation remained the same. Despite the access of power to the British now that the cruisers of 7th Armoured Brigade had come up, they were still facing overwhelming numbers of enemy troops who, however battered they might be, still wanted desperately to get away to the south and had not yet given up hope of doing so. Moreover, the M13s which had been driven by the cruisers through the column to the north had not been destroyed and were now coming down to the Pimple – but on the western side of the road, a direction from which the tired and already over-strained British tank crews were not expecting them.

The Pimple changed hands yet again just before 1800 on the 6th, the three remaining R.T.R. cruisers limping away to the Mosque ridge under cover of the R.H.A.'s fire, again with nearly empty ammunition racks, and leaving one of their number gutted and burnt out. Fortunately, more supply lorries had now arrived and, perhaps even more fortunately, the early desert dusk was upon them. The men of 4th Armoured concentrated around the Mosque, wearily stacked more shells and bullets aboard their battered hulls, the fitters wrestled exhaustedly with vastly overstrained and wrenched tracks, everyone helped with the refuelling of men and machines, and then with the exception of the sentries all fell into varying degrees of coma – while the 7th Armoured Brigade held the ring.

The armour had been holding the ring in the south all day; in the north, the Australians had been closing it. Since well before dawn, with Barce safely in their hands, they had been driving forward against varying opposition. Alan Moorehead was with them during their advance through the Jebel:

A kind of frenzy possessed the Australians now in their utter determination to have Benghazi at once. I cannot conceive that anything would have stopped them from that Wednesday night on. But now hail and rain came that turned the countryside into red mud and slush. Every few kilometres the tracks were blown away by the Italian rearguard, which was fighting only for time and still more time in which to organize and make a stand. Australian engineers slaved at the head of the column until men in their ranks were forced to drop out through sheer exhaustion, while others came forward to take their places. Soon it developed into a contest between the engineers and the squads of Italian minelayers and dynamiters. All that first day after Barce, while the storm still gathered force, the Australians kept flinging boulders into craters along the roads or breaking open new roads along the goat tracks. Kilometre by kilometre – yard by yard sometimes – the troops moved forward. It was a forty-mile-long column of vehicles that crashed over tank-traps and plunged headlong into valleys and across ruined gaps in the railway line. Nowhere could the Italians destroy the way sufficiently to hold them more than an hour or two . . . [7]

Throughout the whole of that day, while 4th Armoured Brigade were hanging on desperately around Beda Fomm, the Australians moved forward. 'Push on! Push on!' was the order everywhere and no one needed further spurring, however exhausted he felt, however hungry or thirsty. Whenever the men paused for a bite or a brew-up of tea, they found themselves surrounded yet again by the incredible disorder of incontinent retreat – the same tangle of gorgeous uniforms, broken swords and abandoned offices and quarters, the same shambles of half-eaten meals, half-emptied wardrobes, rifled cellars; and all the time columns of weary and disheartened prisoners trudged back past them, incredulous at the array of vehicles, however battered, possessed by this enemy they had been so frequently assured was a broken power, old, out-of-date and unprepared for war.

One of their most frequently expressed bewilderments was that anyone should want to fight in such appalling weather, anyway.

El Abiar was entered by the Australians unopposed; then there was a bad hold-up on the icy, treacherous slope of a hill, another detour on a hastily buttressed goat-track, a stretch of road flanked by the chaos of bombed-out railyards; then the brow of another hill and at last a long line of roof-tops by the sea with smoke drifting across from a fire in the middle – Benghasi. It had been a long trip – 500 miles from Cairo, 400 miles from Sidi Barrani – fighting all the way.

Just before dusk, the first Australians drove into the town with an escort of carriers and were greeted by a huge crowd of Greeks, Jews and Arabs (together with what afterwards proved to be a large contingent of Italian soldiers who had judiciously demobilised themselves during the preceding hour), who clapped and cheered and referred to them in the speeches which followed as 'Our Brave Allies' – somewhat to the surprise of those who listened.

Brigadier Robertson had sent a message to the mayor that he intended to enter the town the following morning and that he expected the Italian authorities to keep order until then; and he also issued orders to the commander of the 2nd/11th Battalion to take under his command a squadron of the 6th Cavalry, four armoured cars, a battery of field guns and a troop of anti-tank guns, and get them and his men down towards Ghemines and whatever lay beyond as quickly as possible.

During the night, Combeforce had little to deal with except patrol activity and an attempt by some more M13s to slip by along the seaward flank. Callum Renton's riflemen dealt with these problems efficiently, driving the Italian skirmishers to ground and bagging a brace of M13s when one of their platoon sergeant-majors and a rifleman ran down close on them and fired in through the drivers' slits; but all were aware of the fact that dawn on February 7th would bring their greatest test. They were very cold, thirsty and hungry, but if their morale was reduced from its high peak of a few days before by the evident numerical odds now against them, it also received a solid buttressing from the harsh realities of the situation itself.

There was nowhere for Combeforce to go, for a retreat would sweep them deeper into enemy territory; anyway, with the only petrol which had come their way going to the R.H.A., the infantry still had no choice but to stay where they were and fight it out.

Such practicalities breed resolution and when the Italian artillery opened up on the British lines as soon as the light was strong enough to see the fall of shot, the riflemen huddled deep into their slit trenches and waited, listening to the crash of shell around them and to the scream of sliver and shrapnel above. Then came the roar of engines as some thirty M13s approached, the sharp exchange of fire between the tanks and their own portée'd anti-tank guns, and as the tanks passed through their forward positions, the riflemen rose from their trenches and the infantry battle opened.

Behind them the anti-tank guns were suffering casualties and being pressed further and further back, as the M13s lunged forward and the Italian artillery concentrated against the guns with their customary efficiency. Desperately, the R.H.A. battery commanders to the rear asked for and received permission to fire on the Italian tanks although they were now well into the British lines.

The whole area of Combeforce was now a battlefield with M13s trading shot for shot with the anti-tank guns in this culminating drive towards the escape route, infantry fighting it out in vicious close-quarter mêlées and the artillery on both sides shooting into the growing murk of battle with more hope than certainty that their aim was directed at enemies and not friends. Now, in this cauldron of growing turmoil – almost the perfect illustration of the chaos of battle – the only element which might rescue the result from the random decision of blind fortune was professionalism. As tank after tank was hit, as gun-crew after gun-crew was wiped out, as battery after battery ceased fire in the face of the total obscurity which cloaked the field, it came down to the cold proficiency of the men engulfed in the close confines of the battle itself.

Gradually, the Italian tanks pushed forward, overrunning more rifle platoons huddled in their trenches, seeing the British anti-tank guns overturned, their portées wrecked or blazing, the white mess-tent which had been their target coming closer minute by minute; and although their own numbers were down to five, surely the break-out must be theirs in but a little longer.

The R.H.A. Anti-tank Battery commander, Major Burton, was coming to the same conclusion as he watched the crew of his last gun wiped out by machine-gun fire which, however, left gun and portée undamaged. Collecting his batman and the battery cook, he reached the gun, drove it briefly into the shelter of a dune while he checked the traversing and elevating wheels, the sights and ammunition, and then came out on the flank of the last Italian tanks as they drove for the mess-tent and the centre of the defence positions.

He must have been an extraordinarily good gunner. Within the next few minutes, he and his scratch crew accounted for the last five M13s in a fury of fire which blew one tank turret off its chassis, wrecked the bogey-wheels and tracks of three more and killed the driver of the fifth who had by then driven his tank to within a few yards of the mess-tent; and when Burton looked quickly around to see where danger next threatened, all that met his eyes were Renton's riflemen rising up out of the ground to chase after the rapidly retreating Italian and Libyan infantry who had escorted the M13s on their last gallant charge.

And it *was* the last, for the 7th and 4th Armoured Brigades, refuelled, recuperated and with their ammunition racks full, were again threatening the flanks of Bergonzoli's main column and finding nothing much left to stand against them except the exhausted and now demoralised Italian artillery.

Such was the fact, though not apparently the appearance. Lieutenant Joly had been watching the Combeforce battle:

> For a time there was silence on both sides. For all the efforts of the previous day, the Italian column still looked huge and threatening. I watched with apprehension the movements of the mass of vehicles before me. On either side of me, hidden behind the crests of other dunes and ridges, I knew that there were other eyes just as anxious as mine, surveying the scene before them. In the mind of each one of us was the sure knowledge that we were well outnumbered. Each of us knew by what slim margin we still held dominance over the battlefield. Our threat was but a façade

– behind us there were no more reserves of further troops. Even the supplies of the very sinews which could keep us going had almost run out. If we lost now we were faced with capture or a hopeless retreat into the empty distances of the inner desert. It was a sobering thought. I felt that the day, with all its black, wet dullness, was heavy with ominous foreboding. The scene before me was made gloomy enough to match my mood by the black clouds of acrid smoke which shrouded the battlefield like a brooding pall.

Gradually I became aware of a startling change. First one and then another white flag appeared in the host of vehicles. More and more became visible, until the whole column was a forest of waving white banners.[8]

Not able to believe their eyes, the tank crews for some time thought that it might be a trap; but the Italian Tenth Army had had enough and was laying down its weapons. Groups of Italians of all ranks and of all arms walked out towards the British tanks with their hands in the air, while the British crews, with good reason but an apparent lack of good manners, ignored them and drove quickly through their uncertain ranks towards the main body of vehicles and guns behind them, to disarm and marshal those Italians who had preferred to remain in the column.

The scene which therefore met the eyes of Robertson's Australians, now arriving just south of Ghemines, was that of a film director's battlefield. For a stretch of some fifteen miles the desert bordering the road was littered with the debris of battle – overturned lorries and trucks, abandoned Fiat staff cars and runabouts, field-guns with their barrels splayed out and drooping like banana-skins, or occasionally just left, their barrels pointing nowhere, in perfect condition but usually with broken or empty racks. Dozens of dark green tanks lined the roads, often blackened by fire, sometimes empty but too often still the grim coffins of charred and twisted bodies; rifles, machine-guns, ammunition and grenades were everywhere, boxes of food, torn blankets, bedraggled clothing lay in heaps where it had been thrown by overturned lorries and then further disarrayed by disconsolate men providing themselves with some degree of warmth and sustenance for the trials to come.

On every side, the scene was of dank desolation. Rain lanced down in fitful showers, enough to turn the clay to mud but not enough to keep down the sand or put out the smouldering fires which sent black stains of oily smoke drifting along the line of misery and hopelessness. Even the victors were affected, their first surge of relief at the realisation that battle was over for the time being dispersed, their thirst and hunger still with them even if they had found water or food, still desperately tired and now depressed by the dirt, the dead, the dying, the dispossessed.

The immediate taste of victory is very sour.

Generale Tellera, who had commanded the fighting during this last battle, had been wounded during one of the tank skirmishes and died during the day; but scores of colonels and brigadiers were collected and taken to a farmhouse in the drab village of Soluch, together with the captured generals – Generale di Corpo Cona who had taken over when Tellera was wounded; Generale di Divisione Bignani who had commanded at Sceleidima; Generale di Corpo Villanis who at least had some reason to be proud for he had commanded the Italian artillery; Generale di Divisione Negroni; Generale di Divisione Bardini; Generale di Divisione Giuliano; and in the yard outside, Alan Moorehead found a soft-spoken, swarthy little man, wrapped in a blanket for he was ill, his neat, silvery beard parted as usual immaculately in the middle. 'Barba Elettrica' was caught at last.

'You were here too soon, that is all,' he replied to the questions put to him. 'But we gave battle at once . . . And always, here as everywhere else, we were grossly outnumbered. So when our second attack was unable to prevail we had no choice but to make an honourable surrender.'

Two days later, he was flown to Cairo on a stretcher and taken to hospital suffering from suspected appendicitis. He thus had no opportunity then of talking to General O'Connor, who might have disabused him of some of his illusions.

To O'Connor, the moment was obviously one of relief and triumph, and also one of concern and doubt for the future. Where would they go from here?

He and Dorman-Smith had spent the day of the main battle between Corps Headquarters and Msus, aware that all now lay in the hands of the fighting men and that there was nothing, for the moment, for them to do. After breakfasting on a cold sausage each on the morning of February 7th, they drove on to Creagh's headquarters, arriving at about 0900, just in time to be greeted with the news of the Italian surrender all along the line. After checking the details to an extent which later allowed him to write, 'I think this may be termed a complete victory as none of the enemy escaped,' O'Connor turned to Dorman-Smith and said, 'We'd better send a message to Archie. What shall we say?'

Between them they concocted a signal, redolent of the close, county-family atmosphere of dogs and horses, of large houses, of trim lawns and open fields in which all three of them, and indeed the majority of British Army officers, had grown up and to which they hoped to return.

'Fox killed in the open . . . ' it began, and was sent in clear for Mussolini's benefit, though whether Il Duce understood the reference is unlikely.

They then went forward to review the battlefield and were as shaken by the scene as the others who came across it unprepared. Another 25,000 prisoners milled about awaiting collection and organisation; over 100 M13s were counted around Beda Fomm, some of them completely wrecked and burnt out, some totally undamaged and the majority recoverable; no one bothered to take a tally of the light tanks, but there were some 200 guns and over 1,500 wheeled vehicles in various states of serviceability – and as O'Connor would need every one of them if he obtained permission to press on with the advance towards Tripoli, one of the first orders he gave that day was to Strafer Gott to move north and halt the main Australian advance down to the battlefield, in case they felt inclined to help themselves to too much of it.

Another problem which faced O'Connor (but which he quickly passed for solution to one of his subordinates) was presented by a busload of Italian ladies powdering their noses and brewing tea in the middle of the battlefield, protected by a lone priest in a soutane – 'a highly inappropriate figure', as Dorman-Smith commented.

In all, O'Connor's command – first the Western Desert Force and then XIII Corps – had advanced 500 miles in ten weeks, from Sidi Barrani and Nibeiwa to Beda Fomm, during which time it had totally destroyed the Italian Tenth Army. It had captured 130,000 prisoners, 180 medium tanks and well over 300 light tanks, 845 pieces of artillery; and killed and destroyed uncounted numbers more. As for soft-skinned, wheeled vehicles, the tally will never be known.

But the count of British losses was quickly made. Over 80 per cent of the tracked and wheeled vehicles in which they had ridden to battle had either been destroyed or were now too worn for much further use, and of the remainder only the armoured cars of the King's Dragoon Guards which had joined at Mechili had not grossly exceeded their service mileage – indeed, practically all original Western Desert Force transport was written off when eventually it got back to the workshops. The guns of the R.H.A. batteries, however, remained with them until replacements came out, or the batteries were re-formed.

As for the human casualties, in these ten weeks 500 British and Australians had been killed, 1,373 wounded and 55 were missing, later posted 'believed killed'.

It was certainly a moment for celebration, and as the morning progressed and food and drink became available, a festive note was struck. About mid-morning, O'Connor and Dorman-Smith found their way to the Combeforce area where the Rifle Brigade Officers' Mess was at last in some form of operation, 'like rather badly-organised catering at a point-to-point' as Colonel Renton put it, continuing the strain of sporting metaphor. Later O'Connor visited the farm at Soluch and talked to Italian generals there, his corduroy trousers, leather jerkin, tartan scarf and battered officer's cap in some contrast to the continuing immaculacy (complete with spurs) of his prisoners.

'I'm sorry you are so uncomfortable,' he apologised. 'We haven't had much time to make proper arrangements.'

'Thank you very much,' Generale Cona replied politely. 'We do realise you came here in a very great hurry.'

Sympathy is catching.

The situation which now faced O'Connor required decisions on both a tactical and a strategic level; the tactical ones he would take himself but the most vital – whether to press on into Tripolitania and perhaps even further to Tunisia, thus ridding the whole of the North African coastline of Axis troops – must be referred to a higher command. Surely Wavell would realise the immense opportunities now open to XIII Corps, and appreciate the wave of enthusiasm and confidence which now swept through them all as rest, relaxation, and the awareness of achievement overcame the effects of battle fatigue? Within thirty-six hours of the surrender of Tenth Army, O'Connor's men were raring to go – no Italian force could hold from Tripoli the men who had stormed into Benghasi.

No Italian force was in fact making much of an effort even to regroup. Scarcely had the noise of battle died down in front of Combeforce before C Squadron of the 11th Hussars was re-forming and driving south along the coast road to Agedabia, where two troops under command of Second Lieutenant Crankshaw took the surrender of the garrison, including the colonel of one of the Italian light tank regiments who had managed to slip past Combeforce during the previous day, but then got his tanks stuck in the salt-pans. He was most affable, spoke perfect English and was anxious for news of friends in the 12th Lancers with whom, apparently, he had spent many enjoyable weeks hunting in Leicestershire.

Hastily handing over the prisoners to the Rifle Brigade company which followed them up (O'Connor had detached the whole of the Support Group as quickly as possible and sent them forward, leaving the rest of 7th Armoured to clear the battlefield and instructing General Mackay to employ his Australians on getting

Benghasi harbour and town ready for use as an advance supply port
and base as quickly as possible), the Hussars moved out that
afternoon, rendezvoused with B Squadron the following day, and in
driving rain moved on to the fort and barracks of El Agheila
marking the border between Cyrenaica and Tripolitania.

Wet, cold, weary, but immensely grateful for this almost forgotten luxury of a night in dry bedding under a stout roof upon
which the rain was drumming, officers and men were about to turn
in when the guard commander announced the approach of two
mounted figures who, when challenged, revealed themselves as a
Libyan sergeant-major and his orderly. There were, according to
the interpreter, some 400 Libyan cavalrymen in the sand-dunes
around them complete with weapons and mounts (but minus their
officers, for these had departed for Tripoli) and would the English-
men be so kind as to come out and accept their surrender?

There was a resigned pause while a hundred or so half-undressed
Hussars awaited the verdict, distastefully regarding the prospect of
sorting out yet another large batch of prisoners in pitch dark and
pouring rain. Then, to their enormous relief, they heard John
Combe say, 'Tell them to come back again in the morning,' adding
sternly, 'and if they don't, they'll all be shot!'

Punctually at ten o'clock the following morning, a strange assortment rode up, some on horses, some on camels. Most of them were
Libyan, but there were about twenty Italians including an air force
officer and some sailors; there was also an Arab lady of indeterminate status, but by this time it was impossible to surprise the
Hussars.

That afternoon, their first patrols drove some ten miles into
Tripolitania where the only sign of enemy life was an abandoned
remount depot, full of unfed and unwatered horses, some wounded
and all showing signs of sad neglect; such was their state that the
immediate demands of duty were forgotten and one troop spent the
afternoon making up feeds and leading relays of desperately thirsty
horses to a nearby well. Many of the Hussars that afternoon lost
some of the affection they were beginning to feel for their Italian
enemy, and the repeated requests to John Combe for news of when
they were going to push on had an extra edge that night.

This was still the question to which General O'Connor urgently
required an answer. He and Dorman-Smith had spent much time
marshalling their arguments for a further advance. They were both
well aware of the existing intentions to call a halt in North Africa
and send as many men and as much equipment as could be spared
to the Balkans, to succour the Greeks and block any German
encroachment towards the eastern Mediterranean; but they were

determined not to allow the advantages of their own situation to be lost by default on their part.

They were quite certain that despite the battering and unceasing strain put on their equipment, it could be made to function well enough to get them at least to Tripoli, chiefly because the men would not allow its malfunction to stop them. Tobruk was now in full use as a port and Benghasi soon would be – and if the Luftwaffe's attempts to mine the harbours which started on February 4th were combated with the drive and enthusiasm which enlivened XIII Corps, they could easily handle the supplies necessary to keep not only the units already at the front moving, but also 2nd Armoured Division which had been ordered up to help at Mechili, and at least one more Australian brigade which had arrived in the Delta. Perhaps, in view of the promise opening in front of them all, New Zealand would let its 6th Brigade take part in the chase after all without waiting for the rest of the division?

But there was now a reconstructed chain of command for requests for action and orders to travel up and down; Wavell had appointed Maitland Wilson as Governor of Cyrenaica and the latter was already installed at Barce. Dorman-Smith arrived in Barce on February 9th and soon persuaded Wilson of the feasibility and indeed desirability of a further advance; but there were no signalling facilities set up there yet, so Dorman-Smith was faced with another drive to Tobruk in order to send the message on to Cairo. He left Tobruk on the afternoon of February 11th for Cairo in order to be available to buttress the argument in person if necessary, arrived there at 0400 on the morning of the 12th and at 1000 was ushered into Wavell's office.

All the maps of the desert which had previously covered the long wall were gone; in their place was a huge map of Greece.

'You see, Eric,' said Wavell, gesturing towards it, 'I am planning my spring campaign!'

The die had been cast; XIII Corps were to stay where they were in Cyrenaica.

7 · 'In all directions . . .'

The authors of the *Official History*, at one point in their description of the situation facing Wavell and his fellow Commanders-in-Chief during the early months of 1941, write that it must have seemed to them 'that this war was not "one damned thing after another": it was everything in all directions at once'.

One of the great problems, of course, was that so far as material was concerned 'everything' at that moment, despite the Italian booty, did not amount to very much when compared with the tasks to be carried out. Not only had the Greek front already absorbed much of the exiguous R.A.F. strength in the area, together with a great deal of the Middle East anti-aircraft capability and a large part of the captured Italian transport, but Mr Churchill and the War Cabinet were increasingly anxious that a firm Balkan Front against the Axis should be formed which would include not only Greece and Yugoslavia, but Turkey as well; and to this end – as Wavell had good reason to suspect – there were feelings in high places that perhaps some of the forces and equipment now under his command or en route to the area, should be used to fill the evident gaps in Turkey's defences.

In particular, Turkey would need a bolstering of her air defences – and if Air Chief Marshal Longmore's expression when he heard suggestions that yet more of his precious squadrons might leave the Delta for northern destinations was one of bleak incredulity, attempts made to alleviate his sufferings with the announcement that 500 Tomahawk fighters purchased from America would soon be reaching him, probably via the newly opened Takoradi Air Route, did nothing, in fact, to lighten it. Longmore was only too well aware that not only was there no American ammunition to fit the Tomahawks' armament in the Middle East, but there were also no pilots with experience or even theoretical knowledge of the Tomahawks' operational capabilities.

Admiral Cunningham, for his part, had long been pointing out that any attempt to reinforce or supply the Balkan States by sea would encounter enormous difficulties while the Dodecanese

Islands remained in Italian hands – an obstacle which could be rendered well-nigh insuperable if German Luftwaffe units moved into Rhodes as they had already moved into Sicily. A solution suggested by Whitehall was that a Special Service Brigade of newly-trained commando units, earmarked for an assault on the island of Pantelleria in the Sicilian Channel, should instead be diverted around the Cape and into Wavell's command, and these could capture Rhodes and the surrounding islands.

But this idea underlined yet another task which still faced the Commanders-in-Chief. Although the R.A.F. had managed to retain air supremacy over the Red Sea and the approaches to Suez, a third of the Red Sea western coastline – from just south of Port Sudan to the narrows – and the whole of the southern coastline of the Gulf of Aden was in Italian hands, and however ineffective that control might be, in the eyes of President Roosevelt it rendered the entire area a combatant zone. As such, no American shipping was allowed into it to alleviate the desperate shortage of British shipping – in itself a factor adversely affecting supplies.

Indeed, it was in this especial regard that many recent cables from London had been worded; how quickly did the Commander-in-Chief think that he could eliminate the Italian East African Empire? Because once this happened, many more men and much more material could be sent to plug the gaps which would be left in his ranks by the fulfilment of immediate needs – succouring the Greeks, perhaps bolstering the Turks, and certainly demonstrating to the Balkan nations that those who cared to withstand Axis pressure would be assured of British support, *material as well as moral*. This Balkan commitment was, in the light of most of the messages and directives from Whitehall, likely to be given the highest priority, and in order to examine its ramifications in detail and perhaps to advance its course the Foreign Secretary, Mr Eden, and the C.I.G.S., Sir John Dill, would shortly be arriving in the Middle East for discussions and a lightning tour of the relevant capitals. But in the meantime, how about East Africa?

This in fact was the time when, to quote again from the *Official History*, Wavell, Longmore and Cunningham

had to achieve a workable and appropriate balance of forces while doing their best to comply with a rapid succession of in-structions and suggestions, such as to part with forces from Kenya, to capture Kismayu quickly, to capture Eritrea quickly, to deter the Japanese by 'liquidating Italian East Africa', to treat as a 'first duty' the air defence of Malta, to be prepared to send ten squadrons to Turkey, to regard the capture of Rhodes as 'of first importance', and to 'let their first thoughts be for Greece'.[1]

All in all, it is therefore hardly surprising that on the morning of February 12th the view across the Cyrenaican border as seen by Wavell differed markedly from the same view as seen by Dorman-Smith. If to the latter it appeared as one of infinite promise beckoning on into Tripolitania and offering the enticing prospect of clearance from the southern Mediterranean coast of all Axis forces to the man across the desk from him it appeared instead as little more than a welcome relief from one of his many problems. A welcome and blessed relief, certainly; and indeed from what eight weeks ago had been the most urgent and pressing of his problems with the added bonus of a display of military expertise which by its superb execution promised well for the future.

But other fronts and other theatres were now demanding attention – and another of the benefits which would accrue from O'Connor's magnificent victory would be the reservoir of experienced fighting troops upon which, after a period of rest and re-equipment, Wavell could draw for dispatch to the other fronts where, for reasons both military and political, their presence was needed. In respect of which, Eric would doubtless be interested to know that the withdrawal of 4th Indian Division from Western Desert Force and its dispatch to the Sudan was already showing benefits and could easily bring fame and honours to that division to equal those already won at Nibeiwa and Sidi Barrani.

The reduction of the Duke of Aosta's fief had, in fact, already commenced. Wavell was later to judge that the development was 'an improvisation after the British fashion of war rather than a set piece in the German manner' but be that as it may, it was promising to develop very satisfactorily.

Its principal blow against the Italians was an uprising in the centre of their empire by Ethiopian patriots, led by Emperor Haile Selassie, fomented by a Colonel D. A. Sandford who had spent some years before the war farming in Ethiopia and whom Wavell had sent back in the previous September for just this purpose, and guided by a young and eccentric English officer who had already made something of a reputation for himself as a guerrilla leader in Palestine, named Orde Wingate. Already Patriot Forces had been assembled, two of the most powerful but hitherto hostile chieftains in the central Gojjam area, Dejesmach Mangasha and Dejesmach Nagash, reconciled sufficiently at least for them to agree to act together for the time being and – most important of all – Emperor Haile Selassie himself had returned to his native country, flown in by the R.A.F. on January 20th.

This central uprising was being assisted and protected by a pincer

Map 10   The East African campaign

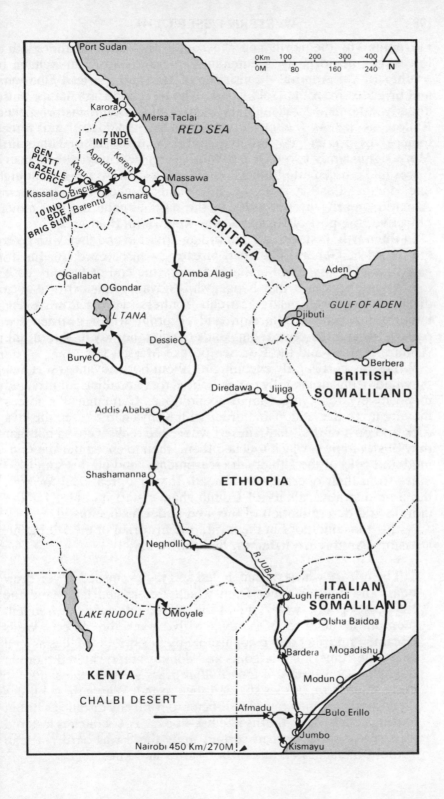

Port Sudan

0Km 100 200 300 400
0M 80 160 240
N

Karora

Mersa Taclai

RED SEA

7 IND
INF BDE

GEN
PLATT
GAZELLE
FORCE

Keru
Agordat
Keren

Kassala   Biscia
Barentu
10 IND
BDE   Asmara
BRIG SLIM

Massawa

Gallabat

Amba Alagi

Aden

Gondar

L TANA

GULF OF ADEN

Djibuti

Dessie

Berbera

Burye

**BRITISH
SOMALILAND**

Diredawa   Jijiga

Addis Ababa

Shashamanna

ETHIOPIA

Negholli

R JUBA

**ITALIAN
SOMALILAND**

LAKE RUDOLF   Moyale

Lugh Ferrandi

Isha Baidoa

Bardera   Mogadishu

KENYA

Modun

CHALBI DESERT

Afmadu   Bulo Erillo

Jumbo
Nairobi 450 Km/270M   Kismayu

movement to the north and the south. In Kenya to the south, forces commanded by Lieutenant-General Alan Cunningham – brother of the Admiral – consisting of 1st South African Division and brigades from the Gold Coast, Rhodesia and East Africa, had already established full military control of the area east of Lake Rudolf as far as the borders of Italian Somaliland and were themselves probing up into the southern provinces of Ethiopia. More significantly two days previously – on February 10th – other forces had crossed into Italian Somaliland, and in twenty-four hours one of the East African brigades had reached and occupied Afmadu, nearly seventy miles to the east; already the first main objective, the port of Kismayu, was well within their grasp.

In the north, first with the 5th Indian Division and then with both 5th and 4th, General Platt had already so threatened the Italian garrisons at Kassala and Gallabat that by the end of January both towns were back in British hands, while advanced elements of both divisions were well inside Eritrean frontiers, driving towards the important centres of Barentu and Agordat which guarded the passes through the central highlands barring the way to Keren, the Asmara Plateau and the Red Sea port of Massawa.

What was particularly encouraging about both advances was that they had been successfully carried out across appalling country and in positively terrifying climatic conditions. Cunningham's forces moving up to the Ethiopian border with Kenya had crossed the lava rock and dust of the Chalbi desert where the rocks were so hot that they blistered flesh which touched them, then to encounter the rain, mud and cold of the Ethiopian escarpment – and all this some 400 miles from their operational railhead. It said a great deal for both the administrative ability of Cunningham's staff and also for the morale and determination of the men under his command.

As for the conditions in the north, the historian of the 5th Indian Division, Antony Brett-James, had this to say:

> The mirage whose outline faded and then vanished as you drew near, the heat shimmer from which tree-ringed lakes and the likeness of still water might be stared at, were a frequent memorable feature of many a drive over the desert. Wells became important and recognizable by the swarms of flies as well as by the camels, cows, goats and donkeys that watered there in daylight . . . Patches of long *tubbas* grass grew on the sand . . . and camel-thorn bushes studded the ground. Where these bushes flourished . . . men found it difficult to walk any distance without getting caught up in thorns like fish-hooks. The scratches festered into septic sores, and in certain units there was hardly a man without bandages on one or both arms and knees.[2]

There are few less accessible places on earth than the Asmara Plateau, especially from the west. At first the Indian Brigades drove across a rolling plain as desolate as those of the Western Desert but more scarred by water-courses and rock shelving; dust enveloped them, to choke their eyes, their noses and throats, while waves of heat beat up from the arid rock. And when they reached the first foothills they found conditions if anything worse – for now they were in defiles which could be blocked, or which would channel them all into narrow streams of sweating men and overheating machines where they could be bombed by the Regia Aeronautica (2nd Camerons suffered twelve casualties on the first day) – and the heat was intensified by reflection back off the craggy walls.

The actions they were called upon to fight had characteristics all their own, too. One force under command of Colonel F. W. Messervy had reached a small village named Keru, about thirty miles across the Eritrean border, to find it abandoned, the defile beyond it blocked and substantial enemy forces on the crests above. As the force began to organise for the next stage of the advance, a patch of scrub about half a mile away suddenly erupted and a squadron of Eritrean cavalry – Askari natives officered by Italians – charged towards them, their small, shaggy ponies at a furious gallop, the riders standing in their stirrups and hurling in front of them a veritable mist of small percussion grenades.

Once the sheer astonishment at the sight in 1941 of a genuine horsed cavalry charge had evaporated (it didn't take long) the result was foregone. Sepoy riflemen and machine-gunners dropped into the nearest cover of thorn bush or fold in the ground and opened up, and even the light artillery had time to swing and virtually blow the

Map 11   Gazelle Force

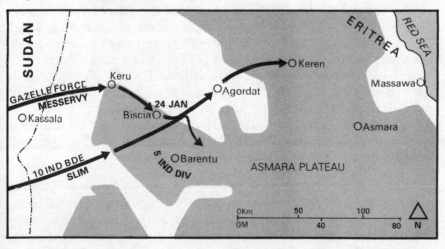

horsemen back from the muzzles of their guns; within ten minutes it was all over, dead and wounded men and beasts strewn about, dust clouds covering the survivors as they galloped frantically for the shelter of the scrub from which they had so dramatically appeared.

During the rest of the day, Gazelle Force (as Messervy's command was known) edged its way forward up the seamed and broken slopes towards the defenders at the top, who withstood the artillery harassment stoutheartedly and kept up a heavy though not very accurate fire on those below. The climbing Sikhs spent the daylight hours edging up and over innumerable false crests and suffering quite a few casualties (and the appalling trauma of manhandling wounded down precipitous and open hillsides was to be a feature of this campaign) but by nightfall were still pinned below the final crest. Then a midnight patrol brought back evidence of enemy withdrawal and by morning the heights commanding what had been demonstrably a formidable defensive position were found to be empty.

All next day the Sappers and Miners laboured at clearing rock from the defiles, opening the way forward, fighting off with their Bren-guns the pestiferous attentions of the Regia Aeronautica and on one occasion waving frantically at R.A.F. fighters who were mistakenly making aggressive passes above them. In the late afternoon the 1st/6th Rajputana Rifles who had come up to take the place of the Sikhs broke clear and went on forward, eventually to take the railhead of Biscia during the morning of January 24th. Again, the opposition had melted away.

Almost simultaneously, 10th Indian Brigade which had been attached to the 4th Indian Division from the 5th and was at that time commanded by Brigadier W. J. Slim, later to become famous as the commander of Britain's Fourteenth Army in Burma, had swung across on a line to the south of that driven by Gazelle Force, fought a brisk action with some Italian colonial battalions in which they took some 700 prisoners, and driven the rest northwards into the Gazelle Force net, after which the combined force closed up on Agordat, the first major objective inside Eritrea. Slim's brigade then swung away to cut the road down to Barentu, along which other Italian forces were by now trying to retreat.

Agordat presented 4th Indian Division with its greatest challenge so far in the Second World War. According to the divisional history:

> This colonial marketing town lay in the plain a mile south of the Baraka river bed, with bunkers of high ground on all sides. To the south-west the approach was barred by the long steep ridge of Laquetat, with forts on either tip. To the north, across

the sandy palm-clad watercourse (itself an obstacle), the terrain rose in a series of jumbled terraces. To the east, four abrupt hillocks stood sentry over the road to Keren. To the south, four miles across the plain, these moderate eminences were dwarfed by Mount Cochen, a steep and involved ridge system which sprang to a height of 1,500 feet, its rugged barrier extending into the east until it ended above a defile four miles long through which the road to Keren passed. From the northern shoulder of Mount Cochen a long tongue of high ground, known as Gibraltar, thrust into the plain. The low ground between Laquetat and Gibraltar was defended by a line of trenches and an anti-tank ditch. The position therefore offered serried obstacles near at hand, while on the southern and eastern horizons the misty outlines of the main Eritrean massif stood into the sky, revealing the Agordat terrain to be the shape of more ominous things to come.[3]

The Italian 4th Colonial Division holding Agordat consisted of three brigades and three additional Blackshirt units, making sixteen battalions in all, and they had ten medium tanks and a scattering of L3s in reserve. Against them the 4th Indian were putting into action two brigades totalling seven battalions – but the last battalion to join had brought the news that four R.T.R. Matildas were making their laborious way forward over the potholed and debris-covered roads.

The action began as all such set-piece battles do, with probing attacks and stealthy attempts to feel for ways around the main defences – and these took until the afternoon of January 28th. By this time Beresford-Peirse knew that there was no passable route for wheeled traffic on either side of the objective and that wherever action was joined, the scene would be dominated by the long straggling outline of Mount Cochen. That night, a company of Sikhs occupied the crest of the Laquetat ridge and held on under heavy fire while 5th Brigade battalions slipped into the re-entrant between the ridge and Mount Cochen where the trench line and anti-tank ditch lay, and waited there the next day.

Meanwhile, 11th Brigade battalions had circled around to the south and east of the mountain. Soon after dark on January 29th, 3rd/14th Punjabis began to climb the rocky slopes and to their surprise encountered no opposition on their first lift to the frontal crest. Up behind and passing through them came the 1st/6th Rajputana Rifles to pad softly on towards the ominous and lowering summit, then suddenly to find themselves in the middle of enemy positions. The night erupted in tracer and rifle fire, the Punjabis came up swiftly to help and from then until dawn bitter and confused fighting rose and fell up and down the mountain side, all

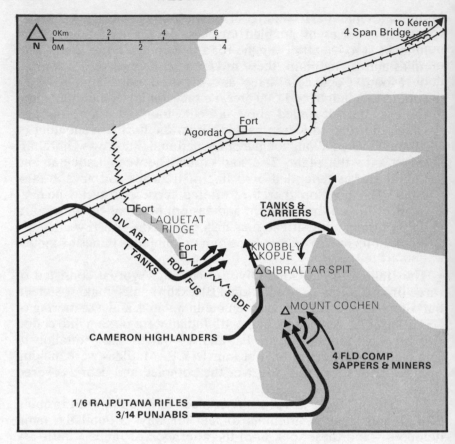

Map 12   The battle of Agordat

the time a matter of countless personal fights between warriors of
African and Indian races wielding arms provided by European
officers – few of whom took much part in the battle.

But in the morning, the defenders were still in possession of their
stronghold and the attackers lay wearily below the first crest, awaiting reinforcement, resupply and the agonising evacuation of their
wounded. Above them, they could hear the sounds of Italian
reinforcements arriving, and the extension of the enemy line across
their front until it overlapped them at both ends, and they were
faced with a crescent of enemies who by the afternoon were edging
forward and harassing them with grenades and petrol bombs. The
Indians clung to the ground and thanked their various deities for the
deep clefts around them which had caused them so much anguish on
the way up, but which now afforded them shelter.

While 11th Brigade had been fighting dourly on the sides of

Mount Cochen, 5th Brigade, attempting to clear the trenches in the re-entrant, had found to their cost that they were held by large numbers of determined troops. Moreover, every move they made on the plain was under full view of an extremely alert force which held the high tip at the end of the Gibraltar spit, and effectively pinned any major attempt by the Fusiliers (who had been given this particular task) to cross the barren and inhospitable ground.

There was nothing for it but for Beresford-Peirse to mount another indirect attack, which he did by sending the Cameron Highlanders around to infiltrate between the eastern end of the Laquetat ridge and the foothills of Cochen, then to climb under good cover along the spit to take the Gibraltar tip from behind. In this they were aided – as were the Rajputana Riflemen on the mountain itself – by the deep nullahs and cracks in the escarpment sides, but much hindered by the Italian artillery in the forts back on Laquetat; nevertheless, they hung on grimly, beat off two counter-attacks launched against them by enemy forces from both the Gibraltar tip and the nearest slope of Mount Cochen, and during the night of January 30th/31st dug themselves a little deeper into the ground against the sniping and machine-gun fire which was directed at them in sporadic bursts. Both sides then waited for whatever the morning would bring.

It was to a very great extent up to General Beresford-Peirse to decide this, and he quickly made up his mind. During the rest of that night, he carefully and quietly removed the remnants of the Rajputana Rifles from their confined position below the first crest of the southern slope of Mount Cochen, relocated them with their comrades of the 3rd/14th Punjabis and added to their company the 4th Field Company of Sappers and Miners, now about to relearn their basic infantry training. This group sidestepped inconspicuously to their right and by morning were half-way up the south-eastern slope of the hill, behind the apparently unsuspecting left flank of the enemy crescent which had so bedevilled the Rajputanas during the previous afternoon.

Behind Laquetat, he marshalled and briefed his divisional artillery and moved the four 'I' tanks up as close as he could behind the Royal Fusilier positions without breaking their cover. All, then, waited for the dawn.

It came with a quite astonishing explosion of military energy and expertise on the part of the 4th Indian Division. At 0500, while the mountain was still wrapped in mists, the riflemen and sappers on the slopes of Mount Cochen began their ascent to the first crest, reached it without being discovered and charged with terrifying violence along the line of Askaris who had lain there all night, confident that their prey was still penned below them. The sheer speed of the charge, as lines of disciplined infantry swept through the ranks with bayonet and bullet, boot and rifle-butt, chanting their weird and petrifying war-cries, struck terror into the hearts of the astonished enemy, many of whom were skewered to the ground where they had lain all night; as the attackers fought their way to the peak, the surviving defenders broke and fled. It was all over in less than an hour, by which time the mists had cleared and the victors could see the scene spread below them in the plain. It was quite a sight.

The action there had been triggered by the first sounds of battle coming from Mount Cochen at 0520 as the 11th Brigade swept over the false crest in their first charge. Hardly had the chatter of machine-guns and rifles echoed down into the plain than the divisional artillery crashed out in the heaviest concentration they could shoot on to the Gibraltar escarpment and the lower adjacent slopes of the mountain. Under its cover, four companies of Camerons rose from their various concealments along the length of the escarpment and swept along towards the tip, two companies on top and two at the bottom; and despite the undoubted courage of the defenders, they were utterly submerged within a matter of minutes. Highland fury was such, in fact, that having cleared the length of the ridge the Camerons swept down and across the plain to take what their history calls a 'knobbly kopje' standing about 500 yards out on the plain.

At this, two things happened. The artillery abruptly shortened range to blanket the trenches in front of the Fusiliers, and the commander of the Italian forces on the lower slopes of Mount Cochen, overlooking the Gibraltar spit, suddenly became aware of the fact that the summit of the mountain behind him was now in hostile hands. Hurriedly dispatching a masking company to contain them, he was still assembling the rest of his command to move down to the plain to join the battle there, when he was violently assaulted from the rear by the very force which he had ordered to be held.

Under command of a Major Holloway, A Company, 1st/6th Rajputana Rifles together with the attached Sappers and Miners from 4th Field Company had apparently been so fired by their morning's victory – perhaps also by the sight below of the Camerons in action – that they had charged down through the masking company with such force that they had destroyed and scattered it. Carried by their own impetus, they then fell upon the luckless and still unorganised force below them with the bayonet to such effect that after the battle, 104 bodies were found in the path of these avenging furies, none of them showing a single bullet wound. What survivors there were had fled away into the tangled country behind the mountain.

Below, as the smoke and dust of the bombardment of the trenches died away, the four Matildas lumbered around the corner of the Laquetat ridge and escorted by carriers, made directly for the trench lines, with the Fusiliers rising from the ground and following in skirmishing order.

There was a brief moment when the defenders stood and hoped that their parapets might be of some use to them, but nothing could halt the implacable 'I' tanks which turned as they reached the trenches and crunched along the line, followed by the Fusiliers, as expert with bomb and bayonet as the Sepoys on the slopes above. It was all over by 0900, the prisoners being led away, the Fusiliers searching the trenches, the tanks lurching back and forth in the area between the Fusiliers and Gibraltar, and the Camerons on the 'knobbly kopje'. And from the Camerons came the sudden announcement that there was some Italian armour concealed in a defile just behind Mount Cochen.

Brigadier Lloyd, who was the senior officer in the neighbourhood at that moment, quickly recalled the Matildas from what the divisional history delicately calls 'their freebooting behind the trenches on the plain', attached them to the Camerons' carriers and sent them off to winkle out the enemy tanks. It was, as one of the officers present afterwards admitted, rather like taking candy from a child. The carriers went first, rather breezily swanning across the plain, around the corner of the defile and into sight of the M13s and L3s, whereat they abruptly halted and reversed out of sight. They then turned and sped away – followed enthusiastically by the Italian armour past a large and thick clump of thorn bushes at which the crews would have been well advised to take a closer look.

From it emerged the four Matildas to take the Italians from the rear and at virtually point blank range. Six medium and five light tanks were quickly ablaze, and as the others scuttled back behind the mountain for safety, they were followed by both tanks and carriers who soon discovered the presence of an entire Blackshirt battalion lying in another defile further back, presumably intending to pounce on the flank of any attacking force moving along the road leading from Agordat, thus threatening the principal fortress of Keren.

Lightly armed infantry, except under most unusual circumstances and then only of exceptional quality, cannot stand against heavy armour, and this Blackshirt battalion was no exception. It broke immediately and fled, but unfortunately the first wave of panic led them down on to the plain instead of up and away into the mountains; their scurrying figures proved too much of a temptation to the riflemen and machine-gunners around them, already stirred by the sights and sounds of the morning and the immediate exultation of victory. There were not many Blackshirts left among the prisoners when the final count was made.

The town of Agordat was then occupied, an end put to the looting which had begun as soon as it had become evident that the Italian military would no longer be in control, and plans for the immediate future considered. From the south came news that 5th Indian Division was now firmly in control at Barentu and that survivors of the Italian garrison there had escaped away into the hills to the south-east and would thus present no problems to the commander of 4th Indian Division.

General Beresford-Peirse very soon found that he had quite enough other problems to worry about, so far as that large and phlegmatic man ever worried about anything. Even while the main body of his division was securing the position at Agordat, his reconnaissance units – the chief of which was the romantically named Skinner's Horse – were off probing forward to discover what lay ahead in the general direction of the Eritrean central highlands, and in the particular direction of the only crack in its bleak and forbidding façade, the Dongolaas Gorge leading up to Keren, the key to the Asmara Plateau.

A few miles from Agordat along the Keren road, the highway crossed a four-span steel bridge over the Baraka watercourse – and the Italian retreat had not been carried out in such a hurry that it had not received attentions from their engineers. It took the indefatigable Miners and Sappers eight hours to clear the mines, neutralise the demolition charges and repair the gaps in the trellises, so the leading vehicles of the reconnaissance party covered only twenty miles that day. Let the divisional historian tell what happened next:

> At 1000 hours next morning [February 2nd] the leading troops of Skinner's Horse reached the southering bend in the Ascidera valley, two miles south of the entrance to the Gorge. From the canyon came dull booms; clouds of smoke and dust curled upwards in the still, hot air. The last Italian rearguards had passed through and on a stretch of several hundred yards demolition squads were blowing away the retaining walls which pinned the road to the cliffsides. Two 'I' tanks crossed the valley to reconnoitre and reported the ravine to be blocked by barricades of huge boulders covered by anti-tank and machine guns. The eastern gateway of the Eritrean fortress was bolted and barred.[4]

Even Beresford-Peirse's placidity was ruffled by this event, and his state of mind further disturbed the following day when his Commander-in-Chief's reaction to the capture of Agordat arrived in the shape of a congratulatory cable, ending, 'Now go on and take Keren and Asmara!'

It was not to be as simple as that, and now began an ordeal for the 4th Indian Division, and later for the 5th as well, which was to have no comparison until three years later at Cassino. There was no way for a force large enough to capture Keren and take control of the Asmara Plateau to reach their objectives other than through the Dongolaas Gorge, and in the opening days of February 1941 the obvious tactic was for the nearest troops to try to take the heights commanding the Gorge by storm.

The first battle raged for three days – from February 4th to the 7th, and it bore little similarity to the one being fought at exactly the same time 1,500 miles away at Beda Fomm. By the end of the three days, two peaks had been won and lost, a col taken and lost and only the first objective, a low ridge already known to the division as Cameron Ridge, was still held – and that at tremendous cost. But much had been learned, perhaps the chief lesson being that Italian troops such as the Savoy Grenadiers now facing them, well-officered and adequately supplied, were as grim in defence as the Indians themselves, and just as ready and expert when it came to mounting a counter-attack. The force which had hurled the 3rd/14th Punjabis back from Brig's Peak to Cameron Ridge had earned the grudging respect of their antagonists, and when three nights later the 4th/6th Rajputanas were pinned below the Acqua Col (on a ridge which then took their name) they faced a night of combat reminiscent of the worst battles fought for the Passchendaele Ridge twenty-four years before; and were quite prepared to agree the following day that they had lost it.

Map 13   The approach to Keren

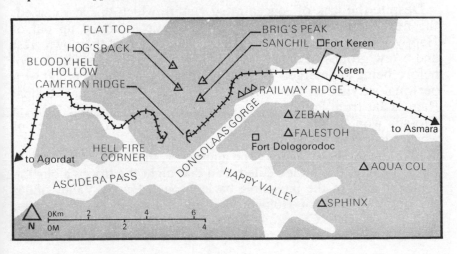

The pattern of the battle was now established. Whatever change in detail the future might show, it was going to be a matter of first storming and then holding, against as fierce counter-attacks as had been mounted to date in the Second World War, the main heights on each side of the gorge – Cameron Ridge, Brig's Peak, Flat Top, Railway Ridge and especially Sanchil on the north; Fort Dologorodoc, Falestoh and Zeban on the south. And some indication of the bitterness of the fighting was already indicated by the names being allocated to some of the vales and hillocks in between – Mole Hill, Pinnacle, Cameron Tunnel, Rajputana Ridge, Bloody Hell Hollow, the Sphinx, Hell Fire Corner (inevitably), and the trapped and exposed basin below Dologorodoc which after only two days became known to the sardonically minded troops as Happy Valley.

A second attack was mounted on the afternoon of February 10th in which the 3rd/1st Punjabis swept upwards from Cameron Ridge, across Brig's Peak and the following morning even across a col to seize the lower slopes of Sanchil. But there the Punjabis found themselves short of men both because of casualties and because as much as a third of the battalion had perforce to be employed as porters, bringing up ammunition and desperately trying to carry away the wounded (no thought was given to such inessentials as food or water). In the early hours of the following morning, a heavy attack fell on the front of the Punjabis' line while another struck them in the flank, sweeping the battalion away from all the ground they had won and back to Cameron Ridge, with a loss of their commanding officer, two company commanders and some 280 others killed. With them went artillery observation crews stationed temporarily on Brig's Peak to direct fire on Acqua Col, the objective of the next planned step in the offensive.

Despite the lack of concentrated gunfire which this loss caused, the next step still went ahead. 5th Brigade swarmed up out of Happy Valley, the Rajputana Rifles again captured their own crest and a few groups of dauntless individuals actually reached the col before being submerged in a sea of enemies, as unconcerned with personal survival as themselves. It was here that Subadar Richpal Ram, a Jat from Patiala State, earned the first of the four Victoria Crosses won by 4th Indian Division during the war, another of which also went to the 4th/6th Rajputana Rifles.

Like the attack on Sanchil and another by the Sikhs on the Sphinx the same day, this attack failed, and that night the troops along the southern side of the pass stole back through Happy Valley under the ominous bulk of Dologorodoc into the main Ascidera Pass, while those on Cameron Ridge were relieved and General Beresford-Peirse and his staff considered the next step – just twenty-four hours after Wavell had told Dorman-Smith that XIII Corps were not to advance further into Tripolitania.

It was quite evident by now that courage and physical toughness were not enough to take the Indians to Keren. Such an attempt must be backed by a well-stocked supply base, launched under cover of massive artillery bombardments, supported by adequate reserves and kept in movement by transport other than weary feet and porterage other than aching backs; one of the enormous advantages enjoyed by the Italian defenders was an efficiently run pack-mule service forward to practically every defence point, and it was particularly galling for the Indian troops carrying everything on their backs to reflect that they had left the best mule transport in the world back at home.

So the main task of building a solid base began and the fighting troops took what rest they could, alternating battalions on Cameron Ridge, while the Central Indian Horse (who had taken the place of Skinner's Horse when Gazelle Force was disbanded and returned to Kassala) guarded the flanks.

During the whole of February, the labour went on. Water holes were bored, disused wells found and cleared; mountain tracks were surveyed, widened and lengthened where considered likely to be useful. Electric generators were brought up, installed and kept going to produce the power for water sterilisation and for ice plants; walls were built out of stone along the approach routes to the pass at night to guard against defilade fire during the day. Wrecked and captured enemy machinery and vehicles were serviced and the railway line which ran back along the Ascidera Valley to Agordat was repaired, rolling stock brought up or dragged out from the tunnels into which the Italians had crashed it during their retreat, the tops sawn off and their platforms blocked to take guns or to bring up equipment. Lorries were fitted with axles long enough for the wheels to run outside the rails and in low gear they could then drag trains of goods vans up the steep gradients; a captured enemy diesel truck was adapted to form a genuine locomotive which then could not only drag water-tanks forward, but could also tow back with some degree of smoothness the trucks carrying the wounded.

While the build-up was proceeding, diversionary threats were made against the objectives by other forces and other arms. A Brigade Group was formed around a 7th Indian Infantry Brigade nucleus under Brigadier H. R. Briggs, consisting of two infantry battalions, a field battery and the Free French Brigade d'Orient of the 14th Battalion of the Foreign Legion and the 3rd Battalion of the Chad Regiment. In January this force had moved from Port Sudan down to Karora on the Eritrean frontier, then down to Mersa Taclai on the coast through which minor port a tenuous line of sea-communication was opened. With this to support them, they now moved south along a thread-like track down towards Keren, their presence sufficient at least to hold the attention of two Italian colonial brigades which might otherwise have been used to buttress the defences above Dongolaas.

And with the capture of both Agordat and Barentu, R.A.F. fighter and bomber squadrons could come forward both to give cover to the troops working in the Gorge and to harass and destroy the Italian rear bases. Eight Wellesleys bombed the Caproni workshops at Mai Edega one night, and two days later a mixed bomber and fighter force struck again, leaving all the main buildings on fire. Asmara airfield was attacked, the railway between Asmara and Keren damaged and even the port installations at Massawa hit – a strike which was repeated a few days later when the aircraft-carrier H.M.S. *Formidable* steamed up the Red Sea towards the Mediterranean to take the place of the damaged *Illustrious*, and flew off two of her Albacore squadrons to attack the harbour workshops.

By March 1st, General Platt had decided on the main form of his next attack – but by this time, there had been startling developments down in the south as well.

General Cunningham had presented his plan for an advance into Italian Somaliland (on a pencilled note, by hand of officer) to Wavell on February 7th and, as has been related, four days later one of his brigades was at Afmadu. The first main objective of the drive was the port of Kismayu, but Cunningham had his eyes firmly fixed on a more valuable prize further east – the provincial capital, Mogadishu. The problem which faced him here was that the river Juba ran into the sea just a few miles east of Kismayu, between two small seaside villages with the unlikely names of Gobwen and Jumbo, and he knew that unless he could cut off the garrison of Kismayu, the river crossings there would be wrecked and the advance on the main objective thus delayed.

With the occupation of Afmadu, therefore, he leap-frogged his second brigade (24th Gold Coast) through the first one (22nd East African) and pitched them forty miles forward to Bulo Erillo, some ten miles short of the river and fifty miles from the estuary. They arrived so quickly that they caught up with the retreating garrison from Afmadu, who then had no choice but to stand and fight. This resistance caused the deaths of eight British officers and N.C.O.s with the men from the Gold Coast as well as over 20 native other ranks, for which price they captured 141 prisoners, four armoured cars and a great deal of fuel and miscellaneous equipment.

Meanwhile, the 1st South African Brigade had also passed through

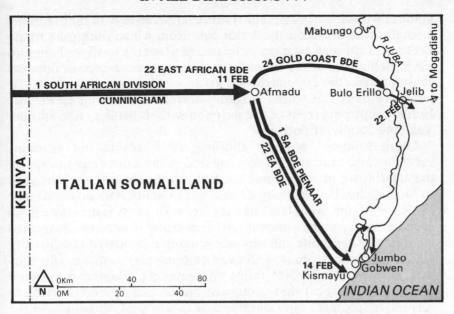

Map 14   Cunningham's advance

Afmadu, turned south and advanced cautiously down towards
Gobwen, where it intended to seize the river crossings and take
Jumbo on the other side. Brigadier D. H. Pienaar and his men were
within striking distance of Gobwen when they heard what sounded
suspiciously like the explosions of demolition charges in Kismayu
port, but as he was under strict orders to maintain radio silence he
continued his advance during the early night of February 13th/14th,
his twelve light tanks encountering traffic problems with what were
quite obviously streams of evacuees from the main objective. The
next morning, Pienaar led his men into Gobwen to find it empty,
but the essential pontoon bridge had been destroyed and a strong
and evidently determined enemy was entrenched on the opposite
bank.

Meanwhile, naval units which had been watching Kismayu had
signalled Cunningham on the previous evening of the developments
in the port and he had in turn instructed the 22nd East African to
get down from Afmadu 'at the double'. They entered the port on
the evening of February 14th – six days ahead of schedule – and
despite the demolitions carried out twenty-four hours before, the
first supply convoys were streaming up from Mombasa within a
week.

By this time, the Royal Natal Carbineers of Pienaar's brigade had
found a crossing twelve miles upstream and carried it in grand

manner by assault boats. The Transvaal Scottish with them formed a small bridgehead on the other side from which during February 17th and 18th they beat off determined attempts to wipe them out, while behind them the brigade engineers threw a second pontoon bridge across the 200-yard-wide river – under fire all the time; on February 19th the whole brigade stormed across and down into Jumbo, capturing most of the garrison with its artillery and another welcome supply of petrol.

There followed a hasty shuffling of forces to net as many survivors and evacuees as possible and at the same time to capture the small town of Jelib, opposite Bulo Erillo and blocking the road to Mogadishu. By February 22nd it was in South African hands with evidence of the complete disintegration of local Italian forces all around. Such was the atmosphere of control in the hastily constituted headquarters, despite the now thoroughly dilapidated condition of all vehicles, tanks, guns, and even clothing and footwear (for they had advanced over 500 miles of appalling country from their railhead at Nairobi) that groups of armed enemy troops trying to surrender, some of considerable size, were sent off back into the bush with orders to come in again in one, two or even three days' time when arrangements might be made to attend to their wishes. So far as was ever known, all groups obeyed – thankfully, for the surrounding country was wild, arid and inhospitable.

In this regard, Cunningham sent a message to Wavell suggesting that in view of the promise opening before him, could something be done about retaking the port of Berbera in British Somaliland in order that his own lines of communication would be shortened if his momentum took him that far? – a request to which Wavell replied that a force from Aden *could* be spared to attack the port, but that Cunningham would have to man the base with his own units if he wanted it to be operational – a somewhat dampening proposal, as Cunningham was as short of base units as everyone else.

Moreover, he still had his left or northern flank to guard. There was no point in jorrocking off on a 250-mile gallop along the coast to Mogadishu if it left the force there with vulnerable lines of communication, in danger of investment followed by a highly embarrassing evacuation by the Navy. One should not take unnecessary chances even with an enemy who showed every sign of disorganisation – and in any case, it was becoming evident that other races than the Italian were finding the presence of the invading forces unwelcome.

The first signs of this had appeared during the attempts to infiltrate into southern Ethiopia in January when it was found that the tribal chiefs there had no love at all for the Amharic Christian Emperor's somewhat feudal rule, and having been left more or less alone by the Italians saw no reason for the *status quo* to be disturbed. Their somewhat primitive customs with prisoners, too, although useful in influencing Italians to give themselves up when cut off, indicated that it might not be wise to leave lines of communication unguarded, or pickets unsupported or too isolated. It was therefore not until Moyale was taken and a line held along the southern Ethiopian frontier from which a strong advance northwards could be launched if necessary, that Cunningham felt reasonably safe on that front, and even then a holding force installed at Mabungo, ten miles north of Bulo Erillo and on the Juba, had to fight off quite a heavy attack made by a mixed and unidentifiable force on the same evening that Jelib fell.

None the less, he felt confident enough to send off the 22nd East African Brigade the following day on the road to the capital. They reached Modun before encountering any opposition, and this was overcome with the aid of naval units who bombarded the town just before it was entered; then the 23rd Nigerian Brigade passed through them and were in Mogadishu, unopposed, by February 25th. As Cunningham pointed out in his triumphant cable to Wavell, on this latest leap forward, his troops had advanced 235 miles in three days.

But the Commander-in-Chief's thoughts were no longer on East African affairs. Mr Anthony Eden and Sir John Dill had arrived, and Balkan politics were engaging all attentions.

To Mr Eden, just beginning his third and what was to prove his longest term as Britain's Foreign Secretary, it appeared that great changes had taken place in the strategic situation in the Middle East since his previous visit in October. Then he had felt strongly that his task was to curb the Prime Minister's enthusiasm for the Balkan Front, to support the Commanders-in-Chief in their wish to build up their forces in Egypt, and even to abide by General Wavell's concern for secrecy to the extent of giving Mr Churchill no hint of the plans for *Operation Compass* until he got home and could do so in person, despite the tone of the cables he had been receiving from London during the visit.

If his attitude on that occasion had been in any way influenced by his position as Secretary of State for War (elevation to Foreign Secretary had only taken place two days before Christmas) then it had also been backed by the attitude of the Greek Prime Minister, General Ioannis Metaxas, who was quite explicit in his views that he did not want a conspicuous British military presence in his country, unless it was also large enough to repulse the German aggression it was almost certain to provoke. And the three or four regiments of artillery, the anti-tank regiment, the pair of anti-aircraft batteries and the single regiment of cruiser tanks which were all that Britain was offering him as late as mid-January were not, in the General's view, enough to check the force which an incensed Führer might dispatch down through Yugoslavia and/or Bulgaria into Greece for much longer than it would take to organise a hasty retreat. A few squadrons of aircraft to help push the Italians further back into Albania was one thing; an army to confront the Wehrmacht was something entirely different.

But now, suddenly and dramatically, Metaxas was dead – struck down by a heart attack on January 20th, five days after his last meeting with Wavell; and although the new Prime Minister M. Koryzis had at first proclaimed that his attitude in all things was practically indistinguishable from his predecessor's, he had now suggested that perhaps a closer look at the kind of defence line which could be held in Greece by joint Anglo-Greek forces might be desirable.

Mr Eden felt very strongly that this examination should be carried out and, if M. Koryzis asked for it, as much military aid – men, guns, tanks, aircraft – as could be assembled in the Middle East should be sent to him. Britain, in Mr Eden's opinion, had of late broken or at least left unfulfilled far too many promises, had renegued on too many obligations – to the League of Nations over sanctions against Italy during the Abyssinian War, to Czecho-slovakia at the time of Munich, to Poland when the war broke out. Over the first, he had resigned from the position of Foreign Secretary in Mr Chamberlain's government, over the others he had been deeply disturbed; and if M. Koryzis now wished to invoke the terms of the agreement made with Britain on April 13th, 1939, under which Britain would come to Greece's aid if her independence was in any way threatened, then he, Anthony Eden, would exert all his influence to see that this time his country honoured her obligations, despite the fact that it might be very inconvenient, despite the fact also that the agreement had been made originally by Mr Chamberlain.

There was, indeed, much more than just his own feelings to support his attitude. On February 10th, four days before he and Sir John Dill had left England, there had been a meeting of the Defence Committee at which the whole situation in the Middle East was thrashed out. The advantages of an advance by General O'Connor's forces to Tripoli were obvious – but even if the port were captured at once and at minimum cost, its subsequent defence would make heavy demands on the resources which might be better used in preventing a German encroachment into the Balkans.

In previous discussions on possible developments in the Middle East, the Chiefs of Staff had always argued that Britain's most advantageous first ally in the area would be Turkey – from whose airfields bombers could attack Rumanian oil, and within whose boundaries armies could either block Axis aggression down towards the vital oilfields in Iraq or in the course of time mass for their own aggression 'up' – to use one of Mr Churchill's favourite expressions – 'through the soft underbelly of Europe'.

But M. Koryzis's recent inquiry, backed by his explicit affirmation that whatever support or lack of it was granted his country, Greece would defend her national soil against German aggression even if she had to do so alone, had caused a shift of opinion. Turkey's attitude was still uncertain and so, come to that, was Yugoslavia's; Greece's attitude was a rock upon which plans could be based. As evidence accumulated during January of an ever greater German build-up in Rumania, coupled with reports from agents of the sinister appearance of hordes of German civilians and officials in Bulgaria similar to that which had preceded all previous occupations of neighbouring countries by the Nazis, the question which had to be answered was – what would Turkey's reaction be if, in the face of a German invasion of Greece, Britain did nothing to help?

It was unlikely to be favourable to British interests – certainly not as favourable as if Britain honoured her agreement and demonstrated that when she *could* do so, then she *would* aid those who stood up to the Axis Powers. If an Anglo-Greek defence proved successful, then perhaps Turkey would come in on the Allied side quickly; if it did not prove successful, then Turkey could still become an ally when the tide at last turned against the Axis. The first thing to find out was the most advantageous way for British military capacity in the Middle East to be co-ordinated with Greek defence capabilities, and this was the main purpose of Mr Eden's journey. Talks with Turkish and perhaps with Yugoslav leaders would follow, but Greece was to be the primary and immediate recipient of British attentions.

In the meantime, Middle East Commanders-in-Chief were instructed to initiate such plans – including the collection of shipping – as would enable them to move the maximum forces to Greece at the earliest possible moment. Just before Mr Eden left England, he was given figures which seemed to indicate that General Wavell would be able to supply a force consisting of three infantry divisions and two armoured brigades, while Air Chief Marshal Longmore could promise at least another three bomber squadrons and an army co-operation squadron.

Mr Eden was also given with appropriate solemnity what the Prime Minister referred to as his 'sealed orders', which he opened during a stopover at Gibraltar to find that he had been granted a freedom of action and judgment which few envoys have enjoyed since the invention of the telephone or the radio, and which was a gratifying indication of the regard, and indeed affection, in which he was held. He was to initiate any action he felt desirable with the Commanders-in-Chief, with the Greek, Yugoslav and Turkish Governments, to judge himself what was the minimum garrison necessary to ensure the safety of the western frontier of Cyrenaica and what were the necessary steps to be taken to make Benghasi a practical and efficient naval and air base . . . Above all, his main objective was to provide Greece with speedy and effective help.

The journey from England was delayed by very bad weather conditions but when they eventually arrived, Wavell was waiting with the British Ambassador to greet them. He regarded them briefly with the contemplative expression he sometimes wore, murmuring, 'You have been a long time coming.'

There was a short explanation, at which Wavell nodded and continued, 'As you were so long I felt I had to get started, and I have begun the concentration for the move of troops to Greece.'

Co-operation on all sides could not have been greater.

One simple, immutable fact had to be faced by all in this situation. If troops, aircraft, tanks, trucks, field-guns, anti-aircraft guns and signal equipment went to Greece in the quantities required to stem a German invasion, then the rest of Wavell's command would have to go short. As his biographer John Connell put it so cogently:

> One soldier could, for a time, do the duty of two; one radar set could be overworked till it fell apart; but neither man nor radar set could do the same job at the same time in two different theatres of operations many hundreds of miles apart.[5]

In order to put the Greek expeditionary force together, Wavell began by crossing some total impracticabilities off the list of theoretical possibilities.

For instance, no matter how high the demand for troops in the Balkans, the 4th and 5th Indian Divisions could not be withdrawn from East Africa without a prolonged disengagement operation which would not only throw away their recent gains, but also so disorganise both formations that they would be virtually useless for any purpose other than random reinforcement of individual units for some time to come. In addition, visions of quickly withdrawing the experienced 7th Armoured Division from the desert and whisking them away to perform prodigies of valour in the Greek mountains must also be discarded; the division was, in fact, already back in Cairo, gazing affectionately after the twelve cruiser and forty light tanks which were all that was left to them disappearing into the work-shops, wondering when and where they would get some replacements. As for the 11th Hussars, they too were back in Abbassia, their last Rolls-Royce cars gone for ever, their Morrises in the repair shops and the few new Marmon-Harringtons which they had received from South Africa being regarded with some scepticism by the old hands, who could spot fundamental insufficiencies a pistol shot away.

All that was left, then, of the formations which had already seen action was the 6th Australian Division which, with the totally unblooded 9th Australian, had been intended to form the 1st Australian Corps under Lieutenant-General T. A. Blamey, to take XIII Corps's place in Cyrenaica. In reserve there was still the New Zealand Division at last up to three brigades, the newly arrived, virtually untrained and poorly equipped 7th Australian Division, a Polish Brigade formed in the Middle East from soldiers who had escaped when their country was overrun, and a British infantry division hastily formed around the nucleus of the British 16th Infantry Brigade by the addition of garrison troops scraped from Mersa Matruh and Palestine. This motley collection had been given the number and name of 6th British Division and earmarked, in the absence of the promised Special Service Brigade, for the attack on Rhodes and the subsequent garrisoning of the rest of the Greek islands.

As for armour, only the untried 2nd Armoured Division had any tanks at all, its cruisers already worn when they arrived in Egypt and now in need of new tank tracks, as a result of training in the desert plus the wear and tear of the journey up into Cyrenaica. No spare tracks had been sent out with them and a supply quickly manufactured and rushed out from Australia were proving impractical in desert conditions.

The three divisions for Greece must therefore comprise the New Zealand Division plus two of the Australian divisions; the armoured brigades must come from the 2nd Armoured, somehow. But what would this leave to protect the Benghasi flank, the hard-won gains in Cyrenaica?

It would *not* leave General Maitland Wilson and his staff, for one of the earliest decisions taken after the arrival of Mr Eden and Sir John Dill was that in order to convince the Greeks that the British were serious in their wish to support them against aggression, any force sent to their country must be commanded by a senior and preferably well-known general – and except for General Wavell himself, Maitland Wilson was the only military figure known to the public at all. Thus he would go to Greece.

The obvious choice to take over the governorship of Cyrenaica and military control of the area was, of course, General O'Connor, but he had been unwell with stomach trouble during the last days of the Beda Fomm campaign, and had been sent off for a well-deserved rest in Palestine – happily with his wife who was still in the area. Upon his return he would take up Maitland Wilson's old position as Commander, British Troops in Egypt at the Cairo Headquarters, though much to his dismay when he discovered it, his well-trained and experienced staff organisation had already been broken up and its individual members allocated to other formations. Brigadier Harding was to go as B.G.S. to Maitland Wilson (who at least promised O'Connor that he could have him back when next he received a corps command), his chief engineer and transport officers were earmarked for Greece, his chief gunner for Rhodes. Dorman-Smith was back in Palestine. O'Connor was later to write:

> A Corps staff is a most complex affair and does not begin to work well, even if the individuals are well trained, until it has been running for some time . . .
> A battalion is not put into battle without being trained in its duties, yet the authorities never seem to hesitate to land a campaign with an entirely new staff, who may never have met before and know nothing of each other's peculiarities.[6]

The only senior officer left in the area to take command in Cyrenaica at that moment was Lieutenant-General Philip Neame, V.C., of whom Wavell later wrote:

> I did not know him well; he had had the 4th Indian Division and had then gone to Palestine to replace George Giffard. He was a Sapper, and had been an instructor at the Staff College, and was the author of a book on strategy, so I accepted him as a skilful and educated soldier; and his V.C. was a guarantee of his fighting qualities. He was at this time a great friend of Dick O'Connor's for whose judgment I had much respect.[7]

But even a winner of the Victoria Cross cannot be expected to hold a newly conquered province without adequate forces, and as day followed day, General Neame saw more and more of his command being whittled away. The first to go was General Blamey and the Australian Corps Headquarters, followed shortly afterwards by the whole of the experienced 6th Australian Division. Moreover, even the unblooded 9th Australian Division which came up to take its place was not complete, two of its relatively well-equipped brigades changing places with two from the raw 7th Division, thus endowing Neame with an infantry component totally inexperienced and mostly ill-equipped.

As for armour, all he eventually retained was just one of the 2nd Armoured's brigades – the 3rd – and a part of the division's Support Group; and of the 3rd Armoured Brigade's 86 tanks (out of a full complement of 156), those allocated to the 6th Royal Tank Regiment were captured M13s, hastily repaired and adapted at the Abbassia workshops, without radio and therefore unable to carry out the tactics in which the crews had been so painstakingly trained.

At least he was left with the King's Dragoon Guards up in the 11th Hussars' old pitch around El Agheila, with their Marmon-Harringtons.

Mr Eden spent his time in Cairo in earnest conference not only with the Ambassador and Generals Wavell and Wilson, but also with the American Colonel William (Big Bill) Donovan who had been touring the Balkans on behalf of his Government. He had much of interest to tell Mr Eden of local morale and opinion and promised to retail to Mr Roosevelt one special plea. The moves to Greece during the next few weeks would throw an enormous strain on British shipping capabilities in the Mediterranean, and anything the President could do to help would be most gratefully received.

Needless to say, Mr Eden was also the recipient of cables from the Prime Minister during his two days in the Egyptian capital, mainly spurring him on to efforts to bring about the longed-for Balkan Front, but one containing an unexpected passage:

Do not consider yourselves obligated to a Greek enterprise if in your hearts you feel it will be only another Norwegian fiasco. If no good plan can be made, please say so. But of course you know how valuable success would be.

This strangely hesitant note in the Prime Minister's missive left Eden unmoved. He had already talked over all possible courses of action with practically every senior military figure in the British service, and his diary entry for February 20th reads:

Met three Commanders-in-Chief and Dill at Wavell's office where we went into a three-hour session. There was agreement upon utmost help to Greece at earliest possible moment. There is grave risk in this course and much must depend on speed and secrecy with which it can be carried out. But to stand idly by and see Germany win a victory over Greece, probably a bloodless one at that, seems the worst of all courses. If we are to act we must do so quickly and we decided at a conference at Embassy later in the day that we would propose ourselves for a secret conference in Greece on Saturday.[8]

But it did seem as though responsibility for the decision to go to Greece had subtly shifted from London to Cairo.

They flew to Athens on February 2nd – Eden, Dill, Wavell,

Longmore and a Captain Dick, R.N., as Cunningham's representative. There they were met by senior Greek generals all muffled in civilian clothes and motored discreetly to the Royal Palace at Tatoi, where it was considered that their conferences could be held in appropriate comfort and security. The first meeting was between Eden and M. Koryzis alone, at which the Greek Prime Minister handed over a note which stated again, quite unequivocally, Greece's determination to continue the war at Britain's side until final victory and that she would defend her native soil against any invasion, if necessary alone. The King wished the British Government to know of this resolution before any conversations took place, and before he or his Government knew whether any British help would be available or not.

With so clear an affirmation of purpose as foundation, it only remained to examine the military situation and make plans to integrate the British and Greek armies to their greatest mutual benefit – and the first note of complete accord was struck by the pleasure and appreciation shown by the Greek Commander-in-Chief, General Papagos, when Mr Eden announced that Maitland Wilson would command the British and Commonwealth force.

From then on it was almost a matter of simple mathematics. The bitterly cold winter had caused enormous suffering and casualties among the Greek troops fighting in Albania, where the evident build-up of Italian forces had drawn troops away from the Bulgarian frontier. There were thus far too few troops left in the eastern sector to hold back a German invasion force driving south down through eastern Macedonia or Thrace towards Salonica, especially if a large-scale Italian drive out of Albania was mounted at the same time, while if the Germans instead came down through a compliant Yugoslavia, then there would be nothing in the middle to stem the tide except the British – if they arrived in time. And every indication was that time was of the essence.

What forces did the Greeks have? What forces could the British send?

The sum was not encouraging. Grasping the nettle, General Papagos admitted that his forces along the Bulgarian frontier were a waste of strength as they could never hope to defend Salonica against any worthwhile attack, in view of the lack of depth between the enemy frontier and the sea, plus the extremely vulnerable east–west communications running along the coast. Work on defence lines along the valleys of both the Nestos and the Struma had commenced, but these would be completely outflanked and useless unless the Yugoslavs successfully stemmed any German advance down through their country – and as Yugoslavia's attitude was uncertain, the wise course would be to assume the worst, abandon the Nestos and Struma lines and build another one down from the Yugoslav frontier through Edessa and along the Vermion Mountains, south across the valley of the Aliakmon and then on to the sea across the northern face of the Pieria-Olympus range.

Into this line, Papagos could put thirty-five battalions, mostly withdrawn from eastern Macedonia and Thrace, but some from the Albanian front which he was prepared to shorten. He could hold one division back in reserve, perhaps two if the Greek hospitals could clear enough rested and recovered casualties, and with the British and Commonwealth forces this defensive position would prove quite formidable, even against Generalfeldmarschall List's Twelfth Army and General Freiherr von Richthofen's Fliegerkorps VIII which, according to Allied intelligence, was massing against them.

General Papagos would need twenty days to withdraw his forces to that line; how quickly could the British forces close up, realising that they would now have to be landed at Piraeus and Volos as Salonica would be far too vulnerable to German air attack?

As the answer to this question would depend upon shipping factors which had not yet been worked out, no firm response could be given then – but as some consolation it was pointed out that when the British did arrive their mobile units would be able to act in front of the Aliakmon Line as a delaying force. And they would come!

In the meantime, could work start immediately upon improving communications so that the British armour could move up as quickly as possible once it had landed?

At a final plenary session late on February 22nd, total agreement was reached upon the military plans, and as far as the political side was concerned, Mr Eden would approach Prince Paul, Regent of Yugoslavia, and endeavour to persuade him to harden his attitude to the dictators. If he would, all well and good, but preparations should at once be made and put into execution to withdraw the Greek advanced troops in Thrace and Macedonia to the line the allied force would be obliged to hold if the Yugoslavs did not come in.

The conference ended with expressions of trust and the utmost goodwill between all parties, and pledges of mutual co-operation until victory was secured. Mr Eden and his party returned to Cairo the next day, deeply impressed by the courageous attitude of the Greek leaders, and after a brief exchange of signals the War Cabinet in London approved the scheme – subject to agreement with the Governments of Australia and New Zealand. Mr Churchill's final exhortation on the subject read, 'Therefore while being under no illusions we all send you the order "Full steam ahead".'

It is always easy to be wise after the event, and no explanation has ever been given of the fact that no written version of the agreements reached between the British and Greek military leaders was drawn up and signed by both parties. Mr Eden made the agreed approach to Prince Paul, then on February 26th went to Ankara where he had friendly discussions with the Turkish leaders at which it was decided that, as things stood, it would be better for Turkey to remain out of the war unless she was herself deliberately attacked – at least until her many military deficiencies were made good. She guaranteed, however, to remain loyal to her alliance with Britain.

On the evening of February 27th, while still at Ankara, Mr Eden received a reply to his inquiry to Prince Paul, which was friendly – but uncertain enough in tone to make it quite clear that neither Greece nor Britain would be wise to depend upon Yugoslavia offering much resistance to an invading force; in the circumstances, all felt they had been wise to plan the retreat to the Aliakmon Line as a matter of urgency.

The events of the next few days seemed to confirm this feeling, for on March 1st, German troops crossed the Danube and moved in large numbers to positions around Sofia and Varna – with the agreement of the Bulgarian Government which at the same time announced itself wholeheartedly on the side of the Axis Powers. The danger to Greece was apparent to all; but for the moment there was nothing that Mr Eden could do, for appalling weather conditions marooned his party at Ismid on the Sea of Marmara.

They did not arrive in Athens until the afternoon of March 2nd – there to be told to their horror that no orders had yet been given for the transfer of Greek troops back from Thrace or Macedonia, apparently because General Papagos was under the impression that it had been agreed that such moves would not be made until a reply had been received from Yugoslavia to Mr Eden's approach. Moreover, in view of the German advance into Bulgaria, it was now too late for such manoeuvres, for not only would they have a disastrous effect on the morale of the Macedonian people, but they would lay the whole force open to the danger of destruction en route by German armies catching them in the flank.

The next few days were spent in talks sadly much less agreeable than the ones of two weeks previously, and no one would claim that the compromise finally achieved was in any way satisfactory in form – and certainly not in outcome. No one was happy, least of all the Commanders-in-Chief, Middle East.

But as it happened, when eventually Wavell did return to Cairo he was greeted by one piece of excellent news, and although it came from the same direction as all the best news had come of late – from Libya – it concerned a location of great importance over 400 miles from Beda Fomm, and it also concerned a special force which Wavell had sponsored since the previous July, and which promised to be of exceptional value.

Despite the recent birth of this force, its roots lay in the past – in the fighting which had taken place in the Western Desert twenty-four years before.

In the First World War, Italy had been an ally of Great Britain while the Senussi Arabs of Marmarica were, via the Turks, allied to the Central Powers. During 1915 the border areas between Libya and Egypt had been the scene of several minor skirmishes, and at the end of that year the Senussi, aided by Turkish money and German efficiency, had invaded Egyptian territory as far as Mersa Matruh. Quite a large number of British and Australian horsed cavalry units were engaged in holding back this incursion, but – like their successors in 1940 – had soon found their theatre of action limited to the coastal strip by problems of supply, especially of forage and water. The use of camels went only a little way towards solving the problems, for the Senussi were not only far more knowledgeable than their adversaries in the ways of the beasts, but they also knew far more about the terrain – virtually unmapped – away from the coastal belt.

It was in order to neutralise both these enemy advantages that Yeomanry Light Car Patrols had been set up in 1916. Using Model T Fords with 'oversize three and a half inch tyres' these patrols ranged well down into the desert, learning the basic techniques of existence there, inventing methods of both navigation and movement for wheeled transport in such conditions, carrying out surveys and map-making, eventually clearing the frontiers and nearer oases of the enemy presence, and then keeping them clear.

In 1917 that phase of the war ended and the following year the Light Car Patrols were disbanded, the men returned to their various more conventional units, the desert to its 10,000-year-old calm.

But it was not to remain undisturbed for very long.

Egypt was the overseas station for several British regiments including those of the Household Brigade, and not all of their officers were content with a social circle limited to the polite confines of Embassy, Officers' Mess and Gezira Sporting Club, varied occasionally by uncharacteristic forays into the Levantine worlds of Greek business or Alexandrine sophistication. Moreover, there was other employment in the Middle East between the wars for the adventurous or curious-minded – with the Sudan Forest Commission or the Egyptian Desert Survey for instance, or with one or other of the archaeological expeditions at work in Egypt, or further afield in the deserts of Sinai and beyond the Jordan.

From among the men and women who thus found themselves in the area had grown up a body of enthusiasts who, learning of the activities of the Light Car Patrols, had ventured out themselves along uncharted ways and into unmapped spaces to acquire again the techniques which the Yeomanry had pioneered, to refine them and to invent new ones – and in so doing had fallen under the spell of that empty, harsh, desolate landscape, which demands so much of its devotees and whose rewards are so fleeting; but unforgettable.

The acknowledged leader of this group was Major R. A. Bagnold of the Royal Corps of Signals, and between the late 1920s and the outbreak of war he organised and led many small parties thousands of miles across the lunar landscape between the Mediterranean and the Sudan, between the Red Sea and the Tibesti Mountains. What began as weekend trips from Cairo to Siwa and back in the 1920s, had by 1938 grown into safaris lasting three weeks and covering a thousand miles or more in trips to Kuffra, 'Uweinat or Wadi Halfa.

When war broke out, Bagnold had been on leave in England and in October had been on his way back to East Africa to a new and unexceptional posting. En route through the Mediterranean (still controlled by the French and British navies and with Italy still neutral) his ship was involved in a collision so the captain put into Alexandria for repairs. During the delay, Bagnold travelled to Cairo to visit old friends. Gossip flew as rapidly as only in the Middle East it can and within a few hours Wavell had learned of his presence; within twenty-four the East African appointment had been cancelled and Bagnold was on the staff at H.Q. Cairo – simply as a communications officer, however, for the political injunction against activity which might offend Mussolini's sense of Mediterranean proprieties was still in force and Bagnold's first suggestion for the formation of a unit capable of carrying out reconnaissance deep into Libyan territory was firmly pigeon-holed.

The Italian declaration of war on June 10th, 1940, quickly put an end to this situation.

On June 19th Bagnold submitted another, and even more deeply considered scheme, four days later it had been approved and by the end of the month he was collecting together the most immediately available of his pre-war collaborators. Their objective was to create a formation which could penetrate deep into the deserts of both Egypt and Libya – to carry out, in fact, the kind of journeys for which they had each lately been paying some £20 per head per thousand miles of their own hard-earned money; now they would be encouraged to do so at Government expense. No one turned the offer down, though some were prevented from joining by superior edict for as long as it took to circumvent it.

W. B. Kennedy Shaw resigned from the Colonial Service in Palestine (where, despite his intimate knowledge of Egypt and the Sudan and his repeated pleas to be allowed to return there, he had been retained since the outbreak of war on the stultifying duties of censoring newspapers) and joined Bagnold in Cairo within a fortnight; P. A. Clayton, one of the few men who had been to Kuffra in the course of duty (with the Egyptian Government Survey Department) came up from Tanganyika, and Captain E. C. Mitford who had also been to Kuffra was posted in from the 6th Royal Tank Regiment, somewhat to his surprise as he had been expecting fairly early action as one of the 4th Armoured Brigade's officers under 'Blood' Caunter.

As they began planning the composition of the force, it quickly became clear what its first assignment would be. Just because the enemy were Italian, it was not enough to assume that they were doing nothing. Italians had already colonised Cyrenaica and Eritrea, had kept in subservience the indigenous though sparse population of Libya for twenty years and had apparently done the same in Ethiopia for four. This could not have been achieved without martial talents and administrative abilities of some order, and if the leadership in the north appeared somewhat hesitant for the moment (and this was still at the time when Balbo was in command) it did not necessarily ensure that the same applied in the south.

The Italians controlled Kuffra and it was known that they had a garrison and landing grounds near Jebel 'Uweinat, the 6,000-foot massif marking the junction point of Egypt, the Sudan and Libya. From Kuffra, they might be planning for an advance down into Chad Province which would influence the French there, still hesitant between Vichy and de Gaulle; from 'Uweinat they could launch a raid across to Wadi Halfa where they could wreck the dockyard and railway workshops, sink the river and lake steamers and thus cut the inner link between Cairo and Khartoum. If at the same time the Italian Navy in the Red Sea – perhaps aided by Italian submarines which would have made the journey around the Cape – could block the narrows north of Djibuti, then there would be no way in which South Africa, Rhodesia, Kenya or the Sudan could send up aid to the Middle East command if and when an Italian advance towards the Delta took place.

These were the possibilities; was the Comando Supremo about to exploit them?

Answers to that and similar questions would obviously be required quickly, and Bagnold and his assistants were spurred to utmost effort – to which end Wavell, who took a close and personal interest in them from the beginning, ordered that the needs of the new force were to be met with the minimum of fuss, opposition or red tape.

The first requirement was for men – and men of a certain type. The British soldier is, almost by definition, a man of infinite adaptability but the necessity for speed dictated that the first teams should be formed from men born and bred to country life as opposed to urban, to the outback as opposed to English pastoral. Australian formations were not immediately available in the summer of 1940 but the first New Zealanders had arrived in the Middle East and from them came the men for the first patrols, possibly – in view of their Government's later attitude – because of the comparative smallness of the numbers required. About a hundred men, mostly from the New Zealand Divisional Cavalry and in civilian life farmers or otherwise independently minded professionals, made up the first patrols – to be followed fairly soon afterwards by Rhodesians and in due course by men from the British Yeomanry Regiments comprising the Territorial Division which had arrived in Palestine. Eventually, too, there would be patrols made up of men from the Guards Brigade.

While the recruitment was proceeding, the problems of transport and supply were also being tackled. Trucks of somewhat greater engine-power and capacity than those used in peacetime would obviously be needed if only to carry the extra weight of weapons and ammunition, of explosives, signal sets and an allocation of medical equipment rather in advance of a motorist's first aid kit. Fords were unavailable, but there were Chevrolet 30-cwt trucks capable of adaptation to take a load of at least two tons with extra leaves fitted to the springs, and doors, windshields and main body tops stripped off. Racks were then fitted for radio sets, water containers, jerricans (when they became available) and mountings welded on for light and heavy machine-guns. All these adaptations and a couple of dozen others had to be carried out not only rapidly, but also with some degree of secrecy. It was fortunate that the American and Greek technicians at Chevrolet in Alexandria and at Fords in Cairo were not only well disposed towards the British, but discreet as well.

One of the most valuable additions to each truck was a radiator condenser, usually in the form of a steel tank bolted to the step. Sealed and half-filled with water, it was connected by tube to the top of the radiator which was itself sealed, the overflow blocked off. When the radiator boiled – which it did with monotonous regularity several times during every day of a patrol – the steam would be condensed in the water of the condenser tank and when the radiator cooled the vacuum thus formed would suck water back until the original balance was regained. If all seals were perfect (which by the

nature of things they rarely were) there would be no need to top the
radiator up from the beginning of the patrol to the end.

Problems of desert navigation had also to be solved, and techniques mastered. From the English Schools in Cairo and Alexandria
logarithm tables were scavenged; theodolites were borrowed from
Egyptian Survey or bought in obscure second-hand shops in half-
forgotten back-streets of Khartoum, binoculars cadged from the
Gezira Sporting Club membership. From the Egyptian Army came
the essential 'sun-compasses' with which direction could be maintained despite the magnetism of the metal truck chassis, which
could throw an ordinary compass ten degrees out. And a ten-degree
error on a 500-mile journey would mean missing the objective by 87
miles; even a two-degree error would miss it by 17 miles, which at
daybreak behind enemy lines might be serious.

Desert navigation was not just a matter of map-reading, for maps
of the major part of the region either did not exist or were
hopelessly inaccurate. A small part of the Egyptian desert was well
mapped (often as a result of the work of the Light Car Patrols or of
members of the pre-war Bagnold parties), a large proportion of it
was indicated on maps by vacant white spaces marked 'Unknown' –
and far too much of the Libyan Desert was splattered on captured
maps with considerable detail which proved on investigation to
have but a tenuous connection with geography. Kennedy Shaw,
who as Intelligence Officer for the newly born formation had to deal
with such problems, later wrote of these Italian creations:

There was no nonsense about the petty details of topography
on these sheets. Many of them were obviously based on air
observation (but not on air survey), and after a few flights across
the country the cartographer had roughed in a range of mountains
here and a sand sea or two there. The mountains were all high as
became the dignity of Fascist Italy. Making our way anxiously
towards an obviously impassable range of hills, we would find
that we had driven over it without feeling the bump. But I have a
certain grudging admiration for Captain Marchesi of the Istituto
Geografico Militare, the equivalent of our Ordnance Survey,
who made the 1/100,000 map of Jalo. Marchesi, I am sure, was a
realist. Jalo, he felt, was a one-eyed hole of which no map was
really needed. The sand was soft and the day hot, so why worry?
Marchesi put his feet up on the mess table shouted for another
drink, and drew his map. It is just possible that the absurd
inaccuracies were a deep plot to mislead our attacking forces, but
it seems hardly likely that the Italians had thought of that as long
ago as 1931.[9]

Eventually, the formation was joined by a professional survey officer, Captain K. H. Lazarus, who would disappear for weeks on end with two or three trucks and reappear with sheaves of pencilled notes and drawings from which, in due course, detailed maps of yet another thousand square miles of enemy territory could be printed. The present rulers of Libya owe a great, though unacknowledged, debt to Captain Lazarus and his assistants in the Long Range Desert Group.

This was the title assumed by the formation gradually taking shape under Major Bagnold's expert guidance. It is possible that only he possessed both the practical knowledge of the problems which the new unit would have to overcome, and the understanding of British Army practice and regulation into which the unit would have to fit. In all corporation life, it is a great advantage to know which is the right form to fill in.

Clayton was the first of the group to venture out, taking six trucks borrowed from the Egyptian Frontier Administration complete with Sudanese crews (the L.R.D.G. trucks and men were still in the process of adaptation and assembly). During the first days of August 1940, he pushed his way south across the Great Sand Sea along a line parallel with the Libyan border to a location known as Two Hills, then westwards and across the border over a gravel plain of excellent going until he reached another sand sea, later to be identified as the Kalansho but at that moment marked on no maps and completely unknown to anyone in Cairo. For two days, they laboured to cross this new obstacle, over range after range of high and convoluted dunes, eventually to reach the Serir of Kalansho along the edge of which ran the main Jalo–Kuffra route.

This he watched for three days – unavailingly, for it had broken up under regular traffic and the Italians had abandoned it in favour of a new track some twenty miles to the west – but by the time he returned, he had learned some valuable new facts and relearned some old ones. Among the first was the discovery of the level plain to the north of Kuffra within the horseshoe of sand seas, and among the second was the desirability of examining footwear for scorpions and other night visitors before trying to put them on in the morning. It is incredible how easily and quickly such habits are forgotten in the cushioned luxury of town life.

In the meantime training was continuing, and as a part of it a vital preliminary chore was carried out. The main routes south-westwards out of Cairo and down past Baharia, either to 'Ain Dalla and across the Sand Sea to Two Hills, or down even further to Pottery Hill and around to the Gilf Kebir, were safe routes still in Egyptian territory and secure except for an occasional marauding enemy aircraft. It was thus possible for dumps to be formed along them and emergency posts set up between the main dumps with supplies of water and food, boots, clothing and medical supplies for victims of accident or attack. In the establishment of such posts much valuable experience was gained in navigation, driving, unsticking trucks and lorries from soft sand, keeping in wireless touch with headquarters despite the vagaries of the radio sets, the problems of 'skip distances' and the infuriating obscurity of ciphers which would not come out.

By the end of August 1940, hundreds of gallons of petrol and water had been cached between Baharia and the western edge of the Great Sand Sea, and an investigation carried out into Italian activities at 'Uweinat. As this revealed that the Italians were doing nothing – nothing offensive, that is – Bagnold decided it was time for his men to venture further afield and tackle the job of crossing the Sand Sea. Kennedy Shaw's description of the obstacle and the task can hardly be bettered:

> There is nothing like these sand seas anywhere else in the world. Take an area the size of Ireland and cover it with sand. Go on pouring sand on to it till it is two, three or four hundred feet deep. Then with a giant's rake score the sand into ridges and valleys running north-north-west and south-south-east, and with the ridges, at their highest, five hundred feet from trough to crest.
> Late in the evening when the sands cool quickly and the dunes throw long shadows the Sand Sea is one of the most lovely things in the world; no words can properly describe the beauty of those sweeping curves of sand. At a summer midday when the sun beats down all its shapes to one flat glare of sand and the sand-drift blows off the dune crests like the snow-plume off Everest, it is as good an imitation of Hell as one could devise. It was across 150 miles of this dead world that Bagnold was proposing to take for the first time a force of heavily loaded trucks.[10]

It took them two days to cross from opposite 'Ain Dalla to Big Cairn, two days of excruciating physical effort in a world full of heat and blown sand, of continual hunting for gaps in the dune ranges, of labouring trucks fighting their way up to uncertain summits, there to be greeted at worst by an unacceptably steep drop in front, at best by a mile-long plough down a treacherous slope spotted with patches of soft sand. Then it all had to start again . . . and for the trail-breaking leading trucks the stops and starts were endless. At one moment you would be steadily forging ahead to the encouraging hum of tyres on hard sand and the thump of gear-changes, the next stopped dead with the back wheels spinning and the truck quickly down to the differential in soft and apparently bottomless dust.

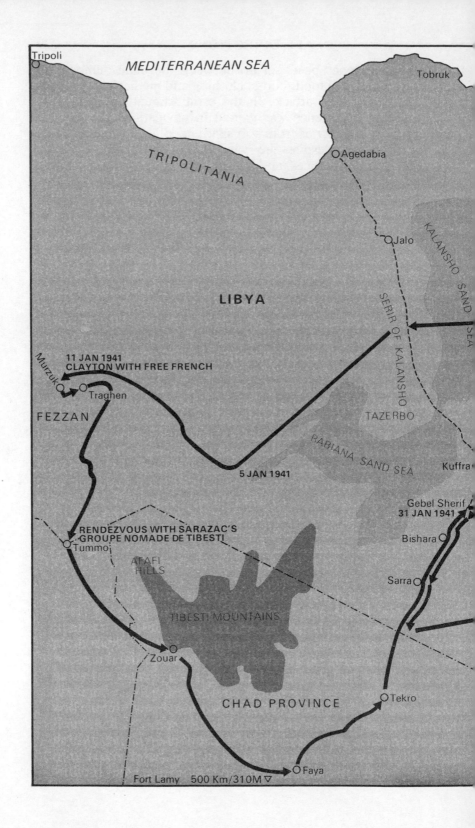

MEDITERRANEAN SEA

Tripoli

Tobruk

TRIPOLITANIA

Agedabia

Jalo

LIBYA

KALANSHO SAND SEA

SERIR OF KALANSHO

TAZERBO

RABIANA SAND SEA

Kuffra

Murzuk

11 JAN 1941
CLAYTON WITH FREE FRENCH

Traghen

FEZZAN

5 JAN 1941

Gebel Sherif
31 JAN 1941

Bishara

Tummo

RENDEZVOUS WITH SARAZAC'S
GROUPE NOMADE DE TIBESTI

AFAFI
HILLS

Sarra

TIBESTI MOUNTAINS

Zouar

CHAD PROVINCE

Tekro

Faya

Fort Lamy   500 Km/310M ▽

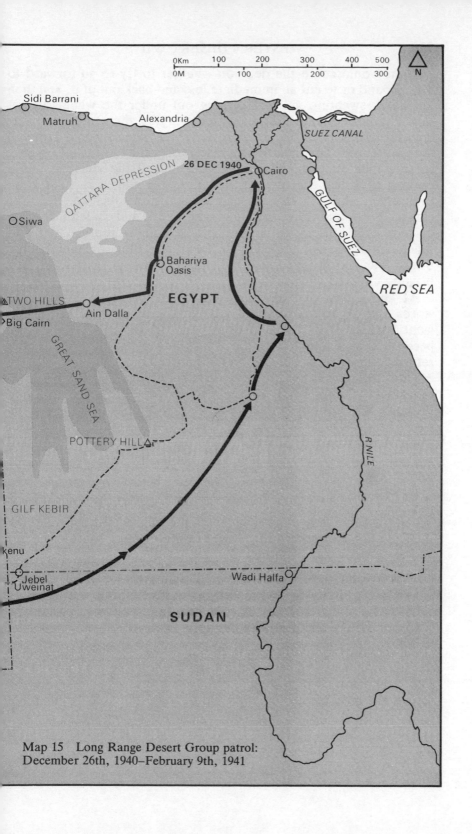

Map 15 Long Range Desert Group patrol:
December 26th, 1940–February 9th, 1941

Then would come the decision whether to try to go forward to firm ground or to cut an immediate loss and back out of it; and then the hard, sweating graft of digging out under the wheels to get sand-channels or canvas strips under the tyres, the gentle and ever-hopeful letting in of the clutch to see if the wheels would grip and not just tear the channels or strip back under the tyres, while twenty cursing men tugged and shoved and rocked the truck to get it moving back just the two-yard length of the mat; then to start all over again. After a day of such labour, every inch of flesh was clogged with sand caked into mud with sweat, and chafed further in by shirt and trousers, collar and belt, all equally impregnated with sand. And it was not helped by the fact that at times the metal of the trucks was too hot to touch with bare hands, at least until they became covered with calluses.

At Big Cairn, virtually on the Libyan border, they unloaded stores and began marking out a landing ground, while one group went back to 'Ain Dalla to bring forward another load . . . and because they could follow the tracks and avoid the pitfalls, the return journey took only six and a quarter hours!

Then the patrols split, Clayton circling Kuffra and driving down the track leading south to the French post at Tekro in Chad Province where he was to investigate possibilities of co-operation with the pro-De Gaulle troops there, while another patrol with Mitford and Kennedy Shaw searched the tracks north of Kuffra and a third made yet another trip back across the Sand Sea to bring forward yet another load of supplies.

At first Mitford's patrol made excellent going across the gravel plain but they hit the edge of the newly discovered Kalansho Sand Sea at the same time as a Libyan *gibli*, the transborder equivalent of the Egyptian *khamsin*, but as it was further south it was also fiercer and even more dehydrating:

> You don't merely feel hot, you don't merely feel tired, you feel as if every bit of energy had left you, as if your brain was thrusting its way through the top of your head and you want to lie in a stupor till the accursed sun has gone down.[11]

All day they fought their way through the Kalansho, emerging in the evening near the Jalo–Kuffra track where the *gibli* developed into a sandstorm which stung their hands and faces unbearably and forced them to button up their clothes and thus secure no relief from the heat. But at least no enemy would be abroad in such revolting weather, so they visited two of the Italian landing grounds along the track and wrecked the petrol pumps and fuel tanks.

The next day they moved even further west in heat which brought men to the edge of delirium, one of the navigators afterwards confessing that for over twenty miles following behind the leading truck he had found himself repeating endlessly to the rhythm of the tyres, 'If he doesn't stop I shall go mad. If he doesn't stop I shall go mad. If he doesn't . . . '

Conditions improved the next day, and three days later the L.R.D.G. went into action for the first time, capturing two six-ton lorries belonging to the firm of Trucci and Monti with their civilian drivers under contract to supply stores and mail to the garrison at Kuffra. A few days afterwards the patrol joined up with Bagnold again in the Gilf Kebir east of Kuffra, hid the lorries in a cave where as far as is known they remain to this day, kept rendezvous with the returning Clayton who brought excellent news from Chad Province and then moved south to take a closer look at the Italians around Jebel 'Uweinat. There was nothing of note to delay them there, and by October 1st all were back at base to receive Wavell's congratulations as soon as their reports, and the contents of the captured mail-bag, had been thoroughly examined.

Other, less tangible but equally important results from the trip had been the impressions brought back from Tekro by Clayton, for the French were enthusiastically for De Gaulle and against Vichy, and uncomfortably anxious to recover the military prestige which had been lost by the sorry misadventures at home four months before. Since the outbreak of war there had been French plans for raids up into the Fezzan if ever Italy showed herself more aggressively committed to the Pact of Steel than she did at the beginning, and French eyes had been fixed upon Kuffra as an objective for attack well before British Headquarters in Cairo had been made particularly aware of its existence.

It was this potential for French co-operation which took Bagnold down to Fort Lamy in November 1940 (when O'Connor was setting up his first Field Supply Depots between Matruh and Sidi Barrani) to explore possibilities, the most significant of which was help with supplies – especially petrol – for an L.R.D.G. raid to the far side of Libya below Tripolitania, culminating in an attack on the town of Murzuk. And if the French wished to send troops to take part in the attack they would be most welcome, as would aid and refuge in French territory for the patrols on their way home.

Colonel Jacques Leclerc, who had assumed command of the French troops in Chad as soon as the governor, M. Eboué, had declared unequivocally for De Gaulle, was more than anxious to collaborate, and indeed suggested that this could well be the time for the attack on Kuffra, with the L.R.D.G. patrols on their way home helping the French in comradely exchange for the French help received on their way out.

This was obviously a situation full of promise, and while it was being thoroughly explored the now-thriving L.R.D.G. grew in both size and experience. Both Rhodesian and New Zealand patrols, each consisting of two officers and about thirty men, were trained and active and two Guards patrols had been formed, one from the 3rd Coldstream Guards and one from the 2nd Scots Guards. During October and November they were all out on separate forays, mining roads leading up from Jalo to Agedabia in the north and between 'Uweinat and Arkenu in the south, attacking isolated garrisons, blowing up explosive and fuel dumps, on one occasion destroying a Savoia bomber caught on a distant landing ground; but chiefly they were learning the duties of reconnaissance – penetration, observation, communication and, above all, survival. No one, inside or outside the Long Range Desert Group, ever gained the impression that it was a suicide squad.

On December 26th, 1940 – while the Australians outside Bardia were recovering from their Christmas dinners and the British were still waiting for supplies – G (Guards) and T (New Zealand) patrols, consisting of seventy-six men travelling in twenty-three vehicles, left Cairo under overall command of Captain P. A. Clayton. On the way past Mena, they picked up Sheikh 'Abd el Galil Seif en Nasr, of the family of paramount chiefs of the Awlad Suleiman nomad tribe who had fought against Italian occupation of Tripolitania since its beginning, and who was himself the veteran of many desert battles. Not only would he act as guide at the crucial junctures of the expedition, but he would also lend an air of Arabic respectability to what might otherwise be seen as a piece of marauding brigandage, by one foreign race against another. Which is what it was . . . but then the sheikh himself was no pillar of polite society, being majestic in girth, fierce in temperament, crippled in arm and leg in some long-forgotten desert skirmish and much given to chewing tobacco and spitting, which could be unfortunate for his travelling companions if the wind was in the wrong direction.

They reached 'Ain Dalla, crossed the Great Sand Sea and the Kalansho beyond, and ten days after leaving Cairo were at the rendezvous point 150 miles north of the Tibesti Mountains. Clayton drove off south to meet the French and collect the essential petrol which had come by camel across from Bardai, while Kennedy Shaw, that indefatigable explorer, tried to ferret out a hitherto unknown route from the west to Kuffra through a rumoured but unidentifiable pass across the Eghei Hills; he was unsuccessful this time, but the route did exist and was to prove useful.

Meanwhile, Clayton had collected the French party consisting of the commander of the French troops at Fort Lamy, Lieutenant-Colonel d'Ornano, a monocled figure, tall, hawk-featured and clad in turban and burnous; Capitaine Massu and an Alsatian lieutenant with two French sergeants and five native troops. There was no doubt that these French meant to fight.

Two days later, on the morning of January 11th (by which time the Australians were moving up to complete the investment of Tobruk) they were ten miles north of Murzuk and from a nearby ridge could see the white roofs, the palms, the radio masts above the fort and the roof of a hangar. It was quite evident that total security had blanketed their 1,500-mile journey throughout its entire eighteen days and that no one in the enemy camp ahead had the slightest inkling of their presence.

They drove into Murzuk after lunch, being greeted by natives around a well with casual 'Buon Giorno's and kidnapping the post-master to act as guide to the fort; then half the trucks peeled off to attack and pin down the garrison, while the rest swung away towards the airfield which constituted the main objective. By the time the second party was in sight of the main hangar the sounds of mortar and machine-gun fire from the fort had alerted the airfield troops, and it became a race towards the machine-gun posts between guards and trucks.

The result was mixed. Kennedy Shaw and Bruce Ballantyne with one group won their race and took prisoner the crews of the nearest machine-gun posts, but Clayton's truck, screaming round a corner of the hangar, ran full tilt into a post as the crew opened up, and as Clayton frantically threw the gears into reverse, the Vickers gun alongside him jammed. There was a short intensive burst of firing, the truck shuddered as Breda bullets ripped along the sides, and then Clayton was back in the shelter of the hangar with d'Ornano dead behind him with blood streaming from a gaping throat wound, and beside him the body of an Italian Air Force sergeant who had also been forcibly co-opted as a guide.

Then the truck with the patrol Bofors came up and quickly put out of action the responsible post and its courageous crew, then turned its heavier metal on to the hangar itself, whose inhabitants were thus caught between Shaw and Ballantyne's machine-gun fire and the Bofors. They quickly surrendered. Inside, Shaw found three Ghibli Bombers which he soaked with petrol, sluicing more over the floor and walls of the hangar and then laying a petrol trail out and across the airfield. The patrol vehicles drew clear, a match was applied and the results were practically instantaneous and dramatic in the extreme. The hangar erupted like a giant torch and, as the L.R.D.G. men watched, the roof collapsed on to the aircraft below while bombs and ammunition exploded in a highly satis-factory display of pyrotechnics. And with the smoke and flame as a background, a string of old African women with bundles of firewood on their heads shuffled with half-bent knees across the airfield exhibiting not the slightest interest in the happenings around them.

Meanwhile, the Guards patrol attack on the fort had set the main tower and flagstaff alight and successfully penned the majority of the garrison inside, as was intended. The exception was the Italian commander who had been out to lunch, apparently with a lady friend and her child; they drove up to the main gate in the middle of the battle and the Guards Bofors was unfortunately turned on the car before it was realised what its cargo was.

Within two hours of the beginning of the attack the patrols were clear of the town again on the route by which they had come in, leaving behind them a burning fort, an airfield with all installations totally wrecked, and some twenty dead bodies. They had also caused such a state of panic and confusion among the Italian command throughout Tripolitania that from then on all garrisons on this unimportant front were to be strengthened, and all vehicle movement along the thousands of miles of desert tracks would be in convoys, guarded by extra armed patrols and as much air cover as could be spared. Italian soldiers and aircraft of the Tripolitania command were henceforth to wear out their boots and engines on sentry go.

The attackers, however, had by no means got off scot free. In addition to d'Ornano, one of the New Zealand sergeants had been killed and four men had been wounded, one of them seriously. (It was later discovered that Capitaine Massu had also been wounded by a bullet through the calf; but he had merely cauterised both entrance and exit wounds with the end of a lighted cigarette and not bothered to mention it to anyone. When questioned as to what he had done with the cigarette end, he replied gravely that he had thrown it away, 'but of course, I had practically finished it beforehand . . . ') In the light of such an episode, his later career is hardly surprising.

They were not pursued by any force from Murzuk, and their fears of air attack proved empty. Moreover, when they approached the small post of Traghen about thirty miles from Murzuk it was evident that nothing was known there of earlier events, and there was no sign of opposition from the garrison who trailed sheepishly out to surrender almost as soon as demands were made. At the next post, however, this pusillanimity was not repeated – and as the fort was of stone construction and the defence resolute, Clayton decided that it was not worth the risk of further casualties. Moreover, it was time to move back into friendly country so he led them south to a rendezvous with a French Camel Corps unit – Sarazac's Groupe Nomade de Tibesti – at Tummo on the border of Libya and French West Africa.

23 The M13 which nearly got there. Rifle Brigade Officers' Mess tent beyond, Lieutenant-Colonel Renton on the left.

24 *Above*, Arabs searching for loot among the abandoned Italian transport after Beda Fomm. 25 *Below*, captured Italian M13s, some in mint condition.

26 The East African campaign: 'Happy Valley'. Fort Dologorodoc is over the ridge to the left.

27 Armoured car manhandled up through Dongolaas Gorge

28 Rommel temporarily in amiable mood. Generale Gariboldi on his left.

29 One of Rommel's dummy tanks on the way up towards El Agheila

30 *Left*, soldier in the field: Rommel signals the advance. 31 *Centre*, the theoreticians: Halder poses with von Brauchitsch. 32 *Right*, the defeated: the Duke of Aosta after the surrender at Amba Alagi.

33 Tactical discussion as Rommel's Feiseler Storch waits to whisk him to another part of the battle

There is a widespread though somewhat insular belief that love affairs with deserts are an English prerogative, and that the only European feet to leave footprints in the burning sand belong to people with names like Doughty, Shakespear, Gertrude Bell, Lawrence, Thesiger and, more lately, Hillaby. This is not so. One of the first and greatest of the camel explorers at the end of the last century was the German Gerhard Rohlfs, and both the Spanish and the Italians have produced notable travellers into the empty, arid wastes of the world. As for the French, after their first incursion into the African continent, they practised desert travel to such an extent as to make it almost an accepted and even unremarkable profession.

Kennedy Shaw was most impressed:

> At times in L.R.D.G. we used to consider ourselves tough, but the life of those French Méhariste officers made one think again. With nothing more than a roll of bedding to spread on the ground they were away for months on end even from the small comforts of their desert posts. We knew that in a few weeks we would be back in the civilisation of Cairo. But the life of the Groupe Nomade is the life of its camels. Camels must follow the changing grazing and the men must follow them, and Sarazac, having finished his operations, would move at once to the scanty pasturage of the Afafi Hills. Added to this – Pétain and Laval being what they were – these men were outlaws from their own country, lost after years of service in the most desolate area of the Central Sahara, having had no home leave for years and with no prospect of leave for years to come. And, perhaps worst of all, with never a word of news from their families in France. Mail day roused no interest in Tibesti.[12]

These were the men who now escorted Clayton's men back through Zouar to Faya, where plans were discussed with Colonel Leclerc, an officer completely in the mould of d'Ornano and Massu, for a joint attack on Kuffra.

It was not until January 26th (the night on which to O'Connor's fury, Babini's armour escaped from Mechili) that Clayton's two patrols left Faya to act as advance guard for the attack, for a great deal of preparation was necessary, especially in view of the distances to be covered. Chad Province main base at Fort Lamy lay 450 miles back behind Faya, while the first stage towards Kuffra would be to Tekro, 200 miles ahead. Moreover, Tekro was the nearest water supply to Kuffra, for both intermediate wells – at Sarra 165 miles and Bishara 270 miles on – had been filled in by the Italians. Water, and indeed everything else, for the 365 miles between Tekro and Kuffra must therefore be carried in the trucks and the ration reduced considerably below the six pints per man per day upon which the trip so far had existed.

Unfortunately, if French military enthusiasm and desertworthiness was admirable, the same did not apply to their security. 'Vers Koufra' had been the toast in the messes and the gossip in the streets for some time, and too much loose chatter on the wireless had taken place for the enemy in the target area to be as unaware of their situation as those at Murzuk had been.

The result was that when, on January 31st, Clayton with T patrol reached Jebel Sherif, sixty miles south of Kuffra, he found himself neatly ambushed in a narrow valley by men of an Italian Auto-Saharan Company, supported by four 20mm. Breda guns and three aircraft. The action which followed was short, sharp and decisive; at the end of it, three of the L.R.D.G. trucks had been burnt out, a New Zealand corporal and two of the Italian prisoners were dead, Clayton and two others taken prisoner (Clayton had been wounded), four men were missing and the remainder of the patrol was in rapid retreat to Sarra where, fortunately, the Guards patrol had been left in reserve. They joined up later that day, and after a brief conference and rest, fell back towards the main French force at Tekro. What none of them realised was that the four men 'missing' had decided not to give themselves up and were following them out on foot.

Trooper Moore from New Zealand, Guardsmen Easton and Winchester and an R.A.O.C. fitter named Tighe had run for cover as soon as their truck had erupted in flame, and had spent the rest of the afternoon crouching among the rocks of Jebel Sherif (accompanied by the remaining Italian prisoner) in a situation aptly described as 'far from pleasant'.

They watched the end of the action, the departure of their surviving comrades, the collection of Clayton and the other two prisoners by the victors, and the Italians' return towards Kuffra without any attempt either to search or to clear up the battlefield. During the extremely cold night which followed the four discussed what to do, and despite the fact that Easton had been wounded in the throat and Moore in the foot, that they had no food and only one and three-quarter gallons of water contained in a two-gallon tin with a bullet-hole through it (fortunately near the top), they overrode the opinion of the Italian prisoner and decided not to surrender. Thus began the first of the series of epic desert walks with which the story of the North African campaign is punctuated.

Three days later, on February 4th, they had reached and passed Bishara, but Tighe was feeling the effects of an old operation and beginning to lag. (Not surprisingly, the Italian prisoner had disappeared during the first day, and eventually made his way to

Kuffra.) On the fourth day the men found some lentils which had been thrown away during a meal on the way up which gave them back a little strength, but next day they decided that they must press ahead leaving Tighe to follow at his own, slower pace. They left him with his share of water in a bottle they had found.

On February 6th, a sandstorm blew up and virtually obliterated the car tracks they were following, but they forced their way on until they reached the mud huts around the blocked well at Sarra. Here the three spent their first night in shelter (the previous ones had been freezing and it had been very difficult to get any sleep in the open, clad only in thin khaki drill), and they found some waste motor oil in which they soaked their feet.

On February 7th, they walked on, and behind them during the evening Tighe arrived at Sarra, took refuge in one of the huts and decided to rest there the whole of the next day. During that day and February 9th the first three slogged on, but the pace had slowed and the gaps between the staggering figures were widening, with Moore always out in front despite the wound in his foot, and Easton now gradually dropping behind. Then during that day, they were seen by a French aircraft which circled around and dropped some food and water; they never found the food and the cork burst out of the bottle as it hit the ground and only a mouthful remained. But late that night a French patrol, sent up to carry out a reconnaissance for another attempt on Kuffra, called at Sarra and found Tighe.

The patrol set out after Moore and his companions at first light on the 10th, found Easton still just alive about fifty miles south of Sarra, Winchester ten miles further on, delirious but just able to struggle to his feet as he heard the trucks – and Moore ahead of him, having walked 210 miles from Jebel Sherif in ten days, on a wounded foot with virtually no food and half a gallon of water. He was quite confident that he could have covered the eighty miles to Tekro in another three days, and according to the Frenchmen who picked him up, seemed rather put out that they had prevented him. He was awarded the Distinguished Conduct Medal – the first won by the L.R.D.G. – but Easton died the evening he was found.

Back in Tekro, Leclerc decided that the conditions for the attack on Kuffra had changed irrevocably, for it would now obviously lack any element of surprise. Moreover, the L.R.D.G. contingent had lost too many trucks and what were left were showing signs almost of disintegration after the battering they had received since leaving Cairo – so except for the best truck and its crew which remained behind to help the French with their navigation, he released the rest. Led now by Captain Bruce Ballantyne after the loss of Clayton, the L.R.D.G. men arrived back at base on February 9th, two days after Beda Fomm, having travelled 4,300 miles in forty-five days, mostly behind Italian lines.

Leclerc wasted little time. He assembled a force consisting of 100 Europeans and about 300 natives, 30 machine-guns, two 37mms, four mortars and a portée 75mm. cannon. They left Sarra on February 17th and during the next two days fought what must have been the first mobile battle of the desert war – between Bedford lorries and Lancia diesel trucks crewed by infantry firing rifles and machine-guns. They were taut, close-fought battles of manoeuvre and counter, of swift pounce and covered retreat – and at the end of the second day, an impartial observer would have been hard put to say whether the French or the Italians were winning.

But as had happened before and was to happen again, when Leclerc's men drove out on the morning of February 20th to renew the action, they found that the Auto-Saharan Company had departed for Tazerbo and left the field to them. By that evening, the French had fully invested the fort at Kuffra, and the 75mm. was lobbing shells into its courtyard while offensive patrols were roaming at will over the entire oasis – for without their mobile screen the garrison were virtually helpless.

During the next week, a curious pattern developed whereby the native inhabitants would leave their homes each morning and spend the day watching the battle, then return home through the investing lines each evening to prepare the evening meal. On February 28th the Italians suggested that the wounded on both sides be placed in an agreed area out of the firing line, but during the consultations which then took place, one of the Italians inquired as to what the surrender terms were likely to be.

Realising that the end was therefore near, Leclerc stepped up the shelling and increased the patrolling and at dawn on March 1st, a white flag was flying from the tower. The Italian rule over Kuffra was at an end.

8 · Enter Rommel

Unfortunately for Wavell – and indeed for the British Army in the Middle East as a whole – as he was reading the cheering reports of the events of March 1st down in Kuffra, other reports, this time on the situation along the most southerly curve of the Gulf of Sirte, were being assessed by a new arrival on the desert scene – one, moreover, who was to stamp his imprint upon the North African campaign to such an extent that no mention of it can fail to evoke his name.

Generalleutnant Erwin Johannes Eugen Rommel had arrived at Castel Benito airfield south of Tripoli on the morning of February 12th and spent the intervening time giving all who came into contact with him an exhibition of the extraordinary mental and physical energy which was to be the hallmark of his command. At this time, Rommel was just nine months short of his fiftieth birthday, a stocky, compact man with no excess flesh, lean features and grey-blue eyes which generally sparkled with both humour and friendliness but which could crackle into blazing fury in an instant.

He had been informed of his new appointment by the Führer himself on the afternoon of February 6th (thus making that week one of the most significant in the history of the campaign) and despite the strict limitations placed upon his activities by the Commander-in-Chief of the Army, Generalfeldmarschall von Brauchitsch, during a subsequent interview, he was quite determined not only that the British advance must be held, but that it must also be thrown back at least as far as the Egyptian border, and preferably further.

Moreover, in view of what he quickly discerned as 'the sluggishness of the Italian command' he had also decided 'to depart from my instructions to confine myself to a reconnaissance and to take the command at the front into my own hands as soon as possible' – a decision which he had imparted to Generalleutnant von Rintelen in Rome, who earnestly advised against it. That was the way, von Rintelen warned, to lose both reputation and honour; but it was a risk Rommel was prepared to take.

Another warning he received within an hour of his arrival in North Africa was from Generale d'Armata Italo Gariboldi, who had taken over command from Graziani upon the latter's not unexpected resignation a few days previously and who now, after listening unenthusiastically to Rommel's plan for the immediate establishment of a strong defence line in the Sirte area – some 200 miles in advance of the lines around Tripoli which Gariboldi had envisaged – gloomily pointed out that Rommel lacked any vestige of experience of desert warfare and had no idea of the difficulties presented by the terrain. To this, Rommel replied crisply that he had every intention of repairing any gaps in his knowledge as quickly as possible, and suiting the action to the word, took off in a Heinkel 111 that same afternoon to fly over the soil of Africa for the first time.

He was by no means discouraged, appreciating immediately the truth behind the remark that the desert was fit for nothing except war. There was a long stretch of undoubtedly difficult country immediately east of Tripoli which would help the defence if and when the British reached that far, but beyond that there was a level plain in which he would be able to deploy his mobile forces, when they arrived, to best effect; while beyond Buerat as far as Sirte lay a stretch of salt marshes which could again provide sound defences if held by stolid infantry. And as Rommel was a great believer in Napoleon's maxim that there are no bad men, only bad officers, he was not unduly concerned at the fact that the only infantry immediately available were Italian, as he intended to command them himself.

When he returned to Tripoli that first evening, he had already made up his mind upon a number of subjects – and his road to success had been smoothed by the arrival of the Chief of Staff of the Italian Army, Generale d'Armata Roatta, bearing with him a directive from Il Duce instructing Gariboldi to place all Italian motorised units in the area at Rommel's disposal. As Rommel was both liberal in his interpretation of the adjective 'motorised', and forceful in argument, the Italian X Corps, consisting of the Brescia and Pavia Divisions, were soon moving up towards Sirte to reinforce the scanty defences already there, while the tanks of the Ariete (only sixty of them, mixed M13s and L3s) were following in its wake.

Moreover, Rommel's first explosion of anger in the Mediterranean theatre was already taking effect. On the day before his arrival in North Africa, Rommel had visited the Commander of the X Luftwaffe Korps at Catania in Sicily, General der Flieger Geissler, and asked him to concentrate his bombing attacks upon Benghasi and the British columns to the south – a request which Geissler had

turned down with some force. He was, he explained, virtually a
visitor to Italy and a none too popular one at that; and he had
recently received strong representations from his hosts to the effect
that he should not bomb Benghasi, as so many high military and
civilian officials owned houses there.

'I had no patience with this,' Rommel later reported with some
understatement, and messages flowed between Rome and the
Führer's Headquarters on the subject. The bombing of Benghasi
started that night and when, six days later, the first British supply
convoy for O'Connor's forces arrived, it found the port under such
strong attack that it had to return to Tobruk with its cargoes still in
the holds.

Rommel's main concern in those first few days was, of course, to
get German formations ashore and up into the forward areas and it
was with considerable relief that he learned that the first convoy had
arrived in Tripoli on the afternoon of February 14th. His immediate
instructions that unloading was to continue throughout the night by
lamplight, despite the dangers of attack by the R.A.F., were
accepted with resignation by the port authorities and the following
afternoon the first contingent of the Afrika Korps, glistening with
self-confidence, paraded through the streets of Tripoli before their
dispatch to the front.

One of the observers was Leutnant Heinz W. Schmidt, newly
arrived in Libya from Eritrea where he had been commanding a
small unit of Germans stranded in the area by the outbreak of war,
and even more newly appointed as Rommel's aide-de-camp. His
account reveals some interesting facets of the Italo-German
alliance:

> It was a bright sunny day, but the Italian population did not
> seem to show a great deal of interest in this display of might. The
> only dense group of civilian spectators was round the platform,
> where Rommel, who was accompanied by several Italian
> generals, took the salute. I stood close to my new chief.
>
> Singly and at regular intervals the Panzers clattered and rattled
> by. They made a devil of a noise on the macadamized streets. Not
> far past the saluting base the column turned into a side-street with
> mighty squeaks and creaks. I began to wonder at the extra-
> ordinary number of Panzers passing, and to regret that I had not
> counted them from the beginning. After a quarter of an hour I
> noticed a fault in one of the chains of a heavy Mark IV Panzer,
> which somehow looked familiar to me although I had not
> previously seen its driver. Only then did the penny drop, as the
> Tommies say, and I could not help grinning. Still more Panzers
> passed, squeaking and creaking round that bend. The road

surface was beginning to show serious signs of damage from the caterpillar tracks. The Italians stared with wide-open eyes, but otherwise were dumb. Where, I wondered, was their proverbial animation and enthusiasm? But I soon understood.

After the Panzers had passed – really passed – the saluting base there was a gap in the column. Then followed, not quite so fast, not quite so noisily, a long line of Italian tanks. The tank commanders showed themselves as conspicuously as they could. Their expressions were bold, daring, audacious. There was an immediate cheer from all sides. The crowd waved and chattered wildly. There were cries of 'Viva Italia!'

With my Staff comrades I pondered over the cool reception of the German troops who had come, after all, as allies to assist in the defence of the city. It seemed that we were tolerated rather than popular.[1]

By the following day, the 3rd Reconnaissance Battalion was at Sirte to be quickly joined by 39th Anti-tank Battalion, while behind them a stream of Volkswagen cars, mocked up to resemble panzers from the air, trundled along the Via Balbia; and if the last element was bluff, the first two were highly efficient, well-equipped and battle-toughened formations. Moreover, they were to be well supplied. Despite more warnings from the Italian command (despite also the difficulties experienced by the Royal Navy in supplying O'Connor's forces by sea), Rommel's quartermaster, Major Otto, successfully organised a flotilla of small cargo boats which carried fuel and ammunition along the coast between Tripoli and Sirte, and later between Sirte and Ras el Ali, greatly easing the pressure on the Via Balbia, not to speak of the lorry columns of which Rommel was suffering from the same shortage as was plaguing his opponents.

Not that Rommel concerned himself greatly with matters of supply. When, much later, he proposed that his command in Africa be augmented by another two divisions in order to allow him to conquer Egypt and then sweep down to East Africa, the Army Chief of Staff Oberstgeneral Halder acidly inquired how, even if he could be spared the divisions, he would supply and feed them, Rommel replied, 'That's quite immaterial to me; that's your problem!' Supply problems in his opinion were the concern of the Staff and the Staff were the servitors of the soldiers in the field; how else did they justify the comfort in which they lived, the regard in which they were held?

It was an attitude at which the Staff-trained purist might well purse his lips and the quartermaster raise his fists to heaven in vain supplication to the insensate gods; but the uncharted capacities of humanity under stress could often make it work, especially when fired by some extra quality of spirit such as loyalty to an inspiring commander.

Every day, as the men and supplies were found and ferried forward, Rommel would follow the hours spent encouraging, persuading, bullying, with more hours in the air above the scene of action, studying the lie of the ground, the capacity of the routes to the front, the areas most advantageous for defence – and more especially, the potential assembly points for the launch of an offensive. For no matter what his orders said or his masters in Rome or Berlin believed possible, Rommel's thoughts were for ever directed towards the attack.

In such a mood, he observed extra British activity between El Agheila and Ras el Ali on February 17th, and the following day the movement of a sizeable British force down from Agedabia towards El Agheila – and to discourage any thoughts which Wavell or his subordinates might have (but hadn't) about a further advance towards Tripoli, he moved his German troops and one Italian battalion under command of Maggiore Santa Maria who had already much impressed him by his aggressive attitude, forward to a new defence line past Nofilia.

These troops were then instructed to move even further forward and let the enemy know of their presence, with the result that during the morning of February 20th two patrols drove past each other along the Via Balbia, only one of which was in any way expectant of the meeting. Both skidded to an abrupt halt and the eight-wheeler armoured car of the 3rd Reconnaissance Battalion promptly swung across the road to block it. On the British side, there was a long moment of question and incredulity ('My God! Weren't those Germans?') and after the briefest exchange of shots the armoured cars of the K.D.G.s, mindful of their chief duty to get back with information, circled around to the south and hastened back to report.

Four days later, at dawn, seven panzers, three armoured cars and a section of motor-cycle grenadiers were waiting by the abandoned fort at Agheila for the early morning British patrols, and as these probed forward across the frontier opened fire on the leading armoured car, badly wounding one of the crew and taking two others prisoner. The second K.D.G. troop swung around to report and an Australian anti-tank troop came up at the same time – and in the general confusion, the anti-tank officer received the impression that it was German prisoners who were being taken and climbed out of his car to assist. Ten minutes later the Germans were roaring back towards Nofilia with their three prisoners, towing one damaged Marmon-Harrington and leaving another in flames behind them, plus a burnt-out lorry and the officer's wrecked staff car. And a number of very red and anxious faces.

On March 4th, Generalleutnant Streich, commanding the 5th Light Division – of which the bulk was still in transit – took immediate command at the front, and on Rommel's prompting moved a mixed force of engineers and infantry up as far as Mugtaa where they sowed the defile with mines – and as salt marshes here extended almost twenty miles south from the coast and across the road, this meant that there now existed a firm block against any British advance at a point already 500 miles east of Tripoli. Three weeks beforehand there had been little or nothing to stop an aggressive task force reaching the outskirts of the port, had they attempted to do so.

One of the most attractive facets of Rommel's character was his total devotion to his wife and son. He had first met Lucie Maria Mollin in 1911, they had become engaged in 1915 and married a year later – and it seems likely that he had cast no significant glances at any other girl or woman before or since. The years which he later claimed to have been his happiest were spent with her and their son, born in 1928, and when they were separated – even by the exigencies of battle – he endeavoured to write to her every day, sometimes twice or even three times. These letters are a valuable barometer of the daily strains and stresses to which he was to be subject:

5 March 1941

Dearest Lu,

Just back from a two-day journey – or rather flight – to the front, which is now 450 miles away to the east. Everything going fine.

A lot to do. Can't leave here for the moment as I couldn't be answerable for my absence. Too much depends on my own person and my driving power. I hope you've had some post from me.

My troops are on their way. Speed is the one thing that matters here. The climate suits me down to the ground. I even 'overslept' this morning until after 6 . . . [2]

At last, the main bulk of the first division of the Deutsche Afrika Korps was well on its way, and although even this was but an offshoot of a complete armoured division – the 3rd Panzer – it nevertheless constituted a solid and hard-hitting force. The 5th Light Division, as it was called, consisted of 3rd Reconnaissance Battalion (already at the front), a 12-gun battery of field artillery, two anti-tank battalions amongst whose weapons were numbered a few 88mm. guns of the class which had already made a name for themselves in Spain and were to emerge from the war as one of the most famous pieces of artillery of all time; and two motorised machine-gun battalions.

These were the ancillary troops; the main striking power of the division lay in its two panzer battalions comprising the 5th Panzer Regiment, with 120 tanks of which half were Marks III and IV, which were certainly the equal in armour and gun-power to everything the British had except the Matilda, whose speed they exceeded by nearly ten miles per hour. But the main advantage 5th Light Division would hold against anything facing it in March 1941 was its practical experience of mechanised warfare, its doctrine of total co-operation between all arms, and its well-developed and intensively practised battle-drill.

There were inevitably some adaptations to be made in view of the unfamiliar conditions the division was now facing – extra air and oil filters to be fitted, carburettors adjusted to take Italian lower-grade petrol, clothing redesigned and rations modified to include more fresh vegetables – but the heart of the division was sound and its attitude young, eager and willing to learn. Rommel's spirits bounded as he watched it move forward along the Via Balbia towards the front where both the division's name and his own would become famous.

Just as valuable from the point of view of an attacking general was the arrival of the first units of Fliegerkorps X under command of Generalleutnant Fröhlich who had been appointed Fliegerführer Afrika. By the time the Reconnaissance Battalion was at Nofilia, Fröhlich had nearly fifty dive-bombers and twenty fighters based on North African airfields and thus available to cover ground operations, and he could also call upon longer-range aircraft based in Sicily. Already they had inflicted casualties on the British troops around El Agheila, who were learning that air attack nowadays could no longer be greeted with sardonic comment or fought off if it came too close with a few bursts from a Bren-gun. The 11th Hussars had lost one of their old armoured cars and its crew to an attack by twenty Junkers 87s, on the day before they moved back to Cairo.

Reports from Fröhlich's pilots were also confirming Rommel's growing conviction that the British were not only devoid of intention for the moment to advance further, but were actually in some disarray, possibly owing to their need to find troops for Greece – a factor of which German Intelligence had kept Rommel quite well informed – but possibly also for another reason, which was beginning to look uncommonly like unimaginative or even unrealistic leadership at a high level.

The more information that came in, the more inviting the

situation appeared; but there were a few minor matters to be dealt with before he could take the necessary steps to exploit it to the full.

On March 15th, at the request of the Italians and with the added intention of both gaining experience and testing equipment in desert conditions, he dispatched a mixed German and Italian column under command of Oberst Graf von Schwerin south towards Murzuk where, it was reported, some of De Gaulle's troops had been making nuisances of themselves; and he also sent young Schmidt, his aide-de-camp, off down to the oasis of Marada with instructions that if he found it unoccupied, he should then make his way some 150 miles further eastwards and discover if the oasis at Jalo was similarly devoid of enemy troops. About this time, he also moved his own headquarters forward to Sirte and in doing so underwent a thoroughly chastening experience:

My original intention was to fly to Sirte in a Ghibli aircraft with my Chief of Staff. After taking off, however, we ran into sand-storms near Tauorga, whereat the pilot, ignoring my abuse and attempts to get him to fly on, turned back, compelling me to continue the journey by car from the airfield at Misurata. Now we realised what little idea we had had of the tremendous force of such a storm. Immense clouds of reddish dust obscured all visibility and forced the car's speed down to a crawl. Often the wind was so strong that it was impossible to drive along the Via Balbia. Sand streamed down the windscreen like water. We gasped in breath painfully through handkerchiefs held over our faces and sweat poured off our bodies in the unbearable heat. So this was the Ghibli [wind]. Silently I breathed my apologies to the pilot. A Luftwaffe officer crashed in a sandstorm that day.[3]

He also gave General Streich instructions to prepare an attack to be carried out by all available elements of the 5th Light Division against British positions at El Agheila, with the object of capturing both airfield and fort and establishing the front line for the Afrika Korps hard up against the entrance to Cyrenaica; the attack to be ready for launching on the morning of March 24th.

Then, on March 19th, after taking another hard look at the British dispositions facing his troops, he flew off to Berlin to obtain permission to take more offensive action, and to ask for sufficient reinforcement to ensure its success.

Rommel was not the only person to be surprised by the state of the British defences along the western flank of Cyrenaica. Wavell paid his first visit to the area on March 16th and was appalled by what he found.

Since the conclusion of O'Connor's offensive, Wavell's hands had been full. Not only had there been the offensive in East Africa to watch and nurture, but also growing evidence of Nazi infiltrations into Iraq, and schemes for Free French activities in Syria – both of which would significantly affect the eastern border of his command. Most demanding of all, however, was the developing situation in the Balkans, the stream of instructions from Whitehall to direct his fullest attention towards every sector on the northern flank from Malta to Turkey, and especially the Eden mission and its decision to send the greater part of his military strength to Greece.

He had had little time to spare for purely tactical matters and had been content to leave these to his subordinate generals. He now discovered this to have been a mistake. From Maitland Wilson he had obtained a totally false picture of the escarpment running south from Benghasi and parallel to the coast, believing it to be similar to the land-cliff running westwards from Sollum and thus impassable except at a few easily guarded points. Had this been so, then mobile forces could have held the passes and flooded down to take any enemy advance on Benghasi in flank, while artillery shelled it from above.

But the escarpment south of Benghasi is in fact not so much a cliff as a line of sloping hills, and a strong enemy force could ascend them almost anywhere and then sweep along the top to wipe out any less efficient or powerful force in its path. And the British armoured force now left in the area lacked both the training and the experience to qualify for the adjective efficient, and it was certainly not powerful.

The core of the defence was the fifty-two cruiser tanks of the 2nd Armoured Division (of which there was only one brigade as the other had been sent to Greece) and of these fifty-two, half were already in the workshops and the rest liable to break down at regular intervals having already grossly exceeded both their track and engine mileages. Some idea of the state of the armour is given by the fact that the 6th R.T.R. men who crewed the captured Italian M13s were comparatively satisfied with their vehicles, which at least kept moving.

Ill luck had contributed yet another deplorable feature to the condition of the 2nd Armoured Division for it had come out from England under command of Major-General J. C. Tilley, but he had died suddenly in January to be succeeded by Major-General M. D. Gambier-Parry, who was thus trying to fit an incomplete force which he did not know at all well into a defence system which was unrealistic to say the least.

General Neame was not living up to Wavell's hopes – perhaps grown too exorbitant on O'Connor's excellences. Wavell later wrote:

I found Neame pessimistic and asking for all kinds of reinforcements which I hadn't got. And his tactical dispositions were just crazy; he had put a brigade of Morshead's 9th Australian Division out into the middle of the plain between Agheila and Benghazi, with both flanks exposed, immobile with no transport, completely useless and an obvious prey to any armoured vehicles that broke through at Agheila. I ordered it to be moved back to the heights above (east of) Benghazi, where there was at least a defensible position . . . I told Neame that if his advanced troops were driven back, he was not to attempt the direct defence of Benghazi, but to pull his Armoured Brigade back on to the left flank of the Australians . . .

I was also appalled at the size and unwieldiness of the 2nd Armoured Division headquarters. Gambier-Parry, though he had only one brigade to handle, had brought forward the whole of his headquarters, with the idea of getting them exercised in the field. All right if they were not attacked but a dangerous encumbrance if they were.

I came back anxious and depressed from this visit, but there was nothing much I could do about it. The movement to Greece was in full swing and I had nothing left in the bag. But I had forebodings and my confidence in Neame was shaken.[4]

One factor which depressed Wavell more than any other was the realisation of the strength of the defensive position in the salt marshes west of Agheila at Mugtaa, which Neame had felt beyond the supply capabilities from Tobruk 300 miles back, but which Rommel apparently considered well within the supply capabilities for his troops from Tripoli 400 miles back; and the Afrika Korps was now immovably entrenched there. Certainly the Via Balbia was a much smoother run for supplies than the Mechili–Antelat tracks or the Trig el Abd – but in March 1941 a touch of Rommel's ruthless attitude towards supply officers would not have come amiss on the Allied side of the border.

However, there was no point in an excess of despondency, and there was always some comfort to be extracted from consideration of the enemy's problems, together with plans to increase them. As Wavell wrote in a directive to Neame:

The enemy's supply and maintenance problem will be a most difficult and precarious one, and do everything in your power to render it more so. Forward dumps of stores are likely to be the surest indication of the offensive intentions of the enemy and should be attacked by air action as far as possible. Similarly, during the advance, attack on his maintenance system will be one of the best methods of bringing him to a standstill . . . Time is pressing and you must put all necessary moves and work in hand without the least delay.[5]

These instructions Neame endeavoured to carry out but, ever mindful of his own supply difficulties and knowing the crucial value which his friend O'Connor had placed upon the Field Supply Depots during his great advance, Neame used what transport he had available firstly to build these up, especially the forward ones at Barce, Benghasi and El Magrun. The problems of troop movement must await their turn, as must those of clearing the battlefield and scavenging the vast quantities of abandoned Italian equipment and supplies.

Back in Cairo, Wavell pondered the situation which would be facing this new opponent, Generalleutnant Rommel, of whom reports were so uniformly flattering, but in view of detailed information now arriving from England in ever-increasing volume, he concluded that Neame and his troops still had some time in hand. Station X, the highly secret decoding organisation at Bletchley Park in Buckinghamshire, was now producing its 'Ultra' intelligence by almost daily reading of Axis wireless traffic, and G.H.Q. Cairo had been warned not only of Rommel's arrival and of the formations already in North Africa, but also of the acceleration of plans for the dispatch forward to Nofilia of the 5th Light Motorised Division, to be followed by the 15th Panzer Division when it arrived in May.

The motorised division was apparently intended to be at the front by March 24th, but as its support would be the Italian Ariete Division with only half its allotted number of tanks and at the most four Italian infantry divisions whose morale would still be suffering from the recent setbacks during *Compass*, Wavell considered that no real threat as yet existed beyond El Agheila. Even the warnings he received from his chief intelligence officer, Brigadier John Shearer, to the effect that an enemy commander of the first rank prepared to take risks and display imagination could already wreak havoc among Neame's dispersed and inexperienced force, were discounted by Wavell as nothing more than the pessimistic presentation by a conscientious staff officer of a 'worst possible situation' report, of the type he had himself occasionally prepared.

It would take at least thirty days to dump into the forward areas the supplies necessary to maintain any forward movement even for the force now available to Rommel, so Neame must have at least until April 16th to make his defences ready for an attack on a comparatively small scale . . . and as Rommel's main reinforcement – the panzer division for which he would surely wait – would not be

arriving until May, after which it would need time for acclimatisation and absorption into the existing force at the front, was it not
more likely that Neame's men would have in fact until June to make
themselves ready to throw back an attack on Cyrenaica?

It would be a serious attack of course, delivered by a mainly
German striking force of almost two divisions, but by that time not
only should Neame and Gambier-Parry have welded their present
command into a strong defensive nucleus, but Keren should have
fallen and Wavell would have one and perhaps two Indian divisions
available as reinforcement, and perhaps a South African division as
well.

Time, for the moment, appeared to be on the British side;
however imaginative, aggressive or daring the enemy commander
might be, he could not ignore the iron laws of logistics.

But Wavell did not yet know Rommel.

Neither, come to that, did his own Commander-in-Chief, von
Brauchitsch, nor even Hitler.

Rommel's brief stay in Berlin was not a particularly satisfactory
one from anybody's point of view. True, the Führer received him
kindly, pressed upon him the Oakleaves to the Knight's Cross in
recognition of his outstanding performance as commander of the
7th Panzer Division during the Blitzkrieg through France, briefly
discussed his report on the situation in Africa and then passed him
rapidly on to the General Staff.

First von Brauchitsch and then Halder listened coldly to his plans
and requests, then made it quite clear that he could expect no extra
reinforcements, no larger scale of supplies than already indicated,
and also that despite the marks of the Führer's favour which
Rommel had in the past received, his command in Africa was not
one of overwhelming importance in the eyes of the High Command.

They did not go as far as to say that the campaign in Africa was
little to them but an unimportant sideshow, for this might have
necessitated revealing their nascent plans: first, for an attack down
through Yugoslavia and Greece to the eastern Mediterranean to be
launched almost immediately; and even more important and thus
secret, those for the Reich's most ambitious and indeed awe-
inspiring project, *Operation Barbarossa*, the invasion of Russia.
But they were quite firm in their declarations that Rommel could
expect no increase in the establishment of the force under his
command, pointing out that its only *raison d'être* was to sustain
Italian morale and to protect their Libyan empire from further
incursions by the British.

Agreed – the best defence might well be to attack the British
forces around El Agheila and push them back perhaps as far as

Agedabia; even Benghasi might be taken. But no further advance should be considered, and obviously even so limited an operation could not be undertaken until the rest of the 5th Light Division and the whole of the 15th Panzer Division had arrived in Africa, and had been given time for acclimatisation. Had they known of it, they might have buttressed their position by pointing out that the opinion of so eminent a soldier as General Wavell almost exactly coincided with their own.

Rommel's protestations that it would be impossible just to advance as far as Benghasi and then stop there were listened to without comment, for both Brauchitsch and Halder were sufficiently realistic to see when it was pointed out to them that geographic factors dictated either the total occupation of Cyrenaica, or its total abandonment; it could not be held by either side *in part*. And their silence indicated that in such circumstances, perhaps Rommel would do best to leave well alone and commit his forces to nothing more than a defensive role.

Certainly, he must not attempt to re-enact his spectacular feat of arms with the 7th Panzer Division in France, which had spear-headed the breakthrough to the Channel coast, earned the division the questionable nickname of the Ghost Division, and brought the High Command to a state of extreme nervous tension. There must be no repetition of that sort of escapade; the Afrika Korps was intended basically as a blocking force, a *Sperrverband*, and its commander – bearer of the Oakleaves to the Knight's Cross though he might be – must obey orders and restrict himself and his troops to the duties which had been allocated to them.

According to Rommel's first biographer, Brigadier Desmond Young, Rommel once called Halder a bloody fool and asked him what he had ever done in war except sit on his backside in an office chair – but it is not recorded if this was the occasion. Whether it was or not, explicit instructions handed to Rommel on March 21st made it quite clear that he was not to consider moving forward until after the arrival of the 15th Panzer Division in May, that Agedabia must be the limit of the first advance and only when the result of that offensive had been carefully analysed would any further action be sanctioned. And he had better report back again in a month's time, in case his superiors should decide that even that first advance was inadvisable or unnecessary.

Rommel arrived back in Africa on March 23rd, and proceeded to disobey his orders with a diligence which compels the admiration of all who have ever cocked a snook at Authority.

The attack on the fort and landing ground at El Agheila which he had ordered for the 5th Light Division before his departure for

Berlin duly took place the following morning, the few British and Australian troops there withdrawing in the face of obviously superior strength. Last to leave was the duty troop of the King's Dragoon Guards, the troop leader only getting out of the fort by the skin of his teeth.

Rommel's description of what then faced him is as transparent a piece of special pleading as one is likely to come across among the literary outpourings of the military commanders of the Second World War, the only difference between it and the vast majority of them being that this is an excuse for action – action moreover which was to prove successful:

> The defile at Mersa el Brega was the first objective for the attack which we were due to launch in May on the enemy forces around Agedabia. After the British had been driven out of El Agheila, they established themselves on the commanding heights at Mersa el Brega and south of the salt marsh at Bir es Suera, and began to build up their position. It was with some misgivings that we watched their activities, because if they had once been allowed time to build up, wire and mine these naturally strong positions, they would then have possessed the counterpart of our position at Mugtaa, which was difficult either to assault or to outflank round the south. The country south of the Wadi Faregh, some 20 or 30 miles south of Mersa el Brega, was extremely sandy and almost impassable for vehicles. I was therefore faced with the choice of either waiting for the rest of my troops to arrive at the end of May – which would have given the British time to construct such strong defences that it would have been difficult for our attack to achieve the desired result – or of going ahead with our existing small forces to attack and take the Mersa el Brega position in its present undeveloped state. I decided for the latter.[6]

An extra reason he gave for the decision to move even further forward was the availability of a better water supply at Mersa el Brega – and another was that Mersa el Brega would give his forces just as suitable a forming-up area 'for the May attack' as the one they already occupied at Mugtaa, an opinion with which both Wavell and Neame would have disagreed had they known of it.

The first probing attacks by 3rd Reconnaissance against the forward British posts at Mersa el Brega began about 0800 on the morning of March 31st, and by 1015 they had driven them back to the main infantry defence positions which were then dive-bombed. The leading tanks of 5th Panzer Regiment then moved up and the rest of the morning was occupied by a brisk tank versus 25-pounder battle, each side feeling out the other's strength, the panzer crews sweating it out for the first time in the close confines of battened-down tanks in the desert at noon. During the early afternoon, the panzers withdrew behind a low rise called by the British Cemetery Hill, which had in the meantime been occupied by some of the 5th Light Division's infantry and artillery, who thus dominated the British infantry positions below. As these were new Territorials (1st Battalion Tower Hamlets Rifles) in their first battle, their position was by no means enviable.

Just after 1400, another wave of dive-bombers struck the British infantry positions and then at about 1630 Generalleutnant Streich, commanding 5th Light, put in an infantry attack through the sand-hills along the coast, backed by more panzers and a machine-gun company, which by dusk had won through to a position completely outflanking the British infantry and threatening their artillery as well. More panzers rolled down from Cemetery Hill towards the main defences, overrunning some forward sections, setting alight some of the British carriers, and through the flame and smoke their gunners sent a few derisory shots after the rapidly retreating British infantry and guns. No British armour had been seen, for when the unfortunate commander of this forward section of 2nd Armoured Support Group appealed for protection, Gambier-Parry withheld it on the grounds that insufficient daylight was left for tank deploy-ment; in view of the reluctance that the far more experienced 7th Armoured Division had always shown to operate in darkness, he was probably right to do so – but it meant that from now on he danced to Rommel's tune.

Rommel, needless to say, had spent the day at the front and in fact, accompanied by his personal aide Oberleutnant Hermann Aldinger and his Chief of Staff Oberstleutnant von dem Borne, he had personally reconnoitred the route through the sandhills along which Streich later sent the infantry attack. He had also kept a close eye on the speed and efficiency with which his panzers and vehicles had been refuelled and restocked, and a far-ranging eye on what lay beyond.

Nothing, he quickly concluded, lay beyond for at least twenty-five miles – and very little there. And as both air and ground reconnais-sance next day (April 1st) revealed little but emptiness back as far almost as Agedabia, he immediately gave orders for all forces to close up to Mersa el Brega and Maaten Giofer, while 5th Light were to be ready to advance and take Agedabia sixty miles ahead the following morning. So much for the value attached to the area around Mersa el Brega as a 'forming-up area for the May attack'.

General Streich had no doubts or hesitations about the advance on April 2nd. The reconnaissance units on their motor-cycle combinations (three men and a machine-gun plus personal arms) rode well forward abreast the Via Balbia, while the panzers and infantry carriers followed on each side, in well-balanced and flexible battle formations capable of rapid switch towards any recognised danger. Those on the southern flank ran into some British armour – and unexpectedly, for these suddenly emerged from under the curious but innocent-looking black folds of some bedouin tents – but the British cruisers were either inexpertly handled or broke down, for seven of them were left blazing in as many minutes; and by evening, somewhat to their surprise, the main body of the Afrika Korps were in and around Agedabia with their advanced units twelve miles further on, and the small port of Zuetina already in their hands.

The following day, April 3rd, Rommel moved his own head-quarters up to Agedabia and then gave perhaps his most classic demonstration of the advantage to be reaped from the occasional disregard of established principles. Faced by an as yet unbroken enemy, he should by all orthodoxy have kept his own forces concentrated; Rommel split his three ways, thereby bewildering his opponents and thoroughly astonishing his Italian superior, Generale Gariboldi.

Divining the disarray which was already loosening control among the British, Rommel sent the Santa Maria Battalion with some German anti-tank units, all under command of Graf von Schwerin who had returned from the expedition to Murzuk, off eastwards first of all to Giof el Matar and then to Ben Gania, with orders to penetrate even further up through Tengeder towards Mechili – thus swinging in a semicircle even wider than that of 7th Armoured's in the opposite direction two months before – to find out if the British really were evacuating Cyrenaica, as appeared possible, and to trap as many of them as they could.

At the same time, he took the armoured cars and motor-cycle troops of 3rd Reconnaissance under his own immediate command and sent them off up to Soluch and Ghemines, and ordered the main bulk of 5th Light to improve their positions forward of Agedabia for an advance to Antelat and Msus. General Streich voiced doubts that morning about the serviceability of some of his panzers, and after brushing aside these objections ('I could not allow this to affect the issue. One cannot permit unique oppor-tunities to slip by for the sake of trifles,') Rommel then dealt in his own fashion with yet another dire prediction by another Italian general.

Warned by Generale di Divisione Zamboni that the track to Giof el Matar along which he had just dispatched the Schwerin Force was a 'death-trap', Rommel, accompanied by Aldinger and Schmidt, set

off and within a comparatively short time had overtaken the head of
the column and thoroughly satisfied himself that the Italians were
trying to place non-existent obstacles in his path. In such a mood he
returned to Agedabia about 1600 hours to be confronted by Streich
maintaining that 5th Light – who had given up some of their petrol
to 3rd Reconnaissance for the probe northwards – were now so
short of fuel that it would be another four days before they would be
able to move forward.

> This seemed to me to be utterly excessive and I immediately
> gave orders for the division to unload all its vehicles and send
> them off at once to the divisional dump at Arco dei Fileni,
> whence they were to bring up sufficient petrol, rations and
> ammunition for the advance through Cyrenaica inside 24 hours.[7]

This would undoubtedly mean that the enemy would remain
unmolested on the central front for the following day, so Rommel
went north to investigate possibilities up there. There he found that
3rd Reconnaissance had made no contact with the British during
that day but had been informed by an Italian priest that they had
evacuated Benghasi, whereat Rommel ordered Oberstleutnant
Freiherr von Wechmar to drive straight into the port – which he did,
to receive a delirious welcome from the inhabitants who could not
offer their gallant allies too warm a hospitality.

3 April 1941

Dearest Lu,
> We've been attacking since the 31st with dazzling success.
> There'll be consternation amongst our masters in Tripoli and
> Rome, perhaps in Berlin too. I took the risk against all orders
> and instructions because the opportunity seemed favourable . . .
> We've already reached our first objective, which we weren't
> supposed to get to until the end of May. The British are falling
> over each other to get away . . . You will understand that I can't
> sleep for happiness . . . [8]

Rommel was certainly right about the consternation in Tripoli, for
Generale Gariboldi had already protested once over the advance
beyond the first agreed objectives at Agheila, had then been
thoroughly outraged by the day's dispersion of effort along three
distinct and divergent paths and now, upon Rommel's return to
Agedabia on the evening of April 3rd, was waiting to bring the full
weight of his superior rank and more ebullient personality to bear
upon his errant subordinate.
It was not a successful venture. Rommel secure in achieved
success might have been amenable to gentle reproof about his

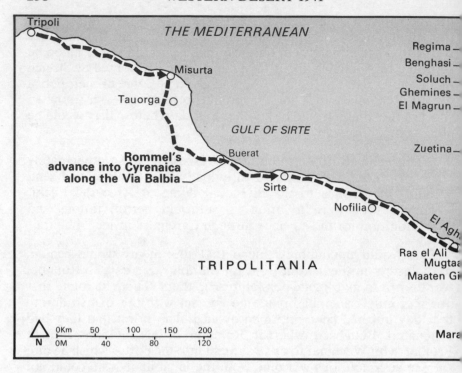

Map 16   Rommel's first advance

methods; Rommel on the flood tide of potential success and clearly perceiving it within his grasp was uncontrollable. He swept aside Gariboldi's warning about the insecurity of his flanks and his supply situation, he totally rejected Gariboldi's claim that as his superior officer he had the authority to forbid any further aggressive operations, and as for the Italian's amended demand that permission for any further advances must at least be obtained from Rome, it was demolished in language which, to quote one observer, 'only generals would use to each other!'

Into the climactic atmosphere thus generated walked, like Mercury, one of the headquarters communications staff bearing a signal from the German High Command. Whatever Halder's reaction to the latest news from the North African front might be, Hitler's had been immediate and enthusiastic; Rommel was granted the fullest freedom of action to exploit the situation which faced him, and there was no room for doubt in the wording of the message that Mussolini's agreement would be forthcoming, should anyone be interested in obtaining it.

It would seem that there may be some truth in the belief that during periods of success, people make their own luck.

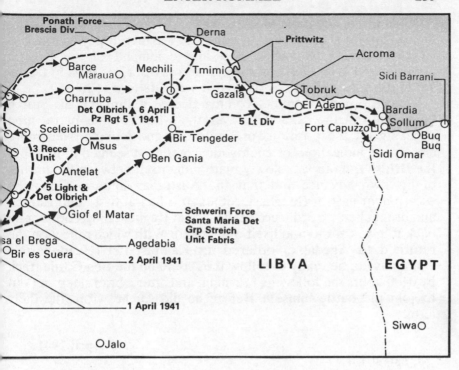

Freed now from all restraint, Rommel became a positive fount of energy. He spent the first few hours of April 4th harrying the 5th Light transport to ensure the division's mobility the following day, then pushed the Brescia Division up and into Benghasi to release 3rd Reconnaissance, whom he then ordered to make their way eastwards through Regima and Charruba towards Mechili, where he had decided that the crucial battle would be fought. He then instructed General Streich, still at Agedabia, that once his division was refuelled – at the latest by that evening – he should split his forces, himself taking the more mobile section along the track used by von Schwerin towards Ben Gania and eventually Tmimi, the remainder consisting of 5th Panzer Regiment and some forty Italian tanks under command of Oberstleutnant Friedrich Olbrich to drive up to Msus and then across to Mechili along the tracks made by 7th Armoured. The main Italian forces – the Santa Maria Battalion, followed by the rest of the Ariete Division in two sections, one commanded by a Colonello Fabris and consisting of motor-cyclists and light guns in advance, and the main bulk coming up behind – were to follow the Streich Group as far as Tengeder, after which they could either join the battle at Mechili or cut across towards El

Adem and Tobruk if the Mechili garrison had escaped. He then met Generalmajor Heinrich Kirchheim (who was merely paying a visit to North Africa), shanghaied him into command of the Brescia Division and instructed him to get it across from Benghasi to Derna along the coastal route as soon as it was safe to do so.

That afternoon Rommel commandeered a Junkers, his Storch being unavailable, and flew over the whole of the battle area checking on the positions of his troops and looking even more closely for indications of enemy movements. It seemed to him that the British armour was slowly marooning itself between the prongs of his own advance and that the Australian infantry along the escarpment east of Benghasi, although it had at first administered an abrupt check to 3rd Reconnaissance at Regima, must shortly pull back if it was not to find itself outflanked. With which reflection, he returned to Agedabia, ordered his Kampfstaffel (Headquarters Company) to be ready to follow the Ariete on the Ben Gania track by 0400 hours the following morning, and after a brief sleep, set out to join the battle himself. Before he did so, he wrote the daily letter:

5 April 1941

Dearest Lu,

Off at 4 this morning. Things are happening in Africa. Let's hope the great stroke we've now launched is successful. I'm keeping very fit. The simple life here suits me better than the fleshpots of France. How are things with you both?[9]

He was over Ben Gania in the Storch during the morning, at noon on the ground again sending Olbrich away northwards towards Msus, and back at Ben Gania in early afternoon. Here he received information that Mechili appeared empty, so von Schwerin, who was the nearest, was instructed to drive hard for the fort while all other forward troops were ordered to close up towards it. Rommel took off again to fly over the area and check where all his forces were (they were getting badly strung out and would undoubtedly have been in danger had there been any coherent British force in the area to threaten them), then returned to Ben Gania to drive forward in what became known as his 'Mammoth' – a captured British headquarters vehicle reputedly originally used by O'Connor – to find out what conditions on the ground were like. Two and a half hours later, he learned that his chief Intelligence officer had been shot down and taken prisoner, that Mechili, far from being evacuated, was full of British forces, and that Streich's force having reached Tengeder had therefore been switched towards Mechili by his Chief of Operations, Major Ehlert, acting independently:

It was now night and too late to fly back to Agedabia. In view of the new and rather less favourable situation, I decided to drive up to the 5th Light Division and take over command of the operation myself.[10]

They drove forward through the night at first with headlights on until they were attacked by British aircraft, and then without – picking their way along the edges of minefields by the light of burning vehicles which had not been so fortunate as themselves – until at about three o'clock in the morning they found the head of the 5th Light Division column, together with the uncomfortable knowledge that they were lost.

But luck had not deserted him. Shortly after dawn on April 6th he was discovered by two aircraft which had been out on a special mission, and given not only his own position but the latest report on Mechili as well. By 0730 two columns had been sent off to block escape routes to the east of the fort and another under Oberst-leutnant Ponath dispatched even further north to do the same across the Via Balbia east of Derna, while Rommel now waited impatiently for the Fabris and Olbrich forces to arrive and close the ring around Mechili.

He had some time to wait, and his account of the next few days offers some comfort for a chauvinistic British reader. Everybody was running out of petrol; Olbrich's force had run into sandstorms stirred up from the surface of the desert, ground to dust by innumerable tank tracks, every time the wind rose; and people got lost, including Rommel again. On one occasion he ran into the rear of a British outpost consisting of several Bren-carriers, but escaped by driving hard at it in three cars and enormous clouds of dust, which so deceived the enemy as to his strength that they hurriedly decamped – allowing him to reach the Fabris column with the only petrol reserve in the area (thirty-five cans stowed in staff cars), enough to bring them up into position but certainly not enough to get them out again.

But there was still no sign of Olbrich, so Rommel set off in the Storch to find him and very nearly landed alongside a British column which had cannily laid out a landing cross to entice him down; but alas for them, he recognised their helmets in time. He found the 3rd Reconnaissance Battalion south of their route and set them on their way, then found a stray section of the Streich Force which had been misled by a mirage and which caught the rough edge of his tongue as a result . . . but still not the 5th Panzer Regiment which would be necessary for any powerful attack on the British at Mechili.

Rommel did not in fact locate them until after dark on the

evening of April 7th, because the same appalling ground which had held up Lieutenant Joly and his companions of 4th Armoured Brigade now proved just as difficult to the panzers – not that this soothed Rommel's temper or saved the hapless Olbrich from a tongue-lashing. Not until 5th Panzer were rerouted and well on their way did Rommel leave them to fly back to his advanced air base, where he found that the R.A.F. had delivered a low-level attack and shot up several of his Junkers.

April 7th had not been a good day for Rommel.

But it had been an even worse one for the British.

Wavell had flown up to Barce on April 2nd, as soon as he realised the seriousness of Rommel's intentions, but his first intervention in the battle had not been of the happiest. Neame had ordered Gambier-Parry to move to the agreed deployment area near Antelat from whence he could cover either the routes to Benghasi or those across the desert to Mechili, but Wavell countermanded this instruction, still convinced that Rommel could not possibly have organised, in the short time in which he had been in North Africa, a force capable of occupying the whole of Cyrenaica. Benghasi itself must surely be the objective for so hastily organised a force, so all of Gambier-Parry's armour could be deployed to block it.

But although this countermanding order was issued at nine o'clock on the evening of April 2nd, signals were being so badly delayed by the increasing chaos that Gambier-Parry did not receive it until half-past two the following morning, by which time his armour was scattered, running very short of petrol and breaking down at the rate of about one tank every ten miles. As the Support Group infantry were also down to half strength through casualties and sheer loss of direction, he felt that he had little option but to disobey this order and collect whatever force remained to him around Sceleidima, setting the first example of a habit which was to grow among British divisional commanders in the desert over the next eighteen months, bitterly described by one aggrieved senior officer as regarding orders from above more as subjects for discussion than as instructions to be obeyed.

But now Wavell made what was to prove the most unfortunate move in his long military career. Feeling the need for stronger and more experienced direction in control, and already somewhat disillusioned with Neame, he sent for O'Connor to come up and take command; and the latter arrived obediently early the following morning, accompanied by John Combe who only hours before had handed over the 11th Hussars upon his appointment to take command of the 6th Cavalry Brigade in Palestine.

O'Connor quickly persuaded Wavell to leave Neame in charge –
for he felt most unhappy about taking over in the middle of any
battle, let alone one which promised as dismally as this one – but he
agreed that he should stay at Neame's headquarters to offer his
advice when asked; upon which note Wavell left for Cairo to
organise further reinforcements, and to put an immediate stop to
the dispatch of troops and equipment to Greece.

It soon became obvious that O'Connor could best occupy his time
by organising rear positions upon which the troops could fall back if
necessary while Neame direct the battle being fought, but already
what one observer has called 'the *danse macabre* of military reverse
– changes of command, role and deployment, planned by commanders and staffs frantic to plug gaps, which never in the event
take place' was in process. And with it went, hand in hand, the bad
luck of defeat which was the obverse of Rommel's fortune at that
moment.

Some extra reinforcement had already made its way to the
various scenes of action. An Indian motorised brigade (without its
armoured vehicles, artillery or anti-tank weapons; but with its
rifles) had arrived at Mechili and was rapidly organising its defence,
and a squadron of the Long Range Desert Group was sent up from
Siwa to play any useful role which could be found for it. It was this
unit, unorthodox in establishment and virtually unknown at that
time in its career, accompanied by some light tanks which had
become lost and now attached themselves to someone who seemed
to have both form and purpose, which on the morning of April 3rd
was seen approaching Msus, the main supply base of 3rd Armoured
Brigade's fuel, and was presumed in the panic to be hostile.

Reports of supposed enemy armour so close to a focal supply
point spread ripples of alarm and confusion across the whole area,
but long before detachments from 3rd Armoured Brigade could get
across to investigate the threat, a Free French motor battalion
which had also come up as reinforcement and had been stationed at
Msus had hastily revictualled their own vehicles, burnt all the
remaining petrol and a substantial amount of other stores, and
smartly withdrawn. From then on, 3rd Armoured's tanks dropped
out of the battle at an ever-increasing rate as their fuel ran out.

Neame and O'Connor moved the headquarters from Barce to
Maraua, tried with but mediocre success to remain in contact with
their troops in the ever-growing chaos, and watched with dismay
the disintegration of 2nd Armoured Division, its isolation and
defeat in detail. The only solid achievement during those days was
by the Australian infantry who had the advantage of being commanded by a resolute and highly intelligent commander, Major-
General Leslie J. Morshead, and despite their inexperience they

twice flung back solid attacks by 3rd Reconnaissance and later by Ponath's force.

But nothing would halt the grotesque palsy of the *danse macabre*. After two days trying to organise 3rd Armoured Brigade to stem the advance, O'Connor and Neame decided that it should instead be fed into Mechili to reinforce the Indians and thus to hold as a solid bastion the fort which had already achieved the cognomen of the 'heart of Cyrenaica' – but this was frustrated by what O'Connor later referred to as the 'complete disobedience of orders on the part of the [2nd] Armoured Division' which became 'absolutely incomprehensible'. Instead of acting as additional protection to the Australian Division, and later as a much needed reinforcement to the Indian Motorised Brigade at Mechili, it had apparently sought its own safety by relinquishing its tanks and joining in the route by which the main withdrawal was to take place.

Such are the consequences of hasty training, inadequate equipment and uncertain command. Worse was to follow, for unalloyed misfortune was now to overtake the British.

During April 6th, Neame had spent most of the day searching fruitlessly for Gambier-Parry in the Got Derva area east of Charruba (Gambier-Parry had already retired to Mechili but had been unable to inform Neame) and he returned to H.Q. at Maraua in the evening. With all lines falling back to the east, it was evident that the time had come for H.Q. to go as well, but O'Connor, still without official appointment and position, was also still without transport. Neame therefore offered to take both him and John Combe in his own staff car and they set out following the main flow of traffic, with Neame at the wheel as his driver was exhausted.

Shortly before dusk it became obvious that they had missed the way and were on one of the northern tracks, but as this seemed anyway a safer route, Neame handed over to his driver and told him to carry on towards Derna. Well after midnight, O'Connor and Combe, who had been asleep in the back of the car, were woken to find the car stationary and voices shouting in front. Combe got out to investigate, quickly realised that the voices were not British and on asking the driver what was happening, received the classic answer: 'I expect it's some of them bloody Cypriot drivers, sir!'

But it wasn't. It was part of the Ponath Force, which had made its way with commendable speed and unerring accuracy north to the Derna road, and now collected as its reward the most valuable car-load of booty to fall to the Afrika Korps during its entire existence.

It is typical of General O'Connor that the only regret he ever recorded was of the abrupt curtailment of the promising career of John Combe who, he wrote, would quickly have won fame as a great cavalry leader had he not been taken prisoner so early in the war. It is at least arguable that a lot of other young men were to suffer curtailment of their careers, and indeed of their lives, by the loss to Britain of so talented a commander as Sir Richard O'Connor.

One person whom the Afrika Korps were not to capture (and they were to bag quite a collection of generals, brigadiers and colonels in this first offensive) was Brigadier John Harding, who had after all remained behind as Neame's B.G.S. when Wilson went to Greece, and who had been travelling with Neame's A.D.C. a few hundred yards ahead of the car carrying O'Connor and Combe. Such is the confusion and random chance of battle that he arrived at Tmimi in the early morning of April 7th without a hint of what had happened behind him, and it was not until 0630 that he became worried enough about the dearth of generals to communicate his fears to Wavell.

He did not, however, hesitate to take on the responsibilities of the senior officer in the area, encouraged by the continuous and well-organised stream of dour and sardonic Australians pouring back along the coast road under Morshead's firm direction. Together, Harding and Morshead formed a line with the Australians stretching from Gazala back to Acroma, with a small force detached to El Adem for observation of the southern approaches to Tobruk, and in the Fortress itself, the 18th and 24th Brigades hard at work on the defences.

Back through this line and into the base were at first to trickle, and later to flood, platoons, sections, half-companies, isolated and random groups of British and Indian soldiers – exhausted, bewildered, parched with thirst, still resolute but often very angry. It was a phenomenon to be observed on two or three later occasions in the desert campaign, and sprang apparently from a deep-rooted objection on their part to being beaten, even by men for whom they later developed the greatest respect.

Mechili fell to the Afrika Korps on the morning of April 8th and Rommel very nearly fell with it.

He had taken off in the Storch early in the morning to ensure that all escape routes to the east were blocked, and in doing so flew low over a Bersaglieri battalion with the Ariete, who failed to recognise the aircraft as friendly; and Rommel's annoyance over the episode was substantially increased by the fact that although they were only some 300 feet above the frantically firing Italians, the Storch wasn't hit even once.

From 3,000 feet, to which height they had rapidly ascended,

Rommel could see that the attack from the east of the fort was going well, but also that quite a large force of British was moving out to the west, obviously intent upon circling around and either catching his own force in flank or escaping altogether. Here Olbrich's panzers should have been waiting, but despite his efforts of the previous night, there was still no sign of them – though on flying off in that direction, he did spot a stationary 88mm. gun about two miles in front of the advancing British.

Thinking that the rest of Olbrich's force must be somewhere near – for the morning wind was raising its usual sandscreen – Rommel ordered the pilot to put down by the gun, which he managed to do extremely efficiently considering the conditions; but as the Storch taxied towards the gun it ploughed into a sandhill and smashed its propeller. It was then that Rommel discovered that the gun had been put out of action the previous day, that it could not even fire from its isolated position as the firing-pin had been taken by the crew member sent to bring aid, and that the British columns were driving closer every minute.

Fortunately for him, the gun crew had retained a lorry and in it they all drove off at great speed, arriving back at H.Q. to find that there was still no sign of Olbrich but that more and more of the Ariete were arriving to be fed into the battle. Within an hour, Rommel was on his way again, but now he and his party ran into a violent sandstorm which delayed their arrival in Mechili until noon, where they found that Gambier-Parry, having authorised the early morning breakout, had then concluded that the smoke and sand to the east denoted an overwhelming force against him and that the Mechili garrison should surrender.

Olbrich's force had arrived at about the same time, and neither Rommel nor Streich was particularly impressed by his presence at the subsequent capitulation ceremony. He was quickly ordered to refuel his panzers and take them off after von Schwerin's light forces towards Derna, while Streich and the Italians held Mechili and looked after the prisoners. These were already proving an encumbrance.

At Derna himself by 1800, Rommel first congratulated Ponath upon his recent exploits, thanked Kirchheim who had brought the Brescia Division up from Benghasi, then welcomed Generalmajor Heinrich von Prittwitz und Gaffron, commander of 15th Panzer Division, the advanced party of which had landed at Tripoli a few days previously. Handing command of the 3rd Reconnaissance Battalion, the 8th Machine-gun Battalion and the 605th Anti-tank Battalion to Prittwitz, he instructed him to follow the Australians along the coast road and take part in the operation designed to 'bounce them out' of Tobruk, the other details of which Rommel would now organise. There was no room for idle hands, of whatever rank, in Rommel's theatre of operations.

It took two days to bring up the forces for the first attack on Tobruk, two days during which Rommel hardly rested for an hour, and during which he had to inform the commander of 5th Light Division coldly that when he gave orders for the division to move immediately, it did not imply that they had two days for rest and vehicle maintenance. They must be in position to the south of Tobruk within twenty-four hours, their advanced units were to push on east and then north, to reach the coast, cut the Bardia road and seal in the Tobruk garrison by the morning of April 11th – Good Friday – at the latest. Move now!

In the meantime, Prittwitz was to send 3rd Reconnaissance away to the south through Acroma to take El Adem, then launch his main attack straight up alongside the main Derna–Tobruk road, driving through the perimeter and into the town from the west. This attack was to start in the early hours of April 10th, and by 0900 the crash of artillery – rather heavier than had been expected – told Rommel that battle had been joined. The machine-gun and anti-tank battalions were obviously having a rough time, but speed was of the essence and Rommel was soon at the front urging them on, then away after the 3rd Reconnaissance to check their progress; and with news at last that the Ariete were moving from Tengeder towards El Adem he could harry 5th Light to move even further around towards the Bardia road. Then, at about 1030, a sinister shimmer came to the air, the daily sandstorm blew up, visibility was abruptly reduced to twenty feet and news came through that General Prittwitz, driving forward to control the battle more closely, had been killed by a shot from an anti-tank gun.

It was a portent. For the first time the Afrika Korps was meeting a resistance which had had time to organise, in a defensive position which was not to be given up. Although by April 11th the encirclement was complete and the country to the south, west, and as far east as the Egyptian border (where the 11th Hussars had resumed their old watch) was clear of British troops, Tobruk was fast hardening into a rock-solid enclave, based on the well-conceived defences built by the Italians (who were apologetically unable to provide Rommel with a map of them for some time) but manned now in great part by Australians of the 9th Division, grimly determined that no one would be able to call them the division which lost all that the 6th had won.

That afternoon the first attack was delivered from the west by the Brescia Division and from the south-east by the panzers of the 5th Light, in a blinding sandstorm which should have given them some protection from the enemy artillery, but which instead so robbed the attack of impetus that it stalled along the perimeter wire and anti-tank ditch until, reluctantly, Rommel broke it off. Again, the British artillery had proved more concentrated and more accurate than had been expected, and so hammered the panzers that their commanders were beginning to lose confidence and raise objections to their battle orders – 'which I had to brush aside', as Rommel was to write rather tetchily. He was becoming as angry with some of his own troops as he had previously been with the Italian generals.

By noon on April 14th, he was even more angry. The previous evening 8th Machine-gun Battalion with ancillary troops, all under command of the excellent Oberst Ponath, had crossed the anti-tank ditch just west of the El Adem track and filled part of it in, then crossed the wire and formed a bridgehead under a well-coordinated artillery cover. Just after midnight, the panzers of 5th Light formed up to move forward and by daybreak Ponath was reporting excellent progress though to Rommel it seemed that flank support for the penetration was weak; so he drove away to find and bring up the Ariete in support. But when he returned to the focal point of the battle he found that the advance had come to a stop under murderous British artillery and Australian rifle fire about two and a half miles from Tobruk itself, and that the panzers had withdrawn leaving the infantry exposed – and probably lost. In the violent outburst which followed this news, both Streich and Olbrich were given clearly to understand that they were to go in and get the infantry out, and Rommel went off again to harry the Ariete into position – only to return to find that the panzers were still immobile under the hail of British shelling.

Rommel then decided to bring the Ariete up himself to a position on the left of 5th Light, had got them up just south-east of Gasr el Gleicha when a salvo of shells came over from beyond the perimeter – and total confusion ensued, the division turning tail and fleeing off in streams back towards Derna and Mechili. As it was by now almost dark, the divisional commander could do little to regain control and Rommel had to organise a small assault force from his own troops to try to break through and release the now encircled Ponath force.

They were too late. Although they broke through into the area which the machine-gunners had occupied, they found that most of the battalion had been wiped out, including their commander – who had just been awarded the Knight's Cross by Rommel.

A further attack by Ariete on April 16th and 17th also failed, accompanied by the humiliating sight of troops under heavy artillery fire throwing down their arms and running en masse *towards* the British and Australian lines in order to give themselves up. In addition the Italian armoured force was reduced from over a

34 *Above*, Panzer IIs on the way past Tobruk. 35 *Below*, soft-skinned transport between Belhammed and Gambut.

36 75mm. flak gun bound for the frontier

37 *Left*, German mortar-post outside Tobruk

38 *Below*, the Germans reach Halfaya Pass

39 *Top right*, Rats of Tobruk

40 *Far right*, 'Cock the bastard up a bit!'

41 *Centre right*, Major-General Morshead

42 *Far right*, 'Let 'er go, mate!'

43 *Below right*, Northumberland Fusiliers covering an attack

44 Long Range Desert Group patrol

45 *Above*, 'unsticking' a loaded Chevrolet in soft sand

46 *Below*, 7th Armoured Brigade cruisers moving up. Many of them would be
destroyed at Sidi Rezegh.

hundred tanks to less than ten in the matter of a few days and two of
the remainder were wrecked in error by German anti-tank guns.
This brought about the final acceptance by Rommel that nothing
could be done to reduce the Fortress before the arrival of a
substantial number of reinforcements, preferably German, and of
replacements for destroyed panzers; and that those panzers which
remained were in dire need of maintenance. He also required some
more senior officers as he had decided to dispense with the services
of both Generalmajor Streich and Oberst Olbrich.

In the meantime, there was the rest of the front to clear up.

The front line east of Tobruk was by this time an indeterminate area
between the line held by the Germans from Bardia down through
Fort Capuzzo towards Sidi Omar, and the positions held by the only
force Wavell could move up in a hurry from the Delta, basically the
7th Armoured Division's Support Group, still commanded by
Brigadier Strafer Gott and with Colonel Jock Campbell as second in
command.

Gott had been sent up to El Adem after the collapse at Mechili to
form some sort of screen to the south and east of Tobruk, and one
of the first units to join him there had been the 11th Hussars who
found themselves at one time desperately trying to hold a fifty-mile
semi-circle around Tobruk on their own. They were inexorably
thrown back as first Prittwitz's and then Streich's forces came up,
but they kept Gott informed of enemy movements and delivered
some sharp, mosquito-like attacks.

But by April 19th, Gott and his men were back behind the
frontier with the main force consisting of 22nd Guards Brigade on
and around Halfaya Pass, and four Jock Columns, each with a
company of infantry (the 2nd Rifle Brigade had also been rushed up
from Ismailia), one or more troops of 25-pounders and a few
armoured cars or light tanks. These columns operated from
Halfaya, Sofafi, Buq Buq and Sidi Barrani, and there was also a
Free French motor battalion at Halfway House on top of the
Escarpment; between them they endeavoured both to keep their
new overall commander – Lieutenant-General Sir Noel Beresford-
Peirse, who had been promoted, knighted and appointed G.O.C.
Western Desert Force upon O'Connor's disappearance from the
scene – fully acquainted with the situation at the frontier, and at the
same time to make it as uncomfortable as possible for the new
occupants.

Perhaps they tried too hard. During the last week in April, three
troops of the 11th Hussars staged a raid on Fort Capuzzo in which
they attacked it from three sides and so disrupted traffic back to Sidi
Azeiz that the local commander, Oberst von Herff, reported to

Rommel that his forces in the area were in danger of being cut off. Two days later, a strong force under the Oberst swept along the Escarpment as far as Halfaya, drove in the advance posts there and at Halfway House, and effectively pushed the Mobile Force back to the Buq Buq–Sofafi line. In addition, a flight of Messerschmitt 110s caught two Hussar troops in the open and virtually destroyed them, while in Halfaya Pass itself, a German eight-wheeled armoured car caught two more of the 11th's cars and in the resulting skirmish, Vyvyan Gape was killed – the first 11th officer to fall in the Second World War.

The whole pattern of war in the Western Desert had changed.

From Wavell's point of view, the pattern of war in the whole of the Middle East had changed too, and only on one front had the change been anything but disastrous.

During March, matters had at first promised well. The transporting of British and Australian troops was proceeding expeditiously by the end of the first week, while in East Africa Cunningham had advanced 600 miles north of Mogadishu by March 10th, Berbera had been reoccupied by a force from Aden on March 16th and eight days later (on the day that Rommel took El Agheila) the whole of British Somaliland was regained. On March 25th Wavell himself had gone down to pay a visit to General Platt in front of Keren, had agreed the method for the final assault and had not been at all surprised to learn upon his return to Cairo two days later, that success had at last crowned the efforts of 4th and 5th Indian Divisions and the gateway through to the central plateau had been stormed and taken.

What had come as a surprise – though quite a happy one – was the news that a *coup d'état* had taken place in Yugoslavia that very morning and the pro-British King Peter had taken over from his pacific-minded Prime Minister and appointed, to the evident delight of his subjects, a Cabinet of patriots who promptly rejected the Tripartite Pact signed between Yugoslavia and Germany only two days before. This obviously portended a resumption of Mr Eden's attempts to form that Balkan Front about which he was so keen, and Wavell soon learned that both Eden and Dill were returning as quickly as possible (they were still at Malta when the news from Yugoslavia broke) and would be with him tomorrow.

Any lack of warmth which Wavell may by now have been feeling towards the idea of another series of conferences with a senior politician, was dispelled during March 28th as the news came in of the resounding defeat administered by the Royal Navy to Admiral Iachino's fleet off Cape Matapan, thus lessening the threats to the Greek convoys – and the following day, he felt sufficiently secure to be able to end a passage in the directive to Neame quoted earlier with the words, 'But I do not believe that he [Rommel] can make any big effort for at least another month.'

From then on practically everything went wrong.

Eden and Dill went off to Athens on March 31st – and Rommel captured Mers el Brega; then 2nd Armoured Division retreated to Agedabia, and although 5th Indian Division captured Asmara the same day, another cloud the size of a man's hand appeared upon an entirely different horizon, when the pro-British Regent of Iraq, Amir Abdul Illah, was forced to flee from Baghdad, and it became fairly evident that power would fall into the hands of one Raschid Ali el Gailani, whose political stance was well indicated by his friendship for Haj Amin el Husseini, the violently anti-British Mufti of Jerusalem, long a refugee from Palestine.

But Wavell's closest attention was at that moment obviously focused on events in Cyrenaica, and on April 2nd he had gone to Barce where, as has been related, he amended Neame's plans for defence and called O'Connor forward to join him. By the time he returned to Cairo, Benghasi had been abandoned and Raschid Ali was indeed Premier of Iraq.

Three days later, German forces invaded both Yugoslavia and Greece and by the evening Belgrade was in flames and an ammunition ship had been hit by a Luftwaffe bomb in Piraeus harbour, blowing up and almost totally wrecking all the port installations. Moreover, news from Yugoslavia indicated that however hardy in physique and independent in mind the population might be, their army was proving no match for the fourteen infantry and mountain divisions and six panzer divisions which were pouring down through their country; thus it could not be many hours before the flank of the Greek defence was torn open.

During the afternoon of April 6th, there was a conference of the three Commanders-in-Chief in Cairo attended by both Dill and Eden (who had at last abandoned the dream of a Balkan Front), but the best hope to come out of this was a unanimous determination that, however far Rommel might advance towards or even into Egypt, Tobruk must be held; and the following day Eden and Dill left for London, the Yugoslav southern front was broken and Neame and O'Connor were captured.

On April 8th (the day that Mechili fell and the Germans also captured Salonica) Wavell took a very bumpy and uncomfortable flight up to Tobruk, accompanied by the commander of the 7th Australian Division, Major-General J. D. Lavarack, in order to talk to General Morshead and John Harding about the possibilities open to them. As both thought that Tobruk could be held, Wavell confirmed them in their tasks – with, apparently, the memorable comment, 'Well, if you think you can, you'd better get on and do it!' – appointed Lavarack for the time being commander of all troops in Cyrenaica and Libya and Morshead commander of the main force in Tobruk, then wrote out a six-paragraph directive for Lavarack which could serve as a model of brevity and lucidity – and perhaps optimism – for any Staff College course.

It was late afternoon before he was free to leave and a storm was blowing. As the aircraft was about to take off, a wheel brake seized up imposing a delay of about an hour, and then about a quarter of an hour after take-off, oil pressure failed on one engine. The pilot returned to El Adem airfield – by now abandoned by the British and about to be occupied by the Germans – effected a hasty repair and took off again. Twenty minutes later, the oil pressure failed again and the attempt by the pilot to complete the journey with a single and fast overheating engine ended in a forced landing, a shattered port wing and a disintegrated tail.

Fortunately no one was hurt, but the only certainty about their position was that they were still far west of the Egyptian border and thus in imminent danger of capture. A fire was lit, tea was brewed – and just before anyone could enjoy a cup, some vehicles approached out of the murk, halted some fifty yards from the wrecked aircraft and from the first emerged a gigantic figure carrying a rifle, challenging them in a distinctly foreign tongue.

He proved, however, to be a friendly Sudanese and the party were soon bowling happily along towards Sollum from where, about midnight, Wavell was able to contact the Cairo Headquarters – by then distraught with worry at his disappearance. One of the pieces of news they were able to give him was that the British armour in front of the Aliakmon Line was already under attack and that the line itself appeared in considerable danger of being outflanked by German troops moving down towards the Monastir Gap.

Another day to remember was April 11th. To the eventual and enormous relief of the Middle East Command, President Roosevelt that day declared the Red Sea a non-combatant zone and thus open to American shipping, but for Wavell this good news was offset first by reports of the breaking of the Aliakmon Line, and then by the sealing in of his forces in Tobruk. This was followed by a request from Whitehall that he make instant arrangements for the dispatch from Palestine of 'a sizeable force' to Habbaniya, the R.A.F. station some 40 miles from Baghdad (and thus 500 miles from Jerusalem) which with the advent of Raschid Ali to power was presumed – rightly – to be in danger. There was no practical suggestion as to where either the men or the equipment for such a force could be found in Wavell's command (obviously if he had men for such a task they would already be in employment) or recognition of the fact that never in history had Baghdad been captured along any other routes but those of the valleys of the Euphrates or Tigris, neither of which was available to Wavell.

He went back to Athens the following day at Maitland Wilson's request to discuss withdrawal of the British and Australian forces to what was optimistically referred to as the 'Olympus line' and which in fact hardly existed, and upon his return (April 13th) learned of the attack on Tobruk and the occupation of Belgrade by the Germans. He was able to remain in Cairo for the next five days (during which he proposed to Whitehall that approaches should be made to the Italian Government to exchange O'Connor for any six captured Italian generals; a serious suggestion which Whitehall took two weeks to turn down on the egalitarian grounds that exceptions couldn't be made for senior officers!) but on April 16th, with the troops in Greece now pushed back almost as far as Thermopylae, General Papagos put a request through Wilson that the British should be withdrawn as quickly as possible from his country in order to 'save it from devastation' – a request which took Wavell back to Athens for the last time.

On April 17th, the Yugoslav Army laid down its arms, and Wavell issued a warning to the forces on the island of Crete to expect a rapid influx of troops evacuated from Greece followed soon afterwards by a sea and airborne invasion by Germans; and in Athens, he received a cable from Churchill which demanded in imperious language that London be kept in much closer touch with affairs on the Greek front than hithertofore. As neither Wavell nor indeed Wilson had been able to obtain from the Greeks any accurate, up-to-date pictures of events along their portions of the front, and thus had had but a sketchy idea of what was happening on their flanks, there was undoubtedly some cause for concern in London, but a mistaken idea of where the fault lay. The cable marked the beginning of a breakdown in understanding between Churchill and Wavell which had probably been inevitable from the start, although relations had in fact improved lately as a result of Churchill's remarkable sympathy over the reverse in Cyrenaica.

The Greek Government capitulated to the German forces on April 24th and the evacuation of the British and Australian survivors began on the same day – preceded by the virtual destruction of the remaining R.A.F. units in Greece by overwhelming Luftwaffe attacks. Three days later – on the day that von Herff's troops took Halfaya Pass from the Guards Brigade – the Germans were in Athens and evacuation could then only take place from small and isolated ports in the Peloponnese, but it continued until April 30th, by which time Wavell was in Crete discussing its defence with the famous New Zealander Major-General Bernard Freyberg, V.C. Here he learned that on the previous afternoon 350 British subjects had taken refuge in the British Embassy in Baghdad, another 150 in the American Embassy – and that 240 women and children had been given safe conduct to the R.A.F. station at Habbaniya by Raschid Ali, who then ordered the Iraqi Army to invest and attack it.

Somehow, and from somewhere, Wavell had to find the troops to rescue them.

On the same day, Rommel mounted his biggest attack so far on the western face of Tobruk and in a determined action lasting two days carried out by German troops under General Kirchheim, drove in a salient two miles deep towards Fort Pilastrino which then became so well entrenched, despite every Australian attempt to eliminate it, that it remained there like an abscess threatening the heart of the Fortress until the end of the siege.

So much for April.

May was dominated for Wavell by three main events – the first British counter-attack against Rommel, the German airborne invasion of Crete, and the elimination of Raschid Ali with, as a consequence, the end of German influence in Iraq and later in Syria.

Of these, *Operation Brevity* on the Egyptian borders at first bulked largest in Wavell's eyes. Although it was obvious to all that the sooner the Afrika Korps were pushed back at least beyond Tobruk the better, two factors introduced by personalities outside the Middle East theatre determined its timing.

Not altogether surprisingly, one of these personalities was Churchill's. His reaction to the reverse in Cyrenaica had been magnificent. The nagging ceased, there were no recriminations – only sympathy, understanding and an immediate concern to help; and one of the most practical aids which the Prime Minister felt that he could give to his hard-pressed commander in the field was to override the natural apprehensions of his senior Army and Navy advisers in England, strip the Home Defence of every tank and aeroplane that could be spared (and this at the time when the industrial heart of Britain was under heavy attack; Coventry had been virtually destroyed during two nights in early April) and send them by the fastest means possible through the Mediterranean to Alexandria. By April 28th Wavell had been informed that he might expect some 300 new tanks and over 50 Hurricane fighters by mid-May; and generosity was a quality to which Wavell responded far more readily than to truculence.

The second personality concerned was Halder's. Like many another theoretician risen to eminence in a vast organisation, he invariably exhibited signs of outrage when success was achieved by means other than those enshrined in his own dogma; and the fact that they had been thus achieved by a man who had had the temerity to call him a bloody fool did nothing to ease his chagrin. His diary entries covering the period immediately following Rommel's advance contain such passages as:

> Rommel has not sent in a single clear report, and I have a feeling that things are in a mess . . .
> All day long he rushes about between his widely scattered units and stages reconnaissance raids in which he fritters away his strength . . .
> Air transport cannot meet his senseless demands, primarily because of lack of fuel . . .
> It is essential to have the situation cleared up without delay . . .

To this end he dispatched to Africa 'perhaps the only man with enough influence to head off this soldier gone stark mad' – Generalleutnant Friedrich Paulus, as yet supremely unaware of the fate which was to overtake him at Stalingrad.

Paulus arrived at Rommel's H.Q. on April 27th and at first refused permission for the attack on Tobruk planned for April 30th, but two days later relented and remained at the front to watch it. Perhaps because he had himself some responsibility for the action taking place at all, he reported it as 'an important success' – but then went on to state that the Afrika Korps was in a tactically difficult and unbalanced situation, logistically unsupportable and from a strategic point of view (for he knew of *Operation Barbarossa* whereas Rommel still did not) grossly over-extended. No further attempt should be made against Tobruk, he felt, unless the garrison evacuated it voluntarily; and indeed, the principal task for the Afrika Korps should be restricted to the holding of Cyrenaica, irrespective of who held Sollum, Bardia or even Tobruk.

These views he communicated to Berlin by cable and within hours the Bletchley Park organisation were reading them. Churchill's reaction when they arrived on his desk, and Wavell's in the light of Churchill's recent benevolence, were predictable. If the German Command already felt that their forward troops should not be further east than, say, Tmimi or Gazala, then the lightest push might be enough to send them back there and thus relieve not only the Tobruk garrison, but also the hard-pressed Royal Navy from the onerous and increasingly dangerous task of supplying them. Such a move would also cheer up the home population in their tribulations and so ease Churchill's gigantic burden a little.

Operation Brevity began at dawn on May 15th, lasted some thirty-six hours and was from the British point of view a complete failure – compounded later by wrong conclusions drawn from the fighting at almost all levels of command.

Brigadier Gott, who commanded the operation in the field, had planned for a three-pronged advance. Along the coast road the 2nd Rifle Brigade supported by artillery were to take the post at the bottom of Halfaya Pass, and then to push on into Sollum to occupy the village, force their way up the pass there and take the barracks at the top. Parallel with them the infantry of 22nd Guards Brigade plus two squadrons of 4th Royal Tank Regiment in twenty-four Matildas would drive along the lip of the Escarpment, taking the post at the top of Halfaya, then capturing Fort Capuzzo and exploiting northwards, with luck as far as Bardia. Away to the south an Armoured Brigade Group, considerably under strength and consisting of the Support Group with two squadrons of cruiser tanks (twenty-nine in all) were to provide a screen for the slower-moving forces inside them, and also a means of exploitation should all

Map 17   *Operation Brevity*: May 15th–17th, 1941

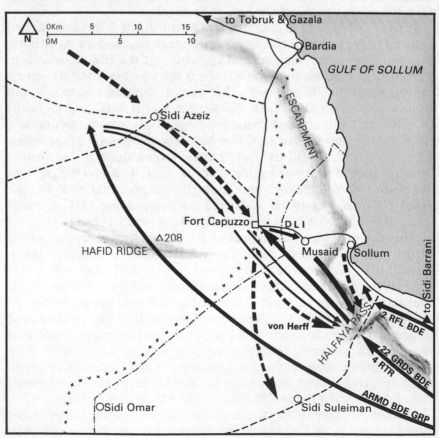

hopes be realised and the Afrika Korps in the area retreat in haste.

In the light of conclusions to be drawn from Paulus's cable, it was not a wildly impracticable scheme – but perhaps unfortunately, neither Rommel nor his local commander Oberst von Herff were as fully aware of the thoughts of the emissary from Berlin as were Whitehall and Cairo. They certainly showed little inclination to abandon their positions and hurriedly decamp towards Gazala, and although the Armoured Brigade did reach around as far as Sidi Azeiz in their screening endeavour, it took the coast group practically all day to capture their first objective at the bottom of Halfaya Pass, and the battle which developed around Fort Capuzzo reached a pitch of intensity new in that particular area.

By 2100 that evening Brigadier Gott was sufficiently worried by the stalemate to signal Beresford-Peirse suggesting a withdrawal to the Halfaya Pass line, and after five hours without a reply ordered the Guards Brigade and their remaining Matildas to fall back – just three-quarters of an hour before receiving Beresford-Peirse's instructions to hang on until morning in the positions attained. By that time, the British infantry who had reached Fort Capuzzo (1st Durham Light Infantry) had been driven back as far as Musaid with heavy loss, and Gott was well aware of the vulnerability of the rest of the Guards Brigade on the top of the Escarpment should von Herff receive armoured reinforcement.

This appeared at Sidi Azeiz in the early morning of May 16th and although it was stranded there through lack of petrol for most of the day, its mere presence was enough to cause the withdrawal of the Armoured Brigade Group, for many of their cruiser tanks had broken down on the way up – and more were to break down on the way back.

By the morning of May 17th, the Afrika Korps stood on the line Sollum–Sidi Suleiman–Sidi Omar, and although the British now held Halfaya Pass, they had bought it at the cost of 160 dead and wounded, five Matildas destroyed and 13 damaged, and extra wear and tear on the already over-worn engines and tracks of their cruisers.

Ten days later, von Herff sent panzers and infantry forces from Capuzzo and Sollum and retook the top and bottom of Halfaya Pass, which he then turned into the anchor point of a strong defensive line swinging back in an arc crossing Hafid Ridge at Point 208 and ending at Sidi Azeiz. The main strong-points in the arc consisted of 88mm. anti-tank guns sunk so deep into the ground that little was visible from the front except the barrels, but each of which commanded a wide field of fire.

'I had great hopes of the effectiveness of this arrangement,' wrote Rommel later, with all the smug security of hindsight.

Few people really expected the defence of Crete to succeed, probably because the pattern of advance, confrontation and early retreat for the British seemed set, and no recent portent in the sky had given hope for a reversal of fortune. Yet it was in Wellington's famous phrase, 'a damned nice thing – the nearest-run thing you ever saw in your life!' Despite the lack of arms and especially of air cover, despite the hastily assembled staffs and scratch formations which were all that could be scavenged from the evacuation from Greece, there were many extended periods when the German Fallschirmjäger – in many ways an elite force – felt that they were facing defeat; and it would have been the first for German arms in the Second World War. Rarely has the difference between defeat and victory apparently been balanced for so long on such a fine knife-edge, when in fact a comparatively minor decision had already decided the issue within hours of the first landing.

In a corner of Maleme airfield the commander of a New Zealand battalion, wise, experienced, brave enough to have won the Victoria Cross during the First World War but in receipt of faulty information and so anxious for the lives of his men, ordered a withdrawal on to supporting battalions. A lodgment in one corner of the airfield was thus given to the German paratroops who, before the significance of the loss was appreciated by Freyberg, widened their area of control until troop-carrying aircraft could bring in reinforcements. From that moment the invader could be regularly supplied and augmented while the defenders' strength was inexorably whittled away. Like the fall of a grain of sand which starts a landslide, the withdrawal of 22nd New Zealand Battalion from that single point eventually gave Crete to the Germans.

Ironically enough, this violent and protracted battle, which left a strategically valuable position in German hands, proved a Pyrrhic victory for the practitioners of the new and apparently successful military technique which had brought it about. General Student, who had raised, trained and commanded the German airborne troops, later wrote, 'Crete was the grave-yard of the German parachutists', and they were never used in an airborne role again.

This, however, was a judgment of the future and no comfort at all to Wavell, watching on the last day of May the Homeric conflict fought out among the orange groves, the scented gardens and across the terraced hills, to reach its dusty and depressing conclusion on the tiny south coast beach of Sphakia; followed by yet another evacuation, another tale of unavailing gallantry, of abandoned equipment and of brave and valuable men killed and taken prisoner. Of the 32,000 British and Commonwealth soldiers on Crete when the battle opened, only 18,000 got back to Egypt and of these over 1,000 would never fight again. Very few could bring back even their rifles, let alone some of the heavier armament which had been sent across the Mediterranean from the theatre which now needed it so desperately.

But at least the whole Greek entanglement was now over, and could no longer drain men and material from the main battlefront in the desert, or distract the Commander-in-Chief's attention from the crucial area.

The bare outlines of the Raschid Ali revolt are quickly told.

At Habbaniya was an R.A.F. flying school and upon investment by the Iraqi Army, the instructors and pupils first dispersed and then armed their aircraft as best they could. Some idea of the problems which faced them in this operation can be gained from the list of aircraft at their disposal – thirty-two Audaxes, eight Gordons, twenty-nine Oxfords, three Gladiators, one Blenheim and five Hart trainers; in the many hundreds of books dealing with the Second World War which the present writer has read, he has only come across mention of two of those types of aircraft in any other context. Nevertheless, they were able to carry out reconnaissance flights and to provide information that the surrounding forces comprised at least two infantry battalions with supporting artillery; and at dawn on May 2nd, augmented by eight Wellingtons which had flown up from Shaiba they were out bombing and strafing the enemy positions.

This action attracted first some scattered rifle and machine-gun fire against them and then sporadic shelling of the cantonment, followed by the arrival over the area of planes of the Iraqi Air Force. By the end of the day, five of the assorted Habbaniya aircraft had been destroyed and their desperately inexperienced pilots killed, several had been damaged and seventeen people inside the camp had been killed by shellfire. The investment force had been increased to brigade strength.

The next two days were spent in similar pattern, but at night patrols carried out by men of the King's Own Royal Regiment who had been flown up from Basra ranged well out on to the surrounding plateau, and their encounters with the Iraqi Army were not marked by any high degree of aggression on the part of those surprised. At dawn on May 6th, a large proportion of the investing army had disappeared, leaving the ground dotted with abandoned equipment which the besieged quickly dragged into the confines of Habbaniya and put to some use.

That afternoon, two brisk actions were fought with Iraqi columns on the road back from Habbaniya towards Baghdad in both of which the enemy was thoroughly routed, for their troops seemed both unwilling to fight and unable to stand. The siege was thus lifted within six days.

However, Habbaniya was an isolated garrison at least 200 miles inside the borders of a potentially hostile country, and British men and women were still penned within the embassies in Baghdad; a flying column was hastily cobbled together from the 1st Cavalry Division in Palestine (still in the process of exchanging its horses for vehicles) and set out under command of Brigadier J. J. Kingstone on its 500-mile dash, crossing the Iraqi frontier on May 13th.

Its size was limited by the extreme shortage of lorries available, and some indication of the lengths to which Wavell had been driven to form it at all is given by the fact that its one experienced formation consisted of eight cars of the R.A.F. Armoured Car Company, withdrawn from the vital co-operation with the 11th Hussars on the Egyptian Frontier.

The column was attacked by German fighters, diverted by floods caused by destruction of bunds as they approached their objective, and much hindered by the problems of digging heavy lorries out of soft sand in temperatures of 120 degrees with inexperienced hands; but they swung around to the south of Lake Habbaniya and reached the road to Baghdad by May 19th (by which time two infantry brigades of 10th Indian Division had reached Basra) and during the next few days all forces in the immediate area were reorganised. During this phase also, rumours reached the Iraqi capital grossly exaggerating the British forces, which in the end were reported to be advancing with an unknown but vast number of tanks – at which Raschid Ali's nerve broke and when the advance did begin on May 28th, he and his supporters fled to Persia.

The armistice was signed on May 31st, the British troops moved into Baghdad the same day and on June 1st the pro-British Regent flew back and was reinstated. On the surface, the episode was over.

But from Wavell's personal point of view, there was far more to it than that.

'I always disliked Iraq – ' Wavell was later to write, 'the country, the people and the military commitment . . . It blew up at the worst possible time for me, when I had the Western Desert, Crete, East Africa and Syria on my hands, and no troops.'

His basic psychological allergy to the country had found expression in early March when he had arranged with the Chiefs of Staff in London that the entire area should come under the India Command, and that any trouble in it should be dealt with by the new Commander-in-Chief there, General Sir Claude Auchinleck – a suggestion with which the Chiefs of Staff then agreed, as did General Auchinleck. To both generals it seemed that hostile control of Iraq would not greatly jeopardise Wavell's defence of Egypt and Palestine whereas, via Iran and Afghanistan, it would affect the entire defence system of the Indian Empire.

Moreover, India could and indeed did supply troops during April as soon as trouble threatened, shipping two trained Indian infantry brigades to Basra at Auchinleck's suggestion, at precisely the time that Wavell was resisting the demands from London that he dispatch the 'sizeable force' to Habbaniya from Palestine on the not unreasonable grounds that with Tobruk just sealed in, Rommel's forces at Bardia and threatening Capuzzo, and the Aliakmon Line breaking, the agreement that India should deal with troubles in Iraq should surely stand. And General Quinan, commanding the Indian troops at Basra, brought with him a directive from Auchinleck beginning, 'You will command all British Empire land forces in Iraq from the time of your arrival. You will be under my orders,' – a sentiment with which Wavell was in complete agreement.

But both Churchill and the Chiefs of Staff now changed their minds again, for reasons partly geographical and partly historical. Baghdad might be 500 miles from Jerusalem but it was 1,500 from Bombay, and although men could and should be rushed up from the vast reservoir of the Indian Army, it seemed obvious and logical that supplies – vehicles, fuel, equipment and ammunition – should come from the Middle East Command, a view which took note of the realities on the map but not on the quartermaster's store-sheet.

The result was a plethora of signals passing between London and Cairo containing such phrases as:

Chiefs of Staff to A. P. Wavell   2nd May, 1941
. . . operational command should now pass temporarily to Mideast whence alone immediate assistance can be given. This will take place forthwith . . .

A. P. Wavell to Chiefs of Staff   3rd May, 1941
I have consistently warned you that no assistance could be given to Iraq from Palestine . . . commitment in Iraq should be avoided.

There are no guns or A.F.V.s in Palestine . . . merely asking for further trouble.

My forces are stretched to limit everywhere . . .

I do not see how I can possibly accept military responsibility.[11]

In this last cable he suggested that the Iraq problem must be solved by diplomatic action and later that either Turkey or the U.S.A. be asked to mediate, courses of action which raised hackles in the Foreign Office and caused a noticeable increase in Churchill's blood-pressure. It also resulted in another long cable from the

Chiefs of Staff to Wavell on May 4th which, while regretting the extra burdens now thrown on Wavell's shoulders, firmly rejected the ideas of diplomatic negotiation for mediation by neutrals and equally firmly ordered him to take specific action – a cable which elicited a reply whose opening sentence read:

A. P. Wavell to Chiefs of Staff   5th May, 1941
Your 88 takes little account of realities. You must face facts.[12]

The cable went on again to list the difficulties facing him, the consequent weakness of any force which he could assemble for dispatch into Iraq, the desirability for mediation and for military operational control of the theatre to reside with India.

As this cable arrived in London at the same time as one from Auchinleck – who was deeply sympathetic with Wavell's problems and anxious to help him – offering to send five complete infantry brigades plus ancillary troops to Basra if London could find ships to carry them, Wavell's stock in London sank and Auchinleck's rose; but the gist of the reply sent to Cairo was to the effect that Wavell should stop bellyaching and get on with it.

A. P. Wavell to C.I.G.S.   5th May, 1941
Nice baby you have handed me on my fifty-eighth birthday. Have always hated babies and Iraqis but will do my best for the little blighter. Am hatching minor offensive in Western Desert but not sure yet can bring it off.[13]

But this last cable was to his old friend Sir John Dill, who had himself been trying to argue Wavell's case and thus found himself becoming increasingly unpopular. On the following day, the Chiefs of Staff sent another cold and formal cable to Wavell, dismissing his objections, informing him that they would take responsibility for the dispatch of the force from Palestine, but nevertheless hedging their bets at the end with the equivocal instruction

Subject to security of Egypt being maintained, maximum air support possible should be given to operation in Iraq . . . [14]

At the same time, they sent a cable to Auchinleck:

C.o.S. to C.-in-C. in India   6th May, 1941
Your bold and generous offer greatly appreciated. Please prepare forces as a matter of urgency. Notify dates by which they will be ready to sail and we will confirm before despatch.[15]

And what the Chiefs of Staff gave expression to, the Prime Minister was at the same time feeling. He had greeted Wavell's statement that there was no worthwhile force in Palestine to send to Habbaniya with the acid comment, 'Fancy having kept the Cavalry

Division in Palestine all this time without having the rudiments of a mobile column organised!' – which was grossly unfair, for if the equipment had been available, that and even more could have been organised, and employed on the most immediately threatened fronts in Egypt or Greece. On the morning of those last cables, Sir John Dill told one of his confrères that he felt that Churchill had now lost all confidence in the Middle East Command.

Churchill's disenchantment with Wavell now seems to have been so great that it was not to be readjusted even by the news of the successful conclusion of at least one campaign in the area – for by the middle of May, Italy's East African Empire had totally collapsed.

As has been mentioned, the two Indian divisions stormed up through the Dongolaas Gorge to take Keren on March 27th, 5th Indian advanced to Asmara four days later and by April 8th the Red Sea port at Massawa was in British hands. To the south, Cunningham's forces had swept up through Harar Province reaching Jijiga by March 17th where they joined the Aden force which had taken Berbera and regained Somaliland, the combined forces then pressing on to take Addis Ababa on April 5th. Emperor Haile Selassie was back in his capital a month later, after an absence of almost exactly five years.

The position of the Duke of Aosta, Viceroy of Ethiopia, was now critical. The large majority of the forces he had commanded consisted of native levies, and as Platt in the north and Cunningham in the south advanced into the heart of their country, these melted away and the Duke found himelf by mid-April penned with his remaining forces into the mountain fortress of Amba Alagi where, although they could undoubtedly repel for some time any attacking force, they could not themselves break out nor, in the circumstances, expect relief from the home country so many miles away across the Mediterranean.

The end was incvitable and began on May 16th with armistice negotiations, to be solemnised three days later by a parade of 5,000 Italian survivors marching past a Guard of Honour, after which they were disarmed and the Duke of Aosta formally surrendered. He was then taken to the villa near Nairobi, his chosen place of incarceration as a prisoner of war where, on the morning of March 3rd, 1942, he died of tuberculosis – mourned by all, for he had been a charming, generous and extremely civilised man. But alas, these are not the qualities of which victorious soldiers are made.

By the end of May, then, three of the major problems which had been facing the Commanders-in-Chief, Middle East, had been resolved, and two of them satisfactorily. True, the incipient animosity against the British which had flared into open hostility in Iraq seemed about to erupt again even nearer, in Syria – but the East African front was now completely closed down and would remain so. As for the northern front, although there the battle had ended in defeat, at least it was no longer a drain on valuable supplies.

On paper the overall situation was more favourable than it had appeared six weeks before, and Britain had demonstrated that against at least one of the Axis partners her armies were invincible. Whether they would be so against the partner who showed strong indications of making up in martial prowess for whatever might be lacking in Latin charm, remained to be seen.

9 · *Battleaxe*

Rommel's problems during May were perhaps not as disparate as those facing Wavell, but they were just as acute; and they all sprang either from the inadequacies of his subordinates or the unconcern of his superiors.

The attack on the western perimeter of Tobruk at the end of April, however deep the salient it had driven towards the port, had revealed a lack of expertise in plain infantry fighting among his own German troops, more unacceptable even than the evident lack of enthusiasm for the battle exhibited by some of the Italians:

> The high casualties suffered by my assault forces were primarily caused by their lack of training. Even in the smallest action, there are always tactical tricks which can be used to save casualties, and these must be made known to the men. It frequently happened that dash was used where caution was really needed, with, of course, casualties as a result. On the next occasion, when boldness really was required, the men would be over-cautious.[1]

The main problem for the German troops, especially the panzer crews, was that it had suddenly become an entirely different sort of war. Their fame, their confidence, their expertise were all concerned with the mystique of Blitzkrieg – the rapid movements, the sharp clash of armour followed quickly by either parry and disengagement or (and more often for them so far) by breakthrough and victory. Their first serious attack on Tobruk had been their first experience of a hard, slogging infantry fight against solid defences which could not be outflanked, and apparently would not be overrun.

There was another aspect of the battle, too, which came as a shock to a large number of Rommel's troops, and awoke unpleasant memories amongst the rest. The most searing experience which comes to a soldier, and the one to which the majority of his early training is directed to help him overcome, is the first moment when he realises that out there is another man intent on killing him – not a far-distant artilleryman blindly firing his huge missiles at random into a target area, but another infantryman like himself, who knows where he is, has his sights on the immediate position and will fire to wound or kill at the first false move. Infantry fighting in such circumstances is a very serious and personal business, and such exhilarating factors as speed and excitement have nothing to do with it. It is cold, destructive and dreadfully exhausting, and an additional shock to the morale of the German troops who found themselves in the Ras el Madauer salient was the realisation that the Australians were for the moment better at it than they were. Rommel, who probably had more first-hand experience of this type of fighting than the rest of his command put together, was most impressed:

A batch of some fifty or sixty Australian prisoners was marched off close beside us – immensely big and powerful men, who without question represented an elite formation of the British empire, a fact that was also evident in battle. Enemy resistance was as stubborn as ever and violent actions were being fought at many points.[2]

These violent actions were being fought by the Afrika Korps troops from slit trenches so shallow in the rocky ground that they often had to lie there pinned down all day, defenceless, under the onslaught of thousands of flies attracted to the site by the awful detritus of war now exaggerated by the effects of the dysentery from which so many of them were suffering. Their days were aeons of agony and the relief of night was punctuated by the shock of battle with Australian patrols – sharp, vicious and invariably bloody.

In such work, the Italian ally was of little account, both for lack of training and total inadequacy of weapons or equipment, and also because, as Rommel wrote, 'Many Italian officers had thought of war as little more than a pleasant adventure and were, perforce, having to suffer a bitter disillusionment.'[3]

Another problem with which Rommel had to grapple was his lack of authority over the Luftwaffe in Africa. Although Fröhlich was amenable to suggestion it was *his* choice whether his aircraft acted in close tactical support of Rommel's troops, or in more wide-ranging tasks of enemy harassment – and his choice did not always coincide with Rommel's. And there was always the basic problem of supply, for the Italians still preferred to sail their convoys into Tripoli, declaring Benghasi far too close to R.A.F. bases to risk either ships or cargoes, which were anyway both in short supply. Even the voyage to Tripoli was proving costly, for British submarines and light naval forces operating from Malta took toll of almost every convoy, and during April two destroyer flotillas, one under command of Captain Lord Louis Mountbatten aboard

H.M.S. *Kelly*, had operated from Grand Harbour with disastrous effect, on one occasion sinking all five ships of a convoy together with its escort. It was thus proving exceedingly difficult to bring in the 1,500 tons of supplies needed every day at the front, let alone enough to build up a reserve against the time when a further advance could be made.

As for the Italian colonists of Cyrenaica, grown used over the years to a certain minimum of sustenance from the homeland, there was little or nothing to spare for them and they were faced with increasingly overt hostility from the indigenous Arabs – by now well aware of the fact that whoever was in control in the area, it was not the previous and much-resented occupants of their land. A number of Italian troops had been found murdered in the rear areas, and punitive expeditions against tribal villages had been fought off with arms evidently salvaged from the recent battle-fields.

But above and beyond all this was the total lack of appreciation exhibited by Berlin for the achievement of the Afrika Korps and their commander. This was not only wounding but also incomprehensible, for Rommel and his troops were still kept in ignorance of the gigantic operation being planned for mid-June in the east, not least because it was shrewdly suspected that had he known of it, he might have attempted to return hotfoot to Berlin to secure a place in *Operation Barbarossa* for himself. Compared with the invasion of Russia, the Desert War to his political and military masters would be an unimportant skirmish, and this attitude was illustrated by the arrival of Generalmajor Alfred Gause with a large staff of appointees from the Oberkommando der Wehrmacht. They were charged officially with a number of liaison duties, but sent out in reality to act as a bureaucratic curb on what Halder considered intransigence bordering on gross insubordination on the part of 'this particularly disagreeable character'.

One significant fact that Rommel quickly elicited was that Gause had received explicit instructions not to place himself under Rommel's command – instructions which did not stand long in the face of Rommel's anger when he heard of them. Cables, orders and counter-orders flew apace, and Gause soon found himself taking von dem Borne's place as Rommel's Chief of Staff, a role he filled for many months with exemplary efficiency; but the circumstances surrounding his arrival could not easily be brushed aside, and they were accompanied by others:

Dearest Lu, 26 May 1941
Yesterday evening I received a considerable rocket from Brauchitsch, the reason for which completely passes my com-

prehension. Apparently the reports I send back, stating the conditions as they exist, don't suit their book.

Dearest Lu,   29 May 1941
Von dem Borne is to take this letter with him to-morrow and I hope it will reach you earlier than usual. I've had a major rocket from the OKH – to my mind unjustified – in gratitude for our previous achievements . . . I'm not going to take it lying down, and a letter is already on its way to von Brauchitsch.
For your peace of mind, I've kept very well so far . . .

Dearest Lu,   2 June 1941
It was 107° here yesterday, and that's quite some heat. Tanks standing in the sun go up to as much as 160°, which is too hot to touch.
My affair with the OKH is under way. Either they've got confidence in me or they haven't. If not, then I'm asking them to draw their own conclusions. I'm very intrigued to know what will come of it. It's easy enough to bellyache when you aren't sweating it out here.[4]

There were a few reasons for satisfaction, though, the first being that by the end of May, the bulk of 15th Panzer Division had become available for deployment at the front and its new commander, Generalleutnant Walther Neumann-Sylkow, was able to take over command in the Capuzzo area in early June. This meant that the majority of troops immediately facing any British threat would be German except along the line Sollum–Musaid–Capuzzo where there were three battalions of the Trento Infantry Division and one regiment of the excellent Italian artillery, with two more Italian artillery regiments back in Bardia.

The German element at the frontier consisted of two battalions of the 8th Panzer Regiment, the 33rd Reconnaissance Battalion, a battalion of lorried infantry and a motor-cycle battalion, an anti-tank battalion with twenty-one 37mm. guns and twelve 50mms – and an anti-aircraft battery with thirteen of the superb 88mm. guns, mostly built into dug-outs to serve in their most effective role as anti-tank guns; and one battery of field artillery. The static elements were concentrated along the Hafid ridge, at Point 206 and Qalala, with the most forward positions at Halfaya well fortified and under command of an extraordinary soldier and clergyman, Major the Reverend Wilhelm Bach, of whose military ability Rommel had the highest opinion.

The 5th Light Division by the end of May had been largely withdrawn for rest and maintenance to the south of Tobruk, while around the perimeter were the tanks of the Ariete Division and the

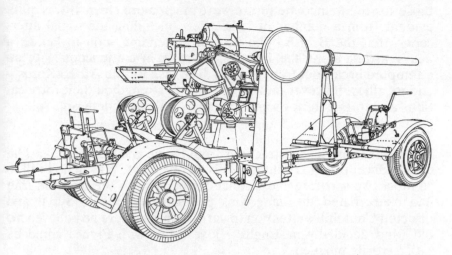

Figure 4   88mm. flak gun: weight in action 5 tons; travelling weight 7·5 tons; traverse 360°; horizontal range 16,200 yards; vertical range 35,100 feet; weight of projectile H.E. 20 lbs, A.P. 21 lbs; rate of fire 15/20 per min.; crew 10

infantry of the Brescia and Pavia Divisions, buttressed by German Rifle Companies, especially in the salient.

One other vitally important unit operating between both battle-fronts was Rommel's signal intercept service, which kept him very well informed indeed about both British and Australian intentions, for neither the Imperial nor Commonwealth formations, from individual tank crews to Headquarter Staffs, had yet learned to curb their inclination to chatter, using on most occasions the simplest codes or the most transparent jargon.

So far as vehicles and artillery were concerned, too, the position was better than Rommel had expected, for from the acres of equipment abandoned by the Italians and left almost undisturbed by the British, the industrious Germans salvaged and repaired a great deal. Italian guns appeared in German positions (with their correct ammunition efficiently stacked alongside), Italian lorries, cars and motor-cycles, all newly adorned with the Afrika Korps insignia of palm tree and swastika, patrolled the roads and tracks with German drivers at the wheels; so it was not long before Rommel was in receipt of a diatribe from Generale Gariboldi to the effect that such equipment was Italian property and must only be put to use by Italians – an instruction which elicited only an extremely acid comment from the Afrika Korps commander.

If, then, prospects for the distant future appeared vague and unsatisfactory as a result of equivocation in both Rome and Berlin, those for the immediate future were much more clear. It was quite evident from a number of indications, including the signal intercepts, that the British opposite were intending soon to launch a heavy attack along the frontier, possibly in conjunction with an attempted break-out from Tobruk. The task for the Afrika Korps – and its allies, however unwilling – was to strengthen their fortifications and train hard for something new to them, a defensive role.

Whatever Rommel's distractions from Rome and Berlin, at least he could concentrate his military skills on one front; Wavell had still to conduct two separate and distinct campaigns, for the revolt in Iraq had exacerbated the dangerous political situation in Syria, and directed Churchill's attention towards an area where he believed his old (and decidedly un-English) love affair with France could be satisfactorily pursued.

Under the terms of the Armistice with France, an Italo-German Commission had arrived in Syria at the end of August 1940 charged with the task of progressively disarming, demobilising and repatriating the 120,000-strong Army of the Levant, which in the early days of the war Wavell had regarded as his strongest bulwark against German aggression in the Middle East, and its commander, Général Weygand, as his staunchest ally. By early 1941, it had been reduced to 35,000 officers and men retained to ensure internal order and security – but these were all hard-core professional soldiers, equipped with a considerable proportion of the war supplies originally sent to Syria for the entire Army of the Levant, and they were commanded by Général Henri Dentz, a soldier who buttressed his pro-Vichy patriotism with a strong personal Anglophobia.

Of this situation Wavell was well aware, but Churchill was not – and the Prime Minister's illusions were fostered and encouraged by the ambitions of Général de Gaulle, together with the glowing optimism of the latter's representative in the Middle East, Général Georges Catroux, aided and abetted by Churchill's old friend and liaison officer with the Free French, Major-General Edward Spears. The situation was thus fraught with possibilities for misunderstanding and resultant friction.

The official British position regarding Syria was quite clear. Britain was not at war with Vichy France, but she could not allow Syria or the Lebanon (both provinces ruled by the French under a mandate granted by the League of Nations after the First World War) to be occupied by any hostile power, or to be used as a base for attacks on neighbouring countries in which Britain had interest; neither could she allow Syria or the Lebanon to become the scene of disorders which might threaten in any way the internal security of such countries.

Unfortunately for Wavell, towards the end of 1940 Général Catroux became convinced that conditions in Syria were ripe for a *coup d'état* in which, so he and his supporters believed, the rump of the Army of the Levant would rise in support of Général de Gaulle, throw off the shameful mantle of Vichy and join the fight against Nazi oppression.

To this opinion Wavell did not subscribe, remembering that during the hiatus immediately after the collapse of France, the only worthwhile body of men to decamp from Syria to Palestine in order to continue the fight had been a brigade of Poles who had escaped from Europe after the tragic defeat of their own country. They had been accompanied by less than a thousand individual Frenchmen, though a Colonel Collet had managed to bring over with him his own picturesque regiment of Circassian Cavalry. Wavell was far closer to the truth of the matter than either the leaders of the Free French or Churchill, appreciating that in the eyes of many Frenchmen – and especially in the eyes of the French professional officers – De Gaulle and his followers represented nothing but a traitorous and dissident faction which, by breaking away from the decisions of the official government of France and by maintaining what was still regarded as a hopeless struggle alongside the pig-headed British, were jeopardising France's prospects of obtaining tolerable peace terms from the eminently reasonable and scrupulously well-behaved Germans.

Général de Gaulle paid a visit to the Middle East in April and one result was that in early May a feverish exchange of cables took place between Wavell and the Chiefs of Staff, the British Ambassador in Egypt and the Foreign Office, Général de Gaulle (who had gone on to French Equatorial Africa) and Général Catroux, General Spears and Mr Churchill. The main burden of the messages from the French was that on the one hand their propaganda bombardment of the Vichy French Forces had now rendered Syria ripe for invasion (later events demonstrated that it had merely irritated both French and Syrian opinion) and on the other hand, the Germans were on the point of invading Syria themselves, so Général Dentz would welcome assistance against them from any source, especially the Free French.

On May 18th, Général Catroux went so far as to announce that secret intelligence sources had informed him that Général Dentz was about to withdraw all Vichy French forces into the Lebanon and present the rest of Syria without battle or even argument to an advancing German occupation force – so as the road to Damascus was now open, would General Wavell please give orders for an immediate advance? General Wavell declined to move – much to Général de Gaulle's indignation – so Catroux then requested permission for the five battalions of Free French troops in the Middle East to go at least as far as the Syrian border in order to test reaction on the other side, pointing out that all he would need from the British would be 300 lorries and a minimum of air support; this at a time when Wavell had to cut down the size of the force he had been ordered to send into Iraq precisely because of lack of lorries. It was also the day after *Operation Brevity* ended and two days before the launching of the German airborne invasion of Crete.

With a restraint which had marked all his actions since his appointment as Commander-in-Chief but which was now showing signs of wearing thin, Wavell cabled Whitehall with his own cogently expressed objections both to the entire scheme and to this harassment by the Free French, and rather pointedly asked if London expected him to accept the French suggestions despite his own objections; to which he immediately received a reply telling him to do as Général Catroux wished!

The heated exchange which then followed culminated in a cable sent direct from Churchill, which ended:

> For this decision we of course take full responsibility, and should you find yourself unwilling to give full effect to it arrangements will be made to meet any wish you may express to be relieved of your command.[5]

The writing was on the wall, plain to read, but as it happened, on the day Wavell received it, Général Catroux discovered that he had been misled by his secret sources, that the information about French withdrawal to the Lebanon was untrue, and that, far from withdrawing, Vichy French forces had in fact moved to key positions in which they could effectively block any attempt to enter Syria from the south or east.

The storm died down but there is no trace of any signal to Wavell apologising for the doubt which had been cast on his judgment, or even for the trouble he had been caused; but then these were the days when the German battleship *Bismarck* was loose in the Atlantic, and Wavell was not alone in having to fight the war on many fronts. It is surprising that more sympathy did not exist between sets of people grappling with similar sets of problems, but the sad fact remains that the impression left in London – especially in Churchill's heart – was not that Wavell had been right, but that he had been obstructive.

So strong was this feeling that despite the collapse of Catroux's case for the invasion of Syria, despite also the myriad tasks with which Wavell and his forces in the Middle East were grappling, he was instructed to make ready the largest force possible – without, of course, endangering the security of the Cyrenaican front or interfering with the launching of an offensive against Rommel at the earliest opportunity – and dispatch it northwards into Syria in order to capture the important airfields from which, undoubtedly, several Luftwaffe squadrons had been operating against Habforce, and from which they might in the future launch operations .against Egypt and especially the Suez Canal.

Operation Exporter began on June 8th when elements of the 7th Australian Division, a brigade of the 4th Indian Division (hastily rushed back from Eritrea), two regiments of 1st Cavalry division (one still on horses), a battalion of the Special Service Brigade now stationed in Cyprus, and a weak Free French Force under Legentil-homme, now promoted Général, crossed the frontier in three drives, one directed towards Damascus through Deraa, one in the centre towards Rayak through Merjayun and one along the coast to Beirut, where Général Dentz's Headquarters lay.

A detailed account of the Syrian Campaign is not part of this history, except in so far as it affected General Wavell and the conduct of the war in North Africa. At this point it is sufficient to say that by the end of the first phase, which lasted until June 13th, all advances were held up and it had become very evident that the Vichy French forces were not only well entrenched and well

Map 18 *Operation Exporter*: June 1941

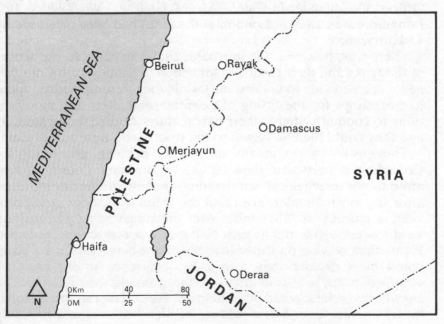

equipped, but that they showed not the slightest sympathy towards Gaullist or Free French ambitions. On the contrary, they greeted all attempts at propaganda or dialogue with their compatriots with contempt and abuse, the fighting between them was amongst the bitterest of the war, there were a number of violations of both the white flag and the Red Cross and the Vichy French treatment of any prisoners they took, especially British or Indian, was abominable.

But by the end of that first phase, not even Churchill expected Wavell to be paying much attention to *Exporter*. During the afternoon of June 14th, three British columns left the area of Sidi Barrani and advanced some twenty-four miles towards the Egyptian frontier.

Operation Battleaxe had begun.

The 'Tiger' convoy, by which Churchill's generosity after the loss of Cyrenaica had been best expressed, arrived at Alexandria on May 12th, and the Prime Minister's courage was rewarded by the fact that of the five fast transports in which vital cargoes travelled, only one had been lost – the *Empire Song* carrying 57 tanks and ten Hurricanes struck mines in the narrows to the south of Malta and had blown up, fortunately with no loss of life. The result was that by mid-May Wavell's armament had been theoretically increased by 135 Matildas, 82 cruisers (of which 50 – enough to re-equip one complete tank regiment – were the new Mark IV 'Crusaders'), and 21 light tanks, while the force at the command of the acting Air Officer Commander-in-Chief, Air Marshal A. W. Tedder (for Longmore was away in London at the time) had been increased by 43 Hurricanes.

There was, however, the inevitable time-gap between the arrival of the tanks and their readiness for action (a hiatus which Churchill never seemed able to understand) while they were unloaded, taken to workshops for the fitting of essential sand-filters and modifications to cooling systems, their new features studied by technicians and they could then be issued to the troops who were to use them.

They were by no means universally popular, the Mark IV Crusaders in particular showing exactly the same defects of thin armour and mechanical unreliability as their predecessors. Even after the most complete overhaul the Delta workshops could provide, a journey of thirty miles over the rough going and drifting sand was enough to put at least 10 per cent out of action. Sir David Hunt, then serving on the Staff, tells of one cavalry officer who so hated his Crusader that with the concurrence of his crew he swopped it for a 3-ton lorry on the grounds that it would go anywhere the tank could go, would not break down so often, and if hit by an anti-tank shell would suffer merely a neat and probably inconsiderable hole in its fabric, instead of brewing up and incinerating the crew.

However, most of the tanks were at last taken over by their crews and joined the reconstituted formations of the 7th Armoured Division – but this was by no means the same division which had won the resounding victories leading up to Beda Fomm. For one thing, they had been without tanks of any sort for four months, and now at least one regiment was to be mounted in this new model which they were seeing for the first time. Moreover, many of the stalwarts of the division, including for instance 'Blood' Caunter, had found other outlets for their energies and enterprise during the interregnum, and were either no longer in Egypt or had been promoted and appointed to duties from which they could now not be spared. Two promising officers and some senior N.C.O.s had joined the Long Range Desert Group and others were attached to various new unorthodox units which were springing up like flowers in April, though a proportion of them were to prove to be weeds. And now Pat Hobart was no longer there to drill the remainder quickly back into shape.

All squadrons had received their new tanks by June 9th, but at O'Moore Creagh's urgent representations they were given another five days for extra training before the onset of *Battleaxe* – the operation whose declared aim was now to destroy Rommel's forces in the frontier area and follow up as far as Tobruk, where the garrison was to be relieved and the enemy forces defeated. The combined forces would then sweep forward as far as the Derna–Mechili line.

The operation was to be commanded in the field by Lieutenant-General Sir Noel Beresford-Peirse, and he had two divisions under his command – the 4th Indian now under Major-General Frank Messervy (who had led Gazelle Force in Eritrea) and 7th Armoured under Creagh. Neither of these divisions, however, was up to full strength, each lacking one brigade.

The 4th Indian Division, which would at the outset push along the coast through Halfaya towards Sollum and Capuzzo, consisted of the 11th Indian Brigade with Rajputana Rifles and Mahrattas at the foot of the Escarpment and the Camerons at the top, and the 22nd Guards Brigade which was motorised and would advance to attack Capuzzo and then exploit if possible up towards Bardia.

Those responsible for the numeration of the units of the 7th Armoured Division carried out their duties with a fine disregard for the problems of the historian. The 7th Armoured Division consisted of two brigades, 4th Armoured and 7th Armoured. The 4th Armoured Brigade consisted basically of two regiments (both at *Battleaxe* armed with Matildas) – 4th Royal Tank Regiment and 7th

Royal Tank Regiment; 7th Armoured Brigade also consisted of two regiments – 2nd R.T.R. in a mixture of A9, A10 and A13 cruiser tanks (to which they were well accustomed although these were new ones), and 6th R.T.R. in the new Crusader tanks. The Support Group, temporarily commanded by Jock Campbell, consisted of four batteries of the Royal Horse Artillery and their old friends, 1st Battalion King's Royal Rifle Corps and 2nd Battalion The Rifle Brigade.

The duties for the 7th Armoured Division were to some extent dictated by their weapons. However indestructible the Matildas had proved to be in the past, their speed was but a trifle more than that of marching infantry, and their capability for co-operation with cruisers, the oldest of which had a speed of 15 m.p.h. while the Crusaders were reputed to be able to move at 27 m.p.h., was thus much restricted. The Matildas of 4th R.T.R. would therefore be used, at least initially, as infantry support, two troops accompanying the Rajputanas and Mahrattas along the coast road, one squadron with the Camerons in their attack on the garrison at the top of Halfaya Pass, the rest shepherding 22nd Guards Brigade on and into Capuzzo and then exploiting towards Sollum if necessary, and then up to Bardia if all went well. Point 206, which was known to be held in strength by the enemy, lay along the axis between Sidi Suleiman and Capuzzo, and the Matildas would certainly be necessary there.

The main bulk of 4th Armoured Brigade would thus be on the southern wing of the infantry advance, and available if necessary to support their brothers in the cruiser tanks of 7th Armoured Brigade, as these swung in an even wider circle to the south aiming up towards the Hafid Ridge where it was believed the bulk of Rommel's armour lay. The Support Group would string out behind the cruisers to form a shield during the battles on the coast and escarpment, against possible enemy intrusion from the direction of Sidi Omar. The main aim of the 7th Armoured Division was to bring the German armour to battle, to destroy it and then prepare to sweep westwards towards Tobruk and the second stage of the battle.

Above the advance would fly 98 Hurricanes and Tomahawks, while ranging beyond them, over and past Tobruk, 105 heavy and medium bombers would attack Rommel's supply routes and the reinforcements which he would undoubtedly move up once he realised the seriousness of the attack – all under the direction of Air Marshal Tedder who was stripping the rest of his command of every possible aircraft to give support to *Battleaxe*. Both Tedder and Beresford-Peirse would direct the operation from well to the rear – Tedder from Maaten Baggush and Beresford-Peirse from Sidi Barrani.

Both Wavell and Beresford-Peirse were pinning their hopes for the success of *Battleaxe* on the toughness and expertise of the Indian and Guards infantry, on the proven durability of the Matildas, and on the capacity of the cruisers to bring the German panzers to battle and then to defeat them.

Dawn on June 15th broke clear and fine, and all troops and vehicles were on the move. Along the top of the Escarpment, 2nd Camerons and their escort of thirteen Matildas of 4th R.T.R., with a battery of 31st Field Regiment, marched or drove stolidly forward towards their first objective, the garrison at the top of Halfaya, aware that to their right and below the lip their comrades of the 1st/6th Rajputana Rifles and 2nd/5th Mahrattas were moving parallel and level with them. The commander of the 4th R.T.R., Lieutenant-Colonel Walter O'Carroll, caught the mood of the moment exactly:

> To start with the tanks moved in double line ahead and slowly so as to make a minimum of noise; they were also ready to shake out in the event of hostile air. By 0530 there was not very much further to go before they might expect fire to open on them and they slowed down and fanned out. The guns [British] should open about 0540, and they did not wish to get mixed up in the 25-pounder concentration. The sun was rising behind and light forward was excellent. No guns sounded. The tanks crept on. At Halfaya the month before, Major Miles had found the enemy still in bed or shaving when he arrived, but they were Italians. Now it seemed almost too good to be true that the garrison should be so caught again . . . [6]

It was indeed. At 0600 when Major Miles – in the absence of the planned artillery cover, for the supporting battery had bogged down in the soft sand over which his tanks and the infantry had advanced with no trouble – gave the orders for the Matildas to fan out and lead the charge towards the top of the pass, it was the last order he was to give. Artillery fire crashed out ahead of them within which could be heard quite clearly the flat, whip-lash crack of the 88mm., and within a minute all but one of the Matildas, including Miles's, were in flames – and their reputation as Queen of the Battlefield gone for ever. The Camerons debussed, opened their ranks into artillery formation and marched steadily on between the lines of blazing tanks, praying for their own guns to open up and that the gap between themselves and their objectives would close more quickly – but long before it was below a thousand yards, German armoured cars and lorried infantry debouched from the head of the pass and charged, overrunning one company and chasing the remainder away into the heads of the wadis seaming the Escarpment, from where they could do little for the rest of the day but wait for darkness and watch the battle being fought out below them.

By 0730, the Mahrattas and Rajputanas were within three miles of the Reverend Bach's post at the bottom of the pass, and they had six Matildas of A Squadron 4th R.T.R. to lead them, and some 25-pounders in support. The Mahrattas moved along the base of the Escarpment and the Rajputanas on the slopes above, and the broken ground gave them excellent cover for the first mile. They then reached a curve in the line of approach, and as they rounded it, came under heavy fire from ahead and above which pinned them down – and the Matildas on the right flank ran into mines upon which four of them promptly blew up while the remaining two were blocked in positions from which they could do little but act as pill-boxes.

Map 19   *Operation Battleaxe*: June 15th–17th, 1941

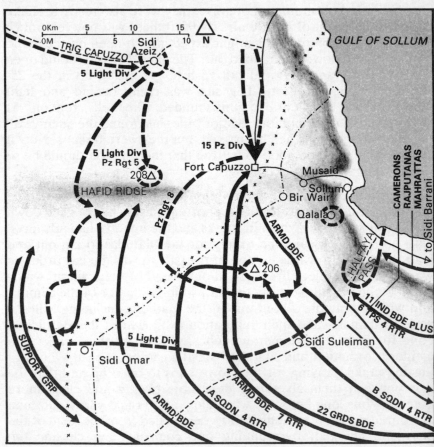

That was virtually the end of the attacks on Halfaya Pass, and Rommel's faith in the military expertise and foresight of his remarkable cleric had been fully justified.

Further south on the upper plateau, however, matters had gone better for the central thrust. Matildas of 7th R.T.R. (4th Armoured Brigade) had by-passed Point 206 which was known to be strongly held, paused by the Wire until the motorised Guards Brigade arrived and then swept on across the frontier at a steady eight miles an hour. They reached Capuzzo just before noon, chased the garrison away into the desert and then, slightly to their surprise, found themselves the object of several well-pressed counter-attacks in which five of their Matildas were knocked out and another four damaged. But the Guards infantry came up and consolidated the position, successfully fought off a much more serious counter-attack about 1830, and the joint forces then prepared for all-round defence during the night and possible exploitation of successes gained the following day.

The news from the most southerly flank, where the cruisers of 7th Armoured Brigade had swung around to Hafid Ridge had been so good so early that the failure to capture Halfaya Pass to the north had not seemed too serious a check. The brigade had been led by the older and lighter cruisers of the 2nd R.T.R. in order that the Crusaders of the 6th R.T.R. should be held as a 'card up the sleeve' until the last possible moment, and shortly after 0900 they had arrived at what the leading squadron commander, partly blinded by the shimmering and ever-growing heat-haze, believed to be the objective.

But Hafid Ridge consisted in fact of three gentle crests and between them lay the German anti-tank guns, including four 88mms. As the A9s and A10s breasted the first rise there was a blast of fire, two violent explosions as a pair of A9s brewed up – and the rest were then retreating rapidly while their crews, especially the gunners, faced up to a very awkward fact: their only armament consisted of machine-guns and 2-pounder anti-tank guns – and however effective their high-velocity solid shot might be against armour, it was useless against gun positions or dug-in infantry which required high explosive to shift them. And the bulk of the British 25-pounders was back with the Support Group.

After consultation, two squadrons of 2nd R.T.R. put in a flank attack just before noon between the first and second ridges, swept along the gun line machine-gunning the artillerymen and their supporting infantry and reached the end of the line for the loss of only one tank; but then the commander realised the presence of more enemy positions behind the second ridge, ordered a hasty retreat away from the danger area but failed to make contact with five of his tanks (owing to shortage of radio sets the allocation had been reduced to only one per troop) – and these swept on and were never seen again.

By this time, messages were coming in from the R.A.F. that long lines of German armour were streaming towards the battle area from the west, so Brigadier Russell, commanding 7th Armoured Brigade, ordered the first wave of Crusaders to clear the enemy posts from the ridge and set the scene for the main armoured battle for which the generals had been planning. They were encouraged by reports from observers at the front that the Germans there appeared to be pulling back anyway and this would seem the ideal moment to attack – so as the lighter tanks of 2nd R.T.R. (among which was one commanded by Lieutenant Joly) drew back, the Crusaders swept forward over the first crest – to see exactly what they hoped and expected, a group of German lorries and towed guns moving up and over the crest beyond.

In less than five minutes, the Crusaders were topping the second crest to be met in their turn by a storm of fire from the waiting anti-tank guns – 88mms as well as 50mm. and 37mm. guns, all of which were quite effective at that range. In their first action, the Crusaders had thus been neatly ambushed, and within minutes eleven had been completely knocked out and six more badly damaged; and now it was seen that over thirty panzers of a battalion from the 5th Panzer Regiment were coming in from the west. Light was failing by this time and, as neither side was particularly anxious to close, a long-range battle ensued during which the surviving cruisers of 7th Armoured Brigade slowly drew back towards the frontier Wire, leaving over half of their tank strength on the field either totally wrecked or, worse still, available for repair and use against them by the indefatigable German recovery teams. The tank returns for the following morning revealed that 2nd R.T.R. had but twenty-eight tanks still fit for action, while of 6th R.T.R.'s fifty Crusaders, only twenty remained.

A significant fact about the performance of the 7th Armoured Brigade on the first day of *Battleaxe* was not discovered until afterwards; it would not have achieved what little success it did, had it not been for the violent battle being fought for most of the day around Point 206 by Matildas of A Squadron of 4th R.T.R. (whose other troops had accompanied the infantry attacks against Halfaya). They had advanced along the Wire in the early morning, then after overrunning two small German posts came up against the very well-fortified Point 206, whose anti-tank guns repeated the successes on the other parts of the battlefield by knocking out eight of the Matildas before the end of the day. Twice the post changed hands and it was not until the sixteen Matildas of B Squadron came up in the evening that Point 206 was firmly held in the British hands; but the fierce fighting which went on during the daylight hours had at least protected the inner flank of 7th Armoured Brigade's advance against the Hafid Ridge.

The details of another event of that epochal day seem not to have been fully known for many months. The Rifle Brigade history contains the following passage:

> Two years later we heard from a German officer prisoner who was an inmate of our prison cage at Hammam Lif after the German surrender in Tunisia that about twenty of our Matildas broke clean through during the fighting [presumably around Capuzzo], and advanced on a defenceless Bardia, which contained only German administrative units. There were German 88-mm. flak guns in Bardia for anti-aircraft defence of the harbour. The officer commanding them stopped a German supply column which was passing through Bardia at the time, waylaid a truck which contained 88-mm. anti-tank ammunition, lined his guns up south of the perimeter defences and gave battle to our tanks. After a short slogging match eleven tanks were left and one 88-mm. gun. This gun destroyed all the remaining tanks . . . The officer was awarded the Ritterkreuz.[7]

It has not proved possible to confirm in every detail the truth of this account, but it is certainly true that a number of Matildas were never accounted for in the final battle analysis. And what is certain is that of the hundred-odd Matildas which went into action with the 4th Armoured Brigade on the morning of June 15th, only thirty-seven were still capable of action when night fell, although the fitters would have eleven more ready by the following morning.

In all, then, by the end of the first day of *Battleaxe* British armour had been reduced to about 50 per cent of its strength, and as yet had failed to bring the main strength of the German panzers to battle.

Rommel, though obviously concerned by the loss of Capuzzo, the isolation of Major the Reverend Bach's forces at Halfaya, the known destruction of artillery and infantry positions along the Hafid Ridge and the suspected loss of Point 206, was sufficiently well informed by his intercept service of losses and problems on the British side to be able, by about midnight on June 15th, quite coolly and confidently to begin planning the battle for the following day.

He had instructed the new commander of 5th Light Division, Generalleutnant von Ravenstein, to put his leading combat group on the road from Tobruk towards Sidi Azeiz as early as the evening of June 14th, and it was a panzer battalion of this group which had arrived to the west of Hafid Ridge on the evening of the 15th and pushed the cruisers of 7th Armoured Brigade back to the Wire. Behind them, the rest of 5th Light Division was coming up and by midnight almost all had arrived at Sidi Azeiz.

Meanwhile, Neumann-Sylkow's 15th Panzer Division had remained more or less where it had been stationed in the morning, its anti-tank and artillery batteries and its infantry taking the brunt of the British attack, while the majority of its panzers – though not all – were held back on Rommel's orders to the north of the battle area. He had no intention of committing them to battle until the situation clarified. Around Capuzzo, panzers had been in the original clash and in the counter-attacks, but as their chief tactic had been to lure the British tanks on to the anti-tank batteries and not to accept action themselves unless it was forced upon them, they had not suffered many losses.

Although Rommel had started the battle with less tanks in the area than the British, and although he had meanwhile obtained an exaggerated idea of British strength, with the arrival of 5th Light and increasing knowledge of British plans for the following day he felt that prospects now favoured him. He knew, for instance, that Beresford-Peirse had ordered the 4th Indian Division both to renew its attacks on Halfaya Pass and to consolidate its hold on Capuzzo; and he was in no way disturbed when he heard that a battalion of the Scots Guards had mounted a successful night attack on the post back at Musaid. He also knew that General Messervy had been ordered to release 4th Armoured Brigade from its duties of protecting the infantry so that its Matildas could join the cruisers of 7th Armoured Brigade to fight that set tank-versus-panzer battle which the British seemed determined to bring about.

Rommel had no intention of allowing such a battle to take place, principally because he did not believe that the role of armour was to fight armour. In his opinion – shared, indeed, by the majority of the German panzer leaders – the task for armour was to find weak places in the enemy defence, which would generally be infantry positions, break through them and then attack the soft-skinned and unprotected rear echelons of the enemy supply organisation. It was the task of artillery to fight tanks, and infantry to capture artillery posts – a case almost of scissors cut paper, paper wraps stone, stone sharpens scissors.

Even without this philosophy, however, he had a more urgent task for his panzers than the destruction of the British armour – a matter which seemed to be progressing quite satisfactorily without their intervention. Bach and his men at Halfaya were trapped and running out of supplies, and the panzers of 5th Light Division must attempt to get through to them as quickly as possible by swinging down to the south from Sidi Azeiz to Sidi Omar, then east and across through Sidi Suleiman. Neumann-Sylkow's 15th Panzer Division could best help this move by a determined attack in the centre against Capuzzo, which would pin down the Guards Brigade and perhaps also the Matildas of the 4th Armoured Brigade, despite Beresford-Peirse's contrary intentions for them.

And as the British apparently intended to begin the day's fighting shortly after dawn, he would anticipate them and strike while it was still dark.

The battle in front of Capuzzo was joined by 0600 (15th Panzer had started their approach an hour before) and it developed in a way which Rommel would have regretted, for it became a copybook pattern of a well-conducted defensive. There was no need for a bait to tempt the German panzers on to the British anti-tank guns, for Rommel had in effect ordered this while Neumann-Sylkow carried it out in detail. Eighty panzers attacked Capuzzo in two columns, one on each side, and they ran into a barrage of artillery and anti-tank guns supported by the guns of Matildas held stationary in hull-down positions, which virtually made anti-tank gun-posts of them.

And owing to the strong infantry element at Capuzzo, there could be little or no possibility of retreat for the British, who thus were forced to stand and fight it out. This they did to such effect that by 1000 Neumann-Sylkow was reporting his tank strength down to but thirty tanks and the morale of his panzer crews falling fast; smoke and flame covered the battlefield and the wreck of the old Italian stone fort was ringed with burning panzers stopped in their tracks by 25-pounders brought up after the fort had been taken, or caught and penetrated in flank by the 2-pounders as they turned. All the time, machine-guns chattered and rifles cracked and German panzer crews and escorting engineers or infantry fell beneath the famous rapid fire of the British infantry. By noon, 15th Panzer Division was drawing back, counting its losses and hastily salvaging whatever they could from the maul, while the British watched and waited again and on the right even felt strong enough for the Scots Guards to move across from Musaid and take the Sollum barracks at the top of the pass.

Meanwhile, behind Capuzzo at Halfaya, the situation was reversed. Mahrattas and Rajputanas below the Escarpment and Camerons above were trying to shift Bach and his men from the vital posts they held, but like the panzers a few miles away the British infantry were trying to advance against prepared positions, manned by men who knew quite well that there was nowhere for them to retreat to – for the Guards Brigade lay between them and their support.

But to the south-west and west an entirely different battle was being fought, for here there was ground for manoeuvre. The panzers of 5th Light had begun their move down past the western edge of the Hafid Ridge at dawn, and all day the remaining cruisers of 7th Armoured Brigade side-stepped with them, at first by themselves as 4th Armoured were indeed tied down at Capuzzo and then, as the battle moved south towards Sidi Omar, aided by the infantry and guns of the Support Group columns which had been shielding the south-western flank.

There had been some unexpected and lucky successes for the British during the early part of the day – a combined charge by tanks of both 2nd and 6th R.T.R. which drove a column of enemy transport thinly escorted by panzers well out into the desert, and an attack on an unescorted column of soft-skinned transport which dispersed it and left a wide expanse of the plateau littered with wrecked and smoking lorries; but when the British cruisers tried to fight it out with the panzers, the results were rarely favourable to them.

The basic reasons for this were technical. Like the British tank school, the Germans had opted for three types of tank, one of which was little more than a light reconnaissance tank. But the other two, instead of being divided in the British way into different types to fight in different battles – in infantry battles in support or in tank battles in manoeuvre – were divided into vehicles with differing armaments to fight in the same battle. Their Panzerkampfwagen IIIs were armed with a 50mm. anti-tank gun which was in fact marginally inferior to the British 2-pounder (40mm.) but the Panzerkampfwagen IVs were armed with a 75mm. gun which could fire both high explosive and smoke at ranges of up to 3,000 yards, and the British tanks carried nothing to equal this. Moreover, the two types of panzers were trained to work together and the effect of their co-operation and armament on the cruisers of 7th Armoured Division that morning, even when the latter were covered by the 25-pounders of the Support Columns, was ominous.

When the panzers of 5th Light turned to attack a line of British cruisers and artillery, they did so at about fifteen miles per hour, and once they had closed to 3,000 yards their 75mm. guns could open fire with high explosive. This could inflict some damage on the tanks – but would annihilate the unprotected 25-pounders and their crews. As it would take the panzers six minutes to cover the 3,000 yards and the guns three minutes to limber up and get out of action, this meant in practice that the guns must cease firing and begin pulling out as soon as shell-fire began exploding around them; and it was quickly found that the 2-pounder anti-tank guns in the cruisers were only really effective against the German panzers at ranges of less than 500 yards.

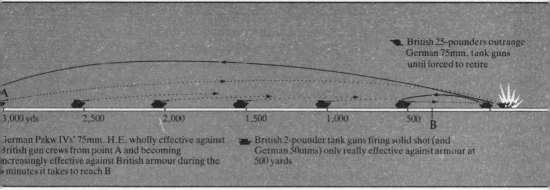

British 25-pounders outrange
German 75mm. tank guns
until forced to retire

A

3,000 yds   2,500   2,000   1,500   1,000   500   B

German Pzkw IVs' 75mm. H.E. wholly effective against   British 2-pounder tank guns firing solid shot (and
British gun crews from point A and becoming   German 50mms) only really effective against armour at
increasingly effective against British armour during the   500 yards
minutes it takes to reach B

Thus, when a squadron of about forty German panzers attacked a
line of ten British cruisers (and by the morning of June 16th, the
entire 7th Armoured Brigade had only forty-eight tanks left and the
first engagements had already taken their toll), even though it was
supported by a troop of four 25-pounders, the only guns which
could engage the panzers before they came within 3,000 yards were
those of the artillery – who would then come under H.E. fire from
which they were virtually unprotected and must, in the light of
simple mathematics, pull out. And from that moment until the
panzers had closed to within the 500-yard range of the cruisers'
2-pounders, there was nothing the British could fire at them which
could do them anything but trivial damage.

Many British tank gunners during that frustrating morning
opened fire at German panzers at ranges of a thousand yards or
more – a futile gesture for not only could their solid shot deliver
little but a glancing blow, but in the shimmer and haze as the heat of
the day increased, their comparatively rudimentary gun-sights were
useless. The panzers had better armament and optical equipment,
sounder engineering and therefore fewer breakdowns and, moreover, their crews had been given more time to get used to their
vehicles in the conditions in which they were operating. Mr
Churchill's impatience for action was wasting the fruits of his own
beneficence.

Thus, as the morning wore on, the strength of 7th Armoured
Brigade was whittled away and by noon when the commander of
6th R.T.R. withdrew his Crusaders to the Wire for refuelling and
replenishment, he found that he had only ten runners left – and the
remainder of 2nd R.T.R. were at that very moment fighting a
desperate rearguard action to enable the Support Group column
which had gone down to Sidi Omar the previous day to get away.
By mid-afternoon both R.T.R.s were back east of the frontier,

about six miles apart and with their supporting artillery further back still, the tank crews watching anxiously the massing of panzers along the Wire, totally incapable of interfering with the preparations for the next stage of the advance which was obviously imminent.

It came about 1900, just as the light was fading – in itself an indication of the high degree of German training – and as on so many occasions that day, the Crusaders had to wait under heavy fire until the approaching panzers came within effective range, watched all the time by men of their Support Group to the rear, paralysingly unable to help them:

> There we first saw that most depressing sight – the tracer of the solid shot from our 2-pounder guns describing graceful parabolas in the air and bouncing anything up to five or six hundred yards short of the enemy tanks, while the tracer from enemy weapons flew on much flatter curves and 'brewed' our tanks up one after the other. When the 7th Armoured Brigade concentrated at Bir Khireigat the next morning they had nine 'runners' left.[8]

After the first attack on the 6th R.T.R. Crusaders, the panzers had turned against the even lighter and older tanks of the 2nd R.T.R. and annihilation of the British cruisers was only averted by the onset of complete darkness. June 16th, 1941, was the day when the British tank crews first realised that their own experts on armoured warfare had been out-thought by Hitler's.

It also marked the beginning of the last twenty-four hours which Wavell was to spend on a desert battlefield, for with the perception which always took him to the place where he was most likely to be needed, he had arrived at Sidi Barrani during that afternoon to find that Beresford-Peirse was away visiting Messervy and Creagh. Despite the trend of the day's events, Beresford-Peirse had confirmed them in their orders to hold on at Capuzzo with the infantry, and to consolidate the armour of 4th and 7th Brigades the following morning for a mass onslaught against Rommel's panzers, and by evening there was perhaps a little more ground for the somewhat spurious hope that this might be achieved. There had been an unexpected easing of pressure against Capuzzo, so perhaps in the morning the Matildas might indeed be able to get away; but the lessons which had been learned that day by the tank crews had obviously not yet percolated to the higher ranks. They would take some time to do so.

Rommel had not needed to learn many lessons that day, and late in the afternoon he gave an excellent example of what his countrymen called his *Fingerspitzengefühl* and which his opponents with wry admiration and perhaps a little more elegance were to call 'The Rommel Touch'.

'It is often possible', he was to write later, 'to decide the issue of a battle merely by making an unexpected shift of one's main weight.'

This he proceeded to do. He had carefully followed the engagement between the 5th Light panzers and the 7th Armoured tanks and watched them clash west of Sidi Omar:

> The violent tank battle which ensued was soon decided in our favour and the division succeeded in fighting its way through to the area north-east of Sidi Omar and continuing its advance on Sidi Suleiman. This was the turning-point of the battle. I immediately ordered the 15th Panzer Division to disengage all its mobile forces as quickly as possible and, leaving only the essential minimum to hold the position north of Capuzzo, to go forward on the northern flank of the victorious 5th Light Division towards Sidi Suleiman. The decisive moment had come.[9]

The switch of thrust from one side of the arena to the other was made during the late afternoon and evening of June 16th, but not appreciated by the British until 0600 the following morning when the full weight of Rommel's remaining panzers – which had been on the move since 0430 – fell upon the weak and exhausted screens west of Sidi Suleiman and began inexorably to press them back towards the Escarpment and the battles around Halfaya.

Creagh was the first to realise the danger which now threatened the entire Battleaxe Force, and at 0930 sent a message to Beresford-Peirse requesting his presence for advice and instructions – a message which was promptly picked up and retailed to Rommel who was not slow to grasp its implications:

> It sounded suspiciously as though the British commander no longer felt himself capable of handling the situation. It being now obvious that in their present bewildered state the British would not start anything for the time being, I decided to pull the net tight by going on to Halfaya.[10]

As Wavell was still with Beresford-Peirse, he took over command, flew up to Halfway House in a light Magister aircraft which hugged the ground the whole way and so escaped the attention of the Luftwaffe fighters who now dominated the sky, arriving at 1145. However, before he had time to issue orders he discovered that General Messervy at Capuzzo had also realised the danger the infantry were in, and had disobeyed his orders of the night before to release the Matildas to augment the Crusaders' attack on the panzers and instructed them instead to hold the southern border of a channel leading back along the edge of the Escarpment through which the survivors of the 22nd Guards Brigade could escape as far as Halfaya at least, and accompanied by the Camerons, perhaps back even further.

It had been obvious to Wavell since the previous afternoon that tactical control of the battle had been exercised almost since the beginning through the co-operation between Creagh and Messervy, with Beresford-Peirse too far back to be in touch. Even the security between the two subordinate generals had been better than that between themselves and Western Desert Force Headquarters, for whenever they had felt the need to communicate directly they had foxed Rommel's intercept service by talking in Hindustani; and now the retreat which neither Wavell nor Beresford-Peirse had sanctioned was well under way.

'I think you were right to withdraw in the circumstances,' Wavell later told Messervy, 'but orders should have come from Western Desert Force' – a remark which underlined the hollowness of a situation in which junior officers could be right in usurping the responsibilities of their seniors.

And now the tactical advantages reverted to the British.

The Matildas came stolidly back from their positions around Capuzzo, the Crusaders fell back on their flank and Campbell's artillery from the Support Group was with them to hold the line – against panzers now with emptying fuel tanks and, more vitally, bereft of the striking power of the 88mms or even their lighter anti-tank guns. From hull-down positions the British tanks with their 2-pounders fought a six-hour battle with the 25-pounders alongside them, both elements of the defence confident at last that the other would not retire – at any rate until the rear columns of infantry scuttling back from Capuzzo and Halfaya had passed, by which time they could all go.

It was mid-afternoon before the crash of battle began dying down from the west, and 1600 before the leading panzers felt their way forward to find that there was now nothing between themselves and the delighted and triumphant men of Major Bach's force. Below them, the last of the Mahrattas and Rajputanas had gone, and as on Rommel's urgent instructions the panzers turned west and swept towards Musaid and Capuzzo it was to find that the trap was empty, the quarry escaped – and their commander furious at what he considered their ineptitude at trying to squeeze out the pocket instead of blocking off the neck.

Rommel could be as unfair to his subordinates as any other high-level commander.

On the last day of *Battleaxe*, Churchill, shaken by the accumulating evidence of the loss of what he had romantically come to look upon as his own 'Tiger Cubs', left London and went down to his home at Chartwell which he had shut up for the duration of the war, to roam disconsolately through the empty rooms and the once-immaculate gardens, now shabbier, now showing the signs of less exact attention. It was not an atmosphere conducive to optimism, impartiality of judgment or even of charity; and while he was there Wavell's report on the events of the last few days arrived, opening with the chilling sentence 'I regret to report failure of "Battleaxe".' During the next few days, the figures of the British losses came in – losses for what the maps showed only too clearly had been no gain at all.

XIII Corps had lost 122 officers and men killed, 588 wounded and 259 missing. The R.A.F. had lost 36 aircraft and the artillery had lost four of their guns; but the figures which rubbed salt into Churchill's wounds were the ones which revealed that of the hundred-odd Matildas with which the battle had opened, 64 had been lost together with 27 of the cruisers. He had not stripped Britain of her defences, ignored the advice of his Chiefs of Staff and braved the dangers of the Mediterranean passage for results such as these. The arrival of a further cable from Wavell strengthened a resolve already firmly in his mind:

A. P. Wavell to Prime Minister   21st June, 1941
Am very sorry for failure of 'Battleaxe' and loss of so many Tiger cubs, especially since I have realised from figures produced by liaison officer how short we are of requirements at home. Fear this failure must add much to your anxieties. I was over-optimistic and should have advised you that 7th Armoured Division required more training before going into battle. Feel I should also have deferred 'Exporter' till we could have put in larger force, but in both places I was impressed by apparent need for im-mediate action.[11]

The fact that both operations had been launched under strong pressure from London was left unsaid by Wavell, and ignored by Churchill.

The Prime Minister had decided: Wavell must go.

But how? It would be better if it could be done with only the faintest hint of censure on Wavell's performance, for too many people would spring to his defence asserting that he was being made a scapegoat for the Government's own mistakes; and it would be better still if matters could be so arranged that Wavell did not return to London where he could well prove an embarrassment, and if questioned by the Press or by some of Churchill's parliamentary opponents, might give answers which would be best not heard.

The solution was, in fact, quite neat and simple. As Churchill wished command of the armies of the Middle East to devolve upon the present Commander-in-Chief in India, General Auchinleck, and as Wavell had considerable experience of military service in India, the generals could simply exchange commands; Wavell would enjoy sitting under the pagoda tree – and he would be a long way from London.

The cables flew between Whitehall and Cairo, Whitehall and Delhi, Delhi and Cairo – polite, flattering, compliant; in due course aircraft bearing the new Commander-in-Chief Middle East and his personal staff arrived in Cairo, and after a few days of meetings and talks, other aircraft flew in the opposite direction bearing the old one away. The talks between the two generals had been very friendly as they knew each other well, but undoubtedly Auchinleck had cause for a great deal of thought on other problems than those of pure military tactics or strategy as he took up the reins of his new command.

As for Wavell, he had been shaving when the news of the Prime Minister's decision was read to him by his C.o.S. on the morning of June 22nd, and he had showed not the slightest emotion.

'The Prime Minister's quite right,' he said. 'This job needs a new eye and a new hand.' And he went on shaving.

He made no complaint when his request for a brief period of leave in London before taking up his new appointment was refused, but one decision by the Chiefs of Staff caused a tightening of the lips and an abruptness of manner which warned those who knew him to keep away for the rest of the morning. Two days before the official announcement of his new post, command of troops in Iraq reverted to India and would thus still be Wavell's responsibility. Churchill was not the only person to have salt in his wounds.

10 · Auchinleck Takes Command

Plus ça change, plus c'est la même chose.

The most fundamental change in the situation in the Middle East as it had faced Wavell and as it now faced Auchinleck, was that brought about by the German invasion of Russia which, indeed, introduced an entirely new dimension into the war. What remained ominously the same was the total divergence of the conclusions drawn from that event in London and Cairo.

To Churchill and the Chiefs of Staff it seemed that Auchinleck was now presented with a golden – but fleeting – opportunity to strike at Rommel immediately while all Germany's attention was held in the east and not one tank, one fighter, one man or one shell could be spared to help the Afrika Korps in any danger which threatened. To Auchinleck it appeared as a heaven-sent release of pressure which would give him time to reorganise his forces, get to know his men and ensure that they were properly equipped and much better trained for the tasks he would set them, once he was confident of their prowess.

The scene was thus set for an immediate head-on clash. The first cable which Churchill sent Auchinleck began with the words, 'You take up your great command at a period of crisis,' and ended, 'The urgency of these issues will naturally impress itself upon you. We shall be glad to hear from you at your earliest convenience' – while Auchinleck's reply, after its opening politenesses, flatly declared, 'No further offensive in the Western Desert should be contemplated until base is secure.' It then went on to state that there was no possibility whatsoever of attacking Rommel until the vexatious affair in Syria had been brought to a successful conclusion.

Churchill, who had pinned all his hopes upon the tall, ruggedly handsome and until this moment apparently forthcoming and aggressive general, was bitterly disappointed. Had he exchanged an exhausted Wavell for an obstinate or pusillanimous Auchinleck? The thought that the second was as unlikely a prognosis as the first was unfair a judgment never crossed the Prime Minister's mind, for one of the qualities which gave him the strength to bear his enormous burdens was a profound belief in the acuity of his own opinions, and the correctness of his decisions. He could hardly have carried on without it.

But to Auchinleck, the barrage of cables he now received from London – urgent, abrupt, indicative of the Prime Minister's inclination to leave the absolute minimum to anybody else's judgment – did little but confirm the warnings he had received from Wavell (and later in a long letter from Sir John Dill) and strengthen him in his determination to exercise his command in his own way and to fight his battles, if not in his own time, at least at times which he himself felt gave the best chances of victory. And he did not consider that the forces now under his command could be welded into an army well-trained and powerful enough to defeat Rommel and expel the Axis forces from Cyrenaica – let alone from the whole of North Africa, which he considered to be his ultimate objective – until the end of the summer at the earliest, and probably not until well into the autumn.

But first of all there was this tiresome business up in Syria – which was, in the event, quite quickly concluded.

The second phase had coincided with *Operation Battleaxe* and by the end of it the Australians on the coast had reached Sidon and the British had reached Damascus – but Merjayun in the centre and Palmyra (under siege by Habforce which had come up from Baghdad) were still in Vichy hands. The fighting had been bitter in the extreme and of the Free French infantry only the Marine Battalion could still be relied upon, the others having lost their enthusiasm for battle against their fellow countrymen.

With the conclusion of *Battleaxe*, however, Air Marshal Tedder could release two fighter and three bomber squadrons to operate with the forces in Syria, and the 10th Indian Division (under Major-General 'Bill' Slim) came up from Baghdad along the valley of the Euphrates to take Deir ez Zor and threaten Aleppo. The Vichy French forces could thus see that odds were mounting against them from all directions, that no help could come to them from metropolitan France and that Germany's attention was elsewhere.

A fierce battle was fought on the coast at Damour during July 7th and 8th, Beirut was under close attack by the night of the 10th and on the evening of July 11th, Général Dentz was asking for an armistice to begin at midnight. The terms were agreed that night – Allied occupation of the country, the handing over intact of ships, aircraft, naval and air establishments, the release of all British, Indian and Free French prisoners; and the choice to be given to the officers and men of the Army of the Levant either to be repatriated to France or to stay and join the Free French.

The immediate results did little to encourage belief in any French desire to see the defeat of Hitler's Germany. Of the 37,736 officers and men offered this choice, only 5,668 opted to join De Gaulle's forces and of these only 1,046 were native Frenchmen, the rest being members of the Foreign Legion (mostly German or Russian), North Africans or Senegalese. Moreover, to the astonishment and disgust of the British and Australian commanders, and of the American Consul-General who had helped with the negotiations, it was discovered that *after the signing of the armistice terms*, Général Dentz had ordered the hasty removal via Athens, Munich and Lyons to the naval fortress at Toulon of thirty-eight captured British and Indian officers, one Free French officer and thirteen N.C.O.s of the Royal Fusiliers.

Cornelius Engert, the American Consul-General, wrote a tirade on the subject to his superiors in Washington containing such phrases as 'gross breach of faith' and 'indecent collusion between Berlin and Vichy', ending, 'The Nazis have found uncommonly apt pupils in the kind of moral turpitude which they themselves have so consistently displayed in their international relations.'

When the deception was discovered, Général Dentz, three other French generals and some thirty colonels and majors were promptly arrested (just as they were packing and ready for repatriation) and it was made clear to them and in due course to the authorities in France, that they would not be released until the missing Allied prisoners were returned – a move which brought violent expostulations from both Dentz and Paris with regard not only to the differences in rank between the French hostages and the Allied prisoners, but also upon the differences in colour, which apparently they felt most keenly.

At first the Vichy Government refused to believe that the British could be so uncouth as to hold French senior officers against exchange for British and Indian junior officers and other ranks, but when the facts of the matter were fully appreciated, they quickly discovered where the prisoners were being 'sheltered' (*hébergés*) and they were soon on their way back to Beirut, travelling in first class cabins.

But it had not been like that on their journey to France, during which they had been herded together in appalling conditions and made to eat with their fingers out of horse-troughs; which resulted in some bitter comments as they watched the French hostages leaving the comforts of a Carmelite convent near Jerusalem where they had been penned.

At a ceremony at Arles in October, Admiral Darlan decorated Général Dentz with the insignia of Grand Officer of the Legion of Honour and the returned hero referred to De Gaulle and his followers as 'the corrupt, debtors, place-seekers, the perpetually dissatisfied, the mismatched, the keepers of mistresses . . . ' and to the British as 'our secular enemies, who think only of finding France when peace comes without a Navy, colonies, or military traditions . . . They represent those things which almost destroyed us; democratic-masonic politics and judaeo-saxon finance.'

With senior officers such as Dentz, it is hardly surprising that France's armies put up so little resistance to Hitler's.

Once the Syrian campaign was successfully concluded, Auchinleck could turn his full attention to the Western Desert which in everyone's mind now appeared the most important theatre – at least until the possible arrival of German troops in the Caucasus. On July 15th, he sent a long and considered cable to Churchill in reply to the Prime Minister's urgent requests for immediate action, in which he stated that in his opinion not only was time needed for training tank crews in the use of their new tanks and in co-operation with both infantry and air forces, but also that a 50 per cent reserve of tanks should be available before any aggressive operations were commenced. In view of their breakdown rate en route to the battle-field this last point was perhaps not as unreasonable as it sounded.

According to his figures, therefore, if – as Churchill was promising him – by the end of July his tank strength in the Delta rose to 500 with another 75 in Tobruk, then by the end of October he should be able to open an offensive against Rommel with a striking force of about 350 tanks, supported by one infantry division. As in one of his first cables to the Prime Minister he had said that he needed two and preferably three armoured divisions plus a motorised infantry division to ensure success, the inference was that the 500 tanks which he had been promised was about enough to supply half the forces he considered necessary. And of course, if he did receive all the tanks he required, he would probably need more time to ensure the proper training of their crews, so the offensive would not be launched until even later.

'Generals only enjoy such comforts in Heaven,' wrote Churchill much later, when his blood-pressure had returned to normal. 'And those that demand them do not always get there.'

Auchinleck's stock at Downing Street after three weeks stood but little higher than Wavell's had after twelve months.

Auchinleck suffered from another disadvantage in addition to that of inexperience in dealing with politicians which he shared with Wavell. He had spent almost his entire military life serving in the Indian Army, and even the years of the First World War had been spent with Indian troops in Mesopotamia. Except for a ten-month period as a corps commander (end of January to mid-December

1940) in England, he had not served with the British Regular Army and he therefore did not know very well the men who made up that comparatively small group of senior officers from whom his immediately subordinate generals would be chosen. He thus had no knowledge of their strengths or weaknesses.

At an intermediate level, he was well acquainted with the officers and men of the 4th Indian Division (he had been commissioned, in 1902, into the 62nd Punjabis, now renamed the 1st/1st Punjab Regiment) and was glad to confirm Frank Messervy in command of it; but except for the personal staff he had brought with him from Delhi he was surrounded at the Cairo Headquarters by almost complete strangers – and perhaps most important of all, as there had been no armoured divisions in India (very few armoured cars even, let alone tanks), his main striking force in the field would be commanded by men of whom he knew little but their names when first they came under his command. The danger of mistaken choice at all critical levels was therefore present from the moment he accepted appointment as Commander-in-Chief.

The same was true at much lower levels, too. Auchinleck had little knowledge of the type of man who was flooding out to crew his tanks, to drive his armoured cars and lorries, to man his guns or to march forward into battle with nothing but his rifle and his trust in his comrades to protect him; but this he had in common with the other generals, for the men now arriving in the Middle East were no longer the professional, regular soldiers. They were the 'hostilities only' soldiers – civilians who had either joined the Territorial Army before the war and spent some of their weekends and two weeks every summer in keen but amateur military endeavour, or who had been called up under the National Service regulations and subjected to hastily organised training in little but the basic elements of their new craft.

The great majority of them were more than willing to serve; they were keen, they were intelligent, they would in time prove to be brave and hardy. But they still had a great deal to learn, especially about open warfare, as much of their preliminary training had been based on a belief that warfare in 1940 would not be markedly dissimilar to that of 1918. A large number of them also suffered from the great disadvantage that they did not believe that regular soldiers had much to teach them.

There was an enormous difference between the civilians who had flooded forward to join the British Army in 1914 and their sons and nephews who did the same in 1939, for the latter had read the books and seen the films which the embittered survivors of that first holocaust had wrung from their sufferings, and the message which stood forth from every page and every frame was that the High

Command from 1914 to 1918 had been incompetent, stupid, callous and unimaginative. Whatever the degree of fabrication or exaggeration in that judgment, there was a great tendency among the first of the hundreds of thousands of civilians who during the Second World War suddenly found themselves in uniform to accept it totally, to assume that the same situation applied now, and thus to regard the regular officers and men with whom they were thrown into contact with thinly veiled amusement, and to listen to their advice or instruction with scepticism. In their eyes, the regular officers were likely to be indolent, aristocratic and brainless, while the other ranks were assumed to have joined the army as a result of their inability to earn their livings amid the more rigorous competitions of civilian life. What could such people teach them that their own bright intelligences would not pick up on their own, probably more accurately and certainly more perceptively than their mentors would ever appreciate?

Evelyn Waugh wrote an account of his voyage aboard the converted merchantman *Glenroy* to the Middle East in February 1941, as a member of Number 8 Commando. The troop commanders were young, high-spirited and eager for adventure and one of the butts for their wit was the *Glenroy*'s captain, to whom they referred, to the extreme annoyance of the other naval officers aboard, as 'the old bugger on the roof'. But Captain Sir James Paget, whatever his shortness of temper or lack of social sophistication, was a long-serving, capable officer who knew exactly how to get a large ship filled with valuable men and materials from Greenock to Suez via the Cape of Good Hope, and 8 Commando should have been grateful to him for it. Instead they nicknamed him 'Booby', and were quite sure that given the shortest time to study the equipment on the bridge, they could do it themselves; and this was the attitude in which they would at first regard practically every professional officer placed in command of them.

The trouble was aggravated by the fact that many of the regular officers, especially at the top, felt a degree of sympathy with them. They had themselves fought in the Ypres and Somme trenches, had agreed with much that had been written between the two wars, and although they were determined themselves not to squander men's lives with the prodigality of Haig at Passchendaele or Mangin at Verdun, they were also aware that Government parsimony coupled perhaps with a degree of personal indolence (and who has worked so hard all his life that he knows for certain that he could not have worked harder?) might have left gaps in their professional competence which these brilliant young men would sense.

Some of them remembered 'Boy' Bradford who had won both the Victoria and Military Crosses by the age of twenty-four and before his death in 1917 had risen meteorically to the rank of brigadier-general. Perhaps one of these young prodigies would do the same?

The fact that by 1945 some of them would have done remarkably well by turning themselves into thorough-going professionals does not alter the fact that in 1941 they were still the veriest amateurs – dangerous amateurs, too, for some of them combined mistaken ideas of their own abilities with aristocratic, social or political influence enough to force those ideas through against the scepticism of more realistic professionals.

One of the results of this, in 1941, was the proliferation of 'private armies'.

There were undoubtedly times during the North African campaign – and to a lesser extent in the later campaigns in Europe and the Far East – when a few small unorthodox units, established upon unusual structures of rank and equipment, carried out valuable work behind enemy lines and thoroughly justified their independence of the more usual, tried and proved line of battle formations of Army Group, Army, Corps, Division, Brigade and Battalion. The Long Range Desert Group was arguably the most successful of these, but the Jock Column was the prototype and what was later to be called the Special Air Service the most enduring.

But there were other irregular units which had neither the professionalism of the Long Range Desert Group nor the necessity for existence of the first Jock Columns, and these were to drain off valuable men and materials from the regular formations by their demands, and lose a quantity of both through their inefficiency. The trouble was that service with them seemed so attractive, especially to the more romantically minded of the new arrivals in the theatre. They offered an escape from the regulation and discipline of battalion life, freedom for the young subaltern or private from the incessant disfavour of adjutant or regimental sergeant-major, and they were all at one time or another gilded with glamour. To have been able to boast in Cairo of taking part in some of the early Jock Column exploits could result in free drinks for an evening, and a place in the Long Range Desert Group was one for which captains would willingly drop to lieutenants and sergeants to privates; and those who failed to get into either, eagerly volunteered for any other formation which promised the same apparent freedom and cachet, however non-existent its record or doubtful its purpose.

From the point of view of the Cairo Headquarters, these formations were allowed to sprout because they seemed to promise a quick return for a minimal outlay, and if they had all performed as successfully as those first ones this could have been a profitable policy; but too often these *ad hoc* units were set up as a result of little but enthusiasm coupled with social salesmanship, and manned by youngsters with cheerfully vague notions of 'swanning around the blue', blowing up enemy dumps with loud bangs and spectacular pyrotechnics, and wearing unorthodox and somewhat flamboyant variations of uniform.

This matter of clothing was, on the surface, quite amusing, but in its way it was symptomatic of a malaise which had begun to infect the forces under Auchinleck's command, and would need the heat of action to burn it out.

The first troops to operate in the desert – the 11th Hussars, the R.H.A. batteries, the Rifle Brigade and K.R.R.C. – quickly found that many well-established ideas of uniform and equipment for hot climates were mistaken. Spine-pads, for instance, supposed to protect the nervous system from the harmful rays of the sun, gave the unfortunate wearers heat-stroke and those with sensitive skins an irritable rash. The solar topees may have given a little protection to the eyes against the desert glare, but proved impractical in the haste of battle, and were invariably crushed to pulp in the chaos of a lorry or truck body as the vehicle rocked and rolled over unmade or non-existent tracks.

Very quickly and to the dismay and frustration of the old-fashioned military medicos, the Australians first and the British afterwards demonstrated that after a comparatively short period of acclimatisation it was possible for men to work in the desert clad in nothing but shorts, boots and beret, with perhaps sun-glasses for those with sensitive eyes; and that in addition to turning mahogany they then exhibited all the other signs of robust good health.

But one very real problem was desert sores, which appeared when the cooler weather came especially around the neck and on wrists and hands. The collar of the serge battledress became impregnated with sand, and when the heat of exertion or midday caused sweat to run down the neck, chafing became unbearable and the tender skin raw and open; only the essential cleanliness of the desert prevented widespread infection. The solution was obviously to wear a scarf, and soon everyone was doing so – ranging from Paisley silks for the wealthy to soft yellow muslin made from illegally opened shell-dressings for those not so well-blessed. The more decorative scarves gave a welcome touch of colour to the drab desert scene and as long as the wearers still carried out their duties with professional efficiency, no one was bothered.

It was also quickly found that the serge battledress trousers were too hot during the day and too absorbent of sand, while khaki drill trousers or shorts were too light once the sun went down; so corduroys were increasingly worn 'up the blue' – and as army boots had a tendency to crunch gravel on a night patrol, these were often replaced by the rubber-soled boots, often of suede, which rejoiced in the name of 'brothel-creepers'.

Clad in beret (rust-coloured in the case of the 11th Hussars), khaki shirt with silk muffler, leather jerkin, corduroy trousers and suede boots, the old desert hand would still bring an admirable efficiency to his duties, an expertise with every weapon in his armoury against the enemy, and a tough realism to the business of war. But his appearance was seized upon with delight by the new arrivals, who added sheepskin coats and eau-de-Cologne, and once they were well sunburned believed – human nature being what it is – that they would be just as effective soldiers, when their chance came, as those they emulated.

In the meantime, a trip behind the Wire with this or that demolition squadron or somebody else's reconnaissance column (usually called a 'shufti-job') would give them experience, and also save them from the dull routine of drills, weapon-training, map-reading and vehicle maintenance under the instructions of those unimaginative fellows at the depot. One series of totally abortive coastal raids carried out in this spirit was most aptly code-named after the famous string of theatrical farces which had run during the 1930s at the Aldwych – Rookery, Nook, Cuckoo – and many of those who took part were to spend the rest of the war in German prison camps wondering what had gone wrong; of the remainder, some died, some obtained desk jobs on the Staff but the rest in time learned what soldiering was about and duly fulfilled their role. As it happened, their sheepskin coats proved excellent value, eau-de-Cologne was found beneficial for treating cuts and abrasions and if inhaled deeply during the stunning heat of a July midday, remarkably revivifying. But neither would replace professionalism.

One place where there were no silk scarves or eau-de-Cologne was in Tobruk. By July, the defences were firm, the tasks understood and accepted, the techniques of living and fighting in severely cramped and arid circumstances both well developed and well learned, and morale as high as anywhere in the Middle East – truly high, too; not just the journalist's delight of wise-cracking optimism and sing-songs around the camp fire, but the mood of grim determination which comes to men who have been told by their commander, 'There'll be no Dunkirk here. If we have to get out, we shall fight our way out. There is to be no surrender or retreat,' and have sufficient knowledge of and respect for him to know that he meant it.

Major-General Leslie Morshead was now in sole command of the Tobruk Fortress, Major-General Lavarack having left to command the Australians in Syria the day after Rommel's first attempt to take

Tobruk at Easter. Morshead was a man in the great civilian-soldier tradition of Australia's famous First World War general, Sir John Monash; a schoolmaster in 1914, a battalion commander in 1918 with the C.M.G., D.S.O. and Légion d'honneur, a shipping executive in 1939 and now in 1941 a major-general holding the most important Allied command in the Middle East after Auchinleck's.

For Britain, it was extremely fortunate that circumstances had combined to bring Morshead to that place at that time, for in addition to being extremely tough in both mind and body (he was known to his troops as 'Ming the Merciless') he was also highly intelligent and very perceptive. For instance, he had very quickly appreciated that however well conceived and soundly constructed the original Italian defences might be – and manned by Australians commanded by Morshead they were to prove very effective – they were essentially static, and if looked upon solely as a defence perimeter, could be cracked open by enemy pressure if this were allowed to come too close.

The defences must therefore be regarded as bases for offensive action and the no-man's-land beyond – as wide as it could be made and dominated by the Australians – was to be the only recognised perimeter.

'I was determined to make no-man's-land *our* land,' Morshead wrote later, and a keynote to his attitude was revealed by his reaction to a newspaper headline declaring 'Tobruk can take it!'

'We're not here to "take it,"' he announced angrily. 'We're here to "give it."'

At the beginning, of course, Rommel had been the first to attack, but after the initial attempt to rush the port, his troops found themselves up against defences growing in depth, manned by infantry who to their astonishment did not surrender as soon as the panzers had broken through, but stayed where they were and destroyed the German infantry and artillery crews trying to follow up the armoured spearhead. Even in the rear areas, the few panzers which got through found themselves furiously attacked by troops normally considered non-combatant, such as batmen, cooks and clerks, who had been told in no uncertain terms that whatever their nominal appointment their basic duty was to fight the enemy wherever they found him and never easily to yield a yard of ground. As a result of such Draconian commandments, many of the Afrika Korps troops who had taken part in the battle of the salient at the end of April regarded it as the most bitterly fought battle of the war.

In general, the Tobruk perimeter was held by Australian infantry, while the reserve positions and the vital defence of the port and harbour installations were in the hands of British tank crews and gunners. This was a combination which in the event proved very satisfactory, though it was the result of historical accident. The Australians had been the only combatant troops to arrive in Tobruk in large and still well-organised formations; the remainder had consisted either of base troops who had been sent up to administer the port after it had fallen to O'Connor's advance, or British and Indian troops who had avoided capture and made their way back piecemeal to Tobruk after the débâcle of Rommel's first advance.

When Morshead and Lavarack first surveyed their command after its hasty construction during the first two weeks in April, they discovered that of the 40,000-odd souls then in Tobruk and its immediate environs, some 15,000 were unlikely to contribute much towards its defence and should be moved out as soon as possible. Chief among these were 5,000 prisoners, but the majority of Corps troops – Ordnance, Pay, even Medical – could leave, and there was not even much point in keeping a strong complement of transport personnel as no one would be going anywhere. Those that did remain, however, were to be prepared to fight – and some Service Corps companies later fought so well as infantry that they won the right to retain the bayonets with which they had equipped themselves, and which are normally not carried by such second-echelon troops.

By the end of April, the garrison had been stripped down to 23,000 men, all armed and capable of fighting, of whom about 15,000 were Australian, 500 Indian and the rest British. The Australians were the men of the 9th Division – the 20th, 24th and 26th Brigades – plus those of the 18th Brigade from the 7th Division (whose other brigades were in Syria) together with divisional engineers, several anti-tank gun units, one artillery unit and an anti-aircraft battery. The British were the tank crews, the majority of the field and anti-aircraft gunners, a third of the anti-tank gunners and a battalion of the ubiquitous machine-gunners of the Royal Northumberland Fusiliers. The Indians occasionally manned the line with the Australians, and they played a vital role in the night patrolling.

Not surprisingly, garrison spirits had been somewhat cast down by the failures of both the *Brevity* and *Battleaxe* operations, so in order to keep everyone's mind off more depressing matters, Morshead immediately instigated a programme of extensive fortification and patrolling. The original Italian complement for each concrete-lined post in the outer defences had been two officers and twenty-five men with an orthodox scale of weapons; now the posts were meticulously cleansed of all the debris and filth of the previous battles and manned by half that number, but with their fire-power doubled and sometimes trebled by captured, reserviced and constantly checked and maintained Italian weapons. This was the Red Line, held by fire-power, continuously strengthened by the construction of new intermediate posts, and covered by an ever-widening band of mines.

Two miles behind it was the Blue Line, a series of platoon-held strong-points with a selection of heavier weapons including mortars, each surrounded by an anti-tank ditch and a zareba of barbed wire, its fire covering the wider and thicker minefields which by mid-summer extended forward almost as far as the Red Line. Behind them were the main field artillery batteries which it was their principal duty to protect, while the guns in their turn would protect the infantry from any panzers which reached this far – though their chances of doing so now were slim in view of the spreading mine-fields. These became eventually so omnipresent that a danger arose of the engineers losing track of them; before the end of the siege, to Morshead's fury, some Allied transport was blown up by Allied mines.

The whole of the defence system was dotted with what became known as the 'Bush Artillery' – Italian 37mm. and 75mm. anti-tank and field guns (there were even a couple of 105mm. guns in the coastal battery) which had been dragged from their original positions, or those in which they had been abandoned, cleaned, serviced and crewed by hard-swearing but enthusiastic infantrymen after but the briefest instruction from helpful gunners, who then retired, amused and somewhat shaken by the unorthodox fire instructions used.

'When they want to increase the elevation', one awed artillery subaltern later told his colonel, 'they say – "Cock the bastard up a bit!" – and the usual fire order is – "Let 'er go, mate!"'

At the beginning, the method of sighting was to peer along the barrel, for most of the Italian artillerymen had at least taken the precaution of destroying the sights before abandoning their pieces five months before, and despite this rough and ready method there is good reason to believe that one of the shells fired in this way killed General Prittwitz during the first enemy approach along the Derna road. By July, however, quite a number of sets of sights had been brought in at the earnest request of these amateur gunners by their infantry friends on patrol, for enemy gun-positions were a favourite objective, especially if they had been plastering the Red or Blue Lines.

The patrolling in no-man's-land went on night after night, and during the day when dust-storms were so thick that the enemy could be closing up unobserved. There were also continuous patrols between the Red Line posts, known as 'Love and Kisses' patrols. Pairs of men from each post would move out at given intervals to an agreed half-way point, where two sticks had been left; many factors could delay a team and the other had no wish to wait around, so if the first team to arrive were from one of the alternate 'Kisses' posts they would leave the sticks crossed. When the other team arrived they would know that their opposite numbers had been and gone and would leave the sticks parallel – the 'Love' position. If one team found the sticks in the same position three times running, there would be some urgent telephoning when they returned to their own post.

Other patrols watched the anti-tank ditches and the wire fences, while 200 or 300 yards further out patrols consisting of an N.C.O. and perhaps half a dozen men would lie in an observation or listening post, or cover a 'beat' of perhaps half a mile to give warning of any large-scale enemy approach or to shoot up any prowling enemy patrols.

These were the defensive patrols; but it was the offensive patrols which kept no-man's land under Australian domination and won for Tobruk its special fame. These could vary from a small patrol of just an officer or sergeant with ten men raiding a gun position, shooting up the crew, wrecking the gun with a grenade down the barrel and removing the sights, to a company-size attack taken out in carriers and accompanied by tanks to destroy a known German or Italian post.

Before a raid the men would have a hot meal and a tot of rum; then, dressed in one-piece patrol overalls reinforced at knee and elbow and either with soft-soled boots or with socks over regulation boots, they would set off, each man with two or three grenades, many armed with Tommy-guns, at least one Bren per section and the rest with rifle, bayonet or club. There was a great deal of personal selection and specialisation in the weapons each man carried, but the commando knife which was now coming into use so much in raids in Europe does not seem to have gained much favour among the Australians. The Indians were prepared to use the knife (although unfortunately there were no Gurkhas present to display their expertise with the kukri) but they patrolled in bare feet or made themselves sandals soled with strips of old tyres, moving down like ghosts upon their unsuspecting prey. One heart-stopping manoeuvre of theirs, to obviate the danger of killing the wrong people, was for two to creep up behind a sitting or standing sentry and while one pinned the subject's arms to his sides with a sudden embrace, the other slid a hand over his shoulder and felt for the collar badge. The only survivors of this chilling experience were Australians wearing their sun-burst badge, who then felt a re-assuring pat on the shoulder perhaps accompanied by a sibilant 'O.K. Aussie', release of the embrace and through the tumult of thudding heart an impression of flocks of large, dangerous birds flitting away into the darkness. One night, the Indians found three Italians asleep by their gun . . . and cut the throats of the two on the outside, deliberately leaving the one in the middle to a dire awakening.

Often the patrols would carry mines and plant them well to the rear of the German or Italian forward posts thereby catching the transport as it came up the following day, but on one occasion a large patrol with a high proportion of Sappers went out, lifted nearly 500 mines from a newly laid German field, brought them back and used them to cover a gap in front of their own southern sector. Mines were also taken at first from Italian fields, but the best hauls were made as a result of observation during the day of new Italian mine-laying, followed by a raid that night with the object of collecting the stocks as yet unlaid; it saved trouble, and occasional casualties.

Sometimes the patrols would lie up all day at carefully selected points, waiting for the enemy working parties or patrols to move at night, and ambush them . . . and sometimes they would themselves be caught by German patrols trying the same trick. Every night was punctuated by bomb-blast and split open with machine-gun and rifle fire . . . and every morning there would be more dead bodies in one uniform or another to lie rotting in the sun until either they were recovered and buried, or they burst and stank.

During the day, for everyone in Tobruk, the main curse was dust; and after dust the plagues of flies and fleas which inhabited every building, shack, strong-point or trench like a perpetual fifth column. The dust at Tobruk was as pervasive and all-encompassing as the mud had been at Passchendaele twenty-four years before, and still lives in the memory of every man who stayed there for more than a week. So much had happened within the confines of the Fortress even before the siege began, and so many men were now crammed inside it, that the surface clay was ground to powder even without the explosion of shell or vibration of gun which now pulverised deeper or shook more thoroughly. On average, at least every fourth day the wind blew and whipped up thick clouds in which men coughed and cursed and choked and wondered if they would ever breathe cool air again, and had hardly enough moisture left in their mouths to spit it out when evening came and the wind died.

Even when the wind dropped, the dust was still everywhere . . . in the food, in the weapons and weapon-pits, in boots, half-filling pockets, between the threads of shirts, under arms and under eyelids. You ate it, breathed it, rubbed it into your hair and scratched it into your flea-bites. And every time you slapped a fly to death, its squashed remains were coated in it.

Few men ever really gave up the fight against the flies, despite their continuous, monotonous pestering; perhaps because they gave you some peace at night (no one ever found out where they disappeared to) and thus you recovered your fury against them. During the day, they were there all the time, covering your food as soon as it arrived, accompanying it to your lips and into your mouth if you weren't careful; settling on every bead of sweat that appeared on your face, neck, hands or legs and trying to suck damp from the corners of your eyes. One particular brand would settle on your arms and legs and if you didn't slap it away quickly, seemed able to sink fangs into your flesh, brace its forelegs like a horse and rock on them until it had torn a lump away . . . at which all its friends would swoop down on the blood.

What was astonishing was that in addition to retaining their sanity, the Rats of Tobruk, as they were soon styled, remained in excellent health. Of course, the majority were young and in the prime of life and had been brought to a degree of fitness by army discipline and training before coming to the desert which, in the case of the British, they may not have known before – but one extra factor which was happily not present, the mosquito, could have nullified all natural advantages as it did later in the Far East theatre. In Tobruk, however, there was little enough water of any sort, so no stagnant pools and thus no malaria.

What water there was, either from the condensation plants by the harbour for those in the vicinity, or from artesian wells, was in short but regular supply – three-quarters of a gallon per man per day for all purposes – either brackish or chlorinated in taste and often medicinal in effect; an effect which if not carefully controlled could lead, ironically, to minor outbreaks of dysentery. After a time, the taste-buds adapted to tea reeking of sulphur or chlorine, but coffee was always a disaster – and the Germans who, after all, were sharing this particular aspect of the Tobruk siege were increasingly sardonic about it.

'Do not bother to try to make coffee,' one of them wrote. 'Just heat the water. The result will look like coffee anyway . . . and taste like sulphur, which every drink does out here!'

Chester Wilmot, an Australian journalist in Tobruk, recorded an occasion when someone arrived from Alexandria with a bottle of 'sweet' water which, after careful sampling by a select band, was shared out among them. Everyone drank his tot neat.

Food during the first few months had consisted of little but bread and bully beef with occasional tinned bacon or herrings; no butter, a little margarine but hardly any sugar or jam and no fresh vegetables at all. Ascorbic acid tablets were issued to combat vitamin deficiency but as soon as the siege settled into a pattern and shipping convoys could run with some degree of regularity, the dietary experts were called in and matters improved. Lime juice came up (and even the Australians would drink it in the absence of beer), fruit and vegetables usually tinned but occasionally fresh, and sometimes there was even real meat. Oddly enough, as the siege went on and boredom began to take its insidious hold, food became of little interest or importance (so long, of course, as there was enough to stave off hunger) and by August many of the front line posts held stocks of tinned bacon or fish because no one could be bothered to open or prepare it. So long as there was a good hot meal at night, the troops would exist during the day on bread and margarine, jam and cheese, washed down with chlorinated water.

What was essential, in almost everyone's mind, was the supply of cigarettes. The issue was fifty a week to each man and after June they were able to buy another fifty from the organised canteen, while the Australian Comforts Fund provided more (when the Navy could bring it in) and from the beginning, to the enormous appreciation of the British troops, it was agreed that everyone in Tobruk was Australian as far as Comforts were concerned.

Living conditions were rougher for the infantry than for the gunners or tank crews, but on the other hand the gunners – especially the ones around the harbour – were bombed and shelled much more often. There was no refuge in the Fortress from Rommel's heavy artillery, and his airfields at El Adem and Sidi Rezegh were so close that sometimes the infantry could hear the bombers take off and follow their entire flight until they had dropped their load over the harbour. Once Rommel had accepted that time must pass before his ground troops could hope to overrun the garrison, he concentrated all possible effort on disrupting the supply lines, and in his opinion the easiest place to do this was at the disembarkation point; as the months went by, the number of wrecks in the harbour grew, the devastation around it spread – but the anti-aircraft batteries thickened and the barrage which greeted the Luftwaffe pilots above the port claimed more and more victims.

At first, the raids had been carried out by dive-bombers in daylight, confident that history would be repeated and the anti-aircraft crews would take cover as soon as the howl of the Stuka dive reached its peak – but they were defeated by the realities of the situation. As there was nowhere for the besieged to run to in the long term, there was no psychological justification for running in the short term. So the gunners stayed at their posts, followed the dive-bombers down all the way and discovered to their astonishment that this was the safer procedure to follow, for it put the equally astonished pilots off their aim and eventually caused them to drop their bombs from a much greater height.

The Luftwaffe then tried different methods – high-level bomb-ing, low-level strafing, both at once, low-level minelaying – and inevitably they scored some successes at the beginning of each new technique. But the officer commanding the artillery, Brigadier J. N. Slater, brought an immense enthusiasm to his command together with a great deal of originality, and so inspired his crews that each man came to regard the conflict as a direct contest between his own team and the Luftwaffe's, whose separate flights and indeed aircraft he quickly began to recognise. The gunners also began to appreciate that basic element of conflict which is so often overlooked in the heat of battle – that the enemy has problems too; and they planned to increase them.

They would vary the height of the barrage – one day at 4,000 feet, the next at 6,000 feet – and when the pilots learned to wait and not to come in until they had judged what that day's height was to be, the gunners mixed the heights so that although the concentra-tion was not great at any one level, it was distributed up through a band. They learned to swing the block of the barrage together so that a pilot hoping to slip along the outer edge to find a place to dive in underneath would suddenly find himself in the middle with shells bursting above, below and all around. And when fighters tried to streak in low across the desert, they put up a barrage of Bofors and Breda fire along fixed lines, quite confident that they were not spraying their own infantry as the arcs of fire had been clearly worked out beforehand.

There was little the troops could do to protect themselves against long-range shelling except dig themselves fox-holes, reinforce their sangars or shelters with concrete slabs, steel beams from destroyed buildings and sandbags – or stake out claims in some of the deep caves with which the area had been honeycombed by the Italians. Quite a high proportion of the Rats of Tobruk lived in holes in the ground.

Protection of the Fortress from the land was therefore in the hands of the Australian and Indian infantry, and from the air in those of the mainly British artillery. From the sea, except for two 105mm. Italian guns, a few light guns and some Brens mounted for the protection of bathing parties, the defence was the responsibility of the Royal Navy – and as Tobruk also relied entirely upon the Navy for their supplies, the role played by the Inshore Squadron in the epic of the siege was critical.

Destroyers carried out the greater part of what became known as the 'Spud Run', for their advantages of both speed and fire-power took them quickly in and out of the danger zones and gave them good protection at the critical times, but a whole flotilla of smaller craft – lighters, South African whalers, captured Italian schooners

– all made their vital contributions. Every ship which visited Tobruk took in stores and took out men – in May 2,593 tons in and 5,918 men out, in June nearly 3,000 tons in and 5,148 men out. From July until September the majority of the men evacuated were wounded, but the supply tonnage mounted and on two occasions the petrol tanker *Pass of Balmaha* made the run, loaded with 750 tons of the vitally needed but appallingly dangerous fuel.

The Spud Run was in itself a very risky operation, without the additional hazard of a highly volatile cargo to escort. Chester Wilmot described a trip he made aboard the destroyer H.M.S. *Decoy* towards the end of the siege, with two other destroyers in company, each carrying some fifty tons of freight and about a hundred replacement or reinforcement troops.

They had left Alexandria early in the morning, were abreast of Mersa Matruh by 1530 and two hours later level with Sidi Barrani but well out to sea to avoid enemy aircraft based on Bardia. All hands were at Action Stations when the first aircraft appeared – to deep sighs of relief when these proved to be escorting Hurricanes – but speed was increased to thirty-two knots and the cramped and crowded decks throbbed as the ships tore through the water.

Air cover remained with them until just before dusk but then had to leave and the ships then ploughed steadily on for another four hours under a silver but waning moon, their crews praying that the enemy aircraft would stay out of sight of their phosphorescent wake until the moon had gone down. But with half an hour to go, the Stukas caught them and the next twenty miles were a journey of wide sweeps and sudden turns as the dive-bombers swooped and the destroyers twisted away. The decks became a chaos of sliding crates and ammunition boxes, of loose stretchers from a consignment which broke away, of cursing soldiers hanging on to stanchions and rails and equally vehement sailors intent on their duties of working the ship and fighting off the attackers.

At last the Stukas left to refill their bomb-bays, the two dim, shaded lights which marked the entrance to Tobruk harbour glowed greenly ahead, engine speed was cut, and slowly and with almost no wake the ships glided between them past a pair of blackly looming wrecks, and as *Decoy* slowed to a halt, two barges and two launches materialised from the shore and came alongside. Immediately, a frenzy of activity seized all aboard, but as most were old hands at this exercise it was an ordered frenzy. Troops clambered over the side, pitching their kitbags ahead of them; unloading parties demonstrated an enviable expertise as they manhandled crates and boxes, a tank track, a spare lorry engine, a new barrel for a Bofors, the stretchers, over the side and safely into a barge; then, from the other side, the wounded began their often pain-wracked lift up and on to the decks, helped by firm but surprisingly gentle hands. And by this time, the Stukas were back, knowing full well that their quarry was now in the tight confines of the harbour and that only the barrage could keep them away:

One stick of bombs screams down on the south shore of the harbour; the next is closer – in the water 500 yards away. The old hands continue working, unworried, but some of the new ones, like us, pause momentarily, shrinking down behind the destroyer's after-screen. From the man with the megaphone comes a sharp rebuke – 'What are you stopping for? Those bloody bombs are nothing to do with you.'[1]

The last man goes overboard, the barges pull away, the engines throb and the destroyer backs, turns and disappears into the blackness. Fifty tons of cargo and a hundred men disembarked, twenty stretcher cases and half a dozen walking wounded taken aboard; in and out in under half an hour.

Such episodes occurred every night during the dark period of the moon, but once the anti-aircraft batteries had demonstrated their ability to keep at bay the majority of the bombers, then the smaller, slower craft joined in, slipping into Tobruk just before dawn, lying close alongside the battered jetty or by one of the wrecks which had been roughly converted into a landing stage all day under heavy camouflage-netting while the cargoes were unloaded, and sailing again as soon as it was dark.

These craft were skippered and manned by a breed of staunch individualists who refused to be daunted by the enemy or restricted in any way by Authority. Their backgrounds were various and rarely respectable, their uniforms picturesque but practical, and their armaments unorthodox and usually of foreign make. The most famous was an R.N.R. lieutenant known as 'Pedlar' Palmer who at one time had commanded a company of Chinese Lancers in the Shanghai Volunteer Reserve, and who now ran a weekly service from Mersa Matruh to Tobruk in a captured Italian schooner, the *Maria Giovanna*. His navigation was of a rough and ready type, and after a wide sweep out to sea he would approach Tobruk preferably during the late evening so that his objective could be suitably illuminated by both bomb-flashes and anti-aircraft fire – through which he was quite content to sail unconcerned. On one dark night there was no air raid and he waxed indignant.

'How do they expect me to get in when there's no moon and no bloody air raid?'

The Italians got him in the end by fixing dummy lights about fifteen miles east of the Tobruk harbour entrance and the *Maria Giovanna* ended her days on the rocks with her skipper and crew in various prison camps; but 'Pedlar' had by this time taken some twenty cargoes into the Fortress and claimed to have shot down three aircraft with his motley collection of machine-guns. His Distinguished Service Cross was well earned.

As for the enemy, by midsummer the Italians were regarded by most with such amused affection that their working parties would be left in peace until they came too close, then sprayed with random machine-gun fire to make them retreat. The nearest Italian posts were visited most nights, and wrecked or despoiled with such regularity that they were soon abandoned; only if a prisoner were needed or if something had happened to anger the Australians in the sector would much blood be shed.

But the atmosphere along German sectors was different. Here, growing professionalism on both sides fostered a competition which relentlessly added to the casualty lists. Around the borders of the salient especially, the watch was never-ending, the thump of mortar-bomb, the crack of the sniper's rifle a continual punctuation. The commander of the 2nd Battalion of the German 115th Motorised Infantry Regiment, Major Ballerstedt, wrote:

Enemy snipers achieve astounding results. They shoot at anything they recognize. Several N.C.O.s of the battalion have been shot through the head with the first bullet while making observations in the front line. Protruding sights in gun directors have been shot off, observation slits and loopholes have been fired on, and hit, as soon as they were seen to be in use (i.e. when the light background became dark). For this reason loopholes must be kept plugged with a wooden plug to be taken out when used so that they always show dark.[2]

On the other hand, such efficiency bred respect, and the adversity in which both sides dwelt produced a degree of fellow-feeling. After one particularly vicious battle at the beginning of August when a force of over a hundred Australians had been driven back to their starting-point, it was realised in the morning that more than thirty were unaccounted for and some of these must be lying wounded out in the minefields. In order to do something to help them, one of the Australian sergeants volunteered to be driven out sitting on the bonnet of a truck and waving a huge Red Cross flag, though no one had attempted such a move before. Some 400 yards short of the nearest German post, the truck stopped and the sergeant, accompanied by a stretcher-bearer and their Roman Catholic padre, walked forward another 100 yards until a German emerged from the post carrying a similar Red Cross flag and shouted to them that they were entering the minefield.

Two German engineers with mine-detectors then appeared and guided an officer and a German doctor towards them, and during the next half hour they all worked together to bring out four wounded and fifteen dead Australians, and the German doctor told them that already four other wounded Australians were being looked after in the German aid posts.

When the last of our dead had been brought to us, the lieutenant told me we were not to move until they were all back in the post and had taken in their flag. He went back; his men went below. He lowered his flag and I lowered mine. I saluted him, and he saluted back, but he gave me the salute of the Reichswehr, not of the Nazis. Our armistice was over.[3]

In some parts of the sector, especially across and east of the El Adem road, a virtual armistice existed for two hours every night while men climbed out of their trenches to stretch their aching limbs, while water and food was brought up, the filth and debris of the day cleared and some relief from the heat enjoyed during the blessed cool of the first few hours of darkness; there would be little firing, and that generally vague and unaimed, and an unspoken agreement existed that this time should not be used for patrolling or even for swift preparation for any especially aggressive operation. That should wait until the signal was given to end the nightly peace – a burst of tracer fired vertically up into the sky, usually about midnight. By such unspoken agreements, life was made just a little less intolerable and respect between two opposing armies deepened.

Whether Rommel knew of such incidents and attitudes is difficult to say; one side of his nature would undoubtedly have sympathised, but on the other hand, the capture of Tobruk had become something of an obsession with him and his singlemindedness in such circumstances might have meant that any hint of compromise in its immediate achievement would provoke him to fury.

His position in North Africa had improved considerably, to a great extent, ironically enough, as a result of Halder's efforts to curb his activities. The arrival of General Gause and the posse of Staff officers had precipitated the change, for not only Rommel but also the Italian commanders had had no warning of the move and were immediately suspicious. Gariboldi as Italian Commander-in-Chief, North Africa (Comandante Superiore), protested vigorously at the introduction of yet another German general into his area of operations without consultation, and Generale Ugo Cavallero, the Chief of Staff in Rome (Comandante Supremo), was quite willing to forward the complaints to Berlin.

Although Hitler's attitude was one of apparent unconcern,

Halder was well aware of the high regard in which the Führer held
Rommel and knew that he must act with caution; his explanation to
Cavallero was subdued and couched in conciliatory tones so that the
Italian Chief of Staff, who had his own ends to further and one
important piece of inside knowledge, seized upon it, ordered
Gariboldi to withdraw his objection and then, to everybody's
surprise, proposed the establishment of a Group Headquarters in
Africa to control the activities of all military formations, both
Italian and German, and insisted that Rommel, despite his com-
parative lack of seniority, should command it.

He then drew Gariboldi's teeth by revealing to him that he was
about to be recalled to Rome and replaced by Generale d'Armata
Ettore Bastico, a close friend of Il Duce's and a man of such
autocratic demeanour that he had made himself highly unpopular in
practically all military circles; both Gariboldi and Cavallero would
be delighted to watch him being ridden over by Rommel in one of
his more implacable moods. As for Halder, he well knew that an
appeal to Hitler to stop the promotion of a German general –
especially one who was in many ways a protégé – to overall
operational command in a theatre held until then to have been of
major Italian concern, would fall on very deaf ears. The only
success which Halder was able to snatch from the ruin of his plans to
bring Rommel to heel was to insist that the new Army Group be
called Panzergruppe Afrika and not, as was at first suggested,
Panzergruppe Rommel.

Panzergruppe Headquarters were first of all set up at Beda
Littoria, but Rommel quickly had them moved up to Ain el Gazala,
with Advanced Headquarters – where, needless to say, he was to
spend most of his time – further forward at Gambut, between
Tobruk and Bardia. From there, by August he commanded all
troops in the operational area and had also assumed territorial and
administrative responsibilities as head of the 'Marmarica Command'. Considering that he had arrived six months before in charge
of little but a single light division and that in mid-June he had been
battling to defend his position as commander of all German troops
in North Africa, his position now in command of all Axis ground
troops facing the original enemy, Britain, was a remarkable
achievement; and one revealing talents not always included among
those expected in a plain, bluff, straightforward soldier. As
Halder's fury increased, so did his sense of personal risk, for
Rommel was proving a far more dangerous opponent in the
convoluted world of Axis military politics than had been anticipated.

Promotion for Rommel had, of course, followed the extra
responsibilities, but with the peculiar inconsequence which warfare
brings about, Rommel first heard that he was a Panzergeneral from

friends writing to congratulate him, having themselves heard it on the Berlin radio. It was mid-August before full confirmation of his new appointment arrived, and by that time the forces under his command, despite Halder's continual injunctions, had grown considerably and were in the process of redistribution and intensive training – especially the German formations, whatever their experience or prestige.

Generalleutnant Neumann-Sylkow's 15th Panzer Division was now complete, based on the coast at Marsa Belafarit and training hard in the desert to the south, while 5th Light Division had been built up, reorganised and renamed 21st Panzer Division, and was being put through its paces by its new commander, Generalleutnant Johan von Ravenstein, in the area just west of Bardia. Each division consisted of a panzer regiment of two battalions, each regiment with about 170 panzers – Marks II, III and IV, and a few captured Matildas – three battalions of infantry, an anti-tank battalion, a regiment of artillery, a reconnaissance battalion and the usual complement of engineer and administrative troops. These two divisions comprised D.A.K. – Deutsches Afrika Korps – Rommel's original responsibility in North Africa, now under command of Generalleutnant Ludwig Cruewell.

Another German formation which began arriving at the end of August and was eventually to win considerable renown as the 90th Light Division, was for the moment known by the cumbersome title of Division Afrika zur besondern Verfügung (shortened, not all that conveniently, to Div zbV Afrika), commanded by Generalleutnant Max Sümmermann and consisting of two infantry regiments, an engineer battalion, an anti-tank battalion and something called a 'Sonderverband' – which seems to translate most nearly to 'Special Service Unit'. What duties were intended for this formation remains uncertain, but some idea of the flavour of the Div zbV Afrika in its earliest days may be gleaned from the fact that one of its infantry regiments, Afrika Regiment 361, consisted mostly of ex-members of the Foreign Legion who had been collected during the sweep through France and had now come to Africa accompanied by the grim hint that this might be their last chance to rehabilitate themselves as 'good Germans'. As between them they had had considerable experience of desert fighting and their service for France had done nothing to promote pro-British sentiments, they were to prove a very valuable addition to Rommel's strength.

Finally, partly as a result of the sweeping success of German arms in Russia and the widening horizons for Hitler's ambition as the Wehrmacht swept down towards the Caucasus, opening his eyes to the possibilities of further advances down through Iran or perhaps

Anatolia to attack the Nile Delta from the north, the Führer ordered that a train of siege artillery was to be sent to Rommel in order to allow him to reduce Tobruk, thus freeing Panzergruppe Afrika to form the western arm of a pincer attack which would completely demolish the only hostile army left in the field after the obviously imminent collapse of Russia. This group, known to the Germans as Artillery Command 104 and to the British when they learned of it as 'Rommel's travelling circus', was centred at Belhammed five miles to the south-east of the Tobruk perimeter, and commanded by Generalmajor Karl Böettcher. It consisted of five artillery units and its armament included nine 210mm. howitzers, twelve French 100mm. guns and forty-six French 150mms, thirty-six Italian 105mms, eighty-four Italian 149mms, and twelve naval 120mm. guns. Once German thoroughness had mastered the problems posed by the diversity of ammunition, the train could lay down a most formidable barrage.

As for the Italian formations under Rommel's direct command in Marmarica, these were the four infantry divisions Bologna, Pavia, Brescia and Savona which made up Army Corps XXI commanded by Generale di Corpo d'Armata Enea Navarrini, three of which were used in the static investment of Tobruk, while Savona was disposed along the frontier. Here they held a line of well-prepared positions stretching from Sollum down past Sidi Omar, buttressed by German artillery posts including several of the precious 88mms and a large number of the salvaged Italian guns, all sheltered behind local and separate minefields while a further wide belt covered the front as a whole. And Major the Reverend Bach and his men still held Halfaya Pass.

Back in Cyrenaica was assembled the only Italian force with any pretensions to independence of Rommel, the Corpo d'Armata di Manovra XX – the Mobile Army Corps, known as C.A.M. – under command of Generale Gastone Gambara, consisting of one armoured division, the Divisione Corazzata Ariete, and a motorised division, the Divisione Motorizzata Trieste. Although the Comandante Superiore, Ettore Bastico (already nicknamed 'Bombastico' by Rommel's Staff), had intimated that it was never to be embroiled in any action without his own express permission, Generale Gambara was both experienced and realistic enough to know quite well where his orders would come from if emergency threatened.

Rommel, of course, was not to be satisfied for long with nothing but training programmes to occupy either his troops or his military ardour, and by early September he and the equally eager von Ravenstein had between them concocted a plan for a raid along the edge of the Escarpment towards what Intelligence believed to be a large British supply dump, possibly set up in preparation for a future attack. There were other reasons, too, for suspecting the British of aggressive intentions; until July, the two Afrika Korps Reconnaissance Battalions, numbers 33 and 3, had experienced no problems in keeping deep watches respectively in front of the Sollum–Sidi Omar line and along the open flank to the south, but recently their activities had been greatly curbed by the appearance opposite them of armoured cars of the 11th Hussars augmented by 4th South African Armoured Car Regiment, and some of the mobile columns which even they were beginning to call 'Jockolmnen'. The British air strength had grown considerably of late, too – thus even further blinding the view across the frontier – and their ground forces had reputedly grown even more. It was therefore imperative that information about British preparations be obtained, and if a solid blow could be delivered against such preparations at the same time, so much the better.

Operation Sommernachtstraum began at dawn on September 14th, as three columns from 21st Panzer Division moved through and past the Sollum–Sidi Omar line into Egypt, the northern column accompanied by Rommel himself, perched high up on the edge of the sunshine roof of his Mammoth, looking, as his A.D.C., Schmidt, recalled, 'like a U-boat commander on his bridge'. Battle Group Schütte was aimed along the line of the Escarpment, Battle group Stephan parallel and some ten miles south along the Bir Sheferzen–El Hamra track, and Reconnaissance Battalion 3 down along the Wire with instructions to raise as much dust as possible, thus creating the impression that the whole of the Afrika Korps was on the move. A large force of lorries followed the two main columns in order to collect the loot.

By midday the pincers had closed around the location of the presumed dump, to find little but a few empty bully-beef tins and some even emptier beer-bottles ('I noticed suddenly that my mouth was parched,' wrote Schmidt later) but one of the small outriding units came racing in with a captured lorry and its disconsolate driver and companion, which examination revealed to be the orderly room staff and truck of the 4th South African Armoured Car Regiment. The lorry was full of quite important documents and cipher material which von Ravenstein delightedly declared a prize quite sufficient to justify the raid on its own.

Rommel, of course, was by no means satisfied and urged the columns further on into Egypt, where they came up against ever-increasing opposition as the armoured cars and Jock Columns fell back upon the Support Group bases. By mid-afternoon both Schütte and Stephan columns were halted, and indeed out of petrol, south-east of Sofafi, where they were found by R.A.F. and

S.A.A.F. fighters and bombers and heavily attacked. As they were also being shelled by the Support Group 25-pounders, they experienced a very uncomfortable time during which they suffered some seventy casualties, including Rommel's driver, and a sliver of steel took off the heel of Rommel's boot.

The bombing and shelling continued and it was not until almost dusk that the columns were refuelled and could turn and make off back to the frontier – and it was during this race to the Wire that a front tyre of Rommel's Mammoth, which had been grazed by another splinter, chose to go flat. There was unspoken agreement among all the senior officers in the vehicle that the job of repairing it should fall to the A.D.C. and for some hours Leutnant Schmidt wrestled with the gigantic wheel while his Commander-in-Chief and staff sat around watching, and the wireless operator gloomily reported chit-chat on the British radio as the vehicles of the Support Group closed up. Rommel dared not send out a cry for help as this would undoubtedly be picked up by the enemy, and he had enough respect for the 11th Hussars to know that they would correctly interpret the situation and move very rapidly indeed to exploit it.

Map 20   *Operation Sommernachtstraum*: September 14th–15th, 1941

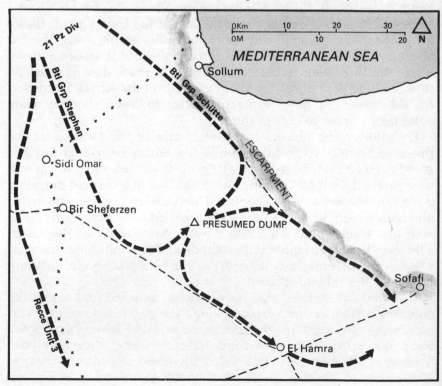

Eventually, with Rommel holding a shaded torch and other seniors helping as best they could ('which really just complicated the task,' as Schmidt rather sulkily reported) the wheel was fixed and, with Rommel driving, the Mammoth tore back through the gap in the Wire, to the evident astonishment of some Italian and German pioneers nearby. It had been a near thing, and Midsummer Night's Dream had at times held elements of a nightmare; but at least there was the consolation of the captured ciphers and orderly room papers. Further examination of these seemed to indicate that British forces in the area were being prepared, not for an advance into Marmarica, but for a retreat back behind Mersa Matruh.

This unexpectedly good news strengthened Rommel's determination to reduce the Tobruk Fortress, and warnings from Halder in Berlin and Bastico in Benghasi, that he should watch his back for an attack across the frontier immediately he began a main assault on the port, were rejected with disdain and a jet of caustic comment. The British in Egypt were not preparing to do anything significant; the Australians in Tobruk were the main enemy.

Rommel was quite wrong, of course, and Midsummer Night's Dream (or the 'El Hamra Scurry' as the British inelegantly dubbed it) did him far more harm than just the German casualties it caused, for it seriously misled him. The orders found in the orderly room truck had been for a temporary unit withdrawal, not a large-scale movement intended to change a strategic or even tactical pattern; and had Battle Groups Schütte and Stephan been allowed to progress much further, they would have uncovered some significant evidence of offensive preparations. General Auchinleck's plans for the Winter Battle were quite well advanced and both men and material were beginning to flood out to the area in unprecedented quantities.

Rommel was not even right in believing that when his attack on Tobruk was eventually launched, the main enemy would be Australian. Public opinion in the Dominion was demanding that their troops be relieved before conditions in the Fortress affected their health, and in July General Blamey had pointed out to General Auchinleck that the clear understanding that Australian troops would generally serve together was not being observed – so could the 9th Division be withdrawn from Tobruk and sent to join the 7th in Syria?

It was not a request which the Middle East Commanders-in-Chief could view with anything except apprehension – Auchinleck because of the risk and difficulty of replacing large numbers of experienced troops with large numbers of inexperienced ones,

Cunningham because of the extra strain which would be thrown on the already hard-pressed ships of the Inshore Squadron, and Tedder because although his air strength was increasing rapidly he would need everything which could fly when the main battle started, and between then and now he must use all available flying hours for training, for harassing the Luftwaffe airfields, for attacking the convoys bringing Rommel his essential petrol and ammunition and, most important of all, keeping the skies over the Western Desert clear of enemy reconnaissance planes, which, from mid-September onwards, would undoubtedly note the growing signs of offensive preparations.

But the Australian Government proved intractable, so during the dark periods of August, September and October the vast majority of the Australians (and the Indians) were replaced by the British 70th Division and the 1st Polish Carpathian Brigade – at some cost, it may be said, for during the operations the Navy lost three ships sunk, and two destroyers, a gunboat and a cruiser were badly damaged. The last attempt to evacuate the Australians was the most costly and had to be curtailed, with the result that the whole of the 2nd/13th Australian Battalion, two companies of the 2nd/15th and some men of the Divisional Headquarters were left behind; but an interesting facet of the siege is revealed by the bald figures of naval achievement during the period April 11th to December 10th. Including wounded and prisoners, the Royal Navy had evacuated 47,280 men and brought in 34,113, plus 33,946 tons of stores; and the price paid was 34 warships and merchantmen sunk, 33 damaged. As during the same period the R.A.F. and S.A.A.F. had provided air cover whenever possible over the sea approaches and the port itself, the Siege of Tobruk provides an excellent demonstration of the interdependence of the three services in modern warfare.

A most curious historical coincidence appeared to underline this. Mr Churchill had been pressing Auchinleck to appoint 'Jumbo' Maitland Wilson as commander of the rapidly growing army in the Western Desert (it had reached a size by the end of September to justify its assumption of the title 'Eighth Army') but either through a reluctance to have such matters dictated to him by Whitehall or through a genuine feeling that the northern front facing up towards the Caucasus might in the end prove more important, Auchinleck insisted on Wilson remaining in Syria in command of what became known as 'Ninth Army' with Headquarters near Beirut. For command of Eighth Army in the forthcoming offensive, Auchinleck chose General Cunningham, fresh from his triumphs in Ethiopia; so the two brothers Lieutenant-General Sir Alan and Admiral Sir Andrew were to hold high appointments in the same area; and as it happened the newly designated Western Desert Air Force at the same time came under a new commander – a New Zealander, Air Vice-Marshal Arthur Coningham. Even the same initial.

For Lieutenant-General Sir Alan Gordon Cunningham the future, in August 1941, appeared very promising indeed. Fifty-four years of age, in excellent health and giving everyone who met him an impression of bouncing, bright-eyed vitality, he had just completed one of the most successful and highly publicised campaigns in British history and was as a result far better known to the British public than O'Connor had ever been.

In eight weeks, Cunningham had led an army seemingly half across Africa, crowning his achievements only the previous month by replacing Haile Selassie, Lion of Judah and King of Kings, on the throne from which the Italians had driven him five years before. The speed and dash of the advance had impressed everyone – even his military contemporaries, one of whom (Alec Gatehouse who was about to serve under him) wrote, 'Cunningham was a magnificent-looking chap. I thought, this is the man . . . ' Even Churchill was prepared to be overridden in his favour.

Now he was to command the best-equipped army Britain had managed to put into the field so far in the Second World War against an opponent who, whatever his reputation or accomplishments, had at his disposal an army known to be numerically inferior in men, armour and aircraft. Surely, Cunningham could not lose.

There were, as always, some flaws behind the impressive façade. Cunningham was a gunner, and the divisions he had commanded as a major-general had been infantry divisions. These quite important factors in his military development had probably been an advantage during his recent campaign through the close and broken country of East Africa, but it was already being assumed that in the desert armour would dominate or at least play the major role, and the armoured formations themselves – especially those of the now-famous 7th Armoured Division – were subtly (and perhaps unconsciously) adopting a superiority of attitude which tended to make those not wearing the black beret feel excluded. As Auchinleck had already voiced the opinion that three armoured divisions and not much else would be needed to win the war in North Africa, Cunningham's lack of experience in handling armour placed him at a psychological disadvantage, which may have been increased by the thought of his elder brother watching his performance – however sympathetically – from a few miles away.

Moreover, upon taking up his command, he found that the main outlines of two plans for the forthcoming offensive had already been drawn up and his first duty would apparently be but to choose between them. This did not take him long. The plan suggesting an

advance deep down in the desert along the northern edge of the
Sand Sea, from Jarabub through Jalo and then up to threaten
Benghasi, would necessitate an unwarrantable logistics risk, however attractive the arrows might look on maps pinned to a Staff
Office wall in Cairo. Moreover, even if the risks were taken, the
difficulties overcome and the Eighth Army spearheads driven
successfully through to their target, it might be some time before
Rommel's supplies in the forward areas ran down, during which he
might well be able to wreak considerable havoc across the Egyptian
border. Being Rommel, he might even choose to ignore the force to
his rear, drive aggressively eastwards and restock the Afrika Korps
from British depots in the Delta.

The second and less imaginative plan was far more practical, and
with some modification was the one which Cunningham eventually
put forward to Auchinleck and upon which *Operation Crusader* was
launched.

Eighth Army consisted of two corps – XIII and XXX – and
detached troops such as those in the Tobruk Fortress (now commanded by Major-General R. M. Scobie), the Matruh garrison,
and forces held in reserve. XIII Corps, now under command of
Lieutenant-General A. R. Godwin-Austen (an appointment looked
upon with some suspicion and resentment by Churchill), consisted
of 4th Indian Division under Frank Messervy, the New Zealand
Division under Bernard Freyberg and 1st Army Tank Brigade (with
135 tanks, half Matildas and half the new, faster infantry tanks, the
Valentines) under Brigadier H. R. B. Watkins.

XXX Corps consisted of 7th Armoured Division now commanded by Strafer Gott promoted Major-General, made up of the
Support Group under Jock Campbell, and two armoured brigades,
7th and 22nd; the 1st South African Division under Major-General
G. E. Brink, the 22nd Guards Brigade whose task would be
basically to protect the Field Maintenance Centres (a development
from O'Connor's Field Supply Depots) set up behind the advance;
and Alec Gatehouse's 4th Armoured Brigade Group.

The basic plan was for the infantry divisions of XIII Corps to
mask, then surround and capture from the rear the static defences
along the frontier between Sollum and Sidi Omar, while the armour
of XXX Corps crossed the frontier south of Sidi Omar, swung up
towards Tobruk where, after defeating the Afrika Korps panzers en
route, they would join hands with the Tobruk garrison and together
sweep westwards, to break through the Axis forces in the Gazala
line defences, and repossess themselves of Cyrenaica.

A detached force known as the Oasis Group was to stage a
demonstration down in the Jarabub–Jalo area to distract Rommel's
attention at the crucial moment, and to this end flocks of dummy

lorries and tanks were already assembled there, while the surrounding atmosphere was filled with fake signal communications and general wireless traffic; and other, smaller-scale diversions had also been organised. But the main passage for the Eighth Army was to be close along the coast, and its main force was assembled there.

During the conferences and deliberations which had preceded the final decisions, there emerged some significant divergences of opinion, the main one concerning the employment of Alec Gatehouse's 4th Armoured Brigade Group. Consisting basically of 4th Armoured Brigade strengthened with extra artillery and infantry, it had at first been cast in the role of a 'Centre Force' charged with the duties of guarding the left flank of the XIII Corps infantry as they advanced across the Wire to get behind the static defences, at the same time maintaining contact with the right wing of XXX Corps. In such a geographic situation, it could also find itself fighting a main engagement with 21st Panzer Division should von Ravenstein choose to bring that formation south from its base area near Bardia. At first, Gatehouse's force had been part of XIII Corps but Cunningham decided that its mobility made it more suitably part of XXX Corps, a decision which brought protests from the infantry commanders. Later, Bernard Freyberg was to write:

> When the Planning Conference was being held at Army Headquarters on the 6th October I listened in cynically. The proceedings bore a close resemblance to the talk I had with the Commander of Western Desert Force . . . before the 'Battleaxe' disaster. I did not take any part in the discussions until the employment of the New Zealand Division was discussed . . . at once I made it clear that I did not agree with the plan to go into the blue against unbeaten armoured formations unless I had tanks under my immediate command.[4]

Cunningham quickly pointed out that 4th Armoured Brigade Group would be alongside in support, but this statement was met with the cold inquiry as to who would give Gatehouse the final order if 4th Armoured was wanted both forward with 7th Armoured Division engaging perhaps Neumann-Sylkow's 15th Panzer Division, and at the same time back on the New Zealanders' wing threatened by von Ravenstein:

> I made it clear that that [support from 4th Armoured] meant nothing to me, as they could be ordered away in a crisis and under the circumstances that unless we had tanks under our immediate command we should not be moved across the wire until the armoured battle had commenced. In this I was quite precise. I was not popular.[5]

Freyberg was by no means alone among infantry commanders in his desire for armour whose duty would be specifically to protect his troops against panzers, so much so that after the war one of the Royal Tank Regiment officers there, Michael Carver, was to write:

> The 'Crusader' operation was fought to an unending accompaniment of screams from one infantry division, headquarters, or field maintenance centre after another for tanks to come and protect them against the presence or threat of enemy tanks.[6]

Perhaps the armoured formations should not have been so loud in their protestations of omnipotence for they now found themselves fighting to maintain the concentration of force vital to their allotted task of destroying Rommel's armour; any requirement for them to act as watch-dogs for helpless flocks of infantry they considered not only a waste of battle-strength, but also something of a slur upon their role as Monarch of the Battlefield.

As the main lesson of *Battleaxe* – that the greatest potential for the destruction of the Afrika Korps panzers the British possessed at that time lay with their artillery, not with their tanks – had apparently not yet permeated upwards even as far as brigade and divisional commanders, it is hardly surprising that it had not reached Cunningham either, and that the basis of his plan remained for 7th Armoured Division to meet and vanquish Rommel's two panzer divisions.

His confidence that his own armour would be strong enough to carry out this vital role was based upon the British superiority in numbers of tanks, and on paper this appeared undeniable. According to Intelligence estimates, Panzergruppe Afrika could put into the field about 240 mixed Marks II, III and IV panzers and an additional 150 Italian M13s; the 160 Italian light tanks, Cunningham was assured, could be safely ignored. Against these figures, XXX Corps alone could field some 475 tanks, while the Army Tank Brigades with XIII Corps and in Tobruk held a total of 261 tanks of which 201 were 'I' tanks – Matildas and Valentines.

But of course such purely quantitative calculations ignored other equally crucial factors. In view of the cavalier attitude adopted towards the Italian light tanks it might, for instance, have been more realistic to discount some of 7th Armoured Brigade's ninety-four cruiser tanks of marks earlier than the Crusader, many of which – as should have been foreseen – would be in the workshops until a few days before the operation began. Moreover, Churchill's habit of assuming that the arrival of a tank at Suez would precede its employment on the battlefield by a fully capable and experienced crew merely by the time taken to transport it there, was here being accepted by men who should have known better. Owing to a continued lack of communication between Cairo and London, all the new Crusaders for 22nd Armoured Brigade had perforce gone straight from ships to engineering sheds, where they spent valuable weeks (to the perturbation of Admiral Cunningham as he considered the effects of a really heavy air attack on Alexandria) undergoing essential modification to air and lubrication systems before they could be sent up into the desert – thus drastically reducing the time in which their crews, straight from England, could adapt to desert conditions and tactics.

However, the dictum remained that British armour should destroy the German panzers and it seemed that the Tank Corps had won the argument; they were thus somewhat bemused when the details of Cunningham's plan emerged to find that they were not maintaining to any great extent that concentration of armour which they had demanded. Although, despite Freyberg's protests, Gatehouse's 4th Armoured Brigade Group remained a part of XXX Corps, it was still ordered to remain in the neighbourhood of the New Zealand Division close to the Wire, while the experienced 7th Armoured Brigade, accompanied by the inexperienced 22nd Armoured Brigade (it was the first brigade of the 1st Armoured Division to arrive in the Delta, the other brigades having been delayed in England by shipping shortages), pressed on up towards Tobruk, with the South Africans to their left rear.

However, they would not drive immediately all the way to Tobruk, but at the end of the first day dispose themselves in a triangle around Gabr Saleh, an insignificant landmark in an otherwise featureless desert about a third of the way between XXX Corps's crossing-point of the Wire and Tobruk itself, the points of the triangle being just over twenty miles apart. The 7th Armoured Brigade (with a high proportion of the early mark cruisers) would be at the apex of the triangle pointing towards Tobruk with the Support Group just behind them, 22nd Armoured Brigade with their 155 newly modified Crusaders and Yeomanry crews on the left, and 4th Armoured Brigade Group, now totally re-equipped with American Stuarts (regarded by the Americans as light tanks and dubbed 'Honeys' by the British tank crews who were delighted by their reliability), held back on the right to afford the protection to XIII Corps.

Here, according to the official 'Preliminary Narrative', 'the enemy armour would be compelled to fight on ground of XXX Corps' choosing' – a piece of casuistry whose hollowness would have been revealed had anyone braved Cunningham's growing irritability by asking who in XXX Corps chose that particular piece of ground, and why? The area around Gabr Saleh was just as flat, stony and open as any other part of the adjacent desert, and if the strategy was to tempt the Afrika Korps forward to its destruction, then 'ground of XXX Corps' choosing' should surely have some natural defensive advantages.

In fact, the area was not 'chosen' by anyone, but dictated by Cunningham's attempt to compromise between the armour's wish to stay concentrated, and the infantry's wish to have armour protection on its flank. Lieutenant- General C. W. M. Norrie, who found himself unexpectedly in command of XXX Corps just six weeks before *Operation Crusader* was launched (owing to the death in an air accident of the intended corps commander, General Pope), was most unhappy about the plan. Not only was there in his eyes an unnecessary dispersion between the brigades at the points of the triangle, but

> . . . in order to make the enemy fight I considered it essential for our forces to secure ground vital to him. I did not consider Gabr Saleh of any real importance to the enemy. In fact, if we went there, there was no real reason why he should attack us and we were in danger of handing him the initiative . . . I suggested we would do better to threaten the enemy L of C about Sidi Rezegh from the word 'Go'.[7]

But Norrie's reservations and suggestions were dismissed and the concept of the clash of armour developed, best described in the most detailed account of *Operation Crusader*, by the South African historians J. A. I. Agar-Hamilton and L. C. F. Turner:

> After 30th Corps had made its penetration, the *Afrikakorps* would present itself at Gabr Saleh and be soundly beaten. The remaining stages would follow decently and in order – the march to Sidi Rezeg, the break-out of the Tobruk garrison (with the seizure of the Sollum–Sidi Omar positions as a picturesque parergon), and the rounding-up of the broken remnants of the *Panzergruppe* between Acroma and Ain el Gazala. It was hoped that the port of Tobruk would be available as a supply base on D3 and the permanent water of the Jebel el Akdar at the end of a week. The smooth flow of events could not possibly be hindered by so perverse a circumstance as a rebuff to the Eighth Army, and even the German armour would not be so ill-mannered as to be late in attending its rendezvous with destiny. The detailed provisions of the Corps Operation Orders . . . confirmed the sense of inevitability, until even those who originally disliked the plan were bemused into acceptance.[8]

The employment of the South Africans on the outer flank of the advance was another matter of doubtful prescience. General Brink's division had arrived in Egypt with an immense reputation as a result of their splendid achievements in Ethiopia, but their first employment in the area had been to restore the fortifications at Mersa Matruh in the face of Rommel's advance to the Wire, for these had been allowed to deteriorate after O'Connor's victories. Even after the immediate threat had died away, 1st South African Division were kept at the task of extending the Matruh defences even deeper, and the time and energy which could and indeed should have been spent learning the differences between warfare in desert and warfare in bush and mountain were instead spent digging. Not only did this affect their efficiency for the coming battle but it obviously affected the morale of men who had volunteered for active military duties, and now found themselves continually employed as static labourers.

Moreover, the reinforcements sent up from the Union to replace the casualties suffered in the Ethiopian campaign were so inadequate in both quantity and training that the decision had to be taken to go into battle with only two instead of three brigades, and for even this weakened division there was not enough transport until early October. Even then, a large number of the lorries and their drivers were commandeered by Eighth Army Q side to help build up the supply dumps in the forward area, and thus were not available for training. This circumstance not only increased the risk of faulty navigation at crucial moments, but allowed little or no time to rehearse the vital and often complex routines of supply under battle conditions.

General Brink on several occasions pointed out these deficiencies in the training of his command to Cunningham, and as late as November 2nd General Norrie after an inspection reported, 'I must again bring to your notice that I am not at all satisfied with the progress of training of 1 SA Div due to factors beyond their own control . . . '9

The South African troops themselves were keen, tough and only too eager to undertake any operations allocated to them, and there is no doubt that they were more than competent to carry out some of the more static duties required in *Operation Crusader* – such as the investment of the defences south of Sollum with which 4th Indian Division, the infantry with more experience of desert warfare than any other, had been charged. But Cunningham had intimated to Brink that he wanted the South Africans in the forefront of the battle, and when Brink reiterated that his men required more time, presented him with a virtual ultimatum. Brink must let him know by a stated hour whether his division was in a fit state to play an important part in the battle or not; if not, its role would be reduced.

This was surely a most unfair burden to place upon the shoulders of a subordinate commander, especially of a Dominion formation anxious to uphold its reputation and again prove its loyalty to the Mother Country. That night Brink wrote in his diary:

> There was no time to ponder or to argue. The Army Commander was applying the acid test. I was not happy about the state of training of my Division and in my heart I felt that it was not in a fit state, tactically, and did not possess the hitting power to engage in serious operations. We have splendid fighting material, well led and ably commanded, but the best human material in the world requires careful moulding and must have the wherewithal to engage a tough and determined enemy such as the *Afrika-Korps*. The die was cast, however, the Division was already on the move to its concentration area and the honour of South Africa was at stake.[10]

Thus the formations given the specific task of seeking out the two panzer divisions of Rommel's Afrika Korps consisted of three armoured brigades of which one – the 22nd – was totally inexperienced but comparatively well-equipped, one – the 7th – was experienced but equipped in large part with out-dated tanks (described by General Norrie as being in a state of 'general debility') and the third – the 4th – was both experienced and equipped with new tanks, but held back from the most likely area of battle by its requirement to protect infantry divisions; all protected on the outward flank of their advance by an understrength division of troops who, in the opinion of their commander, were inadequately trained.

But at least the 4th Indian Division and Bernard Freyberg's New Zealanders were more than capable of discharging their duties of pinning down and then cutting off the Axis troops along the frontier. Perhaps they might also help in the destruction of the panzers.

Moreover, a considerable degree of surprise would be achieved, for not only had the combined R.A.F. and S.A.A.F. kept the skies above the concentration areas clear of German or Italian reconnaissance aircraft, but the British intelligence services under Brigadier Shearer had achieved a coup as remarkable in its way as the repeated cracking of the Enigma codes by the Bletchley Park organisation in England.

It had all begun in July when a Palestinian farm-worker reported that he had seen a parachutist descend to the ground near Ramleh and had later observed him digging holes nearby as though to bury something. The parachutist was eventually caught and upon close investigation proved, despite a remarkably Jewish appearance, to be, of all people, the Gauleiter of Mannheim, dropped into

Palestine by German Intelligence with a view to increasing anti-British sentiment among the Arabs.

In the holes he had dug were found a bundle of Palestinian currency and a short-wave transmitter complete with codes, identification signals and specified times of transmission, and it was not long before Shearer and his team were exchanging routine and fairly harmless messages with what seemed likely to be their opposite numbers in Bari. Then, with more devious ploys in mind, they sent out details of troop movements which they guessed could be adequately confirmed by other espionage networks in the Delta and were soon receiving congratulations upon the accuracy of their information, together with the news that Rommel was most grateful for it and would welcome more.

With the forthcoming major operation in mind, Shearer now decided upon a more ambitious piece of deception.

Auchinleck was persuaded to pay an obviously very official visit to Ninth Army H.Q. in Palestine, dust columns were seen moving east across Sinai and northwards through Palestine giving the impression of heavy traffic driving wide to escape observation – and Bari were dramatically informed by this valued new source that Britain's real immediate intentions were to move as much strength as they could spare up towards the Caucasus to help Russia, and thus safeguard her own oil supplies in the Persian Gulf. The apparent preparations for an attack in the Western Desert were a cover, and could safely be disregarded.

This was indeed news to gladden Rommel's heart, feeding his almost fanatical obsession to capture Tobruk. From then on, no report or suggestion of aggressive intentions by the British against Panzergruppe Afrika was listened to with anything except irritation, and on one occasion he contemptuously threw aerial photographs of the extension of the British rail-line westwards from Mersa Matruh to the floor, refusing even to look at them. On November 14th he telephoned Berlin to complain of continuing harassment by his worried Italian allies (presumably, for security reasons, he could not reveal the source of his own confidence) and he gave the Chief of the Wehrmacht Operations Staff, Oberstgeneral Alfred Jodl, his personal guarantee that no danger existed on his front. He even informed Gambara that his next attempt to reduce Tobruk could begin on November 20th without the slightest risk of serious interference, and at the beginning of that month flew off to Rome to spend a fortnight with Dearest Lu.

Operation Crusader, or the Winter Battle as the Germans were to call it, was not to be distinguished by great perception or even competence at the highest level on either side; only the fighting troops were to win renown.

Shortly before Eighth Army began moving to its battle positions, two small-scale operations were mounted to divert Axis attention from the main fronts, by parties made up from officers and men who had come out from England with the Special Service Brigade, originally intended for the attack on Rhodes. The brigade had played a somewhat inconclusive role in the opening stages of the Syrian campaign and was now being disbanded, many of the men having already returned to their regiments. Some, however, had been retained to form the nucleus of what was to prove the most durable of the private armies.

On the night of November 16th, five Bristol Bombay aircraft took off from a small airfield near Fuka carrying fifty-seven men and three officers, whose aim was to carry out raids on Luftwaffe airfields in the Gazala–Tmimi area, their special targets being the new 109F fighters which were proving a hazard to the R.A.F. Tomahawks and Hurricanes.

Meteorological forecasts were excellent at take-off, visibility perfect, and during the early part of the journey there was little wind to confuse the navigation. But as the five planes droned westwards over the sea, conditions worsened rapidly and by the time they were due to turn south to cross the coastline, they were flying in thick turbulent cloud which bucketed the aircraft around the sky until all were separated and lost. Soon it was evident that even if the correct dropping zone could be found, cloud base was so low that for the parachutists to be dropped at the minimum safe height of seven hundred feet, they would have to be dropped blind in thick fog. One pilot who did venture down to try to pick up a landmark, found cloud base at 200 feet – registered on his altimeter just seconds before it disintegrated in a burst of anti-aircraft fire which came up to greet him. Incredibly, that aircraft survived for the moment, to fly in a gigantic circle as a result of a jammed compass, until it ran out of petrol and after further misadventures was shot down and its passengers and crew either killed or taken prisoner.

But in the meantime, the other four pilots had all pressed on separately through the appalling conditions until they felt that they were over the correct destination, whereupon they dropped their parachutists – disastrously. Many of the men were never seen again, some on landing were dragged by their canopies – caught open by the powerful ground wind – along the bumpy and rock-strewn desert floor to broken and agonising deaths, and no one escaped the ordeal entirely unscathed. Morning revealed not only that the supply chutes were so dispersed over the desert that, for instance, although much explosive was recovered no one could find the fuses, but also that the party had been dropped so far south that there was no chance of any of them reaching their objectives in either time or condition to carry out their allotted tasks.

Tacitly, the operation was abandoned, and the twenty-two survivors set out for their rendezvous with the Long Range Desert Group at the Rotunda Segnale. Fortunately, they arrived there safely and even more fortunately among them were two men – Captain David Stirling and Lieutenant Paddy Mayne – who were able to draw the correct conclusions from their experiences and thus keep alive the basic concept behind the Special Air Service Regiment.

The second operation held, even by 'private army' standards, bizarre elements in both concept and conduct.

Early in October, six officers and fifty-three men from No. 11 Commando (which had taken part in the landings at the mouth of the Litani River in June) had congregated in the Canal Zone and there practised the techniques of landing on open beaches at night, in rubber dinghies and canvas-covered canoes, called 'folboats', launched from the slippery decks of submarines.

On the night of November 13th/14th, they attempted to do this off the coast of the Jebel Akhdar, some twenty miles west of Appollonia, but in a howling gale very different from the calm in which they had continually trained. The result was that it took seven hours instead of the planned ninety minutes to get twenty-eight men (including the operational commander, Lieutenant-Colonel Geoffrey Keyes) ashore from the first submarine, *Torbay*, and when the second submarine, *Talisman*, closed the shore to disembark her commandos, she touched bottom and in the subsequent turmoil seven boats and eleven men were swept overboard and several never seen again. At this, *Talisman* withdrew with many of the raiding force still aboard, so that in the morning when Keyes assembled his force – wet, chilled to the bone and short of vital weapons and equipment – it was already considerably under strength for the operations for which it had been landed. One person who was present, however, was Colonel Robert Laycock, the original commander of the Special Service Brigade, who had accompanied the force as 'observer', and now decreed that in the circumstances the objectives must be curtailed.

These had originally been four in number – to attack the Italian Headquarters at Cyrene and cut all telephone and telegraph installations, to attack the Italian Intelligence Centre at Appollonia, to wreck communications around El Faidia, and to attack the German Headquarters at Beda Littoria and Rommel's personal villa to the west of the village. Who originally proposed this last objective is a mystery lost in time and perhaps the files of the Cairo

Headquarters, but as the only possible reason for attacking a small private villa would be to capture or kill the occupants – and as the improbability of Rommel allowing himself to be captured and then transported from a point so far behind his own lines to Egypt, or even to Tobruk, must have been recognised – there can be little doubt that the purpose behind this part of the Keyes Raid was assassination. Perhaps Laycock's presence was intended to relieve the young man (Keyes was only twenty-four) of an agonising decision should Rommel indeed be taken alive, and then stand in chance of rescue.

In the face of the major depletion of forces, however, it was now agreed that only two of the objectives would be pursued – the attack on the telegraph and telephone systems at Cyrene, and the attack on the German Headquarters at Beda Littoria. Only if the German Commander-in-Chief was in that particular building would he be in danger, and the idea of an attack on his private villa was tacitly dropped.

It took the party until the night of November 16th to reach a small cave some five miles from Beda Littoria, where they passed the whole of that night and most of the following day in uncomfortable and odorous surroundings, but at least sheltered from the torrential rain which had plagued them almost continuously since their landing. They spent the time drying their clothes, cleaning their weapons and gradually thawing out from the debilitating cold which had gripped them from the moment they had emerged from the submarine hatches, wondering what had happened to the blazing, sub-tropical sunshine in which, reputedly, the southern Mediterranean shore was continually bathed.

At about 1800 Keyes, who had carried out a short reconnaissance during the afternoon, briefed the whole party, divided it in two and sent one half off to blow up the communication pylon near Cyrene while the rest listened to his detailed plans for the attack on the German Headquarters. Then, with blackened faces, clad in combat gear and wearing plimsolls, they all set off on the final stage of the attacks.

By midnight, Keyes and his party were at the outskirts of Beda Littoria and the first nerve-shattering experience occurred when one member tripped over a tin can, to produce a frenzied barking from every dog in the neighbourhood and hysterical screams from at least one of the inhabitants. Two of Mussolini's soldiers who investigated the uproar were arrogantly bullied in fluent German by Keyes's second-in-command, Captain Robin Campbell, until they retired wearing a decidedly disgruntled air and doubtless reflecting upon the disagreeable truculence of some of their allies.

Keyes by this time had himself cut through the wire surrounding the Headquarters Building – a six-storey house standing away from the main village – to find that the rain, which had made their journey so uncomfortable so far, now yielded a dividend by confining all of the sentries except one to their tents. This exception Keyes silently killed and the rest of the party now joined him, bringing with them sufficient explosive to wreck both the building and the electric power plant close by.

As investigation revealed no easy access to the building, Campbell hammered on the front door and demanded entry in his excellent German, and when eventually the door opened, Keyes jammed his revolver in the ribs of the startled soldier behind it – who was, however, sufficiently well-trained and brave as to grab the gun, begin wrestling with Keyes and to shout warnings at the top of his voice. Surprise now lost, Campbell shot the struggling German over Keyes's shoulder, Keyes flung the door back and the six men making up the assault party stormed inside. The next few minutes were a chaos of sub-machine-gun and pistol fire, of shouts of anguish and alarm, of slamming doors and running footsteps on stone steps.

On the left of the main hall, a door started opening and Keyes kicked it wide to see inside about ten Germans frozen in startled shock; he was emptying his revolver into the room when Campbell appeared at his elbow with a grenade so Keyes pulled the door shut while the pin was pulled and the fuse burnt down, then opened it again. A crash as the grenade went in, a burst of Tommy-gun fire into the room as well – and then a single shot back from some more than usually quick-witted German and Keyes was flung away by a bullet which hit him just over the heart. He was dead within seconds.

An uncanny silence now fell upon the building as every light went out. Campbell dragged Keyes's body outside, checked back in the house for further signs of hostile activity, then ran around to the rear where a covering party had been left. Too late he remembered he should have shouted a password; sub-machine-gun bullets smashed into his leg and the party at the Rommel-haus was now without an officer capable of leading. Sergeant Terry took over, brought up enough explosive to blow up the entire building – only to discover that the fuses were rain-soaked and unusable and that the only damage the party could still inflict was by way of dropping a grenade down the breather pipe of the main generator, which thus at least kept the place in darkness.

The fit men then withdrew, justifiably believing that the Germans would not ill-treat their wounded, and by the following evening had made contact with Colonel Laycock at the beach. There then followed hours of frustration while their signals to *Torbay* – lying fully surfaced about 400 yards out – were unacknowledged and *Torbay*'s belated signals to them were largely incomprehensible and certainly did not result in boats coming in to fetch them. The twenty-two survivors moved just before dawn into a wadi to lie up for the day, but there they were first attacked by Arabs and then by Italians, so Laycock gave orders for them to split into small groups before a more serious attack by Germans developed.

In the end, all except two were captured; Laycock and Sergeant Terry got clear and after forty-one days made contact with the British near Cyrene. Campbell was well treated by his captors though his leg had to be amputated, Keyes and four Germans were buried with full military honours by Rommel's chaplain, and in due course Keyes was awarded a posthumous Victoria Cross. It had undoubtedly been an operation upon which great courage had been exhibited, and a certain amount of skill.

But not enough, for important aspects of training had been neglected. There is no point in arranging a pick-up from a beach unless each side can read the other's signals, and even less in carrying explosive for miles without two methods of detonating it – and preferably more. And a number of questions yield only unsatisfactory answers.

Why should a party of at maximum sixty men be commanded by a lieutenant-colonel, however young?

Why was a full colonel accompanying the party?

Why, as a full colonel was present, did he allow the landings to continue in the face of such appalling weather conditions, with the consequent loss of time, and the deterioration of both men and material?

Every answer obtainable to these questions, from whatever source, is coloured by reference to such admirable qualities as courage, leadership, imagination, devotion to duty and to one's men; by the sceptical listener the trumpet tones of romantic excitement can clearly be heard. What still seems to have been missing was hard professionalism and an acceptance of the grim realities of war.

And of course, Rommel had moved his headquarters from Beda Littoria weeks before, and that night was nowhere near the place.

11 · Crusader: The Clash of Armour

During the weekend of November 16th and 17th, 1941, the whole of the Eighth Army was on the move – 100,000 men, 600 tanks, 5,000 assorted cars, trucks and lorries; and although the troops accepted the resultant tribulations with their usual sardonic good humour, the administrative staffs were shaken by the ordeal.

The South Africans probably had the worst time of it as a result of their enforced lack of training, and after the last short move to the concentration area, deliberately undertaken at night, General Brink declared, in heartfelt tones, 'Never again!' Units became entangled, men were lost and run over, vehicles overturned; and the tally of broken springs, axles and propeller shafts, for which spares were almost unobtainable, was deeply worrying. The most frightening revelation of all, however, was the figure for petrol consumption. The vehicle average, estimated at eight miles per gallon, proved during that last chaotic phase no higher than two miles per gallon – a situation perceptibly worsened by the fact that three of the overturned vehicles had been petrol carriers and 1,500 gallons of precious fluid had been poured into the sand. The spectre of the division stalled and isolated in the desert haunted the South African command for the rest of the operation.

Even the move forward of the New Zealand Division, by now as well trained and experienced as any in the desert, had not been without difficulties, again due to the absolute aridity of the desert. Even at the low ration of a gallon of water per day per man, each brigade needed to take with it enough to fill a small reservoir – and water was only one of the vital necessities. Each brigade required 1,000 vehicles to carry the men, weapons, ammunition and stores – and spread out at ten vehicles to the mile, this gave a tailback 100 miles long which took six and a half hours to pass any given point. On the last seventy-mile move up to the concentration area the leading vehicles of each brigade arrived at their destination before the last had left the starting-point. It was, indeed a quartermaster's nightmare come to life, and a nightmare unrelieved by any awakening to a world of sanity when morning came.

Altogether there were fourteen brigades of one sort or another on the move, picking their slow, dusty, frustrating and often inexpert ways across the Egyptian desert towards the Wire and the enemy beyond, and it is astonishing that the morale of everybody concerned was as high as it was. Inexperience and the optimism of youth played a very great part (they are qualities of inestimable value to an uncertain military command) and Churchillian rhetoric had also helped. Before the major moves had taken place, a message from the Prime Minister had been read to them all:

> For the first time British and Empire troops will meet the Germans with an ample equipment in modern weapons of all kinds. The battle itself will affect the whole course of the war. Now is the time to strike the hardest blow yet struck for final victory, home and freedom. The Desert Army may add a page to history which will rank with Blenheim and with Waterloo. The eyes of all nations are upon you . . . May God uphold the right![1]

Despite passages in that exhortation which struck a rather hollow note in the minds of some senior officers, the men of the Eighth Army accepted the spirit of the message and even added to it from their own happy confidence. According to one of the New Zealand historians, ' . . . the morale of the Division was at its peak, a level never surpassed,' and Desmond Young, the biographer of Rommel, wrote of this approach march to *Crusader*, 'The battle that ensued was desperately fought by both sides. On ours there was an exhilaration, a will to victory that I had not seen equalled since the final battles at the end of the first war.'

This was as well, for the spirit was to be severely tested almost immediately. That night the hitherto mild November weather broke, the wind rose and at first whipped up a sandstorm distinguished by the perverse quality of being bitterly cold, followed shortly by the most spectacular thunderstorm to burst upon the desert within local memory. Jagged flashes of lightning ripped open the Mediterranean skies, and as the clouds built up thicker and thicker, each acted as both electric pole and light reflector until the entire horizon sparked and crackled, floodlighting the desert with an almost continuous, cold, green, flickering radiance, while overhead the thunder boomed and roared, then crashed out with the startling suddenness of cannon-fire.

And then the rain came. Squalls of bitter sleet swept across the huddled army, lancing down through every tear in fabric, gap in lacing, open windshield or gun-port; soaking inexorably through serge or drill to transform it into icy poultices to chill the flesh and blood beneath – and to turn the desert dust to mud. Along the Escarpment, wadis flooded and cascades washed away not only rocks and clumps of scrub but men who had thought to find cover and shelter in them, and their weapons and equipment too. The rain flooded the whole of the desert from Tobruk across to Sidi Barrani and down in a triangle whose apex was well south of Fort Maddalena, collecting in flat pans, turning sand-stretches into spongy marshes, and totally washing out Air Vice-Marshal Coningham's airfields and any chance of R.A.F. covering operations until they dried. It even put a stop to a proposed bombardment by the Royal Navy of the Reverend Bach's positions around Halfaya, as the spotting planes could not take off.

The only consolation for the Eighth Army was that the Luftwaffe was similarly grounded, and that Rommel's forces, poised for their concentrated attack on Tobruk, were just as severely discomforted as themselves.*

The storm ended before dawn, though all next day the sky remained overcast with dark, sullen clouds; but exercise and movement soon warmed the waiting soldiers. The armoured cars moved first through the Wire – 11th Hussars on the left leading the Yeomanry of 22nd Armoured Brigade (11th had been patrolling on both sides of Fort Maddalena for nearly a week), 4th South African Armoured Car Regiment in the centre leading 7th Armoured Brigade, and the 1st King's Dragoon Guards (less one squadron in Tobruk) on the right; by midday they had all fought brief, sporadic actions with Axis armoured cars which had then retired.

The armour of XXX Corps then followed, 4th Armoured Brigade Group and the New Zealanders wheeling on the inside rim. Despite the conditions of the night before, high spirits quickly returned and confidence surged through the vast procession – though at certain levels, new doubts arose. One of Freyberg's battalion commanders, Howard Kippenberger, wrote:

> This great approach march will always be remembered by those who took part in it though the details are vague in memory. The whole Eighth Army, Seventh Armoured Division, First South African Division, and the Second New Zealand and Fourth Indian Divisions moved westwards in an enormous column, the armour leading. The Army moved south of Sidi Barrani, past the desolate Italian camps of the previous year, along the plateau south of the great escarpment, through the

*For a map of the opening moves of *Operation Crusader*, November 18th–19th, 1941, see the back endpaper.

frontier wire into Libya, south of the enemy garrisons in the Sidi Omars, and wheeled north. Then, just as we were rejoicing in the conception of a massive move on Tobruk, disregarding the immobile frontier garrisons and crushing everything in our path, the whole Army broke up and departed different ways.[2]

Not so many people, however, noticed the fragmentation; besides that extraordinary amalgam of fear and excitement, of frantic activity and tense waiting, of hoarse direction and sweating obedience which makes up the first moves into battle, those who travelled in the midst of the slow swing across the frontier were treated to a memorable series of mirages. Alan Moorehead was there:

At times you could see on the horizon a towered city that floated on a lake and undulated as you watched like a stage back-cloth blown in the wind. Small bushes looked in the distance like great trees, and each truck was a two-storied house passing through the dust. Often we saw groups of castles on the horizon. As we approached, these turned to battleships and then at last from a mile away they resolved into the solid shapes of tanks.[3]

Shortly after midday, it became evident that enemy forces in front were beginning to stand and that the armoured cars could go no further forward on their own (11th Hussars on the outer flank of the advance had by this time driven sixty miles into enemy territory) and the armour came up. In the centre, the cruisers of 2nd R.T.R. came through and before the impressive sight of them moving apparently invincibly forward, the cars of Rommel's Reconnaissance Battalion 33 retired and very soon the spearheads of 7th Armoured Brigade had crossed the Trig el Abd and reached their rendezvous for the day, about ten miles north-west of Gabr Saleh. On their right, Alec Gatehouse's 4th Armoured Brigade Group had also reached their day's objective across the Trig el Abd, level with and about ten miles east of Gabr Saleh, having pushed back elements of Reconnaissance Battalion 3 (which had reported back in some agitation that they were being attacked by over two hundred heavy tanks). Only on the outer rim of the wheel had there been delay, for 22nd Armoured Brigade had had the usual poor luck which accompanies inexperience, and stopped at dusk some ten miles short of their objective. Outside them, 1st South African Brigade had overcome their recent lack of training and covered sixty miles to reach the track running south from Bir el Gubi down to Jarabub at El Cuasc, with 5th South African Brigade another twenty miles south at Elwet el Hamra.

All in all, XXX Corps had advanced very satisfactorily, meeting nothing but armoured screens and suffering very little from enemy action. And if breakdowns had reduced the number of tanks with 7th Armoured Brigade from 141 to 119, and with 22nd Armoured Brigade from 155 to 136, this was set off by a discovery of German inadequacy which heightened even further the air of general euphoria. During the advance of the 2nd R.T.R. cruisers, they had overrun and captured one of the famous German eight-wheeled armoured cars, and during the evening tank enthusiasts flocked in from miles around to inspect it. Brigadier G. M. O. Davy, now commanding 7th Armoured Brigade, was amused:

One used to hear of primitive people being impressed by visiting warships, not because of their speed, armour or fire-power, but for the number of their funnels. The German eight-wheeler had somehow acquired an importance, in the imagination of its opponents, which nothing but its eight wheels could have justified. It was a poor thing, with thin armour and few weapons, and in the light of day the once formidable myth collapsed.[4]

A cold comfort, though, to men such as Sergeant Wood and his crew of the 11th, who in their Marmon-Harrington had been shot to death twelve weeks before by the highly efficient crew of one of these eight-wheelers.

To General Cunningham, the events of the day had been mildly irritating and its very success provided a mixture of both satisfaction and uncertainty; and the uncertainty was growing.

He had set out before first light and it was unfair that a sticky patch of soft sand had so engulfed his car that he arrived at General Norrie's Corps Headquarters (at which he intended to spend this first day of *Operation Crusader*) an hour late. Fortunately, Norrie had allowed a margin for emergencies, and they had moved off on time, crossed the Wire amid the bulk of XXX Corps B Echelon supply vehicles and by evening had settled down at Point 174, south of Gabr Saleh, due east of El Cuasc, and thus central to the northern and western faces – surely the most vital – of the deployment of the armoured force with which he intended to annihilate the Afrika Korps.

As the signals came in – and they were laconic in the extreme, for one lesson at least had been learned from *Battleaxe* and British wireless discipline greatly tightened – he could build up a picture of all that had happened that day, and see how smoothly his plans had gone.

All armoured brigades, including 4th Armoured Brigade Group and Brigadier Campbell's Support Group were, if not in exact

position, certainly in sufficient approximation to give cause for
satisfaction, while the New Zealanders had crossed the Wire south
of Bir Sheferzen, regrouped and were ready to advance northwards
to take the enemy static defences in rear when called upon to do so.
As for the 4th Indian Division, 7th Brigade was closed up around
Bir Sheferzen occupying the doubtless watchful attention of
German and Italian units in the Sidi Omars, 11th Brigade was on
the coast opposite Sollum while between the two the cars and
carriers of Central India Horse kept watch and the Matildas of 1st
Army Tank Brigade waited ponderously for their call to action.

All had gone according to the book.

The only missing element was the enemy.

Where was Rommel?

Rommel was at his advanced headquarters at Gambut and had not
the slightest intention of reacting seriously to what he was certain
was nothing but a diversion staged by the British Command in order
to frighten the Italians at El Gubi and Bir Hakeim, causing them in
their turn to distract his attention from his main purpose, the final
reduction of Tobruk. To suggestions by Cruewell and his Chief of
Staff, Oberstleutnant Fritz Bayerlein, that 15th Panzer Division
should at least be put on the alert and Panzer Regiment 5 from von
Ravenstein's 21st Panzer Division sent down towards Gabr Saleh to
check on the reports of British armour in that neighbourhood, he
replied brusquely, 'We must not lose our nerve' – a rebuke which
ruffled the feelings of the Afrika Korps command, and added to the
tensions at Gambut.

For although the attacks on the south-east face of the Tobruk
perimeter were planned to commence in some sixty hours' time,
there were many at headquarters, especially among the Quartermaster Staff, who felt that insufficient fuel and ammunition had
been collected. Rommel might appear unconcerned about the
intentions and capability of the British Eighth Army, but even he
had to recognise the recent accomplishments of the Royal Air Force
and the Royal Navy. Since September, port installations at Tripoli
and Brindisi had been under constant attack by Wellingtons based
in Egypt and Malta, and the supply convoys across the Mediterranean upon which Panzergruppe Afrika had to rely for existence
just as much as Eighth Army had to rely upon the rail and lorry
trains from the Delta, had been harried mercilessly.

Ten Axis ships had gone down in September, seven in October
and the tally so far in November was already ominous; and of late
the concentration by the R.A.F. on less remote targets such as the
Luftwaffe bases at Derna, Barce, Benina, Berka and Tmimi – and
the roads and tracks in between – indicated not only that the British

were aware of the impending attack on Tobruk (as how could they be ignorant?) but that they also knew the most vulnerable aspect of Afrika Korps's deployment, the jugular vein of communications guarded for the most part by the troops of the uncertain ally, Italy. Twenty per cent of the vital supplies sent from Germany, including the most precious of all, petrol, was ending either in flames or at the bottom of the sea, and if this proportion continued and the battle for Tobruk should be prolonged, then a most critical situation would arise.

In the Oberquartiermeister's offices, Q Branch, then, there was just as great a concentration upon capture of the all-important town and harbour as there was in Rommel's mind; and those who heard of yet another piece of evidence purporting to demonstrate immediate British aggression on land, tended to agree with Rommel's terse disposal of it. On the first night of *Crusader* (November 18th) according to the Afrika Korps War Diary:

> The German Liaison Officer with Savona Division reported results of the interrogation of an English soldier captured at Sidi Omar. It appeared from this that 7th Armoured Division had already advanced west of the Wire, 4th Indian Division was on either side of the Wire and two South African Divisions were moving west from Mersa Matruh.[5]

Obviously, this was a deliberate attempt to deceive, reminiscent of the famous trick played by Colonel Lawrence in the Syrian desert twenty-three years before, when he gulled the Turkish Command into a mistaken view of the axis of the British advance on Damascus. If anything, it confirmed opinion at Gambut that no serious threat to the assault on Tobruk existed, and that the empty manoeuvrings by the British around Gabr Saleh were a bluff which could safely be ignored.

The cloak of secrecy which had been thrown over Eighth Army intentions by a combination of radio discipline and freakish nature, and then perfected by Brigadier Shearer's deception, was making available enormous military advantages for General Cunningham to exploit. It was a pity that this situation was not one for which his plan had provided. In the event, having arrived on the 'ground of their own choosing' XXX Corps was finding itself blandly ignored and in exactly that danger of losing the initiative of which Norrie had warned his superior. There is indeed the faintest suggestion of crocodile tears about Norrie's expressed regrets that, to urgent requests for information upon which to base future plans, he had to reply that evening that he had none.

One result of the uncertainty thus generated was the issue of two sets of orders which although apparently in some agreement, differed in one vital respect. Strafer Gott, who had no intention of allowing 7th Armoured Division to lose the momentum they had acquired during the first day of the operation by hanging about doing nothing on the second, issued orders that on the morrow the armoured car screens were to probe forward both north and west, that the Support Group with the 22nd Armoured Brigade in close attendance should investigate Bir el Gubi where it was known that Bersaglieri of the Ariete Armoured Division were in strength, and that 7th and 4th Armoured Brigades should be prepared for battle with the Afrika Korps to the north.

Two hours later, XXX Corps issued orders upon Cunningham's direction, that 7th Armoured Division would secure *both* Bir el Gubi *and* Sidi Rezegh on the direct line towards Tobruk, and that the 1st South African Brigade would move up to take over Bir el Gubi, with their 5th Brigade moving to Gueret Hamza some ten miles south along the same axis. As the message ended with the statement that bomber support had been requested for the following day above both Ed Duda and El Adem, and that the Army Commander was 'anxious to stage relief' – presumably of Tobruk – it seemed that the decision had been taken to go straight for the port without achieving that 'destruction of the enemy armour' which had previously been considered so vital. But as the message also precluded any move by 4th Armoured Brigade Group much further westwards, it seemed that this amendment to the original *Crusader* plan envisaged two brigades, one totally inexperienced and the other equipped largely with outdated tanks, between them brushing aside the Ariete formations at Bir el Gubi and advancing to Tobruk against whatever resistance Rommel could organise; and presumably the bland indifference with which Afrika Korps had regarded Eighth Army moves to date would not continue once their vital communications between Sidi Rezegh and Ed Duda were threatened.

Whatever the thinking, Gott accepted that 22nd Armoured Brigade's blooding in battle would now be as leaders instead of in support, and that its support in turn would come from the South Africans, while Jock Campbell's more experienced force remained close to Gabr Saleh ready to follow 7th Armoured Brigade north towards Sidi Rezegh and Tobruk beyond. A matter not greatly considered was that however derisory the performance of the Italian M13s might be, they would fight a defensive battle and thus be well supported by their artillery; and another was the inadequacy of the communications system. The orders for the moves of the South African brigades up towards El Gubi only reached General Brink the following morning, and he understood them to mean that his men would only move into and occupy the location *after* the armour had captured it.

The move against Bir el Gubi by 22nd Armoured Brigade began early in the morning, and by noon the Crusaders of 2nd Royal Gloucester Hussars were on the outer defence line, driving the first enemy tanks their crews had ever seen back into the perimeter. It was an exhilarating experience for them. There was then a pause, more Crusaders from the 4th City of London Yeomanry (C.L.Y.) came up on their left, and despite warnings from one of the 11th Hussars' squadron commanders, a full-scale copybook attack was launched against what the Brigade Staff thought was a mobile defence post five miles east of El Gubi, but which proved to be a heavily fortified main line screened by dummies, behind which sheltered, in fact, the whole of the Ariete Armoured Division.

It was extraordinary that the Crusaders did so well. One observer said that the main attack was 'the nearest thing to a cavalry charge with tanks seen during this war', and its very unlikelihood may have given it a first spectacular advantage during which 34 M13s and 12 Italian guns were knocked out, and over 200 of the Bersaglieri killed or taken prisoner – a score which might indeed have been larger. One of the 4th C.L.Y. squadron commanders, Viscount Cranley, later wrote:

> The enemy seemed somewhat daunted by this spirited, if not very professional, attack and were coming out of their trenches in considerable numbers, offering to surrender, but thanks to brigade headquarters not having listened to the 11th Hussars, there was no infantry close enough to take over, and the bulk of my tanks were by now knocked out. The enemy quickly appreciated the position and, bobbing back again, started to shoot us up once more.[6]

By 1630, both the Gloucester Hussars and the 4th C.L.Y. had run into severe trouble against artillery and in minefields, and the 3rd C.L.Y. who had mounted a relieving attack to the north-west, had also suffered heavily in a counter-attack by the main body of the Italian 132nd Tank Regiment; blazing Crusaders littered the area around Bir el Gubi, grounded tank crews ran for shelter towards anything which moved and might be friendly, while isolated tanks, the rest of their troop burnt out or trackless, collected together and moved slowly and uncertainly back out of range of the still efficient and relentless Italian gunners. Wireless communications had long since broken down.

That evening, 22nd Armoured Brigade reported that they had lost half their tanks, though the Italians only claimed that they had destroyed fifty so perhaps the other thirty-two had merely broken

down; but the fact remained that one of the three brigades with
which Cunningham intended to destroy the Afrika Korps armour
had been very roughly handled – and Bir el Gubi was still firmly
held by the Ariete Division.

The advance of 7th Armoured Brigade northwards was, however, attended by success. During the morning they had pushed
away elements of the German Reconnaissance Battalion 33 (which
had leaguered virtually alongside them during the night) and,
preceded by their screen of South African armoured cars, pressed
on over the ridge of what became known as the Southern Escarpment. They saw before them running east–west a sloping valley,
gradually rising on the far side to the Escarpment crest upon which
stood the white, square tomb of Sidi Rezegh, and beyond which lay
the Trig Capuzzo; on the floor of the valley lay the airfield, upon
which were dispersed several aircraft of the Regia Aeronautica
with, for the moment, unsuspecting ground personnel unhurriedly
moving between them.

It looked an enticing and indeed promising prospect and the
events of the next hour or so were to justify the impression. With an
hour to go before sunset, the Crusaders of 6th R.T.R. preceded by
the South African armoured cars swept down and across the valley
to charge the airfield with most satisfying results. Many of the
aircraft were shot down as they tried to take off, some were even
shot down as they gallantly turned and tried to beat off their
assailants, but many were caught on the ground and either crushed
by the tanks or later hacked to pieces by exultant crew members.

One squadron of tanks was ordered further forward to take the
crest of the main Escarpment, but there they found two battalions
of the ex-Foreign Legionnaires of Afrika Regiment 361 well
entrenched, and as there were no accompanying British infantry
(for the Support Group was still beyond the southern escarpment)
the squadron retired back to the airfield, as did the armoured car
patrols which had explored westwards towards the El Adem–El
Gubi track until they ran into fire from the Italian Pavia Division.
By nightfall, therefore, 7th Armoured Brigade was solidly in
leaguer on the Sidi Rezegh airfield.

This was, of course, the location at which Norrie had wanted to
concentrate the whole of XXX Corps armour as soon as possible
after the crossing of the Wire, feeling that Sidi Rezegh was indeed
of vital importance to Rommel; now, if Norrie's judgment proved
correct, he could find himself facing the massed panzers of the
Afrika Korps with the armour of just one brigade – and the most
ill-equipped one at that. Little support could be given it, for as the
evening reports came in it seemed that 22nd Armoured Brigade was
too badly mauled to be of much use, and Cunningham's injunction

against moving up 4th Armoured Brigade was still in force. Not that Gatehouse's command had come through the day unscathed, for at last Rommel was beginning to take notice of the British presence west of the Wire.

During that second morning (November 19th) von Ravenstein had become more and more conscious of strong British forces to his immediate south, and when General Cruewell came to see him he repeated his request of the previous day to be allowed to send a strong panzer force down towards Gabr Saleh. The commander of the Afrika Korps, though he agreed with von Ravenstein's point of view, was still smarting under Rommel's suggestion of weakening nerves so he drove back to Gambut and placed the situation before his commander again. This time Rommel proved more amenable and by 1145 orders had been issued for a reinforced Panzer Regiment 5 (the reinstated Battlegroup Stephan) to attack and destroy 'the enemy threatenjng Reconnaissance Battalion 3'.

It was, in fact, the reports from this reconnaissance unit which had prompted a more reasonable attitude on Rommel's part, for since early morning he had been reading accounts of a delaying action by them against armoured cars of the King's Dragoon Guards and American Stuarts of 3rd R.T.R., who had been endeavouring to push the German patrols back northwards. There were even reports coming in of British armoured cars or light tanks advancing as far north as the Escarpment overlooking Bardia. The British were apparently putting more into this diversionary raid than had been expected.

Battlegroup Stephan, consisting of eighty-five mixed Panzers III and IV plus thirty-five Panzers II, complete with an artillery component of twelve 105mm. howitzers and four 88mm. flak or anti-tank guns, moved off shortly after midday and reached the area north-east of Gabr Saleh by 1430 to find the fifty Stuarts of 8th Hussars deploying rapidly to meet them.

What followed was the infinite confusion of the first purely panzer versus tank encounter on a large scale to take place in the desert, and it bore little relation to any previously held theories on armoured warfare. Instead of troops or squadrons manoeuvring together in mutually supporting teams, it became a frantic scurry of individual tanks fighting individual battles amid a cloud of sand and smoke, which blotted out visibility beyond a few yards and formed a choking fog illuminated sporadically by the flare of exploding ammunition and often by the flash of cannon much too near for comfort.

The Germans relied upon their drill and routine, the British upon the speed and manoeuvrability of their Honeys together with a

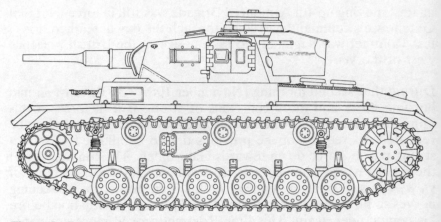

Figure 5   Panzerkampfwagen III (Ausführung F): weight 20 tons; armour 12mm.–30mm.; engine 300 h.p.; maximum speed 25 m.p.h.; armament one 5cm. (L/42), two 7·92 m.g.; crew 5

certain native quickness of reaction, and during the battle no one could tell which combination was proving the more effective. The first charge of the Hussars took them clean through the German formation and they then turned and swept back in again in a manner reminiscent of the charge of the Heavy Brigade at Balaclava, the action being at such close range that the inadequacies of their main armament were unnoticeable. An American observer of the battle (Colonel Bonner Fellers, who had attached himself to XXX Corps Headquarters and was watching with considerable interest the performance of the Honeys) noted that the German anti-tank guns co-operated superbly on the flanks of their panzer columns, but were handicapped by the fog and confusion and suffered losses from the machine-guns of the marauding Hussars as these briefly emerged from the murk, and more later when the Honeys of 5th R.T.R., which had also been detached northwards after the K.D.G.s came hurrying back to join the battle.

It was all, as Alexander Clifford who was also watching it, commented, 'utter, indescribable confusion':

There was something in it of a naval battle, something of a medieval cavalry charge, but all speeded up madly as you might speed up a cinema film . . .

Inside that frantic jumble tanks were duelling with tanks in running, almost hand-to-hand fights, firing nearly point blank, twisting, dodging, sprinting with screaming treads and whining engines that rose to a shriek as they changed gear. As each new tank loomed up ahead gunners were swinging the muzzles of their guns automatically, eyes strained behind their goggles, fighting through the smoke and dust to discriminate friend from foe . . .

Men told me afterwards that they were not even conscious of the two-pounders going off almost in their ears, so tense was their concentration.[7]

But a strange incident towards the close of the battle served to highlight grave and significant deficiencies in the British approach to armoured warfare. Either as a result of wireless requests or of routine practice, a German petrol and ammunition column arrived on the horizon about an hour before sunset, and as if at a signal the panzers drew off and clustered around it like bees around a honey-pot; and the British could do nothing but stand and watch, for the German guns could pick Honeys off long before their own guns could register effectively. As for the British artillery, it was too scattered, it took too long to get into action and out again – and it still lacked the spirit and training of close co-operation with armour.

The battle was renewed briefly before sundown, but the two sides then drew apart, the Germans to remain on the battlefield (and thus to be able more easily to recover their damaged panzers) the British retiring.

They both claimed victory, and both overestimated the number of hostile tanks destroyed – the first example of a persistent habit which was to play havoc with operational planning on both sides for most of the campaign. Colonel Stephan claimed twenty-four Honeys destroyed and although this figure was close for Honeys knocked out, many had been towed away and were repaired and back in action within twenty-four hours, giving an actual loss to 4th Armoured Brigade of but eleven. The British claimed 'between nineteen and twenty-six' panzers knocked out, but in fact Battle-group Stephan left only two Panzer IIIs and one Panzer II wrecked on the battlefield, while their admirable recovery service took away four damaged Panzer IIIs, and any other damage was sufficiently slight either to be reparable by the crews or left until the battle was over.

There is today no doubt as to which side had come off best in the first armoured mêlée between German panzers and British tanks in the desert, but at the time the true facts were not known and thus had no impact on that vital ingredient in battle, morale.

The tank crews of the 4th Armoured Brigade were delighted anew with the performance of their Honeys and were quite certain that they themselves were the equal of Rommel's panzer crews; and as for the reflections of their commander, from the reports coming in he was certain that his brigade was more than holding its own, and that when the fighting was renewed the next morning the destruction of the nearby enemy force was inevitable. By then the 3rd and 5th Royal Tank Regiments which he had sent off to the north that morning towards Sidi Azeiz and Bardia would have rejoined, bringing between them over a hundred more Honeys, and his concentrated brigade would be irresistible.

The idea of a concentrated *corps*, whether at Gabr Saleh or Sidi Rezegh, seems to have disappeared from everyone's mind.

November 20th was surely the day upon which tactical command on the desert battlefield – on both sides – was at its nadir.

Rommel, still the victim of British deception and ignoring the warnings from his intercept service that the whole of 7th Armoured Division was now west of the Wire, was still intent upon the reduction of Tobruk, and in order to protect himself against further interference he most uncharacteristically gave Cruewell a free hand to use his armour to clear up this intrusion behind the frontier. As for the reports of British troops near both Sidi Rezegh and Bir el Gubi, Sümmermann's Div zvB Afrika could deal with the first and the Ariete of Gambara's C.A.M. the second. Meanwhile, the deadline for the great assault – dawn tomorrow – was fast approaching.

Perhaps Cruewell did not see the reports of the intercept service which gave the probable positions of the left and right wings of the 7th Armoured Division at Bir el Gubi and Gabr Saleh respectively but he did know about those of the previous day from Reconnaissance Battalion 3 which had told of British tanks at Sidi Azeiz and above Bardia. Deciding that here must lie his greatest danger, he sent Neumann-Sylkow's 15th Panzer Division eastward along the Trig Capuzzo and ordered von Ravenstein to drive with the rump of 21st Panzer Division south-eastwards to Sidi Omar, rendezvousing en route with Battlegroup Stephan after the latter had disengaged itself from whatever formation it had been fighting that evening. Thus the intrusive British armour close behind the frontier would be encircled from both north and south, and cut off in a classic German military manoeuvre from both its supplies and its escape route.

Gatehouse's detachment of armoured cars and tanks on the previous day was therefore reaping a temporary, and totally undeserved, reward.

As for Cunningham's plans, these too were based upon misconception. Although he had been startled by the reports that 22nd Armoured Brigade had already lost half their tanks, the equally mistaken reports of 4th Armoured that they had administered a trouncing to the Afrika Korps were adequate compensation. At one moment it had even begun to look as though the original plan for *Crusader* – the destruction of the Afrika Korps in the neighbourhood of Gabr Saleh – was to be realised, and the fact that it was now being undertaken by one brigade group instead of by the whole of XXX Corps, does not seem to have perturbed anyone. But it was the success of 7th Armoured at Sidi Rezegh (in doing nothing but occupy a virtually unprotected airfield) which really excited him.

Here, he felt, was where concentration should take place (without exposing the flank of XIII Corps, of course) and success be exploited. The dominant point of the main Escarpment overlooking the airfield was Point 175, and 7th Armoured Brigade should send out a force to capture this as soon as possible. Meanwhile, Campbell's Support Group would cross the southern escarpment and join them on the airfield and 22nd Armoured must disengage themselves from Bir el Gubi and move northwards to add what was left of their strength to the force in the main battle area. In addition, to provide extra infantry for holding the line along the main Escarpment once the Afrika Regiments had been ejected, 5th South African Brigade was to leave Gueret Hamza, swing in a semicircle to the west around Bir el Gubi, cross the southern escarpment and also make for the airfield, while the remaining force in the area, 1st South African Brigade, took over the task first allotted to 22nd Armoured.

This, it will be remembered, had been to occupy and hold Bir el Gubi which, as events had proved, would entail the prior defeat and ejection of the Ariete Armoured Division from well-fortified defences. Even Corps Headquarters admitted that the situation there was 'obscure', but optimism ruled to such an extent that it was felt that the losses sustained by 22nd Armoured *must* be offset by a corresponding weakening of the Ariete, and the destruction of the remainder should be well within the capability of so doughty a formation as 1st South African Brigade. This atmosphere was somewhat chilled by the reaction of its commander, that staunch individualist Dan Pienaar, who forcefully rejected the argument, pointing out that failure by an armoured brigade was no guarantee of success by infantry; his orders were soon modified to that of just 'masking' the stronghold, his protest being perhaps the one note of realism in that night's communications.

The Germans moved first, 15th Panzer duly debouching on to and moving along the Trig Capuzzo, and the infantry of 21st Panzer (Battlegroup Knabe which had remained behind when Battlegroup Stephan had been detached) moving south-eastwards towards the rendezvous with Stephan at Gabr Lachem, prior to the joint advance on Sidi Omar. But by 0830, Knabe was reporting a strong enemy tank force in front and calling for help from both sides, in response to which von Ravenstein ordered a quicker move north by Stephan but Neumann-Sylkow took no notice. In this he was fully

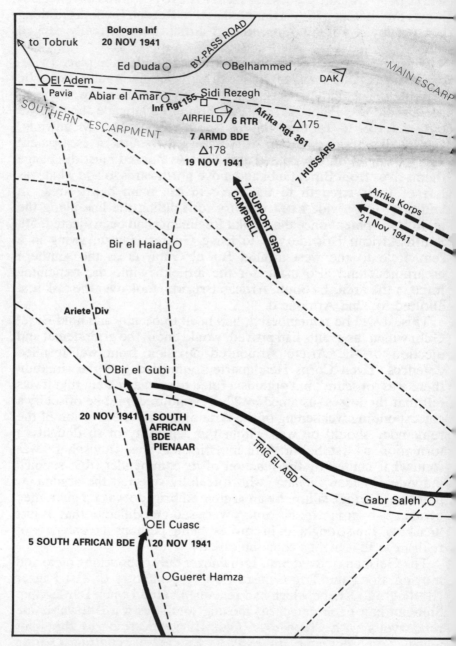

Map 21 *Operation Crusader*: November 20th–21st, 1941

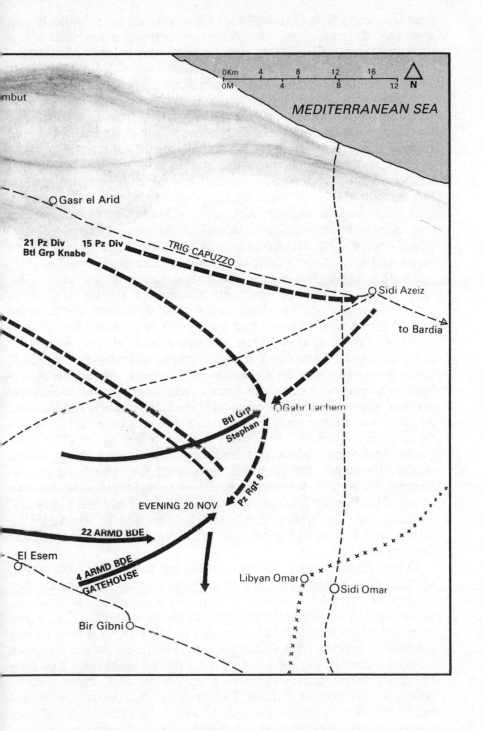

Mediterranean Sea

0Km 4 8 12 16
0M 4 8 12

N

mbut

Gasr el Arid

21 Pz Div 15 Pz Div
Btl Grp Knabe

TRIG CAPUZZO

Sidi Azeiz

to Bardia

Btl Grp
Stephan

Gabr Lachem

EVENING 20 NOV

Pz Rgt 8

22 ARMD BDE

El Esem

4 ARMD BDE
GATEHOUSE

Libyan Omar

Sidi Omar

Bir Gibni

justified, for when Cruewell hurried to the scene, he quickly and correctly diagnosed the opposition as nothing more than a few armoured cars (King's Dragoon Guards) and coldly ordered continued obedience to the morning's orders.

In this, 15th Panzer encountered no opposition at all, but Battlegroup Stephan, having been delayed by late arrival of their fuel and ammunition supplies, was only saved from serious trouble by the equally late arrival of Gatehouse's tank regiments which had failed to join him during the night. The result was a running battle as Stephan first moved across the front of both the 8th Hussars and the 5th R.T.R., followed by the breaking off of the engagement by Stephan on receipt of the hastening order from von Ravenstein to move northwards to meet Knabe – a move which Gatehouse not surprisingly interpreted as a retreat in the face of superior force. Much encouraged, 4th Armoured pursued for about six miles, then leaguered to complete their long-delayed concentration.

By this time, Neumann-Sylkow had reached Sidi Azeiz unmolested and reported the total absence of British armour to Cruewell, who quickly realised his error and concluded that the main axis of the British advance had been the Trig el Abd after all, and not the Trig Capuzzo. Thus the spearhead of 7th Armoured Division must be the force at Sidi Rezegh, and whatever covering force it was at Gabr Saleh was merely a flank guard. Neumann-Sylkow's division had by this time swung south around Sidi Azeiz and met groups Knabe and Stephan at the Gabr Lachem rendezvous, and it was while the combined Afrika Korps was here that Cruewell decided to launch its concentrated strength first against the flank guard and then, when this had been eliminated, back northwestwards across the desert in pursuit of the spearhead at Sidi Rezegh. It was at this point that he was informed that the now united 21st Panzer Division was completely out of both petrol and ammunition, and unless they could be supplied by air would be unable to move until the next day. And the Luftwaffe was already fully committed.

Cunningham in the meantime, beginning to despair of the arrival of that crucial moment in battle upon which the commanding general of one side or another (preferably one's own) can seize and so decide the issue, had early that morning left XXX Corps and returned to his own headquarters east of Maddalena. There he was greeted by reports from Coningham that bombers on the way back from operations over Cyrenaica the previous evening had seen Axis traffic streaming back westwards from Tobruk to Gazala, from El Adem to Acroma and from Bardia towards Tobruk. What this traffic was is now irrelevant, but it could have been anything from empty supply vehicles going back for refill, to Galloway's suggestion that it was Italian administrative troops moving out of critical areas to leave room for operations by German armour; but in the mood of euphoria which had overtaken Eighth Army Headquarters as a result of the advance to Sidi Rezegh and the possibility of the imminent relief of Tobruk, it was interpreted with only the minimum of hesitation as the first move in a general evacuation of Marmarica by Panzergruppe Afrika. This reading of events was to influence thought at the top at several crucial moments during the next few days.

In the immediate future, however, it was to receive something of a setback, for at 1100 Norrie signalled the content of the latest British intercepts of messages between Cruewell and Rommel, which included the exchange setting out Cruewell's new and more accurate understanding of the situation, but not that concerning 21st Panzer Division's enforced immobility. According to these intercepts, 4th Armoured Brigade would by noon be under attack from the entire Afrika Korps, and with sudden appreciation of the fact that Rommel's armour would then be concentrated whilst his own was dispersed, Cunningham sent off urgent signals instructing 22nd Armoured Brigade to ignore its previous orders to join the forces at Sidi Rezegh, and instead to move smartly eastwards and reinforce Gatehouse's brigade. As 22nd Armoured was at this time still embroiled with Dan Pienaar's cautious take-over of the positions around Bir el Gubi and, moreover, itself in need of refuelling and resupply, it would be some while before it could arrive anywhere near Gabr Saleh, so 4th Armoured's fate, had Cunningham's information been correct, might have been sealed; and probably 22nd Armoured's as well, had it run into a combined Afrika Korps just emerging from the triumphant destruction of Gatehouse's force.

Not that this possibility was in any way apparent to Gatehouse or his tank commanders, still brimming with confidence in their own invincibility. Only ten miles away from them to the south-east lay the bulk of 2nd New Zealand Division, its three brigades fully assembled, in battle order and with its full complement of divisional artillery and a battalion of the new Infantry tanks, the Valentines, attached from 1st Army Tank Brigade – all under command of its famous and aggressive commander Bernard Freyberg, already finding the waiting somewhat irksome. But of course, the New Zealanders were an infantry division and a part of XIII Corps, and when the Corps B.G.S., John Harding, suggested that the two formations might find mutual benefit in co-operation, it was an idea which fell on one set of deaf ears.

Freyberg and his men were more than willing to help Gatehouse and the dashing Hussars and tank regiments, but these on their part were unconcerned with the odds which might be against them and wished to fight their own armoured battles without assistance from pedestrians. Cunningham was not entirely to blame for the unco-ordinated lurches into danger of parts of XXX Corps.

As it happened, Cruewell, too, now failed to see the advantages of concentration and co-operation and, ordering 21st Panzer to refuel as quickly as possible and join 15th Panzer the following day in the chase along the Trig el Abd to Sidi Rezegh, he directed Neumann-Sylkow's division south to clear away the 'flanking force' on their own. At 1600, Panzer Regiment 8 set out with two infantry regiments in echelon to the left and a powerful artillery force behind, and half an hour later came upon 4th Armoured Brigade in a sound defensive position on a slight rise, with the sun behind them and full ammunition racks.

For the next thirty minutes a slogging battle between tanks was fought out in which the British advantages of hull-down positions and light were matched by numerical superiority on the German side which gave 15th Panzer an overlap; and then the German artillery component came up and amid the crash of howitzer and 50mm. P.A.K. could be heard the whiplash crack of the 88mms. Soon smoke and flame were erupting from some of the front line Honeys and inevitably the weight of the German attack drove 4th Armoured slowly back down the reverse side of their slope.

Then, as the panzers advanced and light began to fade from the sky, the first hurrying Crusaders of 22nd Armoured appeared to the west, and Neumann-Sylkow threw out an artillery screen to guard his main attack against what might be a strong attack in flank; and by the time the bulk of 22nd Armoured survivors had arrived, darkness had fallen and the night rituals begun. The panzers leaguered where they were, their recovery teams began work on their own casualties while their medical and engineer teams removed the British wounded from the knocked-out Honeys and then blew up the wrecks.

The British brigades withdrew south of the Trig el Abd with 4th Armoured on the right of 22nd Armoured, formed leaguer, reported their tank strengths at respectively 97 Stuarts and 100 Crusaders, and prepared themselves for what the morrow might bring. There was still no thought in anyone's mind of co-operation with the New Zealanders, perhaps because, for the first time since crossing the Wire, two of XXX Corps's brigades were at last within supporting distance of one another.

This meant, however, that the other two components of 7th Armoured Division, 7th Armoured Brigade and the Support Group – the 'spearhead' aimed at what had now become the main target of the operation, Tobruk – although themselves concentrated, were at least thirty miles ahead of the division's best-equipped armoured units and supported only by one infantry brigade, with another held back by its task of 'masking' a hostile armoured division.

Moreover, during the previous night (November 19th/20th), while 7th Armoured Brigade and the South African Armoured Cars had leaguered on the airfield and considered how successfully they had conducted themselves, Panzergruppe Afrika had been making strenuous efforts to reinforce the Afrika Regiments of Sümmermann's Division along the main Escarpment in front of them. Some 100mm. guns had been rushed across from Bardia, a battalion of Bologna infantry with a German engineer battalion and some more artillery were moved up to the eminence at Belhammed from which, although north of the Trig Capuzzo, it could certainly shell the airfield; and the German infantry along the main Escarpment grouped for a dawn attack on 7th Armoured Brigade's positions.

This, covered only by the attackers' anti-tank guns, was quickly beaten back, but at 0800 another attack was launched under cover of a much heavier barrage from the force at Belhammed, and although the German infantry was again held by the British artillery and the tank guns, the position of 7th Brigade on the exposed and open plain clearly left a great deal to be desired. The armoured cars, for instance, if they were not to disperse away from the airfield altogether, could do little or nothing to protect themselves. According to 4th South African Armoured Cars' War Diary:

> R.H.Q. had (rather rashly perhaps) parked next to a battery of 25-pounders, which were severely shelling the enemy position on the Sidi Rezegh ridge to the N.W. This idyllic state of affairs came to an end at 0830 hours when the enemy Artillery got the range of these guns (and incidentally of R.H.Q.) with unpleasant accuracy. A rapid move of a few hundred yards became necessary, and such was the urgency of the case that R.II.Q.'s tea and sausages . . . were left to waste their sweetness on the desert air. The 25-pounders were forced to pull out also, but not so fast but that a gunner (evidently a man of unusual presence of mind), contrived to carry off R.H.Q.'s breakfast with him. He undoubtedly deserved the tea and sausages, but he might perhaps have left (or anyhow returned) the plates and the mugs.[8]

The shelling continued on and off throughout the day, but there were no more attempts at infantry assault on the position, and in their turn 7th Armoured quickly decided that the attack ordered by Cunningham on Point 175 would need more infantry support than they had available – even after the whole of the Support Group had closed up. This should therefore await the arrival of 5th South

African Brigade which would not reach the southern escarpment until late in the afternoon. As its commander, Brigadier B. F. Armstrong, was understandably reluctant to move into the danger area at night, it was obvious that Afrika Regiment 361 would remain undisturbed by anything except minor harassment by light units until the next day.

The rest of November 20th thus passed comparatively uneventfully at Sidi Rezegh. Sporadic shelling by German artillery certainly made the place uncomfortable for the occupants and a Stuka attack during the afternoon added to the noise and fury, but there were few casualties to report at the end of the day.

Then, in the evening, General Gott arrived with plans for the next day – November 21st – and revealed that the decision had been taken to order the break-out of the Tobruk garrison to be launched at dawn. Norrie had in fact given the code-word ('Pop') during the afternoon, and plans were now laid for the infantry on the Sidi Rezegh airfield to clear the ridge to the north so that the armour could then make its way down the Escarpment at Abiar el Amar to the west, to reach and cross the Trig Capuzzo and the Axis by-pass and meet the Tobruk Matildas of 32nd Army Tank Brigade at Ed Duda after their break-out. In due course, they would all be joined by Armstrong's 5th South African Brigade which should have crossed the airfield during the morning, and together the combined armour and infantry would advance westwards and secure the ground between Ed Duda and the main Tobruk–El Adem road.

It all promised very well, and no one there was to know of another factor about to be introduced into the situation. The obvious need for secrecy to shroud all such ploys as Brigadier Shearer's will on occasion itself contribute to their failure or untimely end. That evening in its normal news bulletin, the British Broadcasting Corporation had joyfully announced that the Eighth Army, with some 75,000 excellently armed and equipped men, had invaded Libya with the object of destroying the remainder of the Axis forces in Africa, and that the operation was proceeding successfully; and when Rommel heard of it, the scales dropped from his eyes. He abruptly abandoned the proposed assault on Tobruk, approved Cruewell's orders to the Afrika Korps for the following morning and urged action at the earliest moment and with the greatest speed. As a result von Ravenstein's refuelled division was moving by 0300, and an hour later Cruewell received a further spur to action from his Commander-in-Chief.

> The situation in this whole theatre is very critical. In addition
> to the strong enemy force south-east of Tobruk, 500 or 600

enemy cars are moving through the desert towards Benghazi from the south-east. On 21 November *Afrikakorps* must begin moving in good time and follow the enemy tanks which have advanced toward Tobruk. Objective the centre airfield at Sidi Rezegh.[9]

The feint moves of Oasis Group between Jarabub and Jalo were at last having an effect, and it was rather a pity that it was not – as had been intended – towards a dispersion of Rommel's forces, but towards a greater concentration.

Inside Tobruk, the news that at last the moment for the break-out had come generated immense excitement, lifting the spirits of the garrison, especially those of the crews of the thirty-two cruisers and sixty-nine Matildas who were to lead the sortie, with their attached infantry. Although the patrolling across the no-man's-land on the south-east sector had not been pressed of late quite so vigorously as it had been when the Australians were there, it was felt that sufficient was known of the enemy posts which made up the first objectives – 'Butch', 'Jill', 'Jack', 'Tiger' and 'Tugun' – their surrounding minefields and their Italian occupants, for it to be assumed that they would all be captured within the time schedule. The 'I' tanks would then press on and, despite their lack of speed, most probably reach Ed Duda before the cruisers of 7th Armoured Brigade coming up from the south. Anyway, it would be a healthily competitive race, and in the meantime the hours of darkness must be used by engineers to gap the minefields, open the wire and bridge the anti-tank ditches along the break-out sector.

It all began very well, D Squadron, of 7th R.T.R. leading through the gap, swinging left to assault 'Butch' and – with some losses on minefields of which they had inexplicably received no briefings – completely surprising the occupants who were being marshalled and led back towards the perimeter by 0900. The R.T.R. tank crews were rather surprised, too, for the occupants proved to be Germans from the Afrika Regiment and not Italians from the Bologna Division as they had been led to expect.

Half an hour later, C Squadron of the 4th R.T.R. was in trouble. Not only had they been delayed by a bottleneck on their own side of the break-out gap, but their start line had been laid askew and many of the flank tanks had run on to mines and been variously knocked out of the fight; by the time they had covered the mile and a half approach to their objective, 'Jill', they were not only behind their schedule but also behind their infantry, the 2nd Battalion the Black Watch. These, however, with a fine disregard for the advantages of armoured protection, pressed on through the murk, rushed the minefield surrounding the post, broke through the wire and to the thrilling skirls of their pipes stormed the post at point of bayonet. Such actions exact their price, however, and though the Afrika Regiment survivors here were also soon on their way into Tobruk, white and shaken by the ordeal they had just experienced, they could console themselves with the numbers of dead Highlanders lining their route.

Their blood up, the remnants of the battalion immediately rallied behind the 4th R.T.R. and moved towards the main objective of the first phase of the break-out – 'Tiger'. Among the Highlanders was a

Map 22   Tobruk break-out: November 21st, 1941

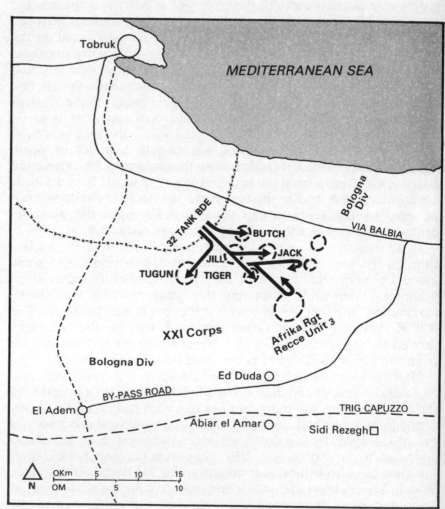

Rhodesian who had chosen to fight with the men from whom his ancestors had come:

> The enemy held his fire until we were past the wire. And then his machine-guns let go. Such of us as survived at once fell flat to take what cover we could; but our Adjutant, who had been wounded, crawled to where we were lying and got to his feet. 'Isn't this the Black Watch!' he cried. 'Then – charge!' He waved us on with his stick and was instantly killed. We rose and took 'Tiger' with the bayonet . . . but of our battalion that evening only 8 officers and 196 men were able to answer to their names.[10]

'Jack' was captured by 1030, but 'Tugun' proved a very hard nut to crack and the assault had faltered by mid-afternoon with tanks held up by minefields or anti-tank guns, and infantry completely pinned down. Moreover, other assaults to take secondary objectives beyond 'Tiger' were thrown back, and by the time set for the final drive to Ed Duda (1430) 32nd Army Tank Brigade was, in fact, bitterly fighting to retain the ground won so far against rapidly assembled and robust German counter-attacks, organised by Rommel who by this time was personally directing the battle alongside four 88mms which he had rushed across from Gambut.

Then just before 1600, a message came through that the juncture with the XXX Corps troops from Sidi Rezegh must be put off at least until the next day. At Sidi Rezegh also, the battle had not gone quite as General Gott had hoped.

As with the break-out, it had started off well enough. One of the artillery commanders wrote of the dawn of that epochal day:

> The slow first light of November 21st, 1941, broke on the usual desert scene at Sidi Rezegh. Leaguers were dispersing. From every quarter came the noise of transport starting up, guns rumbled slowly and cautiously into battle positions; chilled, silent men with sleep-heavy eyes moved mechanically into their appointed places. Everywhere full use was being made of the valuable 30 minutes of half-light, when visibility was too poor for the enemy to pick out a target.
>
> Support Group of the 7th Armoured Division was preparing for battle . . .[11]

Under the cover of a four-minute concentrated barrage by the 25-pounders, three companies of the 1st King's Royal Rifle Corps and one of the 2nd Rifle Brigade, with tanks on each flank and carrier platoons to the front, formed up on the exposed ground to the south of the airfield and at 0830 began their advance, with no more substantial shield than a smokescreen, against Italian and

German infantry well dug in along the line of the Escarpment in positions with excellent fields of fire. The carrier platoons, who had raced forward so fast that they caught up with the tail of the barrage and were fortunate in suffering no casualties at that stage, overran many forward German and Italian gun positions, and then the platoons in the centre reached the lip of the Escarpment to see a 100-yard-wide slope in front of them beyond which the ground dropped almost vertically. The slope was peppered with enemy posts ensconced in small wadis and birs from which came a hail of small-arms fire, so the line of carriers wheeled right and swung sheer across the width of the slope to reach a wadi running across its eastern edge, where the riflemen swarmed out, cleared the wadi and began pouring enfilade fire across the slope; but many of the enemy posts were out of range or covered by dips and bumps in the slope. On one side of this central thrust, carriers of D Platoon had run into concentrated anti-tank fire and been virtually wiped out; on the other side C Platoon reached their objective unscathed.

On the airfield, the main bulk of the riflemen began to march forward. There was still enough dust and fog to screen them from anything but the artillery fire as they crossed the airfield, but once they were in the ground to the north they were in open view of the German and Italian posts along the line of the Escarpment, and the closer they got to the lip the more they were exposed to posts further back on the reverse slope.

Now was fought a pure infantry battle in which platoons edged up to defensive posts under cover of fire from neighbouring platoons and the age-old leap-frog tactics, sparked by leadership, engineered by training and routine, and sustained by unbelievable courage, gradually closed the gap between attackers and objectives until the last charge with bomb and bayonet could be mounted. A posthumous Victoria Cross was won by Rifleman Beeley, who when the time came for the final assault against his platoon's target found himself the only unhurt survivor, so he raced across the last stretch alone firing his Bren-gun from the hip and with that uncanny combination of luck and accuracy which is occasionally bestowed on high enterprise, wiped out seven occupants of the post who between them had been manning an anti-tank gun and two machine-guns. He was himself killed by a grenade when about twenty yards from the post.

By noon, the whole of the lip of the Escarpment was in the hands of the riflemen, some 600 mixed German and Italian prisoners were being led back towards the airfield while the bodies of nearly 400 more littered the battlefield. But of the 300 officers and men who had mustered on the airfield at dawn, 84 were not present at the subsequent roll call.

Now the armour could go forward, and with a great deal of panache the Crusaders of 6th R.T.R. swept across the ridge past the tomb of the prophet, down towards the Trig Capuzzo and Ed Duda beyond; and straight on to the anti-tank guns of Reconnaissance Battalion 3, reinforced by the four 88mm. guns which were later to halt the 'I' tanks breaking out from Tobruk, all under the personal command of Rommel himself.

As on Hafid Ridge during *Battleaxe*, the Crusaders which reached the reverse slope were knocked out to a tank, those lucky ones behind rapidly retiring as soon as the sight of the blazing hulls and the sound of high velocity shell revealed the situation; but in any case they would have had to be recalled, for the leading panzers of the combined 15th and 21st Panzer Division – the entire Afrika Korps, in fact – were in sight to the south-east and 7th Armoured Brigade and the Support Group were in danger of annihilation.

Perhaps the main trouble with the British command of the battle on November 21st was that 7th Armoured Division were fighting two battles thirty miles apart, and however talented General Gott may have been, he could not exercise close control in both places at once.

Brigadiers Gatehouse and Scott-Cockburn (of the 22nd Armoured Brigade) had spent the night preparing their battle positions for what promised to be the long-expected clash of armour the following day, still with undiminished confidence in their ability to fight the whole of the Afrika Korps and destroy it on their own, despite their previous experience against, respectively, one panzer division and one Italian armoured division in which each had suffered casualties and been forced to retire. They certainly felt no need for help from Bernard Freyberg's infantrymen away to the south, and a great deal of their planning was directed towards a relentless pursuit of a beaten enemy once he turned and ran.

It thus came as little surprise to either of them, or to their tank crews, when after a night spent listening to the sounds of armoured movement to the north and to reports from 11th Hussars of a strong concentration of panzers north-east of Gabr Saleh, in the morning the wide spaces in front of them emptied after but the briefest exchange of fire, and the Afrika Korps was seen streaming off over the horizon to the north-west. Scott-Cockburn's Crusaders raced across to catch the enemy in flank but mistimed the strike and hit only a rearguard and then thin air, while Gatehouse's Honeys were a little slow getting away and despite their speed never managed to catch up in force.

The Crusaders did manage to check their first lunge, regroup, swing forward and launch another attack in flank later during the

morning, but they came up against some 88mms with Afrika Korps
H.Q. in the centre of the column and lost, according to Oberst
Kriebel who was with Neumann-Sylkow's H.Q., seven of their
number before the rest retired out of range. For the next hour 22nd
Armoured hung on the flanks of 15th Panzer, during which time
according to their reports they destroyed about 200 German trucks
and cars (there is no mention of these losses in the Afrika Korps
Diary) and then, because of a 'hitch in the petrol supply', they had
to break off the action and refuel. The short range of the Honeys
had already forced a similar check on the 4th Armoured Brigade,
but as they watched what they considered to be a thoroughly beaten
enemy disappearing over the north-western horizon, few doubted
that a great victory had been won or paused to wonder what might
be happening to their comrades-in-arms away towards Tobruk.
Most of them, at that point, had never heard of Sidi Rezegh.

By this time, in fact, one formation of the 7th Armoured Brigade
was already in process of annihilation. In the face of what he at first
thought was but a minor threat, Brigadier Davy had hastily thrown
the thirty-odd old cruisers and twenty Crusaders of the 7th Hussars
in front of the approaching enemy, while he rethought the day's
engagements:

> From the point of view of the 7th Armoured Brigade the
> problem was clear-cut. The sortie from Tobruk . . . had already
> begun, and the leading troops of the 70th Division should now be
> approaching Ed Duda. The attack [to the north] must take place
> as planned. But the arrival of German armour from the south-
> east was a threat to the main project and had to be dealt with at
> once. Other troops, known to be operating farther to the south,
> would soon be able to intervene and it was important that the
> smallest possible number of troops should be diverted from the
> attack towards Ed Duda.[12]

His own H.Q. was still south of point 178 on the southern
escarpment, and having deployed a battery of Royal Horse
Artilley and his reserve force of 2nd R.T.R. cruisers close by, as an
outer shield to the Support Group forces still occupying the ground
around the airfield, Davy accompanied the Hussars on their
allocated task 'to locate and delay the advance of the enemy tanks'.
Although he was sceptical of reports from the south that the Afrika
Korps had been defeated, and somewhat surprised by the continued
absence from the battlefield of both 5th South African Brigade and
22nd Armoured (he had not known of the switch across by
Scott-Cockburn's brigade the previous evening) he still thought that

he was faced at the most with only one panzer division, and that 4th Armoured Brigade would be aggressively snapping at its heels.

As it was, the combined force of the most famous armoured corps in the world at that time was sweeping down upon two regiments of outdated tanks, spread across some ten miles of desert with a single battery of artillery somewhere between them.

Davy and the Hussars first saw the oncoming hordes about 0830, but even then considerable doubt existed as to their identity for the head of the attack was wreathed in lorries of the Support Group's B Echelon, swept up in the course of 21st Panzer's advance and now – ignored by the panzer crews – endeavouring frantically to get out of the way. Among them, coolly and efficiently, the German anti-tank gunners had infiltrated their mobile 50mm. P.A.K. guns and with these they opened fire on the Hussars, who could not reply at that range anyway and were hindered by the swarm of British soft-skinned transport even when the range shortened.

During the holocaust which followed, all but ten of the old cruisers (and these the ones that had broken down before battle had joined) and all the Hussars' Crusaders were destroyed; not just knocked out with some possibility of recovery and repair, but completely wrecked as the panzers rode over their positions and pumped shell after shell into their smoking and immobile hulls until they were reduced to scrap iron. Between the wrecks, surviving crew members dodged from cover to cover, carrying wounded, dragging burnt and pain-wracked comrades out of hatches, falling under the hail of machine-gun fire; 7th Hussars was not to be seen again in the desert, although re-formed, it fought in Burma.

Two miles to the west, Davy's reserve cruiser force from 2nd R.T.R. was held off by the inevitable German anti-tank screen, its early efforts to intervene having merely served to push 15th Panzer to the right so that its weight was added to that of 21st Panzer as they crashed together down on the Hussars. During the morning, therefore, 2nd R.T.R. suffered little damage – a piece of good fortune which they owed, though they did not know it, to what had now become the overriding aim behind the Afrika Korps advance: to sweep down the gentle slope westwards between the southern and main Escarpments to Abiar el Amar obliterating whatever force held the airfield, then across the Trig Capuzzo to Ed Duda, eventually to make contact with Artillery Group Böttcher at Belhammed. In this way they would eliminate the British forces threatening the besiegers of Tobruk, Rommel's command would again be concentrated and could then turn and clear up the remaining Allied units littering the desert between Tobruk and the frontier. But first, the panzer divisions must halt to refuel and replenish their ammunition racks from the supply vehicles now congregating at the head of the valley down which they intended to charge.

The Support Company of 2nd Rifle Brigade were to be the first to feel the weight massing against the British force around Sidi Rezegh, for they occupied the eastern end of the southern escarpment and it was in this direction that the first of the panzers to complete refuelling decided to investigate:

> Sixteen tanks appeared over a ridge moving slowly westwards about eight hundred yards away into the valley to the north-east. The two 2-pounders on the ridge to the north under command of Ward Gunn opened fire on them. The 25-pounders of the 60th Field Regiment engaged them over open sights. Four of them went up in flames. The remainder halted, dodged about and, finding that they could make no headway against our fire, but having had a good look at our positions, withdrew just out of sight. They had returned our fire and the two anti-tank guns had been knocked out. It was quite clear that the enemy's retirement was only temporary . . . Everyone in the Battalion knew that the Germans were choosing their own time and their own place of attack and that not sixteen but sixty tanks might appear at any moment over the ridge.[13]

During the short interval before the onslaught, frantic efforts were made to dig just a little deeper into the unyielding rock, and messages were sent off to Davy's H.Q. warning them of the developing situation and asking for any available tank protection – messages which were greeted with frank incredulity by the brigade major who indignantly accused them of firing on 7th Hussars. This was not a comforting reaction for the riflemen and their gunners, now becoming acutely aware of their isolation in the face of ominous German preparations.

First came a series of Stuka attacks (not very effective once fox-holes were deep enough for men to lie in them), followed by some concentrated shelling – and then the panzers moved in. There was nothing the riflemen could do but shrink lower into their weapon pits, and the only three vehicles still with them – the signals trucks – were soon under fire, two in flames while the other, by some incredible miracle, was driven unscathed out of danger by a quick-thinking and dauntless corporal. They had, however, sent off signals to Brigade Headquarters couched in such terms as to persuade the brigade major that friends were not being mistaken for foes, so five Crusaders arrived on the edge of the battalion area – to be totally destroyed well before their 2-pounders could be brought into effective range. And all the while a little dog ran pathetically from slit trench to slit trench seeking its master and attracting a hail of fire to any spot where it stopped and made obviously friendly overtures to some subterranean figure.

This stage of the battle was thus fought out between panzer crews and gunners who, despite the flimsiness of their gun-shields where they existed at all, remained coolly at their posts until, separately and inevitably, they were killed or too badly wounded to continue serving their weapons. Two 2-pounder anti-tank guns and a Bofors anti-aircraft gun were at one moment the only weapons capable of engaging effectively and one of their officers was Lieutenant Patrick McSwiney:

> At 1130 hrs the enemy came on again and were engaged by the anti-tank guns in front of my troop and were halted after six tanks had been put out of action . . . only one member of the troop survived. A few minutes earlier Colonel de Robeck had appeared and found me lying full length on the ground whilst moving between my guns. He was standing in the front of his truck waving his fly whisk – presumably at the bullets which were flying thick and fast from the machine-guns of the leading enemy tanks! We passed the time of day from our respective positions and I asked for permission to withdraw. I was informed that this was a case for no withdrawal![14]

One of the anti-tank guns commanded by Second Lieutenant Ward Gunn was soon put out of action and when the crew of the other had all been killed or wounded, the driver began backing it away. At that moment, Gunn was joined by Major Bernard Pinney who shouted to him, 'Go and stop that blighter!' – which seemed a little hard on the chap even at the time – and Gunn, the wounded driver and Pinney together cleared the 2-pounder and got it back into action until Ward Gunn was himself killed and the ammunition set alight. Pinney put the flames out and continued firing until another hit finally wrecked the gun, whereat he reversed and drove it out of danger; he was killed the following day in not dissimilar circumstances, and Ward Gunn was later awarded a posthumous Victoria Cross.

But in the meantime, the 25-pounders of the 60th Field Regiment just to the north of the Rifle Brigade positions were themselves being slowly but surely overwhelmed, as panzers of 21st Panzer Division came across from their refuelling point and began the move down the valley between the southern and main Escarpments. Gun after gun fell silent as the crews were picked off, as the guns were hit, as the ammunition blazed or ran out; between the panzers the German infantry were moving insidiously but inevitably forward, and it seemed that all too soon the last artillery screen would be thrust aside and only the Support Group headquarters units and the survivors of 6th R.T.R.'s morning attempt to reach Ed Duda would stand between the Afrika Korps and their objective at the bottom of the valley across the airfield.

And at this point, 21st Panzer ran short of ammunition, while 15th Panzer on their left flank and still south of the southern escarpment became conscious not only of 2nd R.T.R. pressure, but also of 'a fresh armoured force superior to ours' manoeuvring away to the south-west. This was, in fact, 22nd Armoured Brigade who had swung westwards after their pause for refuelling. They had no sense of urgency – for how could there be a crisis to the north with the Afrika Korps so badly beaten that they had turned and run but a few hours before? As for 4th Armoured Brigade, they too were in no haste to move after their quarry, and when they did so found themselves delayed by patches of boggy sand caused by a sudden mid-morning rain storm. In the event, both British brigades were to take several hours in their much faster tanks to cover the same ground that Afrika Korps had covered in just over one, and their comrades in 7th Armoured Brigade and the Support Group were to see little of them before darkness fell; but at least their reported presence now gave respite to the hard-pressed men in the valley.

And one small action fought against the panzers was crowned with success, though its lessons seem not to have been appreciated for far too long. When the panzers withdrew again to cluster around their petrol and ammunition lorries, two troops of South African armoured cars went forward to observe them and on their way up passed a squadron of 2nd R.T.R. tanks lying hull-down behind a ridge:

> Both troops moved closer to the enemy column, in spite of heavy shell fire, and were busy counting enemy tanks when a party of 25 of them detached themselves from the main enemy concentration and came straight for our patrols.[15]

These manoeuvred carefully and with forethought, gradually enticing the panzers forward out of support of their own guns until they suddenly found themselves under those of the hull-down 2nd R.T.R. cruisers. The result was the destruction of five panzers and damage inflicted on six more without the slightest loss or damage to the British or South Africans; and, as the South African history says, 'an object lesson in what could happen if the British tanks caught their opponents without their regular anti-tank screen'.

The fighting for the rest of that day was concentrated around the eastern end of the southern escarpment, where 2nd R.T.R.'s screen of elderly cruisers was gradually whittled away until by nightfall only six were still in action, and the full weight of the attack fell upon the survivors of the Rifle Brigade Support Company. Their attached artillery now destroyed, one platoon totally eliminated and the others all severely reduced in strength, the order was given for the survivors to make their own separate ways out of danger:

> Under cover of a few wisps of smoke from the burning vehicles and the occasional distraction of friendly aircraft flying overhead, most of Battalion Headquarters and subsequently most of 'S' Company crawled away, all being shot at as they did so.[16]

By nightfall, the eastern end of the southern escarpment was in German hands, and with all the evidence now available it can be seen that November 21st, 1941, was a day of some achievement for the Afrika Korps. They had destroyed the 7th Hussars, inflicted considerable damage on two Royal Tank Regiments – the 2nd and the 6th – destroyed a large number of the Support Group's guns and wiped out the Support Company of the Rifle Brigade. Moreover, on the other side of the battlefield, the Afrika Regiment and Reconnaissance Battalion 3 had stemmed both the break-out by the Army Tank Brigade from Tobruk and the attempt by 7th Armoured Brigade to push forward to join hands with them, and as this portion of the day's battle had been under Rommel's personal direction, one would think that he had by evening good cause for satisfaction.

He was, in fact, deeply worried – both by the apparent weight of forces between which he and his immediate command were sandwiched, and by Cruewell's failure to bring the Afrika Korps down through the valley to take some of that weight away. His messages to Cruewell had held during the latter part of that day a note of irascibility which did nothing to ease Cruewell's own problems, or to soothe the worries with which the commander of the Afrika Korps was beset – for he, too, had little idea of the true picture.

In Cruewell's mind, his famous corps was almost completely encircled by forces 'immeasurably superior' – to quote the Afrika Korps Diary – to his own, with an apparently inexhaustible supply of fresh reserves to throw against him whichever way he turned. His route to Ed Duda was blocked by the powerful artillery formations of the Support Group which had beaten back his panzers; to the south-west were the armoured formations of which he had received late intelligence, and beyond them, according to Italian sources, another strong force of British or South African infantry was containing the Ariete Armoured Division and awaiting opportunity to pounce upon his flank if he ventured too far west; while he knew that behind him was the 4th Armoured Brigade Group closing up from Gabr Saleh after the morning's disengagement.

Although he was more than willing to accede to his Commander-in-Chief's instructions to concentrate with the other forces of Panzergruppe Afrika nearer to Tobruk, it seemed to him that he could not, after all, do so by the direct route down the valley. He would have to regroup to the east and then send aid to Rommel along the Trig Capuzzo, having extricated his forces from between the British brigades and regained that freedom of manoeuvre which was the constant desire of the well-trained panzer leader.

Spurred on by another missive from Rommel which reached him at 2240 and opened with the instruction, 'On 22 November, D.A.K. in conjunction with Pavia Division will hold the area reached today, as well as Belhammed. The Corps will prevent enemy tank forces on its front from pushing through to Tobruk,' Cruewell ordered 15th Panzer away eastwards to regroup seven miles due south of Gambut around Point 196, and von Ravenstein to take his 21st Panzer Division down the Escarpment near Point 175 and along the Trig Capuzzo to Belhammed, where he would also assume command of Afrika Regiment 361 and an infantry regiment, Number 155, whose main duty would be to expel the British from the Escarpment as soon as possible.

Thus, during the night of November 21st/22nd, for the third time in three days, the Afrika Korps vacated the field before XXX Corps formations which had little chance of defeating or even resisting them had they stayed. No wonder the British remained confident of victory, only the remnants of 7th Armoured Brigade and the Support Group registering even surprise as they watched the German infantry and armour stream away from the ground they had won so doughtily.

At Eighth Army Headquarters, the atmosphere by the evening of November 21st was filled with that supreme confidence which is based upon solid and predicted achievements. As foretold, XXX Corps had met and thoroughly defeated the Afrika Korps. Simply by adding up the figures of panzers destroyed coming in from the brigade headquarters (and according to that day's figures alone 170 panzers had been 'hit' – a phrase which in that air of euphoria was interpreted as damaged beyond repair), it was evident that Rommel's armour had been reduced by over 50 per cent. This was further borne out by the figures of XXX Corps's casualties – for they could surely not have lost as many tanks as that without inflicting comparable losses on the enemy? In any case, it all fitted in with the belief sparked by the R.A.F. reports of the westward flow of Axis traffic two days before, that Rommel was pulling back out of Marmarica and was more than ready to evacuate the area at least as far back as Gazala.

That evening a Press cable was sent from Cairo which read:

It is authoritatively stated that the Libyan battle, which was at its height this afternoon, is going extremely well. The proportion of Axis tank casualties to British is authoritatively put at three to one. General Rommel, the German commander, is trying to break through, but his situation is becoming more unfavourable . . . [17]

Many people who read it took even greater heart from the slightly guarded tone of the last sentence, confidently assuming that total victory, though not yet fully established, would be consummated within a matter of hours.

The only question causing General Cunningham great concern was the failure of the link-up with the Tobruk break-out. Here there seemed definite indications of a check to his plans (for the schedule still called for the use of the port facilities to fuel the general advance by Day 3) and he had already put measures in hand to help in that area. Since early that morning, XIII Corps had been implementing their portion of the *Crusader* plan, for Cunningham had phoned Godwin-Austen just before 0900 and suggested a move northwards by the New Zealanders and the 7th Brigade of 4th Indian Division, although he emphasised, somewhat uncharacteristically and surely unusually for one in his position, that he 'was not going to press XIII Corps Commander if XIII Corps Commander was against the project'.

But Godwin-Austen was as eager to see his corps into action as Bernard Freyberg was to lead his division, and by noon the New Zealand brigades were all across the Trig el Abd with two-thirds of the Matildas of 1st Army Tank Brigade, while 7th Indian Brigade and the rest of the Matildas were abreast on their right. By late afternoon, New Zealand Division Cavalry had reached Sidi Azeiz where they took fifty-five very surprised Germans and Italians prisoner, 4th New Zealand Brigade were moving up through them across the Trig Capuzzo towards the heights above Bardia, 5th Brigade had swung right along the Hafid Ridge towards the rear of Fort Capuzzo and 6th Brigade had swung the other way towards the Trig Capuzzo in order to concentrate at Bir el Hariga, some ten miles west of Sidi Azeiz.

Meanwhile, the Punjabis, Sikhs and Royal Sussex battalions of 7th Indian Brigade were moving in behind the two Omars, Libyan Omar and Sidi Omar, in order the following morning to attempt to repeat their successes of almost a year before at Nibeiwa, the Tummars and Sidi Barrani. They were imbued now with as much confidence as they had been then, with perhaps more justification than the rest of Eighth Army.

By the evening of November 21st, then, three brigades of XIII Corps were poised to fall on the rear defences of the frontier while one – 6th New Zealand – was pointed away from that battle area towards Tobruk; and with the delay in link-up with the Tobruk garrison in mind, Cunningham had sent a message to Norrie offering this extra infantry reinforcement should he feel he needed it. Unfortunately, there was an ambiguity about the message which gave Norrie the impression that the New Zealanders would be coming up along the Trig el Abd instead of the Trig Capuzzo, and, mindful of the communications of his over-extended corps and conscious of the presence already of the two virtually unemployed South African infantry brigades, he rejected the offer on the grounds that he already had enough infantry above the Escarpment – a rejection which elicited the decidedly huffy comment from Cunningham that if, in that case, Tobruk were not relieved soon, he would 'certainly require to see the Corps Commander tomorrow'!

The armour was beginning to reap the consequences of its own hubris.

Throughout this period – and indeed until the end of the year and well into the next – the troops were living in conditions of acute discomfort. Although in the daytime some warmth was engendered by action and the bright but often watery sun, the nights were bitterly cold and rain always fell at some point, so that during that brief spell of half-light in which every day's 'stand-to' took place, the desert was spotted with clumps of bone-chilled, unshaven, unwashed men groping clumsily for their weapons, for their water-bottles, for any remnant of their rations which they had saved, for their boots if they had cared to take them off before they had fallen asleep.

If their days had not been riven by battle, pain, fear and the deaths of comrades, then they had been spent either in dry, dusty, flea-bitten and scorpion-ridden boredom, or in equally dusty and much more thirst-making hard labour at the wheel of a lorry, at the shaft of a spade or pick-axe, or confined within the shaking, reeling, jolting box of some vehicle or other as it swayed across the lunar landscape with such inconsequential and unpredictable jumps and drops that it was necessary to cling fast all the time to some comparative fixture in order to avoid not only painful knocks but the ever-present risk of broken bones.

Thirst, fleas, grit, sweat-caked clothing, cuts, bruises and desert sores, sanitation at its most rudimentary; this was life in the desert for men of both Eighth Army and Panzergruppe Afrika during the last days of 1941. The only comfort, even for those whose sense of privacy and individuality was the most developed, was the pro-

pinquity of lives circumscribed by the walls of a lorry, the hull of a
tank, or for infantry in defence posts the line of weapon-pits or the
chasm of a wadi. Even for the formations which had not yet seen
action with the enemy, such as those of the 22nd Guards Brigade
organising and watching over the Field Maintenance Centres by
now well established south of the Trig el Abd, the aridity of life
drove men in upon themselves, limiting their horizons to the world
of platoon, battery, tank troop or even just tank crew; and if
memories now recall the comradeship and the flashes of excitement
and occasional triumph, they forget the fear, the cold, the aching
guts, the dreadful sights, the stench, the disgust.

The night of November 21st/22nd was no different from the
others; it rained everywhere almost continuously so that in the
morning hard pans had been converted into large sheets of water
and, according to Alexander Clifford, sandy wastes reduced to the
'consistency of cold cream'. Behind the Omars waited the British
and Indian infantry of the 7th Indian Brigade with the Matildas of
42nd R.T.R., overlooking a minefield of uncertain position and
magnitude.

The attack went in on time with armour and infantry carriers
racing in together, and supporting infantry following:

> But there *was* a minefield! . . . just forward of the enemy's
> foremost posts – a narrow belt of mines hidden in the sand; and
> the first wave of tanks ran slap on to it. It took more than a mine
> to knock out a Matilda but tracks were blown off and sprockets
> damaged, and nearly all the leading tanks were brought to a
> sudden halt in full view of the enemy. Worse was to follow, for
> behind the minefield, carefully sited on rising ground with a good
> field of fire, well dug in so that their muzzles almost rested on the
> sand, was a troop of the dreaded 88 mm. guns. Their first shot
> went clean through the front of Lieutenant Hembrow's tank, set
> it on fire and killed the entire crew; and they followed this up by
> engaging all the first echelon of tanks lying crippled on the mine-
> field. The Matilda carried no H.E. with which to reply; and
> though they engaged them with their Besa machine-guns, they
> were unable to silence them.[18]

But another Matilda squadron found a way through the minefield
and the Royal Sussex then 'poured over the position' which
surrendered early in the afternoon.

This was the post of Sidi Omar, and later that day the 4th/6th
Punjabis with their escorting Matildas repeated the operation at
Libyan Omar a few miles to the west – repeated also the experience
of watching their tanks shot up by well-sited 88mm. guns, and paid
for their victory with the same proportion of casualties.

Away to the north, 5th New Zealand Brigade had stormed into Fort Capuzzo early in the morning and proceeded to rip out the telephone lines and wreck water-pipes and any other permanent installations they could find; 4th Brigade had reached the outskirts of Bardia and captured a German transport park with all its vehicles and personnel, and 6th Brigade – after a hair-raising night journey – reached the Trig Capuzzo about 1000 and an hour after received orders to move further westwards. Cunningham and Norrie had resolved their misunderstandings and XXX Corps could certainly do with more infantry fed into the gap north of the main Escarpment up towards Belhammed, so the New Zealanders should move first of all as far as an obscure point named Bir el Chleta, just six miles south-west of Gambut. As this was the area in which Afrika Korps Headquarters had been stationed for some time, and to which Cruewell had directed 15th Panzer the previous evening, it seemed likely to become crowded.

But not as soon as it might have done, for Rommel was now in control of the battle from the Axis side, his preoccupation with Tobruk for the moment forgotten, replaced by an acute sense of the passage of time and a determination to make up for any that had been lost. The crews of both panzer divisions were quickly disabused of their belief that the morning of November 22nd could be devoted to rest and maintenance, those of 15th Panzer soon finding themselves probing back westwards along the crest of the main Escarpment overlooking the Trig Capuzzo, searching for British armour whose presence around Point 175 had been reported by Reconnaissance Battalion 33.

As for von Ravenstein's 21st Panzer, they had hardly deployed their infantry and artillery (with General Böttcher's) on the southern slope of the Belhammed position – from which defence line they expected to repulse the next attempt by the British on the Sidi Rezegh ridge to link up with the Tobruk break-out – when Rommel was amongst them, issuing orders for an immediate assault by Battlegroup Knabe on the ridge itself to drive the Support Group riflemen from the positions they had so gallantly won the previous morning. In addition Infantry Regiment 155 was sent with supporting artillery and some armour to the southern escarpment around Bir bu Creimisa from where they were to push off any British or South Africans they found there eastwards and into the open desert.

Panzer Regiment 5, having refuelled its tanks and restocked its ammunition racks, was to make its way carefully by the northern route under cover of Belhammed itself on to the by-pass road, then along to Ed Duda, across to Abiar el Amar and thus around the western end of the main Escarpment. From here, with the German infantry holding the attention of the enemy along both flanking escarpments, they would sweep up the valley which the previous day they had failed to sweep down, and this time, under Rommel's eagle eye, they were expected not to halt until the British on and around the airfield had been annihilated.

According to one of the panzer crews, although they were desperately tired, dirty, thirsty, and somewhat shaken by their repeated experience of battering their heads against a wall compounded of British stubbornness and an apparently immense material superiority, they all felt a wave of reassurance sweep over them with the realisation that Rommel was now again firmly in control – even if this meant yet another commitment to a battle they did not seem to be winning.

For the British around the airfield, the morning passed comparatively peacefully. At dawn the South African armoured cars had reported the impending departure of the last of von Ravenstein's panzers (they had been delayed in their movement across and down the Escarpment near Point 175 by lack of fuel) and at 0730 some of 22nd Armoured's Crusaders attempted to close with them but were fought off effectively by the inevitable rearguard anti-tank screen; and 4th Armoured Brigade, having completed the early morning rituals, had moved off to attack German armour which they had seen the previous evening leaguering nearby, only to find that the enemy leaguer was not there. After trouble caused by bogging in the soft ground, 4th Armoured rallied back in its previous night's position. Eventually they received orders to make for Point 175, from where, at about midday, the Honey crews watched the last details of Panzer Regiment 8 making their way down to the Trig Capuzzo – and were themselves seen by men of Reconnaissance Battalion 33.

Other than these activities, the British troops between the two escarpments occupied themselves with nothing more aggressive than reorganising the remnants of their formations, tending their wounded and arranging their evacuation, repairing and refuelling their vehicles as far as was possible, and restocking ammunition racks. And well away to the south of the Trig el Abd, XXX Corps Headquarters made itself ready for what it referred to, even in its report, as 'General Cunningham's threatened visit'.

This, however, proved quite a painless experience, for Cunningham contented himself with expressing guarded satisfaction with progress so far, and delivering himself of the opinion that with the New Zealanders moving along towards Tobruk it seemed likely that *Operation Crusader* would develop more and more into an infantry battle, in which case he hoped that South Africans would soon be able to play a more significant role than they had to date. With this hint in mind, Norrie requested General Brink to concentrate both his brigades and move them up into the Sidi Rezegh area (presumably this meant at least up to and across the southern escarpment) while 22nd Guards Brigade should move in bulk to Bir el Gubi to take over the tasks of 'masking' the Ariete, leaving only token screens with the Field Maintenance Centres. Obviously Pienaar could not move his 1st South African Brigade until this take-over was complete, but Armstrong's 5th South Africans should move as soon as was convenient towards Point 178, on the left flank of the positions held by the survivors of the Rifle Brigade Support Company, now reinforced by some of Jock Campbell's headquarter troops. There were, however, reports of German infantry on the crest of the southern escarpment here, and good grounds for believing that they might be growing in strength – so the South Africans should be prepared for some opposition; it might indeed be a good thing for them to move as soon as possible, for if the enemy were allowed to consolidate there, they would overlook the concentration of the 22nd Armoured Brigade with the remnants of the 7th Armoured Brigade taking place just below them in the ground to the south of the airfield.

This was a point which was exercising Strafer Gott, and shortly after 1300 he held a conference on the landing ground where it was declared that no attempt would be made that day to link up with the Tobruk garrison (which was, of course, the main reason for the British presence in the area) but that everything possible must be done to ensure the progress northwards of 5th South African Brigade so that Armstrong's men would be available, with the riflemen already on the Sidi Rezegh ridge and the Support Group artillery, to undertake the advance to Ed Duda early the following morning. Just before 1400, he left the airfield to drive to Armstrong's H.Q. to make certain that the South Africans themselves appreciated the need for movement.

He thus missed the opening of the first battle of Sidi Rezegh.

The first wave of the panzer attack was seen massing for an advance up the valley even while General Gott's conference was taking place, but warnings only reached the gunners along the western flank who then so busied themselves with preparations to withstand the assault that the message seems not to have been passed on; but by 1415 everyone on the airfield could see what was happening. At least fifty panzers were coming implacably up the slope towards them, more were moving up behind, and the attached and ubiquitous German anti-tank screens were weaving between the column and along the flanks.

The 25-pounders of 4th Royal Horse Artillery were the first to open fire, and soon all the guns of the Support Group were in action, the crews, half-naked, caked in dust runnelled with sweat, crouched either in the open or behind the derisory gun-shields as they slaved with automaton precision to pump their shells out at the advancing panzers. Smoke and the crash of battle engulfed the airfield, shot with the fire of explosion as shells from the Mark IVs erupted among the guns and, as the panzers edged in, machine-gun bullets whined close and too often cut down the unshielded crew members. And now, unlike during the previous day's fighting on the other side of the airfield, there was no sign of an easement of the pressure as panzers, flak guns, the crouching, leap-frogging knots of German infantry edged inexorably forward despite the weight of steel flung against them. Desperately, the gunners waited for help from someone – more gunners, some tanks or even the orderly-room clerks from the Support Group Headquarters who were almost the only infantry left on the airfield.

Suddenly it arrived; Crusaders from 22nd Armoured Brigade had come up from their new positions under the southern escarpment, passed through the waiting gunners of the 60th Field Regiment,

Map 23   The first battle of Sidi Rezegh: November 22nd, 1941

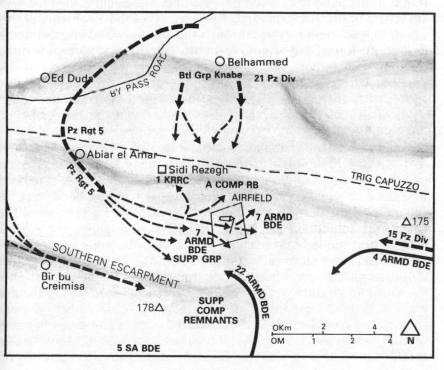

wheeled across the airfield and then through the R.H.A. gun-line and into battle. The exhausted gunners relaxed briefly and used the respite to clear away debris and collect the ammunition from the guns already out of action. But, in the words of one of the official accounts:

> The relief was very short. With horrified eyes they saw tank after tank go up in flames, hopelessly out-gunned. Sadly, but with grim determination, the gunners took up the battle again, while the tanks re-formed under their protection. Bravely our tanks went into the unequal contest again, and for a while armour fought armour. But the end was inevitable, and when the remnant of our tanks limped out of battle, the field was left once more to the gunners.[19]

Now the military exploits of Brigadier Jock Campbell reached their zenith. Not only was it his own command, the 7th Support Group, which was the principal – indeed at times the only – British formation in action, but the most committed arm in the airfield was the artillery and he was himself a gunner, his own regiment the Royal Horse Artillery. That afternoon he was everywhere – standing upright in his unarmoured staff car and holding nothing more lethal in his hand than a red flag, he time and again rallied the few survivors of the 7th Armoured Brigade and of the Yeomanry of the 22nd, to lead them forward through the gun-lines and into the chaos and confusion of the armoured battle. Shells burst alongside him, machine-gun bullets, shell-splinters and pebbles pock-marked his car, but wherever the action was most furious, the tall figure was there, stiff, aristocratic features more and more obscured under the cake of dust and grime, the voice hoarser, but the energy never flagging.

But by now the cumulative tank losses of *Operation Crusader* were taking their toll – of morale. Too many British tanks were now battered and smoking hulks, and too many tank crew members had been shocked by the sight of comrades burnt to death and by the realisation that despite the exhortations of higher authority, there was something lacking in their armoury against the Afrika Korps; they tended now to come out of the battle more quickly than before and were more reluctant to turn and go back in again. In the lengthening time-gaps between their appearances, the panzers and the German infantry were reaching nearer and nearer to the British guns, and these were falling silent or drawing back. As they did so, they were pressed south-east by the first wave of panzers, while the second wave swung north-east against the rear of the British infantry now holding the Sidi Rezegh ridge against the assaults of

Battlegroup Knabe supported by the heavy artillery of Böttcher's siege train on Belhammed.

Overrun unexpectedly from the rear, their ammunition shot away and without protection against panzers, the riflemen of the 1st King's Royal Rifle Corps and of A Company, the Rifle Brigade – many of whom had fought in every major engagement since Sofafi and a host of minor skirmishes with the Jock Columns – were hunted through the wadis as daylight faded and all were either dead or prisoner by 1600. By dusk the length of the Sidi Rezegh ridge was back in German hands.

But the battle in the valley had still to be decided. If by this time the airfield itself seemed to have been lost by the British, the 60th Field Regiment had formed another gun-line to the south and behind it Jock Campbell was still rallying, exhorting, bullying the desperate tank crews to further efforts, often succeeding by nothing more than his own example and refusal to believe they would not follow when he led the way back into the conflict.

'What could we do?' one exasperated Crusader driver said afterwards. 'We couldn't let the bastard go back on his own, could we? Not in that bloody silly little staff car?'

So they went out again and again, and braved the fire of the 50mm. and 88mm. anti-tank guns, and watched their own 2-pounder solid shot ricocheting away from the panzer armour unless a lucky strike gave it a head-on impact. By 1530, help was at hand; 4th Armoured Brigade was moving slowly across from Point 175 (and being rather more slowly followed by the leading panzers of Neumann-Sylkow's division, still searching for them) but were in some doubt as to what was happening. According to the first official account to be written after the battle:

> to 4 Armd Bde, the situation was obscure; 'the aerodrome, which could be seen in the centre of a large depression, was covered with derelicts. The enemy appeared to be on the north-western edge, 7 Sp Gp and 22 Armd Bde on the south.' The strength of 4 Armd Bde at this time was a hundred and eight tanks.[20]

These were, of course, Honeys which were really no match for the panzers – but they were armoured vehicles and as such grist to the battle's mill and strength to Jock Campbell's purpose. Indifferent to other orders which their leading troops (of 3rd R.T.R.) might have been given, Campbell drove up, leapt from his car, hammered on the sides of the tanks until the tank-commanders threw back the hatches and looked out, shouted his orders, leapt back into the car and, according to one observer, 'led them in a sort of cavalry charge waving a red flag . . . '

Among them was Cyril Joly, already shaken by the scenes around him.

> I was appalled at the extent of the devastation and carnage which seemed to spread as far as the eye could see. It was a frightening and awesome spectacle – the dead and dying strewn over the battlefield, in trucks and Bren-carriers, in trenches and toppled over the trails of their guns, some silent and grey in death, others vocal with pain and stained by red gashes of flowing blood or the dark marks of old congealed wounds. Trucks, guns, ammunition, odd bits of clothing were smouldering or burning with bright tongues of fire. Here and there ammunition had caught fire and was exploding with spurts of flame and black smoke . . . [21]

Now, with the other Honeys of his squadron, he followed this 'large man standing unprotected in an open car flying a brigadier' pennant on the bonnet' and found himself almost immediately blinded in 'a vast synthetic sandstorm caused by the medley of charging tanks and bursting shells which soon blotted out the scene . . . '

Nobody has ever been able to describe in detail what happened under that dense cloud, for nobody outside it could do anything but stare in astonishment at the blank phenomenon and nobody inside it could see what was happening beyond a very limited, and itself confused, circle. But one section of the combatants in that extraordinary mêlée was becoming increasingly conscious of a crucial factor; both battalions of Panzer Regiment 5 and their anti-tank batteries were by now short of ammunition, and if the pitch of battle remained as high as this for much longer their racks would soon be empty. Slowly, and almost unbelievably to the watchers, the cloud began to extend northwards back across the airfield, and as it did so it thinned to reveal the panzers withdrawing towards the main Escarpment, now – although this was not yet known to the British – in the hands of Battlegroup Knabe.

On the southern borders of the airfield, the Honeys and the few remaining Crusaders halted and waited while a few guns and infantry came up and the fog dissipated; and just before last light General Gott, who had returned to the sound of the guns, held a conference with Gatehouse, Scott-Cockburn and Campbell (who had at last been slightly wounded, under the right arm, probably as he waved forward yet another attack). Despite the improving visibility the situation was still obscure, for even though the panzers appeared to be withdrawing, Gott and his brigadiers were all too aware of the weaknesses behind them. To all intents and purposes 7th Armoured Brigade no longer existed, its survivors together with

47 The Cunninghams – Andrew and Alan

48 Major-General Freyberg and
    General Auchinleck

49 Brigadier Jock Campbell and Major-General Strafer Gott

50 Infantry waiting along the Sidi Rezegh ridge

51–2 The Corps Commanders: Lieutenant-General Godwin-Austen and Lieutenant-General Willoughby Norrie

53 Rommel, south of Tobruk

54 *Left*, Generalleutnant Cruewell. 55 *Right*, German medium artillery.

56 *Left*, Generalfeldmarschall Kesselring and Oberstleutnant Westphal.
57 *Centre*, Oberst Bayerlein. 58 *Right*, Generalleutnant von Ravenstein.

59 Panzerkampfwagen IV – chief battle-tank of the Afrika Korps

those of 22nd Armoured Brigade mustering only 49 tanks between them; and if 4th Armoured Brigade still had 100 tanks, these were Honeys, outgunned and outranged by the panzers. As for the Support Group, no one yet knew the price they had paid for the fame which was to be theirs once the story of that afternoon became known.

In the circumstances, withdrawal appeared the most sensible course – withdrawal from a position which had never been easily defensible and which now, with an unbeaten enemy panzer force this side of the only natural barrier – the Sidi Rezegh ridge – appeared untenable. Somewhere to the south – surely by now at least on the southern escarpment – lay the virtually unscathed 5th South African Brigade with beyond it the equally sound and unharmed 1st South Africans under Dan Pienaar. These brigades should form the nucleus of a new force with which to continue the battle, and the men and armour in the valley should fall back towards the most northerly of them (Armstrong's 5th Brigade) with the Support Group to the east and the two armoured brigades forming battle positions by 'first light 23 November, to protect the two flanks of this leaguer'.

This apparently logical and wholly reasonable plan would have held greater chance of success had 5th South African Brigade actually been able to clear the German infantry off the southern escarp- ment, and thus to join forces with the Rifle Brigade companies holding the eastern end. As it was, they had been unable even to reach their first objective, Point 178.

The first advance towards this point, by 3rd Transvaal Scottish, had begun at about 1300 with artillery support from eight field guns, across 1,000 yards of open desert against a wadi just to the east of Point 178 which was 'believed to be held by the enemy' – but, they hoped, not in great strength.

The hopes were not justified.

Even before they became fully aware of the strength and determination of the men of Infantry Regiment 155 in front of them, the marching South Africans suffered casualties from a sudden Stuka attack, and when they had approached to within 500 yards of the lip of the wadi, heavy machine-gun fire was opened on them and they soon found themselves pinned to the desert floor by a tremendous concentration of rifle and Spandau fire, supported by both artillery and mortars from well-concealed positions in the other wadis which seamed the escarpment. One observer wrote of the Transvaal Scottish:

These magnificent infantry advanced in widely extended lines

of riflemen followed by man-handled mortars and other weapons
– a text-book show of 1914–15 vintage. Magnificent but not
war.[22]

It was certainly not war in 1941; even the British riflemen who had
taken the Sidi Rezegh ridge the previous morning had been
supported by forty-two field guns, covered by a smoke screen and
preceded by assault platoons in carriers.

There was little the South Africans could do but stay where they
were and endeavour to burrow into the ground, while the only units
which could help them – artillery and a few valiantly manned
armoured cars – drew such sustained and accurate fire on both
themselves and the infantry that their efforts soon petered out.
Transvaal Scottish lost both their colonel and second-in-command
that grim afternoon, and when they were withdrawn after dark their
strength had been whittled down by twenty-five men killed, nine
missing and eighty-three wounded.

The failure to take Point 178 had other repercussions too. Across
the ridge from the South Africans and equally engaged with the
staunch and efficient German infantry, were B Company of 1st
Battalion Rifle Brigade, the remaining guns of 4th R.H.A. and the
batteries at the western end of the 60th Field Regiment line.
Through this line the British troops on the airfield and just south of
it began to withdraw and with that expert sense of opportunity
which characterised units under Rommel's command and with
which the British were to become only too familiar, the refuelled
panzers, artillery and infantry groups came hurrying down to take
the fullest advantage of an enemy in retreat.

The men of the Rifle Brigade had watched the first battle for the
airfield, the cloud which screened the 4th Armoured when they
joined the battle and the return up as far as the southern edge; now
they watched the slow inexorable creep of action back towards
them as the Honeys dropped back through the gun-line, as the
75mm. shells exploded again around the unprotected 25-pounders
and the panzers closed in. One of the artillery observers later
described the scene as darkness fell:

> Under cover of artillery concentrations and supported by tanks
> the German infantry advanced on the gun positions. Orders were
> given for a withdrawal on to the South African Brigade, which
> was in action three miles to the south. Troop by troop, under
> covering fire from the remainder, the guns, or what was left of
> them, moved out as the day drew to a close. Officer casualties
> had been heavy but N.C.O.s rose magnificently to the occasion
> and withdrew in good order. Towards dusk the last remaining
> guns of a troop of 60th Field Regiment and a troop of 3rd R.H.A.

seemed doomed. The advancing German infantry were almost on them. Firing at point-blank range, with apparently no hope of survival, these indomitable men still fought their guns. Suddenly a troop of light British tanks roared out of the gathering gloom, charged straight into the German infantry and, firing with every weapon they had, halted the enemy attack long enough for the gunners to hook in and pull out.

The final scene was awe-inspiring enough. In the light of burning vehicles and dumps our guns slipped out of action, leaving the field to a relentlessly advancing enemy, who loomed in large, fantastic shapes out of the shadow into the glare of bursting shells.[23]

Thus the valley was emptied of British troops as darkness thickened on the evening of November 22nd. Just below the southern escarpment, the 5th South Africans drew together and ruefully considered the day's events while the weary Crusader crews of 22nd Armoured formed a leaguer on their western flank and the grim remnants of the Support Group clustered around Jock Campbell's H.Q. to the east, sure in the knowledge that no one would ever call their military worth into question. Further out in the desert to the east lay the headquarters of 4th Armoured Brigade awaiting the return of their commander, Gatehouse, while the squadrons of the 3rd and 5th R.T.R. sorted themselves out after the confusions of both their advance to the airfield and their withdrawal. Among them, still, was Cyril Joly:

As usual, the leaguer seemed to be ringed with enemy, whose presence was always marked by an astonishing display of coloured Very lights. But it was not these nor the failure of the supply column to arrive that caused my worry. For no accountable reason I felt that something was wrong somewhere . . .

With Kinnaird I was no nearer finding a solution, except that I heard that the Brigade was still not fully accounted for and that tanks, some in fairly large numbers, appeared to be wandering aimlessly about the area in which the units had leaguered. While I stood by Kinnaird's tank and listened to the flurry of orders and information being passed on the Brigade forward control, I suddenly heard, quite distinctly, at no great distance, the muffled note of the engines of a column of tanks and the accompanying clank and creak of tracks. For a moment I nearly shouted . . . But some instinct restrained me, and I listened to the column move past without even disturbing Kinnaird.[24]

This was unfortunate, for what Joly heard were the advance units of Panzer Regiment 8 of Neumann-Sylkow's 15th Panzer Division at last catching up with the British armour they had set out to find some hours before. They had had little contact all day as their progress westward had been no faster than that of the armour they were looking for, except that as daylight faded the noise of battle in front of them had suddenly increased, and their commander, Oberstleutnant Cramer, reacted in the traditional way by driving towards the sound of the guns. But darkness was upon them before they could reach the valley and for some time they probed slowly and carefully forward. At about 1700 they saw in front of them a congregation of dark shapes from which suddenly erupted a white Very light (fired, in fact, to guide Gatehouse back to his H.Q.) and in its glare the battalion commander recognised the vehicles as English tanks at ten yards. According to the War Diary of 15th Panzer:

[Cramer] burst through the enemy leaguer in his command vehicle and ordered No 1 Company to go round the left and No 2 Company round the right to surround the enemy.

The tanks put on their headlights and the commanders jumped out with their machine-pistols. The enemy was completely surprised and incapable of action. Thus far there had been no firing. A few tanks tried to get away, but were at once set on fire by our tanks, and lit up the battlefield as bright as day. While the prisoners were being rounded up an English officer succeeded in setting fire to a tank.

This *coup* on our part got the rest of 4 British Armoured Brigade with light casualties to ourselves. The Brigade Commander, 17 officers and 150 other ranks were taken prisoner. One armoured command vehicle, 35 tanks, armoured cars, guns and self-propelled guns, other fighting vehicles, and some important papers fell into our hands.[25]

This tally of success is not quite accurate, since not Gatehouse but his second-in-command was taken, and it was, in fact, only the headquarters of 4th Armoured Brigade which had been rounded up, the operational squadrons being still dispersed at varying distances away. Nevertheless, from the British point of view it was a devastating blow, for it meant that for the next few vital hours, indeed perhaps days, the only substantial armoured formation left to XXX Corps would be without a head, incommunicado until an emergency signals framework could be set up, and with all its own internal and XXX Corps's codes hopelessly compromised.

There was another spurt of confused action when Cramer and his men stumbled across some 5th R.T.R. tanks as the panzers were feeling their way out of the ring with their captures and the Honeys were groping around to find their own command; but with the lack of directives and the general incomprehension of events on all sides which now shrouded the night's activities, they both broke away for fear of finding when daylight came that they had been firing on their own units. Neither Neumann-Sylkow nor Norrie, at that point, was aware of what had happened – Norrie at least being much more concerned with plans for the following day.

He had already approved Gott's plans for the concentration of the remaining armour around 5th South African Brigade south of the southern escarpment, and indeed was determined to strengthen it further. The New Zealanders and a squadron of Valentines had begun their move along the Trig Capuzzo early in the afternoon and their leading elements, now aware that they might meet strong German forces at Bir el Chleta, were planning to diverge around them when orders came (from Cunningham) that they were to advance as fast as possible to Sidi Rezegh and assist the hard-pressed Support Group. To do this, they must climb the Escarpment (quite gentle this far east), concentrate above it and then move to Point 175 prior to the last step down to the valley. These orders had been received by the New Zealanders at 1615; since then they had been making their way westwards at maximum speed (eight miles per hour), and no further information or instructions had reached them.

And in addition to the New Zealand brigade, Norrie felt that with 22nd Guards Brigade moving up towards Bir el Gubi, the 1st South Africans should get away to join their sister brigade immediately, leaving only the sketchiest masking force behind. General Brink received instructions to this effect by 1445 and duly passed them on to Dan Pienaar, though Brink's acknowledgment to Norrie expressed doubts both as to the speed with which 1st South African Brigade could disengage from the Ariete, and the advisability, in view of this probable delay, of the brigade attempting to move up towards the southern escarpment until daylight the following day.

As for the brigade commander's reactions, as the South African historians put it so delicately:

It was not Brigadier Pienaar's habit to allow the orders of any superior to pass without thorough examination and discussion, and he now proceeded to indicate the difficulties that lay ahead. He

pointed out to Div . . . that, in the light of information regarding enemy dispositions in the intervening area, it would be most dangerous and inadvisable for a motorized infantry column to move during the hours of darkness beyond the 38 Northing Grid Line [i.e. within 15 miles of Sidi Rezegh air-field].[26]

Pienaar requested permission instead to move due east for some eight miles, then to turn north, leaguer for the night and move up towards 5th South African Brigade the following morning (of November 23rd). It has never been ascertained what the 'information regarding enemy dispositions in the intervening area' between Bir el Gubi and 5th South Africans consisted of, for there were no German units there – but Brink loyally supported his brigadier and Norrie, conscious of Dominion susceptibilities, reluctantly agreed but stressed the urgency of the situation.

As a result, the bulk of Dan Pienaar's brigade arrived at their turning-point at dusk and moved about a mile northwards, but orders to stop and leaguer there until the following morning failed to reach the soft-skinned B Echelon supply transport and also the men of the 10th Field Ambulance, and these proceeded happily throughout the night, eventually settling down for breakfast but two miles south of the southern perimeter of 5th South African Brigade, an area also occupied by soft-skinned B Echelon units. With the panzers away to the north and British armour on each side, it seemed quite a sensible arrangement that the dispositions of Armstrong's artillery and anti-tank screens should be along the western, northern and eastern sides of a box with the southern side left open to receive any support which might come up.

Thus, with some degree of concentration but with a vulnerable 'soft' space between the two vital infantry brigades, began for the South Africans and the British the morning of November 23rd. For the New Zealanders some seventeen miles away to the north-east, it was proving rather more exciting.

They had been delayed by minefields during their move along the Trig Capuzzo in the afternoon, and their commander, Brigadier Barrowclough, halted them just after 2000 for a hot meal and rest, for the Valentine crews had been on the move for many hours (they had been late coming up to the start point and had thus delayed the whole brigade) and in any case if battle threatened it would be as well to replenish fuel tanks and feed the men. The supply transport arrived after midnight, a conference was held between the unit commanders and at 0300, shivering with the cold and half asleep, the soldiers climbed back into their lorries and the journey began again. It was very dark, the drivers could hardly make out the jolting, heaving shapes of the vehicles in front and progress was very slow. At dawn the main columns halted while reconnaissance parties were sent out to establish their position. According to the New Zealand history:

> The men were cold, tired, and hungry, and lost no time in dismounting to set up burners, boil billies, and get something to eat.

Daylight always reveals in a great laager an apparent confusion with vehicles of many kinds facing in all directions, each like a domestic household – waking, washing, cooking and not minding its neighbours. And so it was this morning . . . The war could wait until after breakfast.[27]

It was at this point that two important discoveries were made. The first was that the guides had veered off the course during the night and instead of avoiding Bir el Chleta, the brigade was precisely there; and the second was that sitting in the middle of the brigade leaguer were Cruewell's Afrika Korps headquarters, complete with almost all his wireless vehicles and the whole of his cipher staff. There was also part of a German mobile column within the mêlée which promptly developed and this put up most resistance to capture – but the end was certain and swift. Within a few minutes some 200 German prisoners were being rounded up and the staff vehicles ransacked for the vital information they contained.

Gatehouse was not the only commander to face the coming day's trials without a headquarters and, indeed, the loss of Afrika Korps H.Q. was obviously more serious to Rommel than the loss of 4th Armoured H.Q. to Cunningham.

General Cruewell, accompanied by his Chief of Staff, Oberst-leutnant Bayerlein, had only left the headquarters half an hour before the arrival of the New Zealanders, and although the loss of his staff undoubtedly occasioned him much inconvenience, the thought may have crossed his mind that there were advantages to be abstracted from every situation.

Just before he had left his H.Q., according to Bayerlein, 'D.A.K. received a long wireless message for the deciphering of which General Cruewell had not time to wait. He had to act on his own initiative.'

Certainly, the message contained a great deal of administrative detail which was of little interest to the commander of the Afrika Korps, but it began with Rommel's orders for battle on the following day, and whether or not Cruewell knew of the general outline of those orders, it is evident that he disagreed with them. The relationship between Rommel and Cruewell at this time may have borne some resemblance to that between Sir Hyde Parker and Nelson during the Battle of Copenhagen, the loss of Cruewell's cipher staff providing him with a conveniently blind eye, for he now issued orders to 15th and 21st Panzer Divisions which differed in marked degree from Rommel's intentions.

To Rommel, the situation was at last clear and he felt he controlled it. The airfield at Sidi Rezegh was held by Panzer

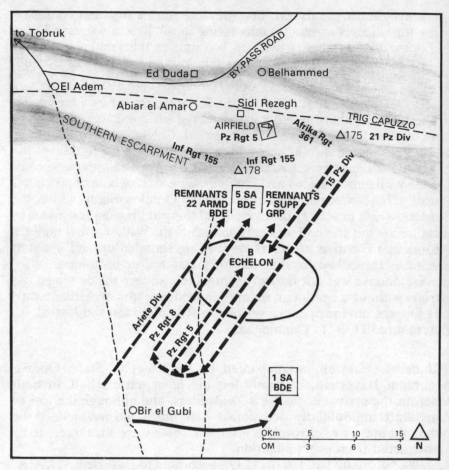

Map 24 *Totensonntag*: November 23rd, 1941

Regiment 5 (21st Panzer Division's armour) with their own divisional infantry of Battlegroup Knabe holding the Sidi Rezegh ridge. The infantry and armour of 15th Panzer Division were grouped south-west of Point 175 which was itself held by Infantry Regiment 361, while Infantry Regiment 155 held the southern escarpment, just to the north of the main British and South African concentration. Accordingly, he issued his orders, beginning:

On 23 November, *Panzergruppe* will force a decision in the area south-east of Tobruk, by means of a concentric attack by *D.A.K.* and parts of Corps Gambara. With this object, Corps Gambara will advance from El Gubi at 0800 hours with elements of Panzer Division Ariete in the direction of Gambut. At 0700 on 23 November, *D.A.K.*, effectively concentrating its forces, will advance in the general direction of El Gubi – with main effort on the left wing, encircle the enemy and destroy them.[28]

Again the classic German manoeuvre of encirclement was intended or, to use a different metaphor, the enemy were to be smashed between the hammer of the German panzer regiments and the anvil of the Ariete.

For reasons at which one can perhaps guess, Cruewell seems to have felt that both hammer *and* anvil required a German component, and his instructions to 21st and 15th Panzer Divisions were to the effect that the panzer regiments should amalgamate south of Point 175 as quickly as possible and, accompanied by the infantry of 15th Panzer Division, cut through the enemy's lines of communication in a drive to Bir el Gubi. There they would join up with the *Ariete*, turn, and *then* crush the opposition against the anvil of Infantry Regiment 155 – with a secondary anvil waiting further back in the shape of Battlegroup Knabe on the Sidi Rezegh ridge in case the overstrained steel of 155 should fracture under the impact.

A glance at the map will reveal the interesting possibilities open to an armoured force following the shortest route on the first leg of that journey.

The combination of Cruewell's modification of Rommel's concept and the German habit of rising and going to work rather earlier than their opponents resulted, from about 0800 onwards on the morning of November 23rd, in some quite extraordinary scenes. Men in every stage of dress and undress, caught at their morning rituals, scampered about the desert racing for their weapons, their vehicles or their slit trenches, and as the armour and infantry carriers of 15th Panzer Division (21st Panzer armour were late off the mark and came through afterwards), with Cruewell, Bayerlein and Neumann-Sylkow in the first wave, crashed through the soft-skinned B Echelon transport which occupied the gap between 5th and 1st South African Brigades, British lorries, staff cars, ambulances, trucks, pick-ups and motor-cycles bolted in all directions like a stampeding herd in a Western film.

Some raced for the security of the two South African Brigade perimeters but others went helter-skelter out into the desert in whichever direction took the fancy of the driver – west, south-east or around and back towards the Wire. The supply vehicles for Jock Campbell's Support Group were the first to see the danger and feel the shock, and quite naturally the majority moved first to rally to that stalwart figure, only to find that he wished them for the moment away and over the horizon while he amassed around his own person whatever fighting force was available.

Sitting on top of his A.C.V. waving alternate red and blue
flags – made from his scarves – for 'Stop' and 'Go' . . . he
started to rally every [fighting] vehicle he could find to turn and
face the German tanks. He had 23 people in the A.C.V., all
urging the driver to go like hell, while Jock kept shouting down
that he was not to go faster than 8 m.p.h. and to stop when he was
told to. To one Troop of guns . . . he gave the classic order:
'Expect no orders. Stick to me. I shall advance soon!'[29]

And advance in due course he did, surrounded by a miscellaneous
collection of old cruiser tanks, a few repaired Crusaders which had
not managed previously to report back to Scott-Cockburn, parts of
both B and C Squadrons of the 11th Hussars, and guns from both
60th Field Regiment and his own beloved Royal Horse Artillery.
However, by the time this motley collection had assembled and
moved into action, the bulk of the panzers were through and
wreaking havoc among the South African supply vehicles – and
with the incongruous perversity of war, Campbell led his force
through the tail of the onslaught, on into a patch of soft ground
where many of his heavier vehicles promptly bogged down.

But the fighting by no means ended with Campbell's temporary
disappearance, for Armstrong had posted artillery out as a screen
for his transport, and this was soon joined by some Support Group
guns which had been north of the axis of Cruewell's advance and
now raced across to attack it in flank.

One of the South African B Echelon sergeants later wrote:

British artillery kept rushing from one side of our lines to the
other. Pandemonium appeared to have broken loose. We all fired
with our rifles and a tommy-gun on German tanks which we saw
not far distant. The firing was passing continually over our heads.
One British tank ran right over the shell slit in which our driver
was crouching, next to the truck, covering him with earth. A
British anti-tank gun took up its position right next to us, firing
over our heads. The ground shook with the reverberations of the
heavy firing and the falling of shells all around us and we saw
German tanks on all sides.[30]

Everywhere, men caught in trenches were blazing away fruitlessly with small arms at the shut-down, implacable panzers as they
drove past, but these – except for a burst of machine-gun fire at
some unusually reckless and exposed figure – were concentrating
their attention and fire on the fleeing trucks and lorries and the
occasional gun or tank which dared to stand in their direct path. But
behind the panzers came the German infantry carriers, and these

had much more time and attention for the men who had not leaped aboard the escaping transport.

Short, fierce infantry fights developed as isolated Bren-guns opened up the carriers, which slowed to a halt to spill their cargoes out in a flood which then rushed the defiant post and wiped it out. Many of the B Echelon units, including 10th Field Ambulance which of course bore no arms heavier than the officers' pistols and the drivers' unbayoneted rifles, were rounded up almost complete and taken prisoner; but many were later to find themselves abandoned by their captors as their growing weight of numbers slowed the advance and menaced the redeployment for the main attack; and in this theatre at any rate, there was to be no indiscriminate slaughter of prisoners.

But the panzers did not have it all their own way. According to 15th Panzer's War Diary, 'Again and again strong enemy battle groups with tanks, anti-tank guns and artillery came out of the desert and tried to take the Division in flank to divert it from its objective.'[31]

One of these 'battle groups' consisted of a detachment of Honeys from 4th Armoured Brigade which had become so hopelessly lost the previous evening that it had leaguered with some South Africans – a happy coincidence as their commander was Major Bob Crisp, a well-known South African cricketer who had elected to join the British Army.

After spending a convivial night with them, he and his tanks had left the leaguer shortly before the German attack developed, and after a brief period of confusion in the opening mêlée, he noticed a battery of four German field-guns for the moment isolated in an otherwise empty patch of desert, firing over the battle area and into 1st South African Brigade zone.

'It seemed to be a monstrous bit of cheek,' related Crisp later, 'and got my back up!' Despite the danger he would face if any of the gunners noticed the Honeys streaking upon them from the rear, he ordered a charge – across nearly a mile of open desert – and fortunately for him, he was not seen until his tanks were within 300 yards of the guns and he could then see the panic on the faces of the Germans as they frantically swung the nearest gun around. There was a flash and a cloud of black smoke, but 'I could afford to laugh at this, and I believe I actually did, as the gun was pointing upwards at a range of about 6,000 yards, and there I was not 100 yards away. I knew I had them.'

But not for long. Although Crisp took the whole battery prisoner and ordered them to march away to 5th South African Brigade area, he had no way of enforcing his order once circumstances distracted his attention from them; and as no member of his command possessed the technical knowledge necessary to wreck the field guns, these were, according to 15th Panzer War Diary, later brought back into action. The morning of November 23rd, though sparkling with myriad deeds of valour and enterprise, was not distinguished by remarkably high military expertise.

Even on the German side, this was so. By 0900 Neumann-Sylkow had watched the chaos spreading in front of him for long enough to sense further opportunity for immediate exploitation; he could see now the southern borders of the 5th South African Brigade area and had a shrewd idea of the confusion which must reign therein. Surely the time had arrived for a change of plan, a decision to do without the Italians at El Gubi entirely, and a switch of course which would take his armour without the slightest check to their momentum straight up through the open side of the South African box into its soft centre?

But Cruewell would have none of this. Perhaps because, having made up his own plan in defiance of Rommel's ideas, he would now brook no interference from a subordinate, or perhaps because of the strength of these isolated (and indeed uncoordinated) flank attacks, he ordered a continuation of the advance towards Bir el Gubi, his only additional instruction being to 21st Panzer infantry which he now ordered to move down towards the southern escarpment to buttress Regiment 155 and increase the threat to the South Africans from the north. To 21st Panzer's armour he sent word that they should hurry along to take up their prescribed position with 15th Panzer and himself for the afternoon attack.

Thus the Afrika Korps armour plus the 15th Panzer's infantry swept on towards Bir el Gubi and the Ariete formations, leaving in its wake the dispersed, badly shaken and in no small part destroyed supply trains of two South African Brigades and Jock Campbell's Support Group, and to the rear two astonished infantry brigades, one on each side, each still virtually untouched so far as its fighting strength was concerned but with one of them at least acutely aware of the danger which would soon be threatening from the south-west. They may have been half asleep when the Afrika Korps first approached that morning, but they were wide awake now, and they knew where their gun-lines must lie if many of them were to see the sun set that evening.

The lull which followed was certainly not wasted by the British and South Africans of 5th Brigade.

The first to move in was D Battery of 3rd R.H.A. from the Support Group, followed shortly by all the remaining artillery from 22nd Armoured Brigade and two more R.H.A. batteries with 25-pounders. These took up positions on the south-west corner of the brigade area, and General Gott, who was now advising Armstrong and at the same time trying to organise a defence of the whole 7th Armoured Division area, brought across the 2nd Battalion of the Scots Guards from 4th Armoured Brigade. He then instructed a reluctant Jock Campbell to release the 4th R.H.A. batteries (originally from 7th Armoured Brigade but collected that morning as a result of what one surely carping critic referred to as the brigadier's 'predatory instincts') to guard the eastern flank of the 5th South Africans, but allowed Campbell to keep the rest of his motley collection of guns and fighting vehicles. With the survivors of the Support Group headquarters, these set off to the south-east, where to Campbell's annoyance many of the heavy vehicles promptly sank up to their axles in yet another bog.

Meanwhile, twelve 25-pounders of the South Africans' own artillery came hurrying down from their previous positions as Armstrong stripped his eastern and northern sectors of as much as he dare, plus two 18-pounders firing solid shot and nine 2-pounder anti-tank guns. But as the ground was so hard and time was so short, many of the 2-pounders remained portée'd on their lorries.

And all the time, with the B Echelon traffic which had found refuge inside the brigade perimeter thickening the target, Böttcher's heavy guns on Belhammed some eight miles away were lobbing their great shells into the area, to explode with shattering force and random effect, sometimes to obliterate lorries and trucks, sometimes scything down anything which stood higher than two feet above the ground in the path of their wayward shards – but quite often doing no more harm than making a big bang. In such circumstances heavy artillery is like a primitive god – uncertain, inconsistent and unjust; and hateful. And very wearing on the nerves.

Away towards Bir el Gubi, Cruewell had by 1235 made contact with the Ariete divisional commander and ascertained that he was willing for nearly two-thirds of his division's armour to take their place in Cruewell's attack. Some explanation and indeed persuasion had been necessary because Ariete was part of Generale Gambara's Corpo d'Armata di Manovra and as such did not come under Panzergruppe Afrika command (though Rommel was, at that moment, engaged upon clandestine manoeuvres which resulted in it doing so on the following day) – but by 1300 clear understanding had been reached and the amalgamated armour of Afrika Korps and Ariete was being marshalled for the attack.

It must have been a remarkable sight. Cruewell's intention was that the three armoured formations would form a long line with 120 panzers of Panzer Regiment 8 grouped in the centre, 40 panzers of

Panzer Regiment 5 on the right and 100-odd M13s of the Ariete on the left; and with them all moving together at their joint maximum speed, they would sweep down on the 5th South African Brigade and the remnants of the 7th Armoured Division, and consign them all to oblivion. Some 200 yards behind the lines of armour, the infantry of Rifle Regiment 115 and Infantry Regiment 200 would follow in their carriers, their orders being that they were to remain in the vehicles at least until they were under heavy fire and preferably until they had followed the panzers well into the enemy positions. Such manoeuvres were, as Panzergruppe's Chief of Intelligence was later to write, with marked reserve, 'an innovation in German tactics', and as the men and vehicles of the assault force lined up almost as though on parade for inspection by a Prussian Generalfeldmarschall, many of them must have wondered whether Rommel would have approved had he been there; and some, what price would have to be paid for so unsophisticated an approach to modern battle.

For the introspective or superstitious there was another cause for thought. Every day is a bad day upon which to fight a battle, but for Christians Sunday is probably the worst; and for those who were sensitive to such matters this particular Sunday was the worst of all.

November 23rd, 1941, fell on the last Sunday of the ecclesiastical year, known in the English Church calendar as the 'Sunday next before Advent'. But for German Protestants it was the Sunday upon which they prayed for the souls of the dead, and its very name of *Totensonntag* holds the chill of sorrow and the grave. Assuredly, it was not a day upon which to fight any battle, let alone one in which the evident intention was the total annihilation of all the combatants on one side or the other.

Whatever the private thoughts of the German soldiers, however, they seem not to have affected their sense of duty and obedience. Even as they formed up for the attack, Panzer Regiment 5 on the right of the line was under fire from artillery with the 1st South African Brigade, who had withdrawn slightly after the events of the morning and were now watching the German deployment with considerable interest. But these harassing tactics made no difference to the forty panzers and at 1500 when Cruewell signalled the order to advance, the whole line moved forward, gradually increasing speed until the ground shook under the massed steel charge.

Almost immediately, it met a storm of fire from the opposing guns, firing over open sights. On the left, the Italian M13s were late off the mark, slow to catch up and suffered such severe casualties when they did so that their line dropped back, exposing the flank of Panzer Regiment 8 which thus became more vulnerable to the

South African fire; but their commander, Oberstleutnant Cramer, in the leading tank held an undeviating course towards the enemy, spurring his armour on with brief exhortations over the air. Oberstleutnant Kriebel was also there:

A terrific fire front of well over 100 guns [*sic*] concentrated on the two attacking panzer regiments and the two rifle regiments following close behind in their vehicles. A concentration of anti-tank weapons unusual in this theatre of war, and cleverly hidden among enemy vehicles which had been knocked out during the morning, inflicted heavy losses . . . [32]

And if the panzers were able to withstand at least some of the shock of the fire, the soft-skinned vehicles crammed with infantry behind had nothing but their speed and good fortune to protect them. Jock Campbell's example of uncaring courage was repeated now on the opposite side by at least one commander, for Oberstleutnant Zintel led his men of Rifle Regiment 115 standing upright in his car, apparently unconcerned by the shot and shell which screamed past him.

Heinz Schmidt had some time before managed to persuade Rommel to release him from his duties as A.D.C. and was now commanding an anti-tank company in Zintel's regiment:

The regimental commander led, standing erect in his open car. The Major's car followed, with me right behind him. We headed straight for the enemy tanks [*sic*]. I glanced back. Behind me was a fan of our vehicles – a curious assortment of all types – spread out as far as the eye could see. There were armoured troop carriers, cars of various kinds, caterpillars hauling mobile guns, heavy trucks with infantry, motorized anti-aircraft units. Thus we roared on towards the enemy 'barricade'.

I stared to the front fascinated. Right ahead was the erect figure of the colonel commanding the regiment. On the left close by and slightly in rear of him was the Major's car. Tank shells were whizzing through the air. The defenders were firing from every muzzle of their 25-pounders and their little 2-pounder anti-tank guns. We raced on at a suicidal pace.

The battalion commander's car lurched and stopped suddenly – a direct hit. I had just time to notice the Colonel steadying himself. He turned sideways and dropped from the car like a felled tree. Then I had flashed past him. The Major was still ahead.

I recognized infantry positions in front of me. There was a tall, thin fellow out in the open, running backwards as if impelled by a jet from a hose. I heard bursts behind me and followed the tracer as it whipped past me into the distance ahead. How slowly tracer seems to travel! The tall fellow dropped . . .

The Major's car lurched and went over on its side. I was alone out ahead in this inferno now. In front I saw nothing but belching guns.

Then suddenly there was a violent jolt, a screeching and a hiss, and my car stopped dead. I saw a trench immediately ahead, leaped from the car, and plunged towards the slit.[33]

Oberleutnant Schmidt was lucky for very few of the officers and N.C.O.s of Regiment 115 had reached even this far alive and unwounded. But the panzers had broken through the gun-line and were now wheeling to the support of their infantry (which in this and other cases had actually beaten the armour to the first enemy positions, so acutely had they realised that in speed lay their only safety) and as the British and South African guns were put out of action or hastily dragged back by their tows, the German infantry could come out of whatever shelter they had found and fight the opposing infantry, by this time attacking the German artillery units as these came up. Fierce, isolated fights broke out along the length of the southern border of the brigade area, confused, shrouded in sand and smoke, fought most often to the death of either or both sides.

On the left, where the Ariete had still failed to catch up, Crusaders of 22nd Armoured Brigade were seen massing for a charge against the left flank of 15th Panzer's infantry, and their anti-tank platoons swung around to help the divisional screen which had ridden as usual along the flank of the charge. And when the British tanks had been fought off, there followed a duel with South African guns on the south-west corner of the box until, tardily, the M13s of Ariete again came up and for a short while relieved the pressure, until they were themselves reduced to smoking hulks.

On the right flank, the outer units of 21st Panzer Division had at first found themselves with apparently no opponents ahead, for their line of march took them past the eastern flank of the box – but Jock Campbell's miscellany, despite its troubles with the desert bogs, regained for itself sufficient mobility to make threatening drives towards its flanks. This in turn drove the forty-odd panzers which were all that Panzer Regiment 5 had left northwards, where they wreaked havoc among the 5th South African B Echelon vehicles now endeavouring to escape the fury developing inside the box.

For by 1600, leading troops of 15th Panzer Division were deep into the heart of the 5th South African Brigade, the gun-line along the southern border smashed, its ammunition gone, its gun crews dead or prisoners, the portées almost all in flames for too little time had been given for digging in. With the disintegration of the opposing artillery the first wave of Panzer Regiment 8 had been able to reassemble and methodically work their way to the north through the inside of the box. The first effect was to start a stampede among the B Echelon vehicles, but when the majority of these had fled or been destroyed some of the Crusaders from 22nd Armoured, having been driven away from the western flank of the attack, came across and tried to delay the implacable advance of the Panzers. One observer of this stage was Major Melzer, command-ing 11th South African Field Ambulance whose Main Dressing Station lay at first behind the screen of Crusaders:

As the battle developed they kept on their patrols, but were gradually being pushed back closer and closer to us. After a while they were about 300 yards away, then 200 yards, then 100 yards . . . Eventually they reached us, and our tanks actually worked their way between the groups of casualties lying on the ground.[34]

The line of British tanks was forced back behind the M.D.S. which then had an uncomfortable time between the two lines of manoeuvring and embattled armour until, inevitably, the panzers were also fighting among the lines of casualties and Melzer became worried about the danger to the wounded men:

My fears, however, were quite unfounded, because the German tanks kept clear of the persons lying on the ground, and not one of the casualties or personnel was run over by a tank. Eventually the front line of the German tanks had the M.D.S. behind them, and they kept on the advance until all their tanks had passed us.[35]

Shortly afterwards German infantry posted guard over the Field Ambulance and all within knew they were prisoners, but no attempt was made to interfere with their ministrations to the wounded. During the two hours when the M.D.S. had been in the front line of the conflict, only two men had been wounded and no one believed that the injuries had been caused by anything except accident; the desert bred a chivalry of its own.

Beyond the Field Ambulance lay the Brigade Headquarters and by 1615 these had been taken – to the astonishment of the Staff who had been curiously out of touch with the German progress. Shortly afterwards Brigadier Armstrong, his brigade major, intelligence officer and signals officer were all taken prisoner, while away to the north near the southern escarpment the last battles were taking place; but even at this stage it was to be by no means a simple roll-over for the panzers. Panzer Regiment 8 found themselves alone in the middle of the enemy, whose fierce, determined resistance still persisted. The shell-fire continued to fall on the tanks without abatement. At this stage the regimental commander personally summoned his last reserves, the regimental engineers, in their troop carriers and what escort tanks were available, to join II/8 and attempt to decide the day without the infantry. This was an epic of courage and soldierly sacrifice. The tanks charged forward ruthlessly: the engineers followed close and dug out of their holes the crews of the field and anti-tank guns which had been overrun by the tanks.[36]

Then there was little but the infantry of the 3rd Transvaal Scottish ahead of the panzers, virtually defenceless against them, especially as they were now being overrun from the rear. Although some groups managed to slip off into the gathering dusk, those nearest the panzers and the German engineers were quickly rounded up and marched back towards the centre of the box, forming in the gloom that saddest and most dispiriting sight of all – amorphous clumps of beaten men deprived of their weapons and for the moment of their purpose.

There was one final burst of action across the desolate scene as the last remaining tanks of 22nd Armoured Brigade made a dash for the haven of a link-up with Campbell, or whoever now lay to the south-east of the battle area. They had watched the gradual disintegration of the South African brigade, the escape of the surviving Scots Guards, the last defiant shots from the few isolated South African guns before ammunition ran out. Now they felt that a surprise burst of energy might cause sufficient confusion for some of the prisoners to slip away:

> The final rush through the camp and the German tanks was thrilling: Lt. Col. Carr was at the head. Towards the end his tank was set on fire, but he and Major Kidston got on to other tanks and went on. Major Kidston's tank again became knocked out and he had to spend the night in the enemy lines, eventually creeping out next morning on Lieut Melville's tank.[37]

But Carr and the others broke through the German agglomeration and emerged on the far side of the box – to see in the gloom ahead dark, looming shapes at which they promptly opened fire. Fortunately, only two hits had registered and no one killed before it was realised that the shapes were those of some 7th Hussar relics, and that the 22nd tanks had broken through to the British forces concentrated around the Support Group. These lay just to the east of 1st South African Brigade, which had taken but little part in the day's fighting and were now anxiously watching the fires to the north and speculating on the fate of their friends.

Away to the north, the leading panzers of 15th Panzer Division had reached the southern escarpment and made contact with Infantry Regiment 155, who had spent their day watching the holocaust to the south and making such threatening moves as were necessary to hold the attention of the South Africans in the northern flank of the box.

They could now look back across a scene of harrowing desolation – harrowing even for those who could count themselves the victors, for if it was evident that the 5th South African Brigade had been destroyed, the litter of smashed panzers and the toll of grey-clad corpses pointed to the fact that the price was so high as perhaps to have been Pyrrhic. Among the groups of battle-tired infantry and disconsolate prisoners, between the burning lorries and exploding heaps of blazing ammunition, around the dark clumps of doctors and orderlies still intent upon their ministrations, the German staff officers walked or drove, muttering between themselves, counting, asking their questions and gradually piecing together the events of the day; and adding up the butcher's bill.

Totensonntag had proved a day of grievous cost to all.

12 · Crusader: The Infantry Take Over

As Rommel was not to become aware of the full cost of the fighting on *Totensonntag* for some days, it is not surprising that on the evening of that fateful day he arrived at the headquarters at El Adem greatly excited, announcing news of a decisive victory over the British.

He had been out of direct touch with Cruewell for nearly twenty-four hours but had gathered from various sources the extent of the fighting and had received via 21st Panzer Headquarters a message from Afrika Korps to the effect that a 'large enemy force' had been destroyed. This news when confirmed and amplified together with the reports of British armour destroyed on previous days surely added up to a tale of the virtual destruction of the larger part of Cunningham's army? On November 21st, the British 7th Armoured Brigade had been wiped out, during the evening of the 22nd the reports from 15th Panzer indicated destruction of the 4th Armoured Brigade, and now came news from Bayerlein that 'the remains of the 7th Armoured Division and the main body of 1st South African Division [*sic*] were destroyed. There is no further danger to Tobruk.'

At El Adem there was also news for Rommel of another, more personal victory. Only that morning he had sent a complaint to Mussolini about Generale Bastico's lack of personal involvement in the battle, with its resultant hesitancy on the part of Italian formations to move into action; already, to his surprise, Il Duce had responded by placing the whole of Gambara's Corpo d'Armata di Manovra at Rommel's disposal and directly under his command. With such an increase in the striking power available, coupled with the day's victories, should it not now be possible, to use his own words when writing of *Battleaxe*, 'to decide the issue of a battle merely by making an unexpected shift of one's main weight'?

As Rommel saw it on the evening of *Totensonntag*, at least half of Cunningham's army – and the important armoured part of it at that – was spread-eagled over the desert, much of it destroyed, the rest disorganised and split into a hundred fragments, all short of the necessities of battle and probably in many cases of life itself – and if he could strike quickly, its total annihilation would be certain. But speed was essential. The British had on previous occasions revealed a power of recuperation and a talent for improvisation which could snatch victory from defeat, and this might still happen if those isolated units were given opportunity to coalesce, and if they could be resupplied.

In supply lay their hope and therein also lay their vulnerability. Now, therefore, was the time to cut their lines of communication and by rapid and violent movement, to increase their disarray and block their withdrawal routes to Egypt. It must not take long, and to his patient staff he announced that he intended to place himself at the head of the Afrika Korps and lead it, with Ariete on the right flank, in a lightning stroke to the frontier which would not only paralyse the enemy forces in between, but relieve the frontier garrisons (including the one at Halfaya still under command of the redoubtable Major Bach) which had been holding out so valiantly during the last four days.

As he intended to take with him his Chief of Staff, General Gause, Headquarters control would remain in the hands of the Operations Chief, Oberstleutnant Westphal. To the latter's protests on the question of British intentions regarding Tobruk, Rommel promised that he would return within twenty-four or at the most thirty-six hours, and said he was sure Westphal was more than capable of managing on his own until then.

To his Quartermaster at El Adem he also announced that he hoped to capture the British supply dumps along the way, and when in his attempts to make contact with Cruewell he arrived at Neumann-Sylkow's headquarters at about 0400, he gave orders for an advance guard to move off as soon as possible towards Sidi Omar, perhaps as a result of a plaintive request for help received from the commander of the Savona Division there the previous afternoon. In the absence of Cruewell, Rommel also assumed command of Afrika Korps – which might have been a cause of tension at Kilo 13 on the Tobruk by-pass two hours later when the two at last made contact.

Not that Rommel was in a mood to notice other people's hurt feelings or even contrary opinions. Cruewell's suggestions that the following day might be better spent reorganising the Afrika Korps and assessing the cost of the recent fighting, in clearing up the litter of enemy units still at large in the space between the Trig Capuzzo and the Trig el Abd and, more especially, in salvaging the vast stocks of captured and abandoned enemy material before the

enemy could reclaim them, were brushed aside as restricted and
unimaginative. According to Bayerlein, who had remained at
Cruewell's side all the time, Rommel summarised the whole
situation in the following words:

> The greater part of the [enemy] force aimed at Tobruk has
> been destroyed; now we will turn east and go for the New
> Zealanders and Indians before they have been able to join up
> with the remains of their main force for a combined attack on
> Tobruk. At the same time we will take Habata and Maddalena
> and cut off their supplies. Speed is vital; we must make the most
> of the shock effect of the enemy's defeat and push forward
> immediately and as fast as we can with our entire force to Sidi
> Omar.[1]

In the van would be 21st Panzer Division which had apparently
suffered less than 15th Panzer during *Totensonntag*'s battles, and
Afrika Korps H.Q. with both Rommel and Gause in attendance
would accompany them; 15th Panzer would bring up the rear, with
Ariete on the flank. As for Cruewell's excellent suggestions regarding salvage, Infantry Regiment 155 and the Afrika Regiment could
undertake this chore, and in so doing motorise themselves – perhaps
in time to follow the main thrust and help exploit it. But at this
moment all that mattered was speed, speed, speed . . . and everything must be sacrificed to it!

Needless to say, both 21st and 15th Panzer Divisions had ended
Totensonntag short of ammunition and fuel and although much had
been done during the night to repair the situation, neither division
was ready to move as soon as their Commander-in-Chief would
have liked. Eventually his patience wore thin and Panzer Regiment
5 was peremptorily ordered off, with von Ravenstein in the lead and
Rommel and Gause urging on the following units. By 1100 the
Mammoth was well up with the leaders, Rommel himself perched
up on the edge of the roof in his usual position, filled with the
excitement of the chase and his hopes for such a victory as would
put the recent conquest of France in the shade and silence once and
for all his critics in Berlin.

From the top of the command vehicle, the view must indeed have
given added zest to his excitement and foundation for his hopes, for
now he was treated to the kind of spectacle which the previous day
had been witnessed by Neumann-Sylkow's staff as they crashed
through the supply trains of the two South African brigades on their
way down to Bir el Gubi. On each side he could watch the British
and South African B Echelon leaguers explode into activity as the
leading panzers drove down on them, the startled crews hurling
partly cooked meals, tins of food, petrol and water-cans, weapons

and clothing into their lorries before leaping into the cabs and driving furiously away from the wrath which threatened.

Isolated figures blazed angrily but unavailingly back with Bren-guns at the oncoming hordes, then ran out of the way and threw themselves into fox-holes or passing vehicles, or into the shelter of the wrecks which littered the area; and the leading panzers ploughed indifferently on, aware only of the spreading chaos in front of them and the eager, eagle eye of their commander immediately behind.

Unknowingly, they crashed through one corner of the 1st South African Brigade box (the brigade had just withdrawn southwards to Taieb el Esem, west of Gabr Saleh and on the Trig el Abd) and for a few unheeded minutes they might have caught Dan Pienaar himself as he careered with considerable panache back through their ranks on his way from General Brink's H.Q. about four miles to the east. They drove straight across the triangle contained within the points Bir Berraneb, Bir Taieb el Esem and Gabr Saleh and in so doing pushed out of their way the headquarter units of XXX Corps, 7th Armoured Division, 1st South African Division (General Brink's H.Q.), 7th Support Group and the relics of 7th Armoured Brigade, and had it not been for that acute sense of survival which marks headquarter personnel and Rommel's own insistence upon speed, there is no doubt that the Afrika Korps could that morning have made a most notable haul of prisoners.

Map 25   Rommel's 'Dash to the Wire': November 24th–27th, 1941

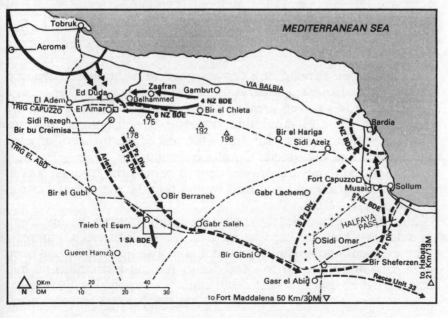

As it was, most of the headquarter units skipped out of the way to find shelter amid the Support Group artillery and some armoured formations which had hastily rallied along the flanks of the advance, and were intent on doing what they could to hinder it.

This was not very much and by noon von Ravenstein and the leaders were past Gabr Saleh and had reached the Trig el Abd, along which they moved with gathering speed towards the frontier. Directly in front of them they could watch, fleeing in chaos and confusion, literally hundreds of British and South African vehicles from mobile workshop pantechnicons to bucking motor-cycles and scurrying pick-up trucks, all bearing frustrated, frightened, angry and bewildered officers and men whose most coherent thoughts were probably best summarised by one exasperated wail overheard emerging from a rapidly accelerating truck:

'Christ Al-bloody-mighty! Not again!'

One officer had been taking advantage of what promised to be a relaxed and peaceful morning to indulge in a complete sponge-down in a basin of carefully saved water when the area he was occupying was deluged with scurrying transport, and when its cause became apparent he had just time to abandon all and leap into his staff car and drive it away. He managed to make two small adjustments to his comfort during the frantic drive which followed, but when several hours later he brought his vehicle to a halt and alighted, he did so wearing nothing but one unlaced boot, his steel helmet and an expression of such unmitigated ferocity that two private soldiers who witnessed his emergence and had been about to offer comment and even some unsolicited advice, instead stiffened to attention and remained rigidly at the salute until he had pulled on another boot and stamped away towards the reporting centre.

To Rommel, driving at a furious pace with the most advanced units of 21st Panzer, exhilaration at the prospect of victory was a continual urge to even greater effort, and by 1600 he was at the Wire near Gasr el Abid directing von Ravenstein up towards Halfaya without waiting for either the rest of the division, or even the presence of the official Corps Commander.

So General Cruewell, travelling well behind the leaders, was in fact both worried and annoyed by the time he arrived at Gasr el Abid an hour later.

He had not had nearly such an exciting journey as his Commander-in-Chief, perhaps because he lacked Rommel's optimistic temperament and flexibility of vision, but also because he had been able to watch those British and South African formations pushed aside by the column's spearhead rapidly reorganizing themselves and, indeed, causing casualties among the panzers in the second and third waves of the advance. Moreover, the further along the route he had travelled, the more evident it had become that whatever confusion the advance might be spreading in enemy ranks, an uncomfortable degree of disorganisation and disarray was now affecting his own.

The Afrika Korps now presented a decidedly ragged appearance, the prime cause being the speed of the head of the column resulting in growing attenuation in the body. In any column, even when speed of march is carefully controlled, concertina-ing is a well-known phenomenon – but when the speed at the head is continually increasing *as a result of direction at the head*, the tailing-out behind becomes more pronounced every minute. Had the distance to the Wire been much greater the separate parts of Afrika Korps would undoubtedly have lost not only contact, but also cohesion, and when Cruewell eventually reached Gasr el Abid it was to find his corps spread out from just south of Halfaya Pass back in a fifty-mile hook to Gabr Saleh, with a vehicle casualty rate for the day's advance to make him blench.

Panzer Regiment 5, which had led the column in the morning, had been forced to halt for refuelling back along the Trig el Abd (the lead had then been taken over, to the armour's mortification, by the infantry and artillery of Battlegroup Knabe now driving on up after von Ravenstein) and its first reports gave a figure of only thirty vehicles still in running order. Worse was to come, and four hours later at von Ravenstein's H.Q. Cruewell was faced with the fact that of the 170-odd panzers with which 21st Panzer Division had entered battle five days before, only four Pz IIs, fifteen Pz IIIs, one Pz IV and a command vehicle could still be considered battle-worthy! Panzer Regiment 8 with 15th Panzer had not suffered so severely, losing only seven tanks during the day's travel, but the division's Reconnaissance Battalion 33 had now lost all its remaining armoured cars – a revelation which threw a light of startling clarity on the effect of two days' violent action.

At last the details of the losses suffered the previous day in the attack on the 5th South African Brigade were emerging, and back at El Adem, Oberstleutnant Westphal was examining them with growing horror.

Over seventy panzers had been knocked out during the fighting on *Totensonntag* and even the Afrika Korps's recovery service could do nothing to help, for they were themselves now part of the 'Dash to the Wire' and (though Westphal did not yet know this) had been badly shot up by South African armoured cars and by low-flying aircraft; and this destruction of armour, in Westphal's opinion, did not even constitute the most crippling loss. It was the cost in senior and experienced officers and N.C.O.s which presented the darkest item in the balance sheet for *Totensonntag*, for Panzer Regiment 8 had lost two battalion commanders and five out of six of its company commanders, while many of the officers and N.C.O.s of Rifle Regiment 115 had been killed including the regimental commander and one battalion commander, and most of the remainder wounded. Figures for 21st Panzer were not so stark for they had been on the fringe of the *Totensonntag* fighting; but today they had been in the lead . . .

Oberstleutnant Westphal was by no means a happy man at the end of his first day as *de facto* commander of Panzergruppe Afrika, and his task of providing support to his Commander-in-Chief, by now some seventy miles away, was made more difficult by another piece of news which filtered through that evening. The Ariete Division, although they had started out more or less on time, had run full tilt into a large and stationary enemy formation well back along the Trig el Abd and were apparently unable to break through it, to push it aside or even to go around it. Il Duce's gesture of co-operation did not, in the circumstances, seem likely to aid the Afrika Korps to any immediately noticeable degree.

Not that Rommel was as yet aware of this. Even as Westphal was absorbing this latest piece of dire information, Rommel was issuing his orders for the following day by which he intended to destroy the remnants of Cunningham's army – an operation in which both Ariete and Trieste Divisions were meant to play crucial parts, as were non-existent cars of Reconnaissance Battalion 33:

> *Afrikakorps'* task is to co-operate with the [Italian] Motorized Corps, bottle up and destroy the enemy east of the Sollum front, west of the Sollum front and at Bardia. For this purpose 21 Panzer Division will swing east from the Sollum front; 15 Panzer will close the enemy's route southward, with half its forces on either side of the Wire and its centre in the Gasr el Abid area. Ariete will adjoin it on the west, with Trieste on the flank of Ariete. 21 and 15 Panzer will force the enemy into the minefields on the Sollum front and compel him to surrender. Reconnaissance Unit 33 will push forward to Habata to block the descent from the escarpment so that the enemy will be unable to use it for withdrawal or replenishment.[2]

Any modifications suggested by Cruewell on the grounds either of exhaustion of German forces or unreliability of Italian support were brushed aside, and he was persuaded to issue orders hurrying 15th Panzer and Reconnaissance Battalion 33 forward to their designated positions and then to set off himself, accompanied again by Bayerlein, to catch up with von Ravenstein and direct him to

concentrate his division in readiness for an attack at dawn next day
(November 25th) to 'drive the New Zealanders into the minefields'.

But of course, the New Zealanders were by now miles away to
the west and Rommel was 'building pictures', totally disregarding
unwelcome intelligence from any source. Convinced that XIII
Corps was still sandwiching his frontier garrisons between its Indian
half to the east and its New Zealand half to the west, and apparently
unaware that the Sidi Omar position, most of the Libyan Omar
position and all of Fort Capuzzo had been lost some thirty-six hours
before, he envisaged the formation of two more outside layers to
the sandwich with which he would squeeze the enemy infantry
between the concrete of the garrisons and the steel of Afrika Korps
and Ariete, blowing up any who might survive the pressure on the
double line of minefields stretching from Sidi Omar to Sollum.

And the state of mind which allowed Rommel to brush aside
unpalatable news and ignore such facts as overstrained logistics would
also not allow him to remain at even his advanced headquarters if
everyone else was further forward; so having dispatched Cruewell
northwards he then took Gause and his A.D.C. to drive eastwards
through the Wire, past a number of the rear units of 4th Indian
Division and in the general direction of Habata, possibly in search of
some of those British supply dumps which he had promised his
Quartermaster but which he had as yet signally failed to discover.

The search proved fruitless, and eventually he ordered a return
through the black, empty, early Egyptian night towards the Wire;
and some miles short of it, at about 2000, the car broke down and
no efforts on the part of any of the occupants could get it moving
again. They now became suddenly conscious of the fact that they
were to all intents and purposes lost in enemy territory, and that the
night, in addition to being dark and starless, was extremely cold.

Fortune, however, had not yet deserted Rommel. After about an
hour's acute discomfort, they heard the approach of a heavy vehicle
and to their gratified astonishment saw Cruewell's Mammoth
lumbering towards them out of the darkness on its way back from
von Ravenstein's headquarters. It was sheer coincidence that
brought them together in that virtually trackless expanse, and it was
with a degree of satisfaction that Bayerlein later related how
Rommel and Gause, shivering with cold, respectfully asked for a
lift.

But the night's adventures were by no means over for when they
reached the Wire they could find no gap through it, and the
Mammoth by itself was not the vehicle to force a passage. An
impatient Rommel then insisted on taking the wheel himself – but
to no purpose, and after spending some hours 'banging fruitlessly
against the Wire like a bewildered bee on a window-pane, even

Rommel gave in, and the accumulated authority of the *Panzergruppe* settled down for a night in the open desert'.[3]

The Mammoth had in fact hit the Wire well south of its destination and even Rommel's legendary sense of direction, according to Bayerlein, was of no effect.

To make matters worse they were in an area completely dominated by the enemy. Indian dispatch riders buzzed to and fro past the Mammoth, British tanks moved up forward and American-built lorries ground their way through the desert. None of them had any suspicion that the highest officers of the German–Italian Panzer Group were sitting in a captured command vehicle, often only two or three yards away. The ten officers and five men spent a restless night.[4]

But when daylight came, they soon established their position and drove sedately northwards to the Gap and through the Wire, doubtless watched on occasion by British and Indian junior ranks who had no intention of approaching a command vehicle of known British design (and the black German crosses had faded to virtual invisibility) and perhaps incurring the wrath of the high-ranking brass within.

Rommel and his senior commanders were back at Gasr el Abid by 0700.

To General Cunningham the events of the last two days had, not surprisingly, now composed themselves into a picture of almost unmitigated disaster made blacker by the euphoria of the previous period. If at midday on November 22nd he could still adopt at Norrie's headquarters an attitude of relative satisfaction with the progress of the battle – despite the criticism of the armour implied by his prognosis that the relief of Tobruk would probably have to be undertaken by the infantry of XIII Corps – by that evening, as news of the massacre of 7th Armoured Brigade at Sidi Rezegh came in, he was becoming sufficiently worried to urge Freyberg to send as much more of the New Zealand Division as he thought wise westwards towards Tobruk, leaving the 'minimum troops necessary' at the frontier to keep the Capuzzo–Bardia area under observation.

Freyberg's reaction to this was to take his 4th Brigade hurriedly after Barrowclough's 6th, leaving the 5th New Zealand Brigade around Bardia and Sollum. By the evening of *Totensonntag* he had established his own H.Q. at Bir el Chleta, the scene of the capture of Cruewell's.

Cunningham now decided to recast the *Crusader* plan fundamentally, giving Godwin-Austen not only responsibility for the relief of Tobruk, but also command of the Tobruk garrison, the 5th South

African Brigade and perhaps also of the 1st South Africans. Norrie's armour should guard the inner flank of the infantry and 'continue the destruction of the enemy armour'. But, even before the events of that Sunday afternoon were to reveal the hollowness of the premises upon which those orders were based, the figures of tank losses at Sidi Rezegh the previous day had so depressed Cunningham that he sent an urgent request to Cairo asking that Auchinleck should fly up at once.

That this request was not totally the result of momentary panic is demonstrated by the fact that Cunningham's B.G.S., the sardonic but undeviatingly resolute Brigadier Galloway, also telephoned his opposite number in Cairo about the same time, indicating that another influence at Eighth Army Headquarters would be necessary if the battle in Libya were not to get out of hand.

In the meantime, Cunningham had held a midday conference with Godwin-Austen at which he suggested that Norrie should be asked to decide either to break off the battle or to retire and stabilise on a line from Point 175 to Bir el Gubi, and even raised the question as to whether it was wise to continue *Operation Crusader* at all. As Godwin-Austen's corps was still virtually untouched, its commander reacted vigorously with the suggestion that now was the time to press forward with his infantry towards Tobruk, and as soon as Cunningham had left he made contact by radio-telephone with Norrie whom he found unruffled by events and confident of his ability to handle any immediately foreseeable situation.

No one on the British side, however, had foreseen the grim battle that took place that afternoon, and the destruction of the 5th South Africans and the immobilisation of 4th Armoured as a result of the amputation of their H.Q. were sufficient to dent (temporarily) even the imperturbability of Generals Freyberg and Godwin-Austen. The effect upon Cunningham was to convince him that *Operation Crusader* had been a failure. When Auchinleck descended from his aircraft at Maddalena that Sunday evening, Cunningham insisted that all forces in Libya should be withdrawn immediately in order to form a shield to keep Rommel from the Nile.

He found himself faced with friendly, cool but quite unyielding opposition from two strong men. Auchinleck had learned many years before the undoubted truth that nothing is either as good, or as bad, as it appears at first sight, and Galloway, as B.G.S. to General Wilson in Greece, had recently seen and weathered far worse situations than the one facing the British on the evening of *Totensonntag*. They could both accept the military realities of enormous tank losses in XXX Corps, but they also both saw that the unscathed XIII Corps – which itself contained over a hundred 'I' tanks in 1st Army Tank Brigade – was certainly capable of driving forward to Sidi Rezegh and Ed Duda and, if given the opportunity, perhaps of breaking into Tobruk and thus releasing the 'I' tanks of the 32nd Tank Brigade. And with Tobruk open both XXX and XIII Corps could be fed with Auchinleck's carefully husbanded reserves, with much greater speed and efficiency than across the open desert as at present.

What was needed, of course, was a firm grip at the top, and Auchinleck's presence was enough to provide it for the time being. By 2230 on *Totensonntag*, Cunningham had been sufficiently reassured as to issue orders instructing Godwin-Austen to push the New Zealanders further westwards (their 25th Battalion had taken Point 175 that afternoon during very heavy fighting with the Afrika Regiment) and to Norrie telling him to reorganise his remaining armour as quickly as possible and to use it to protect Dan Pienaar's South African brigade in the south and the New Zealanders in the north. Nevertheless, he still proclaimed in his instructions to Norrie that the main role of armoured forces was to destroy enemy tanks – an attitude with which both Auchinleck and Galloway agreed at that time – so an element of compartmentalisation was still present in the planning for the next day.

In the event, Rommel's 'Dash to the Wire' put paid to all Cunningham's plans and forced a greater degree of co-operation upon armour and infantry in the immediate neighbourhood than had been achieved before. But it also gave Cunningham's nerves an even more severe jolt, and the unkind ribaldry which greeted the news that many headquarters staffs had been forced to make hurried and undignified scrambles to safety reached its climax when it became known that Cunningham himself had escaped capture by the narrowest of margins.

He had visited Norrie's XXX Corps Advanced Headquarters that morning and then gone further forward to 7th Armoured Division's H.Q. where, in the words of one observer, he, Norrie and Gott settled down to 'cook up the next battle'. They had not been so engaged for very long when shells began to drop among the dispersed vehicles, whistles blew and everyone began throwing equipment into lorries and driving smartly away. Brigadier Clifton, XXX Corps's Chief Engineer, drove Cunningham at furious speed across hummocky desert and through a 'thickening mob of runaways' back to the Advanced H.Q. airstrip, where the pilot was already revving up the engines as Cunningham arrived. He then took off before his passenger was comfortably seated (missing a lorry crossing the airfield by about three inches as he did so) and from that moment the Eighth Army Commander had little to do but watch the stampede of vehicles taking place underneath him and reflect upon the perils of a military career. But not for long afterwards; he arrived back at his own H.Q. to find that Auchinleck had spent the morning in calm analysis of the situation and had drawn up the following document:

To:– Lieut.-General Sir Alan Cunningham,
　　　　　K.C.B., D.S.O., M.C.
　　Commander,
　　EIGHTH ARMY.

1. Having discussed the situation with you and learned from you the weak state to which 7th Armoured Division has been reduced by the past five days' fighting, I fully realize that to continue our offensive may result in the immobilization, temporarily at any rate, of all our cruiser and American M3 tanks.

2. I realize also that should, as a result of our continued offensive, the enemy be left with a superiority of fast moving tanks, there is a risk that he may try to outflank our advanced formations in the Sidi Rezegh–Gambut area and cut them off from their bases in Egypt. I realize also that in this event, there would remain only very weak forces to oppose an enemy advance into Egypt. On the other hand, it is clear to me that after the fighting of the last few days, it is most improbable that the enemy will be able to stage a major advance for some time to come.

3. There are only two courses open to us:
　(i) To break off the battle and stand on the defensive either on the line Gambut–Gabr Saleh or on the frontier. This is a possible solution as it is unlikely that the enemy would be able to mount a strong offensive against us for many weeks and would enable us to retain much of the ground we have gained, including valuable forward landing grounds. On the other hand it would be counted as an Axis triumph and would entail abandoning for an indefinite time the relief of Tobruk.
　(ii) The second course is to continue to press our offensive with every means in our power.
　There is no possible doubt that the second is the right and only course. The risks involved in it must be accepted.

4. You will therefore:
　(i) Continue to attack the enemy relentlessly using all your resources even to the last tank.
　(ii) Your main immediate object will be as always to destroy the enemy tank forces.

    (iii) Your ultimate object remains the conquest of Cyrenaica and then an advance on Tripoli.

5. To achieve the objects set out in para. 4 it seems essential tha you should:

    (i) Recapture the Sidi Rezegh–Duda ridge at the earlies possible moment and join hands with Tobruk garrison. I is to my mind essential that the Tobruk garrison shoulc co-operate to the utmost limit of their resources in thi; operation.

    (ii) Direct the Oasis Force at the *earliest possible momen* against the coast road to stop all traffic on it and if possible capture Jedbaya or Benina, neither of which is strongly held apparently.

    (iii) Use the Long Range Desert Group patrols offensively to the limit of their endurance against every possible objective on the enemy lines of communication from Mechili to Benghazi, Jedbaya and beyond to the west. All available armoured cars should be used with the utmost boldness to take part in this offensive. The advantages to be gained by a determined effort against the enemy lines of communication are worth immense risks which will be taken

C. J. Auchinleck
General
C.-in-C. M.E.F.[5]

In the circumstances reigning at the Maddalena Headquarters a noon on November 24th, even the ebullient Dan Pienaar woulc have hesitated to question so lucid and explicit a direction, and repressing his doubts, Cunningham loyally set about expediting hi; Commander-in-Chief's intentions. Another trip to Godwin Austen's H.Q. reassured all concerned that a XIII Corps drive to Tobruk would be supported at all levels, but the trip back took Cunningham over a triple column of Axis transport moving eastwards from Gabr Saleh, which worried him again until he hac returned to the reflective calm engendered by Auchinleck's presence.

By now, darkness had fallen, Rommel's car had broken down (less than thirty miles from where Auchinleck was sitting), von Ravenstein was planning the drive intended to take him north past Halfaya Pass towards Capuzzo, Cruewell was on his way back to Gasr el Abid; and back in the desert reaches lining the Trig el Abd, Allied and Axis formations were still blundering about trying to avoid each other and find their own friends. Typical among the adventures of that confused night were those of the remnants of 7th

60 Brigadier Armstrong, whose 5th South African Brigade were destroyed on *Totensonntag*, talking to Field Marshal Smuts

61 Brigadier Pienaar, whose 1st South African Brigade could do nothing but stand by and watch

62 The Tobruk Corridor formed – 'for whatever it was worth'. The link-up at Ed Duda.

63 *Above*, the Tomb of Sidi Rezegh. 64 *Below*, Generalmajor Böttcher, Rommel, and his brilliant intelligence officer, Major von Mellenthin.

65 Sidi Rezegh, November 22nd, 1941. The litter of burning trucks and smashed panzers, of grey- and khaki-clad corpses, which made up the desolation of the battlefield.

66 The immediate riposte, January 1942: artillery turning

67 *Above*, the Panzergruppe moving forward again. 68 *Below*, Panzer IV in the lead.

69–70 The heroic figures of *Crusader*. *Above*, Major the Reverend Wilhelm Bach upon his surrender. *Below*, Major-General Jock Campbell talks to Auchinleck after receiving the Victoria Cross.

Support Group and 7th Armoured Brigade, who had been ordered to move south across the Trig el Abd and reach Field Maintenance Centre 62 which, like No. 63 even further south, had been completely missed by Rommel's drive. According to the Rifle Brigade historian, the whole march was a nightmare:

It was pitch dark. The column which formed up, close together and four abreast, contained various extraneous elements. Jock Campbell sat astride the bonnet of his armoured command vehicle, hoarse with energy expended, so that his voice reverberated like a ghost's whenever the engines were turned off. At intervals Very lights would go up, showing that there were parties of Germans in every direction. The column moved by fits and starts. At halts other vehicles would be heard approaching, sometimes the ghastly clanking of tanks, quite unidentifiable until they were right on top of the column. Once a German motor-cyclist shot through the column and away before anyone could engage him. One party of Germans met our column about half-way up and in the confusion and shooting and excitement many vehicles went astray. But as dawn broke the Support Group found themselves on the edge of the vast dump on which the continuance of the offensive depended. The Germans in their rush towards the wire had left it a few miles to their south.[6]

Gradually, during the night, groups sorted themselves out, formations coalesced and attained some degree of internal re-organisation, headquarter units found their subordinate echelons and sometimes even found their generals – though Norrie, who had spent most of the day driving around with Gott, is reported to have remarked pensively that there was much to be said for fighting a battle with only an A.D.C. in attendance as it saved so much paperwork.

But by the morning of the 25th, a great deal of both literal and figurative dust had settled, and if the mixture of German combatant and British non-combatant units east of the Wire was still confused and lacking sound direction, the British, South African and New Zealand fighting units west of the Wire were settling themselves down and making ready to continue the battle. For them, Rommel's 'Dash to the Wire' had been of almost unalloyed benefit.

Two brigades of the New Zealanders – the 4th and the 6th – were by now driving westwards together towards Tobruk, the 4th along the Trig Capuzzo and the valley on each side, and the 6th along the Sidi Rezegh ridge. At dawn on the 25th, the 4th Brigade had reached Zaafran, and the 6th, after a hard battle for a blockhouse some two miles west of Point 175 which had further reduced their strength, already severely diminished by the fighting on *Totensonntag* for Point 175, sent their 26th Battalion on and across the landing-field 'littered with the wreckage of German and Italian planes, burnt-out and abandoned tanks, a few trucks and some field guns'.

Late in the morning came more orders from Godwin-Austen. With Rommel and the Afrika Korps engaged around the frontier, now was the time for the link-up with the Tobruk garrison, and the first move for the New Zealanders would be to occupy the dominating heights in the area – Zaafran itself, Belhammed, Ed Duda and the length of the Sidi Rezegh ridge. General Freyberg, perhaps with memories of infantry fighting in 1918 and certainly with a sceptical attitude towards the tactics adopted so far by the armour, decided that night should provide the cover for his eager troops to go in with the bayonet, leaving Matildas and Valentines to follow in a supporting role. At 2100 six battalions crossed their start lines.

Freyberg's faith in his men's courage was certainly justified, but darkness and broken country over which no reconnaissance had been carried out form a recipe for confusion, and both brigades ran into trouble. Headquarters of 4th Brigade veered too far right and found themselves at one point on the Via Balbia and out of touch with their battle formations which were engaged in vicious (and eventually successful) fighting on the summit of Belhammed; 6th Brigade ran into the Bersaglieri around the Sidi Rezegh tomb, and these fought them off with such determination that two of the attacking battalions found themselves floundering down the Escarpment on to the Trig Capuzzo (from which they had to crawl back up the wadis the following day) while the other two battalions were still pinned down on the landing-ground at dawn. It looked as though 26th November would be a bad day for the Kiwis.

However, General Scobie's men inside the Tobruk perimeter were as anxious as ever to escape the increasing claustrophobia of life within the perimeter, and more especially in the 'appendix' which had been formed during their first break-out attempt. The code-names of the Axis strong-points which had been the targets for the first drive had been changed, for security reasons, to those of the more squashily-sentimental characters of a well-known film, and 'Doc', 'Bashful', 'Happy' and 'Sneezy' had all been bloodily eliminated during the previous week; and while 4th New Zealanders had been wresting Belhammed from Group Böttcher, a combined armour and infantry attack had ejected the Bologna Division from 'Grumpy'. A counter-attack was beaten off during the morning of the 26th, and by midday the thirty-seven Matildas, fourteen cruisers and twenty light tanks of 32nd Army Tank Brigade under Brigadier

Willison, supported by the 25-pounders of 1st R.H.A., were poised on the edge of 'Bashful' for the four-mile plunge across the desert to Ed Duda.

In all, it took them just short of an hour and a half, during which time they were subject to sporadic and almost random shelling from various points in a quadrant from below Belhammed to just west of Ed Duda, but very little from Ed Duda itself where units of Trieste Division seem to have been taken by surprise – and by 1320, muffled in a thick dust-cloud, the Matildas were on top of the feature for which both the Tobruk garrison and Norrie's armour had been aiming for days, with advanced patrols down to the Trig Capuzzo and infantry of the 1st Essex Battalion coming up in support.

From four miles away to the east, the pinned-down New Zealanders watched not only the capture of Ed Duda but also the excellent fighter cover provided by the R.A.F., followed by direct bombing support by Marylands of the S.A.A.F. which, however spectacular it might have been, was misdirected and fell upon the advancing Essex who lost half their carrier platoon as a result.

Nevertheless, the excitement of beating off the inevitable German counter-attacks on Belhammed and the news of the taking of Ed Duda was enough to spur the New Zealanders to even greater efforts, and that night 6th Battalion went in again with the bayonet in what their historian called 'the hardest, bloodiest and most deadly attack ever staged by our unit'. By morning on November 27th, the whole of the Sidi Rezegh ridge was in New Zealand hands, the 9th Bersaglieri were wiped out as a fighting unit and the 26th New Zealand Battalion had lost another eighty-four men.

But their 19th Battalion, accompanied by tanks of the 44th R.T.R., had flanked the main opposition and marched through the night to Ed Duda. Just before midnight, the link-up with the Tobruk garrison was made and the 'Tobruk Corridor' had been formed – 'for whatever', as the South African historians say, 'it was worth'.

Further west at El Adem, Oberstleutnant Westphal was watching developments with ever-increasing anxiety. He had been unable to communicate with either his Commander-in-Chief or the commander of the Afrika Korps for over twenty-four hours, the only wireless link still open being to von Ravenstein who was as ignorant of Rommel's whereabouts as Westphal himself. Aircraft sent out to find Rommel had failed to return or even to report back (they had been shot down by marauding R.A.F. fighters) and Westphal had an uncomfortable feeling that dispatch riders or even escorted Staff Officers sent to establish communication would likewise disappear. All through November 25th and 26th, he had been sending signals via 21st Panzer to Rommel and Cruewell until, apparently despairing of ever receiving answer or even acknowledgment from the highest level, he sent a résumé of the situation to von Ravenstein late on the afternoon of November 26th, suggesting that 21st Panzer Division at least had better move as quickly as possible towards Tobruk and attack the New Zealanders from the rear before the whole of the Tobruk front disintegrated.

Von Ravenstein, tired of sitting in the Egyptian desert out of touch with both Corps and Army Commander, moved with admirable celerity, slipping between 4th Indian formations and the New Zealanders of 5th Brigade at Capuzzo, around and into Bardia where he intended to refuel and refill his ammunition racks before continuing towards Tobruk. To his surprise, he met 15th Panzer just as they were emerging from the fortress, having gone in for exactly the same reasons, and some hours later he discovered that Rommel was there as well. Feeling with some justification that he had done rather well to extricate himself from Egypt so smartly, von Ravenstein reported to his Commander-in-Chief, to be greeted at once with astonishment and rage. Roundly declaring at first that the message von Ravenstein had received had been nothing but an enemy ruse, Rommel then took such strong exception to Westphal's action that that officer's career was undoubtedly in the balance for several days – until, in fact, Rommel reached El Adem and could examine the situation maps and read the reports upon which Westphal's decision had been made; after which he apparently made no comment but went to lie down for a few hours, never mentioning the matter again.

But in the meantime, his attention had been drawn back towards the crucial area, and during the early hours of November 27th he spent some time drawing up plans for the renewal of the Battle of Sidi Rezegh, and the destruction of yet another large formation of Dominion troops. By 0200 the first directives were sent out, ordering the dispatch westward along the Via Balbia of von Ravenstein's H.Q. and Battlegroup Knabe, and Neumann-Sylkow to clear up the situation on the frontier as quickly as possible and then to follow von Ravenstein for a combined attack on the New Zealanders.

A note of protest was struck by Neumann-Sylkow at the time schedules to which he was expected to move but Rommel insisted upon a further attack on the frontier positions before 15th Panzer returned to Tobruk. There then followed such a sequence of events as to cause the student of military affairs to wonder if there is much point in careful planning.

Panzer Regiment 8 moved off towards Sidi Azeiz, again became thoroughly entangled with 21st Panzer Division outside Bardia, extricated itself after the loss of much valuable time and then moved on. At 0600, Neumann-Sylkow received from Westphal an impassioned signal, 'C-in-C cannot be contacted at moment. *Panzergruppe* orders your immediate start to relieve the Tobruk front. Situation grave. *Achtung!*' – which, in the circumstances, he ignored, moving off instead after his panzer regiment who were already, much to his surprise, reporting a strong enemy force in front of them.

There then followed a sharp and bitter fight during which 15th Panzer Division captured some 800 prisoners, a huge supply dump of whose existence Panzergruppe had been unaware, six field guns and the entire headquarters of 5th New Zealand Brigade including its commander, Brigadier Hargest. And while they were counting their spoils, Rommel, at last convinced of the danger threatening to the west, arrived to cancel his previous orders and dispatch the bulk of the division back towards Tobruk. 'Order, counter-order . . . ' had thus resulted not in 'disorder' but in a very handsome profit.

Still stranded much further south at Gasr el Abid, Cruewell was at this time completely in the dark as to even the whereabouts, let alone the objectives, of his armoured divisions, neither had he any late news of the position around Tobruk although he suspected this to be serious. He therefore decided to move up towards Sidi Azeiz where he hoped to find at least some of his units. On the way up he unexpectedly came across the Ariete Division which had the previous evening managed to disengage itself from the force blocking its route down the Trig el Abd (Dan Pienaar's 1st South Africans) and set out towards the frontier. Cruewell found the Ariete artillery busily shelling the post at Bir Ghirba, but on his own responsibility he instructed the division to break off the action and proceed at once towards Tobruk – an order which came as a relief to the headquarters of the Savona Division who had been the only occupants of Bir Ghirba for weeks past.

Later that day the last Afrika Korps detachment – Group Wechmar, which on the morning of the 25th had been ordered south along the Wire to mask the activities of the Oasis group at Jarabub but had never moved because of petrol shortage – after an abortive attack on the Indians at Sidi Omar was also ordered up to Sidi Azeiz, then to follow 15th Panzer westwards; and so the 'Dash to the Wire', 'Rommel's Swan' or 'The Matruh Stakes' as the venture became variously known to the more irreverent of Eighth Army's junior ranks, came to an end, its sole tangible result the fortuitous capture during its dying spasms of 5th New Zealand Headquarters.

It did, however, have another, less concrete but more significant result. To borrow a metaphor from a distinguished authority on the Afrika Korps, Mr Ronald Lewin, the spectacular nature of the Afrika Korps manoeuvrings was itself throwing up its own anti-bodies, first in the form of the grip which Auchinleck had taken on the battle at a crucial juncture, and now in that of a change of command which Auchinleck felt himself compelled to make.

During the morning of the 25th had come news to Maddalena of the advance of a large panzer formation southwards towards them from Gasr el Abid. This was, in fact, Panzer Regiment 5 looking for a gap in the Wire through which it could make its way up to join its commander, but to Cunningham and his staff it looked rather like a direct attack on themselves, and all agreed that Auchinleck's presence there constituted an unnecessary risk. The Commander-in-Chief was therefore hurried away aboard an aircraft, and on the long flight back to Cairo he had had ample time for reflection. Twice he had listened to exhortations from Cunningham in which extreme anxiety had been the keynote, twice he had had to use his authority to calm exaggerated fears, to overrule the Army Com-mander's suggestions and to insist that the battle should continue – and although Cunningham had immediately and loyally accepted the directions which Auchinleck had given him, there was little doubt that those directions were now being obeyed by a man who held reservations as to their wisdom.

Cunningham's mind, in fact, had been set by recent circum-stances into a *defensive* mould and he was endeavouring to obey *offensive* instructions. It was hardly a pattern for success. The atmosphere when Auchinleck had left Maddalena, if not one of panic, was decidedly one of 'flap' – a state of affairs which must be put right and not be allowed to recur, so a new figure must be placed at the head of Eighth Army.

But who? The next senior officer in the theatre was Godwin-Austen and after him was Norrie – but to change Corps Com-mander at this juncture would surely be even more upsetting than changing the Army Commander. One change at that level was bad enough, two could be disastrous.

The ideal of course would be for Auchinleck to take over himself, but, aware that his eyes must continually sweep a wider horizon than just that of the Libyan theatre, he concluded that he must appoint instead a man of his own cast of mind, not only already imbued with his own ideas but also fully cognisant of his plans for the immediate future; someone, in fact, already on his Staff.

His choice fell on Major-General Neil Ritchie, then Deputy Chief of the General Staff at the Cairo Headquarters – a big, cheerful, beefy man of conventional military looks who had already commanded the famous 51st Highland Division after its re-formation after Dunkirk, and had since served very efficiently on the Staff. He would have been a natural choice for promotion to Corps Commander had such an opening been available but now he would have under him two Corps Commanders each of longer service than he was. In the circumstances, they would undoubtedly understand and support him, and his appointment as Army Commander would, at least until he had proved himself, be temporary.

The change-over took place at Maddalena in the early afternoon of November 26th, and General Cunningham flew back to Cairo in the plane which had brought Ritchie up; after which Cunningham went into hospital suffering from severe exhaustion.

It seemed at first that Ritchie had taken over at a most propitious moment, for that evening the link-up at Ed Duda occurred and by the morning of the 27th it had become evident that the tank strength of XXX Corps was higher than could have been expected. Industrious recovery on the battlefield together with some excellent work by the Tank Delivery Section had raised the strength of Gatehouse's 4th Armoured Brigade to 77 Honeys, while 22nd was now possessed of 42 assorted cruisers. These 119 tanks, however, comprised the sum total of 7th Armoured Division's tank strength, for the survivors of 7th Armoured Brigade had retired to the Delta and the formation was not to see action in North Africa again.

But with this reinforcement and reorganisation, both Norrie and Gott felt that the time had come for XXX Corps to re-enter the battle, and for a start the armour should do something about the strong enemy column reported moving along the Trig Capuzzo. From Bir Sciafsciuf 22nd Armoured should move down the Escarpment and form an ambush to stop the head of the column, while from Bir Berraneb twenty miles to the south 4th Armoured's Honeys should race up as quickly as possible and attack the main enemy body which they should catch strung out on the road; and in order to clear up the area behind the frontier and ensure that no significant German force was lurking behind the main battleground, the Support Group should send out various columns from Gabr Saleh in a fan from Sidi Omar up to Gasr el Arid. In other words, a degree of concentration in the north and dispersion to the east was ordered.

Scott-Cockburn's Crusaders were in position by 1330 and in action by 1342, their hulls well screened in wadis, their 2-pounder anti-tank guns effective against the armoured cars and soft-skinned transport at the head of Neumann-Sylkow's force, and their attached eight 25-pounders enough to keep the panzers back for a while; and just as the inevitable and efficient German redeployment was likely to bring overwhelming pressure against them, the

Honeys of 4th Armoured appeared over the ridge and began pouring their shot in against the flank. Further back, Major Crisp even took his troops down the Escarpment and wrought a degree of havoc among the supply train until two *Batterien* swung their barrels around and effectively drove them off; and even while this was happening Hurricanes and Marylands of the R.A.F. and S.A.A.F. arrived overhead and caused many casualties and much damage to 15th Panzer's already exiguous transport.

Ritchie had kept well in touch with developments despite the distance between Trig Capuzzo and Maddalena, and now made his first personal intervention in the *Crusader* operation at 1845 by signalling XXX Corps that it was imperative that the sealing operation by the armour was continued and that 15th Panzer was prevented from all further advance westward and, should they attempt it, southwards as well across the ridge.

Unfortunately, his instruction arrived after darkness had fallen, at which point the British armour had followed their usual practice of breaking off the action and retiring some five miles southwards into the desert. Surprised and extremely gratified, 15th Panzer had pressed forward again and, despite losses during the day (not excessive for six hours of battle) covered another seven miles, thus reaching their day's objective before calling a halt. They were then almost next door to the New Zealanders' B Echelon, and as Cruewell had by this time ordered 21st Panzer to come across from the Via Balbia and Ariete were coming up also from Sidi Azeiz, Freyberg's men were very soon going to find themselves under extreme pressure.

By this time, 4th New Zealand Brigade with the 'I' tanks of 44th R.T.R. were at Belhammed, 6th Brigade held the Sidi Rezegh ridge between Point 175 and the Tomb, while the infantry and tanks of the garrison were at Ed Duda and by a singular coincidence of objective not previously much in evidence at any stage or level during *Crusader*, the headquarters of the New Zealand Division, of XIII Corps and of 1st Army Tank Brigade were all clustered together on the Trig Capuzzo at the eastern end of the New Zealand positions. Much time was being spent trying to eliminate small German units between Belhammed and the Sidi Rezegh escarpment, and 24th and 26th Battalions of 6th Brigade reluctantly concluded that after their quite heavy casualties of the previous two days they were unable to occupy the southern escarpment upon which the regiments and most of the artillery of Group Böttcher were congregated, west of Bu Creimisa. The New Zealanders therefore spent the night of November 27th/28th clearing up their area, burying their dead, resting and preparing for the morrow with a fair degree of confidence. They were for the most part unaware of the danger threatening from the east, and considered that their next move would be either into Tobruk or on towards El Adem. In any case, if serious fighting became necessary again, 1st South African Brigade were somewhere close at hand to the south and would be joining them soon.

During November 28th, in fact, little fighting took place around Sidi Rezegh – an advance from the southern escarpment by the infantry of Group Böttcher collected another 200 New Zealanders and reduced the strength of 24th Battalion to about 100 men, while to the south of Sciafsciuf the British armour, somewhat disgruntled by the manner in which Panzer Regiment 8 had pressed on the previous evening instead of waiting for the next day's play, attacked sporadically in the late afternoon, lost several more of 22nd Armoured's cruisers and then retired again into the desert as darkness fell. Further east, Support Group's Jock Columns felt that they had had a hugely successful day, having made offensive moves against Ariete and the tail of 15th Panzer and watched them both disappear westwards – though Italian reports do not mention the attacks, claiming that they were moving instead in accord with Cruewell's instructions, while Heinz Schmidt, commanding two rearguard companies of the 15th Panzer, remarks:

> The desert was alive with small mobile columns of the enemy – 'Jock Columns' they were called – which were a nuisance, as mosquitoes are, but in the end no more violent in their sting. They were never really strong enough to do irreparable damage.[7]

That night, in view of the evident build-up of German pressure westwards along both the Trig Capuzzo and the ridge, the three British headquarter formations threaded their way along the valley past Belhammed and into the comparative haven of Tobruk, Godwin-Austen signalling his safe arrival to Ritchie, 'Corridor to Tobruk perfectly secure and open to passage our troops and will be kept so. Have arrived there without incident. Press may now be informed that Tobruk is as relieved as I am.'

Conditions were not, however, as cosy as that message may seem to indicate, if only because of the appalling weather conditions. Much further south the 1st South Africans were engaged in a series of peripatetics of which historians have since found difficulty in making much sense:

> We bedded down at night under four blankets and although we were fully dressed and wearing greatcoats and balaclava helmets, the icy wind swept right through us. We got filthier every day. Even if we could have spared water for washing it was too cold to undress . . . rations were finished. We [his section] lived for days

on rice begged from passing Indians, and biscuits ground to powder, with which we made a hot, tasteless porridge that warmed our insides for an hour or two . . . [8]

It was all a far cry from the popular picture of golden sand dunes, green oases and tropical heat.

The day was not totally devoid of significant events, however. After an absence of four days, Rommel had returned to Panzergruppe Headquarters at El Adem and was securely back in command again, intent upon resealing the Tobruk perimeter, reopening the Battle of Sidi Rezegh and destroying the New Zealanders.

The first move in the battle began late the following morning (November 29th) when 15th Panzer, which had climbed the Escarpment east of Point 175, swept down the Sidi Rezegh valley to turn north around Abiar el Amar in a move reversing the sequence with which 21st Panzer had opened their first attack on the airfield seven days before. By mid-afternoon they were facing north-east towards the defences of Ed Duda, which consisted of the infantry of 1st Essex, 2nd/13th Australians, a company of 1st Royal Northumberland machine-gunners and twenty-six 'I' tanks of 4th R.T.R. all under command of Lieutenant-Colonel Walter O'Carroll of the R.T.R. In a three-hour attack, the leading panzers rolled over two companies of the unfortunate Essex infantrymen, destroyed all the anti-tank guns in the area and knocked out fifteen tanks, but fortunately for O'Carroll, just behind his headquarters was a battery of Royal Horse Artillery. When, shortly after 1700, the panzers advanced again, they found themselves pinned down by a storm of fire which took them totally by surprise.

Map 26   The ordeal of the New Zealand division: November 28th–December 1st, 1941

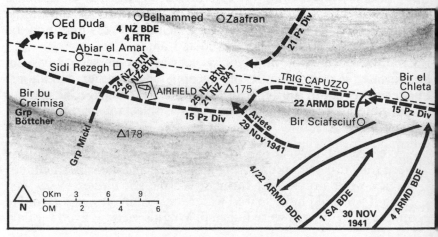

Moreover, the bombardment increased as darkness thickened, for Brigadier Willison arrived and decided that shock tactics alone would rectify the situation. Just before midnight, after yet another crashing barrage from the R.H.A., the eleven remaining tanks of 4th R.T.R. lined up abreast with only a foot between their horns and advanced directly forwards with every gun firing as fast as it could be reloaded and two companies of Australians charging with the bayonet immediately behind. By 0200, the Essex positions were re-established, 167 German prisoners were being led back towards Tobruk and the bodies of many more littered the area. Panzer Regiment 8 had been bloodily repulsed and the Tobruk 'Appendix' still existed.

At the eastern end of the New Zealand pocket, November 29th had brought mixed fortunes to the defenders. Just after dawn they had been astonished by the approach of a convoy of about 200 unidentifiable trucks and lorries which made its last run to the New Zealanders' position under the impartial artillery fire of both sides. It proved then to be a supply column brought up by XXX Corps's indefatigable Chief Engineer, Brigadier Clifton, who had disdained such aids to travel as recognised tracks and driven through the night in a roughly northerly direction, confident that he would hit the Escarpment eventually as long as he avoided the German leaguers, illuminated as usual by their unending flare pattern. When he came to the Escarpment, he just led the convoy straight down it, vehicles crashing from rock to rock and slithering down the scree slopes with remarkably few total catastrophes, though none of the vehicles was ever quite the same again, a qualification also applicable to the drivers. But they brought Freyberg's men much-needed food and ammunition, eight armoured cars, two anti-tank guns and seventeen Honeys intended for Gatehouse's brigade which remained for the moment in the pocket.

Then came an even more unexpected bonus.

Just after 0800, an outpost of 21st Battalion on Point 175 was surprised to see approaching them a German staff car which, when but twenty yards away, obligingly pulled up so that its occupants could make inquiries as to their position from what they obviously expected to be friendly troops. The New Zealanders quickly disabused them of their illusion, and when they inspected their haul, found that they had captured an obviously high-ranking German officer who gave his name and rank, perhaps unimaginatively, as Colonel Schmidt, together with his driver, 'a tin of Aulsebrook's biscuits, some cartons of South African cigarettes, a case of Crosse and Blackwell's tinned delicacies, a bottle of Greek brandy, and a jar of rum' – plus an extensively annotated map showing German and Italian positions and a collection of papers which revealed among other things the daily cipher changes for 21st Panzer Division for the next few days.

Retaining such items as they did not consider of great military significance, the fortunate members of the outpost sent the staff car and personnel onwards to Divisional Headquarters, where German etiquette promptly betrayed the unfortunate 'Colonel Schmidt'. Confronted with General Freyberg, he saluted, clicked his heels together, bowed shortly and announced, 'Von Ravenstein, General!'

He was the first high-ranking Afrika Korps officer to become a casualty of the *Crusader* operation, and proved such a charming and honourable man that everyone who met him was glad that he had not become the victim of a more fatal miscalculation.

Throughout the day, however, there was one continual disappointment for the New Zealanders in the non-arrival of Dan Pienaar's 1st South Africans, whose assistance had been promised and whose appearance was expected hourly by every one of Freyberg's men with some of the eagerness of beleaguered Western pioneers awaiting the U.S. Cavalry. This gave rise in the early evening to an unfortunate and even ludicrous episode when 21st Battalion on Point 175 was informed that a column, 'probably the South Africans', was approaching from the east, and the men swarmed out to give a warm welcome to high-turreted vehicles which they assumed to be Marmon-Harrington armoured cars. These proved, however, to be the leading tanks of the Ariete, the Italian commanders standing in open turrets waving their berets in the equally mistaken belief that Point 175 was held by *their* allies – and it was probably the enthusiasm of the welcome which astonished the Italians and made them the first to appreciate the true situation; another 200 New Zealanders found themselves 'in the bag' as a result.

The Ariete also took over a fully equipped New Zealand field hospital which had been captured the previous day by the Germans. It must be said that their treatment of the 1,000 patients and 400 medical personnel entirely lacked the chivalry with which the original captors had behaved.

As for the 1st South Africans, a curious malaise seems to have affected them, and also the remaining British armour in 4th and 22nd Brigades.

Admittedly the experiences of Dan Pienaar's South Africans so far in *Operation Crusader* had been unlikely to inspire confidence either in the higher direction of the battle or in their own fortune. Their journey across the frontier had been a nightmare, the first operational order they had received after arrival in the battle area had been to undertake a task – the elimination of the Ariete at El Gubi – at which the 22nd Armoured Brigade at its full strength had failed, and of the subsequent modification of the order one of the critics of the battle has since written, 'It would be interesting to have some enlightenment on the tactics which should be adopted by an infantry brigade when called upon to "mask" a hostile armoured division in the desert.'

Nevertheless, they had taken up static positions around Bir el Gubi where they had been subject to sporadic shelling and occasionally fierce Stuka attacks for three days, until given the order to move up close to the 5th Brigade – a night move despite their previous experience, and one which Pienaar again caused to be modified. And from the position in which the modified order left them on the morning of *Totensonntag* they had witnessed the destruction of their brother South Africans – a sobering experience which strengthened Pienaar's determination that his 'boys', as he affectionately referred to the troops under his command, should not be unnecessarily exposed to risk.

Like the 'Pals' Battalions' of the First World War, many South African formations were composed of men all from one district, and when the news of the destruction of the 5th Brigade reached home, there would be many localities plunged into deep mourning. Dan Pienaar had no intention of allowing the same pall of sorrow to blanket the areas of Natal and the Transvaal from which the 1st Brigade men came – a natural feeling with which one can sympathise, though not one likely to lead to speedy victory in battle. As a result of these sentiments, Pienaar repeatedly interpreted orders in such a way as to keep his men away from the battle areas, a course he was enabled to follow both by the astounding degree of ambiguity in the phrasing of the orders he received, and the marked reluctance of British senior commanders at this time to press their demands too hard upon Dominion troops.

After *Totensonntag*, 1st Brigade had moved to Bir Taieb el Esem, south of the Trig el Abd, where they had missed the rush of 'Rommel's Swan' but then found themselves blocking the route of the Ariete, a situation in which both formations appear to have found some satisfaction, for they remained virtually static for twenty-four hours doing little but shell each other at comparatively long ranges, while the Ariete M13s and the South African armoured cars manoeuvred circumspectly between. The appearance of the Italian tanks was enough, however, to cause Pienaar to send out signals indicating heavy engagement and requesting armoured support, with the result that Alec Gatehouse was sent across with Honeys from his brigade and two batteries of R.H.A., arriving, according to one South African account:

. . . just in time . . . in sailed Brig Alex [*sic*] Gatehouse, that gay cavalier of the armour. His top-booted legs dangled from the turret-top, a Scots plaid travelling rug lay across his knees, for the day was cold; later one was to see Gatehouse with that rug belted round his waist like a kilt, riding into battle seated in an arm-chair strapped to the top of a tank. Gatehouse of the heavy head, the hawk nose and deep-set eyes, was a man after Pienaar's heart, and in later days he often remarked: 'Alec Gatehouse is a great tank commander, the best in the Desert – I will fight with him anywhere in tanks.'⁹

This encomium did not, apparently, strike any responsive chord in Gatehouse's breast; much later he was to write of his arrival at Taieb el Esem that he 'could see nothing which justified the prevailing view that we were "just in time". Nor did I see any signs . . . that the 1 S.A. Bde had already been fiercely attacked twice that morning . . . Brigadier Dan Pienaar was, in my opinion, in a highly excitable state, and it was very difficult to discover what he wanted . . . '¹⁰

What he wanted was to get his brigade out of whatever danger they then stood in. That night, despite repeated orders to stand firm and, to use his divisional commander General Brink's words, 'scrag them [the Ariete] hard', he pulled out in pitch darkness, made a highly efficient night march south to the protection of the nearest Field Maintenance Centre – and let Ariete through to the frontier.

This occurred on November 26th, and on the evening of the following day began the series of signals intended to move 1st South African Brigade up to the assistance of the New Zealanders on the Sidi Rezegh ridge.

It is a fascinating and, at this remove, entertaining, exercise to follow the movements of 1st South African Brigade during the next few days (unless, perhaps, you are a New Zealander). Orders to move them nearer to the battle area seem to have arrived almost invariably either too late or not at all, those ordering a change of direction or suggesting a temporary halt being acted upon with remarkable celerity; and there were also several clashes with hostile forces which have found no mention in German or Italian histories but which – according to Pienaar's later accounts – further delayed the South African arrival at Sidi Rezegh.

But no means all the responsibility for the extension of the New Zealanders' ordeal on the ridge rests in South African hands. On one occasion, Norrie halted a South African move on receipt of a signal from Godwin-Austen of which no trace has subsequently been found, and early on the morning of the 29th, Pienaar received the following signal from XXX Corps:

Information Rome [Point 175] area obscure. Your task join Bernard [General Freyberg] earliest but do NOT repeat NOT move from present position until contacted Bernard's boys with own recce and consider move feasible.[11]

It was late in the afternoon before one of the South African armoured cars made contact with the New Zealanders, and Freyberg's immediate request that Pienaar move as quickly as possible to Point 175 was negated by the arrival there instead of the Ariete; so 1st South Africans again remained where they were, despite further instructions from Freyberg (under whose command they had now been placed) that they were to press on and either recapture Point 175 or by-pass it and enter the pocket by another route. Unfortunately, in the early evening, wireless communication between the two bodies of Dominion troops broke down before Pienaar could explain fully the reasons why such a move would be impracticable; and indeed, Freyberg was to die many years later without thoroughly appreciating them.

General Ritchie had also felt that the early presence of 1st South Africans at Sidi Rezegh was essential – so strongly that he sent messages to Norrie suggesting, indeed urging, their immediate move further forward which were in due course passed on to the errant brigade; but as the South African historians delicately remark, 'Pienaar, having braved the wrath of the redoubtable "Bernard", was not likely to be disturbed by the reported sentiments of more remote members of the military pantheon.'[12]

So he remained where he was, his brigade formed into what Norrie referred to as a 'South African huddle', their day's peace disturbed only by their own airmen, who showered them with pamphlets in Italian and German and caused four casualties by indiscriminate machine-gun fire.

The British armour was not acquitting itself much better, either.

Having failed to halt the progress of 15th Panzer along the Trig Capuzzo on the 28th, on the following day it missed all but the tail of the move down over the landing-ground and instead had a brush with what could only have been elements of the Ariete, about which the best which can be said is that the results were inconclusive. As the main 7th Armoured artillery support was still dispersed over the desert in random Jock Columns, they borrowed some of Dan Pienaar's guns and used these to shell the Italians from quite long range, while the Honeys and cruisers milled about between.

Early in the afternoon, Strafer Gott somewhat impatiently ordered a concentration of both guns and armour to carry out a direct assault towards Point 175, but it cannot be said that this

assault was pressed home with any worthwhile degree of determination. The Honeys came to a halt soon after their first move,
upon the appearance to the west of 'a force of up to forty tanks' –
presumably Ariete M13s and as such no opposition to the seventy-
plus Honeys, especially as these were soon joined by the cruisers of
the 22nd. Yet both brigades remained virtually stationary while the
guns continued banging away until light faded – whereupon the
British armour retired as usual some seven miles into their night
leaguer.

The men were undoubtedly very tired, perhaps more tired than
the Italians as they had been moving about much more; and the
tank crews had certainly become much more conscious of short-
comings in their vehicles, and especially their guns, than they had
been when they crossed the Wire ten days before. It also seems that
by this time their disillusionment was spreading upwards to more
senior levels, where officers were questioning the very doctrines in
which they had been trained. Vocal expression of these doubts
came most often in contemptuous remarks about their own
2-pounder solid shot armament, and envious ones about the
German artillery, especially the 88mm. – but underlying these
comments was a growing admiration for the military expertise of
the Afrika Korps and exasperation at the repeated failures of their
own concepts and techniques to beat them.

Perhaps, as Howard Kippenberger had felt at the beginning of
Crusader, the whole of Eighth Army, armour and infantry, should
have remained together, co-operating and concentrated? Perhaps it
was *not* the task of armour to destroy armour? Although the
questions may not have been asked outright, seeds of doubt were
already planted deep in the minds of men who, though willing to
risk their lives in battle for their country, were unwilling to have
them thrown away by incompetence.

On the last day of the month – a week after *Totensonntag* –
Scott-Cockburn handed over the remaining twenty-five cruisers of
22nd Armoured to Gatehouse, and retired with his headquarters
back to Egypt leaving Strafer Gott with but one composite brigade
of 120 tanks in place of the three brigades with which 7th Armoured
Division had crossed the frontier so confidently eleven days before.
Gott's orders to his armour for that day were 'to harass and destroy
the enemy as opportunity occurred and to protect 1 S.A. Inf Bde
Gp which was under orders to advance and regain from the enemy
Point 175 hill' – orders which may have been framed to give tank
commanders an enviable freedom of action, but which, containing
as they did a choice of roles, gave instead to the tired and
disillusioned men the opportunity to avoid the hazards of aggression.

The protection of the 1st South Africans was given priority over the harassment and destruction of the enemy, and as Dan Pienaar was still employing Fabian tactics to avoid confrontation with either Afrika Korps or Ariete, this allowed the British armour to settle down on the South Africans' right flank to ward off enterprising – but in different circumstances surely ineffective – attacks by the Ariete M13s. These continued on and off during the day, and some M13s were destroyed – one account claimed sixteen for no British loss – but Point 175 overlooking the New Zealanders' eastern flank stayed in Italian hands, and darkness found the South Africans and the British armour but little nearer the besieged force than they had been at dawn.

The South Africans had made one move. In the morning, Pienaar had detached an infantry battalion and a field battery off towards Point 178 on the southern escarpment in response to orders from XXX Corps that he should again change direction of advance so that he could attack the flank of 15th Panzer Division (with an infantry brigade!) but after it had run into strong opposition from what was now called Group Mickl (General Böttcher had taken von Ravenstein's place in command of 21st Panzer) it was recalled and by mid-afternoon was safely back inside the 'huddle'.

But Norrie had become so concerned at the lack of movement that he decided personally to 'apply a little ginger' and went down to Pienaar's position where he found the brigadier 'in an affable and

Figure 6   Carro armato tipo M13/40: weight 14 tons; armour 14mm.–30mm.; engine 105 h.p.; maximum speed 20 m.p.h.; armament one 47mm., three 8mm. Breda m.g.; crew 4

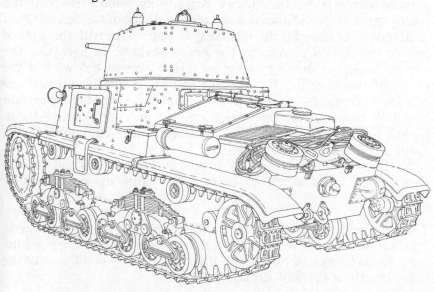

pleasant mood but . . . insufficiently conscious of the urgency of the situation . . . '

After some discussion, it was decided that Point 175 was, after all, the true objective for 1st South Africans, but that instead of proceeding directly there (after all, the armour had failed to get through so how could a soft-skinned infantry brigade?) Norrie should himself lead them to a point overlooking the Trig Capuzzo near Bir Sciafsciuf, and that the brigade should then approach its objective from the east along the line of the Escarpment. By noon, the line of march had been agreed and Norrie led off with his own Battle H.Q. and three armoured cars, only to find after some time that he was out on his own again. Rude but encouraging signals were dispatched and in due course

> the leadings tps of 1 SA Bde came slowly into view and halted, so I sent back Brigadier Aikenhead (my C.C.R.A.) to Brigadier Pienaar with orders that he was to push on immediately . . . The momentum was soon re-established, only to be followed by some quite accurate and heavy shelling of the column from a west and NW direction. This unexpected development again caused the leading tps to pause and some men actually got out of their trucks, with the apparent intention of digging in.[13]

In his efforts to get the column moving forward again, Norrie came to the conclusion that although the troops themselves were anxious and indeed eager to get on, they had been given no idea of what was expected of them.

It was thus nearly dark when, with Norrie himself leading them in a recce car, 1st South African Brigade eventually reached the Escarpment at Bir Sciafsciuf some ten miles east of the nearest New Zealanders, in time for their artillery to join forces with the guns of one of the Jock Columns in the neighbourhood in harassing the enemy transport moving along the Trig Capuzzo below. But the effort of reaching the Escarpment had apparently exhausted the brigade's strength – or perhaps its brigadier's spirit of co-operation – and to Norrie's extreme irritation, yet another South African huddle was soon only too evidently in existence, exhibiting all the familiar signs of gluey immobility.

As for 4th/22nd Armoured Brigade, this was still out in the desert, five miles south of Point 175, taking up night leaguer positions.

The failure of both the South Africans and the British armour to reach Point 175 on November 30th and take the pressure off the New Zealanders had resulted in the loss for the second time of the main length of the Sidi Rezegh ridge.

The last ordeal for the battered 6th Brigade began at about 1400, after a comparatively peaceful morning, when the guns of Group Mickl began a bombardment from their positions on the southern escarpment which by 1500 had become very severe. According to the 26th Battalion history:

> A large-calibre gun was firing and its shells left huge craters in the rocky ground. Eight men had been killed and seven others wounded . . . One soldier who had been blown out of his trench during the morning suddenly went berserk. The men on the higher ground watched with dismay enemy tanks converging on the sector. Infantry were crossing down the southern escarpment and moving northward through the wadis. The 25-pounders had practically ceased firing . . . One by one the anti-tank guns were knocked out. Two more sent up by Brigade HQ suffered a similar fate after they had fired a few shots . . . Enemy infantry moved in from the south. As they neared the sector and crossed the ridges the tanks opened fire . . . Firing as they came, the enemy armour breasted the escarpment and fanned out across the lower ground. The 24th Battalion was overrun, then A and B Coys of 26th Battalion. A few men made a break and escaped.[14]

By dark, the main body of the attackers had swept eastwards along the ridge almost as far as Point 175, while some of the panzers had gone down to the Trig Capuzzo across which, after a brief battle with New Zealand artillery, they could see the rising ground opposite leading up to the summit of Belhammed still in the hands of Freyberg's 4th Brigade. Of 6th Brigade, only the headquarters, the field regiment of artillery, a machine-gun platoon and the battered remnants of 25th Battalion still grimly hanging on just west of Point 175 remained – and Brigadier Barrowclough's request that they all be allowed to retire into Tobruk was refused on the ground that the South Africans had been ordered to join them during the night, and the armour to attack the Ariete at first light. Not surprisingly, this information was greeted with scepticism, and General Godwin-Austen was left in no doubt that he would be held responsible if the gallant survivors of the brigade were not extricated from their perilous positions.

Pienaar did in fact send out three companies of infantry towards Point 175 during the night, but they found themselves being accompanied by unidentified vehicles to the north and as a result managed only to mount a two-platoon attack on their objective, which not surprisingly failed; after which they returned to their huddle. Gatehouse's armour, however, did move up to the rescue at dawn on December 1st. They drove northwards along the eastern edge of the landing-ground, being fired upon by Group Mickl from the west and Ariete from the east to such effect as to give them a distinct feeling of the Light Brigade charge at Balaclava, and several Honeys were knocked out by the time the main body reached Barrowclough's H.Q. – where they found themselves excitedly welcomed by the eighty-odd 'riflemen, drivers, cooks and clerks' who were all that remained of 24th and 26th Battalions, and who now rushed forward to join what they thought would be a victorious break-out charge to regain the lost ground.

There followed a brief interlude of discussion and explanation, but in the end it was realised that discretion would be the better part of valour and the disappointed Kiwis accepted their lot. There was at first some misunderstanding about the precise direction of withdrawal, but eventually the 6th Brigade survivors made their way north-eastwards towards Zaafran, under the noses of both Ariete and the 21st Panzer Division – who had remained curiously muted since the capture of von Ravenstein, despite his replacement by Böttcher. Behind them, 4th/22nd Armoured remained as shield against possible attack by 15th Panzer until just after midday, under sporadic fire from Ariete and occasionally sallying forth against small groups of panzers and armoured cars of one or other of the reconnaissance battalions, which all apparently retired hastily. During the afternoon, the Honeys climbed back up the Escarpment and regained first their night leaguer, and later went even further back to spend the next night at Bir Berraneb.

By now exhaustion was affecting almost everyone in the battle area, and one of the New Zealand historians who had been taken prisoner and was in the hospital wadi now in the hands of Ariete noted that German troops in the neighbourhood were walking like zombies. The 'Dash to the Wire' had not only reduced 21st Panzer to less than half its strength in men and less than a third in equipment, it had also worn what remained down almost to the limits of physical endurance; and General Böttcher does not seem to have been the man to rejuvenate them. During the morning of December 1st he signalled Cruewell complaining of continual harassment on flank and rear (from the Jock Columns) and asking permission to march away from the danger area and find haven with Corps H.Q. at Bir bu Creimisa – a request which brought a sharp rebuke from Cruewell, especially as Böttcher had had the presumption to send a similar signal in clear to Panzergruppe H.Q. over Cruewell's head.

But 15th Panzer still possessed reserves of energy upon which to call, and Rommel, who was in the area, ensured that they did so by assigning to them the attack intended to complete the annihilation of the New Zealanders.

They were on the move by 0400 on December 1st, infantry and

machine-gun units making their way up the southern slopes of
Belhammed under cover of darkness – a cover continued after
dawn by a thick mist. Then as light increased, a heavy barrage
opened behind them both from their own divisional artillery and
that of Group Mickl, the summit of Belhammed disappeared under
a cloud of black smoke, and the armour of Panzer Regiment 8 came
up through the murk. As the panzers rolled forward, crushing the
flimsy sangars which were all the protection the New Zealand
infantry had been able to erect, fierce fighting again broke out – but
only at infantry level, for the New Zealand and British artillery
could see nothing of the battle and even the Valentines and
Matildas on the western flank were blinded by mist and smoke. By
0830, the survivors of Kippenberger's battalion – now reduced to
nine officers and 286 other ranks – were faced with the alternatives
of surrender or slaughter by the panzers (and wisely chose
surrender), 18th Battalion had lost all its anti-tank guns and
retreated westwards into the Tobruk garrison area, while Freyberg
himself had missed capture by a hair's breadth and slid off with his
Battle H.Q. and that of 4th Brigade to Zaafran, where eventually
he was joined by the survivors from 6th Brigade.

The Tobruk corridor had been cut and the port was under siege
again.

Freyberg's position was bitter indeed. His division had been the
instrument by which Rommel's frontier garrisons had first been
bottled up, had been the one by which the siege of Tobruk had been
lifted, and for four days his men had fought to hold a pocket against
increasing pressure from two panzer divisions and a siege train –
while an unscathed infantry brigade and an armoured formation
with over a hundred tanks manoeuvred gravely in the far reaches of
the desert without, as far as he could see, attempting to do anything
to help him. It is not surprising that his opinion of the reliability of
armoured formations had not been raised by the events of the last
few days, that he did not regard Dan Pienaar with much affection,
and that his wireless conversations with his Corps and Army
Commanders were curt and much to the point. That night he talked
to Norrie about plans for the evacuation of the remnants of his
division back across the border, and the history of the New Zealand
Divisional Signals has an enlivening account of the event.

The GOC called up Headquarters 30 Corps by RT and spoke
to General Norrie about his intentions. Sergeant Smith stood by
the set while the General spoke and listened in horrified silence
while he described his plan in the plainest of plain language, quite
unblemished by the merest pretence of RT procedure or security
precautions. Smith bounded over to OC A Section: 'Did you hear

what he said? Did you hear?' he yelled and, without waiting for an answer, 'Tiny said that we are going to break out at dusk – four miles east, nine miles south-east over the escarpment and then flat out for the wire! *And all in clear*!' The last words were almost a shriek. Throwing out his arm in the direction of the sinister black shapes squatting on the distant skyline . . . , he turned and peered earnestly into the face of Lieutenant-Colonel Agar, who had come up to see the fun. 'And what does he think those bastards out there are going to do about it, sir?' As he sauntered off dejectedly, fragments of his mournful soliloquy floated back to his hearers: ' . . . nine miles to Point 192 . . . east to the wire . . . nine miles to Hell, more like.'[15]

There is, however, despite the sergeant's gloom, a Destiny which guards people like 'Tiny' Freyberg (who in the First World War had won three D.S.O.s in addition to his V.C.) and it was still working effectively on December 1st, 1941.

Despite Rommel's clear and forceful instructions to Afrika Korps that the remains of the New Zealand Division were to be found and annihilated, despite also Cruewell's strict injunction that 21st Panzer Division were to stay where they were blocking the Trig Capuzzo at the eastern end of the pocket, General Böttcher decided that the sudden disappearance of all enemy presence immediately in front of him constituted an open invitation for his armour and infantry to advance westwards, towards Afrika Korps H.Q. and home. By dusk, Panzer Regiment 5 had moved five miles along the Trig and were climbing the Escarpment west of the landing-ground, and by 2000 they had ensconced themselves with their protective infantry in defensive positions around the Mosque, while behind them followed the vehicles of their supply echelon.

Much further back, the tired but gratified survivors of the 2nd New Zealand Division, led by their general and including a doubtless sceptical and puzzled signals sergeant, were making their unobstructed way through the gap so obligingly left for them, rendezvousing thirteen miles further east with Norrie just before midnight, and then pressing on as far as Bir Gibni by dawn. They crossed the Wire the same day and reached Baggush before the end of the week – accompanied all the way by sixty Italian prisoners who, once they had realised what was happening, had hastily repaired some trucks and lorries in the neighbourhood of Zaafran so as to ensure that they would not be left behind.

As the South African brigade had also moved on the night of December 1st/2nd and by dawn were safely back in their old leaguer around Taieb el Esem, Tobruk was now isolated once more, with the nearest friendly formations twenty-five miles away, and Ariete, the Afrika Korps, the siege train and General Sümmermann's Division zbV Afrika (retitled that day 90th Light Division) firmly ensconced between.

Thus it would seem that the courage, determination and transcendent military expertise of the Afrika Korps, coupled with the resilience and drive of their redoubtable commander, had in twelve days defeated the far greater numbers and heavier weight of armament which Eighth Army had flung against them in *Operation Crusader*. They had destroyed one South African brigade and two of the three British armoured brigades, and so battered the New Zealand Division that it had retired from the fray; there seemed to be every justification for the jubilant note in a signal which Rommel sent off that night to the High Command:

> In the continuous heavy fighting between the 18th November and the 1st December, 814 enemy armoured fighting vehicles and armoured cars have been destroyed, and 127 aircraft shot down. No estimate can yet be given of the booty in arms, ammunition and vehicles. Prisoners exceed 9,000, including three generals.[16]

Yet that picture was false, the jubilation unwarranted.

In addition to the purely factual error in the signal (brigadiers do not count as generals in the British Army; and one of the supposed generals had been a full colonel), there were other factors to be taken into account before a true balance could be struck, and if Rommel had not as yet appreciated the realities of the situation, there were others who had.

Some hours before Rommel had sent off his signal, Lt-Colonel Howard Kippenberger, wounded and a prisoner in the wadi hospital, was sadly contemplating the scene of the destruction of his own battalion (20th) on Belhammed, when he was approached by a German artillery officer.

'We have taken Belhammed,' he said, 'and our eastern and western groups have joined hands.'

As this was confirmation of Kippenberger's suspicion of the resealing of the Tobruk perimeter, he expressed his regret.

'But it is of no use,' answered the German. 'We have lost the battle.'

To this the New Zealander replied with some reserve, suggesting that if this were true, the Germans could at least console themselves with the reflection that their enemies would judge that they had fought well.

'That is not enough. Our losses are too heavy. We have lost the battle.' And the German officer went despondently on his way.

But to Rommel a victory had been won and must now be exploited
– and there were still the courageous garrisons on the frontier to
whom succour and encouragement must be given; so he now
proposed a second 'Dash to the Wire'. A battalion group was to be
detached from each panzer division and sent off immediately along
the two northern routes towards Bardia and Sidi Azeiz, to be
followed at the latest by dawn on December 3rd by a reinforced
regiment with tanks, and backed up as far as Gasr el Arid by
Ariete, and as far as Bir el Chleta by Trieste. The remainder of the
Afrika Korps would join forces with the Italian XXI Corps divisions
still holding the Tobruk perimeter to the west, in order, with 90th
Light Division attacking from the north, to eliminate the British
positions at Ed Duda; and the reconnaissance battalions would
probe south from Group Mickl positions on the southern escarpment to find out what the recently dispersed British armour was
doing beyond the Trig el Abd.

Even Cunningham would hardly have dispersed his forces wider
than that and it is not surprising that Panzergruppe staff and the
Afrika Korps command were appalled by Rommel's proposals. The
only consolation they could draw would be that enough might be
discovered of the enemy dispositions for them to be able to discern
the intentions behind them.

Little but probing movement therefore occurred during December
3rd, though reports from the first battalion groups to set out
indicated that they had come up against shields barring the way to
their objectives and were awaiting the heavier support, and in the
evening a signal from Gambara reported that Italian units around
El Gubi were being harassed by shell-fire which Rommel interpreted as nothing more than activity by yet another Jock Column.

But the morning of December 4th presented him with an
ominously different picture. For one thing, his staff had been able
to provide him with figures of German losses since the beginning of
the battle, and these made sombre reading indeed. Sixteen commanding officers had now been killed or seriously wounded, the
losses of junior officers had been in proportion, and 3,800 other
ranks were also out of action. In addition, 142 panzers, 25 armoured
cars and 390 lorries had been destroyed, while of the artillery, eight
88mms, 34 anti-tank guns, ten heavy guns, seven medium, 24 field
guns and 60 mortars had been lost, and although at least the
transport position was eased by the capture of vast numbers of
British trucks and lorries (it had long been virtually impossible for
aircraft or reconnaissance patrols to distinguish between Allied and
Axis columns on the move), this potential advantage was limited by
dwindling petrol and diesel stocks.

Moreover, whether the 'harassing' to which every movement was subject was being carried out by formations no more lethal than Jock Columns or not, the effects were cumulative and beginning to assume significant proportions; already Ariete were complaining of shell-fire from the line of the Escarpment which slowed up their movements along the Trig Capuzzo, while that same morning Gambara reported anxiously that one of the largest Italian fuel dumps nearly twenty miles north-west of Bir el Gubi had been blown up, apparently by a squadron of King's Dragoon Guards. This was bad enough, but then came news that *Indian* troops had captured another dump six miles north-west of Bir el Gubi and that Camerons were attacking a position held by a Young Fascist battalion close by. Obviously, 4th Indian Division had moved up from the frontier – but hopes that this might make the relief of the frontier garrisons easier were dashed by news that the 15th Motor-cycle Battalion moving along the Via Balbia had been virtually wiped out by New Zealand Cavalry and a Maori battalion.

To complete the morning's doleful picture, a well-mounted attack by elements of 21st Panzer, Group Mickl and Engineer Battalion 200 on the appendix at Ed Duda had been halted and pinned down by artillery fire, and then after an hour of increasingly heavy bombardment the supporting 21st Panzer artillery had been suddenly blanketed by shell-fire from the *south* – where another Jock Column had attacked Pavia in Group Mickl's place around Bir bu Creimisa, capturing their anti-tank guns and a large number of prisoners.

From what Panzergruppe Afrika could see on the morning of December 4th, Eighth Army was exhibiting some of the more dispiriting characteristics of the Lernean Hydra, and Afrika Korps's recent successes in hacking off heads had nevertheless left the main body active, if not intact. Even Rommel showed signs of frustration that morning, and the final blow fell shortly after midday with the arrival at El Adem of a report that Bir el Gubi itself was being attacked by a brigade group with artillery and over a hundred tanks.

Hastily, the exiguous remains of Panzer Regiment 5 were sent across the Sidi Rezegh landing-ground towards the southern escarpment to regain command of those vital heights, and Rommel – realising that after all the main area of conflict must still remain south of Tobruk – sent orders recalling the patient and long-suffering Neumann-Sylkow and all his mobile forces from the frontier, so that Afrika Korps would be concentrated to deal with this freshly developing menace; and to increase the chances of success, he also ordered 90th Light Division and the Bologna Division down from the north of the appendix, thereby stripping the eastern end of the Tobruk perimeter of besieging forces.

This was indeed a significant development. For the first time in

eight months, one flank of the Tobruk perimeter was open – and i
no one was immediately interested in moving out through it, this
was only because the attentions of the garrison were engaged
elsewhere.

The Duke of Wellington, when talking about the French and British
armies of the Peninsular War, is reputed to have compared
Napoleon's to a superbly balanced team of horses working together
in well-designed linking harness, whereas his own consisted of a
mixture of nags tied together with ropes. But when the French
leather harness broke the team was thrown into confusion, whereas
if the British rope broke – as it frequently did – it was only
necessary to tie another knot and the jumble would carry on
unconcerned.

It was, of course, a parallel which omitted mention of the figure
on the driver's seat, but some of the explanation of the strength still
left in Ritchie's hands after the débâcles of the last days of
November may be found in it. If the destruction of the 5th South
African Brigade had lowered the morale of the 1st Brigade, it had
had little effect upon the New Zealanders – whose destruction in
turn was of little concern to Norrie's armour, to the 4th Indians or
to the 2nd South African Division, already under orders to move up
to relieve the Indians on the frontier. Auchinleck and Ritchie might
have been worried by the arithmetic of the battles (though they had
far less cause than Rommel) but the fragmentation caused by
differences in attitude between Imperial and Colonial troops,
between armoured elite and pedestrian infantry, between regular
officers with private means and 'hostilities only' officers and men
with nothing but their pay, though it badly hindered co-operation
during the build-up for an attack, gave to each isolated – even
'tribal' – section a degree of bloody-minded independence which
was proving useful in the shadow of catastrophe.

'I'm all right, Jack!' was a common attitude at this stage of
Crusader throughout Eighth Army, and if it reflected adversely on
the effectiveness of political and military command, it now provided
Ritchie with a number of formations with which he could at least
keep punching the Panzergruppe Afrika bag, even though the fist
might not be working in conscious co-operation. His instructions to
his Corps and Divisional commanders had been that at all cost
pressure on the Axis forces must be kept up, and his own pressure
on the commanders themselves was strengthened by the arrival
of Auchinleck at his headquarters on December 1st, and the re
assuring presence of the Commander-in-Chief there in the back
ground for the next ten days.

One of the first moves had been the bringing forward of 11th

Indian Brigade and the arrangements for the relief by the 2nd South African Division of the other two Indian brigades, so that they could move up later. Another had been the appointment of 1st South African Brigade to take over protection of the Field Maintenance Centres thus releasing the 22nd Guards Brigade for a more active role, and then the direction of both 11th Indian and the Guards Brigade towards El Gubi. This was in fact intended as a clearing operation which would then allow 4th Armoured Brigade – now up to a strength of 136 Honeys, though the quality of the new crews was suspect – to sweep forward and take El Adem, afterwards driving on towards Gazala if the opportunity arose; and all the while the Support Group Jock Columns would harry and observe the Axis movements.

The result of these arrangements was that by the evening of December 4th the Mahrattas, Camerons and Rajputana Rifles were either in possession of or attacking Italian positions north of El Gubi (from the west, for they had repeated their tactics at Nibeiwa and the Tummars), the Guards Brigade were in reserve to the south, 4th Armoured were manoeuvring to the north-east, while a semicircle of armoured cars screened them all from the north and west and the Jock Columns extended the screen eastwards along the line of the Escarpment.

Below them the screens could watch the Ariete and Neumann-Sylkow's force pouring back along the Trig Capuzzo under gun-fire from the Jock Columns, then swinging south-west outside the armoured car screens and down towards El Adem – while beyond them the 90th Light held the northern lines of their passage against attempts to interfere by the Tobruk garrison. Afrika Korps orders were to concentrate west of El Adem together with all the remaining German and Italian artillery, and be ready either to beat off a strong British attack or, if none developed, to drive south-east and relieve the Italian positions around El Gubi.

It seemed, therefore, that December 5th would see yet another massed conflict – and most probably the one which would prove conclusive. If the Axis forces there were destroyed or even badly mauled, then the way would be open for the Allies as far as El Agheila and perhaps even to Tripoli; if 4th Armoured Brigade suffered the fate which had befallen both the 7th and the 22nd, then only dispersed infantry would bar Rommel's route to Cairo.

But as it happened, 4th Armoured were not even to be allowed to wait and see. Ritchie had become anxious about the reports still coming in of Rommel's second 'Dash to the Wire' and after a slightly acrimonious exchange of signals with Norrie who pointed out that his forces could be better employed carrying out Ritchie's original purpose than reacting over-sensitively to Rommel's,

Ritchie rather irritably ordered that the 'centre of gravity of 7th Armoured Division should be moved back to where it was'. During the night of December 4th/5th, the Honeys therefore drove back to Bir Berraneb, leaving the two infantry brigades around El Gubi to face the combined armour of the Afrika Korps when daylight came. Like the gains of the first 'Dash to the Wire', those for the second had been reaped after it was all over.

The Afrika Korps did not get under way until late afternoon on the 5th, as Rommel was waiting both for the Ariete to close up, and for signs of movement from the British; and when the blow did fall, its recipients were the Mahrattas near Point 182. Just as darkness was falling, twenty-five panzers followed by lorried infantry swept down upon them, and during the confused and bitter fighting which followed, the Indian anti-tank guns were all knocked out and both A and C Companies overrun, though many members of C Company managed to slip away individually to fall back on the Camerons to the rear. From there, somewhat incredulously, they watched the German formations milling around their newly won positions in a state of obvious indecision, then retiring westwards into the desert in a manner distinctly reminiscent of British armoured tactics. They did not even carry out their retirement efficiently, the panzer columns floundering about in the dark, losing one another and often their sense of direction, with the result that some units back-tracked and the survivors of the 11th Indian Brigade spent much of the night emulating mice in the middle of enemy dispositions.

There was thus no overwhelming victory on December 5th, and it seemed at last that sheer exhaustion was blunting the edge of German efficiency, so perhaps Allied victory was within reach.

In fact, it was – but for very different reasons. Out of sight and out of mind, the Royal Navy and the Royal Air Force had been doing just as much at and over the sea to defeat Panzergruppe Afrika as Eighth Army had been doing on land; and in their tasks had been receiving increasingly valuable help from Ultra intelligence, which could now often give them the destination and route of Axis convoys before they left Italy. The results had been spectacular, as Rommel was about to learn.

He had spent an extremely worrying day. Not only had the figures of German losses presented to him on the 4th depressed him considerably, but certain unpleasant aspects of the supply situation were being forced to his attention in a manner which he could no longer ignore.

He had cabled Mussolini on December 2nd to the effect that the fighting efficiency of Panzergruppe Afrika depended upon a continuous stream of reinforcements, fuel, ammunition, and replace ment armour and artillery, and the reply, that sea traffic between Italy and Libya was becoming increasingly dangerous, and that warships were the only vessels capable of getting through – and then with only limited cargoes of fuel and ammunition – had been dismissed by him as just another example of Italian obstructiveness.

His own Q branch had then warned him that stocks of practically everything from shells for the guns to boots for the infantry were down to an alarming level, but his somewhat cavalier attitude to such matters, combined with faith in his Staff's capabilities in emergency and also in his own luck, allowed him to brush these aside.

But on the evening of the 5th, an Italian Staff officer arrived from the Operations Branch of Comando Supremo, Tenente-Colonello Montezemolo, and proceeded to paint so gloomy a view of Rommel's supply position that even he was forced to reconsider his prospects.

The most revelatory fact of Montezemolo's résumé – and the one he produced at the outset of his argument – was that, of the 22 ships of over 500 tons dispatched from Italian ports to North Africa during November, 14 had been sent to the bottom of the sea taking with them 62 per cent – nearly 60,000 tons – of Rommel's supplies. Tankers had been particularly badly hit and only 2,500 tons of aviation or motor spirit had arrived; but it was the loss in Italian shipping which was proving most significant. It had now reached such a level that although Comando Supremo would do everything possible to send such essential supplies as rations, medical equipment and perhaps ammunition, Rommel must understand that shipping of reinforcements in anything but derisory numbers was totally out of the question, at least until the end of December. By that time the German Luftflotte 2 would be operating from Sicily and air protection over convoys would be possible – but until then, he must expect no more men, no more tanks, no more aircraft, much less ammunition – and he would be lucky to get enough fuel to retreat, let alone to advance even further from his bases.

This was a stunning blow and one to which Rommel's reaction was, for the moment, low-keyed. He pointed out that his present position was, to say the least, grave, that of the 250 panzers with which he had begun the battle fewer than 40 were left, and that existing stocks of ammunition were totally inadequate to fight another battle of consequence. Did the Italian Command realise that Panzergruppe Afrika could not hold the positions in which the forces were disposed at that moment, and must either advance to the lines held when the battle began, or retreat? And if they retreated under present conditions there could be no question of holding Cyrenaica, in view of the probability of a British outflanking movement south of the Jebel Akhdar? They would have to go back to Agedabia at least, and probably to El Agheila and into Tripolitania.

Whether in Rommel's mind the questions were rhetorical or not the effects upon the Italian Comandante Superiore when they were put to him were pronounced. Generale Bastico proclaimed himself 'dumbfounded' at the news of the losses suffered by the joint forces under his command, and of the difficulties revealed by his German subordinate. For the moment, he agreed that the defences around Agedabia must be strengthened, and suggested also that a force be sent to recover the Jalo Oasis; after which he returned to his own headquarters near Tmimi to consider the situation further. Left alone, Rommel endeavoured to find out where his main forces were and what they were up to.

According to the Afrika Korps War Diary for December 6th, this was no easy task. The involved movements of the previous few days and the confusions of the night had left British, Indian, German and Italian units thoroughly mixed up, and the dirt and dust of two weeks' battle combined with the interchange of vehicles which had taken place (for quite a number of Axis vehicles had also found employment in British and Commonwealth formations) made it quite difficult for the combatants themselves, let alone their commanders or their staff, to know who was who. The results were sometimes startling, and often ludicrous.

During December 6th and the day which followed, there was a great deal of shelling but very little mobility, but on one occasion the commander of an armoured car stopped all artillery action on both sides in his immediate neighbourhood by waving his beret - dust-covered and totally unrecognisable. On another, a column of Italian vehicles jerked to a halt when one of the 11th Hussars armoured cars, driving somewhat unconcernedly alongside, hoisted a blue flag on its radio antenna, and on yet another, one of the 11th's armoured cars fled for protection into what was quickly demonstrated to be a German lorry column, from what later proved to be a troop of King's Dragoon Guards.

Perhaps the best illustration of both the difficulties of identification and the exhaustion to which everyone had been reduced occurred during the afternoon of December 7th, when the adjutant of one of Rommel's reconnaissance battalions, looking for his commander, found himself driving parallel to a column which at first he regarded with deep suspicion. He then saw, towards the rear, one of his own unit's eight-wheeled armoured cars, so driving close in, he approached the leading vehicle to challenge in German and, receiving no answer, in Italian. There followed a moment's conversational hiatus, broken eventually when the driver, dust-

covered and naked to the waist, looked down and shouted irritably:
   'Oh, piss off, mate . . . for Christ's sake!'
   And he did.
   But by this time, Rommel had made up his mind. That morning
at Afrika Korps Headquarters he had declared that if the British
were not beaten that day, he would abandon the Tobruk front and
go back to the defensive positions south of Gazala, to which he had
already directed the heavy artillery and some of the Italian
divisions, and to which he now sent 90th Light and his own
headquarters. As the day wore on it became evident that neither
side was engaging closely, that the British artillery fire was growing
heavier all the time, and that in the late afternoon the 4th
Armoured was attempting – not very aggressively – an outflanking
movement to the south.
   Accepting the inevitable, Rommel issued the necessary instructions, and after dark the remnants of the two panzer divisions with
their accompanying guns and infantry drew back from Bir el Gubi,
their retirement covered at first by yet another of their spectacular
Brock's Benefits. The cover was not enough, however, to save
elements of the Pavia Division just to the north, for Comando
Supremo in Rome had signalled that after all everything possible
was to be done to hold Cyrenaica, whatever Rommel might feel,
and Gambara as Bastico's Chief of Staff had cancelled one of
Rommel's orders for their withdrawal. As a result, some of the
luckless Italians around El Adem were caught, the Brescia and
Trento Divisions holding the western end of the Tobruk perimeter were roughly handled before they were eventually forced
to disengage, and bitterness between Italian and German staffs
increased.
   Rommel's personal bitterness was increased, too. Not only had
the decision meant the abandonment of the frontier positions and the
gallant Major Bach, but on the previous evening, the argumentative
but faithful Neumann-Sylkow – capable, attractive and half-Scots –
had been severely wounded by a shell which landed beside his
command vehicle. He had been rushed back to a Derna hospital but
no one had any illusions about his condition and he was to die two
days later.
   The bitterness showed. On the morning of December 8th, Bastico
came to see him at his new headquarters just behind Ain el Gazala
and Rommel kept him waiting for fifteen minutes before admitting
him to his Mammoth. He then treated him to an explosion of
Teutonic wrath in which he not only blamed the Italians for the
failure to beat the British, but announced that in view of the
unsatisfactory nature of the co-operation he had received, he
intended to take his divisions not only back into Tripolitania, but on

and into Tunisia where he would give himself up to the French and be interned!

It took some time and great deal of soothing gesture to cool the atmosphere, but Rommel – who was quite capable of staging fits of temper solely in order to aid the winning of arguments – established the point that, once the consequences of Gambara's 'insubordination' and 'interference' had been overcome and the Italian divisions safely withdrawn behind the Gazala defences, the retirement should be continued and Cyrenaica abandoned to British hands. The argument flared up again a few days later, but when Cavallero arrived from Rome to adjudicate, neither Bastico nor Gambara could produce viable alternative strategies and spent most of their time with their Chief of Staff complaining about Rommel's rudeness. This, they were told, they must grin and bear – and in the meantime they had better comply with their overbearing but efficient ally's suggestions.

It cannot be said that Eighth Army pressed very hard on Afrika Korps's heels during the second British advance through Cyrenaica. There were, of course, inevitable logistic problems as the lines of communication and supply lengthened (one of Rommel's arguments for a long Axis withdrawal had been this resultant disadvantage for the Allies) but the fact remains that by the end of *Operation Crusader* the high confidence and optimism with which the British troops had entered the battle had been largely replaced by a cynical wariness which tended to keep them back from German rearguard screens, formed and manned, as now they knew they would be, by soldiers of high professional competence.

An attempt by XIII Corps (which had taken over the pursuit through Cyrenaica while XXX Corps dealt with the frontier garrisons) to outflank the Gazala positions was efficiently beaten back by 15th Panzer at Alam Hamza on December 15th, whereupon plans were laid for an advance by Gatehouse's armour (which had been attached to Godwin-Austen's force for the operation) towards Mechili, and by 4th Indian Division to Lamluda west of Derna. Oasis Force was directed up from Jalo to Agedabia while 22nd Guard Brigade was to be held like an arrow in a bow for a lunge straight through the Jebel, to take Benghasi by a *coup de main* at the critical moment. It was all to begin on December 19th.

Then, during the night of December 16th/17th, Rommel, with consummate timing, slipped away himself sending Afrika Korps and the Italian armour straight down along the edge of the desert, first to Mechili and then to Msus, and the Italian infantry off around the coast roads. Caught off balance, the British armour scrambled after Afrika Korps but petrol shortages and bad going, exacerbated by hastily improvised supply, slowed them badly and it was not until the morning of December 23rd that their spearheads reached Antelat, where they hoped to repeat the successes of Beda Fomm by cutting off the bulk of the enemy still to the north.

They were too late. Facing them was the whole of the Afrika Korps, reinforced, to Rommel's mingled relief and annoyance, by twenty-two new panzers which despite Montezemolo's forecast had arrived two days previously at Benghasi. (Twenty-three more had been delivered to Tripoli, though two ships carrying a further forty-five between them had been sunk en route from Brindisi.) The result was a bloody nose for 3rd R.T.R. and the hurried dispatch forward from Mechili of a reconstituted 22nd Armoured Brigade with eighty cruisers and thirty Honeys – which ran out of petrol at Saunnu and remained stuck there for twenty-four hours.

In the meantime, King's Dragoon Guards and a column from the Support Group had entered Benghasi in time for their Christmas dinner, to find that Brescia Division's rearguard had just moved out, the inhabitants were not quite so enthusiastic in their welcome as they had been a year before (possibly due to the ever-increasing damage being wreaked upon their once pleasant and prosperous town by the R.A.F.) and several chalked messages from the last Germans to leave, suggesting an early return engagement.

By December 27th, 22nd Guards Brigade were moving down on the Afrika Korps positions around Agedabia and the 22nd Armoured driving out wide to the south to outflank them. With an air almost of *déjà vu*, Cruewell – thoroughly appreciating the over-extension in space of the forces attacking him – struck powerfully at Scott-Cockburn's new force on December 28th and reduced it sharply by thirty-seven tanks before returning to base to confront the Guards. Wisely, Marriott held his infantry brigade back and on the pen-ultimate day of the year, Cruewell sallied forth again, knocked out another twenty-three of Scott-Cockburn's tanks and then, with an almost studied insouciance, retired in rain, mist and depressingly cold winds to Rommel's chosen stopping place at El Agheila.

Operation Crusader was over, fizzling out in bad weather and worse temper in the desolate sands from which, nine months before, Rommel had launched the first spectacular advance of the Afrika Korps. He had good reason for anger. His army had been defeated, and he knew it, not by superior military conception, training or even prowess – but by logistic inadequacy on the part of his own government and their allies. He had undoubtedly himself made mistakes (and a more expert adversary might well have taken advantage of them to his own irretrievable undoing) but after his destruction of the New Zealanders, only the inadequacies of his logistic support (he felt) robbed him of victory. He would pay more attention himself to that side of affairs in future, for it was obviously courting disaster to leave such matters in other hands than his own.

As for the British, although Auchinleck and Ritchie had good cause for satisfaction, the troops themselves were aggrieved and disgruntled. The promises made to them by Churchill, by their own press and by many of their senior commanders regarding the superiority of their arms and equipment and the pre-eminence of their leaders had proved empty; and they had developed a dangerous admiration for the leadership of the Afrika Korps and an envy, much of it unfounded, for the enemy's weapons. Though they had been provided with nothing to equal the 88mm., their tanks were not so greatly inferior in power or armour to the panzers, and the British and Commonwealth troops had, in fact, done rather better than many of them realised.

On November 18th, the Allied forces in the operation had numbered 118,000 and the total Axis forces 119,000; and at the end of the month in which the enemy had vacated the field, the British losses had amounted to 17,700 (15 per cent) and the Axis losses to 24,500 (20 per cent), though the British losses in killed and wounded had been the greater. Moreover, when the Axis frontier garrisons surrendered during January, another 13,800 were to be added to the Axis 'missing', and the final casualty figures can be seen in Table 1.

Table 1

	Killed	Wounded	Missing*	Total
British	2,900	7,300	7,500	17,700
German	1,200	3,300	10,100	14,600
Italian	1,100	2,800	19,800	23,700
Axis totals	2,300	6,100	29,900†	38,300

* Generally prisoners of war
† 13,800 taken at Bardia and Halfaya

The British losses in equipment during the land battles were, of course, much greater than the Axis losses, to some extent because they had much more to lose, and also because none of their armoured fighting vehicles could stand up to the 88mm. But if the desert behind them was littered with the debris of smashed British armour, the sea-bed between Sicily and North Africa was dotted with torn ships vomiting panzers and unused Axis artillery through the gaps in their plates; and if the Royal Navy, the Royal Air Force and the diverse elements which made up the Army could ever learn that they were all fighting the same war, they would together constitute a formidable fighting team. As it was, they had all learned from their experience of the last few weeks something of the grim business of war, and no longer regarded it quite so much as an adventurous game for gifted amateurs.

It had been a soldier's battle with even the best generalship – Rommel's – at a second-best level. If Auchinleck's handling of the battle when he had taken charge had temporarily improved the quality of direction, it had still been his choice of Army Commander which had caused the rot which he had had himself to stop; and only the courage and endurance of the fighting men (aided on the German side by the moral courage and competence of Westphal and his staff) had saved commanders on several occasions from the results of their own folly.

This was reflected in many ways, and principally in the fellow feeling shown between the opposing soldiers – in the respect accorded Major Bach and the garrison at Halfaya when, hungry, thirsty, bombed, shelled and short of ammunition they eventually surrendered on January 17th; in the many quite amicable discussions on recent events and tactics between German and British officers at many levels in the various prison-camps which now dotted the North African coasts, and in the general treatment of prisoners and of wounded by both sides.

One event on the British side especially underlined it – the award of the Victoria Cross to Jock Campbell. It was almost unheard-of for so senior an officer to win the Cross, but when the news reached the men who had fought at Sidi Rezegh it was universally applauded through the ranks, from private soldier to general.

No man so epitomised the uncaring, stubborn, slogging resolution of the men who had fought – on both sides – during the closing weeks of 1941.

13 · *Lightning Riposte*

Not all the Allied losses during the period covered by *Operation Crusader* had been borne by the Army, for the Royal Navy had paid a grievous price for the contribution they had made.

Of the five capital ships in the Mediterranean at the beginning of November only one was still afloat at the end of the year, and during the same period the British had also lost two cruisers sunk, two badly damaged and one withdrawn by the Australian Government for service nearer home.

All the physical damage had been wrought by under-sea weapons, the most lethal being newly arrived German U-boats. Twenty of these had been withdrawn from the Atlantic (to the frustration of Admiral Doenitz but to the enormous relief of the hard-pressed Atlantic convoys) and sent to the Mediterranean, and their effect had been immediate and dramatic. On the afternoon of November 13th, U81 had torpedoed the Gibraltar-based aircraft-carrier *Ark Royal* and although she had not sunk immediately, fire had broken out in her boiler-rooms the following morning and she had gone down twenty-five miles from port, fortunately with the loss of only one life.

But twelve days later, at the other end of the Mediterranean, U331 with enormous skill and daring penetrated the destroyer screen escorting Admiral Cunningham's main battlefleet from Alexandria, and put three torpedoes into the battleship *Barham*, which four minutes later blew up with a tremendous explosion and a great loss of life. The underwater tumult was enough to force U331 to the surface almost under the bows of another battleship, the *Valiant*, but her captain coolly took advantage of the confusion to dive again and get clear away – to the extreme fury and embarrassment of all British present.

That had been in November. December 1941 was to be one of the worst months in the history of the Royal Navy, and although the first disaster – the sinking of the huge capital ships *Prince of Wales* and *Repulse* off the Malayan coast – was not of immediate concern to Eighth Army, it was quickly followed by others which were. On December 12th the cruiser *Galatea* was hit by two torpedoes from

U557 as she was entering the swept channel outside Alexandria, and on the 19th, another cruiser, *Neptune*, was caught in a minefield seventeen miles north-east of Tripoli, and had first her propellers blown off and then her back broken, while when the destroyer *Kandahar* went in to try to tow her free, she also hit a mine and had her stern blown away.

But far worse was happening inside Alexandria harbour itself. Three human torpedoes from the Italian Tenth Light Flotilla had been dropped from the submarine *Scirè* five miles from the harbour entrance, crept into the harbour while the boom was raised to admit some destroyers, slid over the protective netting around their quarries and succeeded in attaching their explosive heads beneath them. The six men making up the crews then left the immediate area, two of them being forced to surface almost immediately to find refuge on one of their target's mooring buoys from which they were quickly made prisoner. The others escaped from the immediate area but missed their rendezvous with the rescue submarine, landed in Egypt and were picked up two days later; but in the meantime, as the two early prisoners had resolutely withstood all attempts to make them divulge details of their mission until too late, the three charges had exploded with devastating effect, severely damaging a tanker and the destroyer *Jervis* berthed alongside – and blowing such vast holes in the battleships *Valiant* and *Queen Elizabeth* that they could do nothing but sit on the bottom of Alexandria harbour with their decks only just clear of the water, for the next few months.

It is pleasant to be able to record that the extraordinary bravery of this Italian exploit was recognised, many months later and after Italy had at last joined the Allies, by the award to the leader of the team, Tenente Luigi de la Penne, of the Italian Gold Medal for Valour – and that it was pinned to his chest by the man who had commanded the *Valiant* at the time he blew it up and who by then was Flag Officer, Taranto and the Adriatic, Rear-Admiral Charles Morgan. They had in the meantime become good friends.

But at the end of 1941, this exploit was the culmination of a series of disasters by which in two months the Royal Navy had suffered as heavy losses as might have been expected in a fleet action of the size of Jutland in the past or Midway in the not too distant future – without having inflicted comparable damages on an enemy battle-fleet. Command of the waters of the mid-Mediterranean, and even more importantly of the air above, was now in Axis hands – and Panzergruppe Afrika was the most immediate beneficiary.

Rommel's situation during the four weeks following the diatribe delivered to him by Montezemolo became, ironically, immeasur-

ably strengthened by other factors in addition to that of the
weakening of the Royal Navy.

One of the most important was the recovery in energy and morale
of the Afrika Korps, which had carried out one of the most difficult
of military manoeuvres – retreat in the face of the enemy – without
losing cohesion, without losing vast quantities of stores such as the
British habitually abandoned in retreat, without showing the
slightest signs of the panic which marked – at least among the B
Echelons – the Matruh Stakes, moving always at their own pace,
and with such confidence that at the end they could still turn and
deliver two numbing blows upon the pursuing enemy. They had
therefore every justification in regarding themselves as a first-class
fighting force still capable of giving an excellent account of themselves.

Another and more immediately apparent factor could be seen on
the map – the shortening of the Axis supply lines and the consequent easing of their logistic problems. Not only had the distance
from their main supply port to the front lessened, but with the
decrease of danger to the sea passages, the pre-Christmas convoys
to Benghasi and Tripoli which had so dramatically turned the tables
on 22nd Armoured Brigade had been quickly followed up by an
even larger convoy bringing Rommel a further fifty-five panzers,
twenty armoured cars and a large consignment of fuel.

This was, as Bayerlein remarked, 'as good as a victory in battle'
but its real significance lay in just its safe arrival. Montezemolo's
predictions, though not entirely inaccurate with regard to timing,

Figure 7   Panzerkampfwagen IV (Ausführung C): weight 20 tons; armour
10mm.–30mm.; engine 300 h.p.; maximum speed 26 m.p.h.; armament one
7·5cm. (L/24), one 7·92 m.g.; crew 5

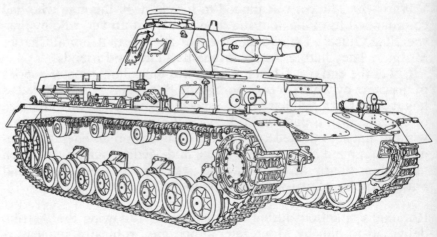

had been too pessimistic in tone, for the onset of the Russian winter had released enough German aircraft for Kesselring's Luftflotte 2 to begin operations on time and to make an immediate impact. Axis convoys to North Africa were now enjoying the immense advantages of efficient air cover.

And in the opinion of Rommel's chief intelligence officer, Major F. W. von Mellenthin, there was a fourth factor to weigh in favour of Panzergruppe Afrika – increasing evidence of disarray in the enemy forces facing them across the frontier at El Agheila, bearing an unexpected resemblance to the weakness and uncertainty of which Rommel had taken such excellent advantage during his first onslaught. By January 12th, von Mellenthin had come to the conclusion that for at least the next two weeks, Panzergruppe forces in the area would be more powerful and much better supplied – in effect, in much better shape for battle – than the British forces facing them.

It only remained for Rommel to choose the moment for attack.

Auchinleck would have been astonished had he known of von Mellenthin's analysis of the situation, for even as Rommel was listening to his intelligence chief, the C.-in-C., Middle East, was in fact composing a letter to Churchill denying views not markedly dissimilar from those of the Germans, apparently held in London:

> I do not think it can be said that the bulk of the enemy divisions have evaded us. It is true that he still speaks in terms of divisions but they are divisions only in name. For instance, we know that the strength of the 90th German Light Division originally 9,000, now 3,500, and has only one field gun left.
>
> . . . These are much disorganized, short of senior officers, short of material and due to our continuous pressure are tired and certainly not as strong as their total strength of 35,000 might be thought to indicate.
>
> I have reason to believe that six ships recently reached Tripoli averaging 7,200 tons.
>
> I am convinced that we should press forward . . . in view of the heartening news from the Russian front I feel that we should do all we can to maintain the pressure in Libya. We have very full and interesting records of daily conversations between our prisoners Generals von Ravenstein and Schmidt. Making all allowances for mental depression natural in prisoners of war there is no doubt that German morale is beginning to feel the strain not only in Libya but in Germany. They speak freely also of great losses in the recent fighting, mismanagement and disorganization and above all of dissatisfaction with Rommel's

leadership. I am convinced the enemy is hard-pressed more than we dared think perhaps.[1]

Nevertheless, his optimism in regard to Rommel's presumed weaknesses had not blinded Auchinleck to defects on his own side – especially those of command, and on January 1st he had replied to Ritchie's account of the closing stages of *Crusader* with a letter which included the following points:

I agree that our tanks are outgunned by the German tanks, but surely superiority in numbers should counter-balance this to some extent, and the number of German tanks with the heavier gun in them cannot be so great?

I agree, too, about the cruiser being too complicated, and delicate a machine for the rough conditions of the Near and Middle East, and that the American M3s, though mechanically excellent, are not comparable to our cruisers or the German medium tanks as fighting machines. Still, we have got to make do with what we have got, and the Boche has got to be beaten! . . . If we are to add to our inferiority in material an apparent inferiority in leadership, then we shall be in a bad way and will not deserve to win . . . I have a most uncomfortable feeling that the Germans outwit and outmanoeuvre us as well as outshooting us . . .

If it is [so], then we must find new leaders at once. No personal considerations . . . must be allowed to stand in the way. Commanders who consistently have their brigades shot away from under them, even against a numerically inferior enemy, are expensive luxuries, much too expensive in present circumstances.[2]

At least one other commander in the area was as aware of British defects as he was.

Godwin-Austen, now commanding troops in Cyrenaica, already considered 22nd Armoured Brigade unfit for further action and had replaced it at the frontier by Jock Campbell's Support Group, with orders to hold the line with the Guards Brigade on their right, and to use their experience to continue harassing Rommel; but of course the Group had been in almost continuous action since November, had suffered serious casualties at Sidi Rezegh, its men were tired and its vehicles and artillery badly worn.

Moreover, Auchinleck, still deeply concerned about his northern flank and the ever-present threat of a German advance down through Turkey or Persia, intended that the whole of 7th Armoured Division, once it had recovered from its *Crusader* losses, should be given a change of scene in Palestine and Syria, and that the newly arrived 1st Armoured Division should take its place; but even in this substitution there were extra complications.

The commander of the 1st Armoured Division, Major-General H. Lumsden, had been wounded in an air attack within a few days of the completion of *Crusader*, and his place was taken by Messervy, who had led 4th Indian Division as far as Benghasi and now handed them over to Major-General Francis Tuker. Why two divisions instead of one needed to suffer a change of commander at this juncture is unknown, but Messervy now found himself with a division which for nearly a year had suffered frustration and fragmentation, and was in a highly unsatisfactory state as a result.

It had been reorganised after Dunkirk, re-equipped with a positively bizarre assortment of tanks of which the most modern had been almost immediately stripped away to make up numbers in the 'Tiger' convoy, after which it had again been re-equipped, this time entirely with Crusaders. It was then decided that the division should go to the Middle East, but as a result of the complaints about the mechanical state of tanks arriving there, the Crusaders were withdrawn for the necessary modifications to be carried out in England – so little if any training had been done on them. Shortly after that, the 22nd Armoured Brigade was removed and dispatched for immediate attachment to 7th Armoured Division as *Crusader* began, and in mid-September the remaining brigade – the 2nd – and the division's Support Group, had set out on the long haul around the Cape.

The experiences and condition of Scott-Cockburn's 22nd Brigade by the beginning of 1942 have already been described, and it must be said that those of 2nd Armoured Brigade were unlikely to render it much more effective. It had been sent forward into Cyrenaica at first as a Brigade Group, with an infantry battalion, an R.H.A. and an anti-tank regiment from its own Support Group incorporated and training en route with it, but as soon as it arrived in the area it lost these units, which rejoined 1st Support Group as this took the place of 7th Support Group. Moreover, 2nd Brigade's tanks had made the journey from the Delta by rail only as far as Mersa Matruh, and had driven the remaining 450 miles on their own tracks which as a result were already in need of replacement; though not quite immediately, as the brigade had used all its petrol allocation on the way up and for some days there was no more with which even to drive to the frontier positions, let alone carry out any advanced training there.

By mid-January, therefore, Godwin-Austen's XIII Corps, occupying Cyrenaica and facing Panzergruppe Afrika (about to be rechristened Panzerarmee Afrika) consisted of two brigades of the 4th Indian Division at Benghasi and Barce respectively (the third

was still back at Tobruk where it had been joined by the remnants
of 22nd Armoured), the 2nd Armoured Brigade hastily training
around Antelat, the Guards Brigade at Mersa el Brega, with the 1st
Support Group to their left in the ground leading down to the Wadi
Faregh – the latter also endeavouring to gain experience, but in
ground so broken and hummocky that wheeled vehicles were
slower than tracked ones, and suffered so much from burst tyres
and broken axles as to be almost useless.

Thus, as had happened after the O'Connor offensive, the
formations expected to hold the gains so lately won were inadequate in both manpower and material. The reasons for the
weaknesses were different, but the effect was the same.

Rommel struck early on the morning of January 21st – just sixteen
days after the last of his rearguards, cautiously pursued by patrols
from the Guards Brigade, had retired to El Agheila. Needless to
say, he had informed neither his own High Command nor his Allies
of his intentions and was thus not very surprised when angry
messages arrived from Bastico, or when Generale Cavallero
appeared on January 23rd in a state of high excitement to order that
the advance must be nothing more than a sortie to be recalled at the
earliest opportunity.

But it had already gone too far for that, and Rommel was
glimpsing victory again. To Cavallero's expostulations he replied
that only the Führer could order a retirement as it was mainly
German troops who were so far engaged, and when Kesselring
voiced opinions which could have been interpreted as backing for
Cavallero, Rommel went so far as to hint that Kesselring's expertise
as an airman was not totally relevant at that moment and invited
him to look at the map.

Already, it revealed a remarkable picture.·

Bad going had held up the advance during the first day, for 15th
Panzer on the right flank had become bogged in the dunes at the
mouth of the Wadi Faregh, and on the left the combined Ariete and
Trieste were content to keep pace; but the bad going which held up
the panzers also bedevilled the British 1st Support Group, who by
the end of the day had left behind sixteen of their 25-pounders, a
number of their lorries and nearly a hundred of their soldiers. And
as the main road back to Agedabia and the line of the Wadi Faregh
diverged, there was by the evening a gap between the Guards
Brigade and the Support Group.

Into this gap, Rommel assumed quite reasonably, the British
would send what they could of the 2nd Armoured Brigade in the
belief that he would lunge for it at dawn the next day – so with
another dislocating shift of weight to his left he instead sent two

lorried infantry battalions from 21st Panzer and 90th Light, augmented by German and Italian artillery and under command of a first-class tactician, Oberst Werner Marcks, straight up through the Italian divisions on the main road to push aside the right flank of the Guards Brigade and reach Agedabia by 1100 on the second day (January 22nd, 1942), then to forge straight on to Antelat and swing east to Saunnu.

As General Messervy had acted almost as Rommel had foreseen (although not exactly, for he had directed 2nd Armoured Brigade down to Giof el Matar, behind the 1st Support Group, and not into the gap), by the evening of January 22nd, Marcks Group and the Italians held the line of the road from Agedabia up to Antelat and across to Saunnu, with all Messervy's command contained in the hook and cut off from its main supplies at Msus. Meanwhile, to the south of the British, 15th Panzer and the armour of 21st Panzer had crossed their front to reach Agedabia and follow the main advance.

Rommel's idea for January 23rd was for a further extension of the hook by Marcks Group down to Maaten el Grara and the strengthening of the main shaft as the panzer regiments came up towards Antelat, from which position they should be able to block the British armour's attempts to reach their stores and perhaps even to drive them southwards into the desert. From the anxious inquiries his intercept services were overhearing from British tank commanders desperately short of petrol it seemed likely they would never make Tengeder, let alone Mechili – and in any case, the Luftwaffe dominated the air above the battlefield this time, as the R.A.F. were too busy evacuating their forward airfields, and were themselves short of fuel.

This, then, was the picture with which Rommel faced Cavallero and Kesselring, and it is easy to see why, at the end of the argument, the former went off growling doubtfully, the latter silent and thoughtful. And except for two slight misjudgments, it might all have come off.

The first misjudgment was the move forward by the Marcks Group from Saunnu to Maaten el Grara which took place too early, with the result that one of the tank regiments of 2nd Armoured Brigade, ordered back to guard the approaches to Msus, arrived at Saunnu to find the place empty; the second was that a direction to 21st Panzer to get across to Saunnu to take Marcks's place was misdirected and so the gap in the net remained open. Through it, after a day of confused actions fought out in the barren country south of the Antelat–Saunnu track, most of 2nd Armoured Brigade, the whole of the Guards Brigade and the survivors of 1st Support Group made their uncertain way, congregating at dawn on the 24th about ten miles north of Antelat in positions from which, in

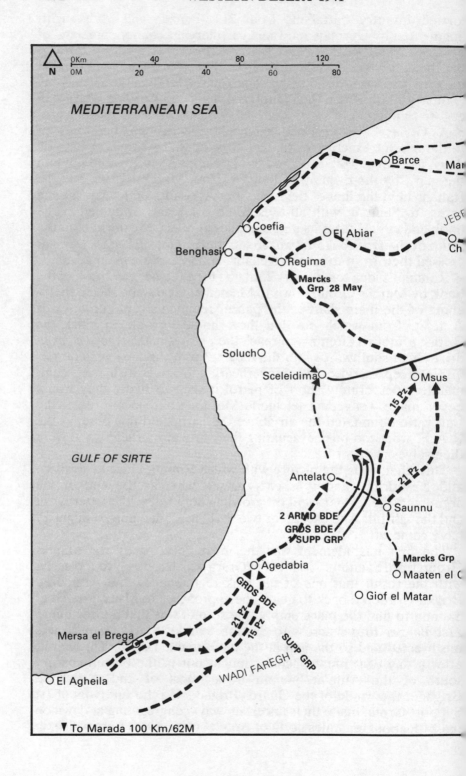

N

0Km 40 80 120
0M 20 40 60 80

MEDITERRANEAN SEA

Barce   Mar

Coefia   El Abiar   JEBE

Benghasi   Regima   Ch

**Marcks
Grp 28 May**

Soluch

Sceleidima   Msus

15 Pz

GULF OF SIRTE

Antelat   21 Pz   Saunnu

**2 ARMD BDE
GRDS BDE
SUPP GRP**

Marcks Grp

Agedabia   Maaten el C

GRDS BDE   Giof el Matar

Mersa el Brega   21 Pz

15 Pz   **SUPP GRP**

El Agheila   WADI FAREGH

▼ To Marada 100 Km/62M

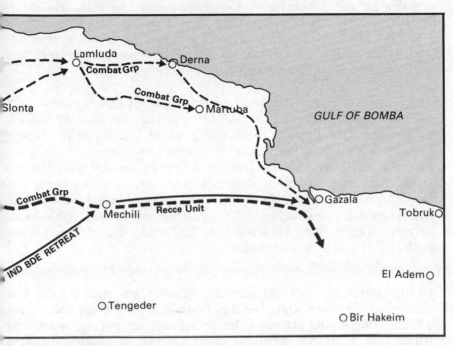

Map 27 Rommel's riposte: January 21st–February 4th, 1942

theory, they should be able successfully to block Rommel's route to the stores dump at Msus.

They were even given extra time in which to prepare for this, for Rommel had not realised the facts of their escape and Afrika Korps spent most of that day (24th) sweeping south-east and finding nothing but abandoned tanks and lorries – many of which their recovery units put back into service; but early on the 25th, the combined panzer divisions attacked north on to Messervy's division and literally drove it from the field. According to von Mellenthin who watched the first onslaught and amassed the details of the battle at the end of the day:

> On the right flank, 21st Panzer met little opposition, but six miles northwest of Saunnu 15th Panzer ran into very superior tank forces. These were overwhelmed by Panzer Regiment 8, closely supported by anti-tank guns and artillery; it soon became apparent that the British tank units had no battle experience and they were completely demoralized by the onslaught of 15th Panzer. At times the pursuit attained a speed of fifteen miles an hour, and the British columns fled madly over the desert in one

of the most extraordinary routs of the war. After covering fifty miles in under four hours 15th Panzer reached Msus airfield at 1100, overwhelming numerous supply columns, and capturing twelve aircraft ready to take off. Further exploitation was impossible as the division was out of fuel, but 96 tanks, 38 guns, and 190 lorries were the booty of the day.[3]

As 2nd Armoured Brigade had already lost nearly seventy of its tanks between January 21st and 23rd, it had thus been effectively eliminated as a fighting force within ninety-six hours of its first contact with the Afrika Korps, which now occupied the road junction at Msus and was happily filling its lockers with English food, drink and cigarettes. Rommel, however, was not so happy as he had hoped to be, for there was very little fuel found there and he could certainly not achieve his greatest immediate ambition of driving straight to Mechili and then to Derna, thus cutting off the entire XIII Corps in Cyrenaica.

In his appreciation of this one fact, Ritchie was right for the first time since January 21st. He had been in Cairo when the enemy advance began, but arrived in the area the following afternoon – by which time Marcks was driving up to Antelat – announcing among other things that Rommel's latest exploit provided a 'God-sent opportunity to hit him really hard when he puts out his neck, as it seems possible that he may be already doing.'

This was, as the *Official History* points out, a robust reading of the situation, but not an accurate one, for if anybody's neck was stuck out, it was his own.

Not all British eyes in the area were so purblind, however, for Godwin-Austen's opinion of the fighting ability of the 2nd Armoured Brigade had been conditioned by that demonstrated by the 22nd, and within thirty-six hours he was pointing out that the defences of Benghasi consisted of but one infantry brigade, to which the British armour could hardly come to the rescue if it was also expected to defend Msus as well as 'cover the eastern flank' – which were Ritchie's latest orders. In the circumstances, he requested permission to order a general withdrawal from Benghasi and eastern Cyrenaica as far as Mechili at least, with administrative units going back to Gazala – a request at which Ritchie baulked on the grounds that Rommel must by now be near the end of his resources and that very soon would come the opportunity to turn and strike him.

But by the evening of the 25th, what little remained of 1st Armoured Division – the shattered remnants of the Support Group and 2nd Armoured Brigade, plus a few headquarter troops – was back at Charruba and so far as Godwin-Austen could see there was nothing to prevent Afrika Korps driving on to Benghasi and capturing at least one Indian brigade, plus the ships, port installations and the accumulated supplies there. He saw no reason to believe that the resistance so far offered to Rommel's advance would have done much to blunt its edge, and in the circumstances he thought it right to use his own discretionary powers to order evacuation – of the Indians to Derna, of the shipping to Alexandria, and of the remnants of 1st Armoured Division to Mechili. He was thus somewhat incensed to learn that Ritchie, divining correctly that Rommel was short of petrol but also leaping over-eagerly to the conclusion that the Afrika Korps must now be at the limits of their strength, cancelled the move, instructed 7th Indian Brigade instead to send raiding columns down to attack Rommel's communications south of Antelat, and 1st Armoured Division to stand and defend Charruba and the approaches to El Abiar. Ritchie also took 4th Indian Division under his own direct command, which in view of the fact that Godwin-Austen had held the acting rank of lieutenant-general rather longer than he had himself, was tactless, and in the end was to prove unwise.

There now followed almost two days of military hiatus, while Tuker and Messervy endeavoured to deploy their divisions in accordance with Ritchie's instructions, and then, in the face of military reality, to try to persuade him that they were impractical – and all the time, Rommel was reading the intercept reports of the squabbling between his opponents, scavenging the field for booty, gradually accumulating supplies, and deciding what he would do next.

As severe sandstorms had blanketed the area during January 26th, nobody in it was much concerned by the general immobility, especially the troops themselves among whom were the 1st Armoured new-comers, 'getting their knees brown', as the saying went, and learning the bitter truth about the desert in which they were to fight their war.

The sandstorms that day had not been dense enough, however, to prevent two Tomahawks of 250 Squadron from spotting a move by some panzers south-eastwards from Msus and reporting it to Ritchie, who delightedly interpreted it as a splitting of Rommel's forces – one half to move on Mechili and the other on Benghasi. He promptly ordered Messervy to send what units he could scrape together south to fall on the rear of the reported panzers and Tuker to send 7th Indian Brigade down to block frontally whatever forces Rommel was sending up towards Benghasi, encouraging them with the statement that, 'The enemy has divided his forces, and is weaker than we are in both areas. The keyword is offensive action everywhere.'

But the movement of the panzers had been a feint (and only Rommel's luck had put the Tomahawks over it at the crucial moment) and, hearing that the main British moves were planned for the 29th, he sent the Marcks Group out on the 28th to sweep around to the north of Benghasi while the Italian divisions and 90th Light came up from the south. The Panzer regiments, after decoying Messervy's scratch armoured force out into the desert, were to remain in the Msus–Charruba area to guard the flank of the attack.

In pouring rain Rommel led the Marcks Group himself across the broken country towards Regima, and by nightfall, Reconnaissance Battalion 33 were blocking the raised causeway at Coefia along which 7th Indian Brigade were endeavouring to escape to join their brother brigade at Barce. There was a frantic confusion of reversing and overturning lorries, a retreat by the Indians into Benghasi and a well-judged decision by the brigade commander that their best way out of a fast-closing trap would be across the front of the approaching Italians, through Sceleidima and flat out for the Trig el Abd and Mechili. Aided by appalling weather and a great deal of luck, the three columns broke through with but few encounters with enemy forces – or at any rate with enemy forces willing to prove obstructive – but they had perforce to jettison a great deal of equipment. At Mechili they found Messervy's units, and all then retreated further – first to El Adem and then into Tobruk – while to their north, the 5th Indian Brigade and the 11th (which had been rushed up from Tobruk to Maraua when danger first threatened) made their joint way back along the roads through Slonta, Lamluda, Derna and Martuba. They were all back into or behind the Gazala defences by February 4th, though during the last sprint home a number of 11th Brigade guns and vehicles blew up on the mines left on the Alam Hamza battlefield, where XIII Corps's attempt to cut off the Afrika Korps retreat had been so roughly handled only seven weeks before.

For many reasons, Afrika Korps did not follow up the British retreat much more closely than they had themselves been followed on their way back to El Agheila. Firstly there was the chronic shortage of petrol, then there was the riveting attraction of the enormous bulk of supplies captured when they entered Benghasi, enough to distract the attention of the most ascetic warrior. The last action of one of the British quartermasters had been to put a match to seven million cigarettes and to organise the evacuation of twelve lorry-loads of rum – but the fire went out and some of the lorries broke down long before they were clear of the hills.

And there were always the constraints of higher command. Mussolini's permission for Rommel to advance and occupy Benghasi with a small mobile force 'if the British saw fit to withdraw voluntarily' arrived shortly after his headquarters had actually taken up residence there, but both Il Duce and Bastico insisted that the forward positions for Panzerarmee Afrika could be no further east than Maraua, in front of which only small mobile forces were to operate; and although Rommel briefly considered incorporating Ariete, Trieste, 90th Light and 15th and 21st Panzer Divisions into what he would be quite prepared to declare was just such a 'small mobile force' in order to drive the British even further back, he reluctantly concluded that there was not enough petrol to make the project feasible.

None the less, his reconnaissance battalions, some anti-tank batteries, and enough infantry to form them into two combat groups followed on the heels of the British retreat and were watching the formation of the Gazala positions as the last fugitives slipped into them, and soon afterwards the bulk of the Afrika Korps and 90th Light were close behind in the Jebel. Italian divisions stayed in Benghasi and around Antelat while a blocking force came out again from Tripoli to hold the border positions, from Mersa el Brega down to Marada.

Weary, weatherworn, thirsty but triumphant, Panzerarmee Afrika under their recently promoted leader, Oberstgeneral Rommel, were well back into Marmarica with Tobruk – for so long their apparently unobtainable objective – again only thirty-five miles beyond their grasp.

On February 2nd when it was evident that the situation had stabilised, Lieutenant-General A. R. Godwin-Austen formally requested that he be relieved of his command in view of the lack of confidence shown in him by the Eighth Army commander, demonstrated by the Army Commander's reversal of his decision to evacuate Cyrenaica on the evening of January 25th, and by the assumption of direct command of one of his divisions by the Army Commander at the same time. General Auchinleck saw fit to accede to this request and, according to the *Official History*, 'this, in the circumstances, was understandable.'

But as the history then goes on to admit that Godwin-Austen's reading of the situation during the retreat had been on the whole more realistic than Ritchie's, the question arises as to *how* Auchinleck's agreement had been 'understandable'. Godwin-Austen had been senior to Ritchie at the time of the changeover of commander during *Crusader* – and although the substance of that changeover had been acceptable in the circumstances which reigned at the time, every account written since stresses the fact that Ritchie's appointment was to be subject to review when the operation ended, and some justification demonstrated for the continuation of Ritchie's command if it were not to be transferred to one or other of the more senior corps commanders.

And what justification was there? Ritchie's performance as Eighth Army commander during the second half of *Crusader* had certainly not been as much at fault as Cunningham's, but on the other hand it had not been so brilliant as to obscure Godwin-Austen's right to consideration for the higher post, especially as it had been New Zealanders from Godwin-Austen's corps who had made the junction with the Tobruk garrison, Indians from his corps who had masked the frontier garrisons and eventually taken Bir el Gubi, and it had certainly not been Godwin-Austen's fault that the British armour had been so severely handled.

If time and circumstance had prevented a cool and just review of the situation between the end of *Crusader* and Rommel's riposte, then the lull when the Gazala Line was reached should provide one – and in view of the validity of Godwin-Austen's prognosis compared with the lack of realism in some of Ritchie's pronouncements, one would have thought the outcome foregone. But perhaps Auchinleck was prompted by one of those qualities which made him so admirable a person – loyalty to his friends and to his personal staff – in which case, he should have omitted that phrase in his letter to Ritchie of January 1st, regarding 'personal considerations'.

Needless to say, the disappointment felt throughout Eighth Army at their sudden reverse was echoed in the British Isles, and cables from Whitehall alternated astonishment with reproof, sympathy with regret. In his replies, Auchinleck made some crucial aspects of the war in the Middle East abundantly clear to Mr Churchill – the 2-pounder gun and the cruiser tanks were, he claimed, both of inferior quality to those in the enemy's service, and went on to observe sombrely that these defects were causing Royal Armoured Corps personnel to lose confidence in their equipment.

He did not, however, add that they were also losing confidence in their leadership – perhaps because he was not aware of it; but the fact remains that the troops were looking askance at their officers at many levels and assessing their abilities with growing scepticism. Cunningham had promised Eighth Army a speedy and complete victory at the beginning of *Crusader*, and if Ritchie had not promised them anything it could have been because he was apparently too busy to visit any formation lower than Corps Headquarters, so the troops felt that not only did they not know him, but he didn't know them. Unfortunately, this set of conditions also applied to the Commander-in-Chief himself, who had not found time to make himself known to a very high proportion of the men under his command. It is difficult for men to believe that the authority under which they serve cares much for them if it remains shrouded in Olympian mystery, especially if its promises prove empty and its directives impracticable.

Their admiration was therefore being increasingly given to the enemy commander, Rommel, who not only won victories but did so by leading from the front where his men could see him – a fact which quickly became well known throughout North Africa. The fact that he led an army with better anti-tank guns was obvious, that it had better tanks was believed – and it was becoming generally accepted that it was also better trained and operated on a more realistic doctrine. In this the men of Eighth Army were undoubtedly correct for German appreciation of the interdependence of all arms was fundamental; but the Afrika Korps had also another advantage which was not yet evident to all.

British reinforcements came out in complete formations – preferably as divisions but, as had happened in *Crusader*, at times in complete brigades – and these went into action as such. Although the officers and men may thus have known each other as a result of training together, when they at last went into action they were all equally inexperienced, at least of local conditions; and in the early years often of any form of battle at all.

But Rommel's reinforcements arrived as individual soldiers and were fed piecemeal into understrength formations – and when they went into action they were accompanied, and most often led, by men who had just come out of it. When the inexperienced men of the 1st Support Group retired in front of the first probe of 15th and 21st Panzer Division on January 21st, they were pursued by formations each with a core of battle-hardened veterans who could not only shrug off the discomforts of desert fighting with accustomed ease, but also recognise danger immediately it appeared, ignore empty sound and irrelevant fury in concentration on the purpose in hand – and teach the newcomers to do the same.

Panzerarmee Afrika Headquarters sent reports on the battles to Berlin, and these contained cool and realistic appraisals of their enemy's performance. As far as *Crusader* was concerned, they praised the general preparations and the manner in which the approach to battle had been concealed, but they were highly critical of the fragmentation of force and the inability ever to concentrate it all at one decisive point. They also praised the steadiness and reliability of the troops, especially the N.C.O.s. But one paragraph directed a criticism which would have come as a shock to many a British heart:

British troops fought well on the whole, though they never attained the same impetus as the Germans when attacking. Officers were courageous and self-sacrificing, but rather timid if they had to act on their own initiative.[4]

Too many of them could still hear ringing in their ears from their days as raw recruits the British drill sergeant's basic precept:

'In the Army, you're not paid to think! You're paid to DO AS YOU'RE BLOODY WELL TOLD.'

At first when there was no one to tell them what to do, many of them were lost.

Thus, in the early days of 1942, the mood throughout Eighth Army was one of frustration, suddenly increased by one of the saddest episodes of the whole campaign.

On February 23rd, a young Hussar officer was driving back towards Matruh from Halfaya Pass when the car he was driving hit a patch of clay newly laid as a temporary covering to the battered road surface, and wet from a recent storm. The wheels began to slip away, there was a shout from the back seat and then the driver found himself flying through the air to land with a crunching shock some yards away; he rolled as he hit the ground and never lost consciousness, but when he had recovered sufficiently to look around he was horrified to see the car lying upside down with spinning wheels, and three unconscious figures beside it.

Two, upon investigation, were revealed to be still alive and not badly hurt – but blood was pouring from the mouth of the third, and it was obvious that if not already dead, he was certainly dying. Only days after promotion to Major-General and appointment to command 7th Armoured Division, and but a few weeks after having the ribbon of the Victoria Cross pinned to his blouse by General Auchinleck, Jock Campbell was killed in one of those senseless accidents which cause men to curse the Fates and question the beliefs inculcated during childhood.

It was an episode which epitomised the fortunes of Eighth Army in that dire spring of 1942. An atmosphere of deep depression engulfed the formations, and only a certain native bloody-mindedness saved them from hopeless resignation; as it was, the continuing tale of misfortunes coming in from all over the globe eventually caused its own backlash, and the troops themselves began to greet every adverse news-flash with jocularity, even competing with each other to fabricate worse ones. Thus their own unquenchable spirits began to undo the ravages of the last few weeks and by March their morale was rising again. Perhaps beneath their scepticism they perceived the reality of their situation, which was that however gloomy the immediate future might seem, victory for the Allies was now assured.

While Rommel had been issuing instructions for the first stage of the withdrawal from Bir el Gubi, Japanese aircraft on the other side of the world had been flying towards Pearl Harbor. A new element was being introduced into the war, and in the desert – as elsewhere – it would never be the same again.

1942 would be a year of tremendous contrast; the year in which the enormous economic and technological resources of the United States would combine with the limitless manpower of Russia to resolve the problems with which European complexities had faced the world.

1942 would provide the turning-point.

Appendix I:
Forces Engaged in Operation Compass

British and Commonwealth Forces

Commander-in-Chief, Middle East   General Sir Archibald Wavell

WESTERN DESERT FORCE (LATER XIII CORPS)
Lieutenant-General R. N. O'Connor

Corps Troops:
7th Royal Tank Regt (Matildas)
1st and 104th Royal Horse Artillery
51st Field Regt R.A.
7th and 64th Medium Regts R.A.

7th Armoured Division – Major-General M. O'Moore Creagh

4th Armoured Brigade – Brig. J. S. L. Caunter
7th Hussars
2nd Royal Tank Regt
6th Royal Tank Regt

7th Armoured Brigade – Brig. H. E. Russell
3rd Hussars
8th Hussars
1st Royal Tank Regt

Support Group – Brig. W. H. E. Gott
1st King's Royal Rifle Corps
2nd Rifle Brigade
1st and 4th Royal Horse Artillery

Divisional Troops:
11th Hussars
3rd and 106th Royal Horse Artillery
2nd Field Squadron, Royal Engineers
141st Field Park Troop, Royal Engineers
No. 2 R.A.F. Armoured Car Company

4th Indian Division – Major-General N. M. de la P. Beresford-Peirse (withdrawn December 11th)

5th Indian Infantry Brigade – Brig. W. L. Lloyd
1st Royal Fusiliers
3rd/1st Punjab Regt
4th/6th Rajputana Rifles

11th Indian Infantry Brigade – Brig. R. A. Savory
2nd Queen's Own Cameron Highlanders
1st/6th Rajputana Rifles
4th/7th Rajput Regt

Divisional Troops:
Central India Horse
1st Northumberland Fusiliers (Machine-gun Battalion)
1st, 25th and 31st Field Regt R.A.
3rd Royal Horse Artillery
4th, 12th, 18th and 21st Field Company (Sappers and Miners)
11th Field Park Company

16th British Infantry Brigade – Brig. C. E. N. Lomax (attached 4th Indian Division until December 11th)
1st Queen's Regt
2nd Leicestershire Regt
1st Argyll and Sutherland Highlanders

Selby Force – Brig. A. R. Selby
3rd Coldstream Guards
W Company Northumberland Fusiliers
A Company 1st South Staffordshire Regt
A Company 1st Cheshire Regt
Detachment 1st Durham Light Infantry
A Troop 7th Hussars
Attached artillery

6th Australian Division – Major-General I. Mackay (joined operation after departure of 4th Indian Division)

16th Australian Infantry Brigade – Brig. A. S. Allen
2nd/1st Battalion
2nd/2nd Battalion
2nd/3rd Battalion

17th Australian Infantry Brigade – Brig. S. G. Savige
2nd/5th Battalion
2nd/6th Battalion
2nd/7th Battalion

19th Australian Infantry Brigade – Brig. H. C. H. Robertson
2nd/4th Battalion
2nd/8th Battalion
2nd/11th Battalion

Divisional Troops:
6th Cavalry Regt
2nd/1st, 2nd/2nd and 2nd/3rd Field Regt, Royal Australian Artillery
2nd/1st, 2nd/2nd and 2nd/8th Field Coys, Royal Australian Engineers

Italian Forces

Comandante Superiore   Maresciallo d'Armata Rodolfo Graziani

TENTH ARMY
Generale d'Armata   Gariboldi   (until November 17th, 1940)
Generale d'Armata   Berti   (until December 23rd, 1940)
Generale d'Armata   Tellera   (died of wounds February 7th, 1941)

XXI Corps – Generale di Corpo d'Armata Bergonzoli (H.Q. Bardia)

1st Libyan Division (at Maktila)
2nd Libyan Division (at Tummar)
4th Blackshirt Division (at Sidi Barrani)
Maletti Group (at Nibeiwa)
63rd Cirene Division (at Rabia/Sofafi)
62nd Marmarica Division (along Escarpment between Sofafi and Halfaya)
64th Catanzaro Division (at Buq Buq)
1st Blackshirt Division (at Bardia)
2nd Blackshirt Division (at Bardia)
Frontier Guard units and Fortress troops in Bardia

XXII Corps – Generale di Corpo d'Armata Petassi Mannella (H.Q. Tobruk)

61st Sirte Division (in Tobruk)
Fortress troops and artillery in Tobruk

XX Corps – Generale di Corpo d'Armata Cona (H.Q. Giovanni Berta)

60th Sabratha Division (at Derna)
27th Brescia Division (at Slonta)
17th Pavia Division (at Cirene)
Babini Armoured Brigade (at Mechili)

Note: Metropolitan Divisions such as Brescia and Pavia usually consisted of approximately 13,000 men; Libyan and Blackshirt Divisions of approximately 8,000.

Appendix II:
Forces Engaged in Operation Battleaxe

British and Commonwealth Forces

Commander-in-Chief, Middle East   General Sir Archibald Wavell

XIII CORPS
Lieutenant-General Sir Noel M. de la P. Beresford-Peirse

7th Armoured Division – Major-General Sir Michael O'Moore Creagh

4th Armoured Brigade – Brig. A. H. Gatehouse
   4th Royal Tank Regt (Matildas)
   7th Royal Tank Regt (Matildas)

7th Armoured Brigade – Brig. H. E. Russell
   2nd Royal Tank Regt (mixed cruisers)
   6th Royal Tank Regt (Crusaders)

Support Group – Brig. J. C. Campbell
   1st, 3rd, 4th and 106th Royal Horse Artillery
   1st King's Royal Rifle Corps
   2nd Rifle Brigade

Divisional Troops:
   11th Hussars
   4th Field Squadron
   143rd Field Park Squadron

4th Indian Division – Major-General F. W. Messervy

11th Indian Infantry Brigade – Brig. R. A. Savory
   2nd Queen's Own Cameron Highlanders
   1st/6th Rajputana Rifles
   2nd/5th Mahrattas

22nd Guards Brigade – Brig. I. D. Erskine
   1st Buffs
   2nd Scots Guards
   3rd Coldstream Guards
   22nd Guards Brigade Attack Company

Divisional Troops:
    Central India Horse
    25th Field Regt
    31st Field Regt
    4th, 12th, 18th and 21st Field Company (Sappers and Miners)
    11th Field Park Company

German and Italian Forces

Comandante Superiore   Generale d'Armata Italo Gariboldi

DEUTSCHES AFRIKA KORPS
Generalleutnant Erwin Rommel

  Corps Troops:
    two regiments Italian artillery in Bardia
    one regiment flak (88mm.)

  15th Panzer Division – Generalleutnant W. Neumann-Sylkow
    Panzer Regt 8
    Reconnaissance Battalion 33
    Battery P.A.K. (anti-tank)
    Battery flak (88mm.)
    Rifle Regt 104
      Battalion lorried infantry
      Battalion motor-cycle infantry
      Battalion foot infantry (under Major the Rev. Wilhelm Bach at Halfaya)
    Divisional artillery at Point 206

  Trento Division
    Three infantry battalions and one artillery regiment in area Sollum–Musaid–Capuzzo

  5th Light Division (later 21st Panzer Division) – Generalleutnant J. von Ravenstein
    Panzer Regt 5
    Reconnaissance Battalion 3

Appendix III:
Forces Engaged in Operation Crusader

British and Commonwealth Forces

Commander-in-Chief, Middle East   General Sir Claude Auchinleck

EIGHTH ARMY
Lieutenant-General Sir Alan Cunningham (until November 26th)
Lieutenant-General N. M. Ritchie

Army Troops:

2nd South African Division – Major-General I. P. de Villiers
    3rd South African Infantry Brigade – Brig. C. E. Borain
    4th South African Infantry Brigade – Brig. A. A. Hayton
    6th South African Infantry Brigade – Brig. F. W. Cooper
    Divisional artillery, machine-gun company and reconnaissance squadron

Oasis Group – Brig. D. W. Reid

Tobruk Fortress
70th Division – Major-General R. M. Scobie
    32nd Army Tank Brigade – Brig. A. C. Willison
    14th Infantry Brigade – Brig. B. H. Chappel
    16th Infantry Brigade – Brig. C. E. N. Lomax
    23rd Infantry Brigade – Brig. C. H. V. Cox
    1st Polish Carpathian Brigade – Major-General S. Kopanski
    Divisional artillery and machine-gun battalion

Matruh Fortress
    2nd South African Infantry Brigade – Brig. W. H. E. Poole
    Fortress artillery

Long Range Desert Group – Lieutenant-Colonel G. L. Prendergast

XIII Corps – Lieutenant-General A. R. Godwin-Austen
Corps Troops:
    Medium, heavy, anti-tank and anti-aircraft artillery

4th Indian Division – Major-General F. W. Messervy
5th Indian Infantry Brigade – Brig. D. Russell
7th Indian Infantry Brigade – Brig. H. R. Briggs
11th Indian Infantry Brigade – Brig. A. Anderson
Divisional artillery, reconnaissance squadrons and Sappers and Miners

1st Army Tank Brigade – Brig. H. R. B. Watkins

New Zealand Division – Major-General B. C. Freyberg
4th New Zealand Infantry Brigade – Brig. L. M. Inglis
5th New Zealand Infantry Brigade – Brig. J. Hargest
6th New Zealand Infantry Brigade – Brig. H. E. Barrowclough
Divisional artillery, divisional cavalry, machine-gun battalion and 28th (Maori) Battalion

XXX Corps – Lieutenant-General C. W. M. Norrie

Corps Troops:
Light anti-aircraft artillery and one reconnaissance squadron

7th Armoured Division – Major-General W. H. E. Gott
4th Armoured Brigade Group – Brig. A. H. Gatehouse
7th Armoured Brigade – Brig. G. M. O. Davy
22nd Armoured Brigade – Brig. J. Scott-Cockburn
7th Support Group – Brig. J. C. Campbell
Divisional medium, anti-tank and light anti-aircraft artillery, and eight reconnaissance squadrons

22nd Guards Brigade – Brig. J. C. O. Marriott

1st South African Division – Major-General G. E. Brink
1st South African Infantry Brigade – Brig. D. H. Pienaar
5th South African Infantry Brigade – Brig. B. F. Armstrong
Divisional artillery, machine-gun battalion and three reconnaissance squadrons

German and Italian Forces

Comandante Superiore   Generale d'Armata Ettore Bastico

PANZERGRUPPE AFRIKA
General der Panzertruppen Erwin Rommel

Deutsches Afrika Korps – Generalleutnant Ludwig Cruewell

15th Panzer Division – Generalleutnant W. Neumann-Sylkow (died of wounds December 9th)
Panzer Regt 8 – Oberstleutnant Cramer
15th Rifle Brigade – Oberst Menny

Reconnaissance Battalion 33 – Oberleutnant Héraucourt
Divisional artillery

21st Panzer Division – Generalleutnant J. von Ravenstein (taken prisoner November 29th)
Panzer Regt 5 – Oberstleutnant Stephan (died of wounds November 25th)
Rifle Regt 104 – Oberstleutnant Knabe (1st Battalion of this regiment was commanded by Major the Rev. Wilhelm Bach at Halfaya)
Reconnaissance Battalion 3 – Oberstleutnant Freiherr von Wechmar
Divisional artillery and engineers

Division zbV Afrika (later *90th Light Division*) – Generalleutnant Max Sümmermann (died of wounds December 10th)
Infantry Regt 155 – Oberst Marks
Afrika Regt 361 – Oberst von Barby
Sonderverband 288 – Oberst Menton
Reconnaissance Battalion 580 – Oberleutnant Hohmeyer
Anti-tank Battalion 605

Corpo d'Armata XXI – Generale di Corpo d'Armata Enea Navarrini (H.Q. El Adem)
Bologna Division – Generale di Divisione Gloria
Trento Division – Generale di Divisione Stampioni
Pavia Division – Generale di Divisione Franceschini
Brescia Division – Generale di Divisione Zambon
Savona Division – Generale di Divisione de Giorgis (H.Q. Bir Ghirba)
Arko 104 (Artillery Group Böttcher) – Generalmajor Karl Böttcher (H.Q. Belhammed)

CORPO D'ARMATA DI MANOVRA XX (under direct command of Comandante Superiore)
Generale di Corpo d'Armata Gastone Gambara

Corps Troops:
Medium and heavy artillery and a reconnaissance unit

Ariete Armoured Division – Generale di Divisione Balotta
132nd Armoured Regt
8th Bersaglieri Regt
132nd Artillery Regt

Trieste Motorised Division – Generale di Divisione Piazzoni
65th Infantry Regt
66th Infantry Regt
9th Bersaglieri Regt
Divisional anti-tank and anti-aircraft artillery, plus machine-gun and mortar companies

Notes

Unless otherwise stated, the place of publication is London.

1 The First Adversaries

1 A. P. Wavell, *Allenby: Soldier and Statesman*, Harrap 1946, p. 245.
2 John Connell, *Wavell, Scholar and Soldier*, Collins 1964, p. 22.
3 Summary of lectures to Staff College candidates, 1930–5, quoted in Connell, op. cit., pp. 161–2, 164.
4 John Masters, *Bugles and a Tiger*, Michael Joseph 1956, Ch. 2.
5 Kenneth Macksey, *Armoured Crusader: Major-General Sir Percy Hobart*, Hutchinson 1967, p. 64.
6 Ibid., pp. 111–12.
7 Quoted in Macksey, op. cit., p. 91.
8 Quoted in Macksey, op. cit., pp. 159–60.
9 Quoted in Macksey, op. cit., p. 160.
10 Quoted in Generale Giuseppe Mancinelli, 'La Preparazione dell'Italia Fascista alla Guerra', in *Storia della Seconda Guerra Mondiale*, Italian edn ed. Angelo Solmi, Rizzoli (Milan) 1967, p. 337.
11 Mancinelli, op. cit., pp. 336–7.

2 Skirmish and Circumspect Advance

1 Brigadier Dudley Clarke, *The Eleventh at War*, Michael Joseph 1952, p. 95.
2 Field Marshal Lord Wilson of Libya, *Eight Years Overseas*, Hutchinson 1950, pp. 20, 21, reproduced by permission of the Estate of the late Field Marshal Lord Wilson of Libya.
3 Quoted in Kenneth Macksey, *Armoured Crusader: Major-General Sir Percy Hobart*, Hutchinson 1967, p. 169.
4 Quoted in Macksey, op. cit., pp. 170–1.
5 Macksey, op. cit., p. 173.
6 Clarke, *The Eleventh at War*, pp. 105–6.
7 Ibid., p. 107.

3 *The Pace Quickens*

1 Quoted in John Connell, *Wavell, Scholar and Soldier*, Collins 1964, pp. 255–6.
2 Winston S. Churchill, *The Second World War, Vol. II*, Cassell 1949, p. 382.
3 Quoted in Connell, op. cit., p. 268.
4 Colonel C. A. H. M. Noble, M.C., unpublished diary.
5 Quoted in Connell, op. cit., p. 277.
6 Churchill, *Second World War*, pp. 483, 484.
7 Quoted in Connell, op. cit., p. 288.
8 Quoted in Connell, op. cit., p. 289.

4 *The 'Five-day Raid'*

1 Cyril Joly, *Take These Men*, Constable Publishers 1955, p. 50.
2 Quoted in John Connell, *Wavell, Scholar and Soldier*, Collins 1964, p. 286.
3 Lieut-Colonel G. R. Stevens, *Fourth Indian Division*, McLaren (Toronto) n.d., p. 18, reprinted by permission of the President, Chairman and Committee of the 4th Indian Division Officers' Association.
4 Joly, op. cit., p. 54.
5 Alan Moorehead, *African Trilogy*, Hamish Hamilton 1944, p. 68.
6 Joly, op. cit., pp. 61–2.
7 Stevens, op. cit., p. 23.

5 *First Battle for Tobruk*

1 Quoted in B. H. Liddell Hart, *The Tanks, Vol. Two*, Cassell 1959, p. 50.
2 General Sir Richard O'Connor, personal account of the Western Desert campaign, unpublished 1941, TS. p. 30.
3 Quoted in Liddell Hart, op. cit., pp. 52–3.
4 Quoted in Liddell Hart, op. cit., p. 53.
5 Gavin Long, *To Benghazi*, Australian War Memorial (Canberra) 1952, p. 148.
6 Ibid., p. 150.
7 Ibid., p. 177.
8 Ibid., p. 193.
9 O'Connor, op. cit., TS. pp. 49–50.
10 Ibid., TS. p. 45.
11 Ibid., TS. p. 46.
12 Ibid.
13 Quoted in Chester Wilmot, *Tobruk*, copyright © Chester Wilmot 1944, reprinted by permission of Angus and Robertson Publishers, Sydney, p. 36.
14 Quoted in Wilmot, op. cit., p. 37.
15 Quoted in Wilmot, op. cit., p. 38.
16 Long, op. cit., pp. 233–4.

17 Lieutenant Hennessy, quoted in Wilmot, op. cit., p. 44.
18 Quoted in Long, op. cit., p. 239.

6 *Beda Fomm: The Narrow Victory*

1 Gavin Long, *To Benghazi*, Australian War Memorial (Canberra) 1952, p. 252n.
2 Major R. H. W. S. Hastings, *The Rifle Brigade in the Second World War*, Gale and Polden (Aldershot) 1950, pp. 54–5.
3 Cyril Joly, *Take These Men*, Constable Publishers 1955, p. 74.
4 Ibid., pp. 74–5.
5 Quoted in George Forty, *Desert Rats at War*, Ian Allan 1975, p. 69, reprinted by permission of Mr A. C. Brown.
6 Quoted in Forty, op. cit., pp. 69, 70.
7 Alan Moorehead, *African Trilogy*, Hamish Hamilton 1944, pp. 106–7.
8 Joly, op. cit., pp. 86–7.

7 *'In all directions . . .'*

1 Major-General I. S. O. Playfair *et al.*, *History of the Second World War*, (hereafter referred to as the *Official History*), *The Mediterranean and Middle East Vol. I*, H.M.S.O. 1954, p. 396.
2 Antony Brett-James, *Ball of Fire: The Fifth Indian Division in the Second World War*, Gale and Polden (Aldershot) 1951, p. 20.
3 Lieut-Colonel G. R. Stevens, *Fourth Indian Division*, McLaren (Toronto) n.d., p. 32, reprinted by permission of the President, Chairman and Committee of the 4th Indian Division Officers' Association.
4 Ibid., p. 36.
5 John Connell, *Wavell, Scholar and Soldier*, Collins 1964, p. 382.
6 General Sir Richard O'Connor, personal account of the Western Desert campaign, part II, unpublished 1941, TS. p. 2.
7 Quoted in Connell, op. cit., p. 383.
8 The Earl of Avon, *The Eden Memoirs: The Reckoning*, Cassell 1965, p. 195.
9 W. B. Kennedy Shaw, *Long Range Desert Group*, Collins 1945, pp. 24–5.
10 Ibid., p. 37.
11 Ibid., p. 42.
12 Ibid., p. 65.

8 *Enter Rommel*

1 Heinz W. Schmidt, *With Rommel in the Desert*, Harrap 1951, pp. 16–17.
2 *The Rommel Papers*, ed. B. H. Liddell Hart, Collins 1953, p. 104.
3 Ibid., p. 105.
4 Quoted in John Connell, *Wavell, Scholar and Soldier*, Collins 1964, pp. 385–6.
5 Quoted in Connell, op. cit., p. 387.

6 *The Rommel Papers*, p. 107.
7 Ibid., p. 110.
8 Ibid., p. 111.
9 Ibid., p. 113.
10 Ibid.
11 Quoted in Connell, op. cit., pp. 434, 435.
12 Quoted in Connell, op. cit., p. 437.
13 Quoted in Connell, op. cit., p. 438.
14 Quoted in Connell, op. cit., p. 439.
15 Quoted in Connell, loc. cit.

9 *Battleaxe*

1 *The Rommel Papers*, ed. B. H. Liddell Hart, Collins 1953, p. 133.
2 Ibid., p. 132.
3 Ibid., p. 134.
4 Ibid., pp. 139, 140.
5 Quoted in Major-General I. S. O. Playfair *et al.*, *Official History, Vol. II*, H.M.S.O. 1956, p. 203.
6 Quoted in B. H. Liddell Hart, *The Tanks, Vol. Two*, Cassell 1959, p. 84.
7 Quoted in Major R. H. W. S. Hastings, *The Rifle Brigade in the Second World War*, Gale and Polden (Aldershot) 1950, p. 72.
8 Quoted in Hastings, op. cit., p. 73.
9 *The Rommel Papers*, p. 144.
10 Ibid., p. 145.
11 Quoted in John Connell, *Wavell, Scholar and Soldier*, Collins 1974, p. 502.

10 *Auchinleck Takes Command*

1 Chester Wilmot, *Tobruk*, copyright © Chester Wilmot 1944, reprinted by permission of Angus and Robertson Publishers, Sydney, p. 255.
2 Quoted in Wilmot, op. cit., p. 205.
3 Quoted in Wilmot, op. cit., p. 200.
4 Quoted in *The Sidi Rezeg Battles 1941*, ed. J. A. I. Agar-Hamilton and L. C. F. Turner, Oxford University Press (Cape Town) 1957, p. 64. This and all subsequent extracts from this title are reprinted by permission of the Government Printer, Pretoria, South Africa.
5 Quoted in *Sidi Rezeg*, p. 64.
6 Quoted in *Sidi Rezeg*, p. 65.
7 Quoted in *Sidi Rezeg*, pp. 110, 66.
8 *Sidi Rezeg*, pp. 110–11.
9 Quoted in *Sidi Rezeg*, p. 90.
10 Quoted in *Sidi Rezeg*, p. 92.

11 *Crusader: The Clash of Armour*

1 Quoted in John Connell, *Auchinleck*, Cassell 1959, p. 336.

2 Major-General Sir Howard Kippenberger, *Infantry Brigadier*, Oxford University Press 1949, p. 81.
3 Alan Moorehead, *African Trilogy*, Hamish Hamilton 1944, p. 220.
4 Brigadier G. M. O. Davy, *The Seventh and Three Enemies*, Heffer (Cambridge) n.d., p. 146.
5 Quoted in *The Sidi Rezeg Battles 1941*, ed. J. A. I. Agar-Hamilton and L. C. F. Turner, Oxford University Press (Cape Town) 1957, p. 136.
6 Earl of Onslow, *Men and Sand*, St Catherine's Press, 1961, quoted in Michael Carver, *Tobruk*, Batsford 1964, p. 53.
7 Alexander Clifford, *Three against Rommel*, Harrap 1943, pp. 131, 132.
8 Quoted in *Sidi Rezeg*, ed. Agar-Hamilton and Turner, pp. 161–2.
9 Quoted in *Sidi Rezeg*, p. 173.
10 Quoted in *Sidi Rezeg*, p. 194.
11 Quoted in *Sidi Rezeg*, p. 175.
12 Davy, op. cit., quoted in *Sidi Rezeg*, p. 177.
13 Major R. H. W. S. Hastings, *The Rifle Brigade in the Second World War*, Gale and Polden (Aldershot) 1950, p. 85.
14 In *The Royal Artillery Commemoration Book 1939–1945*, published for the R. A. Association by Bell 1950, p. 196, quoted in *Sidi Rezeg*, pp. 180–1, and reprinted by permission of the Royal Artillery Institution.
15 Quoted in *Sidi Rezeg*, p. 182.
16 Hastings, op. cit., p. 58.
17 Quoted in *Sidi Rezeg*, ed. Agar-Hamilton and Turner, pp. 199–200.
18 From *42nd Royal Tank Regiment* 1938–1944, published privately by the Regiment 1951, p. 10, quoted in *Sidi Rezeg*, p. 203.
19 Brigadier A. F. Hely, in *R. A. Commemoration Book*, p. 189, quoted in *Sidi Rezeg*, ed. Agar-Hamilton and Turner, p. 211.
20 'Preliminary Narrative', quoted in *Sidi Rezeg*, p. 212.
21 Cyril Joly, *Take These Men*, Constable Publishers 1955, p. 199.
22 Brigadier George Clifton, *The Happy Hunted*, Cassell 1952, pp. 129–30, quoted in *Sidi Rezeg*, ed. Agar-Hamilton and Turner, p. 217.
23 Hely, in *R. A. Commemoration Book*, p. 189, quoted in *Sidi Rezeg*, p. 214.
24 Joly, op. cit., pp. 203–4.
25 Quoted in *Sidi Rezeg*, ed. Agar-Hamilton and Turner, p. 220.
26 Quoted in *Sidi Rezeg*, p. 225.
27 D. Frazer Norton, *History of the 26th Battalion*, War History Branch, Wellington 1952, reprinted by permission of Historical Publications Branch, Department of Internal Affairs, Wellington, New Zealand. Quoted in *Sidi Rezeg*, p. 223.
28 Quoted in *Sidi Rezeg*, p. 233.
29 Quoted in Brigadier Dudley Clarke, *The Eleventh at War*, Michael Joseph 1952, p. 202.
30 Quoted in *Sidi Rezeg*, ed. Agar-Hamilton and Turner, p. 237.
31 Quoted, loc. cit.
32 Quoted in *Sidi Rezeg*, p. 255.
33 Heinz W. Schmidt, *With Rommel in the Desert*, Harrap 1951, p. 108.
34 Quoted in *Sidi Rezeg*, ed. Agar-Hamilton and Turner, p. 261.
35 Quoted, loc. cit.

36 Quoted in *Sidi Rezeg*, p. 262.
37 War Diary of 22nd Armoured Brigade, quoted in *Sidi Rezeg*, p. 264.

12 *Crusader: The Infantry Take Over*

1 *The Rommel Papers*, ed. B. H. Liddell Hart, Collins 1953, p. 163.
2 Afrika Korps War Diary, quoted in *The Sidi Rezeg Battles 1941*, ed. J. A. I. Agar-Hamilton and L. C. F. Turner, Oxford University Press (Cape Town) 1957, p. 305.
3 *Sidi Rezeg*, p. 306.
4 *The Rommel Papers*, ed. Liddell Hart, p. 164.
5 Quoted in John Connell, *Auchinleck*, Cassell 1959, pp. 364–5.
6 Major R. H. W. S. Hastings, *The Rifle Brigade in the Second World War*, Gale and Polden (Aldershot) 1950, pp. 92–3.
7 Heinz W. Schmidt, *With Rommel in the Desert*, Harrap 1951, p. 118.
8 Quoted in *Sidi Rezeg*, ed. Agar-Hamilton and Turner, p. 386.
9 Birkby, Carel, ed., *The Saga of the Transvaal Scottish Regiment 1932–1950*, Howard Timmins (Pty.) Ltd (Cape Town) for Hodder and Stoughton 1950, p. 348, quoted in *Sidi Rezeg*, p. 332.
10 Quoted in *Sidi Rezeg*, p. 332.
11 Quoted in *Sidi Rezeg*, p. 376.
12 *Sidi Rezeg*, pp. 376–7.
13 General Norrie's Report, quoted in *Sidi Rezeg*, pp. 392–3.
14 D. Frazer Norton, *History of the 26th Battalion*, War History Branch, Wellington 1952, quoted in *Sidi Rezeg*, p. 396. This and the following extract, from Borman, *Divisional Signals*, are reprinted by permission of Historical Publications Branch, Department of Internal Affairs, Wellington, New Zealand.
15 C. A. Borman, *Divisional Signals*, War History Branch, Wellington 1954, quoted in *Sidi Rezeg*, p. 412n.
16 *The Rommel Papers*, ed. Liddell Hart, p. 170.

13 *Lightning Riposte*

1 Quoted in John Connell, *Auchinleck*, Cassell 1959, pp. 423–4.
2 Quoted in Connell, op. cit., pp. 420–1.
3 Major-General F. W. von Mellenthin, *Panzer Battles: A Study of the Employment of Armor in the Second World War*, Ballantine (New York) 1971, copyright 1956 by the University of Oklahoma Press, pp. 104–5.
4 Quoted in I. S. O. Playfair, *Official History, Vol. III*, H.M.S.O. 1960, p. 154.

Index